ABOUT THE AUTHOR

EUGENE F. FAMA is Theodore O. Yntema
Professor of Finance at the Graduate School of
Business, University of Chicago. Generally regarded as one of the country's leading experts
in the field of finance, he is the author (with
Merton Miller) of *The Theory of Finance*
(1972) and of numerous articles in scholarly
journals.

FOUNDATIONS

OF

FINANCE

FOUNDATIONS

OF

FINANCE

PORTFOLIO DECISIONS

AND

SECURITIES PRICES

Eugene F. Fama

Basic Books, Inc., Publishers   *New York*

Library of Congress Cataloging in Publication Data

Fama, Eugene F.   1939–
  Foundations of finance.

  Bibliography: p.
  Includes index.
  1. Investments. 2. Securities. 3. Stocks—Prices.
I. Title.
HG4521.F32   332.6   75-36771
ISBN 0–465–02499–8

To my family

Contents

Preface   *xv*

CHAPTER 1

The Behavior of Stock Market Returns   *3*

  I.   Some Statistical Concepts   *3*

      A.   Random Variables   3
      B.   The Mean   4
      C.   The Standard Deviation   5
      D.   Characterization of Normal Distributions by Their Means and Standard Deviations   6
      E.   The Sample Mean and Standard Deviation   7
      F.   Testing for Normality: The Studentized Range   8
      G.   Statistical Models and Reality   11

  II.   The Definition of Return   *12*

  III.   Indexes or Portfolios of Stock Market Returns   *13*

  IV.   Average Return and Variability: A Quick Look   *14*

  V.   The History of Return Variability   *15*

  VI.   Distributions of Stock Market Returns   *17*

      A.   Motivation and Theory   17
      B.   Daily Returns   21
      C.   Monthly Returns   26

  VII.   Conclusions   *38*

CHAPTER 2

The Distribution of the Return on a Portfolio   *41*

   I.   A Portfolio's Return as a Function of Returns
        on Securities   *41*
   II. The Mean and Variance of a Portfolio's Return   *43*

       A.   *The Mean or Expected Value of the Return on a
            Portfolio* *44*
       B.   *The Variance of the Return on a Portfolio* *48*

  III. Portfolio Risk and Security Risk   *58*
  IV. Conclusions   *62*

CHAPTER 3

The Market Model: Theory and Estimation   *63*

   I.   The Multivariate Normal Distribution of Returns on
       Securities   *63*

       A.   *Normal Portfolio Returns and Multivariate Normal Returns on
            Securities* *63*
       B.   *Some Properties of the Multivariate Normal Distribution* *64*
       C.   *Bivariate Normality of Pairwise Security and Portfolio
            Returns* *65*

   II. Bivariate Normality and the Market Model   *66*

       A.   *The Market Model: Fundamental Properties* *66*
       B.   *Some Formal Justification* *69*
       C.   *Some Additional Properties of the Model* *73*
       D.   *The Market Model in the Empirical Literature* *76*

  III. The Estimators   *77*

       A.   *The Generality of the Procedures* *78*
       B.   *The Estimating Equations* *79*
       C.   *Some Algebraic Properties of the Estimators* *81*

  IV. The Sampling Distributions of the Estimators   *84*

       A.   *Unbiasedness* *84*
       B.   *The "t" Distributions of the Standardized Estimators* *87*
       C.   *Why the "t" Distribution?* *89*

   V. The Reliability of the Estimators   *91*

       A.   *Classical Confidence Intervals* *92*
       B.   *Classical Hypothesis Testing* *94*
       C.   *The Bayesian Approach* *96*

  VI. Conclusions   *98*

CHAPTER 4

The Market Model: Estimates 99

I. Estimating the Market Model: A Detailed Example 99

    A. *The Market Model: Summary of Equations and Properties 99*

    B. *Market Model Estimates for IBM 101*

    C. *The Fit of the Estimated Regression 104*

    D. *The Reliability of the Market Model Coefficient Estimates for IBM 106*

    E. *Testing the Assumptions Underlying the Coefficient Estimators 109*

II. Evidence on the Risks or Market Sensitivities of NYSE Common Stocks 121

    A. *Comments on Market Model Estimates for Larger and Smaller Firms 121*

    B. *Evidence on the Assumptions Underlying the Market Model Estimates 124*

    C. *Comparison of Prewar and Postwar Market Model Parameter Estimates 128*

    D. *The Reliability of the Risk Estimates 131*

III. Conclusions 132

CHAPTER 5

Efficient Capital Markets 133

I. An Efficient Capital Market: Introduction 133

II. An Efficient Capital Market: Formal Discussion 134

III. Four Models of Market Equilibrium 137

    A. *Expected Returns Are Positive 137*

    B. *Expected Returns Are Constant 142*

    C. *Returns Conform to the Market Model 151*

    D. *Returns Conform to a Risk-Return Relationship 166*

IV. Conclusions and Some Fine Points of the Theory 167

CHAPTER 6

Short-Term Interest Rates as Predictors of Inflation 169

I. The Market for U.S. Treasury Bills 169

    A. *Treasury Bills: What Are They? 169*

    B. *Real and Nominal Returns on a One-Month Bill 170*

  II.   Inflation and Efficiency in the Bill Market: Theory   *175*

      A. *Market Efficiency in a World of Perfect Foresight* *175*
      B. *Market Efficiency in a World of Uncertainty* *175*

  III.   A Model of Market Equilibrium   *178*

      A. *Why Do We Need a Model of Market Equilibrium?* *178*
      B. *The Model* *178*

  IV.   Testable Implications on Market Efficiency When the Equilibrium Expected Real Return Is Constant Through Time   *179*

      A. *The Real Return* *179*
      B. *The Nominal Interest Rate as a Predictor of Inflation* *180*
      C. *Summary and Reinterpretation of the Proposed Tests* *184*

   V.   The Data   *186*
  VI.   The Major Results for One-Month Bills   *188*

      A. *The Information in Past Inflation Rates* *191*
      B. *Tests of Market Efficiency* *191*
      C. *The Expected Real Return* *192*

  VII.   The Behavior of $\tilde{\Delta}_t$ *197*
 VIII.   Results for Bills with Longer Maturities   *200*
  IX.   Interest Rates as Predictors of Inflation: Comparison with the Results of Others   *204*
   X.   Extension of the Results to the Period of Price Controls   *206*
  XI.   Conclusions   *210*

CHAPTER 7

The Two-Parameter Portfolio Model   *212*

   I.   Introduction   *212*
  II.   Normal Distributions, Risk Aversion, and the Efficient Set   *213*

      A. *The Framework* *213*
      B. *The Simplifications Obtained When Portfolio Return Distributions Are Normal* *214*
      C. *The Simplifications Obtained When Investors Are Risk-averse* *214*
      D. *Geometric Interpretation* *216*

  III.   The Geometry of the Efficient Set   *219*

      A. *The Geometry of Combinations of Two Securities or Portfolios* *219*
      B. *The Efficient Set: No Risk-free Asset* *231*
      C. *The Efficient Set with a Risk-free Asset* *235*

IV. Portfolio Risk, Security Risk, and the Effects of Diversification   *240*

     A. *Portfolio Risk and Security Risk in a Two-Parameter World*   *241*
     B. *Portfolio Risk and Security Risk: Empirical Examples*   *245*
     C. *The Effects of Diversification*   *252*

V. Conclusions   *256*

CHAPTER 8

Capital Market Equilibrium in a Two-Parameter World   *257*

I. Introduction   *257*

II. The Relationship Between Expected Return and Risk in an Efficient Portfolio   *258*

     A. *The Risks of Securities and Portfolios*   *258*
     B. *The Mathematics of Minimum Variance Portfolios*   *260*
     C. *Interpretation of the Results*   *267*

III. Market Relationships Between Expected Return and Risk When There Is Risk-free Borrowing and Lending   *271*

     A. *Complete Agreement*   *271*
     B. *The Efficient Set When There Is Risk-free Borrowing and Lending*   *273*
     C. *Market Equilibrium When There Is Risk-free Borrowing and Lending*   *274*
     D. *Criticisms of the Model*   *277*

IV. Market Relationships Between Expected Return and Risk When Short-Selling of Positive Variance Securities Is Unrestricted   *278*

     A. *The Efficiency of the Market Portfolio*   *279*
     B. *Efficient Portfolios as Combinations of the Market Portfolio* M *and the Minimum Variance Portfolio* Z   *285*

V. Variants of the Model of Market Equilibrium When There Is Unrestricted Short-Selling of Positive Variance Securities   *288*

     A. *Market Equilibrium When There Is a Risk-free Security But It Cannot Be Sold Short*   *288*
     B. *Market Equilibrium When There Is Risk-free Borrowing and Lending But at Different Interest Rates*   *293*
     C. *Market Equilibrium When There Is Risk-free Borrowing and Lending But There Are Margin Requirements*   *295*

VI. Comparison of and Comments on the Various Two-Parameter Models of Market Equilibrium   *298*

VII. Market Equilibrium When There Are No Risk-free
Securities and Short-Selling of Positive Variance
Securities Is Prohibited   *301*

    A.   *Preliminary Discussion 301*
    B.   *The Efficient Set Without Short-Selling or Risk-free*
      Securities 303

VIII. Market Equilibrium: Mathematical Treatment   *305*

    A.   *Consumption-Investment Decisions and Equilibrium*
      Prices 305
    B.   *Counting Equations and Unknowns 313*
    C.   *Market Equilibrium Without Complete Agreement 314*

IX. Conclusions   *319*

CHAPTER 9

The Two-Parameter Model: Empirical Tests   320

I. Introduction   *320*
II. Testing the Model: General Discussion   *321*

    A.   *Hypotheses about Expected Returns 321*
    B.   *Competing Hypotheses 322*
    C.   *The Portfolio Approach to the Tests 323*
    D.   *Least Squares Coefficients as Portfolio Returns 326*
    E.   *Getting the Most Powerful Tests: General Discussion 329*
    F.   *The Reliability of the Least Squares Portfolio Returns 336*
    G.   *Capital Market Efficiency: The Behavior of Returns Through*
      Time 338

III. Details of the Methodology   *340*

    A.   *Application of the Approach to the Equally Weighted Market*
      Portfolio m 341
    B.   *The Portfolio Approach to Estimating Risk Measures 343*

IV. Results   *356*

    A.   *Preliminary Discussion 356*
    B.   *Tests of the Major Hypotheses 362*
    C.   *The Sharpe-Lintner Hypothesis 368*

V. Some Applications of the Measured Risk-Return
Relationships   *370*

    A.   *A Two-Factor Market Model 371*
    B.   *Market Efficiency and the Two-Factor Models 375*
    C.   *Market Efficiency and Company-Specific Information 376*
    D.   *Portfolio Selection and Performance Evaluation 380*

VI. Conclusion   *382*

References   *383*
Index   *389*

Preface

Among the various fields of economics, finance is somewhat unique in terms of the correspondence between theory and evidence. The purpose of this book is to introduce the theory of finance and the empirical tests of the theory. I concentrate on that part of finance which is concerned with portfolio decisions by investors and the pricing of securities in capital markets.

My view is that the student's motivation to master a theory is enhanced when evidence is presented to show that the theory has some power to explain real world phenomena. Moreover, my classroom experience is that pointless squabbles about the realism of a theory or the assumptions from which it is drawn can be avoided if relevant empirical evidence is presented along with the theory. This is the approach taken in this book.

The first four chapters of the book provide the background statistical material. The goals are (a) to review the statistical tools that are necessary for any nonsuperficial study of finance and (b) to familiarize the reader with the descriptive evidence on the behavior of securities prices that forms the empirical foundation for the theory of finance and the formal tests of that theory. The approach in these chapters is to introduce statistical concepts first and then to use them to describe the behavior of returns on securities. Thus, Chapter 1 studies probability distributions and the properties of samples and then uses the concepts to examine distributions of common stock returns. Chapters 2 and 3 take up the statistical tools that are needed to study the relationships between returns on securities and portfolios. To motivate the study of these tools, some of the rudiments of portfolio theory are introduced in Chapter 2. Chapter 4 uses the statistical concepts presented in Chapters 2 and 3 to study empirically the "market sensitivity" of New York

Stock Exchange common stocks, examining evidence on the extent to which the returns on individual securities are related to market returns.

The core of the book is in Chapters 5 to 9. Three related topics are treated: (a) theory and evidence on capital market efficiency, (b) portfolio theory, and (c) theory and evidence on the relationship between expected return and risk. In an efficient capital market, prices of securities "fully reflect" available information. Chapters 5 and 6 discuss theory and empirical work on capital market efficiency; the former is concerned with the stock market, the latter with the bond market. Chapter 7 develops in detail the portfolio model introduced in Chapter 2 and presents empirical evidence on the effects of diversification in reducing risk. Chapter 8 then considers the characteristics of equilibrium security prices when investors make portfolio decisions according to the model of Chapter 7. The relationship between expected return and risk that comes out of the model of capital market equilibrium in Chapter 8 is put to the test in Chapter 9.

Problems for the reader are scattered through the text. The word "scattered" is used advisedly. The problems are not tucked neatly at the ends of sections, but rather appear whenever I want to reinforce a point or give pause for thought. The problems are an integral part of the text; results contained in them are often referred to in later parts of the text. In light of this, fairness and convenience argue that answers to problems follow the problems in the text. This raises the temptation—and thus the probability—that the problems will not be treated as such, but it is in the student's interest to resist this temptation. The problems allow the reader to keep tabs on his understanding of the material and so to avoid unwarranted euphoria.

The technical prerequisites for reading this book are minimal. Mathematics beyond elementary algebra appears only briefly in two chapters and is not critical to understanding the important material in either chapter. Moreover, I try always to supplement even elementary mathematical arguments with verbal discussions; in cases where the details of a mathematical argument can be skipped, this is so indicated. The book is, however, heavy with formal notation, and the reader is well advised to master the notation as quickly as possible.

Although finance is properly regarded as a branch of economics, the ambitious reader could understand this book without previous formal exposure to economics. Financial economics is, however, easier to grasp if one has some familiarity with habits of economic analysis. Thus, although no specific material is needed, some prior exposure to economics is helpful. Likewise, the book reviews the statistical concepts that it uses, but the presentation is more effective if the reader has had some previous exposure to statistics, though not necessarily to the specific statistical concepts that are most useful in finance.

This book is meant to be an introduction to finance, with approximately equal emphasis on theory and evidence. As with any introduction, some picking and choosing of topics is necessary. I have chosen to focus on topics where there is sufficient empirical evidence to draw coherent conclusions about the descriptive power of a theory. I do not claim to cover all the topics that meet this criterion, and one can argue that my choices reflect much personal prejudice. The goal of the book is met, however, if I familiarize the reader with the common methods of analysis in finance sufficiently to tackle original works, both those already available and those yet to come, on his own.

Finally, I am pleased to acknowledge the help of Linda Huegel, who typed several versions of the manuscript; proofreading was provided by Agnes Farris, Vicky Longawa, and Jane Miller. Nicholas Gonedes and Harry Roberts, my colleagues at the University of Chicago, made many valuable comments on the manuscript. My debt to the pioneers of modern finance, who did the original work on which this book is based, is obvious.

FOUNDATIONS

OF

FINANCE

The Behavior of Stock Market Returns

In introducing the theory of finance, our first step is to review some statistical concepts and some of the properties of normal distributions. These are the tools for the empirical work of this chapter, and they are used repeatedly throughout the rest of the book. Next we define what is meant by "return." Then the history of return variability and the nature of distributions of stock market returns are studied. This empirical evidence is important background for the work of later chapters.

I. Some Statistical Concepts

A. Random Variables

When observations of a variable can be thought of as governed by a probability distribution, the variable is called random or stochastic. The idea is that before an observation is generated, the value of the variable to be obtained is to some extent unknown (random or stochastic), and the only way we can characterize what will be observed is in terms of the probability distribution that governs the variable.

For example, the return next month on a share of IBM common stock is unknown now and can only be described in terms of a probability distribution, perhaps normal, of possible values. The form of the distribution of the return depends on the interactions of complex economic phenomena, themselves random variables, and the "drawing" from the distribution of the return is the result of trading among investors. Nevertheless, the return is properly thought of as a variable whose observed value is governed by a probability distribution, and thus the return is a random variable.

To denote a random variable, we include a tilde ($\sim$) over the symbol used to identify the variable. When we refer to a specific value of the variable, the tilde is dropped. For example, the return to be observed next month on a share of IBM might be denoted $\tilde{R}$, while a specific possible value of the return is labeled R.

B. The Mean

Although here and elsewhere one commonly sees the phrase "the normal distribution," the term "normal" in fact refers to a whole family of probability distributions. The two parameters used to distinguish one normal distribution from another are the mean and the standard deviation. We review first the general definition of the mean of a probability distribution (whether normal or not). Since its interpretation is simpler, we consider first the mean of the distribution of a discrete variable.

The mean or "expected value" of a discrete random variable $\tilde{x}$ is

$$E(\tilde{x}) = \sum_x x \, P(x), \tag{1}$$

where the notation $\sum_x$ means "sum over all legitimate values of x," and where $P(x)$ is the probability that a drawing from the distribution of the random variable $\tilde{x}$ will yield the specific value x. Thus, $E(\tilde{x})$, the expected value of the random variable $\tilde{x}$, is the sum, over all possible values of x, of x times the probability of x. Equivalently, the expected value is the weighted average of the different possible values of the variable, with each value weighted by its probability. Note that since the sum is over the specific possible values of x, there are no tildes on the right of the equality in equation (1). Note also that the result of the summation in (1), the mean or expected value of the random variable $\tilde{x}$, is not itself a random variable. It is a unique number whose value is determined by the properties of the distribution of $\tilde{x}$. In short, $E(\tilde{x})$ is a parameter of the distribution of $\tilde{x}$.

The mean or expected value of a continuous random variable $\tilde{x}$ is

$$E(\tilde{x}) = \int_x x \, p(x) \, dx, \tag{2}$$

where $p(x)$ is the probability density function for the random variable $\tilde{x}$ (that is, $p(x)$ assigns positive weights to different possible values of x that reflect the likelihoods of observing these different values in a random drawing), and where, strictly speaking, the integral notation $\int_x dx$ calls for the computation of the area under the function $f(x) = x\,p(x)$. Although it is somewhat non-rigorous, no harm is done and the right idea is conveyed if we interpret (2) in roughly the same terms as (1). Thus, we interpret the mean or expected value of a continuous random variable $\tilde{x}$ as the weighted average of the different possible values of the variable, with each value weighted by its likelihood. Note again that because the expected value is computed over all possible specific values of $\tilde{x}$, there are no tildes on the right of the equality in (2). As in equation (1), $E(\tilde{x})$ is a parameter of the distribution of $\tilde{x}$; that is, it is a unique number whose value is determined by the form of the probability density function $p(x)$.

C. The Standard Deviation

If $\tilde{x}$ is a discrete random variable, its variance is defined as

$$\sigma^2(\tilde{x}) = E([\tilde{x} - E(\tilde{x})]^2) = \sum_x [x - E(\tilde{x})]^2 P(x). \tag{3}$$

Thus the variance is the mean or expected value (again indicated by the symbol E) of the function $g(\tilde{x}) = [\tilde{x} - E(\tilde{x})]^2$, the squared deviation of the random variable $\tilde{x}$ from its mean $E(\tilde{x})$. Equation (3) says that the variance of a discrete random variable $\tilde{x}$ is the weighted average of the different possible values of $[x - E(\tilde{x})]^2$, with each value weighted by its probability $P(x)$.

The variance of a continuous random variable $\tilde{x}$ is

$$\sigma^2(\tilde{x}) = E([\tilde{x} - E(\tilde{x})]^2) = \int_x [x - E(\tilde{x})]^2 p(x)\,dx. \tag{4}$$

We interpret (4) as saying that the variance of $\tilde{x}$ is the weighted average of $[x - E(\tilde{x})]^2$, where the weight assigned to $[x - E(\tilde{x})]^2$ is $p(x)$, the probability density or likelihood of the specific value of x.

The variance is a measure of the dispersion of the probability distribution of $\tilde{x}$. It measures the average variability of successive random drawings from the distribution of $\tilde{x}$ about the mean of the distribution $E(\tilde{x})$. The variance is in units of the variable squared; that is, by definition, the variance measures the squared variability of $\tilde{x}$ about its mean. By taking the square root of the variance, we transform it into a measure of dispersion, the standard deviation $\sigma(\tilde{x})$, which is in the same units as $\tilde{x}$.

$$\sigma(\tilde{x}) = \sqrt{\sigma^2(\tilde{x})}. \tag{5}$$

D. *Characterization of Normal Distributions by Their Means and Standard Deviations*

For any normally distributed random variable $\tilde{x}$, the probability that a random drawing is within one standard deviation of the mean, that is, in the interval

$$E(\tilde{x}) - \sigma(\tilde{x}) \leqslant \tilde{x} \leqslant E(\tilde{x}) + \sigma(\tilde{x}),$$

is .6826 and is the same for all normally distributed variables. Likewise, the probability that a random drawing is in the interval

$$E(\tilde{x}) - 2\sigma(\tilde{x}) \leqslant \tilde{x} \leqslant E(\tilde{x}) + 2\sigma(\tilde{x})$$

is .9550 and is the same for all normally distributed variables. The important general property is that for normal distributions, the probability that a random drawing will be in the range

$$E(\tilde{x}) - \phi\sigma(\tilde{x}) \leqslant \tilde{x} \leqslant E(\tilde{x}) + \phi\sigma(\tilde{x})$$

depends only on ϕ, and not on $E(\tilde{x})$ and $\sigma(\tilde{x})$.

Equivalently, for any normally distributed random variable $\tilde{x}$, the transformed variable

$$\tilde{r} = \frac{\tilde{x} - E(\tilde{x})}{\sigma(\tilde{x})},$$

which is just $\tilde{x}$ measured in units of standard deviations from its mean, has the unit normal distribution, that is, the normal distribution with mean equal to 0.0 and standard deviation equal to 1.0. Thus, if we know the distribution of $\tilde{r}$ (it is shown in Figure 1.1 and tabulated in Table 1.8 at the end of the

FIGURE 1.1

The Unit Normal Distribution

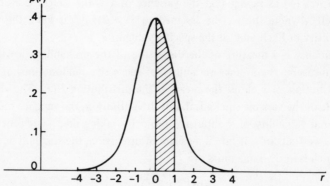

chapter), all we have to know about any other normal variable $\tilde{x}$ is its mean and standard deviation. Given the mean and standard deviation of $\tilde{x}$, the probability associated with any specified interval of $\tilde{x}$ can be determined from the distribution of the unit normal variable $\tilde{r}$. In short, normal distributions are two-parameter distributions; knowledge of the mean and standard deviation of a normal distribution is sufficient to completely characterize the distribution.

This property of normally distributed variables is important in the portfolio model of later chapters. The reason is intuitive. If the probability distributions of returns on portfolios are normal, the portfolio selection problem is simplified, since alternative portfolios can be ranked in terms of the means and standard deviations of the distributions of their returns. These two parameters are sufficient inputs for rational portfolio choice.

E.   The Sample Mean and Standard Deviation

In real-world data analysis, the mean and standard deviation of a random variable are almost never known, but rather must be estimated from a sample. For example, suppose we are willing to assume that month-by-month returns on a share of IBM common stock are random drawings from some, perhaps normal, probability distribution. The population mean and standard deviation of this distribution are unknown. If we want information about them, it must be obtained from sample estimates. The computation of such sample estimates is the next concern.

In this book a sample mean is always computed as

$$\bar{x} = \sum_{i=1}^{T} x_i/T, \tag{6}$$

where T is the sample size (the number of observations in the sample), x_i is the ith observation or drawing in the sample, and $\sum_{i=1}^{T}$ is read "the sum from $i = 1$ to $i = T$." Thus the sample mean is the simple average of the observations in the sample.

It is instructive to compare equation (6) with equations (1) and (2), which define the population means of discrete and continuous variables. In (1), for example, each different possible value of x is weighted by its probability, which is not generally the same for different values of x. In computing the sample mean, however, each sample observation is weighted equally, that is, by $1/T$. In weighting the observations equally, the presumption is not that each different value of x is equally likely, but rather that sample relative frequencies of different values of x approximate population probabilities.

Then, weighting each sample observation by $1/T$ has the effect of weighting observations that have different values by their relative frequencies.

Sample variances are computed in a manner analogous to equation (5); that is,

$$s^2(x) = \sum_{i=1}^{T} (x_i - \bar{x})^2/(T - 1). \tag{7}$$

This is not exactly the average of $(x_i - \bar{x})^2$, since we divide by $T - 1$ instead of T. The reason for this is discussed in Problem II.B.7 of Chapter 2. The sample standard deviation is just the square root of the sample variance:

$$s(x) = \sqrt{s^2(x)}. \tag{8}$$

F. Testing for Normality: The Studentized Range

DEFINITION

In real-world data analysis, not only are the true mean and standard deviation unknown, but the type of distribution that generated a sample is also unknown. For example, if we have a sample of month-by-month returns on a share of IBM common stock, we may be willing to assume that the returns are drawings from some probability distribution, but the type of distribution is unknown. A useful statistic* for judging whether the distribution that generated a sample is normal is the studentized range. The studentized range is

$$SR = \frac{\text{Max}(x_i) - \text{Min}(x_i)}{s(x)}; \tag{9}$$

that is, the studentized range is the range of observations in the sample, the maximum minus the minimum, measured in units of the sample standard deviation.

Since the studentized range depends so much on the extreme observations in a sample, it is sensitive to departures from normality where the probabilities associated with observations far from the mean are either higher or lower than if the variable were normally distributed. This turns out to be relevant for distributions of common stock returns, which are "fat-tailed" relative to normal distributions; that is, where the frequencies of large positive and large negative returns are higher than would be expected from normal distributions.

PROBABILITY DISTRIBUTIONS FOR SAMPLE STATISTICS

Samples of data from a given probability distribution differ from one another, and in general a sample does not reproduce the characteristics of the

*Statistic is the general term for any number calculated from a sample.

distribution completely accurately. Because of variation from sample to sample, any sample statistic (e.g., the sample mean, the sample standard deviation, or the studentized range) is itself a drawing from a probability distribution. The statistic is a random variable. It is common in the statistics literature to conceptualize the distribution of a sample statistic as the distribution generated when values of the statistic are computed from an indefinitely large number of samples of given size from the specified distribution. For this reason, the probability distribution of a statistic is called the sampling distribution of the statistic. However one chooses to dramatize its origins, the distribution of a sample statistic is no different from any other probability distribution.

When we talk about a statistic as a random variable, the tilde notation is used, but when we refer to an observed value of the statistic, the tilde is dropped. Thus, before a sample is drawn, the unknown sample mean, variance, and studentized range are expressed as

$$\tilde{\bar{x}} = \sum_{i=1}^{T} \tilde{x}_i / T, \tag{10}$$

$$s^2(\tilde{x}) = \sum_{i=1}^{T} (\tilde{x}_i - \tilde{\bar{x}})^2 / (T - 1), \tag{11}$$

$$\tilde{SR} = \frac{\text{Max}\,(\tilde{x}_i) - \text{Min}\,(\tilde{x}_i)}{s(\tilde{x})}. \tag{12}$$

The notation is meant to convey the idea that before a sample is drawn, the sample mean, standard deviation, and studentized range are random variables because the T sample observations, $\tilde{x}_i, i = 1, \ldots, T$, are random variables. When we refer to specific values of the statistics obtained from a sample, the notation in (6), (7), and (9) is used; that is, the tildes that appear in (10), (11), and (12) are omitted. This is again just the way that we distinguish any random variable from a specific value of the variable.

INFERENCES ABOUT NORMALITY FROM THE STUDENTIZED RANGE

We see in a later chapter that when samples of size T are drawn randomly from a normal distribution, the distribution of the sample mean is readily determined. The sampling distribution of the studentized range is more difficult to specify. Fortunately, fractiles of the distribution have been computed, and tables of these fractiles are what one uses in applications.

Table 1.9 at the end of the chapter shows fractiles of the lower and upper tails of the sampling distribution of the studentized range when the studentized range is computed from random samples from a normal distribution. The interpretation of the fractiles shown in Table 1.9 is as follows. If

$SR(p, T)$ is the p fractile of the distribution of SR in samples of size T, then the probability of observing a value of SR equal to or less than $SR(p, T)$ in a sample of size T from a normal distribution is p. Alternatively, $1 - p$ is the probability that a sample of size T from a normal distribution will have a studentized range greater than $SR(p, T)$. In intuitive terms, if we take many samples of size T from a normal distribution and compute the studentized range for each sample, then we expect that the proportion p of the sample studentized ranges will be equal to or less than $SR(p, T)$, and we expect that the proportion $1 - p$ of the sample studentized ranges will be greater than $SR(p, T)$.

For example, Table 1.9 says that in a sample of 100 from a normal distribution, the probability that the studentized range will be equal to or less than 6.36 is .99. In intuitive terms, when sample studentized ranges are computed for repeated samples of 100 from a normal distribution, we expect that 99 percent of the sample studentized ranges will be equal to or less than 6.36, and we expect that only 1 percent of the sample studentized ranges will be greater than 6.36.

PROBLEM I.F

1. Table 1.9 shows that any given fractile of the distribution of the studentized range, that is, the value of $SR(p, T)$ for any specific p, is larger the larger the sample size T. Give an explanation for this phenomenon.

ANSWER

1. Values of a normal random variable far from the mean in either direction have low probability. Such extreme observations are more likely to occur in larger samples than in smaller samples. Since the studentized range depends directly on the range of the observations in a sample, that is, the difference between the largest and smallest observations, the distribution of SR shifts toward larger values for larger samples when the samples are from a normal distribution.

Suppose now that we have a random sample of data—for example, month-by-month returns on a share of IBM common stock—and we wish to judge how likely it is that the sample came from a normal distribution. Suppose we compute the studentized range for the sample and that Table 1.9 says it corresponds to a fractile somewhere between .1 and .9. Such a sample studentized range is quite likely if the sample came from a normal distribution. In repeated samples from a normal distribution, the studentized ranges for 80 percent of the samples are expected to be between the .1 and .9 fractiles of the relevant distribution of SR in Table 1.9. On the other hand, if the computed *SR* for IBM corresponds to a fractile far into the tails of the distribution of *SR* in Table 1.9, then the sample studentized range is unlikely if the sample came from a normal distribution. In repeated samples from a normal distribution, only a small fraction of the samples are expected to produce extreme values of *SR*. If the sample *SR* for IBM seems too large, we might reject the normality hypothesis and conclude instead that the sample came from a distribution where the probabilities of observations far from the mean are higher than if the distribution were normal. On the other hand, a low value of *SR* might lead us to conclude that the sample came from a distribution that is "thin-tailed" relative to a normal distribution.

To reject the hypothesis that a sample of data is from a normal distribution always involves some chance of error. To say that very large or very small values of *SR* are unlikely if the distribution is normal is not to say that such values are impossible. On the other hand, to accept the hypothesis that a sample is from a normal distribution also involves some chance of error. Nonnormal distributions can generate samples which, by chance, look much like those from a normal distribution.

It is the nature of empirical research that inferences are made with some degree of uncertainty. A hypothesis is never proved to be true or false with certainty. Rather, the careful researcher always states that a hypothesis is accepted or rejected with some degree of confidence, usually summarized by a probability statement. For example, if the studentized range for a sample of 100 observations is 6.4, the researcher might say something like:

> The probability that the studentized range in a sample of 100 from a normal distribution is 6.4 or larger is less than 1 percent. On the basis of this, the hypothesis that the data are from a normal distribution is rejected.

If the researcher carefully states the conditions under which a sample has been obtained, specifies the assumptions underlying the statistical techniques that have been used, and presents the results obtained in sufficient detail, then the reader can reevaluate the results and conclusions based on his own assessment of the losses involved if a true hypothesis is rejected or a false hypothesis is accepted.

G.   Statistical Models and Reality

Since we are ready to take a look at some stock market data, it is appropriate to end this section with one more methodological point. When a hypothesis or model is suggested as a description of data, the model is not meant to be an exact representation of reality. Rather, the hypothesis or model is proposed as a convenient and useful approximation of the world which explains real-world data better than competing models. Indeed, the word "model" is meant to convey the notion of an approximation.

For example, we hypothesize or propose the normal distribution as a model for the month-by-month returns on New York Stock Exchange common stocks. The usefulness of this model is properly judged by how well it represents samples of returns and by whether it provides better descriptions of such samples than other possible models. This is one of the questions that we now take up. First, however, we must define precisely what we mean by the term "return."

II. The Definition of Return

Important data for the empirical work of this book are the monthly returns on all New York Stock Exchange (NYSE) common stocks from February 1926 through June 1968, as compiled by the Center for Research in Security Prices (CRSP) of the University of Chicago. The return for month t on a given stock is

$$R_{it} = \frac{d_{it} + (p'_{it} - p_{i,t-1})}{p_{i,t-1}} = \frac{d_{it}}{p_{i,t-1}} + \frac{p'_{it} - p_{i,t-1}}{p_{i,t-1}}, \tag{13}$$

where

$\quad d_{it}$ = dividend per share of the common stock of firm i from the end of month $t-1$ to the end of month t;

$\quad p_{i,t-1}$ = price per share of the common stock of firm i at the end of month $t-1$; and

$\quad p'_{it}$ = market value at the end of month t of one share of firm i purchased at the end of month $t-1$.

In words, the return for month t is the dividend plus the capital gain, all divided by the initial price. In this book, returns on securities always include both cash payments and capital gains. The capital gain is included even though the security may not be sold at the end of the period. The reasoning is that the investor can realize the capital gain by selling the security. If he does not sell, this is treated as an implicit decision to sell and then immediately repurchase the security.

The dividend d_{it} and the end-of-month "price" p'_{it} are in terms of an equivalent beginning-of-month share; that is, they are adjusted when necessary to abstract from the effects of capital changes, such as stock splits and stock dividends, that change the number of shares held by a stockholder but do not affect his claims on the firm's assets and earnings. For example, if there is a two-for-one split between the end of month $t-1$ and the end of month t, the end-of-month "price" p'_{it} used in (13) is twice the quoted end-of-month price, p_{it}, so that p'_{it} is the end-of-month market value of one share owned at the beginning of the month. Likewise, d_{it} represents the dividends that accrue during month t on one share of common stock held at the end of month $t-1$.

Finally, equation (13) also can be used to define the return on security i for a day, a week, from transaction to transaction, and so forth, simply by changing the interpretation of the time interval between successive values of t.

III.   Indexes or Portfolios of Stock Market Returns

To get some feeling for the general behavior of securities returns, we examine first an index of the monthly returns on NYSE common stocks. For any month t, the value of the index (call it R_{mt}) is just the average of the returns from the end of month $t-1$ to the end of month t on all securities listed on the exchange at the end of month $t-1$. Equivalently, in Chapter 2 we show that R_{mt} is the return for month t obtained by investing the same proportion of investment funds in each security on the exchange at the end of month $t-1$. The time series of R_{mt}, that is, the sequence of values of R_{mt} for successive months t, is the sequence of returns on a portfolio where each security in the portfolio is given an equal weight at the beginning of each month. As an investment rule, this portfolio implies monthly rebalancing; that is, each month funds must be shifted among securities in order to equalize the proportions invested in each security.

By way of contrast, and for later reference, we can compare the equally weighted index with a value-weighted index or portfolio. The value-weighted portfolio return for month t is again the weighted average of the returns on individual securities but the weight given to a security is the ratio of the total market value of all of its outstanding units at the end of month $t-1$ to the total market value of all securities. Thus, a value-weighted index is the return on a portfolio where each security is weighted by its share of the market. In a value-weighted index, aside from the effects of new issues of securities and delistings of old securities, the changes in weights through time correspond to changes in market value. Thus, if one purchases such a value-weighted portfolio, it is never necessary to rebalance holdings of individual securities.

IV. Average Return and Variability: A Quick Look

Table 1.1 shows the sample means and standard deviations of the monthly returns R_{mt} on the equally weighted portfolio for the overall period February 1926–June 1968, for the periods before and after 1945, and for eight subperiods which, except for the last, cover five years each. The average monthly returns in Table 1.1 are generally high relative to returns on what

TABLE 1.1

Sample Means, $\overline{R}_m$, and Standard Deviations, $s(R_m)$, of R_{mt}, the Monthly Returns
on the Equally Weighted Portfolio, February 1926–June 1968

STATISTIC	PERIOD		
	2/26– 6/68	2/26– 12/45	1/46– 6/68
$\overline{R}_m$	.0138	.0162	.0117
$s(R_m)$	.0853	.1165	.0413

STATISTIC	PERIOD							
	2/26– 12/30	1/31– 12/35	1/36– 12/40	1/41– 12/45	1/46– 12/50	1/51– 12/55	1/56– 12/60	1/61– 6/68
$\overline{R}_m$	–.0019	.0313	.0075	.0274	.0077	.0147	.0090	.0141
$s(R_m)$	.0686	.1822	.1135	.0577	.0520	.0325	.0337	.0433

are usually thought of as less risky securities. For example, the average monthly return on NYSE stocks for the postwar period is 1.17 percent, whereas the average monthly return on U.S. Treasury bills with one month to maturity is .18 percent. This comparison seems consistent with the reasonable hypothesis that, on average, the market compensates investors for bearing risk, a hypothesis that we develop and test in detail in Chapters 7–9.

The high average return on common stocks is matched by correspondingly high variability of returns. In Table 1.1 the average monthly return for the 1926–1968 period is 1.38 percent, and the standard deviation of monthly returns is 8.53 percent. If we assume for the moment that the distribution of $\tilde{R}_{mt}$ is normal and treat the sample mean and standard deviation for the overall period as the population parameters, then for this portfolio of equally weighted stocks, the expected value of the increase in wealth in any given month is 1.38 percent, but the probability is about .32 that the actual change in wealth for the month will be less than $E(\tilde{R}_{mt}) - \sigma(\tilde{R}_{mt}) = .0138 - .0853 =$ $-.0715$ (that is, a decline of 7.15 percent) or greater than $E(\tilde{R}_{mt}) + \sigma(\tilde{R}_{mt}) =$ $.0991$ (that is, an increase of 9.91 percent). The probability is about .045 that in a given month wealth will decline by more than 15.68 percent or increase by more than 18.44 percent; that is, with probability about .045, the return will be outside the interval

$$E(\tilde{R}_{mt}) - 2\sigma(\tilde{R}_{mt}) \leqslant \tilde{R}_{mt} \leqslant E(\tilde{R}_{mt}) + 2\sigma(\tilde{R}_{mt}).$$

V. The History of Return Variability

The results in Table 1.1 indicate that the variability of returns in the post–World War II period is substantially lower than in the prewar period. The postwar standard deviation of R_{mt}, 4.13 percent per month, is about one-third the standard deviation of the war and prewar period, 11.65 percent per month.

King (1966) and Blume (1968) gave the first extensive documentation of the decrease in the variability of NYSE returns from the prewar to the post-war period. Blume reported that of the 251 common stocks listed on the NYSE continuously from December 30, 1926, through December 30, 1960, 247 had higher variances of monthly returns for the period prior to 1944 than for 1944–1960. Thus, the decrease in variability applies to individual securities as well as to the market index.

Officer (1971) later questioned the simple prewar-postwar dichotomy. His suspicions were aroused by the fact, apparent in Table 1.1, that the variability of returns from 1926 to 1929 is more like that of the post–World War II period than like that of the 1930s. He hypothesized that the 1930s was an unusual period and that in the 1940s the variability of returns simply reverted to normal levels. To test this hypothesis, Officer computed the returns on the Dow-Jones Industrial Average (DJIA) from 1897 to 1925. The DJIA was a portfolio of 12 stocks until August 1914, when the number of stocks was increased to 20. Using the returns on the DJIA for 1897–1925 and the returns R_{mt} on the equally weighted CRSP portfolio for January 1926–June 1969, he then computed a time series of standard deviations of monthly returns for overlapping one-year periods. Thus, the first estimate uses the monthly returns for 1/97–12/97, the second uses 2/97–1/98, and so forth. The resulting time series of standard deviations of one-month returns is shown in Figure 1.2. In the figure, each standard deviation is dated, arbitrarily, at the seventh month of the 12 one-month returns from which it is computed.

Figure 1.2 supports Officer's hypothesis. For the entire pre-1929 period,

FIGURE 1.2
Behavior of the One-Year Standard Deviation of the Monthly Returns on the Market Index, 1897–1969

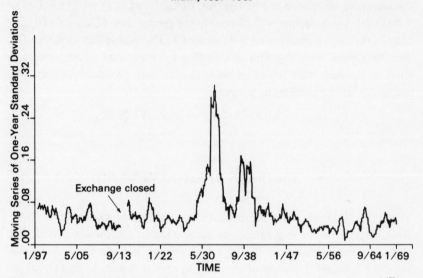

Source: Robert R. Officer, "A Time Series Examination of the Market Factor of the New York Stock Exchange" (Ph.D. dissertation, University of Chicago, 1971). Reprinted by permission.

FIGURE 1.3
One-Year Standard Deviations of the Market Index and of Percentage Changes in Industrial Production, 1919–1968

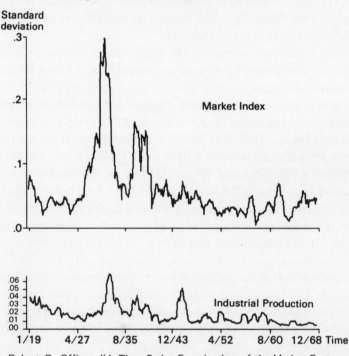

Source: Robert R. Officer, "A Time Series Examination of the Market Factor of the New York Stock Exchange" (Ph.D. dissertation, University of Chicago, 1971). Reprinted by permission.

the variability of returns is more like that of the post-1940 period than like that of the 1930s. Moreover, within the 1930s there seem to be two distinct subperiods, corresponding approximately to the sharp contractions of the two depressions, with the observed increase in the variability of returns more severe in the first. Figure 1.3, also reproduced from Officer (1971), compares the standard deviations of monthly percentage changes in industrial production, computed from overlapping 12-month periods, with the corresponding standard deviations of stock market returns. The periods of greatly increased volatility in stock market returns during the 1930s were also periods of great volatility in industrial production.

Finally, almost everyone is aware that the 1930s was a period of great depression, both in economic activity and in the level of stock market prices. But low levels of economic activity and stock prices do not necessarily imply high variability of returns and changes in production. Thus, Officer's results indicate that the 1930s was not only a period of unusual depression but also a period of unusual uncertainty.

VI. Distributions of Stock Market Returns

A. Motivation and Theory

Evidence on the form of the distributions of returns on securities and portfolios is important for several reasons. For the investor, the form of the distribution is a major factor in determining the risk of investment. For example, although two different possible distributions for returns may have the same mean and standard deviation, the probabilities of returns much different from the mean may be much greater for one than for the other. The form of the distribution is also important from an economic point of view, since, as illustrated by Figure 1.3, evidence on the behavior of stock market returns is indirect information on the underlying economic factors that trigger returns. For example, if very large returns occur quite frequently, one might infer that the economic factors triggering returns on securities are themselves subject to frequent and sudden shocks over time.

The first complete development of a model for distributions of security price changes is credited to Bachelier (1900). Bachelier's work went unnoticed, and his model was derived independently, but much later, by Osborne (1959). Bachelier and Osborne began by assuming that price changes* from transac-

---

*In this paragraph, the term "price change" is meant to include both dividends and change in price. For short intervals, like a day, dividends are relatively infrequent, so that the term "price change" refers to the quantity of interest.

tion to transaction in an individual security are random drawings from the same distribution. In formal terms, this model assumes that successive price changes are independent and identically distributed. The model further assumes that transactions are uniformly spread across time. If the number of transactions per day, week, or month is large, then price changes across these intervals are sums of many independent, identically distributed drawings. The central-limit theorem of statistics leads us to expect that the distribution of a sum of independent, identically distributed drawings generally approaches a normal distribution as the number of items in the sum is increased. Thus, in the Bachelier-Osborne model, distributions of daily, weekly, and monthly price changes are approximately normal.

PROBLEM VI.A

1. Assume that no dividends are paid on security *i*. Convince yourself that if successive price changes are identically distributed, successive returns, as defined by equation (13), are not. Conversely, convince yourself that if successive returns are identically distributed, successive price changes are not.

ANSWER

1. At any time $t - 1$, the price change $\tilde{p}_{it} - p_{i,t-1}$ and the return $\tilde{R}_{it} = (\tilde{p}_{it} - p_{i,t-1})/p_{i,t-1}$ are random variables because $\tilde{p}_{it}$ is unknown. The price $p_{i,t-1}$ is known at time $t - 1$ and can be treated as a constant.

If successive price changes have mean $E(\tilde{p}_{it} - p_{i,t-1})$ and standard deviation $\sigma(\tilde{p}_{it} - p_{i,t-1})$, then the return

$$\tilde{R}_{it} = \frac{\tilde{p}_{it} - p_{i,t-1}}{p_{i,t-1}}$$

has expected value

$$E(\tilde{R}_{it}) = \frac{1}{p_{i,t-1}} E(\tilde{p}_{it} - p_{i,t-1})$$

and standard deviation

$$\sigma(\tilde{R}_{it}) = \frac{1}{p_{i,t-1}} \sigma(\tilde{p}_{it} - p_{i,t-1}).$$

Here we have used the fact that the expected value of a constant times a random variable, in this case $1/p_{i,t-1}$ times $(\tilde{p}_{it} - p_{i,t-1})$, is the constant multiplied by the expected value of the variable. Likewise, the standard deviation of a constant times a random variable is the absolute value of the constant multiplied by the standard deviation of the variable. Such operations with constants and random variables are discussed in Chapter 2.

If successive price changes are identically distributed, this means that $E(\tilde{p}_{it} - p_{i,t-1})$ and $\sigma(\tilde{p}_{it} - p_{i,t-1})$ have the same values for all t, which in turn means that $E(\tilde{R}_{it})$ and $\sigma(\tilde{R}_{it})$ are inversely related to $p_{i,t-1}$. Alternatively, if successive returns are identically distributed, this means that $E(\tilde{R}_{it})$ and $\sigma(\tilde{R}_{it})$ have the same values for all t, which means that $E(\tilde{p}_{it} - p_{i,t-1})$ and $\sigma(\tilde{p}_{it} - p_{i,t-1})$ are directly related to the value of $p_{i,t-1}$.

In later chapters, when we take up portfolio models and more advanced models of price behavior in the stock market, it becomes clear that it makes somewhat more economic sense to formulate models of price determination in terms of returns rather than price changes. A given price change is a different economic quantity, depending on the initial investment. For example, a one-month price change of $1 on a beginning-of-month investment or price of $10 is a different economic quantity than a price change of $1 on an initial price of $100. We now discuss a model for returns analogous to the Bachelier-Osborne model for price changes discussed above.

Whereas the price change for month t is the sum of intermediate daily price changes, the return for month t, as defined by equation (13), depends on the product of the intermediate daily returns, where the daily returns are also as defined by (13). For example, if there are twenty trading days in month t, the return for the month on security i is related to the 20 daily returns (call them $r_1, r_2, \ldots, r_{20}$) as follows:

$$1 + R_{it} = (1 + r_1)(1 + r_2) \ldots (1 + r_{20}). \tag{14}$$

To interpret equation (14), first note that, from equation (13),

$$1 + R_{it} = \frac{p_{i,t-1} + d_{it} + (p'_{it} - p_{i,t-1})}{p_{i,t-1}} = \frac{d_{it} + p'_{it}}{p_{i,t-1}}; \tag{15}$$

that is, $1 + R_{it}$ is the value at the end of month t of $1 invested in security i at the end of month $t - 1$. This end-of-month value of a $1 initial investment is also just the cumulation of the consecutive daily returns. Thus, the value of a $1 initial investment at the end of the first day is $1 + r_1$. If this $1 + r_1$ is reinvested—that is, if the investor continues to hold the security—then the value of his investment at the end of day 2 is $(1 + r_1)(1 + r_2)$, which is also just the value at the end of day 2 of $1 invested at the beginning of the month. The value of a $1 initial investment at the end of day 3 is $(1 + r_1)$ $(1 + r_2)(1 + r_3)$, which leads eventually to equation (14). In general, if R_{it} is the return on an initial investment of $1 for some period of time (e.g., a day, week, month, or year) and if r_k, $k = 1, 2, \ldots, K$, represent the returns for intermediate periods, then

$$1 + R_{it} = (1 + r_1)(1 + r_2) \ldots (1 + r_K). \tag{16}$$

Instead of assuming that successive price changes are independent and identically distributed, suppose successive values of $\tilde{r}_k$ are independent and identically distributed.* Then successive values of $ln(1 + \tilde{r}_k)$ are also independent and identically distributed, where $ln(1 + \tilde{r}_k)$ is the natural logarithm of $1 + \tilde{r}_k$. Since the log of a product is the sum of the logs,

$$ln(1 + \tilde{R}_{it}) = ln(1 + \tilde{r}_1) + ln(1 + \tilde{r}_2) + \ldots + ln(1 + \tilde{r}_K) = \sum_{k=1}^{K} ln(1 + \tilde{r}_k), \tag{17}$$

the cental-limit theorem leads us to expect that for intervals of time where the number of subperiods, K, is large, the distribution of $ln(1 + \tilde{R}_{it})$ is approximately normal.

The quantity $ln(1 + \tilde{R}_{it})$ is the rate of return with continuous compounding for period t, the period covered by the simple return $\tilde{R}_{it}$, while $ln(1 + \tilde{r}_k)$ is likewise the rate of return with continuous compounding for subperiod k of period t.[†] The continuously compounded return $ln(1 + \tilde{R}_{it})$ is always less than the simple return $\tilde{R}_{it}$, although we see later that the two are close when R_{it} is not large—say, less than .15 in absolute value. Note also from (17) that the continuously compounded rate of return for period t, $ln(1 + \tilde{R}_{it})$, is a sum of $ln(1 + \tilde{r}_k)$, the continuously compounded returns for the subperiods of t, whereas, from equation (16), the simple return $\tilde{R}_{it}$ involves a product of the subperiod simple returns $\tilde{r}_k$.

Finally, the central-limit theorem provides some rationalization for why a model that hypothesizes normally distributed returns may be reasonable. But since a model is just a convenient and perhaps temporary way to look at data, and since a model is in any case always just an approximation to the world, we can simply propose the normal distribution as a model for daily or monthly returns and then see what the data say. This is what we do next.

---

*Note that since we are now talking about returns as random variables, tildes are used.
†The rate of return with continuous compounding for period t is the value of ϕ_t such that

$$1 + R_{it} = e^{\phi t},$$

where $e = 2.714 \ldots$ is the base of the natural logarithms and where $1 + R_{it}$ is again the value at the end of period t of \$1 invested in security i at the end of $t - 1$. Thus

$$\phi_t = ln(1 + R_{it}).$$

When we wish to distinguish between the continuously compounded return and the return defined by (13), the latter is called the simple return.

B. Daily Returns

Table 1.2, constructed from Tables 1 and 3 of Fama (1965), shows frequency distributions for continuously compounded daily returns for each of the 30 stocks of the Dow-Jones Industrial Average, for time periods that vary slightly from stock to stock but which usually run from about the end of 1957 to September 26, 1962. Column (1) of the table shows the number of daily returns, T, for each of the 30 stocks in the sample. Columns (2) and (3) show the expected and actual numbers of returns in the interval $\overline{R} - .5s(R) \leqslant R \leqslant \overline{R} + .5s(R)$, that is, within .5 sample standard deviations from the sample mean return. The "expected" frequencies are computed on the assumption that the daily returns are independent drawings from normal distributions with means and standard deviations equal to the sample estimates of these parameters for each security. Columns (4) to (9) of Table 1.2 show the total expected and actual numbers of returns that are within intervals of length $.5s(R)$ both to the right and to the left of $\overline{R}$. For example, columns (4) and (5) show the total expected and actual numbers of returns in the combined intervals $\overline{R} - 1.0s(R) < R \leqslant \overline{R} - .5s(R)$ and $\overline{R} + .5s(R) < R \leqslant \overline{R} + 1.0s(R)$. Finally, columns (10) to (17) show the expected and actual numbers for returns that are more than two, three, four, and five sample standard deviations from the sample mean return. For example, columns (10) and (11) show the expected and actual number of returns greater than $\overline{R} + 2.0s(R)$ or less than $\overline{R} - 2.0s(R)$.

The obvious finding in Table 1.2 is that the frequency distributions of the daily returns have more observations both in their central portions and in their extreme tails than are expected from normal distributions. For every stock the actual number of daily returns within .5 sample standard deviations from the sample mean return is greater than the expected number. Every stock also has more observations beyond three standard deviations from its mean return than would be expected with normal distributions; all but one have more beyond four standard deviations; and all but three have more beyond two standard deviations.

In more vivid terms, if daily returns are drawn from normal distributions, for any stock a daily return greater than four standard deviations from the mean is expected about once every 50 years. Daily returns this extreme are observed about four times every five years. Similarly, under the hypothesis of normality, for any given stock a daily return more than five standard deviations from the mean daily return should be observed about once every 7,000 years. Such observations seem to occur about every three to four years.

Probabilities and relative frequencies must sum to 1.0. If the empirical

TABLE 1.2

Frequency Distributions for Daily Returns on Dow-Jones Industrials

		INTERVALS					
		$\bar{R} - .5s(R) \le$ $R \le \bar{R} + .5s(R)$		$\bar{R} - 1.0s(R) \le$ $R < \bar{R} - .5s(R)$ and $\bar{R} + .5s(R) <$ $R \le \bar{R} + 1.0s(R)$		$\bar{R} - 1.5s(R) \le$ $R < \bar{R} - 1.0s(R)$ and $\bar{R} + 1.0s(R) <$ $R \le \bar{R} + 1.5s(R)$	
	T	Expected no.	Actual no.	Expected no.	Actual no.	Expected no.	Actual no.
	(1)	(2)	(3)	(4)	(5)	(6)	(7)
Allied Chemical	1,223	468.5	562	366.5	349	224.8	
Alcoa	1,190	455.8	521	356.6	343	218.7	
American Can	1,219	466.9	602	365.1	336	224.1	
AT & T	1,219	466.9	710	365.1	285	224.1	
American Tobacco	1,283	491.4	692	384.4	311	235.8	
Anaconda	1,193	456.9	513	357.4	331	219.3	
Bethlehem Steel	1,200	459.6	575	359.5	307	220.6	
Chrysler	1,692	648.0	736	506.9	493	311.0	
Du Pont	1,243	476.1	539	372.4	363	228.5	
Eastman Kodak	1,238	474.2	546	370.9	379	227.5	
General Electric	1,693	648.4	784	507.2	479	311.2	
General Foods	1,408	539.3	632	421.8	423	258.8	
General Motors	1,446	553.8	682	433.2	396	265.8	
Goodyear	1,162	445.0	539	348.1	331	213.6	
International Harvester	1,200	459.6	529	359.5	365	220.6	
International Nickel	1,243	476.1	587	372.4	362	228.5	
International Paper	1,447	554.2	643	433.5	442	266.0	
Johns Manville	1,205	461.5	526	361.0	363	221.5	
Owens Illinois	1,237	473.7	591	370.6	323	227.4	
Procter & Gamble	1,447	554.2	726	433.5	389	266.0	
Sears	1,236	473.4	666	370.3	305	227.2	
Standard Oil (California)	1,693	648.4	776	507.2	468	311.2	
Standard Oil (New Jersey)	1,156	442.8	582	346.3	314	212.6	
Swift & Co.	1,446	553.8	672	433.2	409	265.8	
Texaco	1,159	443.9	533	347.3	311	213.0	
Union Carbide	1,118	428.1	466	335.0	338	205.5	
United Aircraft	1,200	459.6	550	359.5	348	220.6	
U.S. Steel	1,200	459.6	495	359.5	337	220.6	
Westinghouse	1,448	554.6	636	433.8	424	266.1	
Woolworth	1,445	553.5	718	432.9	390	265.6	

Source: Adapted from Eugene F. Fama, "The Behavior of Stock Market Prices," *Journal of Business* 38 (January 19 47–48.

$\overline{R} - 2.0s(R) \leq$ $< \overline{R} - 1.5s(R)$ and $\overline{R} + 1.5s(R) <$ $\leq \overline{R} + 2.0s(R)$		$R < \overline{R} - 2s(R)$ and $R > \overline{R} + 2s(R)$		$R < \overline{R} - 3s(R)$ and $R > \overline{R} + 3s(R)$		$R < \overline{R} - 4s(R)$ and $R > \overline{R} + 4s(R)$		$R < \overline{R} - 5s(R)$ and $R > \overline{R} + 5s(R)$	
Expected no. (8)	Actual no. (9)	Expected no. (10)	Actual no. (11)	Expected no. (12)	Actual no. (13)	Expected no. (14)	Actual no. (15)	Expected no. (16)	Actual no. (17)
07.7	94	55.5	55	3.3	16	.08	4	.0007	2
04.8	85	54.1	69	3.2	7	.07	0	.0007	0
07.4	62	55.5	62	3.3	19	.08	6	.0007	3
07.4	42	55.5	51	3.3	17	.08	9	.0007	6
13.0	73	58.4	69	3.5	20	.08	7	.0008	4
05.1	88	54.3	57	3.2	8	.08	1	.0007	0
05.7	76	54.6	62	3.2	15	.08	4	.0007	1
49.1	117	77.0	87	4.6	16	.11	4	.0010	1
09.5	80	56.5	66	3.4	8	.08	3	.0007	1
09.1	85	56.3	66	3.3	13	.08	2	.0007	2
49.2	111	77.0	97	4.6	22	.11	5	.0010	1
24.0	84	64.1	75	3.8	22	.09	3	.0008	1
27.4	103	65.8	62	3.9	13	.09	6	.0009	3
02.4	71	52.9	57	3.1	10	.07	4	.0007	2
05.7	61	54.6	63	3.2	15	.08	4	.0007	1
09.5	72	56.5	73	3.4	16	.08	6	.0007	0
27.5	100	65.8	82	3.9	19	.09	5	.0009	0
06.2	91	54.8	62	3.2	11	.08	3	.0007	1
09.0	69	56.3	66	3.3	20	.08	3	.0007	1
27.5	71	65.8	90	3.9	20	.09	6	.0009	2
08.9	58	56.2	63	3.3	21	.08	8	.0007	5
49.2	121	77.0	95	4.6	14	.11	5	.0010	1
01.8	70	52.5	51	3.1	12	.07	3	.0007	2
27.4	85	65.8	86	3.9	18	.09	4	.0009	0
02.1	95	52.7	56	3.1	14	.07	2	.0007	0.
98.5	69	50.9	67	3.0	6	.07	1	.0007	0
05.7	77	54.6	60	3.2	11	.08	3	.0007	1
05.7	90	54.6	59	3.2	8	.08	1	.0007	0
27.6	95	65.9	72	3.9	14	.09	3	.0009	2
27.3	91	65.7	76	3.9	23	.09	5	.0009	2

distribution of daily returns on a stock is more peaked than a normal distribution in the immediate vicinity of its mean return, and if the frequency of extreme observations is also higher than would be expected from a normal distribution, then there must be intervals of intermediate distance from the mean for which observed frequencies are less than would be expected with a normal distribution. In Table 1.2, for 24 out of 30 stocks there are fewer observations between .5 and 1.0 standard deviation from the mean return than are expected with normal distributions; in general, the actual numbers of daily returns in the intervals between .5 and 2.0 standard deviations from the mean are systematically less than the numbers expected under the hypothesis of normality.

Although Table 1.2 seems to provide strong evidence against the hypothesis that daily stock returns are drawings from normal distributions, it is well to phrase tests of such hypotheses in terms of probabilities. That is, how likely is it that frequency distributions, like those observed for the daily returns, are generated from normal distributions? To answer this question, Table 1.3 shows the smallest and largest daily returns and the studentized range (SR) of the daily returns for each of the 30 DJIA stocks. From Table 1.9 we find that in repeated samples of 1,000 from a normal distribution, values of SR as large or larger than 7.99 are expected only about once in every 200 samples. Since such a value of SR is so rare in samples from a normal distribution, when a real-world data sample produces a value of SR larger than 7.99, it is fairly safe to conclude that the sample did not come from a normal distribution. All but two of the values of SR in Table 1.3 are greater than 7.99 and most are greater than 10.

The studentized ranges allow us to reject the hypothesis of normality for the daily returns, but based as they are on the two most extreme returns for each stock, the values of SR are not in themselves very informative in the search for alternative distributions. For this purpose, the frequency distributions in Table 1.2 are better. The frequency distributions tell us that any alternatives to the normal distribution that are considered should be more peaked than the normal—that is, they should have higher probabilities for values close to the mean—and the alternatives should also assign higher probabilities to extreme observations. In the jargon of statistics, we must look for distributions that are *leptokurtic* relative to normal distributions.

Finally, some caution in the interpretation of the results in Tables 1.2 and 1.3 is in order. In Chapter 4 we present evidence that successive returns on an individual security are approximately independent, but that returns on different securities for any given period are not independent. There are common "market factors" that cause the returns on all securities to move or covary together. For present purposes, this means that the results for the 30 firms

TABLE 1.3

Extreme Values and Studentized Ranges for Daily Returns on the Dow-Jones Industrials

	(1) SMALLEST RETURN	(2) LARGEST RETURN	(3) STUDENTIZED RANGE (*SR*)	(4) *T*
Allied Chemical	−.0718	.0838	10.83	1,223
Alcoa	−.0531	.0619	7.33	1,190
American Can	−.0623	.0675	11.30	1,219
AT & T	−.1038	.0989	20.07	1,219
American Tobacco	−.0800	.0724	12.62	1,283
Anaconda	−.0573	.0600	7.87	1,193
Bethlehem Steel	−.0725	.0619	10.32	1,200
Chrysler	−.0805	.1008	10.51	1,692
Du Pont	−.0599	.0515	10.79	1,243
Eastman Kodak	−.0443	.0779	9.23	1,238
General Electric	−.0647	.0565	9.59	1,693
General Foods	−.0468	.0625	9.00	1,408
General Motors	−.0976	.0829	14.31	1,446
Goodyear	−.0946	.1743	16.79	1,162
International Harvester	−.0870	.0687	11.17	1,200
International Nickel	−.0592	.0567	9.36	1,243
International Paper	−.0507	.0533	8.67	1,447
Johns Manville	−.0687	.1193	11.96	1,205
Owens Illinois	−.0637	.0606	10.08	1,237
Procter & Gamble	−.0635	.0656	11.06	1,447
Sears	−.1073	.0606	14.48	1,236
Standard Oil (California)	−.0633	.0674	9.85	1,693
Standard Oil (New Jersey)	−.1032	.1007	18.29	1,156
Swift & Co.	−.0675	.0628	9.18	1,446
Texaco	−.0593	.0548	8.84	1,159
Union Carbide	−.0456	.0394	8.17	1,118
United Aircraft	−.1523	.0849	13.81	1,200
U.S. Steel	−.0539	.0555	8.06	1,200
Westinghouse	−.0804	.0863	11.22	1,448
Woolworth	−.0674	.0896	13.63	1,445
Averages	−.0727	.0746	11.28	1,310

Source: Adapted from Eugene F. Fama, "The Behavior of Stock Market Prices," *Journal of Business* 38 (January 1965): 51.

in Tables 1.2 and 1.3 cannot be regarded as 30 independent samples. Because of the covariation of security returns, we can expect some degree of similarity in the results observed for different securities. This weakens the strong impression of nonnormality drawn from Tables 1.2 and 1.3, since departures from normality that arise on a purely chance basis would be expected to appear to some extent in the results for all stocks. The covariation among security returns is, however, far from complete, and the evidence against normality for daily returns is strong and systematically so across stocks. The conclusion that distributions of daily returns are substantially nonnormal seems safe.

C. Monthly Returns

Mandelbrot (1963) was the first to question seriously the hypothesis of normality for distributions of securities returns.* He pointed out that arguments based on the central-limit theorem, like those of Bachelier and Osborne, do not uniquely lead to the normal distribution. In particular, if distributions of sums of variables, such as price changes or continuously compounded returns, approach a limiting distribution as the number of items in the sum is increased, then the limiting distribution must be a member of the stable class of distributions of which the normal is a special case. Moreover, the symmetric nonnormal members of the stable class have the leptokurtic property observed in daily common stock returns; that is, nonnormal symmetric stable distributions are more peaked and assign higher probabilities to extreme observations than normal distributions.

Nevertheless, as models for common stock returns, stable nonnormal distributions also have undesirable properties. Although Mandelbrot's 1963 paper led to much new work on the subject (see, for example, Fama and Roll 1968; 1971; and Blattberg and Sargent 1971), statistical tools for handling data from nonnormal stable distributions are primitive relative to the tools that are available to handle data from normal distributions. Moreover, although most of the models of the theory of finance can be developed from the assumption of stable nonnormal return distributions (see, for example, Fama 1971), the exposition is simpler when the models are based on the assumption that return distributions are normal. Thus, the costs of rejecting normality for securities returns in favor of stable nonnormal distributions are substantial, and it behooves us to investigate the stable nonnormal hypothesis further.

Stable distributions are by definition stable or invariant under addition. This means that if the continuously compounded daily returns on a stock are random drawings from a stable distribution, then weekly and monthly continuously compounded returns, which are just sums of the daily returns, have stable distributions of the same "type" as the daily returns. Operationally, if distributions of daily returns are stable and nonnormal, distributions of returns for intervals longer than a day have about the same degree of

---

*Indeed, Mandelbrot emphasized that frequency distributions for many economic variables have the leptokurtic property observed in distributions of common stock returns.

leptokurtosis as the distributions of daily returns. Thus, if distributions of daily returns are stable nonnormal, distributions of returns for longer intervals should be no closer to normal than distributions of daily returns.

The daily returns for the Dow-Jones Industrials summarized in Table 1.2 do not cover time periods long enough to test the preceding statements in sufficient detail. Thus, we turn to the monthly CRSP returns discussed earlier. Moreover, we work with simple monthly returns as defined by equation (13), even though the preceding theory and empirical work are in terms of continuously compounded returns. The rationale is that in the portfolio models of later chapters, the simple return and not the continuously compounded return is the variable of interest. Moreover, at least in the "low-variance" post–World War II period, simple monthly returns, like simple daily returns, are in general numerically close to their continuously compounded counterparts. Thus, for daily and monthly data, distributions of simple and continuously compounded returns have the same general properties.*

There are three considerations in the choice of a time period for the monthly CRSP returns. First, for comparability the period should include 1957-1962, on which the tests on daily returns are based. Second, the period should include a sufficient number of months to allow construction of meaningful frequency distributions. Third, the choice of period must take account of the earlier finding that the variability of returns was higher in the 1930s than in subsequent periods. One does not want to mix together data from periods characterized by widely different degrees of return variability. With these considerations in mind and after a reexamination of the behavior over time of $s(R_m)$ in Table 1.1, the 210-month period of January 1951– June 1968 has been chosen somewhat arbitrarily.

The frequency distributions of the monthly returns for each of the 30 Dow-Jones Industrials are shown in Table 1.4. The intervals in Table 1.4 are the same as the intervals used for the daily returns in Table 1.2 (that is, the same in terms of units of sample standard deviations from sample mean returns), except that Table 1.4 separately examines intervals to the left and to the right of the sample mean returns. It is convenient to show more intervals for the monthly returns because, with the exception of Alcoa, the monthly data for each stock cover the same period. This means that the expected numbers of observations in different intervals are the same for each stock and can be shown on a single line.† The sample period of daily returns in Table 1.2

---

*The reader will be asked to confirm these statements later.

†Alcoa was listed on the NYSE in June 1951; thus, its returns cover the 204 months beginning with July 1951. The loss of six months of data is not serious enough to require a separate set of expected frequencies for Alcoa.

TABLE 1.4

Frequency Distributions of Monthly Returns on Dow-Jones Industrials, January 1951–June 1968

INTERVALS (IN UNITS OF STANDARD DEVIATIONS FROM THE MEAN)

	<-5	<-4	<-3	<-2	-2.0 to -1.5	-1.5 to -1.0	-1.0 to -.5	-.5 to 0	0 to .5	.5 to 1.0	1.0 to 1.5	1.5 to 2.0	>2	>3	>4	>5
Allied Chemical				2	6	19	44	38	42	27	17	12	3	1	1	1
Alcoa			1	3	11	15	33	42	34	32	21	12	1	1	1	
American Can				5	8	16	37	45	40	25	16	13	5	1		
AT & T				8	1	11	36	56	49	25	11		9	3	1	
American Tobacco				4	8	18	40	41	29	34	24	7	5			
Anaconda				3	12	18	33	42	40	28	15	12	7			
Bethlehem Steel			1		10	19	33	50	42	28	17	5	6	3		1
Chrysler			1	1	6	30	30	39	44	28	17	11	4	1	1	
Du Pont				3	10	19	37	33	48	30	15	10	5	2		
Eastman Kodak				4	10	12	37	46	39	32	12	13	5	1		
General Electric				3	11	23	25	46	35	40	12	10	5	1		
General Foods		1		4	5	19	31	55	34	34	18	3	7	1	1	
General Motors				1	9	20	34	49	40	24	18	8	7	1	1	
Goodyear				4	8	21	30	47	37	36	14	4	9	2		
International Harvester			1	3	3	27	37	41	37	31	15	8	8			
International Nickel			1	5	8	21	28	47	38	30	20	8	5	1		
International Paper				5	7	18	37	42	42	30	11	11	7	1		
Johns Manville				4	6	22	34	46	38	33	12	7	8	2		
Owens Illinois				3	7	31	26	34	48	28	21	4	8	1		
Procter & Gamble			1	7	5	12	41	48	38	27	15	9	8	1		
Sears				7	7	9	31	56	45	24	19	7	5	2		
Standard Oil (California)				5	5	23	26	37	35	34	23	6	6	1		

INTERVALS (IN UNITS OF STANDARD DEVIATIONS FROM THE MEAN)

	≤ −5	≤ −4	≤ −3	≤ −2	−2.0 to −1.5	−1.5 to −1.0	−1.0 to −.5	−.5 to 0	0 to .5	.5 to 1.0	1.0 to 1.5	1.5 to 2.0	> 2	> 3	> 4	> 5
Standard Oil (New Jersey)				1	8	23	41	40	37	29	14	10	7	1		
Swift & Co.				4	9	23	27	46	42	30	17	5	7	1		
Texaco				4	9	26	29	36	36	34	23	11	2			
Union Carbide				2	11	19	35	44	35	24	26	8	6			
United Aircraft				3	8	22	30	48	39	32	15	8	5	3		
U.S. Steel			1	3	4	24	30	49	39	33	18	6	4	3	1	
Westinghouse				2	13	18	34	50	25	30	26	8	4	1		
Woolworth				5	8	11	28	64	47	22	9	7	9	3	2	
Expected frequency	.000	.007	.28	4.78	9.25	19.29	31.47	40.21	40.21	31.47	19.29	9.25	4.78	.28	.007	.000
Average actual frequency	.000	.000	.23	3.60	7.77	19.63	33.47	45.23	39.13	29.80	17.03	8.23	5.90	1.27	.270	.067
Average actual minus expected	−.000	−.007	−.05	−1.18	−1.48	.34	2.00	5.02	−1.08	−1.67	−1.26	−1.02	1.12	.99	.263	.067

varies from stock to stock, so that expected frequencies must be shown separately for each stock.

The expected frequencies in the different intervals, computed under the assumption that the monthly returns are random drawings from normal distributions with means and standard deviations equal to the sample estimates of these parameters for each stock, are shown at the bottom in Table 1.4, following the results for the individual stocks. The table then shows the averages over the 30 Dow-Jones stocks of the observed frequencies in each interval and the differences between these average actual frequencies and the frequencies expected under the hypothesis of normality. The average actual frequencies and average differences provide a convenient summary of the results for individual stocks.

The first thing we can note about the frequency distributions of monthly returns is that they are slightly skewed to the right; that is, the frequency of extreme returns is higher to the right of the mean return than to the left. For example, on average there are 5.90 returns per stock beyond two standard deviations to the right of the mean return and 3.60 beyond two standard deviations to the left. Likewise, on average there are 1.27 returns per stock beyond three standard deviations to the right of the mean return and .23 beyond three standard deviations to the left.

PROBLEM VI.C

1. When a distribution is skewed to the right, its mean is greater than its median. This means that in samples from such distributions there are more observations to the left of the sample mean than to the right. In intuitive terms, the higher frequencies of extreme observations to the right of the mean (as compared to extreme observations to the left of the mean) are balanced by even higher frequencies of small- and intermediate-sized observations to the left of the mean (as compared to small- and intermediate-sized observations to the right of the mean). Check that these statements apply to the frequency distributions in Table 1.4.

Since returns in equivalent intervals on either side of the mean are grouped together, we cannot judge the skewness of the distributions of daily returns from Table 1.2. Other results in Fama (1965), from which Table 1.2 is drawn, indicate that distributions of daily returns are close to symmetric. There is some evidence of this in Table 1.3; for 15 stocks the largest daily return is larger in absolute value than the smallest daily return, while for 15 stocks the reverse is true.

The slight right-skewness of distributions of monthly returns is in part due to the use of simple returns rather than continuously compounded returns in the monthly calculations. Recall that if R is the simple return, then the continuously compounded return is $ln(1 + R)$. The always positive difference between R and $ln(1 + R)$ increases the further R is from 0 in either the positive or negative direction, as in the following table.

R	−.300	−.200	−.150	−.100	−.050	0	.050	.100	.150	.200	.300
$ln(1 + R)$	−.357	−.223	−.162	−.105	−.051	0	.049	.095	.140	.182	.262

Using continuously compounded returns would have the effect of pulling in the right tails of the distributions of monthly returns in Table 1.4 and stretching out the left tails, thus reducing the degree of right-skewness of the distributions.

But the right-skewness of the frequency distributions of simple monthly returns is slight, and we can be comfortable with the assumption of symmetry as a working approximation. We can return to the question of whether non-normal symmetric stable distributions provide good approximations to the daily and monthly returns. A positive answer to this question requires that distributions of monthly returns have about the same degree of leptokurtosis as distributions of daily returns. Rough comparison of Table 1.4 with Table 1.2 suggests that this is not the case. Extreme monthly returns are much rarer in Table 1.4 than extreme daily returns in Table 1.2, and the frequencies of returns close to mean returns seem less excessive in Table 1.4 than in Table 1.2.

Such comparisons of frequencies can be misleading. We can expect larger numbers of extreme daily returns simply because the samples of daily returns are so much larger than the samples of monthly returns. A convenient way to abstract from the effects of differential sample sizes is to compare the distributions of daily and monthly returns in terms of relative frequencies. This is done in Table 1.5, where the intervals shown are those used for the daily returns in Table 1.2. Thus, equivalent intervals of $s(R)$ on either side of $\bar{R}$ in the monthly returns of Table 1.4 are grouped together in Table 1.5. The first line of Table 1.5 shows the probabilities that the normal distribution assigns to the different intervals. The second line shows the averages across the 30 DJIA stocks of the relative frequencies of daily returns in each of the intervals, while the third line shows the differences between these average relative frequencies and the normal probabilities. The next two lines then show the average relative frequencies and the differences between these and normal probabilities for the monthly returns on the DJIA stocks.

Table 1.5 confirms that distributions of monthly returns are less peaked about their means and the relative frequencies of extreme returns are smaller

TABLE 1.5

Comparisons of Relative Frequencies of Daily and Monthly Returns

INTERVALS

	$\bar{R} - .5s(R) <$ $R \leq \bar{R} + .5s(R)$	$\bar{R} - 1.0s(R) <$ $R \leq \bar{R} - .5s(R)$ AND $\bar{R} + .5s(R) <$ $R \leq \bar{R} + 1.0s(R)$	$\bar{R} - 1.5s(R) <$ $R \leq \bar{R} - 1.0s(R)$ AND $\bar{R} + 1.0s(R) <$ $R \leq \bar{R} + 1.5s(R)$	$\bar{R} - 2.0s(R) <$ $R \leq \bar{R} - 1.5s(R)$ AND $\bar{R} + 1.5s(R) <$ $R \leq \bar{R} + 2.0s(R)$	$R \leq \bar{R} - 2s(R)$ AND $R > \bar{R} + 2s(R)$	$R \leq \bar{R} - 3s(R)$ AND $R > \bar{R} + 3s(R)$	$R \leq \bar{R} - 4s(R)$ AND $R > \bar{R} + 4s(R)$	$R \leq \bar{R} - 5s(R)$ AND $R > \bar{R} + 5s(R)$
Normal probability	.3830	.2998	.1838	.0880	.0456	.0027	.00006	.0000006
Average relative frequency (daily; Dow-Jones)	.4667	.2802	.1378	.0631	.0522	.0114	.00304	.0011632
Average relative frequency minus normal probability	.0837	-.0196	-.0460	-.0249	.0066	.0087	.00298	.0011626
Average relative frequency (monthly; Dow-Jones)	.4021	.3015	.1748	.0762	.0453	.0071	.00130	.0003000
Average relative frequency minus normal probability	.0191	.0017	-.0090	-.0118	-.0003	.0044	.00124	.0002994

than for the daily returns. On average, for the daily returns the relative frequency of observations within .5 standard deviation of the mean return is .4667, or .0837 in excess of the corresponding normal probability .3830; for the monthly returns the average relative frequency is .4021, which is only .0191 in excess of the normal probability. For observations beyond two standard deviations from the mean, the average relative frequency of .0453 for the monthly returns is almost precisely equal to the corresponding normal probability of .0456, whereas for the daily returns the average relative frequency of .0522 exceeds the normal probability by .0066. In fact, for every interval shown in Table 1.5, the average relative frequencies for the monthly returns are closer to the corresponding normal probabilities than the average relative frequencies for the daily returns. Thus, contrary to the implications of the hypothesis that daily and monthly returns conform roughly to the same type of stable nonnormal distribution, monthly returns have distributions closer to normal than daily returns.

It is nevertheless clear from Tables 1.4 and 1.5 that distributions of monthly returns are still slightly leptokurtic relative to normal distributions. The frequencies of returns close to mean returns and of extreme returns are still slightly high relative to normal distributions. The impression, however, is that the monthly returns are close enough to normal for the normal model to be a good working approximation. It is well, however, to buttress such a conclusion with formal tests, and again the choice is the studentized range.*

Table 1.6 shows the studentized ranges for the monthly returns of each of the 30 Dow-Jones Industrials. Recall that in the studentized ranges for the daily returns in Table 1.3, all but two of the SR values exceed the value (7.99) of the .995 fractile of the distribution of SR in samples of 1,000 from a normal population. For the monthly returns, only 4 of the SR values exceed the .995 fractile (7.03) of the distribution of SR in samples of 200 from a normal population. Fourteen of the SR values in Table 1.6 exceed the .9 fractile of the distribution of SR in samples of 200 from a normal population, but the remaining 16 values are quite consistent with the hypothesis of normality.

Blume (1968) and Officer (1971) study in detail the distributional properties of returns on portfolios that vary widely in terms of both number of securities per portfolio and risk. Their results confirm both the conclusion that distributions of portfolio returns are of the same type as distributions of returns on securities, and the conclusion that the normal distribution

---

*Fama and Roll (1971) indicate that among the many "goodness-of-fit" tests they try, the studentized range performs well as a formal test of normality when the alternative distribution is nonnormal symmetrical stable. Now that we have studied the properties of stock return distributions, the reader can appreciate why SR is used so much.

TABLE 1.6
Sample Statistics for Monthly Returns on the Dow-Jones Industrials
for January 1951–June 1968; T = 210

	(1) SMALLEST RETURN	(2) LARGEST RETURN	(3) STUDENTIZED RANGE (SR)	(4) $\bar{R}$	(5) s(R)
Allied Chemical	−.1451	.2917	7.75*	.0061	.0563
Alcoa	−.2440	.2912	7.00*	.0113	.0765
American Can	−.1185	.1542	5.86	.0084	.0465
AT & T	−.0855	.1499	7.25*	.0081	.0325
American Tobacco	−.1291	.1619	5.65	.0097	.0515
Anaconda	−.1610	.2031	5.18	.0120	.0703
Bethlehem Steel	−.1178	.3650	7.30*	.0127	.0661
Chrysler	−.2369	.2668	6.51*	.0131	.0773
Du Pont	−.1061	.1873	5.87	.0091	.0500
Eastman Kodak	−.1163	.2289	6.49*	.0175	.0532
General Electric	−.1374	.2431	6.35*	.0123	.0599
General Foods	−.1460	.2388	7.47*	.0140	.0515
General Motors	−.1216	.2520	7.00*	.0139	.0534
Goodyear	−.1465	.2185	5.62	.0169	.0649
International Harvester	−.1474	.1502	6.03	.0088	.0494
International Nickel	−.1702	.2287	6.91*	.0133	.0577
International Paper	−.1296	.2059	5.77	.0097	.0581
Johns Manville	−.1162	.1993	5.68	.0101	.0556
Owens Illinois	−.1420	.1586	5.87	.0096	.0512
Procter & Gamble	−.1379	.1697	6.12	.0117	.0502
Sears	−.1538	.1687	6.49*	.0139	.0497
Standard Oil (California)	−.1081	.1609	5.71	.0106	.0471
Standard Oil (New Jersey)	−.1104	.1511	5.73	.0121	.0456
Swift & Co.	−.1429	.2149	5.99	.0076	.0598
Texaco	−.1226	.1577	5.25	.0148	.0534
Union Carbide	−.1158	.1362	4.82	.0061	.0522
United Aircraft	−.2074	.2903	6.51*	.0159	.0764
U.S. Steel	−.1848	.3004	7.61*	.0092	.0637
Westinghouse	−.1250	.2046	5.13	.0116	.0642
Woolworth	−.1386	.2228	6.88*	.0081	.0526
Averages	−.1421	.2124	6.26	.0113	.0566

*Exceeds the .9 fractile of the distribution of the studentized range.

is a good working approximation for monthly security and portfolio returns in the post-World War II period.

PROBLEMS VI.C

2. In addition to the studentized ranges, Table 1.6 shows the smallest and largest returns and the mean and standard deviation of the monthly returns on each of the 30 Dow-Jones stocks. These numbers allow the reader to develop a deeper understanding of many of the points made in the preceding discussion.

(a) Note that for every stock the largest monthly return in Table 1.6 is larger in absolute value than the smallest return. Recall that in the daily returns of Table 1.3 this was true for only half of the stocks. What do these results imply about skewness in the distributions of daily and monthly returns?

(b) The text claims that the skewness of the distributions of monthly returns can be slightly reduced by using continuously compounded returns rather than simple returns. Convince yourself that this is true by computing the continuously compounded analogues of the largest and smallest returns in Table 1.6. These computations should also convince you that, at least for the period 1951–1968, differences between simple and continuously compounded monthly returns are generally slight. Recall that the differences are larger the further R is from 0, so that in the preceding computations you were looking at the largest differences observed for each stock.

(c) Compute the simple analogues of the largest and smallest continuously compounded daily returns shown in Table 1.3. This should convince you that the observed differences between simple and continuously compounded daily returns are indeed trivial. Why are the differences smaller for daily returns than for monthly returns?

(d) For the period 1951–1968, differences between standard deviations of continuously compounded and simple returns are trivial for both daily and monthly returns. Convince yourself that, in combination with your computations under (b) and (c) above, this means that inferences about normality drawn from studentized ranges are not much affected by whether one uses continuously compounded or simple daily and monthly returns.

3. Fama (1965) does not present tables of the means and standard deviations of the daily returns on the 30 DJIA stocks. The standard deviations can be determined from the information supplied here in Table 1.3. Compute them and compare them to the corresponding standard deviations of the monthly returns in Table 1.6. You will find that the standard deviations of daily returns vary from stock to stock but average about 1.3 percent per day. In comparison, the average of the 30 standard deviations of monthly returns on the DJIA stocks in Table 1.6 is 5.66 percent per month, or approximately 4.4 times the figure for the daily returns.

It is, of course, quite intuitive that monthly returns should show more variation than daily returns, but the number 4.4 (approximately the square root of the number of trading days per month) has an additional significance that the reader will fully appreciate after we discuss distributions of sums of random variables in the next chapter.

ANSWERS

2. Interpreting the data in Table 1.6:

(a) As mentioned earlier in the text, the results suggest that the right-skewness observed in distributions of monthly returns is probably not characteristic of distributions of daily returns.

(b) Table 1.7 shows the largest and smallest simple monthly returns for each of the 30 Dow-Jones stocks (repeated from Table 1.6), the difference between the largest and smallest simple returns, the largest and smallest continuously compounded returns, and the difference between these. For the simple returns, the largest return for every stock is larger than the absolute value of the smallest return; for the continuously compounded returns, however, there are five stocks for which this is not the case. This suggests that using continuously compounded returns reduces slightly the skewness of the distributions of monthly returns, but the fact that most of the largest continuously compounded returns are larger than the absolute values of the smallest continuously compounded returns suggests that the distributions of the continuously compounded returns are still skewed to the right.

(c) The reader can handle this part of the problem without assistance.

(d) Convince yourself.

3. Table 1.3 shows the studentized range and the smallest and largest return for each stock. Since

$$SR = \frac{\text{Max } (R_i) - \text{Min } (R_i)}{s(R_i)},$$

The value of $s(R_i)$ is easily obtained. Go to it!

TABLE 1.7

Comparisons of Largest and Smallest Simple and Continuously Compounded Monthly Returns on the Dow-Jones Industrials, January 1951–June 1968

STOCK	SIMPLE RETURNS			CONTINUOUSLY COMPOUNDED RETURNS		
	SMALLEST RETURN	LARGEST RETURN	DIFFER-ENCE	SMALLEST RETURN	LARGEST RETURN	DIFFER-ENCE
Allied Chemical	−.1451	.2917	.4368	−.1568	.2560	.4128
Alcoa	−.2440	.2912	.5352	−.2797	.2556	.5353
American Can	−.1185	.1542	.2727	−.1261	.1434	.2695
AT & T	−.0855	.1499	.2354	−.0894	.1397	.2291
American Tobacco	−.1291	.1619	.2910	−.1382	.1501	.2883
Anaconda	−.1610	.2031	.3641	−.1755	.1849	.3604
Bethlehem Steel	−.1178	.3650	.4828	−.1253	.3112	.4365
Chrysler	−.2369	.2668	.5037	−.2704	.2365	.5069
Du Pont	−.1061	.1873	.2934	−.1122	.1717	.2839
Eastman Kodak	−.1163	.2289	.3452	−.1236	.2061	.3297
General Electric	−.1374	.2431	.3805	−.1478	.2176	.3654
General Foods	−.1460	.2388	.3848	−.1578	.2141	.3719
General Motors	−.1216	.2520	.3736	−.1297	.2247	.3544
Goodyear	−.1465	.2185	.3650	−.1584	.1976	.3560
International Harvester	−.1474	.1502	.2976	−.1595	.1399	.2994
International Nickel	−.1702	.2287	.3989	−.1866	.2060	.3926
International Paper	−.1296	.2059	.3355	−.1388	.1872	.3260
Johns Manville	−.1162	.1993	.3155	−.1235	.1817	.3052
Owens Illinois	−.1420	.1586	.3006	−.1532	.1472	.3004
Procter & Gamble	−.1379	.1697	.3076	−.1484	.1567	.3051
Sears	−.1538	.1687	.3225	−.1670	.1559	.3229
Standard Oil (California)	−.1081	.1609	.2690	−.1144	.1492	.2636
Standard Oil (New Jersey)	−.1104	.1511	.2615	−.1170	.1407	.2577
Swift & Co.	−.1429	.2149	.3578	−.1542	.1947	.3489
Texaco	−.1226	.1577	.2803	−.1308	.1464	.2772
Union Carbide	−.1158	.1362	.2520	−.1231	.1277	.2508
United Aircraft	−.2074	.2903	.4977	−.2324	.2549	.4873
U.S. Steel	−.1848	.3004	.4852	−.2043	.2627	.4670
Westinghouse	−.1250	.2046	.3296	−.1335	.1861	.3196
Woolworth	−.1386	.2228	.3614	−.1492	.2011	.3503

VII. Conclusions

The frequency distributions in Tables 1.2 and 1.4, the comparisons of average relative frequencies with normal probabilities in Table 1.5, and the studentized ranges in Tables 1.3 and 1.6, all lead to the conclusion that distributions of monthly returns are closer to normal than distributions of daily returns. (This finding was first discussed in detail in Officer 1971, and then in Blattberg and Gonedes 1974.) This is inconsistent with the hypothesis that return distributions are nonnormal symmetric stable, which implies that distributions of daily and monthly returns should have about the same degree of leptokurtosis. Moreover, although the evidence also suggests that distributions of monthly returns are slightly leptokurtic relative to normal distributions, let us tentatively accept the normal model as a working approximation for monthly returns. Later chapters provide many opportunities to judge whether this is warranted. In each case, the judgment can be based on whether the normal model seems to be a useful approximation for the purpose at hand.

Thus, the assumption that distributions of returns on securities and portfolios are normal is used in later chapters first to develop a model for portfolio decisions by individual investors, and then to develop a model of securities prices which derives the implications of the portfolio model for relationships between expected returns on securities and their risks. The usefulness of the portfolio model depends not on whether the normality assumption which underlies it is an exact description of the world (we know it is not), but on whether the model yields useful insights into the essential ingredients of a rational portfolio decision. Likewise, the usefulness of the model for securities prices depends on how well it describes observed relationships between average returns and risk. If the model does well on this score, we can live with the small observed departures from normality in monthly returns, at least until better models come along.

TABLE 1.8
Cumulative Unit Normal Distribution $Pr(\tilde{r} > r)$

u	.00	.01	.02	.03	.04	.05	.06	.07	.08	.09
0	.5000	.4960	.4920	.4880	.4840	.4801	.4761	.4721	.4681	.4641
.1	.4602	.4562	.4522	.4483	.4443	.4404	.4364	.4325	.4286	.4247
.2	.4207	.4168	.4129	.4090	.4052	.4013	.3974	.3936	.3897	.3859
.3	.3821	.3783	.3745	.3707	.3669	.3632	.3594	.3557	.3520	.3483
.4	.3446	.3409	.3372	.3336	.3300	.3264	.3228	.3192	.3156	.3121
.5	.3085	.3050	.3015	.2981	.2946	.2912	.2877	.2843	.2810	.2776
.6	.2743	.2709	.2676	.2643	.2611	.2578	.2546	.2514	.2483	.2451
.7	.2420	.2389	.2358	.2327	.2297	.2266	.2236	.2206	.2177	.2148
.8	.2119	.2090	.2061	.2033	.2005	.1977	.1949	.1922	.1894	.1867
.9	.1841	.1814	.1788	.1762	.1736	.1711	.1685	.1660	.1635	.1611
1.0	.1587	.1562	.1539	.1515	.1492	.1469	.1446	.1423	.1401	.1379
1.1	.1357	.1335	.1314	.1292	.1271	.1251	.1230	.1210	.1190	.1170
1.2	.1151	.1131	.1112	.1093	.1075	.1056	.1038	.1020	.1003	.09853
1.3	.09680	.09510	.09342	.09176	.09012	.08851	.08691	.08534	.08379	.08226
1.4	.08076	.07927	.07780	.07636	.07493	.07353	.07215	.07078	.06944	.06811
1.5	.06681	.06552	.06426	.06301	.06178	.06057	.05938	.05821	.05705	.05592
1.6	.05480	.05370	.05262	.05155	.05050	.04947	.04846	.04746	.04648	.04551
1.7	.04457	.04363	.04272	.04182	.04093	.04006	.03920	.03836	.03754	.03673
1.8	.03593	.03515	.03438	.03362	.03288	.03216	.03144	.03074	.03005	.02938
1.9	.02872	.02807	.02743	.02680	.02619	.02559	.02500	.02442	.02385	.02330
2.0	.02275	.02222	.02169	.02118	.02068	.02018	.01970	.01923	.01876	.01831
2.1	.01786	.01743	.01700	.01659	.01618	.01578	.01539	.01500	.01463	.01426
2.2	.01390	.01355	.01321	.01287	.01255	.01222	.01191	.01160	.01130	.01101
2.3	.01072	.01044	.01017	$.0^{2}9903$	$.0^{2}9642$	$.0^{2}9387$	$.0^{2}9137$	$.0^{2}8894$	$.0^{2}8656$	$.0^{2}8424$
2.4	$.0^{2}8198$	$.0^{2}7976$	$.0^{2}7760$	$.0^{2}7549$	$.0^{2}7344$	$.0^{2}7143$	$.0^{2}6947$	$.0^{2}6756$	$.0^{2}6569$	$.0^{2}6387$
2.5	$.0^{2}6210$	$.0^{2}6037$	$.0^{2}5868$	$.0^{2}5703$	$.0^{2}5543$	$.0^{2}5386$	$.0^{2}5234$	$.0^{2}5085$	$.0^{2}4940$	$.0^{2}4799$
2.6	$.0^{2}4661$	$.0^{2}4527$	$.0^{2}4396$	$.0^{2}4269$	$.0^{2}4145$	$.0^{2}4025$	$.0^{2}3907$	$.0^{2}3793$	$.0^{2}3681$	$.0^{2}3573$
2.7	$.0^{2}3467$	$.0^{2}3364$	$.0^{2}3264$	$.0^{2}3167$	$.0^{2}3072$	$.0^{2}2980$	$.0^{2}2890$	$.0^{2}2803$	$.0^{2}2718$	$.0^{2}2635$
2.8	$.0^{2}2555$	$.0^{2}2477$	$.0^{2}2401$	$.0^{2}2327$	$.0^{2}2256$	$.0^{2}2186$	$.0^{2}2118$	$.0^{2}2052$	$.0^{2}1988$	$.0^{2}1926$
2.9	$.0^{2}1866$	$.0^{2}1807$	$.0^{2}1750$	$.0^{2}1695$	$.0^{2}1641$	$.0^{2}1589$	$.0^{2}1538$	$.0^{2}1489$	$.0^{2}1441$	$.0^{2}1395$
3.0	$.0^{2}1350$	$.0^{2}1306$	$.0^{2}1264$	$.0^{2}1223$	$.0^{2}1183$	$.0^{2}1144$	$.0^{2}1107$	$.0^{2}1070$	$.0^{2}1035$	$.0^{2}1001$
3.1	$.0^{3}9676$	$.0^{3}9354$	$.0^{3}9043$	$.0^{3}8740$	$.0^{3}8447$	$.0^{3}8164$	$.0^{3}7888$	$.0^{3}7622$	$.0^{3}7364$	$.0^{3}7114$
3.2	$.0^{3}6871$	$.0^{3}6637$	$.0^{3}6410$	$.0^{3}6190$	$.0^{3}5976$	$.0^{3}5770$	$.0^{3}5571$	$.0^{3}5377$	$.0^{3}5190$	$.0^{3}5009$
3.3	$.0^{3}4834$	$.0^{3}4665$	$.0^{3}4501$	$.0^{3}4342$	$.0^{3}4189$	$.0^{3}4041$	$.0^{3}3897$	$.0^{3}3758$	$.0^{3}3624$	$.0^{3}3495$
3.4	$.0^{3}3369$	$.0^{3}3248$	$.0^{3}3131$	$.0^{3}3018$	$.0^{3}2909$	$.0^{3}2803$	$.0^{3}2701$	$.0^{3}2602$	$.0^{3}2507$	$.0^{3}2415$
3.5	$.0^{3}2326$	$.0^{3}2241$	$.0^{3}2158$	$.0^{3}2078$	$.0^{3}2001$	$.0^{3}1926$	$.0^{3}1854$	$.0^{3}1785$	$.0^{3}1718$	$.0^{3}1653$
3.6	$.0^{3}1591$	$.0^{3}1531$	$.0^{3}1473$	$.0^{3}1417$	$.0^{3}1363$	$.0^{3}1311$	$.0^{3}1261$	$.0^{3}1213$	$.0^{3}1166$	$.0^{3}1121$
3.7	$.0^{3}1078$	$.0^{3}1036$	$.0^{4}9961$	$.0^{4}9574$	$.0^{4}9201$	$.0^{4}8842$	$.0^{4}8496$	$.0^{4}8162$	$.0^{4}7841$	$.0^{4}7532$
3.8	$.0^{4}7235$	$.0^{4}6948$	$.0^{4}6673$	$.0^{4}6407$	$.0^{4}6152$	$.0^{4}5906$	$.0^{4}5669$	$.0^{4}5442$	$.0^{4}5223$	$.0^{4}5012$
3.9	$.0^{4}4810$	$.0^{4}4615$	$.0^{4}4427$	$.0^{4}4247$	$.0^{4}4074$	$.0^{4}3908$	$.0^{4}3747$	$.0^{4}3594$	$.0^{4}3446$	$.0^{4}3304$
4.0	$.0^{4}3167$	$.0^{4}3036$	$.0^{4}2910$	$.0^{4}2789$	$.0^{4}2673$	$.0^{4}2561$	$.0^{4}2454$	$.0^{4}2351$	$.0^{4}2252$	$.0^{4}2157$
4.1	$.0^{4}2066$	$.0^{4}1978$	$.0^{4}1894$	$.0^{4}1814$	$.0^{4}1737$	$.0^{4}1662$	$.0^{4}1591$	$.0^{4}1523$	$.0^{4}1458$	$.0^{4}1395$
4.2	$.0^{4}1335$	$.0^{4}1277$	$.0^{4}1222$	$.0^{4}1168$	$.0^{4}1118$	$.0^{4}1069$	$.0^{4}1022$	$.0^{5}9774$	$.0^{5}9345$	$.0^{5}8934$
4.3	$.0^{5}8540$	$.0^{5}8163$	$.0^{5}7801$	$.0^{5}7455$	$.0^{5}7124$	$.0^{5}6807$	$.0^{5}6503$	$.0^{5}6212$	$.0^{5}5934$	$.0^{5}5668$
4.4	$.0^{5}5413$	$.0^{5}5169$	$.0^{5}4935$	$.0^{5}4712$	$.0^{5}4498$	$.0^{5}4294$	$.0^{5}4098$	$.0^{5}3911$	$.0^{5}3732$	$.0^{5}3561$
4.5	$.0^{5}3398$	$.0^{5}3241$	$.0^{5}3092$	$.0^{5}2949$	$.0^{5}2813$	$.0^{5}2682$	$.0^{5}2558$	$.0^{5}2439$	$.0^{5}2325$	$.0^{5}2216$
4.6	$.0^{5}2112$	$.0^{5}2013$	$.0^{5}1919$	$.0^{5}1828$	$.0^{5}1742$	$.0^{5}1660$	$.0^{5}1581$	$.0^{5}1506$	$.0^{5}1434$	$.0^{5}1366$
4.7	$.0^{5}1301$	$.0^{5}1239$	$.0^{5}1179$	$.0^{5}1123$	$.0^{5}1069$	$.0^{5}1017$	$.0^{6}9680$	$.0^{6}9211$	$.0^{6}8765$	$.0^{6}8339$
4.8	$.0^{6}7933$	$.0^{6}7547$	$.0^{6}7178$	$.0^{6}6827$	$.0^{6}6492$	$.0^{6}6173$	$.0^{6}5869$	$.0^{6}5580$	$.0^{6}5304$	$.0^{6}5042$
4.9	$.0^{6}4792$	$.0^{6}4554$	$.0^{6}4327$	$.0^{6}4111$	$.0^{6}3906$	$.0^{6}3711$	$.0^{6}3525$	$.0^{6}3348$	$.0^{6}3179$	$.0^{6}3019$

Source: A. Hald, *Statistical Tables and Formulas* (New York: John Wiley, 1952). Copyright 1952 John Wiley & Sons, Inc. Reprinted by permission.

TABLE 1.9

TABLE 1.9
Fractiles SR (p, T) of the Distribution of the Studentized Range in Samples of Size T from a Normal Population

SIZE OF SAMPLE T	LOWER PERCENTAGE POINTS (p)					UPPER PERCENTAGE POINTS (p)					SIZE OF SAMPLE T
	.005	.01	.025	.050	.10	.90	.95	.975	.99	.995	
3						1.997	1.999	2.000	2.000	2.000	3
4						2.409	2.429	2.439	2.445	2.447	4
5						2.712	2.753	2.782	2.803	2.813	5
6						2.949	3.012	3.056	3.095	3.115	6
7						3.143	3.222	3.282	3.338	3.369	7
8						3.308	3.399	3.471	3.543	3.585	8
9						3.449	3.552	3.634	3.720	3.772	9
10	2.47	2.51	2.59	2.67	2.77	3.57	3.685	3.777	3.875	3.935	10
11	2.53	2.58	2.66	2.74	2.84	3.68	3.80	3.903	4.012	4.079	11
12	2.59	2.65	2.73	2.80	2.91	3.78	3.91	4.01	4.134	4.208	12
13	2.65	2.70	2.78	2.86	2.97	3.87	4.00	4.11	4.244	4.325	13
14	2.70	2.75	2.83	2.91	3.02	3.95	4.09	4.21	4.34	4.431	14
15	2.75	2.80	2.88	2.96	3.07	4.02	4.17	4.29	4.43	4.53	15
16	2.80	2.85	2.93	3.01	3.13	4.09	4.24	4.37	4.51	4.62	16
17	2.84	2.90	2.98	3.06	3.17	4.15	4.31	4.44	4.59	4.69	17
18	2.88	2.94	3.02	3.10	3.21	4.21	4.38	4.51	4.66	4.77	18
19	2.92	2.98	3.06	3.14	3.25	4.27	4.43	4.57	4.73	4.84	19
20	2.95	3.01	3.10	3.18	3.29	4.32	4.49	4.63	4.79	4.91	20
30	3.22	3.27	3.37	3.46	3.58	4.70	4.89	5.06	5.25	5.39	30
40	3.41	3.46	3.57	3.66	3.79	4.96	5.15	5.34	5.54	5.69	40
50	3.57	3.61	3.72	3.82	3.94	5.15	5.35	5.54	5.77	5.91	50
60	3.69	3.74	3.85	3.95	4.07	5.29	5.50	5.70	5.93	6.09	60
80	3.88	3.93	4.05	4.15	4.27	5.51	5.73	5.93	6.18	6.35	80
100	4.02	4.00	4.20	4.31	4.44	5.68	5.90	6.11	6.36	6.54	100
150	4.30	4.36	4.47	4.59	4.72	5.96	6.18	6.39	6.64	6.84	150
200	4.50	4.56	4.67	4.78	4.90	6.15	6.38	6.59	6.85	7.03	200
500	5.06	5.13	5.25	5.37	5.49	6.72	6.94	7.15	7.42	7.60	500
1000	5.50	5.57	5.68	5.79	5.92	7.11	7.33	7.54	7.80	7.99	1000

Source: H. A. David, H. O. Hartley, and E. S. Pearson, "The Distribution of the Ratio, in a Single Normal Sample, of Range to Standard Deviation," *Biometrika*, 61 (1954): 491. Reprinted by permission.

CHAPTER

2

The Distribution of the Return on a Portfolio

The next empirical question concerns the relationships between the returns on individual stocks and market returns. To what extent are returns on individual securities associated with or explained by market returns, as represented, for example, by the return R_{mt} on the equally weighted index or portfolio of NYSE common stocks?

Study of this topic requires two chapters of preliminary discussion of statistical concepts. Many of these concepts are also relevant for the model of portfolio selection pursued at length later in the book. Thus, to enliven the discussion of the new statistical tools and to set the stage for the later work in portfolio theory, this chapter introduces some concepts from portfolio theory and uses them as the framework for the discussion of new statistical tools.

The first step is to show how the return on a portfolio is related to the returns on the individual securities in the portfolio.

I. A Portfolio's Return as a Function of Returns on Securities

Consider a particular portfolio (call it p) and let h_{ip} be the number of dollars invested in security i at the end of month $t - 1$ (which, in a discrete time framework, is also the beginning of month t). Let $\tilde{R}_{it}$ be the simple return on the security from the end of month $t - 1$ to the end of month t. The return is as defined by equation (13) of Chapter 1, so that $\tilde{R}_{it}$ is the return from the end of month $t - 1$ to the end of month t per dollar invested in security i at the end of month $t - 1$. As in Chapter 1, the tilde ($\sim$) on $\tilde{R}_{it}$ indicates that the return is a random variable at $t - 1$.

At the end of month t, the dollar value of the investment h_{ip} is

$$h_{ip} + h_{ip}\tilde{R}_{it} = h_{ip}(1 + \tilde{R}_{it});$$

that is, the end-of-month value is the initial investment h_{ip} plus the dollar return $h_{ip}\tilde{R}_{it}$. If n is the number of securities, the end-of-month dollar value of the portfolio is

$$\sum_{i=1}^{n} h_{ip} + \sum_{i=1}^{n} h_{ip}\tilde{R}_{it} = \sum_{i=1}^{n} h_{ip}(1 + \tilde{R}_{it}).$$

The end-of-month value of the portfolio can also be expressed as $h(1 + \tilde{R}_{pt})$, where $\tilde{R}_{pt}$ is the return on the portfolio p for month t and

$$h = \sum_{i=1}^{n} h_{ip}, \tag{1}$$

are the total funds invested at the beginning of the month. It follows that

$$h + h\tilde{R}_{pt} = \sum_{i=1}^{n} h_{ip} + \sum_{i=1}^{n} h_{ip}\tilde{R}_{it} = h + \sum_{i=1}^{n} h_{ip}\tilde{R}_{it},$$

so that

$$h\tilde{R}_{pt} = \sum_{i=1}^{n} h_{ip}\tilde{R}_{it}; \tag{2}$$

that is, the dollar return on the portfolio can be expressed either as the total investment times the return on the portfolio or as the sum of the dollar returns on the investments in each of the securities. If we let

$$x_{ip} = \frac{h_{ip}}{h}, \tag{3}$$

so that

$$\sum_{i=1}^{n} x_{ip} = 1, \tag{4}$$

then dividing through both sides of equation (2) by h, we have

$$\tilde{R}_{pt} = \sum_{i=1}^{n} x_{ip}\tilde{R}_{it}. \tag{5}$$

The quantity x_{ip} is the proportion of total portfolio funds h invested in security i to obtain portfolio p. Thus equation (5) says that the return on portfolio p is a weighted average of the returns on the individual securities in p, where the weight applied to a security's return is the proportion of portfolio funds invested in the security.

One example of a portfolio is the equally weighted index of NYSE stocks studied in Chapter 1. For this portfolio

$$\tilde{R}_{mt} = \frac{1}{n} \sum_{i=1}^{n} \tilde{R}_{it} = \sum_{i=1}^{n} x_{im}\tilde{R}_{it},$$

$$x_{im} = \frac{1}{n}, \quad i = 1, 2, \ldots, n,$$

where n is the number of securities on the NYSE at the end of month $t - 1$.

In describing the collection or set of portfolios from which an investor can choose, it is convenient to let n be the total number of securities that are candidates for inclusion in portfolios. Then, given the returns on the n securities for month t, the only reason that different portfolios have different returns is that the weights or proportions of portfolio funds invested in securities vary from portfolio to portfolio. In this sense, the weights x_{ip}, $i = 1, 2, \ldots, n$, define or characterize the portfolio p. It is understood that some of the x_{ip} can be zero, which means that some securities do not appear in portfolio p.

II. The Mean and Variance of a Portfolio's Return

As indicated by the tilde notation, at the end of month $t - 1$ the returns for month t on securities and portfolios are random variables; that is, the values of the returns that will be observed can be thought of as drawings from probability distributions. Since the return on a portfolio is a weighted sum of the returns on the securities in the portfolio, determining how the distribution of the return on a portfolio is related to the distributions of returns on securities involves, in statistical terms, determining how the distribution of a weighted sum of random variables is related to the distributions of the individual summands.

The problem is simplified by the fact that the portfolio models of this book are based on the assumption, supported by the empirical work of Officer (1971) and Blume (1968), and the data presented in Chapter 1, that, at least for monthly post–World War II data, distributions of portfolio returns, like distributions of returns for individual common stocks, are approximately normal. A normal distribution can be completely characterized from knowledge of its mean and standard deviation. Thus, the problem reduces to one of determining how means and standard deviations of portfolio returns are related to the parameters of distributions of returns on securities. In statistical terms, the problem is to develop expressions for the mean and standard deviation of a weighted sum of random variables.

Since the object of the book is to teach finance, not statistics, most of the relevant results are just stated in the text, with proofs left for the problems.

A.   *The Mean or Expected Value of the Return on a Portfolio*

Since a portfolio's return is a weighted sum of returns on securities, to describe the mean and standard deviation of a portfolio's return we must first know something about the means and standard deviations of weighted random variables. There are two general results. First, the mean (or expected value, or expectation) of a constant times a random variable is the constant times the expected value of the random variable. Thus, for any constant α and any random variable $\tilde{y}$,

$$E(\alpha\tilde{y}) = \alpha E(\tilde{y}). \tag{6}$$

Second, the variance of a constant times a random variable is the constant squared times the variance of the random variable, so that the standard deviation of a constant times a random variable is the absolute value of the constant times the standard deviation of the random variable:

$$\sigma^2(\alpha\tilde{y}) = \alpha^2 \sigma^2(\tilde{y}) \tag{7}$$

$$\sigma(\alpha\tilde{y}) = |\alpha|\sigma(\tilde{y}). \tag{8}$$

The absolute value sign is necessary in (8) since the constant α could be negative and the standard deviation of $\alpha\tilde{y}$, like any standard deviation, must be nonnegative.

PROBLEM II.A

1. Derive equations (6) and (7).

ANSWER

1. Let $f(y)$ be the density function for the random variable $\tilde{y}$, assumed to be continuous. Then

$$E(\alpha\tilde{y}) = \int_y \alpha y f(y) dy$$

$$= \alpha \int_y y f(y) dy$$

$$= \alpha E(\tilde{y}),$$

and

$$\sigma^2(\alpha\tilde{y}) = E\{[\alpha\tilde{y} - E(\alpha\tilde{y})]^2\}$$

$$= \int_y [\alpha y - E(\alpha\tilde{y})]^2 f(y) dy$$

$$= \alpha^2 \int_y [y - E(\tilde{y})]^2 f(y) dy$$

$$= \alpha^2 \sigma^2(\tilde{y}).$$

Although this interpretation is not rigorous, the nonmathematical reader can consider the integral notation $\int_y dy$ as calling for a "sum" over all possible values of $\tilde{y}$. Note that since we are summing over all possible specific values of $\tilde{y}$, in the above equations there are no tildes over the y's that follow an integral sign.

The reader will find it instructive to rewrite the expressions above for a discrete random variable $\tilde{y}$. This involves interpreting $f(y)$ as a probability function rather than as a density function and substituting the summation symbol Σ_y for the integral notation $\int_y dy$. The reader should always interpret what he or she does in words.

The return on a portfolio is a weighted sum of random variables. The mean or expected value of a random variable which is itself a weighted sum of random variables is the sum of the weighted means or expected values of the variables that make up the sum. Thus, if $\tilde{y}_1, \ldots, \tilde{y}_n$ are n arbitrary random variables and $\alpha_1, \ldots, \alpha_n$ are arbitrary weights, then

$$E\left(\sum_{i=1}^{n} \alpha_i \tilde{y}_i\right) = \sum_{i=1}^{n} \alpha_i E(\tilde{y}_i). \tag{9}$$

Expressed verbally, the expectation of a sum of weighted random variables is the sum of the weighted expectations.

Applying (9) to equation (5), the expected return on any portfolio p is

$$E(\tilde{R}_{pt}) = E\left(\sum_{i=1}^{n} x_{ip}\tilde{R}_{it}\right) = \sum_{i=1}^{n} x_{ip}E(\tilde{R}_{it}). \tag{10}$$

Thus, the mean or expected return on a portfolio of n securities is the weighted average of the means of the returns on individual securities, where the weight applied to the expected return on a given security is the proportion of portfolio funds invested in that security.

The results stated in equations (6) through (10) are used repeatedly in this and later chapters.

PROBLEM II.A

2. Establish (9) for the two-variable case; that is, show that for any two constants α_1 and α_2 and any random variables $\tilde{y}_1$ and $\tilde{y}_2$,

$$E(\alpha_1\tilde{y}_1 + \alpha_2\tilde{y}_2) = \alpha_1 E(\tilde{y}_1) + \alpha_2 E(\tilde{y}_2).$$

The answer requires some familiarity with the concepts of joint, conditional, and marginal probabilities, and some familiarity either with multiple integrals or multiple sums.

ANSWER

2. Let $f(y_1, y_2)$ be the joint density for the random variables $\tilde{y}_1$ and $\tilde{y}_2$; that is, $f(y_1, y_2)$ gives the likelihood that a joint drawing of $\tilde{y}_1$ and $\tilde{y}_2$ will yield the particular pair of values of the variables shown as arguments of the function. The expected value of $\alpha_1\tilde{y}_1 + \alpha_2\tilde{y}_2$ is then the weighted average of $\alpha_1 y_1 + \alpha_2 y_2$ over all possible combinations of y_1 and y_2, where the weight applied to any specific combination is its joint density $f(y_1, y_2)$.

$$E(\alpha_1\tilde{y}_1 + \alpha_2\tilde{y}_2) = \int_{y_1, y_2} (\alpha_1 y_1 + \alpha_2 y_2)f(y_1, y_2)dy_1 dy_2,$$

where $\int_{y_1, y_2} dy_1 dy_2$ is loosely read "sum over all possible combinations of y_1 and y_2."

Let $f(y_1|y_2)$ be the density function for $\tilde{y}_1$ conditional on some given value y_2 of $\tilde{y}_2$, and likewise let $f(y_2|y_1)$ be the conditional density function for $\tilde{y}_2$ given that y_1 is observed in the drawing of $\tilde{y}_1$. Let

$$f(y_1) = \int_{y_2} f(y_1, y_2)dy_2$$

be the marginal density function for $\tilde{y}_1$; that is, $f(y_1)$ shows the likelihood that y_1 is observed in the drawing of $\tilde{y}_1$ when no constraint is imposed on what is observed in the drawing of $\tilde{y}_2$. Thus, $f(y_1)$ is just the sum of $f(y_1, y_2)$

over all possible values of $\tilde{y}_2$. Likewise, the marginal density function for $\tilde{y}_2$ is

$$f(y_2) = \int_{y_1} f(y_1, y_2) dy_1.$$

Since the joint density $f(y_1, y_2)$ can always be expressed as

$$f(y_1, y_2) = f(y_1|y_2)f(y_2)$$

or as

$$f(y_1, y_2) = f(y_2|y_1)f(y_1),$$

the equation for $E(\alpha_1 \tilde{y}_1 + \alpha_2 \tilde{y}_2)$ given above can be developed as

(Step 1) $\quad E(\alpha_1 \tilde{y}_1 + \alpha_2 \tilde{y}_2) = \displaystyle\int_{y_1, y_2} \alpha_1 y_1 f(y_1, y_2) dy_1 dy_2$

$$+ \int_{y_1, y_2} \alpha_2 y_2 f(y_1, y_2) dy_1 dy_2$$

(Step 2) $\quad = \alpha_1 \displaystyle\int_{y_1, y_2} y_1 f(y_2|y_1)f(y_1) dy_1 dy_2$

$$+ \alpha_2 \int_{y_1, y_2} y_2 f(y_1|y_2)f(y_2) dy_1 dy_2$$

(Step 3) $\quad = \alpha_1 \displaystyle\int_{y_1} y_1 f(y_1) \int_{y_2} f(y_2|y_1) dy_2 dy_1$

$$+ \alpha_2 \int_{y_2} y_2 f(y_2) \int_{y_1} f(y_1|y_2) dy_1 dy_2$$

(Step 4) $\quad = \alpha_1 \displaystyle\int_{y_1} y_1 f(y_1) dy_1 + \alpha_2 \int_{y_2} y_2 f(y_2) dy_2$

(Step 5) $\quad = \alpha_1 E(\tilde{y}_1) + \alpha_2 E(\tilde{y}_2).$

Step 2 makes legitimate rearrangements of the terms in step 1. Step 4 takes account of the fact that the conditional probability distributions of step 3 are bona fide probability distributions; that is, for any given y_2 the sum of $f(y_1|y_2)$ over all possible values of y_1 is 1:

$$\int_{y_1} f(y_1|y_2)dy_1 = 1;$$

and likewise

$$\int_{y_2} f(y_2|y_1)dy_2 = 1.$$

Again, the reader may want to rework this problem for the case where the random variables $\tilde{y}_1$ and $\tilde{y}_2$ are discrete rather than continuous.

The expected value of a portfolio's return is the weighted sum of the expected values of returns on its constituent securities irrespective of the presence or absence of dependence among the security returns. This is not generally true for the variance of a portfolio's return. The variance of a portfolio's return is in part determined by the variances of security returns, but it is also determined in part and often primarily by the degree of dependence or co-movement in the returns on different securities.

The notation used in the discussions that follow gets rather involved. To simplify things a little, we no longer explicitly include the subscript t on returns and on the parameters (e.g., means and variances) of distributions of returns. This should not cause confusion, since the specific period t to which the various quantities refer is of no particular importance. Thus, we now write equations (5) and (10) for the return and expected return on portfolio p as

$$\tilde{R}_p = \sum_{i=1}^n x_{ip}\tilde{R}_i \tag{11}$$

$$E(\tilde{R}_p) = E\left(\sum_{i=1}^n x_{ip}E(\tilde{R}_i)\right) = \sum_{i=1}^n x_{ip}E(\tilde{R}_i). \tag{12}$$

B.   *The Variance of the Return on a Portfolio*

As for any random variable, the variance of the return on a portfolio is

$$\sigma^2(\tilde{R}_p) = E\left\{[\tilde{R}_p - E(\tilde{R}_p)]^2\right\}.$$

With equations (11) and (12), $\sigma^2(\tilde{R}_p)$ can be rewritten as

$$\sigma^2(\tilde{R}_p) = E\left(\left[\sum_{i=1}^n x_{ip}(\tilde{R}_i - E(\tilde{R}_i))\right]^2\right).$$

This expression calls for the expected value of a sum of weighted random variables. To see what is involved, it is best to begin with the simple case, $n = 2$. Then the preceding expression becomes

$$\sigma^2(\tilde{R}_p) = E([x_{1p}(\tilde{R}_1 - E(\tilde{R}_1)) + x_{2p}(\tilde{R}_2 - E(\tilde{R}_2))]^2)$$
$$= E(x_{1p}^2 [\tilde{R}_1 - E(\tilde{R}_1)]^2 + x_{2p}^2 [\tilde{R}_2 - E(\tilde{R}_2)]^2$$
$$+ 2x_{1p}x_{2p} [\tilde{R}_1 - E(\tilde{R}_1)] [\tilde{R}_2 - E(\tilde{R}_2)]).$$

Since $\tilde{R}_1$ and $\tilde{R}_2$ are random variables, the cross-product $[\tilde{R}_1 - E(\tilde{R}_1)]$ $[\tilde{R}_2 - E(\tilde{R}_2)]$ is a random variable, as are the squared differences from means $[\tilde{R}_1 - E(\tilde{R}_1)]^2$ and $[\tilde{R}_2 - E(\tilde{R}_2)]^2$. In general, the value of any nonconstant function of one or more random variables is itself a random variable. Thus, the preceding equation says that $\sigma^2(\tilde{R}_p)$ is the expected value of a sum of weighted random variables. Since the expectation of a sum of weighted random variables is the sum of the weighted expectations of the component variables, we have

$$\sigma^2(\tilde{R}_p) = x_{1p}^2 E([\tilde{R}_1 - E(\tilde{R}_1)]^2) + x_{2p}^2 E([\tilde{R}_2 - E(\tilde{R}_2)]^2)$$
$$+ 2x_{1p}x_{2p} E([\tilde{R}_1 - E(\tilde{R}_1)] [\tilde{R}_2 - E(\tilde{R}_2)]). \quad (13)$$

The expressions $E([\tilde{R}_1 - E(\tilde{R}_1)]^2)$ and $E([\tilde{R}_2 - E(\tilde{R}_2)]^2)$ are the return variances $\sigma^2(\tilde{R}_1)$ and $\sigma^2(\tilde{R}_2)$. To complete the interpretation of the preceding equation, we need only interpret the quantity $E([\tilde{R}_1 - E(\tilde{R}_1)] [\tilde{R}_2 - E(\tilde{R}_2)])$ called the *covariance* between $\tilde{R}_1$ and $\tilde{R}_2$. The covariance $E([\tilde{R}_1 - E(\tilde{R}_1)]$ $[\tilde{R}_2 - E(\tilde{R}_2)])$ is an expected value which is evaluated by weighting each possible value of $[R_1 - E(\tilde{R}_1)] [R_2 - E(\tilde{R}_2)]$ by $f(R_1, R_2)$, the joint density or likelihood of observing that combination of R_1 and R_2 in a joint drawing of $\tilde{R}_1$ and $\tilde{R}_2$, and then "summing" over all possible combinations of R_1 and R_2. In formal terms, the covariance between the returns on any two securities i and j is denoted either as cov $(\tilde{R}_i, \tilde{R}_j)$ or as σ_{ij}, and is defined as

$$\text{cov}(\tilde{R}_i, \tilde{R}_j) = \sigma_{ij} = E([\tilde{R}_i - E(\tilde{R}_i)] [\tilde{R}_j - E(\tilde{R}_j)])$$

$$= \int_{R_i, R_j} [R_i - E(\tilde{R}_i)] [R_j - E(\tilde{R}_j)] f(R_i, R_j) dR_i dR_j. \quad (14)$$

As in Problem II.A.*2*, the integral notation $\int_{R_i, R_j} dR_i dR_j$ calls for a "sum" over all possible combinations of R_i and R_j.

As its names implies, the covariance is a measure of the degree of covariation (or comovement or association) between the returns on securities i and j. In intuitive terms, the covariance is positive if deviations of $\tilde{R}_i$ and $\tilde{R}_j$ from their respective means tend to have the same sign, and it is negative if the deviations tend to have opposite signs. When the covariance is positive, we say that there is positive association or dependence between $\tilde{R}_i$ and $\tilde{R}_j$; roughly speaking, the returns on the two securities tend to move in the same direction. A negative covariance indicates negative association or dependence; the returns on the two securities tend to move in opposite directions. The covariance concept appears so frequently in future discussions that a thorough understanding evolves naturally.

PROBLEM II.B

1. The random variables $\tilde{y}_1, \tilde{y}_2, \ldots, \tilde{y}_n$ are statistically independent if

$$f(y_1, y_2, \ldots, y_n) = f(y_1)f(y_2) \ldots f(y_n);$$

that is, if their joint density is always the product of their marginal densities. Equivalently, statistical independence says that the likelihoods of different specific values of $\tilde{y}_i$ do not depend on the values observed for the other $n - 1$ random variables. Show that if for all possible y_i and y_j

$$f(y_i, y_j) = f(y_i)f(y_j),$$

then

$$\text{cov}(\tilde{y}_i, \tilde{y}_j) = 0;$$

that is, independence implies zero covariance. Warning: The reverse is not true; zero covariance does not necessarily imply independence.

ANSWER

1. From the general definition of a covariance in equation (14),

$$\text{cov}(\tilde{y}_i, \tilde{y}_j) = \int_{y_i, y_j} [y_i - E(\tilde{y}_i)][y_j - E(\tilde{y}_j)]f(y_i, y_j)dy_i dy_j.$$

Since $\tilde{y}_i$ and $\tilde{y}_j$ are assumed to be independent,

$$\text{cov}(\tilde{y}_i, \tilde{y}_j) = \int_{y_i, y_j} [y_i - E(\tilde{y}_i)][y_j - E(\tilde{y}_j)]f(y_i)f(y_j)dy_i dy_j$$

$$= \int_{y_i} [y_i - E(\tilde{y}_i)]f(y_i)dy_i \int_{y_j} [y_j - E(\tilde{y}_j)]f(y_j)dy_j$$

$$= [E(\tilde{y}_i) - E(\tilde{y}_i)][E(\tilde{y}_j) - E(\tilde{y}_j)]$$

$$= 0.$$

With all the terms in equation (13) now interpreted, the variance of the return on a portfolio of two securities becomes

$$\sigma^2(\tilde{R}_p) = x_{1p}^2\sigma^2(\tilde{R}_1) + x_{2p}^2\sigma^2(\tilde{R}_2) + 2x_{1p}x_{2p}\sigma_{12}, \quad n = 2.$$

Following precisely the same arguments for portfolios of three securities, we obtain

$$\sigma^2(\tilde{R}_p) = x_{1p}^2\sigma^2(\tilde{R}_1) + x_{2p}^2\sigma^2(\tilde{R}_2) + x_{3p}^2\sigma^2(\tilde{R}_3)$$

$$+ 2x_{1p}x_{2p}\sigma_{12} + 2x_{1p}x_{3p}\sigma_{13} + 2x_{2p}x_{3p}\sigma_{23}.$$

The new terms are the variance of the return on security 3 and the covariances between the returns on security 3 and the returns on securities 1 and 2.

PROBLEM II.B.

2. Derive the preceding equation for $\sigma^2(\tilde{R}_p)$ when $n = 3$.

ANSWER

2. Go back to the beginning of Section II.B and retrace the development of the equations, but for the case $n = 3$.

The same arguments also produce the general result that the variance of the return on a portfolio of n securities is the sum of the weighted variances of the returns on the individual securities in the portfolio plus twice the weighted sum of all the different possible pairwise covariances between the returns on individual securities. The weight applied to the variance of the return on security i is the square of the proportion of portfolio funds invested in security i, while the weight applied to the covariance between the returns on securities i and j is the product of the proportions of portfolio funds invested in these two securities. In formal terms, in the n security case, $\sigma^2(\tilde{R}_p)$ is

$$\sigma^2(\tilde{R}_p) = x_{1p}^2\sigma^2(\tilde{R}_1) + x_{2p}^2\sigma^2(\tilde{R}_2) + \ldots + x_{np}^2\sigma^2(\tilde{R}_n)$$

$$+ 2x_{1p}x_{2p}\sigma_{12} + 2x_{1p}x_{3p}\sigma_{13} + \ldots + 2x_{1p}x_{np}\sigma_{1n}$$

$$+ 2x_{2p}x_{3p}\sigma_{23} + 2x_{2p}x_{4p}\sigma_{24} + \ldots + 2x_{2p}x_{np}\sigma_{2n}$$

$$+ 2x_{3p}x_{4p}\sigma_{34} + 2x_{3p}x_{5p}\sigma_{35} + \ldots + 2x_{3p}x_{np}\sigma_{3n}$$

$$\cdot$$
$$\cdot$$
$$\cdot$$

$$+ 2x_{n-1,p}x_{np}\sigma_{n-1,n}; \qquad (15)$$

or equivalently,

$$\sigma^2(\tilde{R}_p) = \sum_{i=1}^{n} x_{ip}^2 \sigma^2(\tilde{R}_i) + 2 \sum_{i=1}^{n-1} \sum_{j=i+1}^{n} x_{ip} x_{jp} \sigma_{ij}, \tag{16}$$

where, as indicated by equation (15), the double sum

$$\sum_{i=1}^{n-1} \sum_{j=i+1}^{n}$$

is read "for each value of i from $i = 1$ to $i = n - 1$, sum over j from $j = i + 1$ to $j = n$; then sum the results over i from $i = 1$ to $i = n - 1$."

Equation (16) is not the only expression for the variance of the return on a portfolio. For example, from (14), it is clear that the order of the terms in the cross-product that defines a covariance is irrelevant:

$$\sigma_{ij} = E([\tilde{R}_i - E(\tilde{R}_i)] [\tilde{R}_j - E(\tilde{R}_j)])$$
$$= E([\tilde{R}_j - E(\tilde{R}_j)] [\tilde{R}_i - E(\tilde{R}_i)]) = \sigma_{ji}.$$

It follows that in equation (16)

$$2x_{ip} x_{jp} \sigma_{ij} = x_{ip} x_{jp} \sigma_{ij} + x_{jp} x_{ip} \sigma_{ji},$$

so that an expression for $\sigma^2(\tilde{R}_p)$ equivalent to (16) is

$$\sigma^2(\tilde{R}_p) = \sum_{i=1}^{n} x_{ip}^2 \sigma^2(\tilde{R}_i) + \sum_{i=1}^{n} \sum_{\substack{j=1 \\ j \neq i}}^{n} x_{ip} x_{jp} \sigma_{ij}. \tag{17}$$

Here the double sum notation

$$\sum_{i=1}^{n} \sum_{\substack{j=1 \\ j \neq i}}^{n}$$

is read "for each value of i from $i = 1$ to $i = n$, sum over j from $j = 1$ to $j = n$, but omitting terms where $j = i$; then sum the results over i from $i = 1$ to $i = n$." Equivalently, the double sum can be read, "sum over all possible combinations of i and j except those where $j = i$."

Equations (16) and (17) still do not exhaust the possibilities. The variance of the return on a security can always be regarded as that return's covariance with itself:

$$\sigma^2(\tilde{R}_i) = E([\tilde{R}_i - E(\tilde{R}_i)]^2)$$
$$= E([\tilde{R}_i - E(\tilde{R}_i)] [\tilde{R}_i - E(\tilde{R}_i)])$$
$$= \sigma_{ii}.$$

With this notation, the security return variances in equation (17) can be included in the double sum, so that

$$\sigma^2(\tilde{R}_p) = \sum_{i=1}^{n} \sum_{j=1}^{n} x_{ip} x_{jp} \sigma_{ij}. \tag{18}$$

The double sum here is read "for each value of i from $i = 1$ to $i = n$, sum over j from $j = 1$ to $j = n$; then sum the results from $i = 1$ to $i = n$"; or equivalently, "sum over all possible combinations of i and j."

Since

$$\sum_{i=1}^{n} \sum_{j=1}^{n} x_{ip} x_{jp} = 1.0,$$

equation (18) expresses $\sigma^2(\tilde{R}_p)$ as a weighted average of the n^2 variances and covariances $\sigma_{ij}(i, j = 1, 2, \ldots, n)$. Equation (17) treats the n security return variances embedded in the double sum of (18) separately from the $n(n-1)$ "true" covariances $\sigma_{ij}, j \neq i$, while equation (16) emphasizes that since $\sigma_{ij} = \sigma_{ji}$, only $n(n-1)/2$ of the covariances in (17) are different.

Finally, at the moment we are concerned with the variance of the return on a portfolio, but the preceding analysis is general. That is, (11) can be regarded as a general expression for a sum of weighted random variables. Equations (16) to (18) are general expressions for the variance of such a sum, expressed in terms of the weights applied to the individual summands, the variances of the individual summands, and their pairwise covariances.

PROBLEMS II.B

3. Show that

$$\sum_{i=1}^{n} \sum_{j=1}^{n} x_{ip} x_{jp} = 1.0.$$

4. For the case $n = 4$, show that equations (16), (17), and (18) are equivalent expressions for $\sigma^2(\tilde{R}_p)$.

5. Let $\tilde{y}_1, \tilde{y}_2, \ldots, \tilde{y}_n$ be arbitrary random variables.

(a) What is the variance of their sum?
(b) What is the variance of their sample mean

$$\tilde{\bar{y}} = \frac{\tilde{y}_1 + \tilde{y}_2 + \ldots + \tilde{y}_n}{n} ?$$

(c) What is $E(\tilde{\bar{y}})$ in terms of $E(\tilde{y}_i), i = 1, 2, \ldots, n$?

  Note that the sample mean is itself a random variable. That is, the value of $\tilde{\bar{y}}$ varies from one sample to another, since each of the $\tilde{y}_i, i = 1, \ldots, n$, varies from one sample to another. Thus, this problem and those that follow are concerned in large part with determining the sampling distribution of the sample mean.

  6. Suppose $\tilde{y}_1, \tilde{y}_2, \ldots, \tilde{y}_n$ are independent random variables. What is the variance of their sum? What is the variance of their sample mean? What is $E(\tilde{\bar{y}})$?

  7. Suppose that $\tilde{y}_1, \tilde{y}_2, \ldots, \tilde{y}_n$ are independent and identically distributed. What is the variance of their sum? What is the variance of their sample mean? What is $E(\tilde{\bar{y}})$?

  8. As an application of the results of Problem II.B.7, suppose successive monthly returns on security i are independent and identically distributed with mean $E(\tilde{R}_i)$ and variance $\sigma^2(\tilde{R}_i)$. What are the mean and standard deviation of the distribution of the average return on security i for T months?

  9. As another application of the results of Problem II.B.7, suppose successive daily continuously compounded returns on security i are independent and identically distributed. What are the mean and standard deviation of the distribution of the continuously compounded monthly return on security i in terms of the mean and standard deviation of the continuously compounded daily return?

  10. As an application of the results of Problem II.B.9, look again at Problem VI.C.3 of Chapter 1.

ANSWERS

  3.

$$\sum_{i=1}^{n} x_{ip} = 1 \quad \text{and} \quad \sum_{j=1}^{n} x_{jp} = 1.$$

Therefore

$$\left(\sum_{i=1}^{n} x_{ip} \right) \cdot \left(\sum_{j=1}^{n} x_{jp} \right) = 1.$$

But

$$\sum_{i=1}^{n} x_{ip} \cdot \sum_{j=1}^{n} x_{jp} = \sum_{i=1}^{n} \sum_{j=1}^{n} x_{ip} x_{jp}.$$

  4. Do it.

5. With $\tilde{y}_1, \tilde{y}_2, \ldots, \tilde{y}_n$ as random variables,

(a)
$$\sigma^2 \left(\sum_{i=1}^{n} \tilde{y}_i \right) = E\left[\left(\sum_{i=1}^{n} \tilde{y}_i - E\left(\sum_{i=1}^{n} \tilde{y}_i \right) \right)^2 \right]$$

$$= E\left[\left(\sum_{i=1}^{n} (\tilde{y}_i - E(\tilde{y}_i)) \right)^2 \right]$$

$$= \sum_{i=1}^{n} \sum_{j=1}^{n} E[(\tilde{y}_i - E(\tilde{y}_i))(\tilde{y}_j - E(\tilde{y}_j))]$$

$$= \sum_{i=1}^{n} \sum_{j=1}^{n} \text{cov}(\tilde{y}_i, \tilde{y}_j).$$

Thus the variance of a sum of random variables is just the sum of all the pairwise covariances, which also includes, of course, the n variances $\sigma^2(\tilde{y}_i), i = 1, \ldots, n$.

(b) From equation (18), with each $x_{ip} = \dfrac{1}{n}$,

$$\sigma^2(\tilde{\bar{y}}) = \sigma^2 \left(\frac{1}{n} \sum_{i=1}^{n} \tilde{y}_i \right)$$

$$= \sum_{i=1}^{n} \sum_{j=1}^{n} \frac{1}{n} \frac{1}{n} \sigma_{ij}$$

$$= \frac{1}{n^2} \sum_{i=1}^{n} \sum_{j=1}^{n} \sigma_{ij}.$$

Alternatively, this result follows from the answer to (a) and the fact that the sample mean is just the sum of random variables treated in (a) multiplied by the constant $1/n$.

(c)
$$E(\tilde{\bar{y}}) = E\left(\frac{1}{n} \sum_{i=1}^{n} \tilde{y}_i \right) = \frac{1}{n} \sum_{i=1}^{n} E(\tilde{y}_i).$$

6. If $\tilde{y}_1, \ldots, \tilde{y}_n$ are independent, $\sigma_{ij} = 0, i \neq j$. Therefore

$$\sigma^2 \left(\sum_{i=1}^{n} \tilde{y}_i \right) = \sum_{i=1}^{n} \sum_{j=1}^{n} \sigma_{ij} = \sum_{i=1}^{n} \sigma_{ii} = \sum_{i=1}^{n} \sigma^2(\tilde{y}_i)$$

$$\sigma^2 \left(\frac{1}{n} \sum_{i=1}^{n} \tilde{y}_i \right) = \frac{1}{n^2} \sum_{i=1}^{n} \sum_{j=1}^{n} \sigma_{ij} = \frac{1}{n^2} \sum_{i=1}^{n} \sigma_{ii} = \frac{1}{n^2} \sum_{i=1}^{n} \sigma^2(\tilde{y}_i).$$

Thus, the variance of a sum of independent random variables is the sum of the variances of the component variables, while the variance of the sample mean is $(1/n)^2$ times the sum of the variances. Finally,

$$E\left(\frac{1}{n} \sum_{i=1}^{n} \tilde{y}_i\right) = \frac{1}{n} \sum_{i=1}^{n} E(\tilde{y}_i).$$

7. If $\tilde{y}_1, \ldots, \tilde{y}_n$ are identically distributed, $\sigma^2(\tilde{y}_i) = \sigma^2(\tilde{y}_j)$ for all i and j; equivalently, $\sigma^2(\tilde{y}_i) = \sigma^2(\tilde{y})$, $i = 1, \ldots, n$. Moreover, $E(\tilde{y}_1) = E(\tilde{y})$, $i = 1, \ldots, n$. Then

$$\sigma^2 \left(\sum_{i=1}^{n} \tilde{y}_i\right) = \sum_{i=1}^{n} \sigma^2(\tilde{y}_i) = n\sigma^2(\tilde{y})$$

$$\sigma^2 \left(\frac{1}{n} \sum_{i=1}^{n} \tilde{y}_i\right) = \frac{1}{n^2} \sum_{i=1}^{n} \sigma^2(\tilde{y}_i) = \frac{n}{n^2} \sigma^2(\tilde{y}) = \frac{\sigma^2(\tilde{y})}{n}$$

$$E\left(\frac{1}{n} \sum_{i=1}^{n} \tilde{y}_i\right) = \frac{1}{n} \sum_{i=1}^{n} E(\tilde{y}_i) = \frac{n}{n} E(\tilde{y}) = E(\tilde{y}).$$

These are important results. Thus, suppose $\tilde{y}_i, i = 1, \ldots, n$ are n independent drawings of a random variable $\tilde{y}$, and we want to use the sample to estimate the population mean $E(\tilde{y})$. If we use the sample mean

$$\tilde{\bar{y}} = \frac{\tilde{y}_1 + \ldots + \tilde{y}_n}{n} \tag{19}$$

as the estimator of the population mean $E(\tilde{y})$, then the preceding results tell us that the estimator is unbiased, which means that $E(\tilde{\bar{y}})$, the mean of the sampling distribution of the sample mean $\tilde{\bar{y}}$, is equal to $E(\tilde{y})$, the mean of the distribution of $\tilde{y}$. Moreover, since $\sigma^2(\tilde{\bar{y}}) = \sigma^2(\tilde{y})/n$, the larger is the sample size n, the more tightly packed the sampling distribution of $\tilde{\bar{y}}$ about its mean $E(\tilde{\bar{y}}) = E(\tilde{y})$. In intuitive terms, the larger the sample size on which $\tilde{\bar{y}}$ is based, the more reliable is the sample mean $\tilde{\bar{y}}$ as an estimator of $E(\tilde{y})$. In the limit—that is, as n becomes arbitrarily large—$\sigma(\tilde{\bar{y}})$ approaches zero, so that the sampling distribution of the sample mean becomes arbitrarily tightly packed about $E(\tilde{\bar{y}}) = E(\tilde{y})$.

The preceding paragraph introduces some new statistical terms whose definitions should be emphasized. A procedure for estimating a parameter from a hypothetical sample is called an estimator. For example, the sample mean $\tilde{\bar{y}}$ defined in equation (19) is an estimator of the population mean $E(\tilde{y})$. The value $\bar{y}$ of $\tilde{\bar{y}}$ obtained from a specific sample $y_1, \ldots, y_n$ is called an estimate of the population mean. The properties of an estimator are described by its probability distribution, which is usually called its sampling distribution. The estimate obtained from a specific sample is a drawing from the distribution of the estimator.

One property that an estimator might have is unbiasedness. This means that the mean or expected value of the estimator is equal to the value of the parameter being estimated. Thus, the sample mean $\bar{\tilde{y}}$ is an unbiased estimator of the population mean $E(\tilde{y})$, since $E(\bar{\tilde{y}}) = E(\tilde{y})$.

Another example of an estimator is the sample variance

$$s^2(\tilde{y}) = \sum_{i=1}^{n} (\tilde{y}_i - \bar{\tilde{y}})^2 / (n-1),$$

which is an estimator of the population variance $\sigma^2(\tilde{y})$. Now that we know what unbiasedness means, we can state (without proof) that the purpose of dividing by $n-1$ rather than n is to ensure that the sample variance is an unbiased estimator of the population variance; that is, dividing the sum of squares by $n-1$ leads to the result that $E[s^2(\tilde{y})] = \sigma^2(\tilde{y})$. We might also note (without proof) that the sample variance has the desirable property that the larger the sample size, the more tightly the sampling distribution is packed about $\sigma^2(\tilde{y})$.

8.
$$E(\bar{\tilde{R}}_i) = E(\tilde{R}_i)$$

$$\sigma^2(\bar{\tilde{R}}_i) = \frac{1}{T}\,\sigma^2(\tilde{R}_i)$$

$$\sigma(\bar{\tilde{R}}_i) = \sqrt{\frac{1}{T}}\,\sigma(\tilde{R}_i).$$

Note again that the distribution of the average return has a smaller standard deviation than the distribution of the return itself; the larger the sample size T, the smaller the standard deviation of the average return.

9. Suppose there are T days in the month. If $\tilde{r}_{it}$ is the simple return for day t, then the continuously compounded return for day t is $ln\,(1 + \tilde{r}_{it})$. From equation (17) of Chapter 1, the monthly continuously compounded return, $ln\,(1 + \tilde{R}_i)$ is related to the daily continuously compounded returns as

$$ln\,(1 + \tilde{R}_i) = \sum_{t=1}^{T} ln\,(1 + \tilde{r}_{it}).$$

Let

$$E(ln\,(1 + \tilde{r}_{it})) = \mu, \qquad t = 1, \ldots, T$$
$$\sigma^2(ln\,(1 + \tilde{r}_{it})) = \sigma^2, \qquad t = 1, \ldots, T.$$

From Problem II.B.7,

$$E(ln\,(1 + \tilde{R}_i)) = T\mu$$
$$\sigma^2\,(ln\,(1 + \tilde{R}_i)) = T\sigma^2$$
$$\sigma(ln\,(1 + \tilde{R}_i)) = \sqrt{T}\,\sigma.$$

10. The answer to Problem II.B.*9* above tells us that if successive daily returns are independent and identically distributed, the standard deviation of the monthly returns is approximately the square root of the number of trading days times the standard deviation of the daily returns. Thus, the results of Problem VI.C.*3* of Chapter 1 are consistent with a world where daily returns are independent and identically distributed.

III. Portfolio Risk and Security Risk

The preceding results allow some simple insights into the measurement of risk when probability distributions of returns on portfolios are normal. In such a world, knowledge of its mean and variance is sufficient to describe completely the probability distribution of the return on a portfolio, and comparisons of portfolios can be made solely in terms of the means and variances of their returns. Thus, a portfolio model for a world where portfolio return distributions are normal is called a *two-parameter model.*

In this book, it is also assumed that investors like expected portfolio return but are risk-averse, which in a two-parameter world means that they are risk-averse with respect to variance of portfolio return; the most preferred portfolio among all those with the same level of expected return is the one with the lowest variance of return. In short, in portfolio models based on normal return distributions, the risk of a portfolio is measured by the variance of its return, and investors are assumed to dislike variance of portfolio return.

It is tempting to jump to the conclusion that the risk of a security is also measured by the variance of its return. In portfolio theory, however, the presumption is that the primary concern in the investment decision is the distribution of the return on the portfolio. Investors look at individual securities only in terms of their effects on distributions of portfolio returns. In a two-parameter world, an investor looks at an individual security in terms of its contributions to the mean and variance of the distribution of the return on his portfolio.

The mean or expected return on a portfolio is just the weighted average of the expected returns on the securities in the portfolio. The contribution of a security to the expected return on a portfolio is $x_{ip}E(\tilde{R}_i)$, the expected return on the security weighted by the proportion of portfolio funds invested in the security.

From inspection of equations (16) to (18), it is clear that the contribution of a security to the variance of a portfolio's return is a somewhat more complicated matter. One important point, emphasized by writing $\sigma^2(\tilde{R}_p)$ as in equation (17), is that when the number of securities n in the portfolio is large, individual security return variances are much less numerous in $\sigma^2(\tilde{R}_p)$ than are covariances. In particular, $\sigma^2(\tilde{R}_p)$ contains only n terms for the security return variances, whereas there are $n(n-1)$ covariances. For example, with a portfolio of 50 securities, $\sigma^2(\tilde{R}_p)$ contains 50 variance terms and 2,450 covariance terms.

The large number of covariances relative to security return variances in $\sigma^2(\tilde{R}_p)$ does not in itself imply that the covariances dominate the variances in the determination of $\sigma^2(\tilde{R}_p)$. Relative magnitudes are also important. This question is studied empirically in Chapter 7, where the portfolio model is presented in detail. To foreshadow the results, at least for NYSE common stocks, pairwise covariances between individual security returns are nontrivial in magnitude relative to variances of individual security returns. In portfolios of 20 or more common stocks, $\sigma^2(\tilde{R}_p)$ is primarily determined by the pairwise covariances of security returns.

All this assumes that the portfolios are diversified in the sense that funds are spread fairly evenly across the securities in the portfolio, or at least that funds are not concentrated in a few securities. For example, if most of the portfolio is in one security, then that security's return variance is important in determining the variance of the return on the portfolio, regardless of how many other securities are also included in the portfolio.

We have strayed. What about the risk of a specific security? What is the contribution of an individual security to the variance of the return on a portfolio? To study this question, it is convenient to work with equation (18) and to rewrite it as

$$\sigma^2(\tilde{R}_p) = \sum_{i=1}^n x_{ip}\left(\sum_{j=1}^n x_{jp}\sigma_{ij}\right). \tag{20}$$

In equation (20), $\sigma^2(\tilde{R}_p)$ can be interpreted as the sum of n terms, one for each security in the portfolio. The term for security i is

$$x_{ip}\left(\sum_{j=1}^n x_{jp}\sigma_{ij}\right), \quad i = 1, 2, \ldots, n.$$

This is the contribution of security i to the variance of the return on portfolio p. This contribution of security i to $\sigma^2(\tilde{R}_p)$ is itself made up of two parts: x_{ip}, the proportion of portfolio funds invested in security i, and

$$\sum_{j=1}^{n} x_{jp}\sigma_{ij}, \tag{21}$$

the weighted average of the pairwise covariances between the return on security i and the returns on each of the n securities (including security i) in the portfolio. If we call this weighted average of covariances the risk of security i in portfolio p, then equation (20) says that the risk of p, as measured by the variance of its return, is the weighted average of the risks of the securities in the portfolio where the risk of security i in portfolio p is weighted by the proportion of portfolio funds invested in this security.

There are two points in this analysis that should be emphasized. First, to be precise we must always say "the risk of security i in portfolio p" since the risk of a given security is different for different portfolios. That is, the pairwise covariances σ_{ij} in (21) are parameters of the joint distribution of security returns and thus are the same for all portfolios. The weights $x_{jp}, j = 1, 2, \ldots, n$, vary from portfolio to portfolio, however, and this is why the risk of security i, as measured by the weighted average of pairwise covariances in (21), is different for different portfolios.

Second, one of the terms in the risk of security i in portfolio p is the variance of the return on that security, $\sigma^2(\tilde{R}_i) = \sigma_{ii}$, which is weighted by x_{ip}. There are, however, $n - 1$ covariance terms in (21). If the covariances are not trivial in magnitude relative to $\sigma^2(\tilde{R}_i)$, then in a diversified portfolio the risk of security i is determined primarily by the covariances of its return with the returns on each of the other $n - 1$ securities in the portfolio.

Finally, expression (21) can be put into a form that provides a natural introduction to the next chapter. In particular,

$$\sum_{j=1}^{n} x_{jp}\sigma_{ij} = \text{cov}\,(\tilde{R}_i, \tilde{R}_p). \tag{22}$$

That is, the risk of security i in portfolio p, as described by (21), is also the covariance between the return on the security and the return on the portfolio.

PROBLEMS III

1. Derive equation (22).

2. Show that, in general, the covariance of a random variable $\tilde{y}$ with a random variable $\tilde{z} = \sum_{i=1}^{n} a_i \tilde{z}_i$ which is itself a sum of weighted random variables is the weighted sum of the pairwise covariances:

$$\text{cov}\,(\tilde{y}, \tilde{z}) = \text{cov}\left(\tilde{y}, \sum_{i=1}^{n} a_i \tilde{z}_i\right)$$

$$= \sum_{i=1}^{n} a_i\, \text{cov}\,(\tilde{y}, \tilde{z}_i).$$

ANSWERS

1. The steps are as follows:

$$\text{cov}\,(\tilde{R}_i, \tilde{R}_p) = \text{cov}\left(\tilde{R}_i, \sum_{j=1}^{n} x_{jp} \tilde{R}_j\right) \tag{22a}$$

$$= E\left([\tilde{R}_i - E(\tilde{R}_i)]\left[\sum_{j=1}^{n} x_{jp}\tilde{R}_j - E\left(\sum_{j=1}^{n} x_{jp}\tilde{R}_j\right)\right]\right) \tag{22b}$$

$$= E\left([\tilde{R}_i - E(\tilde{R}_i)]\left[\sum_{j=1}^{n} x_{jp}\tilde{R}_j - \sum_{j=1}^{n} x_{jp}E(\tilde{R}_j)\right]\right) \tag{22c}$$

$$= E\left([\tilde{R}_i - E(\tilde{R}_i)]\left[\sum_{j=1}^{n} x_{jp}(\tilde{R}_j - E(\tilde{R}_j))\right]\right) \tag{22d}$$

$$= E\left(\sum_{j=1}^{n} x_{jp}[\tilde{R}_i - E(\tilde{R}_i)]\,[\tilde{R}_j - E(\tilde{R}_j)]\right) \tag{22e}$$

$$= \sum_{j=1}^{n} x_{jp}E([\tilde{R}_i - E(\tilde{R}_i)]\,[\tilde{R}_j - E(\tilde{R}_j)]) \tag{22f}$$

$$= \sum_{j=1}^{n} x_j \sigma_{ij}. \tag{22g}$$

In going from (22a) to (22b), we make use of the definition of a covariance as an expected value. The step from (22b) to (22c) makes use of the result that the expectation of a sum of weighted random variables is the sum of the weighted expectations, which is also used to go from (22e) to (22f). The final step from (22f) to (22g) then makes use of the definition of σ_{ij} as an expected value.

2. Except for a trivial change in notation, the steps are (22a) to (22g). The only point of this problem is to get you to recognize the generality of the development of equations (22a) to (22g).

It is also convenient to define

$$\beta_{ip} = \frac{\text{cov}\,(\tilde{R}_i, \tilde{R}_p)}{\sigma^2(\tilde{R}_p)}, \tag{23}$$

which is the risk of security i in portfolio p relative to the risk of the portfolio. From equations (20) and (22),

$$\sigma^2(\tilde{R}_p) = \sum_{i=1}^{n} x_{ip} \, \text{cov}\,(\tilde{R}_i, \tilde{R}_p); \tag{24}$$

that is, $\sigma^2(\tilde{R}_p)$ is the weighted average of the values of cov $(\tilde{R}_i, \tilde{R}_p)$ for all the securities in the portfolio. Thus if β_{ip} is greater than 1.0, then the risk of security i in p is greater than the weighted average risk of securities in p, whereas a value of β_{ip} less than 1.0 implies a security with less than average risk in portfolio p.

Again, bear in mind that β_{ip}, the relative risk of security i in portfolio p, varies from portfolio to portfolio. Indeed, neither component of the ratio that defines β_{ip} is generally the same from portfolio to portfolio.

IV. Conclusions

One measure of the relative risk of security i that appears frequently in the remainder of this book is

$$\beta_{im} = \frac{\text{cov}\,(\tilde{R}_i, \tilde{R}_m)}{\sigma^2(\tilde{R}_m)},$$

where $\tilde{R}_m$ is the return on an equally weighted portfolio of the securities assumed to be available to the investor. Like any other measure of relative risk, β_{im} is the risk of security i in m, cov $(\tilde{R}_i, \tilde{R}_m)$, measured relative to the risk of m, $\sigma^2(\tilde{R}_m)$. If the available securities are all those in the market, or in some market like the NYSE, then β_{im} can be interpreted as a measure of the "market risk" of security i, and this interpretation enhances our interest in β_{im}.

Indeed, much of the material in the next two chapters is concerned with developing the interpretation of β_{im} and with estimating this measure of "market risk." The time is well spent. In the process of studying β_{im}, we can introduce all of the statistical concepts needed for the more interesting theoretical and empirical work in the rest of the book. Thus, β_{im} is the convenient medium through which we complete our technical toolbox.

Finally, the two-parameter portfolio model is developed in detail in Chapter 7. The model is credited to Markowitz (1952; 1959), who is rightfully regarded as the founder of modern portfolio theory.

CHAPTER

3

The Market Model: Theory and Estimation

We now consider the relationships between the returns on securities and portfolios when the probability distributions of returns on portfolios are normal. This chapter studies the statistical foundations of these relationships and considers their estimation from a theoretical viewpoint. Chapter 4 presents the results produced by the estimation procedures when applied to actual data on New York Stock Exchange common stocks.

I. The Multivariate Normal Distribution of Returns on Securities*

A. *Normal Portfolio Returns and Multivariate Normal Returns on Securities*

Let $\tilde{y}_1, \ldots, \tilde{y}_n$ be n continuous jointly distributed random variables with joint density function $f(y_1, \ldots, y_n)$. The value of the joint density function can be thought of as the likelihood that a joint drawing of the random variables $\tilde{y}_1, \ldots, \tilde{y}_n$ will yield the particular combination of the variables shown as arguments of the function. Except for the fact that we are thinking in terms of a joint drawing on n random variables, the notion of a drawing and

---

*The statistical results on multivariate normal distributions that are discussed in this chapter can be found in Anderson (1958, chap. 2) and Cramer (1946, chaps. 21, 29).

a probability distribution on its outcome are the same as in the case of one variable.

Define a new random variable,

$$\tilde{y} = \sum_{i=1}^{n} a_i \tilde{y}_i,$$

which is a linear combination, that is, a sum of weighted values of $\tilde{y}_1, \ldots, \tilde{y}_n$. If every such linear combination of the $\tilde{y}_i$ has a normal distribution (that is, if the distribution of $\tilde{y}$ is normal for any choice of weights $a_1, \ldots, a_n$), then the joint distribution of $\tilde{y}_1, \ldots, \tilde{y}_n$ is multivariate normal, and the joint density function $f(y_1, \ldots, y_n)$ is the density function of a multivariate normal distribution. Conversely, if the joint distribution of $\tilde{y}_1, \ldots, \tilde{y}_n$ is multivariate normal, then the distribution of any linear combination of $\tilde{y}_1, \ldots, \tilde{y}_n$ is normal.

The two-parameter portfolio model introduced in the preceding chapter assumes that probability distributions of returns on all portfolios are normal. The return on any portfolio is a linear combination of the returns on the n securities available for inclusion in portfolios,

$$\tilde{R}_{pt} = \sum_{i=1}^{n} x_{ip} \tilde{R}_{it}, \tag{1}$$

where, following the notation of preceding chapters, tildes are used to denote random variables, $\tilde{R}_{it}$ is the simple return on security i from time $t-1$ to time t, $\tilde{R}_{pt}$ is the return on the portfolio p, and the portfolio p is defined by the proportions $x_{ip}, i = 1, \ldots, n$, of portfolio funds invested in individual securities at time $t-1$. To assume that $\tilde{R}_{pt}$ has a normal distribution for any choice of $x_{1p}, \ldots, x_{np}$ (that is, for any portfolio p) is equivalent to assuming that every linear combination of $\tilde{R}_{1t}, \ldots, \tilde{R}_{nt}$ has a normal distribution. Thus, the joint distribution of $\tilde{R}_{1t}, \ldots, \tilde{R}_{nt}$ must be multivariate normal.

B. Some Properties of the Multivariate Normal Distribution

Multivariate distributions do not lend themselves to facile interpretation. Fortunately, we can use the properties of multivariate normal distributions that we need without getting into the more complicated aspects of multivariate statistics. There are, however, three interesting properties of multivariate normal distributions that we can note briefly.

First, just as a univariate normal distribution (which we have heretofore called a normal distribution) can be described from knowledge of its mean and variance, a multivariate normal distribution can be described from knowledge of the means and variances of the component univariate random variables and the $n(n-1)/2$ pairwise covariances between the component variables. Thus, the multivariate normal distribution of $\tilde{R}_{1t}, \ldots, \tilde{R}_{nt}$ can be described from knowledge of the n expected returns $E(\tilde{R}_{1t}), \ldots, E(\tilde{R}_{nt})$, the n security return variances $\sigma^2(\tilde{R}_{1t}), \ldots, \sigma^2(\tilde{R}_{nt})$, and the $n(n-1)/2$ distinct pairwise covariances, $\sigma_{ij} = \text{cov}(\tilde{R}_{it}, \tilde{R}_{jt})$, between returns on securities.

Second, Problem II.B.*1* in the preceding chapter asked the reader to show that independence implies zero covariances. The multivariate normal distribution is a special case where the reverse is also true. Thus, if $\tilde{R}_{1t}, \ldots, \tilde{R}_{nt}$ have a multivariate normal distribution, then the condition $\sigma_{ij} = 0$ for all i and j, $i \neq j$, implies

$$f(R_{1t}, \ldots, R_{nt}) = f(R_{1t}) f(R_{2t}) \ldots f(R_{nt}).$$

Equivalently, for any i

$$f(R_{it} | R_{1t}, \ldots, R_{i-1,t}, R_{i+1,t}, \ldots, R_{nt}) = f(R_{it}).$$

In words, multivariate normality and zero covariances between all returns imply independence of returns in the sense that the conditional distribution of the return on any security i, $f(R_{it} | R_{1t}, \ldots, R_{i-1,t}, R_{i+1,t}, \ldots, R_{nt})$, is the same for all possible combinations of the returns on other securities, and thus the conditional distribution is identical to the marginal distribution, $f(R_{it})$. Moreover, if returns on securities are multivariate normal and any $\sigma_{ij} = 0$, then $\tilde{R}_{it}$ and $\tilde{R}_{jt}$ are independent, so that

$$f(R_{it} | R_{jt}) = f(R_{it}) \text{ and } f(R_{jt} | R_{it}) = f(R_{jt}).$$

We use this result several times below.

Finally, if $\tilde{R}_{1t}, \ldots, \tilde{R}_{nt}$ have a multivariate normal distribution, then each $\tilde{R}_{it}$ has a univariate normal distribution. Thus, multivariate normality implies that returns on both securities and portfolios have normal distributions. Conversely, our empirical conclusion (see Chapter 1) that distributions of monthly portfolio returns and security returns are approximately normal is consistent with the assumption that the joint distribution of returns on securities is multivariate normal.

C. Bivariate Normality of Pairwise Security and Portfolio Returns

There is one property of multivariate normal distributions that we investigate in some detail. If the joint distribution of $\tilde{R}_{1t}, \ldots, \tilde{R}_{nt}$ is multivariate normal, then the joint distribution of any two different linear combinations of $\tilde{R}_{1t}, \ldots, \tilde{R}_{nt}$ is bivariate normal, which is just the name given to the multivariate normal distribution when it applies to two jointly distributed random variables. This result implies that the joint distribution of the returns on any two different portfolios is bivariate normal. Since securities are special types of portfolios, the result also implies that the joint distribution of the return on any security i and the return on any portfolio p is bivariate normal, as is the joint distribution of returns on any two different securities.

Bivariate normality of security and portfolio returns is the foundation of our theoretical and empirical work on the so-called "market model" relationships between the returns on securities and the return on a portfolio of securities taken to be representative of "the market." The model takes up the rest of this chapter and all of the next. Since we concentrate so exclusively on the market model, it is well to emphasize that the model's statistical properties are a direct consequence of the assumed bivariate normality of the return on a security and the return on the chosen market portfolio. If bivariate normality is assumed—or better, if bivariate normality is implied from the more fundamental assumption that the joint distribution of security returns is multivariate normal—then similar statistical properties hold for the relationship between the returns on any two securities or portfolios.

II. Bivariate Normality and the Market Model

Let $\tilde{R}_{it}$ be the return on any security and let $\tilde{R}_{mt}$ be the return on a "market" portfolio of all securities, where each security is given an equal weight in the portfolio at time $t-1$. If the joint distribution of $\tilde{R}_{it}$ and $\tilde{R}_{mt}$ is bivariate normal, then the conditional distribution of the return on the security has an especially simple form, which in turn implies that the relationship between $\tilde{R}_{it}$ and $\tilde{R}_{mt}$ has an especially simple form. We first summarize the results and then offer some formal justification.

A. The Market Model: Fundamental Properties

The mean or expected value of the distribution of $\tilde{R}_{it}$ conditional on some value R_{mt} of $\tilde{R}_{mt}$ is

$$E(\tilde{R}_{it}|R_{mt}) = \int_{R_{it}} R_{it} f(R_{it}|R_{mt}) dR_{it}.$$

As usual, the mean or expected value is a weighted sum of all possible values of the random variable $\tilde{R}_{it}$; but since we are taking a conditional expected value, the weight given to R_{it} is its conditional density $f(R_{it}|R_{mt})$ rather than the marginal density $f(R_{it})$ which is used in the definition of the unconditional expected value $E(\tilde{R}_{it})$.

Since the conditional density function $f(R_{it}|R_{mt})$ is generally different for different values of R_{mt}, the conditional expected value $E(\tilde{R}_{it}|R_{mt})$ in general depends on the value of R_{mt}. If the joint distribution of $\tilde{R}_{it}$ and $\tilde{R}_{mt}$ is bivariate normal, $E(\tilde{R}_{it}|R_{mt})$ is the linear function

$$E(\tilde{R}_{it}|R_{mt}) = \alpha_i + \beta_i R_{mt}, \tag{2}$$

where the intercept α_i and slope β_i are

$$\beta_i = \frac{\text{cov}(\tilde{R}_{it}, \tilde{R}_{mt})}{\sigma^2(\tilde{R}_{mt})}, \text{ and } \alpha_i = E(\tilde{R}_{it}) - \beta_i E(\tilde{R}_{mt}). \tag{3}$$

Moreover, if the joint distribution of $\tilde{R}_{it}$ and $\tilde{R}_{mt}$ is bivariate normal, the conditional distribution of $\tilde{R}_{it}$ given R_{mt} is normal; that is, the conditional density function $f(R_{it}|R_{mt})$ is that of a normal distribution, with mean given by equation (2) and variance

$$\sigma^2(\tilde{R}_{it}|R_{mt}) = \int_{R_{it}} [R_{it} - E(\tilde{R}_{it}|R_{mt})]^2 f(R_{it}|R_{mt}) dR_{it} \tag{4}$$

$$= \sigma^2(\tilde{R}_{it})(1 - \rho_{im}^2), \tag{5}$$

where ρ_{im} is the correlation coefficient between $\tilde{R}_{it}$ and $\tilde{R}_{mt}$,

$$\rho_{im} = \frac{\text{cov}(\tilde{R}_{it}, \tilde{R}_{mt})}{\sigma(\tilde{R}_{it})\sigma(\tilde{R}_{mt})}. \tag{6}$$

The definitional equation (4) emphasizes that the conditional variance involves weighting squared deviations of R_{it} from its conditional mean $E(\tilde{R}_{it}|R_{mt})$ by the conditional density $f(R_{it}|R_{mt})$. This is in contrast with the unconditional variance $\sigma^2(\tilde{R}_{it})$, which involves weighting squared deviations of R_{it} from its unconditional mean $E(\tilde{R}_{it})$ by the marginal density $f(R_{it})$. Equation (5) then states that with bivariate normality, the conditional variance $\sigma^2(\tilde{R}_{it}|R_{mt})$ has the same value for all values of R_{mt}. This follows from the fact that $\sigma^2(\tilde{R}_{it})$ and ρ_{im} have the same values for all values of R_{mt}. That the conditional variance $\sigma^2(\tilde{R}_{it}|R_{mt})$ is as described in equation (5) is established later.

The results expressed by equations (2) and (5) are summarized in Figure 3.1. As in equation (2), the figure shows the conditional expected return $E(\tilde{R}_{it}|R_{mt})$ as a linear function of R_{mt}. The figure also shows conditional density functions $f(R_{it}|R_{mt})$ for three different values of R_{mt}. Since $E(\tilde{R}_{it}|R_{mt})$ is a function of R_{mt}, the location of these conditional distributions changes with R_{mt}, but otherwise the conditional distributions are the same

FIGURE 3.1

Conditional Distributions for $\tilde{R}_{it}$ Given R_{mt}

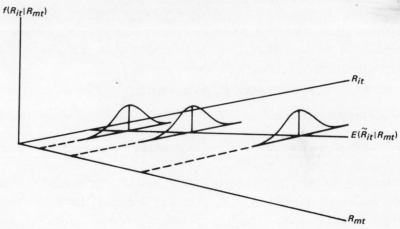

for all values of R_{mt}. The conditional distributions are normal with means given by equation (2) but constant variance given by (5).

Since the conditional distributions of $\tilde{R}_{it}$ are normal with variance independent of R_{mt}, the deviation of $\tilde{R}_{it}$ from its conditional expected value has a normal distribution with mean equal to zero and variance given by equation (5). That is, for any and every value R_{mt} of the return $\tilde{R}_{mt}$, the conditional distribution of

$$\tilde{\epsilon}_{it} = \tilde{R}_{it} - (\alpha_i + \beta_i R_{mt}) \tag{7}$$

is normal with mean

$$E(\tilde{\epsilon}_{it}|R_{mt}) = E(\tilde{\epsilon}_{it}) = 0 \tag{8}$$

and variance

$$\sigma^2(\tilde{\epsilon}_{it}|R_{mt}) = \sigma^2(\tilde{R}_{it}|R_{mt}) = \sigma^2(\tilde{R}_{it})(1 - \rho_{im}^2) = \sigma^2(\tilde{\epsilon}_{it}). \tag{9}$$

Thus the deviation $\tilde{\epsilon}_{it}$ has the same normal conditional distribution for all values of R_{mt}, which means that $\tilde{\epsilon}_{it}$ and $\tilde{R}_{mt}$ are independent.

PROBLEMS II.A

1. Use equations (2) and (7) to show that

$$E(\tilde{\epsilon}_{it}|R_{mt}) = 0.$$

2. Show that

$$\sigma^2(\tilde{\epsilon}_{it}|R_{mt}) = \sigma^2(\tilde{R}_{it}|R_{mt});$$

that is, show that the variance of the distribution of $\tilde{\epsilon}_{it}$ conditional on R_{mt} is the same as the variance of the distribution of $\tilde{R}_{it}$ conditional on R_{mt}.

ANSWERS

1. From equation (7):

$$E(\tilde{\epsilon}_{it}|R_{mt}) = E(\tilde{R}_{it}|R_{mt}) - (\alpha_i + \beta_i R_{mt}).$$

Then from (2):

$$E(\tilde{\epsilon}_{it}|R_{mt}) = (\alpha_i + \beta_i R_{mt}) - (\alpha_i + \beta_i R_{mt})$$

$$= 0.$$

2. The "disturbance" $\tilde{\epsilon}_{it}$ is the difference between $\tilde{R}_{it}$ and its conditional expected value $E(\tilde{R}_{it}|R_{mt})$. For any given R_{mt}, $E(\tilde{R}_{it}|R_{mt})$ is a constant. Subtracting a constant from a random variable has no effect on the variance of the variable.

Bringing all these results together, if the joint distribution of $\tilde{R}_{it}$ and $\tilde{R}_{mt}$ is bivariate normal, the relationship between $\tilde{R}_{it}$ and $\tilde{R}_{mt}$ can be expressed as

$$\tilde{R}_{it} = \alpha_i + \beta_i \tilde{R}_{mt} + \tilde{\epsilon}_{it}. \tag{10}$$

Equation (10) is (7) with a tilde inserted over R_{mt}. This is legitimate, since the results concerning the distribution of $\tilde{R}_{it}$ conditional on R_{mt} hold for all values of R_{mt}. Thus, we can now change our viewpoint slightly (but appropriately) and say that with bivariate normality there is a linear relationship between the jointly distributed random variables $\tilde{R}_{it}$ and $\tilde{R}_{mt}$ with coefficients α_i and β_i defined by (3). This linear relationship is, however, subject to a "disturbance" $\tilde{\epsilon}_{it}$ that has a normal distribution with mean and variance given by (8) and (9). The disturbance $\tilde{\epsilon}_{it}$ is independent of the return on the market portfolio $\tilde{R}_{mt}$.

B. Some Formal Justification

Having stated the form of the relationship between $\tilde{R}_{it}$ and $\tilde{R}_{mt}$ implied by bivariate normality, the next steps are to establish equation (9) and then to interpret the correlation coefficient ρ_{im} between $\tilde{R}_{it}$ and $\tilde{R}_{mt}$. We first show that the bivariate normality of $\tilde{R}_{it}$ and $\tilde{R}_{mt}$ implies that $\tilde{R}_{mt}$ and the disturbance $\tilde{\epsilon}_{it}$ in (10) are independent, which in turn implies (9). We then show that ρ_{im}^2 is the proportion of $\sigma^2(\tilde{R}_{it})$ that can be attributed to the relationship between $\tilde{R}_{it}$ and $\tilde{R}_{mt}$.

From (7), we can see that $\tilde{\epsilon}_{it}$ is a linear combination of $\tilde{R}_{it}$ and $\tilde{R}_{mt}$. Thus, if the joint distribution of $\tilde{R}_{it}$ and $\tilde{R}_{mt}$ is bivariate normal, the joint distribution of $\tilde{\epsilon}_{it}$ and $\tilde{R}_{mt}$ is also bivariate normal. It follows that $\tilde{\epsilon}_{it}$ and $\tilde{R}_{mt}$ are independent if cov $(\tilde{\epsilon}_{it}, \tilde{R}_{mt}) = 0$. Using (7),

$$\text{cov}\,(\tilde{\epsilon}_{it}, \tilde{R}_{mt}) = \text{cov}\,(\tilde{R}_{it} - \alpha_i - \beta_i \tilde{R}_{mt}, \tilde{R}_{mt}) \tag{11}$$

$$= \text{cov}\,(\tilde{R}_{it}, \tilde{R}_{mt}) - \beta_i \sigma^2 (\tilde{R}_{mt}). \tag{12}$$

$$\text{cov}\,(\tilde{\epsilon}_{it}, \tilde{R}_{mt}) = \text{cov}\,(\tilde{R}_{it}, \tilde{R}_{mt}) - \frac{\text{cov}\,(\tilde{R}_{it}, \tilde{R}_{mt})}{\sigma^2(\tilde{R}_{mt})}\,\sigma^2(\tilde{R}_{mt}) = 0. \tag{13}$$

In going from (11) to (12) we make use of three statistical facts: (a) as shown in equations (22a–g) of Chapter 2, the covariance of a random variable (in this case $\tilde{R}_{mt}$) with a linear combination of random variables (in this case $\tilde{R}_{it} - \alpha_i - \beta_i \tilde{R}_{mt}$) is the linear combination of the covariances; (b) by definition, $\text{cov}\,(\tilde{R}_{mt}, \tilde{R}_{mt}) = \sigma^2(\tilde{R}_{mt})$; and (c) as the reader can easily show, the covariance between a constant and a random variable is always 0, so that $\text{cov}\,(\alpha_i, \tilde{R}_{mt}) = 0$. To go from (12) to (13), we just substitute for β_i from (3).

Given the bivariate normality of $\tilde{\epsilon}_{it}$ and $\tilde{R}_{mt}$, the fact that $\text{cov}\,(\tilde{\epsilon}_{it}, \tilde{R}_{mt}) = 0$ implies that these two random variables are independent. Since $\tilde{\epsilon}_{it}$ and $\tilde{R}_{mt}$ are independent, the distribution of $\tilde{\epsilon}_{it}$ conditional on R_{mt} is the same for all values of R_{mt},

$$f(\epsilon_{it} | R_{mt}) = f(\epsilon_{it}).$$

This means that the expected value of $\tilde{\epsilon}_{it}$ conditional on R_{mt} is the same for all values of R_{mt},

$$E(\tilde{\epsilon}_{ij} | R_j) = E(\tilde{\epsilon}_i).$$

In fact, from Problem II.A.*1* above we already know that the expected value of $\tilde{\epsilon}_{it}$ is always zero, so that equation (8) is established. Moreover, since $\tilde{\epsilon}_{it}$ and $\tilde{R}_{mt}$ are independent, the variance of $\tilde{\epsilon}_{it}$ conditional on R_{mt} is the same for all values of R_{mt},

$$\sigma^2(\tilde{\epsilon}_{it} | R_{mt}) = \sigma^2(\tilde{\epsilon}_{it}).$$

To go from here to (9), however, we must first interpret the correlation coefficient ρ_{im} defined by (6).

Since $\tilde{\epsilon}_{it}$ and $\tilde{R}_{mt}$ are independent, equation (10) expresses $\tilde{R}_{it}$ as a weighted sum of the independent random variables $\tilde{R}_{mt}$ and $\tilde{\epsilon}_{it}$, so that

$$\sigma^2(\tilde{R}_{it}) = \beta_i^2 \sigma^2(\tilde{R}_{mt}) + \sigma^2(\tilde{\epsilon}_{it}). \tag{14}$$

PROBLEM II.B

1. Derive equation (14).

ANSWER

1. Since α_i and β_i in (10) are constants and $\text{cov}\,(\tilde{\epsilon}_{it}, \tilde{R}_{mt}) = 0$,

$$\sigma^2(\tilde{R}_{it}) = \sigma^2(\beta_i \tilde{R}_{mt} + \tilde{\epsilon}_{it})$$

$$= \beta_i^2 \sigma^2(\tilde{R}_{mt}) + \sigma^2(\tilde{\epsilon}_{it}) + 2\beta_i \text{ cov } (\tilde{\epsilon}_{it}, \tilde{R}_{mt})$$

$$= \beta_{ij}^2 \sigma^2(\tilde{R}_j) + \sigma(\tilde{\epsilon}_{ij}).$$

If the steps are not clear, the reader should review Section II.B of Chapter 2.

Equation (10) expresses the return on security i in terms of the return on the market portfolio m and the disturbance $\tilde{\epsilon}_{it}$. Equation (14) likewise breaks the variance of the return on security i into two parts: the first part, $\beta_i^2 \sigma^2(\tilde{R}_{mt})$, is due to the term $\beta_i \tilde{R}_{mt}$ in (10); the second part, $\sigma^2(\tilde{\epsilon}_{it})$, is due to the disturbance $\tilde{\epsilon}_{it}$ in (10). To examine the proportion of $\sigma^2(\tilde{R}_{it})$ attributable to each of these two components, we divide through equation (14) by $\sigma^2(\tilde{R}_{it})$ to get

$$1 = \frac{\beta_i^2 \sigma^2(\tilde{R}_{mt})}{\sigma^2(\tilde{R}_{it})} + \frac{\sigma^2(\tilde{\epsilon}_{it})}{\sigma^2(\tilde{R}_{it})} . \tag{15}$$

With the definitions of β_i and ρ_{im} in equations (3) and (6), this equation becomes

$$1 = \rho_{im}^2 + \frac{\sigma^2(\tilde{\epsilon}_{it})}{\sigma^2(\tilde{R}_{it})} . \tag{16}$$

Equivalently,

$$\rho_{im}^2 = 1 - \frac{\sigma^2(\tilde{\epsilon}_{it})}{\sigma^2(\tilde{R}_{it})} = \frac{\sigma^2(\tilde{R}_{it}) - \sigma^2(\tilde{\epsilon}_{it})}{\sigma^2(\tilde{R}_{it})} . \tag{17}$$

In words, the development of equations (14) to (17) tells us that ρ_{im}^2, the square of the correlation coefficient between the returns on securities i and j, is the proportion of the variance of the return on security i that can be attributed to the term $\beta_i \tilde{R}_{mt}$ in (10), while $1 - \rho_{im}^2$ is the proportion of $\sigma^2(\tilde{R}_{it})$ that can be attributed to the disturbance $\tilde{\epsilon}_{it}$ in (10). Intuitively, $\alpha_i + \beta_i \tilde{R}_{mt}$ in (10) is the component of $\tilde{R}_{it}$ that can be attributed to the relationship between $\tilde{R}_{it}$ and $\tilde{R}_{mt}$, and $\tilde{\epsilon}_{it}$ is the disturbance in this relationship. Thus, ρ_{im}^2 can be interpreted as the proportion of the variance of $\tilde{R}_{it}$ that can be attributed to the relationship between $\tilde{R}_{it}$ and $\tilde{R}_{mt}$, while $1 - \rho_{im}^2$ is the proportion of $\sigma^2(\tilde{R}_{it})$ that can be attributed to the disturbance $\tilde{\epsilon}_{it}$.

From equation (17), we determine that

$$\sigma^2(\tilde{\epsilon}_{it}) = \sigma^2(\tilde{R}_{it}) (1 - \rho_{im}^2).$$

Since the independence of $\tilde{\epsilon}_{it}$ and $\tilde{R}_{mt}$ implies that $\sigma^2(\tilde{\epsilon}_{it}|R_{mt})$ is the same for all values of R_{mt},

$$\sigma^2(\tilde{\epsilon}_{it}|R_{mt}) = \sigma^2(\tilde{\epsilon}_{it}),$$

and equation (9) is established.

Finally, from equations (3) and (6), it is clear that the measure of the degree of association between $\tilde{R}_{it}$ and $\tilde{R}_{mt}$ in both the slope coefficient β_i and the correlation coefficient ρ_{im} is the covariance between $\tilde{R}_{it}$ and $\tilde{R}_{mt}$. The slope β_i is $\mathrm{cov}\,(\tilde{R}_{it}, \tilde{R}_{mt})$ scaled by the variance of $\tilde{R}_{mt}$, while ρ_{im} is $\mathrm{cov}\,(\tilde{R}_{it}, \tilde{R}_{mt})$ scaled by the product of $\sigma(\tilde{R}_{it})$ and $\sigma(\tilde{R}_{mt})$. The sign of both coefficients is the sign of the covariance.

PROBLEMS II.B

2. Consider the dollar returns

$$\tilde{D}_{it} = h_i \tilde{R}_{it} \text{ and } \tilde{D}_{jt} = h_j \tilde{R}_{jt}$$

on the dollar investments h_i and h_j in securities i and j. Show that

$$\mathrm{cov}\,(\tilde{D}_{it}, \tilde{D}_{jt}) = h_i h_j \, \mathrm{cov}\,(\tilde{R}_{it}, \tilde{R}_{jt}),$$

whereas the correlation coefficient

$$\mathrm{corr}\,(\tilde{D}_{it}, \tilde{D}_{jt}) = \frac{\mathrm{cov}\,(\tilde{D}_{it}, \tilde{D}_{jt})}{\sigma(\tilde{D}_{it})\sigma(\tilde{D}_{jt})} = \mathrm{corr}\,(\tilde{R}_{it}, \tilde{R}_{jt}).$$

In words, $\tilde{D}_{it}$ and $\tilde{D}_{jt}$ represent a change from proportions to dollars in the units used to measure returns. Your answer to this problem shows that the covariance between random variables depends on the units in which the variables are measured but that the correlation coefficient does not.

3. What are the maximum and minimum possible values of ρ_{im} and when are they attained?

ANSWERS

2. $$\mathrm{cov}\,(\tilde{D}_{it}, \tilde{D}_{jt}) = \mathrm{cov}\,(h_{ip}\tilde{R}_i, h_{jp}\tilde{R}_j)$$
    $$= h_i h_j \, \mathrm{cov}\,(\tilde{R}_{it}, \tilde{R}_{jt}).$$

This step follows from equations (22a–g) of Chapter 2.

$$\mathrm{corr}\,(\tilde{D}_{it}, \tilde{D}_{jt}) = \frac{\mathrm{cov}\,(\tilde{D}_{it}, \tilde{D}_{jt})}{\sigma(\tilde{D}_{it})\sigma(\tilde{D}_{jt})} = \frac{h_i h_j \, \mathrm{cov}\,(\tilde{R}_{it}, \tilde{R}_{jt})}{h_i \sigma(\tilde{R}_{it})h_j \sigma(\tilde{R}_{jt})}$$

$$= \frac{\mathrm{cov}\,(\tilde{R}_{it}, \tilde{R}_{jt})}{\sigma(\tilde{R}_{it})\sigma(\tilde{R}_{jt})} = \mathrm{corr}\,(\tilde{R}_{it}, \tilde{R}_{jt}).$$

If the steps are not clear, the reader should review Section II.A of Chapter 2.

3. Since both terms on the right of the equality in equation (14) are non-negative, $\sigma^2(\tilde{\epsilon}_{it}) \leqslant \sigma^2(\tilde{R}_{it})$. From equation (16), it is then clear that the maximum value of ρ_{im}^2 is 1.0, and this value is attained when $\sigma^2(\tilde{\epsilon}_{it}) = 0$. In this

case, the relationship between $\tilde{R}_{it}$ and $\tilde{R}_{mt}$ of equation (10) is exact; that is, the disturbance $\tilde{\epsilon}_{it}$ is always 0. Since the maximum value of ρ_{im}^2 is 1.0, the maximum and minimum values of ρ_{im} are 1.0 and -1.0. In addition to the condition $\sigma^2(\tilde{\epsilon}_{it}) = 0$, $\rho_{im} = 1.0$ requires cov $(\tilde{R}_{it}, \tilde{R}_{mt}) > 0$, while $\rho_{im} = -1.0$ requires cov $(\tilde{R}_{it}, \tilde{R}_{mt}) < 0$.

C. Some Additional Properties of the Model

In Section III of Chapter 2 we argued that since the risk of the portfolio m, as measured by the variance of its return, is the weighted average

$$\sigma^2(\tilde{R}_{mt}) = \sum_{i=1}^{n} x_{im} \text{ cov } (\tilde{R}_{it}, \tilde{R}_{mt}), \quad x_{im} = \frac{1}{n}, \quad i = 1, \ldots, n, \quad (18)$$

it is appropriate to interpret cov $(\tilde{R}_{it}, \tilde{R}_{mt})$ as the risk of security i in m. Thus, as defined by (3), the slope coefficient β_i in the market model relationship of (10) can be interpreted as the risk of security i measured relative to the risk of the portfolio m. Equivalently, β_i is the risk of security i relative to the average risk of securities in m. A value of β_i greater than 1.0 indicates that security i has higher than average risk, while a value of β_i less than 1.0 indicates a security with less than average risk among securities in m.

PROBLEM II.C

1. Show that, according to the definitions of β_i and α_i of (3),

$$\sum_{i=1}^{n} x_{im} \beta_i = 1 \quad \text{and} \quad \sum_{i=1}^{n} x_{im} \alpha_i = 0;$$

that is, that the weighted average of the β_i is 1.0, and the weighted average of the α_i is 0.

ANSWER

1. From (3) and (18),

$$\sum_{i=1}^{n} x_{im} \beta_i = \sum_{i=1}^{n} x_{im} \frac{\text{cov } (\tilde{R}_{it}, \tilde{R}_{mt})}{\sigma^2(\tilde{R}_{mt})} = \frac{\sigma^2(\tilde{R}_{mt})}{\sigma^2(\tilde{R}_{mt})} = 1.$$

Then, from (3) we have

$$\sum_{i=1}^{n} x_{im} \alpha_i = \sum_{i=1}^{n} x_{im} [E(\tilde{R}_{it}) - \beta_i E(\tilde{R}_{mt})]$$

$$= E(\tilde{R}_{mt}) - \sum_{i=1}^{n} x_{im} \beta_i E(\tilde{R}_{mt}) = 0.$$

An interesting feature of the market model relationship between $\tilde{R}_{it}$ and $\tilde{R}_{mt}$ of (10) is that the average of $\tilde{\epsilon}_{it}$, computed across securities, is always identically zero. To see this, note that with (10) and the answer to the preceding problem we can determine that

$$\tilde{R}_{mt} = \sum_{i=1}^{n} x_{im} \tilde{R}_{it} \tag{19a}$$

$$= \sum_{i=1}^{n} x_{im}(\alpha_i + \beta_i \tilde{R}_{mt} + \tilde{\epsilon}_{it}) \tag{19b}$$

$$= \sum_{i=1}^{n} x_{im} \alpha_i + \sum_{i=1}^{n} x_{im} \beta_i \tilde{R}_{mt} + \sum_{i=1}^{n} x_{im} \tilde{\epsilon}_{it} \tag{19c}$$

$$= \tilde{R}_{mt} + \sum_{i=1}^{n} x_{im} \tilde{\epsilon}_{it}, \tag{19d}$$

which implies that

$$\sum_{i=1}^{n} x_{im} \tilde{\epsilon}_{it} = 0.$$

Thus, in the relationships between returns on individual securities and the return on m that are defined by equations (3) and (10), there are interdependencies among the disturbances $\tilde{\epsilon}_{it}$ for different securities which guarantee that the weighted average of the $\tilde{\epsilon}_{it}$ is always zero.

When $\tilde{R}_{mt}$ is written as in (19b), we can see that the market model disturbance for security i, $\tilde{\epsilon}_{it}$, is part of the return on the portfolio m. Nevertheless, (13) tells us that $\tilde{\epsilon}_{it}$ and $\tilde{R}_{mt}$ are independent. There has been some confusion in the finance literature on this point, for which the author, Fama (1968; 1973) is, unfortunately, to some extent responsible.

Finally, if the joint distribution of the security returns $\tilde{R}_{lt}, \ldots, \tilde{R}_{nt}$ is multivariate normal, the joint distribution of the returns on any two different portfolios is bivariate normal. It follows that the market model can be used to describe the relationship between the return on any portfolio p and the return on the market portfolio m. Thus, repeating only equations (10) and (3), we have

$$\tilde{R}_{pt} = \alpha_p + \beta_p \tilde{R}_{mt} + \tilde{\epsilon}_{pt}, \tag{20}$$

where

$$\beta_p = \frac{\text{cov}(\tilde{R}_{pt}, \tilde{R}_{mt})}{\sigma^2(\tilde{R}_{mt})}, \quad \alpha_p = E(\tilde{R}_{pt}) - \beta_p E(\tilde{R}_{mt}). \tag{21}$$

PROBLEM II.C.

2. Let x_{ip} be the weight of security i in portfolio p. Show that

$$\beta_p = \sum_{i=1}^{n} x_{ip} \beta_i, \quad \alpha_p = \sum_{i=1}^{n} x_{ip} \alpha_i, \quad \text{and} \quad \tilde{\epsilon}_{pt} = \sum_{i=1}^{n} x_{ip} \tilde{\epsilon}_{it}. \tag{22}$$

Interpret these results.

ANSWER

2. For β_p we have

$$\beta_p = \frac{\text{cov}(\tilde{R}_{pt}, \tilde{R}_{mt})}{\sigma^2(\tilde{R}_{mt})}$$

$$= \frac{\text{cov}\left(\sum_{i=1}^{n} x_{ip} \tilde{R}_{it}, \tilde{R}_{mt}\right)}{\sigma^2(\tilde{R}_{mt})}$$

$$= \sum_{i=1}^{n} x_{ip} \frac{\text{cov}(\tilde{R}_{it}, \tilde{R}_{mt})}{\sigma^2(\tilde{R}_{mt})}$$

$$= \sum_{i=1}^{n} x_{ip} \beta_i.$$

Then, for α_p we have

$$\alpha_p = E(\tilde{R}_{pt}) - \beta_p E(\tilde{R}_{mt})$$

$$= \sum_{i=1}^{n} x_{ip} E(\tilde{R}_{it}) - \sum_{i=1}^{n} x_{ip} \beta_i E(\tilde{R}_{mt})$$

$$= \sum_{i=1}^{n} x_{ip} [E(\tilde{R}_{it}) - \beta_{im} E(\tilde{R}_{mt})]$$

$$= \sum_{i=1}^{n} x_{ip} \alpha_i.$$

With these results we can rewrite (20) as

$$\tilde{R}_{pt} = \sum_{i=1}^{n} x_{ip} \alpha_i + \sum_{i=1}^{n} x_{ip} \beta_i \tilde{R}_{mt} + \tilde{\epsilon}_{pt}.$$

Using equation (10), we can also express $\tilde{R}_{pt}$ as

$$\tilde{R}_{pt} = \sum_{i=1}^{n} x_{ip} \tilde{R}_{it}$$

$$= \sum_{i=1}^{n} x_{ip}(\alpha_i + \beta_i \tilde{R}_{mt} + \tilde{\epsilon}_{it})$$

$$= \sum_{i=1}^{n} x_{ip} \alpha_i + \sum_{i=1}^{n} x_{ip} \beta_i \tilde{R}_{mt} + \sum_{i=1}^{n} x_{ip} \tilde{\epsilon}_{it}.$$

It follows that

$$\tilde{\epsilon}_{pt} = \sum_{i=1}^{n} x_{ip} \tilde{\epsilon}_{it}.$$

Taken together, these results imply that the market model equation (20) for portfolio p is just the weighted average of the market model equation (10) for individual securities in p; that is,

$$\tilde{R}_{pt} = \alpha_p + \beta_p \tilde{R}_{mt} + \tilde{\epsilon}_{pt}$$

$$= \sum_{i=1}^{n} x_{ip}(\alpha_i + \beta_i \tilde{R}_{mt} + \tilde{\epsilon}_{it}).$$

D. The Market Model in the Empirical Literature

The market model plays an important role in the empirical literature of finance. In our analysis, the model arises as an implication of the assumption of the two-parameter portfolio model that the joint distribution of returns on securities is multivariate normal. Moreover, we can note again that there are many valid statistical models (one for each possible choice of portfolio p) that describe a statistical relationship between the return on security i and the return on any portfolio p which is similar in form to the market model.

In the empirical literature, however, the market model is interpreted as more than a statistical description of the association between bivariate normal random variables, and this special interpretation accounts for its special place. The return on the market portfolio is assumed to capture the effects of variables that affect the returns on all or at least most securities, whereas the disturbance $\tilde{\epsilon}_{it}$ is presumed to be due to the effects of variables more specific to the prospects of security i. In this view, a type of causation is proposed that is not implied by our purely statistical analysis; part of the return on security i, in particular $\beta_i \tilde{R}_{mt}$, is presumed to be caused by marketwide or common variables. In this interpretation, ρ_{im}^2 measures the proportion of the variance of the return on security i that is explained by marketwide factors, the term $\beta_i^2 \sigma^2(\tilde{R}_{mt})$ in (14) is the component of $\sigma^2(\tilde{R}_{it})$ that is due to marketwide variables, while $\sigma^2(\tilde{\epsilon}_{it})$ is the component of the variability of the return on security i that is due to variables more specific to the prospects of security i. The coefficient β_i, which we earlier interpreted as the risk of security i in m measured relative to the risk of m, is now interpreted as the market sensitivity of the return on security i. That is, β_i summarizes the sensitivity of $\tilde{R}_{it}$ to marketwide factors. A value of β_i greater than 1.0 implies a security with both above average market sensitivity and above average risk in m, while a value of β_i less than 1.0 indicates below average market sensitivity and risk in m.*

In Chapter 5 we shall find that the market model is widely used in studies of the adjustment of securities prices to new information. Most of these studies are concerned with the reaction of returns to company-specific information, such as a stock split or an earnings announcement, rather than to information about marketwide factors. In the market model, the effects of company-specific information should show up in the disturbance $\tilde{\epsilon}_{it}$. Thus, these studies use the market model disturbances to abstract from the effects of marketwide factors on returns in order to concentrate on the reaction of returns to company-specific information.

III. The Estimators

In discussing the market model above, we assume that the parameters—means, variances, and covariances—of the joint distribution of $\tilde{R}_{it}$ and $\tilde{R}_{mt}$ are known. This is never true. The next task is to consider, from a theoretical viewpoint, the estimation of the market model. Chapter 4 examines empirically the properties of the model when fitted to monthly returns on NYSE common stocks.

Most of the material in the remainder of this chapter can be found in Cramér (1946) and Anderson (1958). Other specific references are also given along the way. Since many results are stated without proof, the statistically curious reader may find some of these references interesting.

---

*In the finance literature, β_i is also called the *systematic risk* of security i, and $\sigma^2(\tilde{\epsilon}_{it})$ is called the *unsystematic risk* of the security. The idea is that since $\sum_{i=1}^{n} x_{im}\tilde{\epsilon}_{it} = 0$, the disturbance $\tilde{\epsilon}_{it}$ is "diversified away" in the market portfolio m, and β_i completely captures the contribution of security i to the risk of m. We do not use the terms *systematic risk* and *unsystematic risk* in this book.

Bivariant Normality : (handwritten annotation)

A. The Generality of the Procedures

If the joint distribution of $\tilde{R}_{it}$ and $\tilde{R}_{mt}$ is bivariate normal, then, as stated in (2), the conditional expected value of $\tilde{R}_{it}$ is a linear function of $\tilde{R}_{mt}$, with parameters β_i and α_i defined by (3). Moreover, bivariate normality of $\tilde{R}_{it}$ and $\tilde{R}_{mt}$ implies that the distribution of the disturbance $\tilde{\epsilon}_{it}$ in (10) is normal and that $\tilde{\epsilon}_{it}$ has the additional properties described in equations (8), (9), and (13), which can be summarized by saying that the distribution of $\tilde{\epsilon}_{it}$ is independent of $\tilde{R}_{mt}$. The properties of the procedures for estimating α_i and β_i discussed below follow from the normality of the disturbance $\tilde{\epsilon}_{it}$ and the properties of the disturbance described by equations (8), (9), and (13).

These conditions on the disturbance are, however, all one needs to determine the properties of the estimation procedures. Thus, if instead of assuming that the joint distribution of $\tilde{R}_{it}$ and $\tilde{R}_{mt}$ is bivariate normal, one assumes directly that the conditional expected value of $\tilde{R}_{it}$ is the linear function described by (2), then equation (8) is implied. If the coefficients in (2) are as defined in (3), then (13) is implied; and if the variance of the conditional distribution of $\tilde{R}_{it}$ is independent of $\tilde{R}_{mt}$, then (9) is implied. If we also assume that the distribution of $\tilde{\epsilon}_{it}$ is normal, then all the conditions required below in the discussion of estimation procedures will hold. Equivalently, the properties of the estimation procedures can be based on the assumptions that the conditional distribution of $\tilde{R}_{it}$ given $\tilde{R}_{mt}$ is normal, with mean given by (2) and variance independent of $\tilde{R}_{mt}$. These assumptions about the conditional distribution of $\tilde{R}_{it}$ are less restrictive than the assumption that the joint distribution of $\tilde{R}_{it}$ and $\tilde{R}_{mt}$ is bivariate normal. For example, the assumptions about the distribution of $\tilde{R}_{it}$ given $\tilde{R}_{mt}$ say nothing about the distribution of $\tilde{R}_{mt}$. With bivariate normality, the distribution of $\tilde{R}_{mt}$ is normal.

In the context of the market model, this additional generality of the properties of the estimation procedures is not important. Most of the work in this book is based on the assumption that the joint distribution of returns on securities is multivariate normal, so that bivariate normality of $\tilde{R}_{it}$ and $\tilde{R}_{mt}$ is implied. We do, however, also have occasion to estimate relationships between random variables that are not returns on securities or portfolios and where the assumption of bivariate or multivariate normality is less acceptable. In these cases, we want to know what minimal assumptions are needed to establish the properties of estimation procedures. Thus, although the discussion that follows is in the market model context, for the purpose of applying the results in other contexts we discuss periodically the generality of the properties of the estimation procedures when bivariate normality is not assumed.

Estimation Procedure : (handwritten annotation)

B. The Estimating Equations

In the preceding theoretical presentation of the market model, we omit the time subscript t that might in principle appear on the parameters α_i, β_i, and ρ_{im}. When it comes to estimating the model, this is more than a simplification of notation. Estimation must be based on time series—that is, on successive paired values of $\tilde{R}_{it}$ and $\tilde{R}_{mt}$. If such estimates are to be interpretable without the aid of advanced statistical methods, we must assume that all properties of the relationship between $\tilde{R}_{it}$ and $\tilde{R}_{mt}$ are approximately stationary or constant and thus independent of t. To put it more directly, we now assume that the bivariate normal joint distribution of $\tilde{R}_{it}$ and $\tilde{R}_{mt}$ is constant or stationary during the sample period. This means that the parameters of the joint distribution, $E(\tilde{R}_{it})$, $E(\tilde{R}_{mt})$, $\sigma^2(\tilde{R}_{it})$, $\sigma^2(\tilde{R}_{mt})$, and cov $(\tilde{R}_{it}, \tilde{R}_{mt})$, and any derived parameters, like α_i and β_i, also do not change during the sample period.

Consider a hypothetical sample of T successive months, $t = 1, 2, \ldots, T$, of paired values of the monthly returns $\tilde{R}_{it}$ and $\tilde{R}_{mt}$. Assume that successive monthly returns are statistically independent, so that the sample is a random sample from the bivariate normal distribution of $\tilde{R}_{it}$ and $\tilde{R}_{mt}$. How might such a sample be used to estimate the market model coefficients α_i and β_i? One procedure is to plug sample estimators of $E(\tilde{R}_{it})$, $E(\tilde{R}_{mt})$, $\sigma^2(\tilde{R}_{mt})$, and cov $(\tilde{R}_{it}, \tilde{R}_{mt}) = \sigma_{im}$ into (3). From our previous work, we know that we can estimate $E(\tilde{R}_{it})$, $E(\tilde{R}_{mt})$, and $\sigma^2(\tilde{R}_{mt})$ as

$$\tilde{\bar{R}}_i = \frac{\sum_{t=1}^{T} \tilde{R}_{it}}{T}, \quad \tilde{\bar{R}}_m = \frac{\sum_{t=1}^{T} \tilde{R}_{mt}}{T} \tag{23}$$

and

$$s^2(\tilde{R}_m) = \frac{\sum_{t=1}^{T} (\tilde{R}_{mt} - \tilde{\bar{R}}_m)^2}{T - 1}. \tag{24}$$

The tildes indicate that these equations define methods or procedures for estimating $E(\tilde{R}_{it})$, $E(\tilde{R}_{mt})$, and $\sigma^2(\tilde{R}_{mt})$ from hypothetical random samples of size T. We do not at this point have a specific sample of T observations in mind. Since from this perspective the sample $\tilde{R}_{it}$ and $\tilde{R}_{mt}$ are random variables, the values of $\tilde{\bar{R}}_i$, $\tilde{\bar{R}}_m$, and $s^2(\tilde{R}_m)$ produced by these methods are also random variables. Methods or procedures for estimating parameters are called estimators. For example, $s^2(\tilde{R}_m)$ of equation (24) is an estimator of $\sigma^2(\tilde{R}_{mt})$.

The value of the estimator obtained in a particular sample is called an estimate. An estimator defines a random variable; thus, it has a probability distribution, typically called its sampling distribution. An estimate is then a drawing from this sampling distribution.

In direct analogy with the estimator for $\sigma^2(\tilde{R}_{mt})$ given by equation (24), an estimator of the covariance $\sigma_{im} = \text{cov}(\tilde{R}_{it}, \tilde{R}_{mt})$—call this estimator $\tilde{s}_{im}$—is defined as

$$\tilde{s}_{im} = \frac{\sum\limits_{t=1}^{T} (\tilde{R}_{it} - \tilde{\bar{R}}_i)(\tilde{R}_{mt} - \tilde{\bar{R}}_m)}{T-1}. \tag{25}$$

The covariance σ_{im} is the expected value

$$\sigma_{im} = E([\tilde{R}_{it} - E(\tilde{R}_i)] \; [\tilde{R}_{mt} - E(\tilde{R}_m)]).$$

The estimator $\tilde{s}_{im}$ of (25) estimates this expected value of a cross-product of random variables by the average value of the cross-product in the sample. As in the case of the sample variance, however, $\tilde{s}_{im}$ is not exactly the average of the sample cross-products, since the sum of the cross-products is divided by $T-1$ instead of by T. As in the case of the sample variance, division by $T-1$ ensures unbiasedness*; that is,

$$E(\tilde{s}_{im}) = \sigma_{im}.$$

With equations (23) to (25) we define estimators for β_i and α_i in equation (3), call these estimators $\tilde{b}_i$ and $\tilde{a}_i$, as

$$\tilde{b}_i = \frac{\tilde{s}_{im}}{s^2(\tilde{R}_m)} = \frac{\sum\limits_{t=1}^{T} (\tilde{R}_{it} - \tilde{\bar{R}}_i)(\tilde{R}_{mt} - \tilde{\bar{R}}_m)/(T-1)}{\sum\limits_{t=1}^{T} (\tilde{R}_{mt} - \tilde{\bar{R}}_m)^2/(T-1)} = \frac{\sum\limits_{t=1}^{T} (\tilde{R}_{it} - \tilde{\bar{R}}_i)(\tilde{R}_{mt} - \tilde{\bar{R}}_m)}{\sum\limits_{t=1}^{T} (\tilde{R}_{mt} - \tilde{\bar{R}}_m)^2} \tag{26}$$

$$\tilde{a}_i = \tilde{\bar{R}}_i - \tilde{b}_i\tilde{\bar{R}}_m. \tag{27}$$

An estimator of the disturbance $\tilde{e}_{it}$ (call it $\tilde{e}_{it}$) is then obtained as

$$\tilde{e}_{it} = \tilde{R}_{it} - (\tilde{a}_i + \tilde{b}_i\tilde{R}_{mt}). \tag{28}$$

Such a disturbance estimator is called a residual. The estimated form of the market model is

$$\tilde{R}_{it} = \tilde{a}_i + \tilde{b}_i\tilde{R}_{mt} + \tilde{e}_{it}, \quad t = 1, 2, \ldots, T. \tag{29}$$

In the statistics literature, equation (2) for the conditional expectation of $\tilde{R}_{it}$ as a function of R_{mt} is called the regression function of $\tilde{R}_{it}$ on R_{mt}, and

---

*An estimator of a parameter is unbiased if the mean of the sampling distribution of the estimator is the true value of the parameter (cf. Problem II.B.7 of Chapter 2).

the coefficients α_i and β_i of (3) are called regression coefficients. The $\tilde{a}_i$ and $\tilde{b}_i$ of equations (27) and (26) are then called the regression coefficient estimators, and

$$\tilde{\tilde{R}}_{it} = \tilde{a}_i + \tilde{b}_i R_{mt} \tag{30}$$

is the estimated regression function.

Two comments are in order.

First, note that whereas the regression coefficients β_i and α_i defined by (3) are constants, the estimators $\tilde{b}_i$ and $\tilde{a}_i$ of (26) and (27) are random variables. Since we are talking about a hypothetical sample of unknown values of $\tilde{R}_{it}$ and $\tilde{R}_{mt}$, the values of $\tilde{b}_i$ and $\tilde{a}_i$ to be observed are unknown and are governed by probability distributions. Describing the properties of the sampling distributions of $\tilde{b}_i$ and $\tilde{a}_i$ is the major remaining task of this chapter. When we have a specific sample of known values of $\tilde{R}_{it}$ and $\tilde{R}_{mt}$, we move from the realm of estimators to that of estimates, and all the tildes are dropped.

Second, just as $\tilde{a}_i$ and $\tilde{b}_i$ are estimators of α_i and β_i, the residuals $\tilde{e}_{it}, t = 1, \ldots, T$, observed in a sample are estimators of the disturbances $\tilde{\epsilon}_{it}, t = 1, \ldots, T$. Since one never observes the true coefficients α_i and β_i in (10), one never observes the disturbances. We get to observe returns on security i and on portfolio m, but we only get to compute estimates of the regression coefficients and the regression disturbances.

C. Some Algebraic Properties of the Estimators

The estimated form of the market model has many properties that parallel those of the "true" model. Thus, from (2) we know that

$$E(\tilde{R}_{it}) = \alpha_i + \beta_i E(\tilde{R}_{mt}).$$

Likewise, from equation (27) we know that

$$\tilde{\tilde{R}}_i = \tilde{a}_i + \tilde{b}_i \tilde{\tilde{R}}_m. \tag{31}$$

In short, just as the regression function $E(\tilde{R}_{it}|R_{mt})$ of (2) passes through the point corresponding to the expected values of $\tilde{R}_{it}$ and $\tilde{R}_{mt}$, the estimated regression function of (30) passes through the point corresponding to the sample means of $\tilde{R}_{it}$ and $\tilde{R}_{mt}$.

Equation (31) also implies that

$$\sum_{t=1}^{T} \tilde{e}_{it} = 0, \tag{32}$$

which is somewhat parallel to the condition that the expected value of the disturbance $\tilde{\epsilon}_{it}$ in the market model equation (10) is always zero. To show that (32) holds, note that if we sum equation (29) over t from $t = 1$ to $t = T$ and then divide through by T, we get

$$\tilde{R}_i = \tilde{a}_i + \tilde{b}_i \tilde{\bar{R}}_m + \frac{\sum_{t=1}^{T} \tilde{e}_{it}}{T}.$$

If (31) holds, then (32) must also hold.

The estimated form of the market model has three additional properties parallel to those of the true model, whose proofs are left as problems for the reader. Thus, the condition $\text{cov}(\tilde{R}_{mt}, \tilde{e}_{it}) = 0$ of (13) also holds for the sample covariance between $\tilde{R}_{mt}$ and $\tilde{e}_{it}$:

$$s(\tilde{R}_m, \tilde{e}_i) = \frac{\sum_{t=1}^{T} (\tilde{R}_{mt} - \tilde{\bar{R}}_m)\tilde{e}_{it}}{T - 1} = 0. \tag{33}$$

With equation (33) it is then easy to show that

$$\sum_{t=1}^{T} (\tilde{R}_{it} - \tilde{\bar{R}}_i)^2 = \tilde{b}_i^2 \sum_{t=1}^{T} (\tilde{R}_{mt} - \tilde{\bar{R}}_m)^2 + \sum_{t=1}^{T} \tilde{e}_{it}^2, \tag{34}$$

which is parallel to the market model condition (14). In words, just as the population variance of $\tilde{R}_{it}$ can be divided into one component, $\beta_i^2 \sigma^2(\tilde{R}_{mt})$, attributable to the linear market model relationship between $\tilde{R}_{it}$ and $\tilde{R}_{mt}$, and a second component, $\sigma^2(\tilde{e}_{it})$, attributable to the random disturbance $\tilde{e}_{it}$, so the sample sum of squares $\Sigma(\tilde{R}_{it} - \tilde{\bar{R}}_i)^2$ can be split into a sum of squares, $\tilde{b}_i^2 \Sigma(\tilde{R}_{mt} - \tilde{\bar{R}}_m)^2$, attributable to the estimated market model relation and the sum of squared residuals from the fitted relation, $\Sigma \tilde{e}_{it}^2$. Finally, equation (34) can in turn be shown to imply that just as the square of the population correlation coefficient between $\tilde{R}_{it}$ and $\tilde{R}_{mt}$ is the proportion of $\sigma^2(\tilde{R}_{it})$ attributable to the linear relationship between $\tilde{R}_{it}$ and $\tilde{R}_{mt}$, so the square of the sample correlation coefficient $\tilde{r}_{im}^2$, where

$$\tilde{r}_{im} = \frac{\tilde{s}_{im}}{s(\tilde{R}_i)\,s(\tilde{R}_m)} = \frac{\sum_{t=1}^{T} (\tilde{R}_{it} - \tilde{\bar{R}}_i)(\tilde{R}_{mt} - \tilde{\bar{R}}_m)}{\sqrt{\sum_{t=1}^{T} (\tilde{R}_{it} - \tilde{\bar{R}}_i)^2} \, \sqrt{\sum_{t=1}^{T} (\tilde{R}_{mt} - \tilde{\bar{R}}_m)^2}}, \tag{35}$$

is

$$\tilde{r}_{im}^2 = \frac{\tilde{b}_i^2 \sum_{t=1}^{T} (\tilde{R}_{mt} - \bar{\tilde{R}}_m)^2}{\sum_{t=1}^{T} (\tilde{R}_{it} - \bar{\tilde{R}}_i)^2} , \tag{36}$$

the proportion of the sum of squares $\Sigma(\tilde{R}_{it} - \bar{R}_i)^2$ attributable to the fitted linear relationship.

PROBLEMS III.C

1. Derive equation (33). Hint: substitute for $\tilde{e}_{it}$ from (28) and then for $\tilde{a}_i$ and $\tilde{b}_i$ from (27) and (26).

2. Derive equation (34).

3. Derive equation (36).

ANSWERS

1. Substituting from equation (28):

$$\sum_{t=1}^{T} (\tilde{R}_{mt} - \bar{\tilde{R}}_m)(\tilde{e}_{it}) = \sum_{t=1}^{T} (\tilde{R}_{mt} - \bar{\tilde{R}}_m)(\tilde{R}_{it} - \tilde{a}_i - \tilde{b}_i \tilde{R}_{mt})$$

From (27)
$$= \sum_{t=1}^{T} (\tilde{R}_{mt} - \bar{\tilde{R}}_m)(\tilde{R}_{it} - \bar{\tilde{R}}_i + \tilde{b}_i \bar{\tilde{R}}_m - \tilde{b}_i \tilde{R}_{mt})$$

$$= \sum_{t=1}^{T} (\tilde{R}_{mt} - \bar{\tilde{R}}_m)(\tilde{R}_{it} - \bar{\tilde{R}}_i) - \tilde{b}_i \sum_{t=1}^{T} (\tilde{R}_{mt} - \bar{\tilde{R}}_m)^2$$

From (26)
$$= 0.$$

2. First substitute (27) into (29) to get
$$\tilde{R}_{it} = \bar{\tilde{R}}_i - \tilde{b}_i \bar{\tilde{R}}_m + \tilde{b}_i \tilde{R}_{mt} + \tilde{e}_{it}.$$

Then proceed as follows:
$$\tilde{R}_{it} - \bar{\tilde{R}}_i = \tilde{b}_i (\tilde{R}_{mt} - \bar{\tilde{R}}_m) + \tilde{e}_{it}$$

$$(\tilde{R}_{it} - \bar{\tilde{R}}_i)^2 = \tilde{b}_i^2 (\tilde{R}_{mt} - \bar{\tilde{R}}_m)^2 + \tilde{e}_{it}^2 + 2\tilde{b}_i (\tilde{R}_{mt} - \bar{\tilde{R}}_m)\tilde{e}_{it}$$

$$\sum_{t=1}^{T} (\tilde{R}_{it} - \bar{\tilde{R}}_i)^2 = \tilde{b}_i^2 \sum_{t=1}^{T} (\tilde{R}_{mt} - \bar{\tilde{R}}_m)^2 + \sum_{t=1}^{T} \tilde{e}_{it}^2 + 2\tilde{b}_i \sum_{t=1}^{T} (\tilde{R}_{mt} - \bar{\tilde{R}}_m)\tilde{e}_{it}$$

From (33)
$$= \tilde{b}_i^2 \sum_{t=1}^{T} (\tilde{R}_{mt} - \bar{\tilde{R}}_m)^2 + \sum_{t=1}^{T} \tilde{e}_{it}^2.$$

3. From equation (26):

$$\frac{\tilde{b}_i^2 \sum_{t=1}^{T} (\tilde{R}_{mt} - \bar{\tilde{R}}_m)^2}{\sum_{t=1}^{T} (\tilde{R}_{it} - \bar{\tilde{R}}_i)^2} = \frac{\left(\sum_{t=1}^{T} (\tilde{R}_{it} - \bar{\tilde{R}}_i)(\tilde{R}_{mt} - \bar{\tilde{R}}_m)\right)^2}{\sum_{t=1}^{T} (\tilde{R}_{it} - \bar{\tilde{R}}_m)^2 \sum_{t=1}^{T} (\tilde{R}_{mt} - \bar{\tilde{R}}_m)^2}$$

$$= \tilde{r}_{im}^2.$$

IV. The Sampling Distributions of the Estimators

The coefficient estimators $\tilde{a}_i$ and $\tilde{b}_i$ are random variables. The next task is to discuss the probability or sampling distributions of these estimators.

A. *Unbiasedness*

Our understanding of the statistical work of this section will be enhanced if we first study in some detail the reasons why the regression coefficient estimators $\tilde{b}_i$ and $\tilde{a}_i$ are random variables. To this end, let us rewrite equation (26) for $\tilde{b}_i$ as

$$\tilde{b}_i = \frac{\sum_{t=1}^{T} (\tilde{R}_{mt} - \bar{\tilde{R}}_m)\tilde{R}_{it}}{\sum_{t=1}^{T} (\tilde{R}_{mt} - \bar{\tilde{R}}_m)^2}. \tag{37}$$

PROBLEM IV.A

1. Derive equation (37) from (26).

ANSWER

1.

$$\sum_{t=1}^{T} (\tilde{R}_{mt} - \bar{\tilde{R}}_m)(\tilde{R}_{it} - \bar{\tilde{R}}_i) = \sum_{t=1}^{T} (\tilde{R}_{mt} - \bar{\tilde{R}}_m)\tilde{R}_{it} - \bar{\tilde{R}}_i \sum_{t=1}^{T} (\tilde{R}_{mt} - \bar{\tilde{R}}_m).$$

But

$$\sum_{t=1}^{T} (\tilde{R}_{mt} - \bar{\tilde{R}}_m) = T\bar{\tilde{R}}_m - T\bar{\tilde{R}}_m = 0.$$

The general result is that in any sample, the sum of the deviations of a variable from its sample mean is always zero.

If we substitute the market model equation (10) for $\tilde{R}_{it}$ in (37) and then make use of the general result stated in Problem IV.A.*1*, we get

$$\tilde{b}_i = \frac{\displaystyle\sum_{t=1}^{T} (\tilde{R}_{mt} - \bar{\tilde{R}}_m)(\alpha_i + \beta_i \tilde{R}_{mt} + \tilde{\epsilon}_{it})}{\displaystyle\sum_{t=1}^{T} (\tilde{R}_{mt} - \bar{\tilde{R}}_m)^2}$$

$$= \beta_i \frac{\displaystyle\sum_{t=1}^{T} (\tilde{R}_{mt} - \bar{\tilde{R}}_m)\tilde{R}_{mt}}{\displaystyle\sum_{t=1}^{T} (\tilde{R}_{mt} - \bar{\tilde{R}}_m)^2} + \frac{\displaystyle\sum_{t=1}^{T} (\tilde{R}_{mt} - \bar{\tilde{R}}_m)\tilde{\epsilon}_{it}}{\displaystyle\sum_{t=1}^{T} (\tilde{R}_{mt} - \bar{\tilde{R}}_m)^2}.$$

Then

$$\tilde{b}_i = \beta_i + \frac{\displaystyle\sum_{t=1}^{T} (\tilde{R}_{mt} - \bar{\tilde{R}}_m)\tilde{\epsilon}_{it}}{\displaystyle\sum_{t=1}^{T} (\tilde{R}_{mt} - \bar{\tilde{R}}_m)^2}. \tag{38}$$

The estimator $\tilde{b}_i$ is a random variable because in a hypothetical sample the values of $\tilde{R}_{it}$ and $\tilde{R}_{mt}$ are random variables. Equation (38) implies, however, that it is equivalent to say that $\tilde{b}_i$ is a random variable because the sample values of $\tilde{R}_{mt}$ and the market model disturbances $\tilde{\epsilon}_{it}$ are random variables.

Much of the later discussion deals with the conditional distribution of $\tilde{b}_i$, conditional on fixed values $R_{m1}, \ldots, R_{mT}$. We then rewrite (38) as

$$\tilde{b}_i = \beta_i + \frac{\displaystyle\sum_{t=1}^{T} (R_{mt} - \bar{R}_m)\tilde{\epsilon}_{it}}{\displaystyle\sum_{t=1}^{T} (R_{mt} - \bar{R}_m)^2}; \tag{39}$$

that is, the tildes on $\bar{\tilde{R}}_m$ and the $\tilde{R}_{mt}$ in (38) are dropped. One can think of the conditional distribution of $\tilde{b}_i$ as resulting from repeated samples of size T of the disturbances $\tilde{\epsilon}_{it}$, but where the values $R_{m1}, \ldots, R_{mT}$ are the same from sample to sample. Although the values $R_{m1}, \ldots, R_{mT}$ are fixed, the estimator $\tilde{b}_i$ is still a random variable, since the disturbances are random variables.

There is, however, a more relevant interpretation of the conditional distribution of $\tilde{b}_i$. Although the sampling scenario involves random drawings from the joint distribution of $\tilde{R}_{it}$ and $\tilde{R}_{mt}$, when a sample is to be drawn, the uncertainty in the estimator of β_i that arises because we do not know the values of $\tilde{R}_{mt}$ that will turn up is unimportant. The sample will resolve this uncertainty. The primary interest is in the uncertainty about β_i that cannot be resolved by the sample. To characterize the uncertainty about β_i that will remain after a sample is drawn, we examine the distribution of $\tilde{b}_i$ when only the $\tilde{\epsilon}_{i1}, \ldots, \tilde{\epsilon}_{iT}$ in (38) are treated as random variables. From (39) we can see that this is equivalent to looking at the distribution of $\tilde{b}_i$ conditional on $R_{m1}, \ldots, R_{mT}$.

Expressions similar to (38) and (39) can be obtained for the coefficient estimator $\tilde{a}_i$ of (29). Skipping the tedious details, we write

$$\tilde{a}_i = \alpha_i + \sum_{t=1}^{T} \left(\frac{1}{T} - \tilde{\bar{R}}_m \frac{\tilde{R}_{mt} - \tilde{\bar{R}}_m}{\sum_{t=1}^{T} (\tilde{R}_{mt} - \bar{R}_m)^2} \right) \tilde{\epsilon}_{it}. \tag{40}$$

This equation, which is similar in form to (38), says that the estimator $\tilde{a}_i$ is a random variable because the values of $\tilde{R}_{mt}$ and $\tilde{\epsilon}_{it}$ in a hypothetical sample are random variables. To concentrate on the uncertainty that will remain after the sample is drawn, we again work with the distribution of $\tilde{a}_i$ conditional on $R_{m1}, \ldots, R_{mT}$. Thus, (40) becomes

$$\tilde{a}_i = \alpha_i + \sum_{t=1}^{T} \left(\frac{1}{T} - \bar{R}_m \frac{R_{mt} - \bar{R}_m}{\sum_{t=1}^{T} (R_{mt} - \bar{R}_m)^2} \right) \tilde{\epsilon}_{it}. \tag{41}$$

Unbiased

With equations (38) to (41) it is easy to establish that the coefficient estimators $\tilde{b}_i$ and $\tilde{a}_i$ of (26) and (27) are conditionally and unconditionally unbiased. In words, conditional on any combination of $R_{m1}, \ldots, R_{mT}$, the expected values (the means of the sampling distributions) of $\tilde{b}_i$ and $\tilde{a}_i$ are β_i and α_i. Since this is true for any combination of $R_{m1}, \ldots, R_{mT}$, the unconditional expected values of the estimators are also β_i and α_i. Thus:

$$E(\tilde{b}_i | R_{m1}, \ldots, R_{mT}) = E(\tilde{b}_i) = \beta_i \tag{42}$$

$$E(\tilde{a}_i | R_{m1}, \ldots, R_{mT}) = E(\tilde{a}_i) = \alpha_i. \tag{43}$$

PROBLEM IV.A.

  2. Derive (42) and (43).

ANSWER

  2. The bivariate normality of $\tilde{R}_{it}$ and $\tilde{R}_{mt}$ implies that $E(\tilde{\epsilon}_{it}|R_{mt}) = 0$ for all values of R_{mt}. Since random sampling is also assumed (that is, successive pairs of values of $\tilde{R}_{it}$ and $\tilde{R}_{mt}$ are assumed to be independent), $\tilde{\epsilon}_{it}$ is independent of all market returns in the sample, and

$$E(\tilde{\epsilon}_{it}|R_{m1},\ldots,R_{mt}) = E(\tilde{\epsilon}_{it}) = 0. \tag{44}$$

It follows that the expected values of all the terms in the summations of equations (39) and (41) are zero, and (42) and (43) are established.

B. The "t" Distributions of the Standardized Estimators

  The next step is to discuss the distributional properties of $\tilde{a}_i$ and $\tilde{b}_i$. We first state the results and then provide some justification.

THE STANDARD ERRORS OF THE COEFFICIENT ESTIMATORS

  When the estimators $\tilde{b}_i$ and $\tilde{a}_i$ of (26) and (27) are based on a random sample of size T from the assumed stationary bivariate normal distribution of $\tilde{R}_{it}$ and $\tilde{R}_{mt}$, the standard deviations of the conditional distributions of $\tilde{b}_i$ and $\tilde{a}_i$, conditional on $R_{m1},\ldots,R_{mT}$, are

$$\sigma^2(\tilde{b}_i|R_{m1},\ldots,R_{mT}) = \frac{\sigma^2(\tilde{\epsilon}_{it})}{\sum_{t=1}^{T}(R_{mt}-\bar{R}_m)^2} \tag{45}$$

$$\sigma^2(\tilde{a}_i|R_{m1},\ldots,R_{mT}) = \sigma^2(\tilde{\epsilon}_{it})\left(\frac{1}{T} + \frac{\bar{R}_m^2}{\sum_{t=1}^{T}(R_{mt}-\bar{R}_m)^2}\right). \tag{46}$$

The conditional variances of $\tilde{b}_i$ and $\tilde{a}_i$ both involve the one unknown parameter $\sigma^2(\tilde{\epsilon}_{it})$, the variance of the market model disturbance. The unbiased estimator of $\sigma^2(\tilde{\epsilon}_{it})$ is

$$s^2(\tilde{\epsilon}_i) = \frac{\sum_{t=1}^{T}\tilde{\epsilon}_{it}^2}{T-2}. \tag{47}$$

To get estimators of the conditional variances of $\tilde{b}_i$ and $\tilde{a}_i$, we substitute $s^2(\tilde{\epsilon}_i)$ into (45) and (46):

$$s^2(\tilde{b}_i | R_{m1}, \ldots, R_{mt}) = \frac{s^2(\tilde{\epsilon}_i)}{\displaystyle\sum_{t=1}^{T} (R_{mt} - \bar{R}_m)^2} \tag{48}$$

$$s^2(\tilde{a}_i | R_{m1}, \ldots, R_{mT}) = s^2(\tilde{\epsilon}_i) \left(\frac{1}{T} + \frac{\bar{R}_m^2}{\displaystyle\sum_{t=1}^{T} (R_{mt} - \bar{R}_m)^2} \right). \tag{49}$$

The conditional standard deviations of $\tilde{b}_i$ and $\tilde{a}_i$, the square roots of the variances described by (45) and (46), are typically called the standard errors of the regression coefficient estimators $\tilde{b}_i$ and $\tilde{a}_i$; the estimators of these standard deviations, the square roots of the variances described by (48) and (49), are the estimators of these standard errors. The idea is that $\tilde{b}_i - \beta_i$ or $\tilde{a}_i - \alpha_i$ is the error in the estimator of the regression coefficient, so the standard deviation of the error is called the standard error of the estimator. Likewise, the standard deviation of the market model residuals, $s(\tilde{\epsilon}_i)$, is typically called the sample standard error of residuals, while $\sigma(\tilde{\epsilon}_{it})$ is called the standard error of the disturbances. The idea here is that the disturbance $\tilde{\epsilon}_{it}$ is the "error" of the regression function (2); it is the deviation of $\tilde{R}_{it}$ from its conditional expected value $E(\tilde{R}_{it} | R_{mt})$, and the residual $\tilde{e}_{it}$ is the error in the estimated regression function.

THE MAJOR RESULT

Consider now the random variables

$$\tilde{t} = \frac{\tilde{b}_i - \beta_i}{s(\tilde{b}_i | R_{m1}, \ldots, R_{mT})} \tag{50}$$

$$\tilde{t} = \frac{\tilde{a}_i - \alpha_i}{s(\tilde{a}_i | R_{m1}, \ldots, R_{mT})}. \tag{51}$$

The $\tilde{t}$ random variable of (50) can be interpreted as a standardized version of $\tilde{b}_i$ where one first subtracts β_i (the conditional expected value of $\tilde{b}_i$) from $\tilde{b}_i$ and then divides this difference by the estimator of the conditional standard deviation of $\tilde{b}_i$. There is, of course, an analogous interpretation of (51). When the estimators $\tilde{b}_i$ and $\tilde{a}_i$ are based on a random sample of size T from the assumed bivariate normal distribution of $\tilde{R}_{it}$ and $\tilde{R}_{mt}$, which is also assumed to be stationary during the sampling period, then the $\tilde{t}$ random variables of (50) and (51) have the student or "t" distribution with $T - 2$ degrees of freedom.

A few comments are in order concerning the class of "t" distributions. A "t" distribution is symmetric about 0 and can be completely characterized from knowledge of its one parameter, the degrees of freedom. The degrees-of-freedom parameter can take any positive value. The "t" distribution for infinite degrees of freedom is the unit normal distribution, the normal distribution with mean equal to 0 and standard deviation equal to 1.0. Like the nonnormal symmetric stable distributions discussed in Chapter 1, nonnormal "t" distributions are thick-tailed relative to the unit normal; that is, a nonnormal "t" distribution assigns higher probabilities to extreme observations, and the lower the degrees-of-freedom parameter, the more thick-tailed the "t" distributions. Most statistics books contain tables of fractiles of "t" distributions for various degrees of freedom. Such tables are not necessary here. The "t" distribution is close to the unit normal distribution when the degrees-of-freedom parameter is greater than 30, and we rarely work with less than $T = 60$ observations.

C. Why the "t" Distribution?

In the conditional distributions of $\tilde{b}_i$ and $\tilde{a}_i$, the sample values of R_{mt} are taken as given; that is, they are treated as constants. The coefficient estimators are random variables because the disturbances $\tilde{\epsilon}_{i1}, \ldots, \tilde{\epsilon}_{iT}$ are random variables. With random sampling from the assumed stationary bivariate normal distribution of $\tilde{R}_{it}$ and $\tilde{R}_{mt}$, the values of $\tilde{\epsilon}_{it}$ are independent identically distributed normal variables. A weighted sum (or linear combination) of independent normal random variables itself has a normal distribution. From inspection of equations (39) and (41), we can see that, conditional on $R_{m1}, \ldots, R_{mT}$, $\tilde{b}_i$ and $\tilde{a}_i$ are weighted sums of the $\tilde{\epsilon}_{it}$. Thus, the conditional distributions of $\tilde{b}_i$ and $\tilde{a}_i$ are normal with conditional means β_i and α_i and conditional variances given by equations (45) and (46). It follows that

$$\frac{\tilde{b}_i - \beta_i}{\sigma(\tilde{\epsilon}_i) \bigg/ \left(\sum_{t=1}^{T} (R_{mt} - \overline{R}_m)^2 \right)^{1/2}} \quad \text{and} \quad \frac{\tilde{a}_i - \alpha_i}{\sigma(\tilde{\epsilon}_i) \left(\dfrac{1}{T} + \dfrac{\overline{R}_m^2}{\sum_{t=1}^{T} (R_{mt} - \overline{R}_m)^2} \right)^{1/2}} \quad (52)$$

have unit normal distributions. That is, as usual, when we take the difference between a normal random variable and its mean and divide the difference by the standard deviation of the variable, the variable that results has the normal distribution with mean equal to 0 and standard deviation equal to 1.0. (See Section I.D of Chapter 1.)

It is an interesting and important statistical fact (which, like most of the others in this section, we state without proof) that when normal random variables are transformed into unit normal random variables in the manner of (52), then the same transformation, but with the population standard deviation in the denominator replaced by the sample standard deviation, yields a random variable that has a "t" distribution. For example, if $\tilde{y}$ has a normal distribution with mean $E(\tilde{y})$ and variance $\sigma^2(\tilde{y})$, then the distribution of the sample mean $\bar{\tilde{y}}$ in random samples of size T is normal with expected value $E(\tilde{y})$ and variance $\sigma^2(\tilde{y})/T$. (See Problem II.B.7 of Chapter 2.) Thus,.

$$\frac{\bar{\tilde{y}} - E(\tilde{y})}{\sigma(\tilde{y})/\sqrt{T}}$$

has the unit normal distribution, while

$$\tilde{t} = \frac{\bar{\tilde{y}} - E(\tilde{y})}{s(\tilde{y})/\sqrt{T}} \tag{53}$$

has a "t" distribution.

The value of the degrees-of-freedom parameter of the $\tilde{t}$ random variable is the degrees of freedom of the standard deviation in the denominator. Without going into details, it is generally the case that the value of the degrees-of-freedom of the sample standard deviation is just the denominator of the unbiased estimator of the standard deviation. For example, in equation (53), $s^2(\tilde{y})$, the unbiased estimator of $\sigma^2(\tilde{y})$, is

$$s^2(\tilde{y}) = \frac{\sum_{t=1}^{T} (\tilde{y}_t - \bar{\tilde{y}})^2}{T-1},$$

and $s^2(\tilde{y})$ has $T-1$ degrees of freedom. The random variable $\tilde{t}$ of (53) has the "t" distribution with $T-1$ degrees of freedom. Likewise, the unbiased estimator of the disturbance variance $\sigma^2(\tilde{\epsilon}_{it})$ is (47), and the $\tilde{t}$ random variables of (50) and (51) have the "t" distribution with $T-2$ degrees of freedom.

Two points about this analysis should be noted.

First, the properties of the conditional distributions of $\tilde{b}_i$ and $\tilde{a}_i$ do not require any particular combination of $R_{m1}, \ldots, R_{mT}$; the results apply to any combination of $R_{m1}, \ldots, R_{mT}$. For example, the result summarized in equation (50) is that if, in any sample to be drawn, the estimator $\tilde{b}_i$ is to be transformed by first subtracting from $\tilde{b}_i$ its conditional mean β_i, and then dividing this difference by the conditional standard deviation of $\tilde{b}_i$ (which is conditional on whatever values of $R_{m1}, \ldots, R_{mT}$ turn up in the sample), then the resulting variable $\tilde{t}$ of equation (50) has the "t" distribution with $T-2$ degrees of freedom.

Second, the properties of the conditional distributions of $\tilde{b}_i$ and $\tilde{a}_i$ are implied by the assumption that there is random sampling from the bivariate normal distribution of $\tilde{R}_{it}$ and $\tilde{R}_{mt}$, which is stationary during the sample period. But all of the distributional properties of the estimators hold if (a) the regression function $E(\tilde{R}_{it}|R_{mt})$ is the linear function of equation (2), with regression coefficients α_i and β_i that are constant during the sampling period; (b) the distribution of the disturbance $\tilde{\epsilon}_{it}$ is likewise stationary; (c) there is random sampling from the distribution of $\tilde{\epsilon}_{it}$; and (d) the distribution of $\tilde{\epsilon}_{it}$ is normal. Assumptions (a) to (c) are sufficient to establish that $\tilde{b}_i$ and $\tilde{a}_i$ are unbiased estimators of the regression coefficients β_i and α_i, with conditional variances given by (45) and (46). Normality of the disturbances then produces the result that the $\tilde{t}$ random variables of (50) and (51) have the "t" distribution with $T - 2$ degrees of freedom.

Indeed, econometrics textbooks—for example, Theil (1971)—develop the properties of the estimators from assumptions (a) to (d). In our frame of reference, the market model, it is simpler to develop the properties of the estimators as implications of bivariate normality. Rigorous examples of this approach can be found in Anderson (1958) and Cramer (1946).

V. The Reliability of the Estimators

In an application of the market model, a sample of values R_{it} and R_{mt}, $t = 1, \ldots, T$, is available; regression coefficient estimates b_i and a_i are computed, as are sample standard errors $s(b_i|R_{m1}, \ldots, R_{mT})$ and $s(a_i|R_{m1}, \ldots, R_{mT})$. The preceding analysis tells us that the sample

$$t = \frac{b_i - \beta_i}{s(b_i|R_{m1}, \ldots, R_{mT})} \quad \text{and} \quad t = \frac{a_i - \alpha_i}{s(a_i|R_{m1}, \ldots, R_{mT})}$$

are drawings from the "t" distribution with $T - 2$ degrees of freedom.* This result allows us to make probability statements concerning how far the estimates b_i and a_i are from the true values β_i and α_i. In short, our analysis of the sampling distributions of the estimators $\tilde{b}_i$ and $\tilde{a}_i$ has given us the means to evaluate the reliability of estimates, and this is always important in applications.

There are two formal approaches, "classical" and "Bayesian," and we shall discuss both of them shortly. In both approaches, the determinant of reliability is the magnitude of the conditional variances of the regression coefficient

---

*Note again that when we talk about estimates obtained from a specific sample, tildes disappear.

estimators. The smaller these variances, the more tightly packed the distributions of the estimators about the true values of the regression coefficients. Equations (45) and (46) tell us that the variances of the estimators depend directly on the strength of the relationship between $\tilde{R}_{it}$ and $\tilde{R}_{mt}$, as measured by the disturbance variance $\sigma^2(\tilde{\epsilon}_{it})$; the larger the value of $\sigma^2(\tilde{\epsilon}_{it})$, the larger the conditional variances of the estimators. Equations (45) and (46) also tell us that the variances of the estimators depend on the sample size; the larger the value of T, the smaller the conditional variances.*

Although we can do nothing about the magnitude of $\sigma^2(\tilde{\epsilon}_{it})$, it would seem that the variances of the coefficient estimators can be made as small as one likes by taking larger sample sizes. There are, however, two problems. First, the time period for which we have samples of $\tilde{R}_{it}$ and $\tilde{R}_{mt}$ may be limited. Second, the properties of the estimators depend on the assumption that the joint distribution of $\tilde{R}_{it}$ and $\tilde{R}_{mt}$ is stationary during the sample period. This assumption may be acceptable for "reasonable" periods of time, but it is unlikely to be acceptable for a period of indefinite length. These issues arise naturally in the empirical work of Chapter 4. We turn now to a discussion of the two approaches, classical and Bayesian, for judging the reliability of the regression coefficient estimators.

A. Classical Confidence Intervals

If there is random sampling from the joint distribution of $\tilde{R}_{it}$ and $\tilde{R}_{mt}$ which is bivariate normal and stationary during the sampling period, the $\tilde{t}$ random variable of equation (50) has the "t" distribution with $T-2$ degrees of freedom. For the rest of the discussion, we assume that T is large (say, greater than 40), so that the "t" distribution with $T-2$ degrees of freedom is well approximated by the unit normal distribution.

From Table 1.8 at the end of Chapter 1, the .975 fractile of the unit normal distribution, which we write as $t_{.975}$, is $t_{.975} = 1.96$. This means that

$$\Pr\left[\tilde{t} = \frac{\tilde{b}_i - \beta_i}{s(\tilde{b}_i | R_{m1}, \ldots, R_{mT})} > 1.96\right] = .025. \tag{54}$$

In words, if we consider taking a sample from the bivariate normal distribution of $\tilde{R}_{it}$ and $\tilde{R}_{mt}$, the probability that the sample will generate a value of $\tilde{t}$ greater than 1.96 is .025. Equivalently, in repeated samples of size T, we can expect values of $\tilde{t}$ equal to or less than 1.96 in 97.5 percent of the samples.

---

*Typically, the variance of an estimator grows smaller as the sample size increases. For example, this result appears (but without comment) in the brief discussion above of the sampling distribution of the sample mean. See also Problem II.B.7 of Chapter 2.

The probability statement of (54) can be rewritten as

$$\Pr[\tilde{b}_i - 1.96s(\tilde{b}_i | R_{m1}, \ldots, R_{mT}) > \beta_i] = .025. \tag{55}$$

In words, if in a hypothetical sample we compute the point that is $1.96s(\tilde{b}_i | R_{m1}, \ldots, R_{mT})$ to the left of $\tilde{b}_i$, the probability that the value of this point will be greater than β_i is .025. Alternatively, in repeated samples we expect the sample values of the point to be equal to or less than β_i in 97.5 percent of the samples.

From the symmetry of the normal distribution, if $t_{.975} = 1.96$, then $t_{.025} = -1.96$. Thus, following the arguments of (54) and (55),

$$\Pr\left[\tilde{t} = \frac{\tilde{b}_i - \beta_i}{s(\tilde{b}_i | R_{m1}, \ldots, R_{mT})} < -1.96\right] = .025, \tag{56}$$

$$\Pr[\tilde{b}_i + 1.96\, s(\tilde{b}_i | R_{m1}, \ldots, R_{mT}) < \beta_i] = .025. \tag{57}$$

The interesting probability statement comes, however, from combining (55) and (57). It follows from (55) and (57) that the probability that in a hypothetical sample, the interval

$$[\tilde{b}_i - 1.96\, s(\tilde{b}_i | R_{m1}, \ldots, R_{mT})] \text{ to } [\tilde{b}_i + 1.96\, s(\tilde{b}_i | R_{m1}, \ldots, R_{mT})] \tag{58}$$

will include β_i is .95. Alternatively, in repeated samples we expect the sample values of the interval defined by (58) to include β_i in 95 percent of the samples.

The interval defined by (58) is the 95 percent confidence interval for β_i. It is just the interval from the point that is $1.96\, s(\tilde{b}_i | R_{m1}, \ldots, R_{mT})$ less than $\tilde{b}_i$ to the point that is $1.96\, s(\tilde{b}_i | R_{m1}, \ldots, R_{mT})$ greater than $\tilde{b}_i$. Such confidence intervals are one way to judge the reliability of $\tilde{b}_i$, and they are the way usually suggested in the classical approach to statistics.

In interpreting and applying (58), one must choose words carefully. Since $\tilde{b}_i$ and $s(\tilde{b}_i | R_{m1}, \ldots, R_{mT})$ are random variables, the confidence interval defined by (58) is a random variable. Thus, in making a probability statement, one talks either about a hypothetical sample or about expected frequencies in repeated samples. One can say that in a hypothetical sample, the probability that the 95 percent confidence interval will contain β_i is .95; but in applying (58) to a sample in hand, one cannot say that the probability that the .95 confidence interval observed includes β_i is .95. The .95 confidence interval computed from a particular sample is a drawing from the probability distribution of the interval; it either does or does not include β_i. Alternatively, an appropriate probability statement is that if repeated drawings are made from the probability distribution of the .95 confidence interval, then we expect 95 percent of the sample intervals to include β_i.

To make these statements more concrete, let us poach a little from the empirical results of Chapter 4, where we find that for the five-year period July 1963 to June 1968, monthly returns on a share of the common stock of IBM and on the equally weighted portfolio of NYSE stocks produce the estimates $b_i = .67$ and $s(b_i|R_{m1}, \ldots, R_{mT}) = .13$ for IBM. Thus, the sample value of the .95 confidence interval for β_i for IBM is

$$\tilde{b}_i - 1.96 \, s(\tilde{b}_i|R_{m1}, \ldots, R_{mT}) = .42 \text{ to } .92 = \tilde{b}_i + 1.96 \, s(\tilde{b}_i|R_{m1}, \ldots, R_{mT}).$$

We would like to be able to say that the probability that β_i is in this interval is .95, but β_i either is in the interval or it is not. All the theory of classical confidence intervals allows us to say is that the sample interval is a drawing from the distribution of the .95 percent confidence interval for IBM and that, in repeated samples, 95 percent of such sample confidence intervals can be expected to include the true value of the parameter.

This is a rather unsatisfying way to calibrate uncertainty about β_i, but such are the limitations of the classical approach to probabilities as long-run frequencies in repeated samples. We see later that the Bayesian approach provides more direct probability statements to summarize uncertainty about β_i.

There is no magic in .95 confidence intervals. The choice of degree of confidence is arbitrary, and if confidence intervals are to be used, it is well to look at several of them. The mechanics of the procedure are always the same, as is the interpretation of the numbers obtained. Moreover, it should be clear that the same development of the theory of confidence intervals applies to α_i and its estimator $\tilde{a}_i$.

B. Classical Hypothesis Testing

Closely related to the classical theory of confidence intervals is the classical theory of hypothesis testing. Suppose we want to test the hypothesis that for IBM, $\beta_i = 1.0$. Thus, the hypothesis is that the risk of a share of IBM in m, the equally weighted market portfolio of NYSE shares, is equal to the average risk of shares in m. In order to test this hypothesis, we must specify an alternative hypothesis. A simple alternative is $\beta_i \neq 1.0$.

The next step is to specify what sort of sample result would cause us to reject the hypothesis $\beta_i = 1.0$, usually called the null hypothesis, in favor of the alternative hypothesis $\beta_i \neq 1.0$. This amounts to choosing the chance we are willing to take of rejecting the null hypothesis when it is in fact true. To see what is involved, note that if $\beta_i = 1.0$,

$$\tilde{t} = \frac{\tilde{b}_i - 1.0}{s(\tilde{b}_i|R_{m1}, \ldots, R_{mT})}$$

has the "t" distribution with $T - 2$ degrees of freedom. Since such a $\tilde{t}$ random variable is continuous and unbounded, any value is possible for $\tilde{t}$ (and thus for $\tilde{b}_i$), no matter how far from 1.0. For example, if we decide that we will reject the null hypothesis $\beta_i = 1.0$ if the sample value of $\tilde{t}$ turns out to be less than -1.96 or greater than 1.96, then we are saying that we are willing to take a 5 percent chance of rejecting the null hypothesis when it is in fact true. That is, even when the null hypothesis $\beta_i = 1.0$ is true, there is a 5 percent probability that a sample will yield a value of $\tilde{t}$ that is either less than -1.96 or greater than 1.96.

Although the choice is arbitrary, suppose we decide that the hypothesis $\beta_i = 1.0$ for IBM will be rejected for values of t less than -1.96 or greater than 1.96. Then, from the sample estimates for the period July 1963–June 1968, we determine that

$$t = \frac{\tilde{b}_i - \beta_i}{s(\tilde{b}_i | R_{m1}, \ldots, R_{mT})} = \frac{.67 - 1.00}{.13} = -2.54.$$

Since this is less than the chosen critical value -1.96, we reject the null hypothesis that $\beta_i = 1.0$. Indeed, from Table 1.8 we determine that $t = -2.54$ corresponds to about the .005 fractile of the unit normal distribution; in samples from the unit normal distribution, a value of t equal to or less than -2.54 is expected in only about 5 of every 1,000 samples. Since the sample value of t is so extreme, we can conclude that the sample is truly unlikely if $\beta_i = 1.0$.

Once we choose critical values of t that will cause us to reject a null hypothesis, there are in fact intervals of values of the parameter of interest that a given sample will reject as null hypotheses. For example, suppose we say that we will reject a null hypothesis about β_i on the basis of a sample value of t that is less than -1.96 or greater than 1.96. Then, any hypothetical value of β_i in the interval

$$[b_i - 1.96 \, s(b_i | R_{m1}, \ldots, R_{mT})] \text{ to } [b_i + 1.96 \, s(b_i | R_{m1}, \ldots, R_{mT})]$$

could not be rejected, while any value of β_i outside the interval would be rejected. This interval is precisely the .95 confidence interval discussed earlier. When we decide to reject a hypothesis about β_i if the hypothetical value is outside the interval, we are deciding to accept a 5 percent chance of rejecting a true hypothesis. The basis of the 5 percent chance of error is the fact that in repeated samples we can expect that the .95 confidence interval will not include the true β_i in 5 percent of the samples.

There is an important insight to be gained here. The fact that a test is consistent with a null hypothesis does not always mean that the test provides much support for the hypothesis. Once we choose the values of t that will cause us to reject hypotheses about β_i, then in a sample there will be a range of values of β_i that cannot be rejected, so that the sample is consistent with any number of hypotheses about β_i. For example, in the case of IBM, when the (arbitrarily) chosen rejection values of t are -1.96 and 1.96, then any null hypothesis about β_i cannot be rejected so long as the hypothetical β_i is in the interval [.42 to .92]. Since there is a wide range of possible values of β_i that cannot be rejected on the basis of the July 1963–June 1968 data, the fact that we cannot reject a specific hypothesis (for example, $\beta_i = .5$) is not really positive evidence in support of this hypothesis. In general, appropriate conservative statements are that the null hypothesis cannot be rejected on the basis of the data at hand, or that the data are consistent with the hypothesis. Any conclusions about the merits of the hypothesis that are more positive than this must be justifiable from the specifics of the case.

C. The Bayesian Approach

Having computed the 95 percent confidence interval for β_i for IBM, we would like to be able to say that the probability that the sample confidence interval [.42 to .92] contains β_i is .95. To the classical statistician, however, such a statement is anathema. The statement assigns a probability to a specific interval of possible values of β_i and thus implies a probability distribution on β_i. The classical statistician argues that since β_i is a constant, any assignment of probabilities to different possible values is illogical.

In contrast, the Bayesian argues that the fact that β_i is a constant is irrelevant, since its value is unknown. To the Bayesian, the essence of the problem of making inferences about β_i is to assign probabilities to the possible values of $\tilde{\beta}_i$ in such a way that the resulting probability distribution on $\tilde{\beta}_i$ is the best possible summary of his uncertainty about $\tilde{\beta}_i$.

When the Bayesian goes through the process of summarizing his uncertainty about $\tilde{\beta}_i$, his first step is to assess a prior distribution on $\tilde{\beta}_i$. This can be based on anything, other than the sample at hand, that the Bayesian considers relevant. His prior distribution may, for example, be based on previous samples of $\tilde{R}_{it}$ and $\tilde{R}_{mt}$ and on his judgments concerning the implications of nonmarket, that is, nonreturn evidence for the value of β_i. The idea of a probability distribution based in any way on judgments is again anathema to the classical statistician. For him, the only probability distributions are those from which samples can be drawn. In contrast, the goal of the Bayesian is to get the best possible summary of his uncertainty about $\tilde{\beta}_i$, and from this viewpoint his judgments are relevant. The next and final step in the Bayesian analysis is to combine the prior distribution with the evidence from the sample at hand to get what is called the posterior probability distribution on $\tilde{\beta}_i$. This posterior distribution is what the Bayesian regards as the best possible summary of his uncertainty about β_i.

Although the personal judgments of the Bayesian are certainly relevant for assessing his uncertainty about the value of the unknown parameter, there are circumstances where personal judgments are not relevant. This is probably generally true in scientific investigations. I may agree that uncertainty about the value of an unknown parameter should be stated in terms of a probability distribution on the parameter, but I would prefer that the posterior distribution on the parameter which is the end result of a scientific investigation is a reflection primarily of the evidence from the sample. The way the Bayesian satisfies my preferences is to assign his prior distribution in such a way that, as long as the sample at hand is reasonably large, the posterior distribution is dominated by the sample evidence. Prior distributions that have this property are called diffuse.

In the case of the market model coefficients β_i and α_i, the use of diffuse priors leads to simple results with respect to posterior distributions. In "large" samples, the posterior distributions of $\tilde{\beta}_i$ and $\tilde{\alpha}_i$, conditional on $R_{m1}, \ldots, R_{mT}$, are normal with means equal to b_i and a_i, the estimates of the parameters obtained from the sample at hand, and with variances $\sigma^2(\tilde{\beta}_i | R_{m1}, \ldots, R_{mT})$ and $\sigma^2(\tilde{\alpha}_i | R_{m1}, \ldots, R_{mT})$, equal to $s^2(b_i | R_{m1}, \ldots, R_{mT})$ and $s^2(a_i | R_{m1}, \ldots, R_{mT})$, the usual sample estimates of the conditional variances of $\tilde{b}_i$ and $\tilde{a}_i$. Thus, the standardized variables

$$\tilde{t} = \frac{\tilde{\beta}_i - E(\tilde{\beta}_i | R_{m1}, \ldots, R_{mT})}{\sigma(\tilde{\beta}_i | R_{m1}, \ldots, R_{mT})} = \frac{\tilde{\beta}_i - b_i}{s(b_i | R_{m1}, \ldots, R_{mT})} \qquad (59)$$

$$\tilde{t} = \frac{\tilde{\alpha}_i - E(\tilde{\alpha}_i | R_{m1}, \ldots, R_{mT})}{\sigma(\tilde{\alpha}_i | R_{m1}, \ldots, R_{mT})} = \frac{\tilde{\alpha}_i - a_i}{s(a_i | R_{m1}, \ldots, R_{mT})} \qquad (60)$$

have the unit normal distribution.

Note that in the $\tilde{t}$ random variables of (59) and (60), the roles of $\tilde{\beta}_i$ and b_i are reversed vis-à-vis the classical approach, summarized in the corresponding $\tilde{t}$ variables of (50) and (51). In the classical approach, β_i is always treated as a constant, and probability statements derive from the characteristics of variation from sample to sample in b_i and $s(b_i | R_{m1}, \ldots, R_{mT})$. In contrast, in the Bayesian approach one is concerned with judging the uncertainty about β_i that remains in light of the given sample. Thus, $\tilde{\beta}_i$ is treated as the random variable, and probability statements derive from the fact that, with a diffuse prior, the posterior distribution of $\tilde{\beta}_i$ is normal with mean $E(\tilde{\beta}_i) = b_i$ and standard deviation $\sigma(\tilde{\beta}_i | R_{m1}, \ldots, R_{mT}) = s(b_i | R_{m1}, \ldots, R_{mT})$.

For example, with equation (59) and Table 1.8 we can determine that

$$\Pr\left[\tilde{t} = \frac{\tilde{\beta}_i - b_i}{s(b_i | R_{m1}, \ldots, R_{mT})} < -1.96\right] = .025,$$

which implies that

$$\Pr\left[\tilde{\beta}_i < b_i - 1.96\, s(b_i | R_{m1}, \ldots, R_{mT})\right] = .025. \qquad (61)$$

In words, the uncertainty that remains about the value of β_i, summarized by the posterior distribution of $\tilde{\tilde{\beta}}_i$, is such that we assign probability .025 to the possibility that β_i is less than $b_i - 1.96\, s(b_i|R_{m1}, \ldots, R_{mT})$. Likewise,

$$\Pr\left[\tilde{t} = \frac{\tilde{\tilde{\beta}}_i - b_i}{s(b_i|R_{m1}, \ldots, R_{mT})} > 1.96\right] = .025,$$

or

$$\Pr\left[\tilde{\tilde{\beta}}_i > b_i + 1.96 s(b_i|R_{m1}, \ldots, R_{mT})\right] = .025, \qquad (62)$$

so that we assign probability .025 to the possibility that β_i is greater than $b_i + 1.96 s(b_i|R_{m1}, \ldots, R_{mT})$. Finally, combining equations (61) and (62), the posterior uncertainty about β_i is such that we assign probability .95 to the possibility that β_i is in the interval

$$[b_i - 1.96 s(b_i|R_{m1}, \ldots, R_{mT})] \text{ to } [b_i + 1.96 s(b_i|R_{m1}, \ldots, R_{mT})]. \quad (63)$$

Expression (63) is numerically identical to the classical .95 confidence interval of (58) when applied to a specific sample. When one takes the Bayesian viewpoint, however, the probability statement made from the sample confidence interval is more direct than in the classical approach. In the Bayesian approach, there is no talk about a hypothetical sample or repeated samples. One simply says that the probability that β_i is in the interval given by (63) is .95.

If there is some special interest in a particular possible value of β_i, then the Bayesian can use the posterior distribution of $\tilde{\tilde{\beta}}_i$ to make a direct probability statement about the value of interest. For example, if for IBM there is special interest in the possibility that $\beta_i = 1.0$, the Bayesian computes

$$t = \frac{\beta_i - b_i}{s(b_i|R_{m1}, \ldots, R_{mT})} = \frac{1.0 - .67}{.13} = 2.54. \qquad (64)$$

From Table 1.8 he then determines that the posterior probability that β_i is greater than 1.0 is about .005. In other words, the posterior distribution assigns low probability to the possibility that β_i is as large as 1.0. Again, unlike the classical approach, the probability statement is made without reference to repeated samples.

VI. Conclusions

We have spent much time discussing the market model and its estimation from a theoretical viewpoint. We pass on now to the data.

CHAPTER

4

The Market Model: Estimates

The first step in applying the estimation techniques of Chapter 3 to stock market data is to give a detailed example for an individual stock. Then summary results for two samples of 30 stocks are presented, after which we examine some of the practical problems associated with fitting the market model.

I. Estimating the Market Model: A Detailed Example

A. *The Market Model: Summary of Equations and Properties*

It is helpful at this point to summarize the market model equations. Bivariate normality of $\tilde{R}_{it}$ and $\tilde{R}_{mt}$ implies that the regression function of $\tilde{R}_{it}$ on $\tilde{R}_{mt}$, the expected value of $\tilde{R}_{it}$ conditional on R_{mt}, is

$$E(\tilde{R}_{it}|R_{mt}) = \alpha_i + \beta_i R_{mt}, \quad t = 1, \ldots, T, \tag{1}$$

with

$$\beta_i = \frac{\text{cov}(\tilde{R}_{it}, \tilde{R}_{mt})}{\sigma^2(\tilde{R}_{mt})} \text{ and } \alpha_i = E(\tilde{R}_{it}) - \beta_i E(\tilde{R}_{mt}), \quad t = 1, \ldots, T. \tag{2}$$

The relationship between $\tilde{R}_{it}$ and $\tilde{R}_{mt}$ implied by bivariate normality can be described as

$$\tilde{R}_{it} = \alpha_i + \beta_i \tilde{R}_{mt} + \tilde{\epsilon}_{it}, \quad t = 1, \ldots, T, \tag{3}$$

where the disturbance $\tilde{\epsilon}_{it}$ has mean zero and is independent of $\tilde{R}_{mt}$, so that

$$E(\tilde{\epsilon}_{it} | R_{mt}) = E(\tilde{\epsilon}_{it}) = 0.0, \quad t = 1, \ldots, T, \tag{4}$$

$$\sigma^2(\tilde{R}_{it} | R_{mt}) = \sigma^2(\tilde{\epsilon}_{it} | R_{mt}) = \sigma^2(\tilde{\epsilon}_{it}) = \sigma^2(\tilde{\epsilon}_i), \quad t = 1, \ldots, T, \tag{5}$$

$$\text{cov}(\tilde{\epsilon}_{it}, \tilde{R}_{mt}) = 0.0, \quad t = 1, \ldots, T. \tag{6}$$

It is also helpful to restate the properties of the correlation coefficient ρ_{im} between $\tilde{R}_{it}$ and $\tilde{R}_{mt}$ that are described in Chapter 3. Thus,

$$\rho_{im} = \frac{\text{cov}(\tilde{R}_{it}, \tilde{R}_{mt})}{\sigma(\tilde{R}_{it})\,\sigma(\tilde{R}_{mt})}, \quad t = 1, \ldots, T \tag{7}$$

and

$$\sigma^2(\tilde{\epsilon}_{it}) = \sigma^2(\tilde{R}_{it})(1 - \rho_{im}^2), \quad t = 1, \ldots, T, \tag{8}$$

so that

$$\rho_{im}^2 = \frac{\sigma^2(\tilde{R}_{it}) - \sigma^2(\tilde{\epsilon}_{it})}{\sigma^2(\tilde{R}_{it})}, \quad t = 1, \ldots, T. \tag{9}$$

Since the independence of $\tilde{\epsilon}_{it}$ and $\tilde{R}_{mt}$ implies

$$\sigma^2(\tilde{R}_{it}) = \beta_i^2 \sigma^2(\tilde{R}_{mt}) + \sigma^2(\tilde{\epsilon}_{it}), \quad t = 1, \ldots, T, \tag{10}$$

the square of the correlation coefficient, henceforth called the coefficient of determination,

$$\rho_{im}^2 = \frac{\sigma^2(\tilde{R}_{it}) - \sigma^2(\tilde{\epsilon}_{it})}{\sigma^2(\tilde{R}_{it})} = \frac{\beta_i^2 \sigma^2(\tilde{R}_{mt})}{\sigma^2(\tilde{R}_{it})}, \quad t = 1, \ldots, T, \tag{11}$$

is the proportion of the variance of $\tilde{R}_{it}$ that can be attributed to the market—that is, to the term $\beta_i \tilde{R}_{mt}$ in the market model relationship between $\tilde{R}_{it}$ and $\tilde{R}_{mt}$ of equation (3)—while $1 - \rho_{im}^2$ is the fraction of $\sigma^2(\tilde{R}_{it})$ that can be attributed to $\tilde{\epsilon}_{it}$, the error or disturbance of the market model relationship between $\tilde{R}_{it}$ and $\tilde{R}_{mt}$.

Since the estimation techniques of Chapter 3 are based on the assumption that the joint distribution of $\tilde{R}_{it}$ and $\tilde{R}_{mt}$ is the same for each month of the sampling period, the assumption is maintained in this chapter. We indicate this in the preceding statement of the properties of the market model by appending the notation $t = 1, \ldots, T$ to each equation. Since all properties of the joint distribution of $\tilde{R}_{it}$ and $\tilde{R}_{mt}$ are constant or stationary during the sampling period, there is no need for a subscript t on any parameters. We make use of this prerogative in writing α_i, β_i, and ρ_{im} without t subscripts, but in other cases the prerogative goes unused.

B. Market Model Estimates for IBM

The estimators of the market model coefficients β_i and α_i involve substituting unbiased estimators of $E(\tilde{R}_{it})$, $E(\tilde{R}_{mt})$, $\sigma^2(\tilde{R}_{mt})$, and cov $(\tilde{R}_{it}, \tilde{R}_{mt})$ into (2). The unbiased estimators of these parameters are

$$\tilde{\bar{R}}_i = \frac{\sum_{t=1}^{T} \tilde{R}_{it}}{T} \quad \text{and} \quad \tilde{\bar{R}}_m = \frac{\sum_{t=1}^{T} \tilde{R}_{mt}}{T} \tag{12}$$

$$s^2(\tilde{R}_m) = \frac{\sum_{t=1}^{T} (\tilde{R}_{mt} - \tilde{\bar{R}}_m)^2}{T-1} \tag{13}$$

$$\tilde{s}_{im} = \frac{\sum_{t=1}^{T} (\tilde{R}_{it} - \tilde{\bar{R}}_i)(\tilde{R}_{mt} - \tilde{\bar{R}}_m)}{T-1}, \tag{14}$$

so that the estimators of β_i and α_i are

$$\tilde{b}_i = \frac{\tilde{s}_{im}}{s^2(\tilde{R}_m)} = \frac{\sum_{t=1}^{T} (\tilde{R}_{it} - \tilde{\bar{R}}_m)(\tilde{R}_{mt} - \tilde{\bar{R}}_m)}{\sum_{t=1}^{T} (\tilde{R}_{mt} - \tilde{\bar{R}}_m)^2} \tag{15}$$

$$\tilde{a}_i = \tilde{\bar{R}}_i - \tilde{b}_i \tilde{\bar{R}}_m. \tag{16}$$

Recall that techniques or procedures for estimating parameters, like those described in equations (12) to (16), are called estimators. When such techniques are applied to particular samples of data, the numbers that they produce are called estimates. An estimator is a random variable, which we indicate with the usual tilde. An estimate is a drawing from the sampling distribution of the estimator, so that when an estimate is referred to, the tilde is dropped. The reader should check that these words and notation are used consistently in what follows.

Suppose now that the common stock i of interest is the common stock of IBM, and we wish to estimate β_i and α_i from the monthly returns on IBM and the equally weighted market portfolio m for the five-year period from July 1963 through June 1968. In this chapter, m includes only NYSE common stocks. The monthly returns, R_{it} and R_{mt}, are shown in Table 4.1. From equation (15) we can see that to estimate β_i and α_i, we must first compute

TABLE 4.1

Monthly Returns, R_{it}, on IBM and on R_{mt}, the Equally Weighted
Version of the Market Portfolio, for the Period
July 1963–June 1968

MONTH	R_{it}	R_{mt}	MONTH	R_{it}	R_{mt}
7/63	−.0040	−.0095	1/66	−.0060	.0435
8/63	.0259	.0506	2/66	.0413	.0109
9/63	.0163	−.0184	3/66	.0019	−.0219
10/63	.0929	.0163	4/66	.0804	.0337
11/63	−.0152	−.0068	5/66	−.0220	−.0724
12/63	.0448	.0075	6/66	−.0296	−.0048
1/64	.0690	.0201	7/66	−.0278	−.0127
2/64	.0521	.0270	8/66	−.0562	−.0931
3/64	.0444	.0314	9/66	−.0094	−.0143
4/64	−.0404	−.0031	10/66	.0457	.0127
5/64	.0549	.0116	11/66	.1358	.0382
6/64	−.0063	.0154	12/66	−.0120	.0162
7/64	−.0314	.0277	1/67	.0754	.1428
8/64	−.0438	−.0090	2/67	.0791	.0209
9/64	−.0091	.0370	3/67	.0488	.0520
10/64	−.0378	.0170	4/67	.1009	.0365
11/64	−.0149	.0007	5/67	−.0352	−.0179
12/64	−.0073	−.0069	6/67	.0670	.0516
1/65	.0952	.0587	7/67	.0206	.0709
2/65	.0195	.0278	8/67	−.0136	.0028
3/65	−.0033	.0053	9/67	.0970	.0378
4/65	.0677	.0359	10/67	.0825	−.0359
5/65	−.0113	−.0079	11/67	.0330	.0067
6/65	−.0418	−.0743	12/67	.0245	.0554
7/65	.0459	.0291	1/68	−.0518	−.0035
8/65	.0449	.0451	2/68	−.0222	−.0416
9/65	.0271	.0308	3/68	.0560	−.0045
10/65	.0400	.0474	4/68	.1061	.1164
11/65	−.0122	.0300	5/68	.0558	.0586
12/65	−.0495	.0327	6/68	−.0091	.0192

the sample means $\overline{R}_i$ and $\overline{R}_m$. Applying (12) to the returns in Table 4.1 (and the reader may find it instructive to check the calculations that follow), we get

$$\overline{R}_i = \frac{1.2694}{60} = .0212, \qquad \overline{R}_m = \frac{.9739}{60} = .0162.$$

Thus, the average monthly return on IBM is 2.12 percent, while the return on the market portfolio is 1.62 percent per month. During this period the shareholders of IBM did quite well, but the market portfolio also had a substantial average monthly return. The sample mean returns, the returns in Table 4.1, and equations (13) to (16) can now be used to compute

$$s^2(R_m) = \frac{.089421}{59} = .001516$$

$$s_{im} = \frac{.060315}{59} = .001022$$

$$b_i = \frac{.06031}{.08942} = .6745$$

$$a_i = .0212 - .6745(.0162) = .0103.$$

Thus, corresponding to the regression function of equation (1), we have the estimated regression function

$$\hat{R}_{it} = a_i + b_i R_{mt}.$$

$$= .0103 + .6745R_{mt}.$$

Corresponding to equation (3), we have the estimated market model equation

$$R_{it} = a_i + b_i R_{mt} + e_{it}$$

$$= .0103 + .6745R_{mt} + e_{it}.$$

The results of the computations are perhaps best appreciated from Figure 4.1, which presents a plot of the sample points (the sample paired values

FIGURE 4.1

Plot of Sample Points and Estimated Market Model Regression Function for IBM for July 1963–June 1968

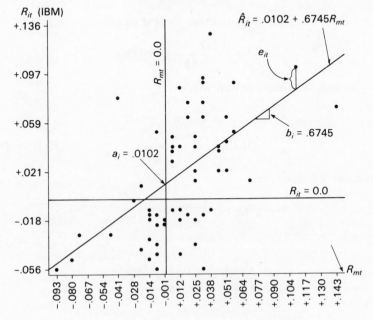

of R_{it} and R_{mt}), indicated by stars, and of the estimated regression function. The slope of the line is b_i, and a_i is the point on the line where $R_m = 0.0$. The residual e_{it} for any sample point is the vertical distance from the dot corresponding to that sample point to the point on the estimated regression function along the (imaginary) line from the dot that is perpendicular to the R_m axis. One such residual is indicated in the figure.

C. The Fit of the Estimated Regression

The impression given by Figure 4.1 is that there is a relationship between the monthly returns on a share of IBM and the monthly returns on the market portfolio m, and the relationship appears to be linear. But it does not seem to be strong, since the dispersion of the sample points around the estimated regression function is substantial. There are several ways to give formal content to this visual impression.

First, from the equation (10), the disturbance variance $\sigma^2(\tilde{\epsilon}_{it})$ measures that part of the variance of the return on security i that cannot be attributed to the market model relationship between $\tilde{R}_{it}$ and $\tilde{R}_{mt}$. The unbiased estimator of $\sigma^2(\tilde{\epsilon}_{it})$ is

$$s^2(\tilde{e}_i) = \frac{\sum_{t=1}^{T} \tilde{e}_{it}^2}{T-2}. \tag{17}$$

Applying this estimator to the residuals for IBM we get

$$s^2(e_i) = \frac{.09164}{58} = .00158.$$

Using the unbiased estimator of $\sigma^2(\tilde{R}_{it})$,

$$s^2(\tilde{R}_i) = \frac{\sum_{t=1}^{T} (\tilde{R}_{it} - \bar{\tilde{R}}_i)^2}{T-1}, \tag{18}$$

we can also determine that

$$s^2(R_i) = \frac{.13260}{59} = .00225.$$

Since

$$\frac{s^2(e_i)}{s^2(R_i)} = \frac{.00158}{.00225} = .702,$$

the sample estimate is that slightly more than 70 percent of the variance of $\tilde{R}_{it}$ is unexplained by the market model relationship between $\tilde{R}_{it}$ and $\tilde{R}_{mt}$. Conversely, since

$$1.0 - \frac{s^2(e_i)}{s^2(R_i)} = \frac{s^2(R_i) - s^2(e_i)}{s^2(R_i)} = .298, \tag{19}$$

slightly less than 30 percent of the sample variance of $\tilde{R}_{it}$ can be attributed to the estimated market model relationships between $\tilde{R}_{it}$ and $\tilde{R}_{mt}$.

There is another approach to the same question, and it gives a slightly different answer. Just as equation (10) says that the variance of $\tilde{R}_{it}$ has two components, so we know from Section III of Chapter 3 that

$$\sum_{t=1}^{T} (\tilde{R}_{it} - \bar{\tilde{R}}_i)^2 = \tilde{b}_i^2 \sum_{t=1}^{T} (\tilde{R}_{mt} - \bar{\tilde{R}})^2 + \sum_{t=1}^{T} \tilde{e}_{it}^2; \tag{20}$$

that is, in any sample the sum of squared deviations of $\tilde{R}_{it}$ from its sample mean can be split into "explained" and residual sums of squares. Moreover, from Section III of Chapter 3 we also know that the sample coefficient of determination (the square of the sample correlation coefficient), which is defined as

$$\tilde{r}_{im}^2 = \left(\frac{\tilde{s}_{im}}{s(\tilde{R}_i) s(\tilde{R}_m)}\right)^2, \tag{21}$$

can be expressed as

$$\tilde{r}_{im}^2 = \frac{\tilde{b}_i^2 \sum_{t=1}^{T} (\tilde{R}_{mt} - \bar{\tilde{R}}_m)^2}{\sum_{t=1}^{T} (\tilde{R}_{it} - \bar{\tilde{R}}_i)^2} = \frac{\tilde{b}_i^2 s^2(\tilde{R}_m)}{s^2(\tilde{R}_i)}. \tag{22}$$

Thus, $\tilde{r}_{im}^2$ can be interpreted as the fraction of the sample variance of $\tilde{R}_{it}$ that can be attributed to the fitted market model relationship between $\tilde{R}_{it}$ and $\tilde{R}_{mt}$.

When equation (21) or (22) is applied to the monthly returns on a share of IBM, the sample coefficient of determination is

$$r_{im}^2 = .307.$$

Thus, slightly more than 30 percent of the sample variance of $\tilde{R}_{it}$ can be attributed to the estimated market model relationship between $\tilde{R}_{it}$ and $\tilde{R}_{mt}$.

Note that (19) gives a slightly lower measure of the strength of the relationship between $\tilde{R}_{it}$ and $\tilde{R}_{mt}$ than (21) or (22), even though the equations purport to measure the same thing. Indeed, (19) and (22) are just the sample counterparts of the two versions of the population coefficient of determination given in equation (11).

Although they are closely related, (19) and (22) are not identical sample quantities. The reason is that although equations (10) and (11) hold for the population variances and although (20) holds for the sample sums of squares, nevertheless

$$s^2(\tilde{R}_i) < \tilde{b}_i^2 s^2(\tilde{R}_m) + s^2(\tilde{e}_i). \tag{23}$$

To see this, simply note that the estimators $s^2(\tilde{R}_i)$ and $s^2(\tilde{R}_m)$ involve dividing the sample sums of squares $\Sigma(\tilde{R}_{it} - \bar{\tilde{R}}_i)^2$ and $\Sigma(\tilde{R}_{mt} - \bar{\tilde{R}}_m)^2$ by $T-1$, whereas in $s^2(\tilde{e}_i)$ the sum of squared residuals $\Sigma\tilde{e}_{it}^2$ is divided by $T-2$. Note also that if we define

$$\tilde{r}_{im}^{*2} = \frac{s^2(\tilde{R}_i) - s^2(\tilde{e}_i)}{s^2(\tilde{R}_i)} = 1.0 - \frac{s^2(\tilde{e}_i)}{s^2(\tilde{R}_i)}, \tag{24}$$

then it follows from (23) that

$$\tilde{r}_{im}^2 = \frac{\tilde{b}_i^2 s^2(\tilde{R}_m)}{s^2(\tilde{R}_i)} > \frac{s^2(\tilde{R}_i) - s^2(\tilde{e})}{s^2(\tilde{R}_i)} = \tilde{r}_{im}^{*2}. \tag{25}$$

Because $\tilde{r}_{im}^{*2}$ takes account of the fact that the unbiased estimator $s^2(\tilde{e}_i)$ has fewer degrees of freedom than the unbiased estimators $s^2(\tilde{R}_i)$ and $s^2(\tilde{R}_m)$, $\tilde{r}_{im}^{*2}$ is usually called the sample coefficient of determination, adjusted for degrees of freedom, whereas $\tilde{r}_{im}^2$ is called the sample coefficient of determination. In applications of the market model, the difference between these two measures of fit is usually negligible. Since the sample size T is generally large, a correction involving one degree of freedom has a trivial effect on the estimator.

For example, for IBM, the choice between $r_{im}^{*2} = .298$ and $r_{im}^2 = .307$ is of no consequence. In either case only about 30 percent of the sample variance of the stock's return can be attributed to the estimated market model relationship between $\tilde{R}_{it}$ and $\tilde{R}_{mt}$. Thus, the impression given by Figure 4.1— that the estimated regression function leaves much of the variation in the sample points unexplained—receives formal confirmation.

D. The Reliability of the Market Model Coefficient Estimates for IBM

The estimate of β_i for IBM from the monthly returns for July 1963–June 1968 is .67. From Chapters 2 and 3 we know that β_i can be interpreted as the risk of security i in the market portfolio m measured relative to $\sigma^2(\tilde{R}_{mt})$, the risk of m, which is also the average risk of all the securities in m. Since m includes all the common stocks on the NYSE, the estimate $b_i = .67$ suggests that the risk of a share of IBM is substantially less than the average risk in m of all stocks on the exchange. Alternatively, if one interprets β_i as the market sensitivity of security i, then the estimate $b = .67$ suggests that the return on a share of IBM has substantially less than average sensitivity to marketwide factors.

An estimate like $b_i = .67$ is, however, just a drawing from the probability distribution of possible values of the estimator $\tilde{b}_i$ of equation (15). To draw any conclusions from a specific estimate, one must measure its reliability. The first step is to compute the sample estimate of the variance of $\tilde{b}_i$. From Chapter 3, the variance of the estimator $\tilde{b}_i$, conditional on $R_{m1}, \ldots, R_{mT}$, is

$$\sigma^2(\tilde{b}_i | R_{m1}, \ldots, R_{mT}) = \frac{\sigma^2(\tilde{\epsilon}_{it})}{\displaystyle\sum_{t=1}^{T} (R_{mt} - \bar{R}_m)^2} = \frac{\sigma^2(\tilde{\epsilon}_{it})}{(T-1)s^2(R_m)}. \qquad (26)$$

The variance of the estimator depends on the strength of the relationship between $\tilde{R}_{it}$ and $\tilde{R}_{mt}$, as measured by the disturbance variance $\sigma^2(\tilde{\epsilon}_{it})$; the weaker the relationship—that is, the larger the value of $\sigma^2(\tilde{\epsilon}_{it})$—the larger the conditional variance of the estimator. The variance of the estimator also depends on the sample size; the larger the value of T, the smaller the conditional variance of $\tilde{b}_i$. Analogous statements apply to the sample estimator of the conditional variance,

$$s^2(\tilde{b}_i | R_{m1}, \ldots, R_{mT}) = \frac{s^2(\tilde{e}_i)}{\displaystyle\sum_{t=1}^{T} (R_{mt} - \bar{R}_m)^2} = \frac{s^2(\tilde{e}_i)}{(T-1)s^2(R_m)}, \qquad (27)$$

where $s^2(\tilde{e}_i)$ is the estimator of $\sigma^2(\tilde{e}_i)$ given by (17).

For IBM the estimate of the conditional variance of $\tilde{b}_i$ for July 1963–June 1968 is

$$s^2(b_i | R_{m1}, \ldots, R_{mT}) = \frac{.00158}{.08942} = .0177,$$

so that

$$s(b_i | R_{m1}, \ldots, R_{mT}) = .1331.$$

This number seems to say that there is substantial uncertainty about the value of β_i for IBM, but let us try to give more formal content to this impression.

Recalling the discussion in Section V.C of Chapter 3, from the Bayesian viewpoint, the uncertainty about β_i that cannot be resolved by the sample at hand is summarized by the posterior distribution on $\tilde{\beta}_i$. For a large sample and given a diffuse prior distribution on $\tilde{\beta}_i$, the posterior distribution on $\tilde{\beta}_i$, conditional on the sample values $R_{m1}, \ldots, R_{mT}$, is approximately normal, with mean

$$E(\tilde{\beta}_i | R_{m1}, \ldots, R_{mT}) = b_i = .6745$$

and standard deviation

$$\sigma(\tilde{\beta}_i | R_{m1}, \ldots, R_{mT}) = s(b_i | R_{m1}, \ldots, R_{mT}) = .1331.$$

If we standardize $\tilde{\beta}_i$ as

$$\tilde{t} = \frac{\tilde{\beta}_i - E(\tilde{\beta}_i | R_{m1}, \ldots, R_{mT})}{\sigma(\tilde{\beta}_i | R_{m1}, \ldots, R_{mT})} = \frac{\tilde{\beta}_i - b}{s(b_i | R_{m1}, \ldots, R_{mT})}, \qquad (28)$$

then we can use the unit normal distribution tabulated in Table 1.8 to compute some fractiles of the posterior distribution and so get a more concrete feeling for the uncertainty about the value of β_i that the sample does not resolve. For example, the .025 and .975 fractiles of the posterior distribution on $\tilde{\beta}_i$ (corresponding to $t_{.025} = -1.96$ and $t_{.975} = 1.96$) are $\beta_i = .414$ and $\beta_i = .935$. Likewise:

Some Fractiles of the Posterior Distribution of $\tilde{\beta}_i$ for IBM

Cumulative probability	.025	.05	.10	.25	.50	.75	.90	.95	.975
Fractile	.414	.455	.504	.585	.674	.764	.845	.893	.935

These fractiles suggest that there is substantial remaining uncertainty about the value of β_i. The posterior probability is .25 that β_i is less than .585, and the probability is .25 that β_i is greater than .764. Thus the probability is .5 that β_i is outside the interval from .585 to .764. Alternatively, the Bayesian 50 percent confidence interval on β_i is from .585 to .764; that is, the posterior probability that β_i is in this interval is .5. Likewise, the interval from .504 to .845 covers a fairly wide range of possible values of β_i, but the probability that the true β_i is outside this interval is .2, so that the interval is the 80 percent Bayesian confidence interval for β_i. If one prefers the classical to the Bayesian approach to measuring reliability, the fractiles of the Bayesian posterior distribution shown above are nevertheless relevant, since sample estimates of Bayesian and classical confidence intervals are identical.

We soon see that the results for IBM are typical. With samples of five years of monthly returns, there is always substantial uncertainty about the values of β_i for individual common stocks.

E. Testing the Assumptions Underlying the Coefficient Estimators

With either the classical or the Bayesian approach, there are two major assumptions from which the properties of the market model regression coefficient estimators derive. The first assumption is that the joint distribution of $\tilde{R}_{it}$ and $\tilde{R}_{mt}$ is bivariate normal. The second assumption is that there is random sampling from the stationary joint distribution of $\tilde{R}_{it}$ and $\tilde{R}_{mt}$. The purpose of this section is to describe how one might judge the validity of these two assumptions. This is an important task. The validity of the inferences from estimates of parameters depends on whether the assumptions that underlie the statistical techniques used are a good approximation to the data at hand. It is always well to check that this is true.

THE IMPLICATIONS OF BIVARIATE NORMALITY

The assumption that the joint distribution of $\tilde{R}_{it}$ and $\tilde{R}_{mt}$ is bivariate normal has three major implications that are the basis of the market model and of the properties of the market model coefficient estimators. First, bivariate normality implies that the regression function $E(\tilde{R}_{it}|R_{mt})$ is a linear function of R_{mt}. Second, the market model disturbance $\tilde{\epsilon}_{it}$ has a normal distribution, as do the returns $\tilde{R}_{it}$ and $\tilde{R}_{mt}$. Third, the expected value of $\tilde{\epsilon}_{it}$ is zero, and $\tilde{\epsilon}_{it}$ is independent of $\tilde{R}_{mt}$; that is, the conditional distribution of $\tilde{\epsilon}_{it}$ is the same for all values of R_{mt}. The first and third implications are summarized in equations (1) to (6).

Using the sample results for IBM for July 1963–June 1968, let us examine first the implication of bivariate normality that the distributions of $\tilde{R}_{it}$, $\tilde{R}_{mt}$, and $\tilde{\epsilon}_{it}$ are normal. We rely on the studentized range introduced and used extensively in Chapter 1. Recall that the studentized range is the difference between the largest and smallest of the sample values of a random variable, divided by the sample standard deviation. From the sample results for July 1963–June 1968, we get

	Studentized Ranges	
R_{it}(IBM)	R_{mt}	e_{it}
4.05	6.06	4.56

From Table 1.9 we determine that the sample studentized range (*SR*) for R_{mt}, 6.06, is between the .99 and .995 fractiles of the distribution of the studentized range in samples of size 60 from a normal population. Thus, in sampling from a normal population, there is less than a 1 percent chance that a sample will yield a studentized range as large as or larger than 6.06. On the other hand, the studentized range for the monthly returns on IBM is 4.05, which is between the .05 and .10 fractiles of the distribution of the studentized range, while the studentized range of the residuals is 4.56, which is almost midway between the .10 and .90 fractiles. The range of the returns on m is unusually large for a sample from a normal population; the range of the returns on IBM is slightly small for a sample from a normal population, while the range of the market model residuals is not at all unusual for a sample from a normal population. One might conclude that the sample returns for R_{it} and e_{it} are consistent with normality but those for R_{mt} are not.

From one viewpoint, nonnormality of $\tilde{R}_{mt}$ is not critical. Recall from Chapter 3 that the distributional properties of the market model coefficient estimators do not require that the distribution of $\tilde{R}_{mt}$ be normal. The critical assumptions are random sampling and normality for the disturbances $\tilde{\epsilon}_{it}$, and the studentized range of IBM's residuals is consistent with the hypothesis of normality for $\tilde{\epsilon}_{it}$. From the viewpoint of the two-parameter portfolio model, however, which is based on the assumption that all portfolio return distributions are normal, it is disturbing if the market portfolio m, which is representative of a diversified portfolio, has a return distribution that is substantially nonnormal.

There is the possibility that the extreme studentized range for R_{mt} for July 1963–June 1968 is due to chance, so that the distribution of $\tilde{R}_{mt}$ is not so nonnormal as this five-year period might suggest. To check this possibility, we examine the studentized ranges for R_{mt} for various subperiods from February 1926 to June 1968:

Period	2/26–12/30	1/31–12/35	1/36–12/40	1/41–12/45	1/46–12/50
$SR(R_m)$	4.75	5.29	5.94	4.42	4.46
T	59	60	60	60	60

Period	1/51–12/55	1/56–12/60	1/61–12/65	1/66–6/68
$SR(R_m)$	4.42	5.12	5.78	4.83
T	60	60	60	30

Two of these studentized ranges, those for 1/36–12/40 and 1/61–12/65, are extreme in the sense that they exceed the .975 fractile of the relevant sampling distribution of SR in Table 1.9; and two, those for 1/31–12/35 and 1/66–6/68, are also extreme (but less so) inasmuch as they exceed the .90 fractile of the relevant sampling distributions of SR. On the other hand, the studentized ranges for the remaining five periods are quite consistent with what would be expected from normal populations. Three of them, those for the three five-year periods 1941–1955, might even be said to fall slightly into the left tail of the relevant sampling distribution of SR.

In short, the results are consistent with a distribution for $\tilde{R}_{mt}$ that is slightly leptokurtic relative to a normal distribution, but much less nonnormal than one might infer from the one studentized range for July 1963–June 1968. This is, of course, similar to the conclusion that we draw with respect to distributions of monthly returns on securities and portfolios in Chapter 1, where frequency distributions and studentized ranges of monthly returns are studied in detail, and where we conclude that for monthly returns normal distributions are a workable approximation.

Next we consider the implications of bivariate normality that there is a linear relationship between $\tilde{R}_{it}$ and $\tilde{R}_{mt}$ and that the disturbances $\tilde{\epsilon}_{it}$ from this linear relationship are independent of $\tilde{R}_{mt}$, so that the conditions of equations (1) to (6) hold. Perhaps the best—or, at least in practice, the most common—way to judge the validity of these propositions is by inspection of a plot of the sample combinations of R_{it} and R_{mt} like that shown in Figure 4.1, with the estimated regression function also included on the graph. Obviously, visual inspection can only lead to impressionistic judgments about the validity of the propositions.

Thus, to judge the validity of the proposition that the regression function $E(\tilde{R}_{it}|R_{mt})$ is a linear function of R_{mt}, which is what we mean when we say that there is a linear relationship between the two variables, we can visually inspect a graph like Figure 4.1 and judge whether some nonlinear function might provide a better fit to the sample points. If, as in Figure 4.1, a linear function seems appropriate, then we can conclude that linearity of the regression function is an appropriate approximation. This allows us to conclude that the proposition of equation (4), that the conditional expected value of $\tilde{\epsilon}_{it}$ is independent of R_{mt}, is also an appropriate approximation to the data; that is, if the regression function $E(\tilde{R}_{it}|R_{mt})$ is a linear function of R_{mt}, then $E(\tilde{\epsilon}_{it}|R_{mt})$ must be zero for all values of R_{mt}.

A graph like Figure 4.1 can also be used to judge the validity of the statement of equation (5) that the variance of $\tilde{\epsilon}_{it}$ is independent of R_{mt}, but a combination of care and artistry is needed. In terms of its implications for a sample, equation (5) says that the dispersion of the sample points about the estimated regression function should be about the same for different values of R_{mt}. But one must be careful in interpreting the word "dispersion." Extreme values of R_{mt} are, after all, much less likely than values close to the mean of R_{mt}. Thus, in a sample there are likely to be fewer drawings from the distribution of $\tilde{\epsilon}_{it}$ corresponding to extreme values of R_{mt} than there are for more moderate values of R_{mt}. As a consequence, even though $\sigma^2(\tilde{\epsilon}_{it}|R_{mt})$ may be the same for all values of R_{mt}, more extreme observations on $\tilde{e}_{it}$ should be more numerous the closer one is to .016, the mean of R_{mt}, since the expected frequency of sample points is higher for intervals closer to the mean of R_{mt}. The range of sample points about the estimated regression function should, however, be about the same at points that are equal distances to the left or right of the mean of R_{mt}, and extreme deviations of sample points from the estimated regression function should be less numerous the further one looks away from the mean of R_{mt}. To my eye, the results for IBM shown in Figure 4.1 are consistent with these qualitative statements.

A more formal approach to examining the proposition that $\sigma^2(\tilde{e}_{it}|R_{mt})$ is the same for all values of R_{mt} is to divide the sample range of R_{mt} into intervals that contain the same number of sample observations and then to compute the standard deviations of the residuals in each interval. If the proposition that $\sigma^2(\tilde{e}_{it}|R_{mt})$ is the same for all R_{mt} is valid, these sample standard deviations should be approximately the same for all the intervals of R_{mt}. Note that, according to the comments of the preceding paragraph, if each of the intervals of R_{mt} contains the same number of sample points, then the closer the interval is to $\overline{R}_m$, the smaller the range of values of R_{mt} it will cover.

Finally, recall from Section III.C of Chapter 3 that the sample mean residual cannot be used to test the proposition of equation (4) that the unconditional expected value of the disturbances $E(\tilde{e}_{it}) = 0$, since the coefficient estimates b_i and a_i are defined in such a way that in any sample

$$\overline{e}_i = \frac{\sum_{t=1}^{T} e_{it}}{T} = 0.$$

Moreover, it is also always true that in any sample,

$$\sum_{t=1}^{T} (R_{mt} - \overline{R}_m) e_{it} = 0,$$

so that the sample covariance between R_{mt} and e_{it} cannot be used to test the proposition of equation (6) that $\text{cov}(\tilde{e}_{it}, \tilde{R}_{mt}) = 0.0$.

STATIONARITY AND RANDOM SAMPLING

Having examined the implications of bivariate normality, we now turn to the questions of whether the joint distribution of $\tilde{R}_{it}$ and $\tilde{R}_{mt}$ is constant or stationary during the sampling period, and whether successive paired values of the monthly returns can be regarded as independent drawings from the joint distribution of the returns.

Time series plots of returns and residuals. Figures 4.2 to 4.4 present plots against time of the monthly IBM returns, the monthly returns on the market portfolio m, and the monthly residuals from the estimated market model regression function. Such time series plots allow us to judge whether the distributions of the returns and residuals remain constant during the sampling period. Specifically, the time series plots are excellent for judging whether

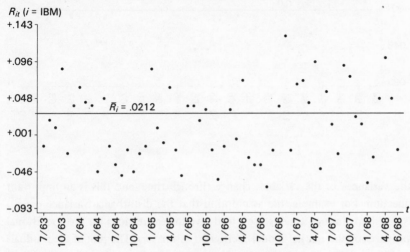

FIGURE 4.2

Time Series Plot of Monthly Returns on IBM for July 1963–June 1968

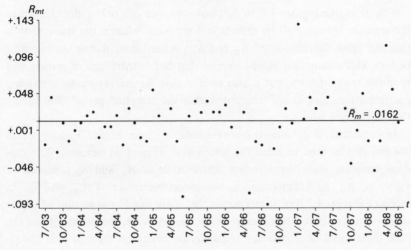

FIGURE 4.3

Times Series Plot of Monthly Returns on the Market Portfolio m for July 1963–June 1968

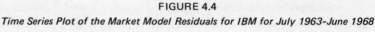

FIGURE 4.4

Time Series Plot of the Market Model Residuals for IBM for July 1963-June 1968

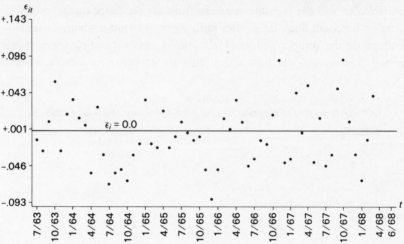

the variances of the variables change through time, and this is an important question. For example, the assumption that the disturbance variance $\sigma^2(\tilde{\epsilon}_{it})$ is constant through time is used to derive the expressions for the conditional variances of the market model coefficient estimators. The plot of the residuals in Figure 4.4 does not seem to raise serious doubts about this assumption. The plots of R_{it} and R_{mt} likewise do not suggest any obvious changes during the sampling period in the behavior of the monthly returns on IBM and on the market portfolio m.

With plots like Figures 4.2 to 4.4, however, one can only judge changes in the separate behavior of the returns and residuals, whereas the assumption is that the joint distribution of $\tilde{R}_{it}$ and $\tilde{R}_{mt}$ is stationary during the sampling period. This assumption indeed implies that the distributions of returns and residuals are stationary, but it also implies that the market model regression coefficients α_i and β_i are constant during the sampling period. We discuss this proposition later.

Autocorrelations of returns and residuals. To some extent, Figures 4.2 to 4.4 can also be used to judge the assumption of random sampling. With random sampling from the bivariate distribution of $\tilde{R}_{it}$ and $\tilde{R}_{mt}$, successive values of $\tilde{R}_{it}$ are independent, as are successive values of $\tilde{R}_{mt}$ and $\tilde{\epsilon}_{it}$. In terms of Figures 4.2 to 4.4, this means that there should not be runs of higher than average or lower than average returns or residuals, above and beyond the runs that would be expected by chance. Equivalently, through time the returns and residuals should be randomly scattered about their respective means.*

Although the plots always provide valuable insights and familiarity with the properties of the data, some amount of bunching through time of high or low returns or residuals is to be expected on a purely chance basis. This makes visual inspection of the behavior of the variables a tricky procedure for judging whether any patterns observed are consistent or inconsistent with the assumption of random sampling. However, quantitative procedures for testing the assumption of random sampling are also available. Fortunately, these procedures are based on statistical concepts that we have already studied.

Let us illustrate the approach in terms of the returns $\tilde{R}_{it}$. The goal is to measure the relationship between the returns $\tilde{R}_{it}$ and $\tilde{R}_{i,t-\tau}$, that is, returns τ months apart. Suppose we are willing to limit attention to a possible linear regression function relationship of the form

$$E(\tilde{R}_{it} | R_{i,t-\tau}) = \delta_\tau + \gamma_\tau R_{i,t-\tau} \tag{29}$$

so that the return can be expressed as

$$\tilde{R}_{it} = \delta_\tau + \gamma_\tau \tilde{R}_{i,t-\tau} + \tilde{\xi}_{it}. \tag{30}$$

Finally, we assume that the process generating the returns is stationary through time; that is, the process is the same for all t, so that, as indicated in (29), the coefficients δ_τ and γ_τ in the relationship between $\tilde{R}_{it}$ and $\tilde{R}_{i,t-\tau}$ are the same for all t.

From Section II of Chapter 3, we know that if δ_τ and γ_τ are defined in the usual way as

$$\gamma_\tau = \frac{\text{cov}\,(\tilde{R}_{it}, \tilde{R}_{i,t-\tau})}{\sigma^2(\tilde{R}_{i,t-\tau})} \quad \text{and} \quad \delta_\tau = E(\tilde{R}_{it}) - \gamma_\tau E(\tilde{R}_{i,t-\tau}), \tag{31}$$

then

$$\text{cov}\,(\tilde{\xi}_{it}, \tilde{R}_{i,t-\tau}) = 0.0, \tag{32}$$

so that

$$\sigma^2(\tilde{R}_{it}) = \gamma_\tau^2 \sigma^2(\tilde{R}_{i,t-\tau}) + \sigma^2(\tilde{\xi}_{it}). \tag{33}$$

---

*The statistical properties of the market model coefficient estimators discussed in Chapter 3 require random sampling from the distribution of the disturbances $\tilde{\epsilon}_{it}$. But when the properties of the estimators are not based on assumed bivariate normality for $\tilde{R}_{it}$ and $\tilde{R}_{mt}$, random sampling from the distributions of $\tilde{R}_{mt}$ and $\tilde{R}_{it}$ is not necessary. We find in Chapter 5, however, that independence through time of security and portfolio returns is an important issue in its own right. Thus, it helps to set up our later work if we now discuss testing for time series independence both for the returns $\tilde{R}_{it}$ and $\tilde{R}_{mt}$ and for the disturbances $\tilde{\epsilon}_{it}$.

It then follows that if we define the correlation coefficient between $\tilde{R}_{it}$ and $\tilde{R}_{i,t-\tau}$ as

$$\rho(\tilde{R}_{it}, \tilde{R}_{i,t-\tau}) = \frac{\mathrm{cov}\,(\tilde{R}_{it}, \tilde{R}_{i,t-\tau})}{\sigma(\tilde{R}_{it})\sigma(\tilde{R}_{i,t-\tau})}, \tag{34}$$

then the coefficient of determination

$$\rho^2(\tilde{R}_{it}, \tilde{R}_{i,t-\tau}) = \left(\frac{\mathrm{cov}\,(\tilde{R}_{it}, \tilde{R}_{i,t-\tau})}{\sigma(\tilde{R}_{it})\sigma(\tilde{R}_{i,t-\tau})}\right)^2 = \frac{\gamma_\tau^2\sigma^2(\tilde{R}_{i,t-\tau})}{\sigma^2(\tilde{R}_{it})} \tag{35}$$

is the proportion of the variance of $\tilde{R}_{it}$ that can be attributed to the linear relationship between $\tilde{R}_{it}$ and $\tilde{R}_{i,t-\tau}$—that is, to the term $\gamma_\tau\tilde{R}_{i,t-\tau}$ in (30)— while $1 - \rho^2(\tilde{R}_{it}, \tilde{R}_{i,t-\tau})$ is $\sigma^2(\tilde{\xi}_{it})/\sigma^2(\tilde{R}_{it})$, the proportion of the variance of $\tilde{R}_{it}$ that can be attributed to the disturbance $\tilde{\xi}_{it}$ in (30).

The correlation coefficient between $\tilde{R}_{it}$ and $\tilde{R}_{i,t-\tau}$ is given a special name: it is called the autocorrelation for lag τ. It is also sometimes called the serial correlation for lag τ. The assumption that the statistical process is the same for all t implies that the standard deviation of $\tilde{R}_{it}$ is the same for all t,

$$\sigma(\tilde{R}_{it}) = \sigma(\tilde{R}_{i,t-\tau}) = \sigma(\tilde{R}_i). \tag{36}$$

It follows from (36) that the autocorrelation for lag τ is also the linear regression coefficient γ_τ. Under the latter interpretation, it is called the autoregression coefficient for lag τ.

The sample estimators of δ_τ, γ_τ, and $\rho(\tilde{R}_{it}, \tilde{R}_{i,t-\tau})$ are defined in the usual way: we simply plug in sample estimators of the covariance, the means, and the standard deviations that appear in (31) and (34). We have

$$\tilde{g}_\tau = \frac{s(\tilde{R}_{it}, \tilde{R}_{i,t-\tau})}{s^2(\tilde{R}_{i,t-\tau})} = \frac{\sum\limits_{t=\tau+1}^{T} (\tilde{R}_{it} - \bar{\tilde{R}}_{it})(\tilde{R}_{i,t-\tau} - \bar{\tilde{R}}_{i,t-\tau})}{\sum\limits_{t=\tau+1}^{T} (\tilde{R}_{i,t-\tau} - \bar{\tilde{R}}_{i,t-\tau})^2} \tag{37}$$

$$\tilde{d}_\tau = \bar{\tilde{R}}_{it} - \tilde{g}_\tau\bar{\tilde{R}}_{i,t-\tau} \tag{38}$$

$$\bar{\tilde{R}}_{it} = \frac{\sum\limits_{t=\tau+1}^{T} \tilde{R}_{it}}{T-\tau}, \tag{39}$$

$$\bar{\tilde{R}}_{i,t-\tau} = \frac{\sum\limits_{t=\tau+1}^{T} \tilde{R}_{i,t-\tau}}{T-\tau}. \tag{40}$$

To see the logic in these expressions, note that a sample of T observations on $\tilde{R}_{it}$ only yields $T - \tau$ paired observations on $\tilde{R}_{it}$ and $\tilde{R}_{i,t-\tau}$ that can be used to estimate the coefficients of (30). That is, the sample points, the paired values of R_{it} and $R_{i,t-\tau}$, that can be used to estimate the coefficients are the $T - \tau$ pairs

$$(R_{i,\tau+1}, R_{i1}), (R_{i,\tau+2}, R_{i2}), \ldots, (R_{iT}, R_{i,T-\tau}).$$

The estimators of the sample means, variances, and covariances then simply reflect the fact that the sample observations on $\tilde{R}_{it}$ are $R_{i,\tau+1}, \ldots, R_{iT}$, while the sample observations on $R_{i,t-\tau}$ are $R_{i1}, \ldots, R_{i,T-\tau}$.

One consequence of this way of looking at the sample is that although the assumed stationarity of the process implies

$$E(\tilde{R}_{it}) = E(\tilde{R}_{i,t-\tau}) = E(\tilde{R}_i),$$

this equality does not hold for the sample estimators; that is,

$$\bar{\tilde{R}}_{it} \neq \bar{\tilde{R}}_{i,t-\tau}.$$

Likewise, although stationarity implies (36), nevertheless in any sample

$$s^2(\tilde{R}_{it}) \neq s^2(\tilde{R}_{i,t-\tau}).$$

Finally, if the sample estimator of the autocorrelation coefficient for lag τ is defined as

$$\tilde{r}(\tilde{R}_{it}, \tilde{R}_{i,t-\tau}) = \frac{s(\tilde{R}_{it}, \tilde{R}_{i,t-\tau})}{s(\tilde{R}_{it})s(\tilde{R}_{i,t-\tau})} \tag{41}$$

$$= \frac{\sum_{t=\tau+1}^{T} (\tilde{R}_{it} - \bar{\tilde{R}}_{it})(\tilde{R}_{i,t-\tau} - \bar{\tilde{R}}_{i,t-\tau})}{\sqrt{\sum_{t=\tau+1}^{T} (\tilde{R}_{it} - \bar{\tilde{R}}_{it})^2} \sqrt{\sum_{t=\tau+1}^{T} (\tilde{R}_{i,t-\tau} - \bar{\tilde{R}}_{i,t-\tau})^2}},$$

then

$$\tilde{g}_\tau \neq \tilde{r}(\tilde{R}_{it}, \tilde{R}_{i,t-\tau});$$

that is, although $\gamma_\tau = \rho(\tilde{R}_{it}, \tilde{R}_{i,t-\tau})$, the sample estimators of the two quantities are not the same.

This last result seems to cause a problem, since either $\tilde{g}_\tau$ or $\tilde{r}(\tilde{R}_{it}, \tilde{R}_{i,t-\tau})$ can be regarded as an estimator of the autocorrelation for lag τ. In practice, however, as long as the sample period T is long—more specifically, as long as τ is small relative to T—then $\tilde{g}_\tau$ and $\tilde{r}(\tilde{R}_{it}, \tilde{R}_{i,t-\tau})$ will be nearly identical.

The property of the sample autocorrelation that we use most in later discussions is the fact that, like any sample coefficient of determination, $\tilde{r}(\tilde{R}_{it}, \tilde{R}_{i,t-\tau})^2$ can be shown to be

$$\tilde{r}^2(\tilde{R}_{it}, \tilde{R}_{i,t-\tau}) = \frac{\tilde{g}_\tau^2 \sum_{t=\tau+1}^{T} (\tilde{R}_{i,t-\tau} - \bar{\tilde{R}}_{i,t-\tau})^2}{\sum_{t=\tau+1}^{T} (\tilde{R}_{it} - \bar{\tilde{R}}_{it})^2} , \tag{42}$$

which can always be interpreted as the proportion of the sample sum of squares

$$\sum_{t=\tau+1}^{T} (\tilde{R}_{it} - \bar{\tilde{R}}_{it})^2$$

that can be attributed to the estimated linear relationship between $\tilde{R}_{it}$ and $\tilde{R}_{i,t-\tau}$. Alternatively, $\tilde{r}^2(\tilde{R}_{it}, \tilde{R}_{i,t-\tau})$ is an estimator of $\rho^2(\tilde{R}_{it}, \tilde{R}_{i,t-\tau})$, which, from (35), can be interpreted as the proportion of the variance of $\tilde{R}_{it}$ that can be attributed to the linear relationship between $\tilde{R}_{it}$ and $\tilde{R}_{i,t-\tau}$. In applications, we commonly rely on this "proportion of variance explained" interpretation of $r^2(\tilde{R}_{it}, \tilde{R}_{i,t-\tau})$ as an indication of the degree of dependence between values of $\tilde{R}_{it}$ that are τ months apart. If the proportion of variance explained by the linear relationship between $\tilde{R}_{it}$ and $\tilde{R}_{i,t-\tau}$ is close to zero, then we conclude that the assumption that returns which are separated by τ months are independent is a reasonable approximation to the data.

As usual, we generally want to judge the reliability of $\tilde{r}(\tilde{R}_{it}, \tilde{R}_{i,t-\tau})$ as an estimator of $\rho(\tilde{R}_{it}, \tilde{R}_{i,t-\tau})$. Like any other estimator, $\tilde{r}(\tilde{R}_{it}, \tilde{R}_{i,t-\tau})$ is a random variable with a sampling distribution; as always, we want to know how tightly concentrated the distribution is about the true value of the parameter of interest. The analysis of this problem is in general quite difficult, but fortunately there are some simple results for the case of most interest. In the applications of this and later chapters, we are almost always interested in the distribution of $\tilde{r}(\tilde{R}_{it}, \tilde{R}_{i,t-\tau})$ under the hypothesis that $\tilde{R}_{it}$ and $\tilde{R}_{i,t-\tau}$ are independent, so that $\rho(\tilde{R}_{it}, \tilde{R}_{i,t-\tau}) = 0.0$. When $\rho(\tilde{R}_{it}, \tilde{R}_{i,t-\tau}) = 0.0$, the distribution of $\tilde{r}(\tilde{R}_{it}, \tilde{R}_{i,t-\tau})$ in large samples is approximately normal, with mean and standard deviation

$$E[\tilde{r}(\tilde{R}_{it}, \tilde{R}_{i,t-\tau})] \doteq -\frac{1}{T-\tau} \tag{43}$$

$$\sigma[\tilde{r}(\tilde{R}_{it}, \tilde{R}_{i,t-\tau})] \doteq \sqrt{\frac{1}{T-\tau}}. \tag{44}$$

An individual sample autocorrelation $r(\tilde{R}_{it}, \tilde{R}_{i,t-\tau})$ allows us to judge whether returns τ months apart are independent. The discussion above applies to any τ, however, so we can compute the values of $r(\tilde{R}_{it}, \tilde{R}_{i,t-\tau})$ for $\tau = 1$, $\tau = 2$, etc., and use these to judge the degree of dependence between values of $\tilde{R}_{it}$ that are separated by one month, by two months, and so forth. If there does not seem to be an important amount of dependence for any τ, then we can conclude that the assumption of random sampling—that is, the assumption that successive values of $\tilde{R}_{it}$ are independent—is a reasonable approximation to the data.

Moreover, although for purposes of illustration the preceding discussion has been carried out in terms of the returns $\tilde{R}_{it}$, the analysis and results apply to any random variable that can be regarded as a time series. Thus, they can be used now to help us decide whether the assumption of random sampling is a reasonable approximation for the monthly returns on IBM, the monthly returns on the market portfolio m, and the market model residuals for IBM for July 1963–June 1968. Table 4.2 shows the sample autocorrelations of

TABLE 4.2

Autocorrelation Estimates for the Monthly Returns on IBM,
the Market Portfolio m, and the Market Model Residuals
for IBM for July 1963–June 1968

LAG τ	$R_{it}(i = \text{IBM})$	R_{mt}	e_{it}	$\sigma(r_\tau)$
1	.139	.111	.213	.130
2	.022	.013	−.071	.131
3	−.003	.103	−.114	.132

the three variables for lags $\tau = 1, 2, 3$. The standard deviations of the coefficients, computed from (44), are also shown. For example, the table says that the sample correlation between values of the return on IBM one month apart is .14. Thus, we estimate that approximately $(.14)^2 \cong .02$, or only 2 percent, of the variance of $\tilde{R}_{it}$ for IBM can be attributed to the linear relationship between $\tilde{R}_{it}$ and $\tilde{R}_{i,t-1}$, which is consistent with the proposition that $\tilde{R}_{it}$ and $\tilde{R}_{i,t-1}$ are independent. Indeed, all of the sample autocorrelations shown in Table 4.2 are in this sense small, as are the coefficients for lags greater than 3, which are not shown. We conclude that the assumption of random sampling is consistent with the data.

We close by noting that since the interpretation of an autocorrelation is linked to a linear regression function relationship like (29), the autocorrelation is a measure of linear dependence. A linear relationship is just one possible form for the relationship between lagged values of a random variable. In practice, however, autocorrelations are the primary tool used to measure serial dependence.

PROBLEM I.E.

1. Below are the monthly returns on a share of Xerox common stock for July 1963–June 1968. For convenience, the returns on the market portfolio m are also shown. Fit the market model to these data. Specifically, compute b_i, a_i, $s(b_i|R_{m1}, \ldots, R_{mT})$, $s(a_i|R_{m1}, \ldots, R_{mT})$, r_{im}^2, the studentized ranges of R_{it} and e_{it}, and the autocorrelations of R_{it} and e_{it} for lags $\tau = 1, 2, 3$. The estimating equation for $s(a_i|R_{m1}, \ldots, R_{mT})$ is (49) of Chapter 3.

MONTH(t)	R_{it}	R_{mt}	MONTH(t)	R_{it}	R_{mt}
7/63	.2471	−.0095	1/66	.0755	.0435
8/63	.1653	.0506	2/66	.0834	.0109
9/63	−.0075	−.0134	3/66	.0454	−.0219
10/63	.2954	.0163	4/66	.0269	.0337
11/63	.0274	−.0068	5/66	−.0406	−.0724
12/63	.1389	.0075	6/66	.0155	−.0046
1/64	−.0772	.0201	7/66	−.0738	−.0127
2/64	.0095	.0270	8/66	−.2191	−.0931
3/64	.0784	.0314	9/66	−.0148	−.0143
4/64	.1141	−.0031	10/66	−.0736	.0127
5/64	.2228	.0116	11/66	.2670	.0382
6/64	−.0013	.0154	12/66	−.0366	.0162
7/64	−.0935	.0277	1/67	.1703	.1428
8/64	−.0420	−.0090	2/67	.0784	.0209
9/64	.2213	.0370	3/67	.1250	.0320
10/64	−.1221	.0170	4/67	.0228	.0365
11/64	−.1168	.0007	5/67	−.0506	−.0179
12/64	.0450	−.0069	6/67	.0055	.0516
1/65	.1255	.0537	7/67	−.0183	.0709
2/65	.1239	.0278	8/67	−.0173	.0028
3/65	−.0311	.0053	9/67	.0551	.0378
4/65	.1253	.0359	10/67	.0531	−.0359
5/65	.0791	−.0079	11/67	−.0022	.0067
6/65	−.0358	−.0743	12/67	.0395	.0554
7/65	.0947	.0291	1/68	−.1650	−.0035
8/65	.1022	.0451	2/68	−.0253	−.0416
9/65	−.0088	.0308	3/68	−.0183	−.0045
10/65	.0356	.0474	4/68	.1489	.1164
11/65	.1219	.0300	5/68	.0904	.0586
12/65	.0313	.0327	6/68	−.0182	.0192

ANSWER

1. The values of the coefficients, their standard deviations, and so forth are shown in Tables 4.3 and 4.5.

II. Evidence on the Risks or Market Sensitivities of NYSE Common Stocks

A. Comments on Market Model Estimates for Larger and Smaller Firms

Table 4.3 shows the market model coefficient estimates b_i and a_i, computed from monthly returns for July 1963–June 1968, for the thirty common stocks that account for the largest fractions of the total market value of outstanding shares on the NYSE at the end of 1971. The estimates of the conditional standard deviations of the coefficients are also shown. Henceforth we refer to these as the standard deviations or standard errors of the coefficients; that is, we no longer explicitly include the word conditional, and the estimates are denoted as $s(b_i)$ and $s(a_i)$. For each of the stocks, Table 4.3 also shows the sample standard deviation of the market model residuals, $s(e_i)$; the sample coefficient of determination, r_{im}^2; and the sample mean and standard deviation, $\overline{R}_i$ and $s(R_i)$, of the stock's return. Table 4.4 shows the corresponding results for a random sample of NYSE stocks.

The first thing to note is that in the results for the larger firms in Table 4.3, only two of the b_i (Xerox and Ford) are greater than 1.0, and most are substantially less than 1.0. The average of the b_i in Table 4.3 is only .61. Interpreting β_i as the risk of security i measured relative to the average risk of securities in m, the estimates imply that the risks of the common stocks of larger firms tend to be substantially less than the average risk of stocks in m. Alternatively, interpreting β_i as the sensitivity of the return on security i to marketwide factors, the larger stocks seem to have less than average market sensitivity. In contrast, in Table 4.4, 15 of the randomly selected stocks have $b_i > 1.0$, 15 have $b_i < 1.0$, and the average of the b_i is 1.00. Thus, these stocks do not tend to have either systematically more or less risk than the average risk in m of all common stocks on the exchange. This is, of course, exactly what we expect from a random sample.

The second point to note from Tables 4.3 and 4.4 is that there seems to be a relationship between $s(R_i)$ and b_i. Generally, the larger the value of b_i, the larger the sample standard deviation of the security's returns. This result has two causes, one algebraic and one that is just an empirical finding. First, the sample sum of squares from which $s(R_i)$ is computed can be expressed as

$$\sum_{t=1}^{T} (R_{it} - \overline{R}_i)^2 = b_i^2 \sum_{t=1}^{T} (R_{mt} - \overline{R}_m)^2 + \sum_{t=1}^{T} e_{it}^2. \tag{45}$$

TABLE 4.3

Market Model Parameter Estimates for 30 Largest Firms for July 1963–June 1968

NAME	% OF 1971 MARKET VALUE	b_i	$s(b_i)$	a_i	$s(a_i)$	r_{im}^2	$\bar{R}_i$	$s(R_i)$	$s(e_i)$
International Business Machines	5.473	.67	.133	.010	.0056	.31	.0212	.047	.040
American Telephone and Telegraph	3.477	.19	.110	−.002	.0046	.05	.0008	.033	.033
General Motors	3.275	.87	.145	−.006	.0061	.39	.0081	.055	.043
Exxon	2.336	.24	.121	.000	.0051	.06	.0043	.037	.036
Sears, Roebuck	2.244	.45	.150	.003	.0063	.13	.0105	.048	.045
Eastman Kodak	2.222	.65	.147	.011	.0062	.25	.0215	.050	.044
General Electric	1.609	.78	.187	−.007	.0079	.23	.0055	.063	.056
Xerox	1.389	1.20	.310	.021	.0130	.20	.0400	.103	.093
Texaco	1.324	.43	.134	−.001	.0056	.15	.0059	.043	.040
Ford Motor	1.087	1.04	.151	−.012	.0063	.45	.0054	.061	.045
Minneapolis Mining and Manufacturing	1.073	.79	.158	.001	.0066	.30	.0133	.056	.047
Coca-Cola	1.027	.38	.147	.016	.0062	.10	.0221	.046	.044
Du Pont	.969	.65	.134	−.009	.0056	.29	.0013	.047	.040
Procter and Gamble	.907	.30	.129	.001	.0054	.08	.0063	.040	.038
Gulf Oil	.848	.24	.137	.009	.0057	.05	.0124	.042	.041
Mobil Oil	.784	.27	.161	.005	.0068	.05	.0095	.049	.048
Johnson and Johnson	.777	.91	.176	.007	.0074	.31	.0222	.063	.053
Standard Oil (California)	.688	.35	.126	−.001	.0053	.12	.0046	.040	.038
Standard Oil (Indiana)	.679	.42	.184	.007	.0077	.08	.0140	.057	.055
Royal Dutch Petroleum	.659	.62	.180	−.000	.0075	.17	.0099	.059	.054
Shell Transport and Trading	.649	.55	.178	.008	.0075	.14	.0173	.057	.053
American Home Products	.639	.83	.161	.003	.0068	.32	.0166	.058	.048
Merck and Company	.639	.60	.159	.011	.0066	.20	.0212	.053	.047
International Telephone and Telegraph	.594	.99	.160	.001	.0067	.40	.0168	.061	.048
J. C. Penney	.578	.89	.177	.000	.0074	.30	.0145	.063	.053
Westinghouse Electric	.539	.99	.207	.001	.0087	.28	.0169	.072	.062
Dow Chemical	.533	.70	.173	−.003	.0072	.22	.0085	.058	.052
Kresge, S. S.	.513	.49	.220	.033	.0092	.08	.0410	.068	.066
General Telephone and Electronics	.497	.48	.136	.004	.0057	.17	.0116	.044	.040
Atlantic Richfield	.460	.40	.149	.014	.0063	.11	.0203	.047	.045
Averages	1.282	.61	.161	.004	.0068	.20	.0141	.054	.048

TABLE 4.4

Market Model Coefficient Estimates for 30 Randomly Selected Firms for July 1963–June 1968

NAME	b_i	$s(b_i)$	a_i	$s(a_i)$	r_{im}^2	$\bar{R}_i$	$s(R_i)$	$s(e_i)$
IPL	1.20	.340	−.013	.0142	.18	.0070	.111	.102
Lehigh Portland Cement	1.07	.207	−.014	.0087	.32	.0034	.074	.062
Hotel Corporation of America	1.60	.338	.009	.0142	.28	.0356	.118	.101
Portec	1.51	.272	−.005	.0114	.35	.0196	.100	.081
Richardson Merrill	.69	.245	.002	.0103	.12	.0128	.078	.073
Van Raalte	.73	.179	.009	.0075	.22	.0208	.060	.054
Ex-Cell-O	1.11	.191	−.002	.0080	.37	.0157	.071	.057
Keebler	1.14	.202	.002	.0085	.36	.0201	.075	.060
Canadian Breweries	.08	.259	.024	.0108	.00	.0253	.077	.077
Gulf, Mobile and Ohio Railroad	1.30	.201	.004	.0084	.42	.0247	.078	.060
Dana Corporation	.84	.123	−.007	.0051	.45	.0066	.049	.037
Union Pacific Railroad	.66	.140	−.002	.0059	.28	.0086	.050	.042
Cyclops Corporation	.87	.177	−.005	.0074	.30	.0095	.063	.053
Ohio Edison	.28	.128	.002	.0053	.07	.0069	.039	.038
Central Foundry	2.24	.413	−.018	.0173	.34	.0188	.150	.124
United States Gypsum	1.01	.180	−.011	.0076	.35	.0053	.066	.054
Eversharp	1.22	.334	−.017	.0140	.19	.0032	.110	.100
Dayton Power and Light	.58	.145	−.002	.0061	.22	.0072	.049	.043
Cluett, Peabody and Company	.67	.196	.009	.0082	.17	.0197	.064	.059
Washington Gas Light	.14	.028	−.002	.0039	.04	−.0001	.028	.028
Lowenstein, M., and Sons	1.21	.214	−.001	.0089	.36	.0189	.079	.064
International Telephone and Telegraph	.99	.160	.001	.0067	.40	.0168	.061	.048
Carpenter Steel	.83	.227	.006	.0095	.19	.0197	.075	.068
Greyhound	.93	.176	−.008	.0074	.32	.0074	.063	.053
Allegheny Ludlum Steel	.66	.184	.004	.0077	.18	.0142	.060	.055
United Air Lines	1.30	.286	.000	.0120	.26	.0210	.099	.086
Adams Express	.40	.087	.006	.0036	.27	.0122	.030	.026
Ambac Industries	2.03	.265	−.004	.0111	.50	.0287	.111	.079
Masonite	1.39	.224	−.006	.0094	.40	.0170	.086	.067
Lehigh Valley Industries	1.34	.522	.032	.0219	.10	.0533	.163	.156
Averages	1.00	.221	.000	.0093	.27	.0158	.078	.067

Since $\Sigma(R_{mt} - \overline{R}_m)^2$ is the same for every security, we can see that the larger the value of b_i, the larger the value of $s^2(R_i) = \Sigma(R_i - \overline{R})^2/T - 1$. Second a universal empirical finding in the literature is that larger values of b_i tend to be associated with larger values of $s^2(e_i) = \Sigma e_{it}^2/(T-2)$. This relationship can be seen in Table 4.3, but it is more evident in Table 4.4, where there are more pronounced differences in the b_i of different securities.

Although both components of $\Sigma(R_{it} - \overline{R}_i)^2$ in (45) tend to increase with b_i, the residual sum of squares, Σe_{it}^2, must increase less (in percentage terms) than $b_i^2 \Sigma(R_{mt} - \overline{R}_m)^2$. This conclusion is implied by the observation that the sample coefficients of determination, r_{im}^2, seem also to increase with b_i. For example, the average values of b_i and r_{im}^2 for the stocks in Table 4.3 are .61 and .20, whereas the average values of b_i and r_{im}^2 for the randomly selected stocks in Table 4.4 are 1.00 and .27. Since r_{im}^2 can be written as

$$r_{im}^2 = \frac{b_i^2 \sum_{t=1}^{T} (R_{mt} - \overline{R}_m)^2}{\sum_{t=1}^{T} (R_{it} - \overline{R}_i)^2},$$

a positive relationship between r_{im}^2 and b_i implies that the numerator of this equation, $b_i^2 \Sigma(R_{mt} - \overline{R}_m)^2$, increases with b_i more (in percentage terms) than the denominator, $\Sigma(R_{it} - \overline{R}_i)^2$, which in turn implies that Σe_{it}^2 does not increase with b_i as much (in percentage terms) as $b_i^2 \Sigma(R_{mt} - \overline{R}_m)^2$.

The final point to note from Tables 4.3 and 4.4 is that for July 1963–June 1968, marketwide factors always explain 50 percent or less of the sample variances of the returns on the individual stocks shown in the tables. The sample coefficients of determination r_{im}^2 are all .5 or less.

B. Evidence on the Assumptions Underlying the Market Model Estimates

Table 4.5 shows sample statistics that can be used to test the assumptions underlying the market model regression coefficient estimates in Table 4.3. For each stock in Table 4.3, Table 4.5 shows the studentized ranges, $SR(R_i)$ and $SR(e_i)$ of the stock's returns and of its market model residuals for July 1963–June 1968, along with the sample autocorrelations $r(R_{it}, R_{i,t-\tau})$ and $r(e_{it}, e_{i,t-\tau})$, $\tau = 1, 2, 3$. Table 4.6 shows the corresponding studentized ranges and sample autocorrelations for the randomly selected securities in Table 4.4.

Interpreting the squared sample autocorrelations as estimates of the proportion of the variance of $\tilde{R}_{it}$ or $\tilde{e}_{it}$ that can be attributed to a linear rela-

Studentized Ranges and Autocorrelations of Returns and Residuals for 30 Largest Firms, July 1963–June 1968

COMPANY	$SR(R_i)$	$SR(e_i)$	$r(R_{it}, R_{i,t-1})$	$r(R_{it}, R_{i,t-2})$	$r(R_{it}, R_{i,t-3})$	$r(e_{it}, e_{i,t-1})$	$r(e_{it}, e_{i,t-2})$	$r(e_{it}, e_{i,t-3})$
International Business Machines	4.05⁻	4.56	.139	.022	-.003	.213	-.071	-.114
American Telephone and Telegraph	5.52⁺	5.97⁺	-.111	.096	.173	-.088	.161	.099
General Motors	4.52	5.83⁺	-.091	-.060	.254	-.013	-.132	.192
Exxon	4.60	4.88	-.025	-.032	.242	.030	-.036	.125
Sears, Roebuck	5.81⁺	6.27⁺	-.105	-.020	.253	-.114	-.055	.204
Eastman Kodak	3.98⁻	3.98⁻	.098	-.175	.088	.057	-.067	.055
General Electric	5.58⁺	5.49⁺	-.028	-.093	-.006	.078	-.119	-.089
Xerox	4.99	4.71	.039	.065	-.067	.063	-.026	-.021
Texaco	5.00	5.02	.076	-.148	.004	.169	-.103	-.113
Ford Motor	4.64	4.17	-.083	-.183	.115	-.067	-.151	-.025
Minnesota Mining and Manufacturing	4.30	4.14	-.062	-.055	-.071	.034	.047	.054
Coca-Cola	4.16	6.06⁺	-.085	-.027	-.044	-.159	-.041	-.178
Du Pont	4.79	4.56	-.076	-.023	.234	.036	-.039	.038
Procter and Gamble	5.52⁺	5.15	-.193	.192	-.077	-.162	.269	-.107
Gulf Oil	4.13	4.17	-.019	.016	-.065	.045	.027	-.126
Mobil Oil	4.49	4.24	-.234	.023	-.296	-.190	.059	-.348
Johnson and Johnson	4.32	5.15	-.056	-.056	-.033	-.084	-.109	-.184
Standard Oil (California)	4.74	4.98	-.111	.093	.207	-.127	.074	.098
Standard Oil (Indiana)	4.72	4.71	-.210	-.117	.175	-.056	-.126	.103
Royal Dutch Petroleum	4.81	4.87	-.032	-.321	.271	-.031	-.337	.162
Shell Transport and Trading	4.77	5.00	.171	-.044	.288	.118	-.081	.175
American Home Products	3.97⁻	5.07	-.080	.108	.115	-.171	.005	.026
Merck and Company	4.34	4.24	-.159	-.065	-.090	-.146	-.044	-.078
International Telephone and Telegraph	4.28	4.79	.005	-.065	-.015	.017	-.222	-.087
J. C. Penney	4.05⁻	4.23	-.159	-.051	.171	-.088	-.048	.053
Westinghouse Electric	4.32	4.36	.099	-.005	-.094	.114	-.085	-.199
Dow Chemical	4.96	5.43⁺	-.049	-.046	.100	-.174	-.108	-.013
Kresge, S. S.	4.71	4.57	-.156	.033	-.059	-.209	.029	-.076
General Telephone and Electronics	4.47	4.28	-.022	.000	.083	.053	.098	.065
Atlantic Richfield	4.13	4.08	-.030	-.284	.088	.035	-.287	.025
Averages	4.62	4.83	-.051	-.041	.064	-.027	-.051	-.009

⁻The sample studentized range is less than 4.07, the .1 fractile of the distribution of the studentized range in samples of size 60 from a normal population.
⁺The sample studentized range exceeds 5.29, the .9 fractile of the distribution of the studentized range in samples of size 60 from a normal population.

TABLE 4.6

Studentized Ranges and Autocorrelations of Returns and Residuals for 30 Randomly Selected Firms, July 1963–June 1968

COMPANY	$SR(R_i)$	$SR(e_i)$	$r(R_{it}, R_{i,t-1})$	$r(R_{it}, R_{i,t-2})$	$r(R_{it}, R_{i,t-3})$	$r(e_{it}, e_{i,t-1})$	$r(e_{it}, e_{i,t-2})$	$r(e_{it}, e_{i,t-3})$
IPL	5.46[+]	5.71[+]	−.050	.114	.009	−.240	.076	.034
Lehigh Portland Cement	6.47[+]	5.50[+]	.092	−.047	−.080	.021	−.186	−.096
Hotel Corporation of America	4.73	5.06	.026	.258	−.012	−.061	.181	−.101
Portec	6.19[+]	5.75[+]	−.192	.011	.386	−.195	−.066	.213
Richardson Merrill	4.38	5.55[+]	−.066	.018	−.276	−.157	.083	−.307
Van Raalte	5.20	4.05[−]	−.093	−.117	.127	−.185	−.106	.029
Ex-Cell-O	5.18	4.37	−.101	.138	.165	−.124	.012	.008
Keebler	4.64	4.34	.322	.218	.038	.124	.292	−.047
Canadian Breweries	5.33[+]	5.24	−.011	−.140	.348	−.025	−.157	.357
Gulf, Mobile and Ohio Railroad	4.40	3.93[−]	−.056	.098	.113	−.182	−.056	.171
Dana Corporation	6.19[+]	4.92	−.053	−.125	.269	−.099	−.161	.109
Union Pacific Railroad	4.67	4.41	.064	.040	.010	.028	−.028	.006
Cyclops Corporation	4.22	4.73	.044	−.010	.038	−.154	.017	.279
Ohio Edison	4.29	4.54	−.142	−.071	−.075	−.162	−.048	−.118
Central Foundry	5.65[+]	5.91[+]	−.120	−.003	−.061	−.335	−.039	.029
United States Gypsum	5.59[+]	5.55[+]	.004	.169	−.058	−.010	.106	−.056
Eversharp	4.30	4.62	−.028	.054	−.059	−.060	.097	−.085
Dayton Power and Light	4.47	4.87	−.074	−.025	−.116	−.014	−.016	−.156
Cluett, Peabody and Company	5.74[+]	5.59[+]	.105	.215	.129	−.049	.246	.034
Washington Gas Light	4.52	4.53	−.121	−.096	.123	−.074	−.127	.037
Lowenstein, M., and Sons	4.22	4.23	−.022	−.159	.342	−.019	−.139	.144
International Telephone and Telegraph	4.29	4.80	.005	−.065	−.015	.017	−.223	−.087
Carpenter Steel	4.99	4.97	−.198	−.016	−.182	−.225	.031	−.175
Greyhound	4.23	4.21	.027	−.025	.175	−.006	.005	.014
Allegheny Ludlum Steel	4.47	4.41	−.203	.027	.092	−.136	.029	.079
United Air Lines	5.23	5.40[+]	.111	.042	.020	.154	−.012	.199
Adams Express	5.41[+]	4.71	−.198	.110	.039	−.181	.052	−.090
Ambac Industries	5.34[+]	5.07	.089	.144	.152	.163	−.069	−.089
Masonite	5.57[+]	4.34	−.117	−.031	.082	−.109	−.105	.186
Lehigh Valley Industries	6.49[+]	6.50[+]	−.288	.166	−.017	−.266	.206	−.014
Averages	5.06	4.92	−.030	−.030	.057	−.085	−.004	.017

[+] The sample studentized range exceeds 5.29, the .9 fractile of the distribution of the studentized range in samples of size 60 from a normal population.

tionship between $\tilde{R}_{it}$ and $\tilde{R}_{i,t-\tau}$ or between $\tilde{\epsilon}_{it}$ and $\tilde{\epsilon}_{i,t-\tau}$, the autocorrelation estimates for both R_{it} and e_{it} seem consistent with the assumption that successive values of $\tilde{R}_{it}$ and of $\tilde{\epsilon}_{it}$ are independent. The largest measured autocorrelations are in excess of .3 in absolute value, implying a 9 percent estimated explanation of variance, but most of the measured autocorrelations are much closer to zero. Moreover, when so many autocorrelations for so many different securities are computed, one can expect a few extreme values to be observed on a purely chance basis. Attributing the large measured autocorrelations to chance seems reasonable, since their signs are not systematically positive or negative.

The studentized ranges shown in Table 4.5 are consistent with the hypothesis that the returns and market model disturbances for the large firms are from normal distributions. As would be expected under the hypothesis of normality for $\tilde{R}_{it}$, most of the values of $SR(R_i)$ in Table 4.5 fall into the central portion of the sampling distribution of SR; and of the "extreme" values of $SR(R_i)$, four are less than 4.07, the .10 fractile of the sampling distribution of SR, and four are greater than 5.29, the .9 fractile of the sampling distribution of SR. The average of the $SR(R_i)$ is 4.62, which is just about halfway between the .1 and .9 fractiles of the sampling distribution of SR. Similar comments apply to the studentized ranges $SR(e_i)$ for the market model residuals of the companies in Table 4.5.

A slightly different picture emerges for the randomly selected firms in Table 4.6. For 12 of the 30 firms, the values of $SR(R_i)$ exceed 5.29, the .9 fractile of the sampling distribution of SR in samples of 60 from a normal population. The distributions of returns for these firms show slightly higher frequencies of extreme returns than would be expected under the hypothesis of normality. The studentized ranges for the market model residuals of the firms in Table 4.6 likewise suggest slight leptokurtosis; nine of the $SR(e_i)$ exceed the .90 fractile of the sampling distribution of SR, while only two of the $SR(e_i)$ are less than the .10 fractile of the sampling distribution of SR. Thus, the assumption of normality is a better approximation for the returns of larger firms than for those of randomly selected firms, but even for the latter we shall continue to see how far the normality assumption can take us in our theoretical and empirical work.

It would be well to use plots like Figures 4.1 to 4.4 to check the assumptions that the joint distribution of $\tilde{R}_{it}$ and $\tilde{R}_{mt}$ is bivariate normal and that the return distributions are stationary through time for each of the 60 securities in Tables 4.3 to 4.6. This would, however, consume much space. Suffice it to say that the graphs for IBM are typical. For other common stocks, plots of R_{it} against R_{mt}, like Figure 4.1, seem roughly consistent with the implications of bivariate normality; and time series plots, like Figures 4.2 to 4.4, seem consistent with the assumption that return distributions are stationary, at least for five-year subperiods.

Finally, the essence of the market model is that, to a greater or lesser extent, depending on the value of β_i, the returns on all securities are related to the return on the market portfolio m. That is, the market model equation (3) says that part of the return on any security i for which $\beta_i \neq 0$ is the return on m. Thus, although we have 60 different firms in Tables 4.3 to 4.6, we do not have 60 independent samples of returns. One implication of this is that there can be much interdependence across firms in the sample values of a given statistic. For example, from equation (45) we can determine that as long as b_i is nonzero, the sample variance of the return on the market portfolio is a component of the sample variance of the returns on any common stock. Thus, the sample estimates of return variances for individual firms are interdependent because each depends on the sample variance of the return on the market. Likewise, the values of other sample statistics, such as $SR(R_i)$ and $r(R_{it}, R_{i,t-\tau})$, are interdependent across firms when there are common factors that affect the returns on all firms.

One might suspect that there is little or no dependence across firms in the values of sample statistics, such as $SR(e_i)$ and $r(e_{it}, e_{i,t-\tau})$, which are computed from the market model residuals. However, this is only true if the return on the market portfolio m does a good job in capturing the effects of common factors on the returns of individual firms, so that there is little dependence across firms in the market model disturbances $\tilde{\epsilon}_{it}$. We shall return to this point in Chapter 9.

C. Comparison of Prewar and Postwar Market Model Parameter Estimates

In Chapter 1 we found that there is a dramatic downward shift in the variance of the return on the market portfolio m sometime in the late 1930s. We stated there, without evidence, that a similar downward shift in the variances of the returns on individual stocks can also be observed at about the same time. We now present some evidence on this point. We also discuss some interesting changes in the properties of the market model.

Table 4.7 shows estimates of the market model parameters for 1934–1938 for those securities of Table 4.3 that were listed on the NYSE throughout the 1934–1938 period. Table 4.8 reproduces the results in Table 4.4 for those firms in Table 4.4 that were on the NYSE throughout the 1934–1938 period. The decline in the variability of returns on individual securities from 1934–1938 to 1963–1968 is evident. Only one firm, Richardson Merrill, shows a higher value of $s(R_i)$ in the later period than in the earlier period. There is

TABLE 4.7

Market Model Parameter Estimates for Larger Firms for January 1934–December 1938

COMPANY	b_i	$s(b_i)$	a_i	$s(a_i)$	r^2_{im}	$\bar{R}_i$	$s(R_i)$	$s(e_i)$
International Business Machines	.27	.051	.006	.0054	.32	.0112	.050	.041
American Telephone and Telegraph	.33	.039	.005	.0042	.55	.0115	.048	.032
General Motors	.77	.072	.001	.0077	.66	.0154	.100	.059
Exxon	.54	.064	-.001	.0068	.55	.0087	.077	.052
Sears, Roebuck	.73	.076	.005	.0081	.62	.0183	.099	.062
Eastman Kodak	.38	.061	.012	.0065	.40	.0193	.064	.050
General Electric	.72	.062	.007	.0066	.70	.0203	.091	.050
Texaco	.68	.094	.009	.0101	.47	.0211	.105	.077
Coca-Cola	.32	.079	.029	.0084	.22	.0345	.072	.064
Du Pont	.50	.055	.004	.0059	.59	.0133	.069	.045
Procter and Gamble	.38	.070	.005	.0075	.34	.0119	.070	.057
Mobil Oil	.63	.080	-.007	.0086	.52	.0043	.093	.065
Standard Oil (California)	.54	.068	-.009	.0073	.51	.0003	.079	.056
American Home Products	.48	.057	.008	.0061	.56	.0165	.069	.046
International Telephone and Telegraph	.89	.118	-.015	.0126	.49	.0016	.134	.096
J. C. Penney	.57	.068	.005	.0072	.55	.0151	.081	.055
Westinghouse Electric	.86	.082	.013	.0087	.65	.0283	.112	.067
Kresge, S. S.	.53	.073	.006	.0078	.47	.0154	.081	.059
Atlantic Richfield	.63	.066	-.008	.0071	.61	.0033	.086	.054
Averages	.56	.069	.004	.0074	.52	.0142	.082	.057

TABLE 4.8

Market Model Parameter Estimates for Randomly Selected Firms for January 1934–December 1938

COMPANY	b_i	$s(b_i)$	a_i	$s(a_i)$	r^2_{im}	$\bar{R}_i$	$s(R_i)$	$s(e_i)$
Lehigh Portland Cement	1.13	.114	.001	.0122	.63	.0210	.151	.093
Hotel Corporation of America	1.54	.148	.002	.0158	.65	.0305	.203	.121
Portec	1.54	.125	−.001	.0133	.72	.0266	.192	.102
Richardson Merrill	.34	.053	.009	.0057	.41	.0154	.056	.043
Van Raalte	1.01	.115	.026	.0123	.57	.0440	.142	.094
Keebler	.50	.073	−.006	.0078	.44	.0030	.079	.060
Gulf, Mobile and Ohio Railroad	1.57	.161	−.009	.0171	.62	.0197	.211	.131
Dana Corporation	1.18	.157	.008	.0167	.49	.0293	.178	.128
Union Pacific Railroad	.65	.068	−.005	.0072	.61	.0063	.088	.055
United States Gypsum	.79	.108	.010	.0116	.48	.0245	.121	.088
Cluett, Peabody and Company	1.02	.155	.014	.0166	.43	.0326	.165	.126
International Telephone and Telegraph	.89	.118	−.015	.0126	.49	.0016	.134	.096
Allegheny Ludlum Steel	.90	.099	−.000	.0106	.58	.0163	.124	.081
Adams Express	1.22	.085	−.004	.0090	.78	.0184	.146	.069
Ambac Industries	1.43	.171	−.003	.0183	.55	.0234	.205	.139
Lehigh Valley Industries	1.26	.150	−.030	.0160	.55	−.0067	.180	.122
Averages	1.06	.119	.000	.0127	.56	.0191	.135	.093

also a clear-cut decline in residual standard deviations from the earlier to the later period. Given that $s(R_m)$ also declined, we can use these results and equation (45) to conclude that the decline in the variability of a security's return generally reflects a decline both in the variability of marketwide factors, as summarized by $\tilde{R}_{mt}$, and in the variability of the disturbance $\tilde{\epsilon}_{it}$.

Perhaps the most interesting evidence is that the decline in the variability of $\tilde{R}_{mt}$ is sharper, in percentage terms, than the typical decline in the variability of $\tilde{\epsilon}_{it}$. The evidence on this point is in the substantial decline in the coefficients of determination, r_{im}^2, from the earlier to the later period. On average, marketwide factors account for 56 percent of security return variances in 1934-1938 for the securities in Table 4.8, whereas for July 1963–June 1968, the corresponding average value of r_{im}^2 in Table 4.4 is only .27. Likewise, in the later period the average value of r_{im}^2 for the stocks of larger firms in Table 4.3 is .20, as compared to .52 for the earlier period (Table 4.7). Thus, a much smaller fraction of the variance of the return on a security can typically be attributed to its market model relationship with $\tilde{R}_{mt}$ for July 1963–June 1968 than for 1934-1938.

The decline in the explanatory power of the market model was first documented by King (1966); Blume (1968) later documented the declines in r_{im}^2, $s^2(R_i)$, $s^2(R_m)$, and $s^2(e_i)$ in more detail and suggested that the declines are best interpreted as a shift that took place sometime around 1940. Finally, Officer (1971) corroborated Blume's results and investigated several possible reasons for the decline in r_{im}^2. None of the explanations turned out to be supported convincingly by the evidence.

D. The Reliability of the Risk Estimates

In discussing the detailed results for IBM for July 1963–June 1968, we concluded that the sample estimate $b_i = .67$ left substantial uncertainty with respect to the value of β_i. The same conclusion holds for the other common stocks we have examined. Thus, from the Bayesian viewpoint, the uncertainty that remains about β_i after a sample has been analyzed is summarized by the posterior distribution on the parameter. With a diffuse prior, a large sample, and under the assumption that the joint distribution of $\tilde{R}_{it}$ and $\tilde{R}_{mt}$ is bivariate normal, the posterior distribution on the parameter is approximately normal, with mean $E(\tilde{\beta}_i) = b_i$ and standard deviation $\sigma(\tilde{\beta}_i) = s(b_i)$. The values of b_i and of $s(b_i)$ for July 1963–June 1968 for each of the stocks in the two samples discussed above are in Tables 4.3 and 4.4. The impression is the same as for IBM. The values of $s(b_i)$ are large, so that the sample estimates leave substantial uncertainty about the values of β_i for the individual stocks. We leave it to the reader to buttress this impression by computing some fractiles of the posterior distributions of β_i for each of the stocks, as was done for IBM.

One apparently direct solution to this problem is to work with a sample period that covers more than five years of monthly data. We can see from equations (26) and (27) that in sampling from the assumed stationary bi-variate normal distribution of $\tilde{R}_{it}$ and $\tilde{R}_{mt}$, the variance of the sampling distribution of b_i decreases as the sample size increases. Thus a larger sample would seem to be the most direct way to reduce uncertainty about β_i. The validity of this approach depends, however, on the assumption that the joint distribution of $\tilde{R}_{it}$ and $\tilde{R}_{mt}$ is stationary through time, and especially on the implication of this assumption that β_i itself is stationary through time. If this is not true, then a larger sample does not necessarily imply a more reliable estimate of the value of β_i at the end of the sampling period.

The evidence of Blume (1968), Gonedes (1973), and L. Fisher (1970) indicates that over long periods, the β_i values of individual stocks do indeed change. The work of Gonedes and Fisher further indicates that with monthly data, the assumption that β_i is constant is a reasonable approximation for periods of up to seven years. With more than seven years of data, the estimates of the β_i of individual securities are likely to be less reliable than if shorter periods are used. With monthly data, the optimal estimation period is apparently five to seven years.

III. Conclusions

It seems that, at least for individual securities, we must learn to live with substantial uncertainty about the values of β_i. For many purposes, the problem is not serious. When we conduct tests requiring estimates of β_i, it is often possible to work with estimates for portfolios rather than individual securities, and it turns out that the β_p's of portfolios can be estimated far more reliably than those of individual securities. This is a matter we shall study in more detail when the need arises.

CHAPTER
5

Efficient Capital Markets

Much of the recent literature in finance is concerned with capital market efficiency. This chapter introduces the theory and discusses tests. The ideas and tests of them reappear in later chapters.

I. An Efficient Capital Market: Introduction

An efficient capital market is a market that is efficient in processing information. The prices of securities observed at any time are based on "correct" evaluation of all information available at that time. In an efficient market, prices "fully reflect" available information.

An efficient capital market is an important component of a capitalist system. In such a system, the ideal is a market where prices are accurate signals for capital allocation. That is, when firms issue securities to finance their activities, they can expect to get "fair" prices, and when investors choose among the securities that represent ownership of firms' activities, they can do so under the assumption that they are paying "fair" prices. In short, if the capital market is to function smoothly in allocating resources, prices of securities must be good indicators of value.

The statement that prices in an efficient market "fully reflect" available information conveys the general idea of what is meant by market efficiency, but the statement is too general to be testable. Since the goal is to test the extent to which the market is efficient, the proposition must be restated in a testable form. This requires a more detailed specification of the process of price formation, one that gives testable content to the term "fully reflect."

The process of price formation described below is far from the most general model that can be used to give testable content to the theory of capital market efficiency. The goals are (a) to present a simple model but one that is nevertheless sufficient to illustrate the problems that arise in testing market efficiency and (b) to describe and give some critical perspective on the types of tests that are commonly done.

II.   An Efficient Capital Market: Formal Discussion

Assume that all events of interest take place at discrete points in time, $t-1$, $t, t+1$, etc. Then define

ϕ_{t-1} = the set of information available at time $t-1$, which is relevant for determining security prices at $t-1$.

ϕ_{t-1}^m = the set of information that the market uses to determine security prices at $t-1$. Thus ϕ_{t-1}^m is a subset of ϕ_{t-1}; ϕ_{t-1}^m contains at most the information in ϕ_{t-1}, but it could contain less.

$p_{j,t-1}$ = price of security j at time $t-1$, $j = 1, 2, \ldots, n$, where n is the number of securities in the market.

$f_m(p_{1,t+\tau}, \ldots, p_{n,t+\tau} | \phi_{t-1}^m)$ = the joint probability density function for security prices at time $t + \tau (\tau \geqslant 0)$ assessed by the market at time $t-1$ on the basis of the information ϕ_{t-1}^m.

$f(p_{1,t+\tau}, \ldots, p_{n,t+\tau} | \phi_{t-1})$ = the "true" joint probability density function for security prices at time $t + \tau (\tau \geqslant 0)$ that is "implied by" the information ϕ_{t-1}.

To keep the notation manageable, the security prices $p_{1,t+\tau}, \ldots, p_{n,t+\tau}$ that appear as arguments in f and f_m are taken to be the prices of the securities at time $t + \tau$, plus any interest or dividend payments at $t + \tau$. The prices $p_{1,t-1}$, $\ldots, p_{n,t-1}$, are just actual prices at time $t-1$.

The set of information ϕ_{t-1} available at time $t-1$ includes what might be called the "state of the world" at time $t-1$: e.g., current and past values of any relevant variables, like the earnings of firms, GNP, the "political climate," the tastes of consumers and investors, etc. Since ϕ_{t-1} includes the past history of all relevant variables, ϕ_{t-1} includes ϕ_{t-2}; equivalently, ϕ_{t-2} is a subset of ϕ_{t-1}. In addition to current and past values of relevant variables, ϕ_{t-1} is also assumed to include whatever is knowable about relationships among variables. This includes relationships among current and past values of the same or different variables, and also whatever can be predicted about future states of the world from the current state. In short, ϕ_{t-1}, the information available at $t-1$, includes not only the state of the world at $t-1$, but also whatever is knowable about the process that describes the evolution of the state of the world through time. We assume that one of the things that is knowable about the process is the implication of the current state of the world for the joint probability distributions of security prices at future times. Thus ϕ_{t-1} is assumed to imply the joint density functions $f(p_{1,t+\tau}, \ldots, p_{n,t+\tau}|\phi_{t-1})$, $\tau = 0, 1, 2, \ldots 2$.

The process of price formation at time $t-1$ is then assumed to be as follows. On the basis of the information ϕ_{t-1}^m, the market assesses a joint distribution of security prices for time t, $f_m(p_{1t}, \ldots, p_{nt}|\phi_{t-1}^m)$. From this assessment of the distribution of prices at t, the market then determines appropriate current prices, $p_{1,t-1}, \ldots, p_{n,t-1}$, for individual securities. The appropriate current prices are determined by some model of market equilibrium—that is, by a model that determines what equilibrium current prices should be on the basis of characteristics of the joint distribution of prices at t. The term "equilibrium" has its usual economic meaning. A market equilibrium at time $t-1$ is achieved when the market sets prices $p_{1,t-1}, \ldots, p_{n,t-1}$ for individual securities at which the demand for each security by investors is equal to the outstanding supply of the security. In other words, a market equilibrium implies a market-clearing set of prices for individual securities.

When we say that "the market" assesses a joint distribution of security prices for time t and then uses the characteristics of its assessed distribution to determine equilibrium prices for securities at $t-1$, we speak metaphorically. To say that "the market" does something is just a convenient way of summarizing the decisions of individual investors and the way these decisions interact to determine prices. The metaphor allows us to save for the end of the chapter, when the issues can be better appreciated, the discussion of some of the subtle and not too subtle simplifications of the world that are built into the model.

In our model of price formation, the hypothesis that the capital market is efficient is stated as

$$\phi_{t-1}^m = \phi_{t-1}; \tag{1}$$

that is, ϕ_{t-1}^m, the information that the market uses to determine security prices at $t - 1$, includes all the information available. Market efficiency also implies that

$$f_m(p_{1t}, \ldots, p_{nt} | \phi_{t-1}^m) = f(p_{1t}, \ldots, p_{nt} | \phi_{t-1}); \tag{2}$$

that is, the market understands the implications of the available information for the joint distribution of returns. Since ϕ_{t-1}, the set of available information, includes whatever is knowable about the process that describes the evolution of the state of the world through time, equation (1) can be taken to imply (2). Stating the two conditions separately, however, emphasizes that market efficiency means that the market is aware of all available information and uses it correctly.

Having correctly assessed the joint distribution of prices for t, the market then uses some model of equilibrium to set prices at $t - 1$. The model says what the current prices of securities, $p_{1,t-1}, \ldots, p_{n,t-1}$, should be in light of the correctly assessed joint distribution of security prices for t. In this sense, both the joint density function $f_m(p_{1t}, \ldots, p_{nt} | \phi_{t-1}^m)$ and the current prices $p_{1,t-1}, \ldots, p_{n,t-1}$ that are based on this joint density function "fully reflect" all the information available at $t - 1$.

Tests of market efficiency are concerned with whether or not the market does correctly use available information in setting security prices. Most common are tests that try to determine whether prices fully reflect specific subsets of information. For example, one possible source of information about future prices is the history of past prices and returns on securities. A nontrivial segment of the empirical literature on efficient markets is concerned with whether current security prices fully reflect any information in past prices and returns. Other sources of publicly available information are also fertile ground for tests of market efficiency. For example, there are studies of the adjustment of stock prices to the information in a stock split, a merger, an earnings announcement, the announcement of a new issue of securities by a firm, and so forth. In these tests, the goal is to determine whether prices adjust fully and instantaneously to the public announcement of the event of interest. Finally, another sort of test of market efficiency is concerned with whether there are individuals or groups—for example, managers of mutual funds—who are adept at investment selection in the sense that their choices reliably provide higher returns than comparable choices by other investors. If prices always fully reflect available information, this sort of investment adeptness is ruled out. For if such adeptness exists, it implies that some investors either have access to information that is not utilized by the market in setting prices or that they are better able to evaluate available information than the market. In either case, the market is not efficient.

The process of price formation in an efficient market, as described so far, is not sufficient for such tests of market efficiency. All we have said is that an efficient market correctly uses all available information in assessing the joint distribution of future prices, which is the basis of current equilibrium prices. Since we cannot observe $f_m(p_{1t}, \ldots, p_{nt}|\phi_{t-1}^m)$, we cannot determine whether (2) holds, and so we cannot determine whether the real-world capital market is efficient. Equations (1) and (2) are formal notations for the statement that prices in an efficient market fully reflect available information, but this is not sufficient to make the statement testable.

What the model lacks is a more detailed specification of the link between $f_m(p_{1t}, \ldots, p_{nt}|\phi_{t-1}^m)$ and $p_{1,t-1}, \ldots, p_{n,t-1}$. We must specify in more detail how equilibrium prices at $t-1$ are determined from the characteristics of the market-assessed joint distribution of prices for t. Some model of market equilibrium, however simple, is required. This is the rub in tests of market efficiency. Any test is simultaneously a test of efficiency and of assumptions about the characteristics of market equilibrium. If the test is successful— that is, if the hypothesis that the market is efficient cannot be rejected—then this also implies that the assumptions about market equilibrium are not rejected. If the tests are unsuccessful, we face the problem of deciding whether this reflects a true violation of market efficiency (the simple proposition that prices fully reflect available information) or poor assumptions about the nature of market equilibrium.

It turns out that a few simple models of market equilibrium produce many successful tests of market efficiency or, more precisely, many successful joint tests of market efficiency and of the models of market equilibrium. We now discuss the most popular models and tests of market efficiency derived from them.

III. Four Models of Market Equilibrium

Four basic models of market equilibrium are used in tests of market efficiency. We discuss them in order of complexity.

A. *Expected Returns Are Positive*

The joint distribution $f_m(p_{1t}, \ldots, p_{nt}|\phi_{t-1}^m)$ of security prices for time t assessed by the market at time $t-1$ implies a marginal distribution $f_m(p_{jt}|\phi_{t-1}^m)$ for the price at t of any security j. This marginal distribution has mean or expected value $E_m(\tilde{p}_{jt}|\phi_{t-1}^m)$.* The first model of market equilibrium simply says that at any time $t-1$ the market sets the price of any security j in such a way that the market's expected return on the security from time $t-1$ to time t is positive.

Formally, the one-period return on security j from time $t-1$ to t is

$$\tilde{R}_{jt} = \frac{\tilde{p}_{jt} - p_{j,t-1}}{p_{j,t-1}}. \tag{3}$$

At time $t-1$ the market assesses a probability distribution on $\tilde{p}_{jt}$ given by the density function $f_m(p_{jt}|\phi_{t-1}^m)$. A distribution for the return $\tilde{R}_{jt}$ is not defined, however, until the market sets $p_{j,t-1}$. The model of market equilibrium which we are discussing posits that the market always sets $p_{j,t-1}$ so that the mean of the resulting distribution of $\tilde{R}_{jt}$ is strictly positive. That is, the market always sets $p_{j,t-1}$ so that, given its assessment of the expected price at t, $E_m(\tilde{p}_{jt}|\phi_{t-1}^m)$,

$$E_m(\tilde{R}_{jt}|\phi_{t-1}^m) = \frac{E_m(\tilde{p}_{jt}|\phi_{t-1}^m) - p_{j,t-1}}{p_{j,t-1}} > 0. \tag{4}$$

Equivalently, the market sets $p_{j,t-1}$ at a value less than its assessment of the expected future price, $E_m(\tilde{p}_{jt}|\phi_{t-1}^m)$.

Suppose now that we join this model of market equilibrium with the proposition that the market is efficient. Market efficiency says that in assessing distributions of future prices, the market uses all available information and uses it correctly:

$$f_m(p_{jt}|\phi_{t-1}^m) = f(p_{jt}|\phi_{t-1}), \tag{5}$$

which implies

$$E_m(\tilde{p}_{jt}|\phi_{t-1}^m) = E(\tilde{p}_{jt}|\phi_{t-1}) \tag{6}$$

$$E_m(\tilde{R}_{jt}|\phi_{t-1}^m) = E(\tilde{R}_{jt}|\phi_{t-1}). \tag{7}$$

In words, market efficiency says that at time $t-1$ the market correctly assesses the distribution of the price of any security for time t, which means that the expected value of the future price assessed by the market is the true expected value, which in turn means that when the market sets the prices of securities at time $t-1$, its assessment of the expected return on any security is the true expected return. If the market sets prices so that equation (4) holds, then the true expected return on any security is always positive:

---

*Tildes (~) are used to denote random variables. When referring to any specific value of a random variable, the tilde is dropped. Thus, $E_m(\tilde{p}_{jt}|\phi_{t-1}^m)$ is the expected value of the random variable $\tilde{p}_{jt}$, but we write $f_m(p_{jt}|\phi_{t-1}^m)$ to denote the density function for specific values of the variable.

$$E(\tilde{R}_{jt}|\phi_{t-1}) > 0. \tag{8}$$

This is not to say that a positive return on security j will be observed at t. The return observed at t will be the result of a drawing from $f(p_{jt}|\phi_{t-1})$, and the drawing may yield a negative return. Rather, the hypothesis that the market is efficient (prices correctly reflect available information), when combined with a model of market equilibrium which says that $E_m(\tilde{R}_{jt}|\phi_{t-1}^m) > 0$ (the market sets current prices so that its expected returns on securities are positive), implies that at time $t - 1$ the true expected return on any security j, $E(\tilde{R}_{jt}|\phi_{t-1})$, is positive.

If the market is efficient and if this model of market equilibrium is correct, then any investor or market analyst who disagrees with the market and posits a negative expected return on a security is incorrect. Many stock market analysts feel that they can identify times when expected returns on individual securities or on the market, as represented by some portfolio of securities, are negative. These analysts would agree with the proposition that the market always sets prices so that its assessed expected returns $E_m(\tilde{R}_{jt}|\phi_{t-1}^m)$ are positive. But they would disagree with the proposition that the market is efficient. They feel that in setting prices, the market sometimes neglects relevant information or draws incorrect inferences from it, so that sometimes the true expected returns $E(\tilde{R}_{jt}|\phi_{t-1})$ are negative. They feel that they see more information or are better able to analyze available information than the market.

Such analysts are potentially a fertile source of tests of market efficiency. If they record the times when they assess negative expected returns on securities, then one can simply compute the returns that are later realized. One or a few such observations are not much evidence for or against market efficiency; but as a history of the predictions of an analyst is built up, a reliable average return for periods when he assesses negative expected returns can be obtained. If the average is negative and if the sample of predictions is sufficiently large to make the negative average return a low-probability event if true expected returns are positive, then we can conclude that the analyst is able to identify periods when true expected returns $E(\tilde{R}_{jt}|\phi_{t-1})$ are negative. If we are willing to stick by the model of market equilibrium which says that the market always sets prices so that its expected returns $E_m(\tilde{R}_{jt}|\phi_{t-1}^m)$ are positive, then the predictions of the analyst establish that the market sometimes either neglects available information in setting prices or analyzes information incorrectly. In either case, the analyst is living evidence for the existence of market inefficiency.

The model summarized by equations (4) to (8) has been used to test the claims of one group of analysts about market inefficiency. This group, collectively known as chartists or "technical" analysts, claims that market prices only react slowly and over fairly long periods to new information. If new information implies a price increase, the increase will be spread across time, as will any decrease in prices that is implied by negative information. This slow adjustment process posited by the chartists is in sharp contrast to the theory of efficient markets. When the market is efficient, prices fully reflect available information, which means that the market adjusts prices fully and instantaneously when new information becomes available.

The chartists further claim that the reaction of the market to new information is so slow that one need not be concerned with the information itself. By studying patterns in the sequence of past prices, they argue, one can learn how the price of the security tends to react to new information. The patterns in the price sequence will be strong enough and will recur frequently enough for a trained eye to predict the future price movement of a security on the basis of its recent past movement and knowledge of the typical patterns in the price behavior of the security. In short, the chartists claim the market is inefficient in the sense that in setting prices, the market does not even take full account of the obvious information in the historical behavior of prices.

Given the expected return model summarized by (4), an empirical confrontation between the claims of the chartist and those of the theory of capital market efficiency is easily devised. The basic proposition of the chartist is that because the market adjusts slowly to new information, price movements tend to persist. When prices have moved up in the recent past, one can expect them to continue to move up, and there is likewise persistence in downward price movements. Consider the following trading rule, suggested by Alexander (1961; 1964) and close in spirit to the various trading rules proposed by chartists. If the price of a security moves up at least y percent, buy and hold the security until its price moves down at least y percent from a subsequent high, at which time simultaneously sell and go short.* The short posi-

---

*In the jargon of the capital market, when one buys a security, this is known as going long. When one owns the security, this is called a long position in the security. The opposite of a long position is a short position. Selling short involves borrowing a security from someone who has a long position in the security, with the borrower promising to return the security to the lender at some future date and to pay to the lender any dividends or interest that are paid on the security while the short position is "open," that is, before the securities are returned. Upon borrowing the security, the borrower or short-seller immediately sells the security in the market. He then repurchases the security in the market when it comes time to return it to the lender, and in this way "closes" or "covers" his short position. If the price of the security falls during the period the short position is open, and if it falls by more than the amount of any dividends or interest paid on the security, then the short-seller profits. Otherwise he loses.

A short sale is equivalent to issuing a security with precisely the characteristics of the security that is sold short. Short-selling is thus a device whereby investors can issue securities that are identical to those issued by firms—assuming, of course, that the investor can deliver on the promises involved in the short sale. These concepts are discussed in Chapter 7.

tion is maintained until the price rises at least y percent above a subsequent low, at which time one covers the short position and goes long. Moves less than y percent in either direction are ignored. Such a system is called a y percent filter. Its sequence of successive long and short positions formalizes the proposition of the chartists that upward price movements tend to persist and to be followed by downward movements, which also tend to persist and to be followed by upward movements, and so on.

If the capital market is efficient and if the market sets prices so that its expected returns are positive, then filter rules are nonsense. If the market correctly uses available information and if it sets prices so that expected returns are positive, then the best trading rule for any security is to buy and hold. If the market is efficient, then the buy-and-hold strategy has higher expected returns or profits than any strategies that involve periods when the security is not held or, like the filter rules, involve periods when the security is sold short. In contrast, the chartist would say that because the market does not correctly use available information, there are periods when true expected returns are negative. This implies that there are strategies for trading in a security that have higher expected returns or profits than the buy-and-hold strategy. Most chartists would believe that some of the filters could systematically beat a buy-and-hold strategy.

Tests of filter rules are reported by Alexander (1961; 1964) and by Fama and Blume (1966). To present their results would involve a long discussion of technical details, none of which would be useful in any of our future work. We shall simply discuss conclusions and let the reader check the original sources. Thus, Alexander (1961; 1964) reports extensive tests of filter rules using daily data on price indexes from 1897 to 1959 and filters from 1 to 50 percent. In his final paper on the subject, Alexander concludes (1964, p. 351):

> In fact, at this point I should advise any reader who is interested only in practical results, and who is not a floor trader and so must pay commissions, to turn to other sources on how to beat buy and hold.

Further evidence is provided by Fama and Blume (1966), who compare the profitability of various filters to a buy-and-hold strategy for daily data on the individual stocks of the Dow-Jones Industrial Average. (The data are those discussed in Chapter 1.) Fama and Blume conclude that for the most part their evidence is in favor of buy and hold, and they reject the hypothesis that there is any important information in past prices that the market neglects in setting current prices.

Looking hard, however, one can find evidence in the filter tests of both Alexander and Fama–Blume that is inconsistent with capital market efficiency, if efficiency is interpreted in a strict sense. In particular, the results for very small filters (1 percent in Alexander's tests and 0.5, 1.0, and 1.5 percent in the tests of Fama–Blume) indicate that it is possible to devise trading schemes based on very short-term (preferably intraday, but at most daily) price swings that on average outperform buy and hold. The average profits on individual transactions from such schemes are minuscule, but they generate transactions so frequently that over longer periods and ignoring commissions they outperform buy and hold by a substantial margin. These results are evidence of persistence in very short-term price movements of the type posited by the chartists.

When one takes account of even the minimum trading costs that would be generated by small filters, however, their advantage over a buy-and-hold strategy disappears. For example, even a floor trader—that is, a person who owns a seat on the New York Stock Exchange—must pay clearinghouse fees on his trades that amount to about 0.1 percent per turnaround transaction (sale plus purchase). Fama and Blume show that because small filters produce such frequent trades, these minimum trading costs are sufficient to wipe out the advantage of the small filters over buy and hold. Strictly speaking, then, the filters uncover evidence of market inefficiency, but the departures from efficiency do not seem sufficient for any trader to reject the hypothesis that the market is efficient so far as his own activities are concerned.

Remember that no null hypothesis, such as the hypothesis that the market is efficient, is a literally accurate view of the world. It is not meaningful to interpret the tests of such a hypothesis on a strict true-false basis. Rather, one is concerned with testing whether the model at hand is a reasonable approximation to the world, which can be taken as true, at least until a better approximation comes along. What is a reasonable approximation depends on the use to which the model is to be put. For example, since traders cannot use filters to beat buy and hold, it is reasonable for them to assume that they should behave as if the market were efficient, at least for the purposes of trading on information in past prices.

B. *Expected Returns Are Constant*

The filter tests are the only tests of market efficiency based on the model of market equilibrium which simply assumes that expected returns are positive. Somewhat more common are tests based on a model in which the expected return is assumed to be constant through time. Specifically, at time $t - 1$ the market assesses a joint distribution for security prices at time t, $f_m(p_{1t}, \ldots, p_{nt}|\phi_{t-1}^m)$, which implies a distribution $f_m(p_{jt}|\phi_{t-1}^m)$ for the price of security j at t, and this distribution has mean or expected value

$E_m(\tilde{p}_{jt}|\phi_{t-1}^m)$. Having assessed $E_m(\tilde{p}_{jt}|\phi_{t-1}^m)$, the market then sets the price of the security at $t-1$ so that the expected return on the security from $t-1$ to t is equal to some constant, call it $E(\tilde{R}_j)$, which is the same for every period. Formally, at every time $t-1$, the market sets the current price of security j so that, given its assessment of the expected value of the future price $E_m(\tilde{p}_{jt}|\phi_{t-1}^m)$,

$$E_m(\tilde{R}_{jt}|\phi_{t-1}^m) = \frac{E_m(\tilde{p}_{jt}|\phi_{t-1}^m) - p_{j,t-1}}{p_{j,t-1}} = E(\tilde{R}_j). \tag{9}$$

The model says that $E(\tilde{R}_j)$ is constant through time, but different securities are allowed to have different expected returns, based perhaps on differences in risk, and some may even have negative expected returns.

If the market is also efficient—that is, if it correctly uses all available information to assess $f_m(p_{jt}, \ldots, p_{nt}|\phi_{t-1}^m)$—then this assessed distribution is the true distribution $f(p_{jt}, \ldots, p_{nt}|\phi_{t-1})$, which implies that equations (5) to (7) hold. Combining (7) with the assumption of a constant expected return, we have

$$E(\tilde{R}_{jt}|\phi_{t-1}) = E_m(\tilde{R}_{jt}|\phi_{t-1}^m) = E(\tilde{R}_j). \tag{10}$$

In words, at any time $t-1$ the market sets the price of security j in such a way that its assessment of the expected return on the security, $E_m(\tilde{R}_{jt}|\phi_{t-1}^m)$, is the constant $E(\tilde{R}_j)$. Since an efficient market correctly uses all available information, $E(\tilde{R}_j)$ is also $E(\tilde{R}_{jt}|\phi_{t-1})$, the true expected return on the security.

This particular combination of a model of market equilibrium with market efficiency has a directly testable implication. There is no way to use any information available at time $t-1$ as the basis of a correct assessment of the expected return on security j which is other than $E(\tilde{R}_j)$. If the market is efficient and sets prices so that the expected return on security j is constant through time, then any market analyst who assesses an expected return for security j that is different from $E(\tilde{R}_j)$ is necessarily incorrect. But if the analyst systematically shows an ability to identify periods when the expected return on security j is not equal to $E(\tilde{R}_j)$, and if we insist on the model of market equilibrium which says that the market sets prices so that its expected return on security j is always $E(\tilde{R}_j)$, then the predictions of the analyst are evidence that the market does not correctly use all available information in setting prices. In this case, equation (7) does not hold, and the market is inefficient.

For the statistically sophisticated, equation (10) implies that for all ϕ_{t-1}, $E(\tilde{R}_{jt}|\phi_{t-1})$, the regression function of $\tilde{R}_{jt}$ on ϕ_{t-1} is the constant $E(\tilde{R}_j)$. Thus, if one takes any elements from the set of information available at $t-1$ and then estimates the regression of $\tilde{R}_{jt}$ on these information variables, all the coefficients except for the intercept should be indistinguishable from zero. If some of the variables have nonzero coefficients, (10) must be rejected; that is, the joint hypothesis that the market is efficient and that it sets prices so that equilibrium expected returns are constant through time is rejected.

Tests of market efficiency based on the assumption that equilibrium expected returns are constant have focused primarily on one subset of ϕ_{t-1}, the potential information about current expected returns that appears in time series of past returns. If the market is efficient and equilibrium expected returns are constant through time, the past returns on security j are a source of information about $E(\tilde{R}_j)$, which, after all, is unknown.* If the market is efficient, however, the past returns are not a source of information about the expected value of the deviation of $\tilde{R}_{jt}$ from $E(\tilde{R}_j)$. For any sequence of past returns $R_{j,t-1}, R_{j,t-2}, \ldots$, the conditional expected value

$$E(\tilde{R}_{jt}|R_{j,t-1}, R_{j,t-2}, \ldots) = E(\tilde{R}_j).$$

In words, if the market is efficient, there is no way to use any information available at time $t-1$ as the basis for a correct assessment of an expected value of $\tilde{R}_{jt}$ which is different from the assumed constant equilibrium expected return $E(\tilde{R}_j)$. Since part of the information available at $t-1$ is the time series of past returns, there is no way to use the past returns as the basis for a correct assessment of the expected return from $t-1$ to t which is other than $E(\tilde{R}_j)$.

This proposition is easily tested with a tool introduced in Chapter 4. If the correct assessment of the expected value of $\tilde{R}_{jt}$ is $E(\tilde{R}_j)$, then for any $R_{j,t-\tau}$

$$E(\tilde{R}_{jt}|R_{j,t-\tau}) = E(\tilde{R}_j); \tag{11}$$

that is, there is no way to use the past return $R_{j,t-\tau}$ as the basis of a current assessment of an expected value of $\tilde{R}_{jt}$ which is other than $E(\tilde{R}_j)$. In formal terms, the regression function of $\tilde{R}_{jt}$ on $R_{j,t-\tau}$, $E(\tilde{R}_{jt}|R_{j,t-\tau})$, is the constant $E(\tilde{R}_j)$.

To test this proposition, we introduce an alternative hypothesis which says that the regression function is linear in $R_{j,t-\tau}$:

$$E(\tilde{R}_{jt}|R_{j,t-\tau}) = \delta_\tau + \gamma_\tau R_{j,t-\tau}. \tag{12}$$

From Chapter 4 we recognize γ_τ as the autoregression or autocorrelation coefficient for lag τ, also denoted $\rho(\tilde{R}_{jt}, \tilde{R}_{j,t-\tau})$. Thus market efficiency, in

---

*If we are willing to assume that the distribution of $\tilde{R}_{jt}$ is constant through time, then frequency distributions of historical returns are information about the distribution of $\tilde{R}_{jt}$. This is the basis of the empirical work in Chapter 1. The assumption that the distribution of $\tilde{R}_{jt}$ is constant through time is, of course, stronger than the assumption that the mean of the distribution is constant.

combination with the assumption that equilibrium expected returns are constant through time, implies that the autocorrelations of the returns on any security j are zero for all values of the lag τ.

In Chapter 4 we looked at sample autocorrelations of monthly returns for common stocks on the NYSE and concluded that the autocorrelations were close to zero. There we used the sample autocorrelations to test the assumption of random sampling that underlies the statistical inferences drawn from market model coefficient estimates. Now that we want to examine sample autocorrelations to test the hypothesis that the market is efficient, it is well to look at more of them.

Table 5.1, taken from Fama (1965), shows sample autocorrelations of daily returns for each of the 30 Dow-Jones Industrials, for time periods that vary slightly from stock to stock but usually run from about the end of 1957 to September 26, 1962. (The data are discussed in Chapter 1.)* For each stock, the table shows sample autocorrelations for lags of from one to ten days. Recall from Chapter 4 that when the true autocorrelation is zero, the sampling distribution of the sample autocorrelation, $r(\tilde{R}_{jt}, \tilde{R}_{j,t-\tau})$, is approximately normal, with approximate mean and standard deviation

$$E[r(\tilde{R}_{jt}, \tilde{R}_{j,t-\tau})] \doteq -1/(T - \tau)$$
$$\sigma[r(\tilde{R}_{jt}, \tilde{R}_{j,t-\tau})] \doteq \sqrt{1/(T - \tau)} ,$$

where T is the number of returns in the sample.

In Table 5.1 the sample autocorrelations that are at least two standard deviations to the left or to the right of $-1/(T - \tau)$ are indicated by asterisks. The values of sample autocorrelations so marked might be regarded as extreme in the sense that they are low-probability events if the true autocorrelations are zero. Of the 30 sample autocorrelations between successive daily returns ($\tau = 1$), 11 are extreme in this sense and 9 of these 11 are positive. Moreover, 22 of the 30 sample autocorrelations between successive daily returns are positive. Since market efficiency says that the true autocorrelations between successive returns are zero, one might interpret the results as evidence against market efficiency: there seems to be positive autocorrelation between successive daily returns.

There are several reasons why one might conclude that the results in Table 5.1 are not sufficient to overturn the hypothesis of market efficiency. First, the 30 autocorrelations for lag $\tau = 1$ (or for any other specific lag) are not independent. From our study of the market model in Chapter 4 we know that returns on individual securities are all related to the return on the mar-

*These are continuously compounded returns, but recall from Chapter 1 that continuously compounded daily returns are numerically close to simple returns.

TABLE 5.1

Sample Autocorrelations of Daily Return on the Dow-Jones Industrials for Lags τ = 1, 2, . . . , 10

STOCK	LAG (τ)										T
	1	2	3	4	5	6	7	8	9	10	
Allied Chemical	.017	-.042	.007	-.001	.027	.004	-.017	-.026	-.017	-.007	1223
Alcoa	.118*	.038	-.014	.022	-.022	.009	.017	.007	-.001	-.033	1190
American Can	-.087*	-.024	.034	-.065*	-.017	-.006	.015	.025	-.047	-.040	1219
AT&T	-.039	-.097*	.000	.026	.005	-.005	.002	.027	-.014	.007	1219
American Tobacco	.111*	-.109*	-.060*	-.065*	.007	-.010	.011	.046	.039	.041	1283
Anaconda	.067*	-.061*	-.047	-.002	.000	-.038	.009	.016	-.014	-.056	1193
Bethlehem Steel	.013	-.065*	.009	.021	-.053	-.098*	-.010	.004	-.002	-.021	1200
Chrysler	.012	-.066*	-.016	-.007	-.015	.009	.037	.056*	-.044	.021	1692
Du Pont	.013	-.033	.060*	.027	-.002	-.047	.020	.011	-.034	.001	1243
Eastman Kodak	.025	.014	-.031	.005	-.022	.012	.007	.006	.008	.002	1238
General Electric	.011	-.038	-.021	.031	-.001	.000	-.008	.014	-.002	.010	1693
General Foods	.061*	-.003	.045	.002	-.015	-.052	-.006	-.014	-.024	-.017	1408
General Motors	-.004	-.056*	-.037	-.008	-.038	-.006	.019	.006	-.016	.009	1446
Goodyear	-.123*	.017	-.044	.043	-.002	-.003	.035	.014	-.015	.007	1162
International Harvester	-.017	-.029	-.031	.037	-.052	-.021	-.001	.003	-.046	-.016	1200
International Nickel	.096*	-.033	-.019	.020	.027	.059*	-.038	-.008	-.016	.034	1243
International Paper	.046	-.011	-.058*	.053*	.049	-.003	-.025	-.019	-.003	-.021	1447
Johns Manville	.006	-.038	-.027	-.023	-.029	-.080*	.040	.018	-.037	.029	1205
Owens Illinois	-.021	-.084*	-.047	.068*	.086*	-.040	.011	-.040	.067*	-.043	1237
Procter and Gamble	.099*	-.009	-.008	.009	-.015	.022	.012	-.012	-.022	-.021	1447
Sears	.097*	.026	.028	.025	.005	-.054	-.006	-.010	-.008	-.009	1236
Standard Oil (Calif.)	.025	-.030	-.051*	-.025	-.047	-.034	-.010	.072*	-.049*	-.035	1693
Standard Oil (N. J.)	.008	-.116*	.016	.014	-.047	-.018	-.022	-.026	-.073*	.081*	1156
Swift and Co.	-.004	-.015	-.010	.012	.057*	.012	-.043	.014	.012	.001	1446
Texaco	.094*	-.049	-.024	-.018	-.017	-.009	.031	.032	-.013	.008	1159
Union Carbide	.107*	-.012	.040	.046	-.036	-.034	.003	-.008	-.054	-.037	1118
United Aircraft	.014	-.033	-.022	-.047	-.067*	-.053	.046	.037	.015	-.019	1200
U.S. Steel	.040	-.074*	.014	.011	-.012	-.021	.041	.037	-.021	-.044	1200
Westinghouse	-.027	-.022	-.036	-.003	.000	-.054*	-.020	.013	-.014	-.008	1448
Woolworth	.028	-.016	.015	.014	.007	-.039	.013	.003	-.088*	-.008	1445

*Sample autocorrelation is at least two standard deviations to the left or to the right of its expected value under the hypothesis that the true autocorrelation is zero.

ket. For current purposes, this means that the sample autocorrelations of the returns on individual securities all reflect to some extent the sample autocorrelation of the return on the market. Thus, it is not necessarily surprising that for a given lag the sample autocorrelations in Table 5.1 are predominantly positive or negative.

Even if we are willing to conclude that there is evidence in Table 5.1 of positive dependence between successive daily returns, it is reasonable to argue that the evidence is not sufficient to reject the hypothesis that the market is efficient. With 1,200 to 1,700 observations per stock, a sample autocorrelation as small as .05 is for some stocks more than two standard deviations to the right of its expected value under the hypothesis that the true value of the coefficient is zero. Thus, a sample coefficient as small as .05 is extreme in the statistical sense, and so is fairly convincing statistical evidence against the hypothesis that the true value of the coefficient is zero. Suppose, however, that the true value of an autocorrelation is as much as twice .05, or $\rho(\tilde{R}_{jt},$ $\tilde{R}_{j,t-\tau}) = .10$. The square of the autocorrelation between $\tilde{R}_{jt}$ and $\tilde{R}_{j,t-\tau}$ is the proportion of the variance of $\tilde{R}_{jt}$ that can be attributed to the linear regression function relationship between $\tilde{R}_{jt}$ and $\tilde{R}_{j,t-\tau}$. Thus, the squared autocorrelation can be interpreted as a measure of the information that $\tilde{R}_{j,t-\tau}$ carries for $\tilde{R}_{jt}$; it tells how much we can reduce the variance of $\tilde{R}_{jt}$ if we have exact knowledge about the linear regression function relationship between $\tilde{R}_{jt}$ and $\tilde{R}_{j,t-\tau}$. In these terms, an autocorrelation $\rho(\tilde{R}_{it}, \tilde{R}_{j,t-\tau}) = .10$ says that $\tilde{R}_{j,t-\tau}$ doesn't carry much information about $\tilde{R}_{jt}$, since only 1 percent of the variance of $\tilde{R}_{jt}$ can be attributed to the linear relationship between $\tilde{R}_{jt}$ and $\tilde{R}_{j,t-\tau}$. Thus, even though the true autocorrelation is nonzero, it is close enough to zero for us to conclude that market efficiency is a reasonable description of the world.

The evidence in Table 5.1 is actually good support for the hypothesis that the market is efficient. The sample autocorrelations are close to zero in magnitude and in terms of "proportion of variance explained." Although the true autocorrelations might be nonzero, given the large sample sizes and the small observed autocorrelations it is unlikely that the true autocorrelations are much different from zero, which means that is is unlikely that the deviation of $\tilde{R}_{j,t-\tau}$ from $E(\tilde{R}_j)$ carries much information about the deviation of $\tilde{R}_{jt}$ from $E(\tilde{R}_j)$. Thus, at least with respect to potential information in past daily returns, the hypothesis that the market is efficient seems to be a good approximation to the world.

For each of the 30 Dow-Jones Industrial stocks, Table 5.2 shows sample autocorrelations of monthly returns for lags $\tau = 1, 2, 3$, that is, for returns one, two, and three months apart. The time period is July 1963–June 1968. Although the sample autocorrelations in Table 5.2 are generally close to zero, they are also more variable and thus larger in absolute value than those for the daily returns in Table 5.1. This is to be expected, since the sample size in Table 5.2 is only $T = 60$, whereas in Table 5.1 the samples include from 1,200 to 1,700 daily returns. As a consequence, the standard deviations for the autocorrelations in Table 5.2 are about .13, while those for the autocorrelations in Table 5.1 are generally less than .03. Thus, the results in both tables are consistent with market efficiency, but those for the larger samples in Table 5.1 give a much more precise feeling for how close the true autocorrelations of returns are to zero.

TABLE 5.2

Autocorrelations of Monthly Returns on the Dow-Jones Industrials for July 1963–June 1968

COMPANY	$r(R_{jt}, R_{j,t-1})$	$r(R_{jt}, R_{j,t-2})$	$r(R_{jt}, R_{j,t-3})$
Allied Chemical	.017	−.236	.144
Alcoa	−.306*	.076	.172
American Can	−.061	.003	.162
AT&T	−.117	.096	.173
American Tobacco	−.282*	−.058	.156
Anaconda	−.097	−.170	.156
Bethlehem Steel	−.034	−.044	−.101
Chrysler	.207	−.020	−.093
Du Pont	−.076	−.023	.234
Eastman Kodak	.098	−.175	.088
General Electric	−.028	−.093	−.006
General Foods	−.001	−.023	.070
General Motors	−.091	−.060	.254
Goodyear	−.034	−.294*	−.114
International Harvester	−.050	.236	.140
International Nickel	−.196	−.043	−.058
International Paper	−.010	−.367*	.089
Johns Manville	.080	−.128	−.113
Owens Illinois	.139	−.176	−.288*
Procter and Gamble	−.193	.193	−.077
Sears	−.105	−.020	.253
Standard Oil (Calif.)	−.111	.093	.207
Standard Oil (N. J.)	−.025	−.032	.242
Swift and Co.	.020	.005	−.020
Texaco	.076	−.148	.004
Union Carbide	−.080	.022	.047
United Aircraft	−.143	.136	.159
U.S. Steel	−.113	.023	.067
Westinghouse	.099	−.005	−.094
Woolworth	.078	.062	.098
Averages	−.044	−.016	.065

*Sample autocorrelation is at least two standard deviations to the left or to the right of its expected value under the hypothesis that the true auto-correlation is zero.

The success of the tests of market efficiency based on autocorrelations is somewhat fortuitous. The tests derive from a model of market equilibrium in which the equilibrium expected return on any security is constant through time. If this assumption is incorrect, tests of market efficiency based on autocorrelations could fail even though the market is efficient. For example, suppose the equilibrium expected return on security j, $E_m(\tilde{R}_{jt}|\phi^m_{t-1})$, instead of being constant at the value of $E(\tilde{R}_j)$, tends to wander around $E(\tilde{R}_j)$, which we now interpret as the long-run average value of $E_m(\tilde{R}_{jt}|\phi^m_{t-1})$. Moreover, suppose, as indicated in Figure 5.1, $E_m(\tilde{R}_{jt}|\phi^m_{t-1})$ tends to stay above

FIGURE 5.1

Hypothetical Behavior of Returns in an Efficient Market Where Equilibrium Expected Returns Wander Substantially Through Time

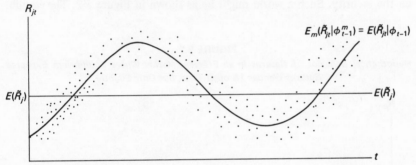

or below $E(\tilde{R}_j)$ for fairly long periods. If the market is efficient, then $E_m(\tilde{R}_{mt}|\phi^m_{t-1}) = E(\tilde{R}_{jt}|\phi_{t-1})$, the equilibrium return expected by the market is the true expected return. With an efficient market, the deviations of $\tilde{R}_{jt}$ from $E(\tilde{R}_{jt}|\phi_{t-1})$ would be more or less as shown in Figure 5.1; the current deviation is unpredictable from the past deviations. In this example, however, the deviation of $\tilde{R}_{jt}$ from $E(\tilde{R}_j)$ is quite predictable from the behavior of the most recent past deviations. Thus, if we used autocorrelations computed from an assumed constant average return to test market efficiency, we would conclude that the market is inefficient, when in fact the high autocorrelations in the returns would be due to the wandering of the equilibrium expected return. This sort of behavior of the equilibrium expected return is in no way ruled out by market efficiency.

The point, of course, is that any test of market efficiency is simultaneously a test of assumptions about market equilibrium. Since tests based on autocorrelations yield evidence consistent with the hypothesis that the market is efficient, the tests can also be interpreted as evidence consistent with the assumption that, at least for common stocks, equilibrium expected returns are constant through time. This does not say, however, that the evidence proves the assumption. Like any statistical evidence, it is at best consistent with the general model in the sense that it does not lead to rejection either of the hypothesis that the market is efficient or of the hypothesis that equilibrium expected returns are constant through time. This just means that, at least as far as the evidence from the autocorrelations is concerned, the hypotheses are reasonable models of the world. Like any models, however, they are just approximations that are useful for organizing our thinking about the phenomena of interest. They do not necessarily rule out other models which might also be reasonable and useful approximations.

For example, the evidence from the autocorrelations is also consistent with a world where the equilibrium expected return is not literally constant but where its variation is trivial relative to other sources of variation in the return on the security. Such a world might be as shown in Figure 5.2. The equilib-

FIGURE 5.2
Hypothetical Behavior of Returns in an Efficient Market Where Equilibrium Expected Returns Wander Through Time, but Only Slightly

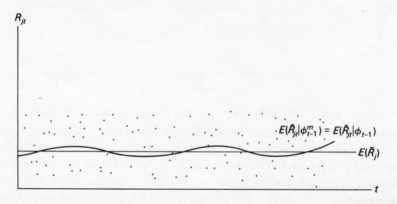

rium expected return $E_m(\tilde{R}_{jt}|\phi_{t-1}^m)$ wanders through time about its long-run average value $E(\tilde{R}_j)$, but its wanderings are slight compared to those pictured in Figure 5.1. In Figure 5.2, the deviations of $E_m(\tilde{R}_{jt}|\phi_{t-1}^m)$ from $E(\tilde{R}_j)$ are so small relative to the deviations of $\tilde{R}_{jt}$ from $E_m(\tilde{R}_{jt}|\phi_{t-1}^m)$ that the wanderings of $E_m(\tilde{R}_{jt}|\phi_{t-1}^m)$ would only be a source of slight positive autocorrelations in successive values of $\tilde{R}_{jt}$.

Thus, autocorrelations of $\tilde{R}_{jt}$ that are close to zero are consistent with a world where the market is efficient and equilibrium expected returns are constant through time. But they are also consistent with a world where the market is efficient and where equilibrium expected returns wander over time, but not sufficiently to have any important effect on the autocorrelations of $\tilde{R}_{jt}$. Since we are primarily concerned with testing market efficiency, the choice between these two models of equilibrium expected returns is not important. All we need to say about equilibrium expected returns is that apparently they do not wander enough or in such a way as to invalidate autocorrelations as a tool for testing the hypothesis that the market is efficient, at least with respect to any information in historical returns.

C. Returns Conform to the Market Model

The tests of market efficiency discussed above are concerned with whether prices of securities fully reflect any information in past prices or returns. Historically, this was the first concern. When the results seemed to support the market efficiency hypothesis (see, for example, the various studies reported in Cootner 1964), attention turned to tests in which the concern was the speed of price adjustment to other publicly available information, like announcements of stock splits, earnings reports, new security issues, mergers, and so forth. As the tests of market efficiency moved in the direction of new information subsets, the models of market equilibrium on which the tests were based also became more complex.

THE MARKET MODEL AND MARKET EQUILIBRIUM

One of the models used extensively in more advanced tests of market efficiency is the market model of Chapters 3 and 4. In these chapters the market model is treated as an implication of the assumption that the joint distribution of security returns is multivariate normal. For current purposes, we formulate the model in part as an outgrowth of the process by which market equilibrium is attained.

The return on security j from time $t-1$ to time t is

$$\tilde{R}_{jt} = \frac{\tilde{p}_{jt} - p_{j,t-1}}{p_{j,t-1}} = \frac{\tilde{p}_{jt}}{p_{j,t-1}} - 1.0. \tag{13}$$

If the true distribution of $\tilde{p}_{jt}$, $f(p_{jt}|\phi_{t-1})$, is normal, then for any given price set by the market at time $t-1$, the distribution of $\tilde{R}_{jt}$, $f(R_{jt}|\phi_{t-1})$, will also be normal, since $\tilde{R}_{jt}$ is just a linear transformation of $\tilde{p}_{jt}$. Moreover, if the true joint distribution of the prices of different securities at time t, $f(p_{1t}, \ldots, p_{nt}|\phi_{t-1})$ is multivariate normal, the joint distribution of security returns, $f(R_{1t}, \ldots, R_{nt}|\phi_{t-1})$, is multivariate normal. According to Chapter 3, this implies that the market model holds. Thus,

$$E(\tilde{R}_{jt}|\phi_{t-1}, R_{mt}) = \alpha_j + \beta_j R_{mt} \tag{14}$$

with

$$\beta_j = \frac{\text{cov}\,(\tilde{R}_{jt}, \tilde{R}_{mt})}{\sigma^2(\tilde{R}_{mt})} \text{ and } \alpha_j = E(\tilde{R}_{jt}|\phi_{t-1}) - \beta_j E(\tilde{R}_{mt}|\phi_{t-1}). \quad (15)$$

As in earlier chapters, the market portfolio m contains all common stocks on the NYSE, and R_{mt} is just the average of the returns on these stocks from $t - 1$ to t. The return on security j at time t will not, of course, be equal to its conditional expected value as given by (14). The returns at t can be described in terms of the market model equation

$$\tilde{R}_{jt} = \alpha_j + \beta_j \tilde{R}_{mt} + \tilde{\epsilon}_{jt}, \quad (16)$$

where the disturbance $\tilde{\epsilon}_{jt}$ is the deviation of $\tilde{R}_{jt}$ from its conditional expected value, and equation (14) implies

$$E(\tilde{\epsilon}_{jt}|\phi_{t-1}, R_{mt}) = 0.0. \quad (17)$$

Equations (14) to (17) describe properties of the true bivariate normal joint distribution of $\tilde{R}_{jt}$ and $\tilde{R}_{mt}$, $f(R_{jt}, R_{mt}|\phi_{t-1})$, implied by the assumption that the joint distribution of security prices for time t, $f(p_{1t}, \ldots, p_{nt}|\phi_{t-1})$ is multivariate normal, and given the security prices set by the market at time $t - 1$. The market is assumed to set prices at time $t - 1$ in the usual way. That is, on the basis of the information ϕ_{t-1}^m, the market assesses a joint distribution on prices at time t, $f_m(p_{1t}, \ldots, p_{nt}|\phi_{t-1}^m)$, and then sets equilibrium prices at time $t - 1$ on the basis of characteristics of $f_m(p_{1t}, \ldots, p_{nt}|\phi_{t-1}^m)$. If $f_m(p_{1t}, \ldots, p_{nt}|\phi_{t-1}^m)$ is the density function of a multivariate normal distribution, then $f_m(R_{jt}, R_{mt}|\phi_{t-1}^m)$ is the density function of a bivariate normal distribution, and the market's assessments imply market model equations, which, by analogy with (14) to (17), are

$$E_m(\tilde{R}_{jt}|\phi_{t-1}^m, R_{mt}) = \alpha_j^m + \beta_j^m R_{mt} \quad (18)$$

$$\beta_j^m = \frac{\text{cov}_m(\tilde{R}_{jt}, \tilde{R}_{mt})}{\sigma_m^2(\tilde{R}_{mt})}, \text{ and } \alpha_j^m = E_m(\tilde{R}_{jt}|\phi_{t-1}^m) - \beta_j^m E_m(\tilde{R}_{mt}|\phi_{t-1}^m) \quad (19)$$

$$\tilde{R}_{jt} = \alpha_j^m + \beta_j^m R_{mt} + \tilde{\epsilon}_{jt}^m \quad (20)$$

$$E_m(\tilde{\epsilon}_{jt}^m|\phi_{t-1}^m, R_{mt}) = 0.0. \quad (21)$$

To indicate that equations (18) to (21) describe the market model as seen by the market, subscript and superscript m's are included in the notation for the various parameters. As usual, if the market is efficient, the market's view is the correct view, so that $\phi_{t-1}^m = \phi_{t-1}$ and $f_m(p_{1t}, \ldots, p_{nt}|\phi_{t-1}^m) = f(p_{1t}, \ldots, p_{nt}|\phi_{t-1})$. Then the various parameters in equations (18) to (21) are identical to those in (14) to (17).

With all of the additional interpretation in terms of the process by which market equilibrium is attained, we still have only presented the market model as an implication of multivariate normality. In tests of market efficiency, an interpretation in economic terms is also given. The market return $\tilde{R}_{mt}$ is presumed to reflect information that becomes available at time t that, to a greater or lesser extent, affects the returns on all securities. When security prices are set at time $t-1$, $\tilde{R}_{mt}$ is unknown. It has a true distribution $f(R_{mt}|\phi_{t-1})$ which, in formal terms, is implied by the joint distribution of security prices, $f(p_{1t}, \ldots, p_{nt}|\phi_t)$, and the prices of securities set at $t-1$. But in economic terms, $f(R_{mt}|\phi_{t-1})$ is presumed to capture the uncertainty at time $t-1$ about information that will become available at time t which will affect the returns on all securities. The market model coefficient β_j in (14) to (16) therefore measures the sensitivity of the return on security j to $\tilde{R}_{mt}$ and thus, indirectly, to information about marketwide factors.

While $\tilde{R}_{mt}$ is presumed to reflect new information at time t that affects returns on all securities, the disturbance $\tilde{\epsilon}_{jt}$ in (16) is presumed to reflect information that becomes available at t that is more specifically relevant to the prospects of security j. The disturbance $\tilde{\epsilon}_{jt}$ has a true distribution $f(\epsilon_{jt}|\phi_{t-1}, R_{mt})$ that summarizes the uncertainty about the company-specific information which will become available at time t. The value of $\tilde{\epsilon}_{jt}$ observed at t will be a drawing from this distribution. Tests of market efficiency based on the market model are primarily concerned with the adjustment of prices to company-specific information, like earnings announcements, new issues of securities, stock splits, and so on. Thus, the tests concentrate on the behavior of $\tilde{\epsilon}_{jt}$ or, more precisely, on the behavior of estimates of $\tilde{\epsilon}_{jt}$.

Specifically, in empirical tests of market efficiency based on the market model, it is (implicitly) assumed that during each period the market sets prices so that $f_m(R_{jt}, R_{mt}|\phi_{t-1}^m)$, its perceived bivariate normal joint distribution of $\tilde{R}_{jt}$ and $\tilde{R}_{mt}$, is constant through time. This means that the market sets prices so that α_j^m, β_j^m, and its perceived distribution on $\tilde{\epsilon}_{jt}$ are the same, period after period. Moreover, it is assumed that it is possible for the market to set prices so that the true joint distribution of $\tilde{R}_{jt}$ and $\tilde{R}_{mt}$, $f(R_{jt}, R_{mt}|\phi_{t-1})$, is constant through time, which means that α_j, β_j and the true distribution of $\tilde{\epsilon}_{jt}$ are the same, period after period.

Suppose now that the market is efficient, so that $f_m(R_{jt}, R_{mt}|\phi_{t-1}^m)$ and $f(R_{jt}, R_{mt}|\phi_{t-1})$ coincide. If the joint distribution of security returns is stationary through time, then the market model can be estimated from time series data on $\tilde{R}_{jt}$ and $\tilde{R}_{mt}$, using the least squares procedures of Chapters 3 and 4. The result is the estimated version of (16),

$$\tilde{R}_{jt} = \tilde{a}_j + \tilde{b}_j \tilde{R}_{mt} + \tilde{e}_{jt},$$

where $\tilde{a}_j$, $\tilde{b}_j$ and $\tilde{e}_{jt}$ are unbiased estimators of $\alpha_j = \alpha_j^m$, $\beta_j = \beta_j^m$, and $\tilde{\epsilon}_{jt} = \tilde{\epsilon}_{jt}^m$ in (16) and (20). Thus, when the market is efficient and the joint distribution of security returns is constant through time,

$$E(\tilde{e}_{jt} | \phi_{t-1}, R_{mt}) = E(\tilde{e}_{jt} | \phi_{t-1}, R_{mt}) = E_m(\tilde{\epsilon}_{jt}^m | \phi_{t-1}^m, R_{mt}) = 0.$$

In words, with an efficient market and stationary return distributions, the deviation of $\tilde{e}_{jt}$ from zero results solely from new information that becomes available at t; there is no way to use information available at $t - 1$ as the basis of a correct nonzero assessment of the expected value of $\tilde{e}_{jt}$. For example, if new information about the earnings of firm j is available at $t - 1$, this affects the price of the security set at $t - 1$, which in turn determines $\tilde{e}_{j,t-1}$. But in an efficient market, the earnings information available at $t - 1$ is fully utilized in setting the price of the security at $t - 1$. This means that at t, the deviation of $\tilde{e}_{jt}$ from zero cannot be due to the earnings information that was available at $t - 1$. On the other hand, if the market is inefficient, and in particular if there is some lag in the adjustment of prices to new company-specific information, then the residual for period t is to some extent predictable for information available at $t - 1$; that is, ϕ_{t-1} and ϕ_{t-1}^m no longer coincide, so that

$$E(\tilde{e}_{jt} | \phi_{t-1}, R_{mt}) \neq 0.$$

Rather than continuing this general and excessively formal discussion of how tests of market efficiency can be approached in the context of the market model, we let the details of the approach arise naturally in the course of a discussion of a specific study, the work on stock splits by Fama, Fisher, Jensen, and Roll (1969), henceforth FFJR, which is the first study that uses the market model as the basis of a test of market efficiency.

SPLITS AND THE ADJUSTMENT OF STOCK PRICES TO NEW INFORMATION

Since the only apparent result of a stock split is to multiply the number of shares per shareholder, without changing any shareholder's claims on the firm's assets, splits in themselves are not necessarily sources of new information. The presumption of FFJR is that splits may be associated with more fundamentally important information. The idea is to examine security returns around split dates to determine whether there is any unusual behavior and, if so, to what extent it can be accounted for by relationships between splits and more fundamental variables.

The FFJR sample includes all 940 stock splits (involving 622 different common stocks) on the NYSE during 1927–1959 where the split was at least 5 new shares for 4 old shares, and where the security was listed for at least 12 months before and after the split. Since any information in a split is likely to be company-specific, the search for unusual behavior in the returns on split securities is confined to market model residuals. Thus, the first step is to obtain estimates of the market model coefficients α_j and β_j of (16) for each of the 622 different securities in the sample. To estimate α_j and β_j, FFJR use all of the monthly return data available for security j during the 1926-1960 period. They then compute the market model residuals for each security for the period from 29 months before to 30 months after any split of the security.

FFJR are concerned with generalizations about the types of return behavior typically associated with splits, rather than with the effects of a split on any individual common stock.* To abstract from the eccentricities of specific cases, they rely on the process of averaging. They concentrate attention on the behavior of cross-sectional averages of estimated regression residuals in the months surrounding split dates. The procedure is as follows: For a given split, define month 0 as the month in which the effective date of a split occurs. Thus, month 0 is not the same chronological date for all securities. Some securities split more than once and hence have more than one month 0. Month 1 is then defined as the month immediately following the split month, month -1 is the month preceding, and so forth. Now define the average residual for month s, with s measured relative to the split month, as

$$\bar{e}_s = \frac{\sum_{j=1}^{N_s} e_{js}}{N_s}$$

where e_{js} is the sample market model residual for security j in month s and N_s is the number of splits for which data are available in month s. The principal tests involve examining the behavior of $\bar{e}_s$ for s in the interval $-29 \leqslant s \leqslant 30$, that is, for the 60 months surrounding the split month. Since FFJR are also interested in the cumulative effects of abnormal return behavior in months surrounding the split month, they also study the behavior of the cumulative average residual U_s, defined as

$$U_s = \sum_{k=-29}^{s} \bar{e}_k.$$

The average residual $\bar{e}_s$ can be interpreted as the average deviation, in month s relative to the split month, of the returns of split stocks from their normal relationships with the market. Similarly, the cumulative average residual U_s can be interpreted as the cumulative deviation from month -29 to month s; it shows the cumulative effects of the wanderings of the returns of split stocks from their normal relationships with the market.

Since the hypothesis about the effects of splits on returns developed by FFJR centers on the dividend behavior of split shares, in some of their tests

*Much of the discussion that follows is taken directly from FFJR.

they separately examine splits that are associated with increased dividends and splits that are associated with decreased dividends. In order to abstract from general changes in dividends across the market, "increased" and "decreased" dividends are measured relative to the average dividends paid by all securities on the New York Stock Exchange during the relevant time periods. The dividends are classified as follows: Define the dividend change ratio as total dividends (per equivalent unsplit share) paid in the 12 months after the split, divided by total dividends paid during the 12 months before the split. Dividend "increases" are then defined as cases where the dividend change ratio of the split stock is greater than the ratio for the NYSE as a whole, while dividend "decreases" include cases of relative dividend decline. FFJR then define $\bar{e}_s^+$, $\bar{e}_s^-$ and U_s^+, U_s^- as the average and cumulative average residuals for splits followed by "increased" ($^+$) and "decreased ($^-$) dividends.

The most important empirical results of the FFJR study are summarized in Table 5.3 and Figures 5.3a–b and 5.4a–d. Table 5.3 presents the average residuals, cumulative average residuals, and the sample size for each of the two dividend classifications ("increased" and "decreased") and for the total of all splits for each of the 60 months surrounding the split. Figures 5.3a–b.

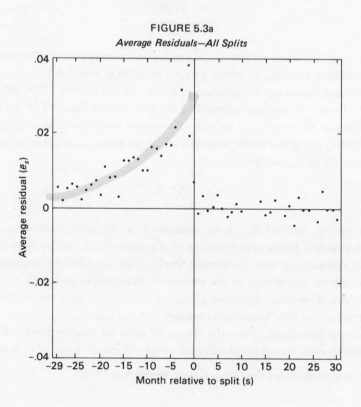

FIGURE 5.3a

Average Residuals—All Splits

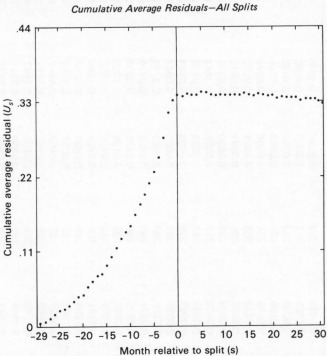

FIGURE 5.3b
Cumulative Average Residuals—All Splits

Source: Eugene F. Fama, Lawrence Fisher, Michael Jensen, and Richard Roll, "The Adjustment of Stock Prices to New Information," *International Economic Review* 10 (February 1969): 1–21. Reprinted by permission.

present graphs of the average and cumulative average residuals for the total samples of splits, and Figures 5.4a–d present these graphs for each of the two dividend classifications.

Figures 5.3a, 5.4a and 5.4b show that the average residuals in the 29 months prior to the split are uniformly positive for all splits and for both classes of dividend behavior. This can hardly be attributed entirely to the splitting process. FFJR cite evidence that in only about 10 percent of the splits was the time between the announcement date and the effective date greater than four months. Thus, it seems safe to say that the split cannot account for the behavior of the residuals as far as $2\frac{1}{2}$ years in advance of the split date. Rather, FFJR suggest that there is probably a sharp improvement, relative to the market, in the earnings prospects of a company sometime during the years immediately preceding a split.

Note from Figure 5.3a and Table 5.3 that when all splits are examined together, the largest positive average residuals occur in the three or four months

TABLE 5.3

Analysis of Residuals in Months Surrounding Stock Splits on the NYSE, 1927-1959

(1) MONTH s	SPLITS FOLLOWED BY DIVIDEND "INCREASES"			SPLITS FOLLOWED BY DIVIDEND "DECREASES"			ALL SPLITS		
	(2) AVERAGE $\bar{e}_s^+$	(3) CUMULATIVE AVERAGE U_s^+	(4) SAMPLE SIZE N_s^+	(5) AVERAGE $\bar{e}_s^-$	(6) CUMULATIVE U_s^-	(7) SAMPLE SIZE N_s^-	(8) AVERAGE $\bar{e}_s$	(9) CUMULATIVE U_s	(10) SAMPLE SIZE N_s
−29	0.0062	0.0062	614	0.0033	0.0033	252	0.0054	0.0054	866
−28	0.0013	0.0075	617	0.0030	0.0063	253	0.0018	0.0072	870
−27	0.0068	0.0143	618	0.0007	0.0070	253	0.0050	0.0122	871
−26	0.0054	0.0198	619	0.0085	0.0155	253	0.0063	0.0185	872
−25	0.0042	0.0240	621	0.0089	0.0244	254	0.0056	0.0241	875
−24	0.0020	0.0259	623	0.0026	0.0270	256	0.0021	0.0263	879
−23	0.0055	0.0315	624	0.0028	0.0298	256	0.0047	0.0310	880
−22	0.0073	0.0388	628	0.0028	0.0326	256	0.0060	0.0370	884
−21	0.0049	0.0438	633	0.0131	0.0457	257	0.0073	0.0443	890
−20	0.0044	0.0482	634	0.0005	0.0463	257	0.0033	0.0476	891
−19	0.0110	0.0592	636	0.0102	0.0565	258	0.0108	0.0584	894
−18	0.0076	0.0668	644	0.0089	0.0654	260	0.0080	0.0664	904
−17	0.0072	0.0739	650	0.0111	0.0765	260	0.0083	0.0746	910
−16	0.0035	0.0775	655	0.0009	0.0774	260	0.0028	0.0774	915
−15	0.0135	0.0909	659	0.0101	0.0875	260	0.0125	0.0900	919
−14	0.0135	0.1045	662	0.0100	0.0975	263	0.0125	0.1025	925
−13	0.0148	0.1193	665	0.0099	0.1074	264	0.0134	0.1159	929
−12	0.0138	0.1330	669	0.0107	0.1181	266	0.0129	0.1288	935
−11	0.0098	0.1428	672	0.0103	0.1285	268	0.0099	0.1387	940
−10	0.0103	0.1532	672	0.0082	0.1367	268	0.0097	0.1485	940
−9	0.0167	0.1698	672	0.0152	0.1520	268	0.0163	0.1647	940
−8	0.0163	0.1862	672	0.0140	0.1660	268	0.0157	0.1804	940
−7	0.0159	0.2021	672	0.0083	0.1743	268	0.0138	0.1942	940
−6	0.0194	0.2215	672	0.0106	0.1849	268	0.0169	0.2111	940
−5	0.0194	0.2409	672	0.0100	0.1949	268	0.0167	0.2278	940
−4	0.0260	0.2669	672	0.0104	0.2054	268	0.0216	0.2494	940
−3	0.0325	0.2993	672	0.0204	0.2258	268	0.0289	0.2783	940
−2	0.0390	0.3383	672	0.0296	0.2554	268	0.0363	0.3147	940
−1	0.0199	0.3582	672	0.0176	0.2730	268	0.0192	0.3339	940

	SPLITS FOLLOWED BY DIVIDEND "INCREASES"			SPLITS FOLLOWED BY DIVIDEND "DECREASES"			ALL SPLITS		
(1) MONTH s	(2) AVERAGE $\bar{e}_s^+$	(3) CUMULATIVE U_s^+	(4) SAMPLE SIZE N_s^+	(5) AVERAGE $\bar{e}_s^-$	(6) CUMULATIVE U_s^-	(7) SAMPLE SIZE N_s^-	(8) AVERAGE $\bar{e}_s$	(9) CUMULATIVE U_s	(10) SAMPLE SIZE N_s
0	0.0131	0.3713	672	-0.0090	0.2640	268	0.0068	0.3407	940
1	0.0016	0.3729	672	-0.0088	0.2552	268	-0.0014	0.3393	940
2	0.0052	0.3781	672	-0.0024	0.2528	268	0.0031	0.3424	940
3	0.0024	0.3805	672	-0.0089	0.2439	268	-0.0008	0.3416	940
4	0.0045	0.3851	672	-0.0114	0.2325	268	0.0000	0.3416	940
5	0.0048	0.3898	672	-0.0003	0.2322	268	0.0033	0.3449	940
6	0.0012	0.3911	672	-0.0038	0.2285	268	-0.0002	0.3447	940
7	0.0008	0.3919	672	-0.0106	0.2179	268	-0.0024	0.3423	940
8	-0.0007	0.3912	672	-0.0024	0.2155	268	-0.0012	0.3411	940
9	0.0039	0.3951	672	-0.0065	0.2089	268	0.0009	0.3420	940
10	-0.0001	0.3950	672	-0.0027	0.2062	268	-0.0008	0.3412	940
11	0.0027	0.3977	672	-0.0056	0.2006	268	0.0003	0.3415	940
12	0.0018	0.3996	672	-0.0043	0.1963	268	0.0001	0.3416	940
13	-0.0003	0.3993	666	0.0014	0.1977	264	0.0002	0.3418	930
14	0.0006	0.3999	653	0.0044	0.2021	258	0.0017	0.3435	911
15	-0.0037	0.3962	645	0.0026	0.2047	258	-0.0019	0.3416	903
16	0.0001	0.3963	635	-0.0040	0.2007	257	-0.0011	0.3405	892
17	0.0034	0.3997	633	-0.0011	0.1996	256	0.0021	0.3426	889
18	-0.0015	0.3982	628	0.0025	0.2021	255	-0.0003	0.3423	883
19	-0.0006	0.3976	620	-0.0057	0.1964	251	-0.0021	0.3402	871
20	-0.0002	0.3974	604	0.0027	0.1991	246	0.0006	0.3409	850
21	-0.0037	0.3937	595	-0.0073	0.1918	245	-0.0047	0.3361	840
22	0.0047	0.3984	593	-0.0018	0.1899	244	0.0028	0.3389	837
23	-0.0026	0.3958	593	0.0043	0.1943	242	-0.0006	0.3383	835
24	-0.0022	0.3936	587	0.0031	0.1974	238	-0.0007	0.3376	825
25	0.0012	0.3948	583	-0.0037	0.1936	237	-0.0002	0.3374	820
26	-0.0058	0.3890	582	0.0015	0.1952	236	-0.0037	0.3337	818
27	-0.0003	0.3887	582	0.0082	0.2033	235	0.0021	0.3359	817
28	0.0004	0.3891	580	-0.0023	0.2010	236	-0.0004	0.3355	816
29	0.0012	0.3903	580	-0.0039	0.1971	235	-0.0003	0.3352	815
30	-0.0033	0.3870	579	-0.0025	0.1946	235	-0.0031	0.3321	814

SOURCE: Eugene F. Fama, Lawrence Fisher, Michael Jensen, and Richard Roll, "The Adjustment of Stock Market Prices to New Information," *International Economic Review* 10 (February 1969): 10–11. Reprinted by permission.

FIGURE 5.4a
Average Residuals for Dividend "Increases"

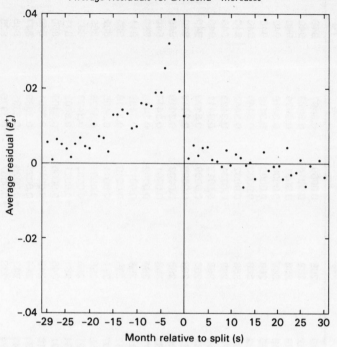

Month relative to split (s)

FIGURE 5.4b
Average Residuals for Dividend "Decreases"

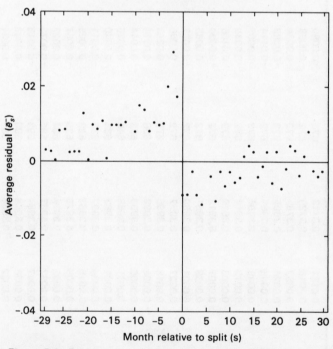

Month relative to split (s)

Source: Figures 5.4a–5.4d from Eugene F. Fama, Lawrence Fisher, Michael Jensen, and Richard Roll, "The Adjustment of Stock Prices to New Information," *International Economic Review* 10 (February 1969): 1–21. Reprinted by permission.

FIGURE 5.4c
Cumulative Average Residuals for Dividend "Increases"

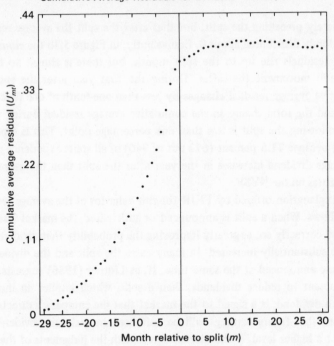

FIGURE 5.4d
Cumulative Average Residuals for Dividend "Decreases"

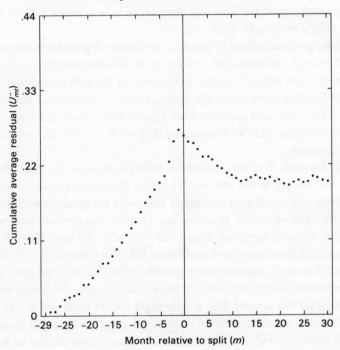

immediately preceding the split, but that after the split the average residuals are randomly distributed about 0. Equivalently, in Figure 5.3b the *cumulative* average residuals rise up to the split month, but there is almost no further systematic movement thereafter. During the first year after the split, the cumulative average residual changes by less than one-tenth of one percentage point, and the total change in the cumulative average residual during the $2\frac{1}{2}$ years following the split is less than one percentage point. This is especially striking because 71.5 percent (672 out of 940) of all splits experience greater percentage dividend increases in the year after the split than the average for all securities on the NYSE.

The explanation offered by FFJR for this behavior of the average residuals is as follows. When a split is announced or anticipated, the market interprets this, and correctly so, as greatly improving the probability that dividends will soon be substantially increased. In many cases the split and the dividend increase are announced at the same time. If, as Lintner (1956) suggests, firms are reluctant to reduce dividends, then a split, which implies an increased expected dividend, is a signal to the market that the company's directors are confident that future earnings will be sufficient to maintain dividend payments at a higher level. If the market agrees with the judgments of the directors, then it is possible that the large price increases in the months immediately preceding a split are due to altered expectations concerning the future earning potential of the firm and thus of its shares, rather than to any intrinsic effects of the split itself.

If the information effects of actual or anticipated dividend increases explain the behavior of common stock returns in the months immediately surrounding a split, then return behavior subsequent to the split should be substantially different in cases where the dividend increase materializes than in cases where it does not. It is apparent from Figures 5.4a–d that the differences are in fact substantial, and FFJR argue that they are in the direction predicted by their hypothesis.

Thus, the fact that the cumulative average residuals for both dividend classes rise sharply in the few months before the split is consistent with the hypothesis that the market recognizes that splits are usually associated with higher dividend payments. In some cases, however, the dividend increase, if it occurs, is declared sometime during the year after the split. Thus, it is not surprising that the average residuals (Figure 5.4a) for stocks in the "increased" dividend class are in general slightly positive in the year after the split, so that the cumulative average residuals for these stocks (Figure 5.4c) drift upward. The fact that this upward drift is only slight can be explained in two ways. First, in many cases the dividend increase associated with a split is declared and the corresponding price adjustments take place before the end of the split month. Second, according to the FFJR hypothesis, when the split is declared, even if no dividend announcement is made, there is some price adjustment in anticipation of future dividend increases. Thus, only a slight additional adjustment is necessary when the dividend increase actually takes place. By one year after the split, the returns on stocks which have experienced dividend "increases" have resumed their normal relationships to market returns, since from this point onward the average residuals are small and randomly scattered about zero.

FFJR contend that the behavior of the residuals for stock splits associated with "decreased" dividends provides the strongest evidence for their split hypothesis. For stocks in the "decreased" dividend class the average and cumulative average residuals (Figures 5.4b and 5.4d) rise in the few months before the split but then plummet in the few months following the split, when the anticipated dividend increase is not forthcoming. These split stocks with poor dividend performance on the average perform poorly in each of the 12 months following the split, but their period of poorest performance is in the few months immediately after the split, when the improved dividend, if it were coming at all, would most likely be declared. The hypothesis is further reinforced by the observation that when a year has passed after the split, the cumulative average residual has fallen to about where it was five months prior to the split, which is probably about the earliest time reliable information concerning a possible split is likely to reach the market. Thus, by the time it becomes clear that the anticipated dividend increase is not forthcoming, the apparent effects of the split seem to be completely wiped away, and the stock's returns revert to their normal relationship with market returns. In sum, FFJR suggest that once the information effects of associated dividend changes are properly considered, a split per se has no net effect on common stock returns.

Finally, and most important, although the behavior of post-split returns is very different depending on whether or not dividend "increases" occur, and despite the fact that a substantial majority of split securities do experience dividend "increases," when all splits are examined together (Figures 5.3a–b), the average residuals are randomly distributed about 0 during the year after the split, so that there is no net movement either up or down in the cumulative average residuals. Thus, the market apparently makes unbiased forecasts of the implications of a split for future dividends, and these forecasts are fully reflected in the price of the security by the end of the split month. After considerably more data analysis than we can summarize here, FFJR conclude that their results are consistent with the hypothesis that the stock market is efficient, at least with respect to its ability to adjust to the information implicit in a split.

One point from the remainder of the FFJR analysis should be mentioned. FFJR especially emphasize that the persistent upward drift of the cumulative average residuals in the months preceding the split is not a phenomenon that could be used to increase expected trading profits. The reason is that the behavior of the average residuals is not representative of the behavior of the residuals for individual securities. In months prior to the split, successive sample residuals for individual securities seem to be independent. But in most cases, there are a few months in which the residuals are abnormally large and positive. The months of large residuals differ from security to security, however, and the differences in timing explain why the signs of the average residuals are uniformly positive for many months preceding the split.

Since one purpose of this book is to encourage the reader to develop a critical eye for discussions of empirical work, some comments about the FFJR analysis are relevant. First, FFJR are somewhat "aggressive" in interpreting their empirical results. In their view, the unusual behavior of the returns on a splitting security in the months immediately preceding a split reflects the information content of the dividend change that usually accompanies a split. There is, however, no direct evidence in their data that dividends or splits convey real information to the market about the future prospects of a firm. For example, an alternative view, completely consistent with their empirical results, is that dividends are a passive variable in the whole process. That is, companies tend to increase dividends when earnings increase and to decrease dividends when earnings decrease. In this view, the FFJR data suggest that splits tend to occur when firms have experienced unusual increases in earnings, which accounts for the positive average residuals of splitting shares in the months preceding the split. As chance will have it, however, the good times do not persist for all firms. Some of them experience earnings declines in the year after the split, which in the FFJR data show up as decreased dividends. Thus, the behavior of dividends is merely a proxy for the behavior of earnings, and neither dividend changes nor splits are a source of information.

It is still the case, however, that in this alternative view the FFJR evidence is consistent with the hypothesis that the market is efficient. Thus, about 30 percent of the firms will come on relatively bad times (decreased earnings) subsequent to splitting their shares, and this will be reflected in decreased dividends. If the market is efficient when adjusting security prices to the high earnings for the period preceding the split, it will take full account of the chances of good and bad times in the period following the split, so that splitting shares will not, on average, experience unusually high or low returns in the period following the split. In Figures 4.3a–b the behavior of the average residuals in the years after the split is consistent with this implication of market efficiency.

OTHER STUDIES OF PUBLIC ANNOUNCEMENTS

Variants of the method of residual analysis developed by FFJR have been used by others to study the effects of different kinds of public announcements, and all of these studies are in most respects consistent with the hypothesis that the market is efficient.

For example, using data on 261 major firms for the period 1946-1966, Ball and Brown (1968) apply the method to study the effects of annual earnings announcements. They use the residuals from a time series regression of the annual earnings of a firm on the average earnings of all their firms to classify the firm's earnings for a given year as having "increased" or "decreased" relative to the market. Residuals from estimates of the market model obtained from monthly data are then used to compute cumulative average return residuals separately for those earnings that "increased" and those that "decreased." The cumulative average return residuals rise throughout the year in advance of the announcement for the "increased" earnings category, and fall for the "decreased" earnings category. Ball and Brown conclude that no more than about 10-15 percent of the information in the annual earnings announcement has not been anticipated by the month of the announcement.

Further evidence consistent with the hypothesis that the market is efficient is provided in the work of Scholes (1972) on large secondary offerings of common stock, that is, large underwritten sales of existing common stocks by individuals and institutions. He finds that, on average, large secondary issues are associated with a decline of between 1 and 2 percent in the cumulative average residual returns for the corresponding common stocks. Since the magnitude of the price adjustment is unrelated to the size of the issue, Scholes concludes that the adjustment is not due to "selling pressure," as is commonly believed, but rather results from negative information implicit in the fact that somebody is trying to sell a large block of a firm's stock. Moreover, he presents evidence that the value of the information in a secondary offering depends to some extent on the vendor. As might be expected, by far the largest negative cumulative average residuals occur where the vendor is the corporation itself or one of its officers, with investment companies a distant second. The identity of the vendor is not generally known at the time of a secondary offering, however, and corporate insiders need only report their transactions in their company's stock to the Securities and Exchange Commission within six days after a sale. By this time, the market on average has fully adjusted to the information in the secondary, as indicated by the fact that the average residuals behave randomly thereafter.

To avoid giving a falsely monolithic appearance to the evidence consistent with the hypothesis that the market is efficient, we should note that although Scholes's work indicates that prices adjust efficiently to the public information in a secondary, his work is also evidence that corporate insiders at least sometimes have important information about their firms that is not yet reflected in prices. This is evidence against market efficiency, since it says that prices do not fully reflect *all* available information.* Moreover, other evidence of the same sort is offered by Neiderhoffer and Osborne (1966), who point out that specialists on the NYSE apparently use their monopolistic access to information concerning unfilled limit orders (orders to buy and sell at given prices) to generate monopoly profits.

Like any null hypothesis, however, the hypothesis that the market is efficient is not likely to be a completely accurate view of the world. We might look at the various tests as providing the evidence that helps us to judge the extent to which the market is efficient and the extent to which it is inefficient. The evidence discussed so far is consistent with market efficiency in the sense that prices fully reflect publicly available information, such as past prices, splits, earnings announcements, etc., but there is also evidence that the market is not completely efficient, since corporate insiders and NYSE specialists apparently have access to information that is not fully reflected in prices. In practical terms, the evidence suggests that if an investor or investment counselor only has access to publicly available information, then the hypothesis that the market is efficient is an appropriate approximation to the world. If prices fully reflect publicly available information, then such information cannot be used to beat the market. On the other hand, market efficiency is an inappropriate view of the world for a corporate insider or an NYSE specialist, since they sometimes have access to and can trade on information that is not fully reflected in prices.

D. Returns Conform to a Risk-Return Relationship

The most recent tests of market efficiency make use of a model of market equilibrium in which the market sets prices at any time $t - 1$ so that there is a positive relationship between the expected return on a security from time $t - 1$ to time t and the risk of the security. For example, one such study, by Mandelker (1974), is concerned with the adjustment of prices to the announcement that two firms will merge. Another, by Jaffe (1974), is concerned with the adjustment of prices to any information implicit in insider trading.

We cannot do justice to tests of market efficiency based on risk-return models of market equilibrium until we consider these models in some detail. This is the topic of Chapters 7–9. Tests of market efficiency that are based on these risk-return models are discussed in Chapter 9.

*Evidence that insiders have monopolistic access to information about their firm is also to be found in the work of Lorie and Neiderhoffer (1968) and Jaffe (1974). Jaffe's work is discussed in Chapter 9.

IV. Conclusions and Some Fine Points of the Theory

In the model of price formation presented in this chapter, at any time $t - 1$ the "market" assesses a joint distribution for security prices at time t, $f_m(p_{1t}, \ldots, p_{nt} | \phi_{t-1}^m)$. The characteristics of this distribution, along with some propositions about the nature of market equilibrium (for example, equilibrium expected returns are positive), are then the basis of the equilibrium prices of securities, $p_{1,t-1}, \ldots, p_{n,t-1}$, set at $t - 1$. This is clearly a simplified view of the world, and we now discuss some of the ways in which it is not completely realistic.

First, in the description of the process of price formation given above, the "market" assesses probability distributions and the "market" sets prices. This can only be a completely accurate view of the world if all the individual participants in the market (a) have the same information and (b) agree on its implications for the joint distribution of future prices. Neither of these conditions is completely descriptive. Nor is it completely realistic to presume that when market prices are determined, they result from a conscious assessment of the joint distribution of security prices by all or most or even many investors.

Pushing this line of attack even further, the two-step process of price formation assumed in this chapter masks some even stronger assumptions about the analytical capabilities of investors. Thus, prices set at $t - 1$ result from an assessment of the joint distribution of prices for time t. But the world is not presumed to end at time t, so the prices that turn up at t must themselves be the consequences of a market equilibrium. That is, pushing the two-step process of price formation one period ahead, prices at time t will be set on the basis of characteristics of the joint distribution assessed at t on prices for $t + 1$. And the process will be repeated at each future point in time. Thus, when at time $t - 1$ the market assesses a joint distribution on prices for t, it must assess what the state of the world at $t - 1$ implies about the likelihoods of different states at t, and it must assume something about how it will respond to different states in setting security prices at t. To do this, it must in turn make assessments about the likelihoods of different states of the world at $t + 1$ and how it will respond to them in setting prices and so forth. In short, the discussion of a two-step process of price formation in the simple model glosses over the fact that the first step, assessment of the joint distribution of prices for time t, also implies assessments of the joint distributions of prices at each future point in time, with all of the judgments about future interactions between the market and the state of the world that these assessments imply.*

Looking at the model in these terms, the student who is newly exposed to scientific research is often tempted to conclude that the model has no value. To draw such a conclusion solely on the basis of the model's unrealistic assumptions is to forget what modeling is all about. The first purpose of a model is to improve understanding of some real-world phenomenon. If the phenomenon is a complicated one, like the adjustment of stock prices to new information, then to abstract from unimportant and potentially confusing details and to focus on the important aspects of the problem, we must impose some simple structure on the world. Since the structure is simplified and is thus not a completely realistic view of the world, we call it a model.

Thus, in deriving testable implications of the hypothesis that the capital market is efficient, we structure the world in terms of a "market" that assesses probability distributions on future prices and then sets current prices on the basis of these assessed distributions. Strictly speaking, this implies that investors have monolithic opinions about available information and act single-mindedly to ensure that their assessments are properly reflected in current prices. What we really have in mind, however, is a market where there is indeed disagreement among investors but where the force of common judgments is sufficient to produce an orderly adjustment of prices to new information. Such an intuitively appealing statement is, however, too unspecific to be the basis for formal tests. Formal tests require formal models, with their more or less unrealistic structuring of the world. And we are, after all, ultimately interested in judging market efficiency on the basis of tests.

The models we have used so far are extreme simplifications of the world. In later chapters we discuss more sophisticated models, which are nevertheless still far short of, and are not meant to be, completely realistic views of the world. The simple models of this chapter have, however, been useful. They seem to lead to meaningful tests of market efficiency, tests which, on the whole, suggest a market that responds well to new information. At the very least, the tests contribute to our understanding of the phenomenon of interest, the behavior of security prices, and this is all we require in order to conclude that the simple models from which they are derived are useful.

---

*Actually, the notation presented in Section II allowed for all this, and the reader who was a bit puzzled then might look back at that discussion now.

CHAPTER

6

Short-Term Interest Rates as Predictors of Inflation

Chapter 5 discussed the theory of an efficient capital market and tests of the theory on common stocks. We turn now to the bond market. First, however, there are a few pages of background material.

I. The Market for U.S. Treasury Bills

A. Treasury Bills: What Are They?

Every week the U.S. Treasury issues at auction certain bonds called Treasury bills, each of which represents a promise to pay $1,000 on the maturity date of the bill. Bills with three months to maturity have been issued since as early as 1935; both three- and six-month bills have been issued since 1959; and one-year bills have been issued since late 1964. A Treasury bill pays no interest, and any return comes from the fact that bills are issued and subsequently sell in the market at "discounts," that is, at prices below their maturity value of $1,000.

This chapter is an expanded version of Eugene F. Fama, "Short-Term Interest Rates as Predictors of Inflation," *American Economic Review* 65 (June 1975): 269–282.

Although Treasury bills are not traded on organized exchanges like the New York Stock Exchange, an active market for them is maintained by dealers. For any given Treasury bill, a dealer stands ready to quote both a "bid" price, the price at which he is willing to buy the bill, and an "asked" price, the price at which he is willing to sell. Thus, although the Treasury issues bills for three, six, and twelve months, there is always an active secondary market for bills that acquire intermediate maturities with the passage of time.

This chapter is concerned with efficiency in the market for one- to six-month Treasury bills, that is, bills that have one to six months before payment of the promised $1,000. Theory and evidence are first presented for one-month bills. The results are then generalized to bills with longer maturities.

B. Real and Nominal Returns on a One-Month Bill

The return on a one-month Treasury bill from the end of month $t-1$ to the end of month t is

$$R_t = \frac{v_t - v_{t-1}}{v_{t-1}} = \frac{\$1,000 - v_{t-1}}{v_{t-1}}, \tag{1}$$

where v_t is the "price" of the bill at t and v_{t-1} is its price at $t-1$.* Since the bill has one month to maturity, at time $t-1$ we know that its "price" at t will be $1,000. Thus, once v_{t-1} is set, the return R_t on the bill that will be realized at t is known for certain, and R_t can be interpreted as the one-month rate of interest, set in the market at the end of month $t-1$ and realized at the end of month t.

PROBLEM I.B

1. Convince yourself that the return from the end of month $t-1$ to the end of month t on a bill with two or more months to maturity at $t-1$ is uncertain at $t-1$. Convince yourself that if the interval from $t-1$ to t is two (or three, or n) months, then the return from $t-1$ to t on a bill with two (or three, or n) months to maturity is known at $t-1$.

ANSWER

1. The return from $t-1$ to t on a one-month bill is known at $t-1$ only because v_t, the "price" of the bill to be obtained at t, is known to be $1,000. For bills with maturities longer than one month, prices to be observed at the end of month t are uncertain at the end of month $t-1$.

---

*We often say "at time $t-1$" or "at $t-1$" in place of the longer statement "at the end of month $t-1$."

If the interval from $t - 1$ to t is two months, then equation (1) is the two-month return on a two-month bill. Since the price of the bill at the end of two months, $v_t = \$1,000$, is known at time $t - 1$, once v_{t-1} is set, the return on the bill for the two months from $t - 1$ to t is known at $t - 1$. In general, the n-month return on an n-month bill is known once the price of the bill is set at $t - 1$. It is important to keep this in mind when we later generalize the model of bill market efficiency to bills with two or more months to maturity.

The prices v_{t-1} and v_t and the return R_t are in "nominal" terms, which means that they are stated in units of money, or dollars. Investors, however, are assumed to be concerned with the "real" values of securities and returns. The real value of a security is its price in terms of consumption goods and services, and its real return is likewise its return in units of consumption goods and services. Since the concepts are important, we explain them in some detail.

Although prices are stated in terms of money, it is always possible to use these nominal prices to compute prices in units of any specific good or security. For example, on July 31, 1974, the price of a share of IBM was $201 and the price of a bushel of wheat was $4.50. The implied price of a share of IBM in terms of bushels of wheat was $201/4.50 = 44.67$ bushels. That is, one dollar purchased 1/4.50 bushel of wheat. One share of IBM purchased 201 dollars. The exchange value or price of a share of IBM in terms of bushels of wheat was $201(\frac{1}{4.50}) = 44.67$ bushels. One can likewise compute the price of a share of IBM, or anything else, in terms of shares of the common stock of GM or in the units of any other commodity.

The term "real" price or "real" value pushes these ideas one step further. The real price or real value of a commodity is its price in units of some "representative" bundle of consumption goods and services. In this chapter, the bundle of consumption goods and services on which the U.S. Consumer Price Index (CPI) is based is taken as representative. The CPI, which is computed monthly by the U.S. Bureau of Labor Statistics, is the nominal or money value of a "market basket" of consumption goods and services (food, housing, entertainment, etc.), where the weights given to individual items in the bundle are based on the proportions of family budgets allocated to these items by a large sample of primarily urban wage earners.* The proce-

---

*For a complete description of the CPI, see U.S. Bureau of Labor Statistics, *Handbook of Methods for Surveys and Studies*, BLS Bulletin no. 1458 (1971). The CPI is actually an index number; the quoted value of the CPI for time t is the price of the CPI consumption bundle for time t divided by the price of the bundle in 1967. Since this rescaling has no effect on anything we do, we refer to the index as the nominal price of the CPI consumption bundle.

dure for determining the price of a commodity in units of the consumption bundle represented by the CPI is exactly as in the wheat example above. One divides the nominal or money price of the commodity by the CPI.

The real price can also be interpreted as follows. Let p_t be the value of the CPI at the end of month t. Since p_t is the nominal price of a particular bundle of consumption goods,

$$\pi_t = 1/p_t \tag{2}$$

is the number of units of the bundle that can be purchased with one dollar; in other words, π_t is the purchasing power of one dollar in terms of the bundle of consumption goods on which the CPI is based. To get the price or exchange value of a commodity in units of the CPI consumption bundle, one multiplies the nominal or money price of the commodity, which is the number of dollars that it can be exchanged for, by π_t, which is the number of units of the CPI consumption bundle that can be purchased with one dollar.

We now examine what is meant by a real return. If v_{t-1} is the nominal price of a Treasury bill with one month to maturity at the end of month $t-1$, then the real price or value of the bill at $t-1$ is $v_{t-1}\pi_{t-1}$. The real return on the bill from the end of month $t-1$ to the end of month t is the change in its real value during the month, divided by its real value at $t-1$. Thus the real return r_t is

$$r_t = \frac{v_t\pi_t - v_{t-1}\pi_{t-1}}{v_{t-1}\pi_{t-1}}. \tag{3}$$

The real return is the return on the one-month bill in units of the CPI consumption bundle per unit of the bundle invested at the end of month $t-1$. In contrast, the nominal return R_t of equation (1) is the return in units of dollars per dollar invested at the end of month $t-1$. Thus, the difference between nominal and real prices or returns is a difference in units of measurement. Nominal prices and returns are in dollars, while real prices and returns are in units of a representative consumption bundle.

The real return can be given a convenient interpretation in terms of the nominal return R_t and

$$\Delta_t = \frac{\pi_t - \pi_{t-1}}{\pi_{t-1}} = \frac{p_{t-1} - p_t}{p_t}, \tag{4}$$

which we call the rate of change in the purchasing power of money from the end of month $t-1$ to the end of month t. First rewrite (3) as

$$r_t = \frac{v_t}{v_{t-1}} \cdot \frac{\pi_t}{\pi_{t-1}} - 1. \tag{5}$$

From (1) and (4) we then determine that

$$r_t = (1 + R_t)(1 + \Delta_t) - 1$$
$$= R_t + \Delta_t + R_t\Delta_t. \qquad (6)$$

In monthly data the cross-product $R_t\Delta_t$ is generally negligible relative to either R_t or Δ_t.* Thus although the equality only holds as an approximation, no harm is done if (6) is reduced to

$$r_t = R_t + \Delta_t. \qquad (7)$$

In words, the real return from the end of month $t - 1$ to the end of month t on a Treasury bill with one month to maturity at $t - 1$ is the nominal return plus the rate of change in purchasing power from $t - 1$ to t.

Note from (4) that the sign of Δ_t is opposite to the sign of $p_t - p_{t-1}$, the change in the nominal price of the CPI consumption bundle. When there is inflation (the nominal price of the consumption bundle goes up), the purchasing power of money goes down, while deflation (the nominal price of the consumption bundle goes down) implies an increase in the purchasing power of money. In terms of returns, inflation (a decrease in the purchasing power of money), implies that the real return is less than the nominal return, while real returns are greater than nominal returns when there is deflation.

PROBLEMS I.B

2. Convince yourself that the preceding statement about the relationship between real and nominal returns and inflation or deflation applies to any security.

3. Convince yourself that if the interval from $t - 1$ to t is two (or three or n) months and if r_t, R_t, and Δ_t are the returns and the rate of change in purchasing power for two (or three or n) months, then (6) and (7) still hold.

4. Show that if the continuously compounded rate of change in purchasing power and the continuously compounded real and nominal returns are used, then (7) is an exact expression; that is, using asterisks to denote the continuously compounded versions of r_t, R_t, and Δ_t,

$$r_t^* = R_t^* + \Delta_t^*.$$

ANSWERS

2. Just check that the algebra of equations (3) to (7) is the same for any security.

3. The algebra of equations (3) to (7) does not depend on the time interval from $t - 1$ to t. If the interval is two (or three or n) months, then (6) and (7)

*Evidence on this is discussed below in Problem VI.C.*3.*

are appropriate expressions for the relationships among r_t, R_t, and Δ_t for two (or three or n) months.

4. The continuously compounded real return is the value of r_t^* that satisfies

$$1 + r_t = e^{r_t^*},$$

where r_t is the simple real return of (3) or (6) and $e \cong 2.714$ is the base of the system of natural logarithms. Likewise, the continuously compounded nominal return and the continuously compounded rate of change in purchasing power are the values of R_t^* and Δ_t^* that satisfy

$$1 + R_t = e^{R_t^*} \quad \text{and} \quad 1 + \Delta_t = e^{\Delta_t^*}.$$

Thus,

$$1 + r_t = (1 + R_t)(1 + \Delta_t)$$

implies

$$e^{r_t^*} = e^{R_t^*} e^{\Delta_t^*} = e^{R_t^* + \Delta_t^*}$$

and

$$r_t^* = R_t^* + \Delta_t^*.$$

Since the theory and empirical work that follow build on (7), it is clear that everything could be done in terms of the continuously compounded versions of the variables, and the sleight of hand used in going from (6) to (7) would be avoided. Any advantages of one approach over the other, however, are more apparent than real. Although the continuously compounded results are not reported, all tests have been done with both versions of the variables and the results are numerically almost identical. The reason is that for periods of one to six months, the periods we eventually use in the tests, the simple and continuously compounded versions of the variables have almost the same numerical values. If this seems puzzling, the reader might review Section VI of Chapter 1.

We are ready to discuss the theory of market efficiency as it applies to one-month Treasury bills. It is well to note from the outset, however, that the theory applies directly to bills with longer maturities. To "generalize" the theory in this way, one need only change the interpretation of the interval of time from $t - 1$ to t—for example, from one month to two months.

II. Inflation and Efficiency in the Bill Market: Theory

For bills with one month to maturity, the task of the market at time $t - 1$ is to determine an equilibrium nominal price v_{t-1}. As usual, an equilibrium price is a market-clearing price, a price at which the demand for one-month bills by investors is equal to the supply. In analyzing the efficiency of the market, we concentrate on one issue: In setting the nominal price of a one-month bill at $t - 1$, does the market correctly use available information about Δ_t, the rate of change in the purchasing power of money from $t - 1$ to t? If the answer to this question is affirmative, then we say that the price v_{t-1} "fully reflects" available information about Δ_t and that the market for one-month bills is efficient.

A. Market Efficiency in a World of Perfect Foresight

We examine first the case where there is perfect foresight: that is, the unrealistic world where π_t, the purchasing power of money at time t, is costless information available to all investors at time $t - 1$. In such a world, when the market sets v_{t-1}, all quantities in the real return equation (3) are known. In terms of equation (7), when the market sets v_{t-1}, the real and nominal returns r_t and R_t are set. Since v_{t-1} is an equilibrium price, r_t and R_t can be interpreted as the equilibrium real and nominal rates of interest set in the market at $t - 1$ and realized by investors at t.

Although an equilibrium nominal price v_{t-1} sets both r_t and R_t, the nominal rate is a passive variable. The ultimate purpose of investment is assumed to be consumption. Although prices are stated in nominal terms, investors are assumed to make their decisions on the basis of real quantities, that is, on the eventual value of their investments in terms of consumption goods and services. When an equilibrium nominal price v_{t-1} is set at $t - 1$, what is really determined is the equilibrium real rate of interest r_t. In terms of (7), the equilibrium nominal rate is just the value of R_t which ensures that the bill will yield the equilibrium real rate, given that the rate of change in purchasing power from $t - 1$ to t will be Δ_t. Market efficiency then simply says that in setting v_{t-1}, the market does not ignore the costless information about Δ_t, so that v_{t-1} fully reflects the available information about Δ_t.

B. Market Efficiency in a World of Uncertainty

RETURNS AND THE INFLATION RATE IN AN UNCERTAIN WORLD

The world in which we live is uncertain. In an uncertain world, $\tilde{\pi}_t$ is a random variable at $t-1$, indicated by the usual tilde, which means that the real return

$$\tilde{r}_t = \frac{v_t \tilde{\pi}_t - v_{t-1} \pi_{t-1}}{v_{t-1} \pi_{t-1}} \tag{8}$$

is likewise a random variable at $t-1$. Note, however, that $\tilde{r}_t$ is a random variable at $t-1$ only because $\tilde{\pi}_t$ is a random variable. Equivalently, with uncertainty about $\tilde{\pi}_t$,

$$\tilde{r}_t = R_t + \tilde{\Delta}_t; \tag{9}$$

that is, the real return from $t-1$ to t on a bill with one month to maturity at $t-1$ is a random variable at $t-1$ only because $\tilde{\Delta}_t$, the rate of change in the purchasing power of money from $t-1$ to t, is uncertain at $t-1$. The nominal return R_t is known for certain at $t-1$.

This property of bills explains why we focus on them. The goal is to examine how well the market uses information about future inflation in setting bill prices. If investors are concerned with real returns on securities, then since all uncertainty in the real return on a one-month bill is uncertainty about the change in the purchasing power of money during the month, one-month bills are the clear choice for studying how well the market absorbs information about inflation one month ahead. For the same reason, n-month bills are the logical choice for studying how well the market predicts inflation n months ahead.

We pause also to note that the introduction of uncertainty changes slightly our use of words. We use the term "rate of interest" only for rates that represent returns that will be realized for certain over the period covered by the rate. Thus, in a world of perfect foresight, we refer to r_t, which is known at $t-1$, as either the real return or the real rate of interest from $t-1$ to t. In a world of uncertainty, since $\tilde{r}_t$ is unknown at $t-1$, we refer to it only as the real return. Since the existence of uncertainty does not change the fact that R_t is known at $t-1$, we continue to call it either the nominal return or the nominal rate of interest.

GENERAL DESCRIPTION OF AN EFFICIENT MARKET

In an uncertain world, efficiency requires a somewhat more sophisticated market than when there is perfect foresight. In a perfectly certain world, efficiency only requires that in setting the nominal price of a bill at $t-1$, the market uses the information about the known value of Δ_t, the rate of change in purchasing power from $t-1$ to t. In an uncertain world, market efficiency requires that in setting v_{t-1}, the market correctly use all available information to assess the distribution of $\tilde{\Delta}_t$.

In the notation of Chapter 5, if ϕ_{t-1} is the set of information available at

$t-1$, and if ϕ^m_{t-1} is the set of information used by the market to assess the distribution of $\tilde{\Delta}_t$, then market efficiency means that

$$\phi^m_{t-1} = \phi_{t-1}, \tag{10}$$

the information used by the market is all the available information. Moreover, efficiency means that the market understands the implications of any set of information for the distribution of $\tilde{\Delta}_t$, so that

$$f_m(\Delta_t | \phi) = f(\Delta_t | \phi), \tag{11}$$

where $f_m(\Delta_t | \phi)$ is the probability density function for $\tilde{\Delta}_t$ assessed by the market from the information ϕ, $f(\Delta_t | \phi)$ is the true density function implied by ϕ, and ϕ is any set of information. Together, equations (10) and (11) imply

$$f_m(\Delta_t | \phi^m_{t-1}) = f(\Delta_t | \phi_{t-1}), \tag{12}$$

which is the concise, formal way of saying that at $t-1$ the market correctly uses all available information to assess the distribution of $\tilde{\Delta}_t$.

When the market sets the nominal price of a one-month bill at $t-1$, R_t is also set. Given the relationship among $\tilde{r}_t$, R_t, and $\tilde{\Delta}_t$ of equation (9), the market's assessed distribution for the real return $\tilde{r}_t$ is implied by R_t and its assessed distribution for $\tilde{\Delta}_t$. If (12) holds—that is, if the market is efficient—then the market's assessed distribution for $\tilde{r}_t$ is the true distribution

$$f_m(r_t | \phi^m_{t-1}, R_t) = f(r_t | \phi_{t-1}, R_t). \tag{13}$$

In sum, if the market is efficient, then in setting the nominal price of a one-month bill at $t-1$, the market correctly uses all available information to assess the distribution of $\tilde{\Delta}_t$. In this sense, v_{t-1} fully reflects all available information about $\tilde{\Delta}_t$. Since an equilibrium value of v_{t-1} implies an equilibrium value of R_t, the one-month nominal rate of interest set at $t-1$ fully reflects all available information about $\tilde{\Delta}_t$. Finally, when an efficient market sets R_t, the distribution of the real return $\tilde{r}_t$ it perceives is the true distribution.

PROBLEM II.B

1. Why does the conditioning argument R_t appear in (13) but not in (12)?

ANSWER

1. Given equation (9), a distribution for $\tilde{r}_t$ cannot be specified until a value of R_t is specified. It is assumed, however, that the distribution of $\tilde{\Delta}_t$ can be specified without knowledge of R_t. The assumed process of price formation is that the market uses ϕ^m_{t-1} to assess the distribution of $\tilde{\Delta}_t$, and this assessment is the basis of the equilibrium value of R_t.

Note that, as in Chapter 5, the information sets ϕ_{t-1}^m and ϕ_{t-1} do not include prices of securities set at $t-1$. Rather, the prices set at $t-1$ are based on assessments derived from ϕ_{t-1}^m, which, in an efficient market, coincides with ϕ_{t-1}.

III.   A Model of Market Equilibrium

A.   *Why Do We Need a Model of Market Equilibrium?*

The preceding description of an efficient market for one-month Treasury bills is so general that it has no testable implications. All we have said is that in pricing a one-month bill at $t-1$, an efficient market correctly uses available information to assess the distribution of $\tilde{\Delta}_t$. Equations (10) to (13) are formal notation for this statement, but the quantities that would be needed to test the statement are unobservable. Since we cannot directly observe either $f_m(\Delta_t | \phi_{t-1}^m)$ or $f(\Delta_t | \phi_{t-1})$, we cannot determine whether the two are the same. Thus, we cannot, on the basis of what has been said so far, determine whether the bill market is efficient.

What the model lacks is a more detailed specification of the link between $f_m(\Delta_t | \phi_{t-1}^m)$ and v_{t-1}; we must specify how the equilibrium price of a bond at $t-1$ is related to the characteristics of the market-assessed distribution of $\tilde{\Delta}_t$. This is the point made repeatedly in Chapter 5: A test of market efficiency must be based on a model of market equilibrium, and any test is simultaneously a test of efficiency and of the assumed model of equilibrium. Fortunately, a simple model of market equilibrium produces successful joint tests of bill market efficiency and of the model of market equilibrium. We first discuss the model and then, in Section IV, the types of tests that can be derived from it. Finally, in Sections V and VI we turn to the data.

B.   *The Model*

The first assumption is that in decisions concerning one-month bills, the primary concern of investors is the distribution of the real return on a bill. The real return $\tilde{r}_t$, the nominal return R_t, and the rate of change in purchasing power $\tilde{\Delta}_t$ are related according to equation (9). A value of the nominal price v_{t-1} implies a value of R_t. Given R_t and the market's assessed distribution of $\tilde{\Delta}_t$, the market's assessed distribution of $\tilde{r}_t$ is implied. A market equilibrium depends visibly on a market-clearing value of the nominal price v_{t-1}, but it is assumed that what really causes investors to demand exactly the outstanding supply of bills is the nature of the implied "equilibrium distribution" of the real return $f_m(r_t | \phi_{t-1}^m, R_t)$.

Testable propositions about market efficiency require propositions about the characteristics of the "equilibrium distribution" $f_m(r_t | \phi_{t-1}^m, R_t)$ that results from an equilibrium price v_{t-1} at $t-1$. As in Chapter 5, we concentrate on the mean of the distribution, and the proposition about $E_m(\tilde{r}_t | \phi_{t-1}^m, R_t)$ is that for all t and ϕ_{t-1}^m,

$$E_m(\tilde{r}_t | \phi_{t-1}^m, R_t) = E(\tilde{r}). \tag{14}$$

Thus the model of bill market equilibrium is the statement that each month the market sets the price of a one-month bill so that it perceives the expected real return on the bill to be $E(\tilde{r})$. The equilibrium expected real return is $E(\tilde{r})$ for every time $t-1$ and for any set of information ϕ_{t-1}^m that the market might use to set v_{t-1}. In short, the model of equilibrium is the simple statement that the equilibrium expected real return on a one-month bill is the same every month.

The assumption that the expected real return on a bill is constant through time is anathema to many economists. The reasons are many, but there is no need to discuss them here. For our purpose, the assumption is a useful approximation if it leads to meaningful tests of efficiency, and this is a question that can be left to the data.

IV. Testable Implications of Market Efficiency When the Equilibrium Expected Real Return Is Constant Through Time

A. The Real Return

Equation (13) says that in an efficient market, the market's perceived distribution for the real return, $f_m(r_t | \phi_{t-1}^m, R_t)$, is the true distribution $f(r_t | \phi_{t-1}, R_t)$. Since the market-assessed and true distributions are identical, the means of the distributions are identical,

$$E_m(\tilde{r}_t | \phi_{t-1}^m, R_t) = E(\tilde{r}_t | \phi_{t-1}, R_t). \tag{15}$$

If market equilibrium is characterized by (14), then with the efficiency condition (15), we have

$$E(\tilde{r}_t | \phi_{t-1}, R_t) = E(\tilde{r}). \tag{16}$$

In words, at any time $t-1$ the market sets the price of a one-month bill in such a way that its assessment of the expected real return is the constant

$E(\tilde{r})$. Since an efficient market correctly uses all available information, $E(\tilde{r})$ is also the true expected real return on the bill.

The general testable implication of this combination of market efficiency with a model of market equilibrium is that there is no way to use ϕ_{t-1}, the set of information available at time $t - 1$, or any subset of ϕ_{t-1}, as the basis of a correct assessment of the expected real return on a one-month bill which is other than $E(\tilde{r})$. One subset of ϕ_{t-1} is the time series of past real returns. If equation (16) holds, then

$$E(\tilde{r}_t | r_{t-1}, r_{t-2}, \dots) = E(\tilde{r}); \qquad (17)$$

that is, there is no way to use the time series of past real returns as the basis of a correct assessment of the expected real return from $t - 1$ to t which is other than $E(\tilde{r})$. One way to test this statement is with sample autocorrelations of $\tilde{r}_t$. If (17) holds, the autocorrelations of $\tilde{r}_t$ for all lags are equal to zero. The reasoning is the same as that in Section III.B of Chapter 5.

Sample autocorrelations of $\tilde{r}_t$ are presented later, but it is well to emphasize one point now. Like any tests, the autocorrelations are joint tests of market efficiency and of the model for the equilibrium expected real return. If the hypothesis that the autocorrelations of $\tilde{r}_t$ are zero is rejected, then (17) is rejected; such a result would indicate that the true expected real return from $t - 1$ to t is not a constant, but rather varies according to the sequence of past returns. Since the sequence of past real returns is a subset of ϕ_{t-1}, nonzero autocorrelations of real returns imply that (16) can be rejected.

Equation (16), however, is a combination of the market efficiency condition of (15) with the equilibrium expected return model of (14). If we insist on (14), then the hypothetical evidence indicates rejection of (15). In this interpretation, the market sets the price of a one-month bill so that it perceives the expected real return to be the constant $E(\tilde{r})$, but it neglects relevant information, with the result that the true expected real return varies from month to month as a function of the time series of past real returns. Thus, the market is inefficient. On the other hand, nonzero autocorrelations are also consistent with a world where (15) holds but (14) does not; the market may well be efficient, and the nonzero autocorrelations may reflect equilibrium expected real returns that change as a function of the sequence of past real returns. Market efficiency is no way rules out such behavior in the equilibrium expected returns.

B. The Nominal Interest Rate as a Predictor of Inflation

There are tests that distinguish more precisely the hypothesis that the market is efficient from the hypothesis that the equilibrium expected real return is constant through time. Once the nominal interest rate R_t is set at time $t-1$, from (9), the relationship between the market's expectation of the rate of change in purchasing power, the nominal rate of interest, and the market's expectation of the real return is

$$E_m(\tilde{\Delta}_t|\phi_{t-1}^m) = E_m(\tilde{r}_t|\phi_{t-1}^m, R_t) - R_t. \tag{18}$$

If the expected real return is the constant $E(\tilde{r})$, then (18) becomes

$$\left(E_m(\tilde{\Delta}_t|\phi_{t-1}^m) = E(\tilde{r}) - R_t.\right) \tag{19}$$

Since $E(\tilde{r})$ is a constant, this equation says that all variation through time in the nominal rate R_t is a direct reflection of variation in the market's assessment of the expected rate of change in purchasing power. If the market is efficient, then

$$E_m(\tilde{\Delta}_t|\phi_{t-1}^m) = E(\tilde{\Delta}_t|\phi_{t-1}), \tag{20}$$

the market's assessment of the expected value of $\tilde{\Delta}_t$ is the best possible assessment. Equations (19) and (20) then imply that

$$E(\tilde{\Delta}_t|\phi_{t-1}) = E(\tilde{r}) - R_t. \tag{21}$$

In words, if the market is efficient, and if the equilibrium expected real return on a one-month bill is constant through time, then all variation through time in the nominal rate R_t mirrors variation in the best possible assessment of the expected value of $\tilde{\Delta}_t$. In this sense, the nominal rate R_t observed at $t-1$ is the best possible predictor of the rate of inflation from $t-1$ to t.

Tests of (21) are easily devised. Given (21), we can write the true expected value of $\tilde{\Delta}_t$, conditional on ϕ_{t-1} and R_t, as

$$E(\tilde{\Delta}_t|\phi_{t-1}, R_t) = E(\tilde{r}) - R_t. \tag{22}$$

Thus, once R_t is set at $t-1$, the details of ϕ_{t-1}, the information that an efficient market uses to set R_t, become irrelevant. The information in ϕ_{t-1} about the expected value of $\tilde{\Delta}_t$ is summarized completely in the value of R_t.

To build these propositions into separate tests of the market efficiency hypothesis and of the hypothesis that the equilibrium expected real return is constant through time, we introduce a new class of equilibrium models that includes (14) as a special case. Suppose that at any time $t-1$ the market always sets the price of a one-month bill so that it perceives the expected real return to be

$$E_m(\tilde{r}_t|\phi_{t-1}^m, R_t) = \alpha_0 + \gamma R_t. \tag{23}$$

This equation implies that

$$E_m(\tilde{r}_t|\phi_{t-1}^m, R_t) - E_m(\tilde{r}_{t-1}|\phi_{t-2}^m, R_{t-1}) = \gamma(R_t - R_{t-1}),$$

so that γ can be interpreted as the proportion of the change in the nominal rate from one month to the next which reflects a change in the equilibrium expected real return. With the expression for $E_m(\tilde{r}_t | \phi_{t-1}^m, R_t)$ in (23), (18) becomes

$$E_m(\tilde{\Delta}_t | \phi_{t-1}^m) = \alpha_0 + \alpha_1 R_t, \quad \alpha_1 = \gamma - 1.0. \tag{24}$$

Thus, in the new model, γ is the proportion of the variation of the one-month nominal rate that reflects variation in the equilibrium expected real return, and $-\alpha_1 = (1 - \gamma)$ is the proportion of the variation in R_t that reflects variation in the market's assessment of the expected rate of change in purchasing power. In the special case where the equilibrium expected real return is constant through time, $\gamma = 0$, $\alpha_1 = -1$, and all variation in R_t mirrors variation in $E_m(\tilde{\Delta}_t | \phi_{t-1}^m)$.

If the market is efficient, then true expected values can be substituted for market assessments, and (23) and (24) become

$$E(\tilde{r}_t | \phi_{t-1}, R_t) = \alpha_0 + \gamma R_t \tag{25}$$

$$E(\tilde{\Delta}_t | \phi_{t-1}) = \alpha_0 + \alpha_1 R_t, \quad \alpha_1 = \gamma - 1.0. \tag{26}$$

Alternatively, by analogy with equations (21) and (22), equation (26) can be interpreted as saying that once R_t is set at $t - 1$, the true expected value of $\tilde{\Delta}_t$ conditional on ϕ_{t-1} and R_t is

$$E(\tilde{\Delta}_t | \phi_{t-1}, R_t) = \alpha_0 + \alpha_1 R_t, \quad \alpha_1 = \gamma - 1.0. \tag{27}$$

From Chapter 3 we recognize the conditional expected value $E(\tilde{\Delta}_t | \phi_{t-1}, R_t)$ as the regression function of $\tilde{\Delta}_t$ on ϕ_{t-1} and R_t. Thus, estimates of α_0 and α_1 can be obtained by applying least squares to

$$\tilde{\Delta}_t = \alpha_0 + \alpha_1 R_t + \tilde{\epsilon}_t, \tag{28}$$

where the disturbance $\tilde{\epsilon}_t$ is the deviation of $\tilde{\Delta}_t$ from its conditional expected value. Equation (22) tells us that if the equilibrium expected real return is constant through time,

$$\alpha_0 = E(\tilde{r}) \text{ and } \alpha_1 = -1.0. \tag{29}$$

If the regression coefficient estimates are inconsistent with this hypothesis, the model of a constant equilibrium expected real return is rejected. The more general interpretation of (23)—that is, with unrestricted values of the coefficients—can then be taken as the model for the equilibrium expected real return, and other results from the estimates of (28) can be used to test market efficiency.

Thus, like (22), equation (27) says that in an efficient market, R_t summarizes all the information about the expected value of $\tilde{\Delta}_t$ which is in ϕ_{t-1}. In terms of (28), this means that

$$E(\tilde{\epsilon}_t | \phi_{t-1}) = 0.0. \tag{30}$$

That is, since all available information about the expected value of $\tilde{\Delta}_t$ is summarized in the value of R_t set in the market at $t-1$, there is no way to use any information available at $t-1$ as the basis of a correct nonzero assessment of the expected value of the disturbance $\tilde{\epsilon}_t$ in (28). Part of the information available to the market at $t-1$ is the time series of the historical values of the disturbance. Equation (30) implies that

$$E(\tilde{\epsilon}_t | \epsilon_{t-1}, \epsilon_{t-2}, \ldots) = 0.0; \tag{31}$$

that is, there is no way to use the time series of past values of the disturbance as the basis of a correct assessment of a nonzero expected value of $\tilde{\epsilon}_t$. One implication of (31) is that the autocorrelations of the disturbance $\tilde{\epsilon}_t$ are zero for all lags. We can use autocorrelations of the residuals from estimates of (28) to test this proposition.

The approach is easily generalized to obtain other tests of market efficiency. Equation (27) says that when the market is efficient, the nominal rate of interest R_t set in the market at $t-1$ summarizes all available information about the expected value of $\tilde{\Delta}_t$. In formal terms, the regression function of $\tilde{\Delta}_t$ on ϕ_{t-1} and R_t is a function only of R_t. To get a test of this proposition, we formulate an alternative hypothesis which says that the regression function of $\tilde{\Delta}_t$ on ϕ_{t-1} and R_t is a function of elements in ϕ_{t-1} as well as of R_t. In other words, the alternative hypothesis is that R_t does not summarize all the information available at time $t-1$ which is relevant for assessing the expected value of $\tilde{\Delta}_t$. In formulating the regression function for the alternative hypothesis, we could include, in addition to R_t, any variables that might be relevant for assessing the expected value of $\tilde{\Delta}_t$, whose values are known at $t-1$ and might be ignored by the market when it sets R_t at $t-1$.

For example, one item of information available at $t-1$ is Δ_{t-1}, the rate of change in the purchasing power of money from $t-2$ to $t-1$. If periods of inflation or deflation tend to persist, then Δ_{t-1} is relevant information for assessing the expected value of $\tilde{\Delta}_t$. If the information in Δ_{t-1} is not correctly used by the market in setting R_t, then the coefficient α_2 in

$$E(\tilde{\Delta}_t | R_t, \Delta_{t-1}) = \alpha_0 + \alpha_1 R_t + \alpha_2 \Delta_{t-1} \tag{32}$$

is nonzero. On the other hand, if the market is efficient and the equilibrium expected real return is described by (23), then the value of R_t set at $t-1$ summarizes all the information available about the expected value of $\tilde{\Delta}_t$, which includes any information in Δ_{t-1}, so that in (32) $\alpha_2 = 0$. Moreover, if the market is efficient, the analysis of equations (30) and (31) applies to the disturbance $\tilde{\epsilon}_t$ in

$$\tilde{\Delta}_t = \alpha_0 + \alpha_1 R_t + \alpha_2 \Delta_{t-1} + \tilde{\epsilon}_t, \tag{33}$$

so that the autocorrelations of the disturbance are zero for all lags. Finally, if the equilibrium expected real return is constant through time, then $\alpha_0 = E(\tilde{r})$ and $\alpha_1 = -1$.

All of these propositions can be tested with estimates of α_0, α_1, α_2, and the time series of $\tilde{\epsilon}_t$ obtained with a generalization of the least squares methods of Chapter 3. We do not discuss the statistical theory underlying the generalization. It is much the same as that in Chapter 3. For the reader who is unfamiliar with the topic, good outside references are available—for example, Johnston (1972, chap. 3)—that are no more difficult than Chapter 3 of this book.

PROBLEM IV.B

1. Why are there tildes over $\tilde{\Delta}_t$ and $\tilde{\epsilon}_t$ in (33) but not over Δ_{t-1} and R_t?

ANSWER

1. Throughout the development of the model, we are at time $t-1$ looking ahead to time t. At $t-1$, R_t and Δ_{t-1} are known, but $\tilde{\Delta}_t$ and $\tilde{\epsilon}_t$ are random variables. A similar comment applies to equation (28).

C. Summary and Reinterpretation of the Proposed Tests

In sum, the tests outlined are as follows. First, autocorrelations of the real return $\tilde{r}_t$ are joint tests of the hypotheses that the market is efficient and that the equilibrium expected real return is constant through time. In contrast, tests based on (28) and (33) provide separate results on the two facets of the model. Equations (28) and (33) allow for a world where the market sets the price of a one-month bill at any time $t-1$ so that the expected real return on the bill is described by the more general model of (23). Estimates of the coefficients α_0 and α_1 in (28) and (33) allow us to test the hypothesis that the equilibrium expected real return is constant through time, while estimates of α_2 in (33) and of the autocorrelations of the disturbances in (28) and (33) are tests of market efficiency.

The proposed tests of efficiency are limited in scope. In setting R_t at $t-1$, an efficient market correctly uses all available information ϕ_{t-1} to assess the expected value of $\tilde{\Delta}_t$. Like most tests of market efficiency, however, the tests we propose look only at limited subsets of ϕ_{t-1}. The sample autocorrelations of $\tilde{r}_t$ examine whether in assessing the expected value of $\tilde{\Delta}_t$, the market correctly uses any information in the time series of past real returns. Estimates of the autocorrelations of the disturbances from (28) and (33) are concerned with any information in the time series of the past values of the disturbances; and tests based on the estimate of α_2 in (33) are directed at any information in Δ_{t-1} that the market may have underutilized in assessing the expected value of $\tilde{\Delta}_t$.

Even this description of the information that the tests examine overstates the case. All of the proposed tests of market efficiency are different ways to examine whether, in assessing the expected value of $\tilde{\Delta}_t$, the market correctly uses any information in the past values $\Delta_{t-1}, \Delta_{t-2}, \ldots$. The point is obvious with respect to tests based on the coefficient α_2 in (33). It is less obvious with respect to the autocorrelations of $\tilde{r}_t$ and of the disturbances $\tilde{\epsilon}_t$ in (28) and (33); we see now that these different autocorrelations are autocorrelations of the deviation of $\tilde{\Delta}_t$ from different versions of its conditional expected value.

The argument is simplest for the autocorrelations of the disturbance $\tilde{\epsilon}_t$ in (28). If (23) is the model of the expected real return, then (24) describes the market's assessment of the expected value of $\tilde{\Delta}_t$ as a function of R_t. It follows that the disturbance $\tilde{\epsilon}_t$ in (28) is the deviation of $\tilde{\Delta}_t$ from its conditional expected value,

$$\tilde{\epsilon}_t = \tilde{\Delta}_t - E_m(\tilde{\Delta}_t \mid \phi_{t-1}^m) = \tilde{\Delta}_t - (\alpha_0 + \alpha_1 R_t),$$

when $E_m(\tilde{\Delta}_t \mid \phi_{t-1}^m)$ is given by (24). The autocorrelations of $\tilde{\epsilon}_t$ allow us to decide whether the time series of past values of these deviations are used correctly by the market when it assesses the expected value of $\tilde{\Delta}_t$; that is, the autocorrelations of the disturbance in (28) tell us whether the past values of the deviations are part of ϕ_{t-1}^m in $E_m(\tilde{\Delta}_t \mid \phi_{t-1}^m)$, given that this expected value is as described in (24). Nonzero autocorrelations imply that the market is inefficient; one can improve on the market's assessment of the expected value of $\tilde{\Delta}_t$ by making correct use of information in past values of Δ_t. Likewise, the disturbance $\tilde{\epsilon}_t$ in (33) can be interpreted as the deviation of $\tilde{\Delta}_t$ from its conditional expected value when the latter is allowed to be a function of Δ_{t-1} as well as of R_t. Finally, if the equilibrium expected real return is constant through time, then the market's assessment of the expected value of $\tilde{\Delta}_t$ is described by (19). In this world,

from (9) $\qquad \tilde{r}_t - E(\tilde{r}) = \tilde{\Delta}_t + R_t - E(\tilde{r})$ $\qquad\qquad$ (34a)

$\qquad\qquad\qquad\quad = \tilde{\Delta}_t - [E(\tilde{r}) - R_t]$ $\qquad\qquad$ (34b)

from (19) $\qquad\qquad\quad = \tilde{\Delta}_t - E_m(\tilde{\Delta}_t \mid \phi_{t-1}^m).$ $\qquad\qquad$ (34c)

In words, the deviation of $\tilde{r}_t$ from its expected value is the deviation of $\tilde{\Delta}_t$ from the market's assessment of its expected value, when the latter is as described by (19). Thus, tests of market efficiency based on the autocorrelations of $\tilde{r}_t$, like all the other proposed tests, are concerned with whether the market correctly uses any information in the time series of past values

$\Delta_{t-1}, \Delta_{t-2}, \ldots$ when it assesses the expected value of $\tilde{\Delta}_t$, on which R_t is then based. Any such test must assume some model of market equilibrium. That is, it must assume some proposition about the equilibrium expected real return $E_m(\tilde{r}_t | \phi_{t-1}^m)$, which in turn implies some proposition about $E_m(\tilde{\Delta}_t | \phi_{t-1}^m)$, and this is where the tests differ.

There is, however, no need to apologize for the fact that the tests of market efficiency concentrate on the reaction of the market to information in the time series of past rates of change in the purchasing power of money. Beginning with the pioneering work of Irving Fisher (1930), researchers in this area have long contended, and the results below substantiate the claim, that past rates of inflation are important information for assessing future rates. In short, the evidence is that periods of high or low inflation tend to persist. Moreover, previous empirical research almost uniformly suggests that the market is inefficient; in assessing expected future rates of inflation, much of the information in past rates is apparently ignored. (For a summary of the literature, see Richard Roll 1972.)

This conclusion, if true, indicates a serious failure of a free market. The value of a market is in providing accurate signals for resource allocation, which means setting prices that more or less fully reflect available information. If the market ignores the information from so obvious a source as past inflation rates, its effectiveness is seriously questioned. The issue deserves further study.

V. The Data

The one-month nominal return or rate of interest R_t used in the tests is the return from the end of month $t-1$ to the end of month t on the Treasury bill that matures closest to the end of the month t. The data are from the quote sheets of a particular dealer, Salomon Brothers. In computing R_t from (1), the average of the bid and asked prices at the end of month $t-1$ is used for the nominal price v_{t-1}.

The Consumer Price Index, compiled by the Bureau of Labor Statistics, is used to estimate Δ_t, the rate of change in the purchasing power of money from the end of month $t-1$ to the end of month t. The use of any index to measure the level of prices of consumption goods can be questioned. For example, the weights assigned to individual items in the CPI may not yield a "representative consumption bundle," if indeed the notion has any precise meaning in a multigood world where consumers differ with respect to both tastes and resources. But there is no need to speculate about the effects of shortcomings of the CPI on the tests. If the results of the tests seem meaningful, the data are probably adequate.

Note, however, that the model does call for some measure of the prices of consumption goods and services. The focus on real returns and equilibrium expected real returns comes from the assumption that investors invest in order eventually to consume. Thus, although one may legitimately be concerned with shortcomings of the CPI, the price level of interest is the price level of consumption goods.

Some details of the calculations should also be mentioned. First, the bill used to compute the nominal rate generally does not mature on the last day of month t. Thus, if left unadjusted, the nominal rate and the rate of change in purchasing power for "month" t might be for periods that could differ by up to a week. To avoid any problems this might cause, the values of R_t and Δ_t are always adjusted to an equivalent 30.4-day basis. It turns out that this adjustment has little effect on the tests. Second, the prices quoted on bills are for delivery usually two days after the day of the quote. In the adjustment process described above, the number of days covered by a bill is computed from delivery date to maturity.

The first tests reported cover the period from January 1953 through July 1971. Tests for periods prior to 1953 would be meaningless. First, during World War II and on up to the Treasury–Federal Reserve Accord of 1951, interest rates on Treasury bills were pegged by the government. In effect, a rich and obstinate investor saw to it that Treasury bill rates did not adjust to predictable changes in inflation rates. Second, at the beginning of 1953, there was a substantial upgrading of the CPI. The number of items in the index increased substantially, and monthly sampling of major items in major metropolitan areas became the general rule. For tests of market efficiency based on monthly data, monthly sampling of major items in the CPI is critical. Less frequent sampling, as was the general rule prior to 1953, meant that some of the changes in prices for month t showed up in the index in months subsequent to t. Since nominal prices of goods tend to move together, spreading changes in prices for month t into following months induces spurious positive autocorrelations in monthly changes in the index. This gives the appearance that there is more information about future inflation rates in past inflation rates than is really the case. Since the spurious component of the information in measured inflation rates is not easily isolated, tests of market efficiency on pre-1953 data would be difficult to interpret.

There is also a problem with the values of the CPI from August 1971 through mid-1974. During this period, the Nixon administration made a series of different attempts to fix prices; the controls were effective in creating shortages of some important goods. (Who can forget the gas queues of the winter of 1973–1974?) Thus, for this period there are nontrivial differences between the observed values of the CPI and the true costs of goods to consumers. For this reason, we first study the "clean" pre-controls period, January 1953 to July 1971, and then later extend the results through June 1974.

VI.   The Major Results for One-Month Bills

For the pre-controls period and for various subperiods,* Part 1 of Table 6.1 shows sample autocorrelations of the rate of change in purchasing power Δ_t for lags τ of from one to 12 months. Since the symbol r is used for the real return, in this chapter the symbol for sample autocorrelations is $\hat{\rho}_\tau$, where the "hat" ($\hat{\ }$) indicates that $\hat{\rho}_\tau$ is an estimate of the true autocorrelation ρ_τ. Table 6.1 also shows sample means, standard deviations, and studentized ranges of Δ_t, and

$$\sigma(\hat{\rho}_1) = \sqrt{1/(T-1)}, \tag{35}$$

where $T-1$ is the number of observations used to compute $\hat{\rho}_1$ and $\sigma(\hat{\rho}_1)$ is the approximate standard error of $\hat{\rho}_1$ under the hypothesis that the true autocorrelation is zero. From equation (44) of Chapter 4, the expression for the approximate standard error of $\hat{\rho}_\tau$, under the hypothesis that $\rho_\tau = 0$, is

$$\sigma(\hat{\rho}_\tau) = \sqrt{1/(T-\tau)} .$$

Thus, for the longer periods—that is, for periods where T is large—the values of $\sigma(\hat{\rho}_1)$ and $\sigma(\hat{\rho}_\tau)$ are similar. Parts 2 and 3 of Table 6.1 show autocorrelations and other sample statistics for the real return r_t and for $dR_t = R_t - R_{t-1}$. Although, for simplicity, the development of the theory is in terms of the approximation given by (9), the exact expression (8) is always used to compute r_t.

Part 1 of Table 6.2 shows summary statistics for the estimated version of (28),

$$\Delta_t = a_0 + a_1 R_t + e_t. \tag{36}$$

In addition to the least squares regression coefficient estimates a_0 and a_1, the table shows the sample standard errors of the estimates, $s(a_0)$ and $s(a_1)$; the coefficient of determination, adjusted for degrees of freedom; the standard

---

*The rationale for the choice of subperiods becomes clear when the tests are later extended to bills with maturities longer than one month.

TABLE 6.1

Autocorrelations of Δ_t, r_t, and $dR_t = R_t - R_{t-1}$ for One-Month Bills, January 1953–July 1971

PART 1: AUTOCORRELATIONS OF Δ_t

PERIOD	$\hat{\rho}_1$	$\hat{\rho}_2$	$\hat{\rho}_3$	$\hat{\rho}_4$	$\hat{\rho}_5$	$\hat{\rho}_6$	$\hat{\rho}_7$	$\hat{\rho}_8$	$\hat{\rho}_9$	$\hat{\rho}_{10}$	$\hat{\rho}_{11}$	$\hat{\rho}_{12}$	$\sigma(\hat{\rho}_1)$	$\bar{\Delta}$	$s(\Delta)$	$SR(\Delta)$	$T-1$
1/53-7/71	.36	.37	.27	.30	.29	.29	.25	.34	.36	.34	.27	.37	.07	-.00188	.00234	5.26	222
1/53-2/59	.21	.28	.10	.16	.01	-.01	.05	.18	.21	.20	.09	.18	.12	-.00111	.00258	4.56	73
3/59-7/64	-.09	-.09	-.25	-.05	.03	.09	-.06	-.20	.13	.04	-.09	.17	.13	-.00108	.00169	4.04	64
8/64-7/71	.35	.34	.26	.23	.33	.30	.18	.37	.24	.21	.18	.30	.11	-.00321	.00195	5.21	83

PART 2: AUTOCORRELATIONS OF r_t

PERIOD	$\hat{\rho}_1$	$\hat{\rho}_2$	$\hat{\rho}_3$	$\hat{\rho}_4$	$\hat{\rho}_5$	$\hat{\rho}_6$	$\hat{\rho}_7$	$\hat{\rho}_8$	$\hat{\rho}_9$	$\hat{\rho}_{10}$	$\hat{\rho}_{11}$	$\hat{\rho}_{12}$	$\sigma(\hat{\rho}_1)$	$\bar{r}$	$s(r)$	$SR(r)$	$T-1$
1/53-7/71	.09	.13	-.02	-.01	-.02	-.02	-.07	.04	.11	.10	.03	.19	.07	.00074	.00197	6.40*	222
1/53-2/59	.11	.17	-.02	.01	-.14	-.18	-.09	.05	.11	.12	.03	.16	.12	.00038	.00240	5.21	73
3/59-7/64	-.04	.01	-.20	-.06	.00	.07	-.09	-.23	.09	.07	-.10	.19	.13	.00111	.00172	4.65	64
8/64-7/71	.10	.08	-.01	-.10	.08	.07	-.15	.17	.04	-.02	-.07	.15	.11	.00075	.00168	5.25	83

PART 3: AUTOCORRELATIONS OF dR_t

PERIOD	$\hat{\rho}_1$	$\hat{\rho}_2$	$\hat{\rho}_3$	$\hat{\rho}_4$	$\hat{\rho}_5$	$\hat{\rho}_6$	$\hat{\rho}_7$	$\hat{\rho}_8$	$\hat{\rho}_9$	$\hat{\rho}_{10}$	$\hat{\rho}_{11}$	$\hat{\rho}_{12}$	$\sigma(\hat{\rho}_1)$	$\overline{dR}$	$s(dR)$	$SR(dR)$	$T-1$
1/53-7/71	-.25	.06	.01	.15	-.03	-.06	-.13	.10	.06	-.24	-.05	.09	.07	.00001	.00032	6.18	221
1/53-2/59	-.14	.05	.07	.23	-.04	.01	-.35	.17	-.03	-.26	-.16	.13	.12	.00000	.00028	6.17*	72
3/59-7/64	-.41	.07	-.03	.08	.07	-.12	-.11	.13	-.06	-.07	-.10	.06	.13	.00001	.00035	5.68*	63
8/64-7/71	-.18	.06	.00	.18	-.13	-.01	-.05	.02	.18	-.42	.08	.04	.11	.00001	.00033	5.14	82

*Studentized range exceeds the .95 fractile of the sampling distribution of the studentized range in samples from a normal population.

SOURCE: Eugene F. Fama, "Short-Term Interest Rates as Predictors of Inflation," *American Economic Review* 65 (June 1975): 275, 278. Reprinted by permission.

TABLE 6.2

Summary Statistics for Regression Tests on One-Month Bills, January 1953–July 1971

PART 1: $\Delta_t = a_0 + a_1 R_t + e_t$

PERIOD	a_0	a_1	$s(a_0)$	$s(a_1)$	COEFF. OF DET.	$s(e)$	$\hat{\rho}_1(e)$	$\hat{\rho}_2(e)$	$\hat{\rho}_3(e)$	$SR(e)$	T
1/53-7/71	.00070	-.98	.00030	.10	.29	.00196	.09	.13	-.02	6.54*	223
1/53-2/59	.00116	-1.49	.00069	.42	.14	.00240	.09	.15	-.05	5.49	74
3/59-7/64	-.00038	-.33	.00095	.42	-.01	.00168	-.09	-.08	-.26	4.30	65
8/64-7/71	.00118	-1.10	.00083	.20	.26	.00167	.09	.06	-.02	5.13	84

PART 2: $\Delta_t = a_0 + a_1 R_t + a_2 \Delta_{t-1} + e_t$

a_0	a_1	a_2	$s(a_0)$	$s(a_1)$	$s(a_2)$	COEFF. OF DET.	$s(e)$	$\hat{\rho}_1(e)$	$\hat{\rho}_2(e)$	$\hat{\rho}_3(e)$	$SR(e)$	T
.00059	-.87	.11	.00030	.12	.07	.30	.00195	-.05	.13	-.04	6.36*	222
.00108	-1.40	.11	.00069	.44	.11	.14	.00238	-.09	.17	-.07	5.35	73
-.00054	-.30	-.08	.00097	.42	.13	-.02	.00170	-.01	-.11	-.25	4.25	64
.00073	-.89	.14	.00084	.24	.11	.24	.00164	-.04	.05	-.01	5.19	83

PART 3: $r_t = a_0 + g R_t + e_t$

a_0	g	$s(a_0)$	$s(g)$	COEFF. OF DET.	$s(e)$	$\hat{\rho}_1(e)$	$\hat{\rho}_2(e)$	$\hat{\rho}_3(e)$	$SR(e)$	T
.00070	.02	.00030	.10	-.00	.00197	.09	.13	-.02	6.54*	223
.00117	-.50	.00070	.43	.01	.00240	.09	.15	-.05	5.49	74
-.00038	.67	.00095	.42	.02	.00169	-.09	-.08	-.26	4.30	65
.00120	-.11	.00083	.20	-.01	.00168	.09	.06	-.02	5.13	84

*Studentized range exceeds the .95 fractile of the sampling distribution of the studentized range in samples from a normal population.

SOURCE: Eugene F. Fama, "Short-Term Interest Rates as Predictors of Inflation," *American Economic Review* 65 (June 1975): 276. Reprinted by permission.

deviation of the residuals, $s(e)$; the first three residual autocorrelations, $\hat{\rho}_1(e)$, $\hat{\rho}_2(e)$, and $\hat{\rho}_3(e)$; the studentized range of the residuals, $SR(e)$; and T, the number of observations used to compute the regression coefficients. Part 2 of Table 6.2 shows similar summary statistics for the estimated version of (33),

$$\Delta_t = a_0 + a_1 R_t + a_2 \Delta_{t-1} + e_t, \tag{37}$$

while Part 3 of the table shows summary statistics for

$$r_t = a_0 + gR_t + e_t, \tag{38}$$

whose role in the tests is discussed later.

A. The Information in Past Inflation Rates

The market efficiency hypothesis to be tested is that the one-month nominal interest rate R_t, set in the market at the end of month $t - 1$, is based on correct utilization of all the information about the expected value of $\tilde{\Delta}_t$ that is in the time series of past values $\Delta_{t-1}, \Delta_{t-2}, \ldots$. The hypothesis is meaningful, however, only if past rates of change in purchasing power have information about the expected future rate of change. The predominance of large autocorrelations of Δ_t in Table 6.1 indicates that this is the case.

In fact, especially for the longer periods 1/53–7/71 and 8/64–7/71, the sample autocorrelations for different lags are similar in size, with individual estimates in the neighborhood of .30. The implications of this finding are discussed later, when the behavior through time of $\tilde{\Delta}_t$ is studied in more detail.

B. Tests of Market Efficiency

Given that the equilibrium expected real return is constant through time, the market efficiency hypothesis says that the autocorrelations of the real return $\tilde{r}_t$ should be zero for all lags. The sample autocorrelations of r_t in Table 6.1 are close to zero. Recall from (9) that the real return $\tilde{r}_t$ is approximately the rate of change in purchasing power $\tilde{\Delta}_t$ plus the nominal interest rate R_t. The evidence from the sample autocorrelations of $\tilde{\Delta}_t$ and $\tilde{r}_t$ is that adding R_t to $\tilde{\Delta}_t$ brings the substantial autocorrelations of $\tilde{\Delta}_t$ down to values close to zero. This is consistent with the market efficiency hypothesis that the nominal rate set at $t - 1$ summarizes completely the information about the expected value of $\tilde{\Delta}_t$ that is in the time series of past values, Δ_{t-1}, $\Delta_{t-2}, \ldots$.

Table 6.2 gives further support to the market efficiency hypothesis. When applied to (33), the hypothesis says that α_2, the coefficient of Δ_{t-1}, should be zero, and the autocorrelations of the disturbance $\tilde{\epsilon}_t$ should be zero for all lags. The residual autocorrelations reported in Part 2 of Table 6.2 are close to zero. The values of a_2, the sample estimates of α_2 in (33), are also small and always less than two standard errors from zero. When applied to (28), the market efficiency hypothesis is again that the autocorrelations of the disturbance $\tilde{\epsilon}_t$ should be zero. The residual autocorrelations in Part 1 of Table 6.2 are close to zero. Comparing the estimates of (28) and (33) in Table 6.2 shows that dropping Δ_{t-1} from the model has almost no effect on the coefficients of determination. This is consistent with the implication of market efficiency that the value of R_t set at time $t-1$ summarizes any information in Δ_{t-1} about the expected value of $\tilde{\Delta}_t$.

Closer inspection of Tables 6.1 and 6.2 seems to provide slight evidence against market efficiency. Except for 3/59-7/64, the first-order ($\tau = 1$) autocorrelations of r_t, though small, are nevertheless all positive. The estimated regression coefficients a_2 of Δ_{t-1} in the second part of Table 6.2 are likewise small but generally positive, as are the first-order residual autocorrelations for (28) shown in the first part of the table. Even after the upgrading of the CPI in 1953, however, there are some items and cities for which prices are sampled less frequently than monthly; and items that are sampled monthly are not sampled at the same time during the month.* Again, since prices of goods tend to move together, these quirks of the sampling process induce spurious positive autocorrelations in measured rates of change in purchasing power. Since an efficient market does not react to "information" that is recognizably spurious, the small apparent discrepancies from efficiency provide more "reasonable" evidence in favor of the efficiency hypothesis than if the data suggested that the hypothesis does perfectly well.

C. The Expected Real Return

The evidence is also consistent with the hypothesis that the expected real return on a one-month bill is constant for 1953-1971. First, autocorrelations of the real return r_t are joint tests of the hypotheses that the market is efficient and that the expected real return is constant through time. Since the autocorrelations of r_t in Table 6.1 are close to zero, the evidence is consistent with a world where both hypotheses are valid.

The regression coefficient estimates for (28) and (33) in Table 6.2 are,

---

*Indeed some items in the CPI are only sampled annually. The spurious autocorrelations introduced by annual sampling might, to a large extent, explain the apparent seasonals (high autocorrelations at lag 12) in $\tilde{\Delta}_t$ and $\tilde{r}_t$.

however, more direct evidence on the hypothesis that the expected value of $\tilde{r}_t$ is constant. The hypothesis implies that in (28) and (33) the intercept α_0 is the constant expected real return $E(\tilde{r})$ and the coefficient $\alpha_1 = -1.0$. The estimates a_1 of α_1 in Table 6.2 are always well within two standard errors of -1.0. And statistical considerations aside, the estimate $a_1 = -.98$ for (28) for the overall pre-controls period is impressively close to -1.0. Given estimates a_1 of α_1 in (28) and (33) that are close to -1.0, and given the earlier observation that the estimates a_2 of α_2 in (33) are close to zero, it is then not surprising to find that the intercept estimates a_0 of α_0 in (28) and (33) in Table 6.2 are close to the sample means of the real return in Table 6.1.

PROBLEMS VI.C

1. Show that equation (9) and the least squares formulas for a_0 in (36) and (37) guarantee that if the estimates a_1 for (36) and (37) are close to -1.0 and the estimates a_2 for (37) are close to 0.0, then the estimates a_0 for (36) and (37) are close to the sample means of r_t.

2. The results for the longer periods 1/53-7/71 and 8/64-7/71 in Parts 1 and 2 of Table 6.2 are clear evidence in favor of the hypotheses that the market is efficient and that the equilibrium expected real return on a one-month bill is constant through time. The results for the shorter subperiods seem more "erratic." What is the reason for this?

ANSWERS

1. From (9), the sample mean of r_t can be expressed in terms of the sample means of Δ_t and R_t as

$$\overline{r} = \overline{\Delta} + \overline{R}.$$

The least squares estimate a_0 in (36) is

$$a_0 = \overline{\Delta} - a_1 \overline{R}.$$

It follows that if a_1 is close to -1.0, then a_0 must be close to $\overline{r}$. Likewise, the least squares estimate a_0 in (37) is

$$a_0 = \overline{\Delta} - a_1 \overline{R} - a_2 \overline{\Delta}.$$

If a_1 is close to -1.0 and a_2 is close to 0.0, then a_0 must be close to $\overline{r}$.

2. Chapter 3 emphasizes that regression coefficient estimators are more reliable; that is, the larger the sample size, the more tightly their sampling distributions are concentrated about the true values of the parameters. There is clear manifestation of this in Table 6.2. The standard errors of the regression coefficient estimates decrease as the length of the period increases. The same phenomenon is observed in the standard errors of the sample autocorrelations in Table 6.1.

The practical implication is that the best or most reliable tests of the hypotheses are those for the longer periods. The results for the shorter periods provide a check that the world is pretty much the same throughout the sampling period. The check is a rough one, however, since the sample sizes of the shorter periods, a large amount of apparently "erratic" behavior of the estimates from one period to another is consistent with the model.

The sample autocorrelations of r_t and the regression coefficient estimates a_0 and a_1 in Table 6.2 are consistent with the world of equation (21), where the equilibrium expected real return is constant and all variation through time in the nominal interest rate R_t mirrors variation in the expected value of $\tilde{\Delta}_t$. There is, however, another interesting way to look at this conclusion. From the discussion of (34) it follows that the standard deviation of the real return $\tilde{r}_t$ is the standard deviation of the disturbance $\tilde{\epsilon}_t$ in (28) when the coefficients α_0 and α_1 in (28) are constrained to have the values $\alpha_0 = E(\tilde{r})$ and $\alpha_1 = -1.0$, which are appropriate under the hypothesis that the expected real return is constant through time. If this hypothesis is incorrect, letting the data determine values of α_0 and α_1, as in Part 1 of Table 6.2, should produce lower estimates of the disturbance variance than when the values of the coefficients are constrained. Yet the results indicate that, especially for the longer periods, not only are the values of $s(r)$ in Table 6.1 almost identical to the values of $s(e)$ in Part 1 of Table 6.2, but the sample autocorrelations and studentized ranges of r_t and e_t are also nearly identical. In short, the hypothesis that the expected real return is constant fits the data so well that the residuals from (36), the estimated version of (28), are more or less identical to the deviations of r_t from its sample mean.

Finally, the results from (36) on the hypothesis that the expected real return is constant through time can be presented differently. Instead of developing the tests from the regression function $E_m(\tilde{\Delta}_t | \phi_{t-1}^m)$ of (24), one can work directly with the regression function $E_m(\tilde{r}_t | \phi_{t-1}^m, R_t)$ of (23). With (23) the relationship between $\tilde{r}_t$ and R_t can be expressed as

$$\tilde{r}_t = \alpha_0 + \gamma R_t + \tilde{\epsilon}_t. \tag{39}$$

If the expected real return is constant through time, then $\alpha_0 = E(r)$ and $\gamma = 0$. The results obtained when the least squares approach is used to estimate the regression coefficients in (39) are in Part 3 of Table 6.2. The estimated version of (39) is (38).

Given the relationship among $\tilde{r}_t$, $\tilde{\Delta}_t$, and R_t of (9), α_0 in (28) is the same as α_0 in (39), $\gamma = \alpha_1 + 1.0$, and the disturbances in the two equations are identical. From comparison of Parts 1 and 3 of Table 6.2 we can see that the least squares estimates preserve these relationships between the two equations.

Thus, consistent with the hypothesis that the expected real return is constant through time, values of a_1 in (36) that are close to -1.0 imply values of g in (38) that are close to zero and values of a_0 in both equations that are close to the sample average values of the real return r_t. Tests based on the regression coefficient estimates a_0 and g in (38) emphasize the implication of the hypothesis that the expected value of the real return $\tilde{r}_t$ is unrelated to R_t. Tests based on the coefficient estimates a_0 and a_1 in (36) emphasize the converse implication of the hypothesis; that is, if the expected value of $\tilde{r}_t$ is unrelated to R_t, then all the variation through time in R_t mirrors variation in the expected value of $\tilde{\Delta}_t$.

In fact, the only new numbers in Part 3 of Table 6.2 are the coefficients of determination, which are nevertheless interesting. They are for all periods zero or trivially different from zero. In other words, consistent with the hypothesis that the expected real return is constant through time, we observe no relationship between R_t, the nominal interest rate on a one-month bill observed at the end of month $t-1$ and realized at the end of month t, and the real return r_t which is realized on the bill at the end of month t.

PROBLEMS VI.C

3. In all of the empirical work, the real return r_t is calculated from the exact expression (8) rather than from the approximate expression (9) which is used in the development of the theory. Show that if (9) were used to compute r_t, the agreement between the numbers in Parts 2 and 3 of Table 6.2 would be exact; that is, the values of a_0 for (36) and (38) would be identical, the values of g in (38) would be equal to $a_1 + 1.0$ in (36), and the residuals in (36) and (38) would be identical. The fact that the agreement between the observed numbers is almost exact is evidence that, as assumed in (9), no harm is done when the cross-product term $R_t \Delta_t$ in (6) is dropped in the development of the theory.

4. In line with the discussion of Chapters 3 and 4, we can interpret the coefficients of determination in Part 3 of Table 6.2 as the proportions of the sample variances of r_t that can be attributed to the estimated regression function relationship between r_t and R_t. Some of the coefficients of determination in Table 6.2 are negative! Given that

$$\sum_{t=1}^{T} (r_t - \overline{r})^2 = g^2 \sum_{t=1}^{T} (R_t - \overline{R})^2 + \sum_{t=1}^{T} e_t^2,$$

so that

$$\sum_{t=1}^{T} e_t^2 \leqslant \sum_{t=1}^{T} (r_t - \overline{r})^2,$$

how does one explain these negative values?

5. Comment on the magnitude of the average real return $\overline{r} = .00074$ for the 1/53–7/71 period in Part 2 of Table 6.1.

ANSWERS

3. The least squares estimates a_1 and a_0 in (36) are

$$a_1 = \frac{\sum\limits_{t=1}^{T} (\Delta_t - \overline{\Delta})(R_t - \overline{R})}{\sum\limits_{t=1}^{T} (R_t - \overline{R})^2} \tag{40}$$

$$a_0 = \overline{\Delta} - a_1 \overline{R}. \tag{41}$$

The least squares estimate g in (38) is

$$g = \frac{\sum\limits_{t=1}^{T} (r_t - \overline{r})(R_t - \overline{R})}{\sum\limits_{t=1}^{T} (R_t - \overline{R})^2},$$

which, if (9) is used to compute r_t, can be reduced to

$$g = \frac{\sum\limits_{t=1}^{T} (\Delta_t + R_t - (\overline{\Delta} + \overline{R}))(R_t - \overline{R})}{\sum\limits_{t=1}^{T} (R_t - \overline{R})^2}$$

$$= \frac{\sum\limits_{t=1}^{T} (\Delta_t - \overline{\Delta})(R_t - \overline{R})}{\sum\limits_{t=1}^{T} (R_t - \overline{R})^2} + \frac{\sum\limits_{t=1}^{T} (R_t - \overline{R})^2}{\sum\limits_{t=1}^{T} (R_t - \overline{R})^2}$$

$$g = a_1 + 1.0.$$

We can then write the least squares estimate a_0 in (38)

$$a_0 = \overline{r} - g\overline{R} = \overline{\Delta} + \overline{R} - (1.0 + a_1)\overline{R}$$

$$= \overline{\Delta} - a_1 \overline{R}.$$

Finally, the residuals in (38) would then be

$$e_t = r_t - a_0 - gR_t$$

$$= \Delta_t + R_t - a_0 - (1.0 + a_1)R_t$$

$$= \Delta_t - a_0 - a_1 R_t.$$

4. The coefficients of determination in Table 6.2 are adjusted for degrees of freedom. (Review Section I.C of Chapter 4.) The formula for the coefficient of determination, adjusted for degrees of freedom, between r_t and R_t is

$$\hat{\rho}^2 = 1 - \frac{s^2(e)}{s^2(r)} \tag{42}$$

where

$$s^2(e) = \frac{\displaystyle\sum_{t=1}^{T} e_t^2}{T-2}$$

$$s^2(r) = \frac{\displaystyle\sum_{t=1}^{T} (r_t - \bar{r})^2}{T-1}.$$

The sum of squares $\Sigma(r_t - \bar{r})^2$ is necessarily equal to or greater than the sum of squares Σe_t^2, but because of the difference of one degree of freedom in their denominators, $s^2(e)$ can be larger than $s^2(r)$, which means that $\hat{\rho}^2$ can be negative.

5. The average monthly real return $\bar{r} = .00074$ for the 1/53–7/71 period implies an average annual real return of less than 1 percent. Apparently, a large expected real return is not necessary to induce investors to hold one-month bills. On the other hand, although the average real return is small, the evidence in Table 6.1 is quite consistent with the hypothesis that the expected real return is greater than zero. The sample standard error of $\bar{r}$ for the 1/53–7/71 period is

$$s(\bar{r}) = \frac{s(r)}{\sqrt{T}} = \frac{.00197}{\sqrt{223}} = \frac{.00197}{14.93} = .00013.$$

Thus, the average real return $\bar{r} = .00074$ is more than five sample standard errors from zero.

VII. The Behavior of $\tilde{\Delta}_t$

The results above allow some interesting insights into the behavior through time of $\tilde{\Delta}_t$. We can always write

$$\tilde{\Delta}_t = E(\tilde{\Delta}_t | \phi_{t-1}) + \tilde{\epsilon}_t. \tag{43}$$

That is, $\tilde{\Delta}_t$ has two components, its expected value at $t-1$ and the deviation of the value observed at t from this expected value. Since the data are consistent with the hypotheses that the market is efficient and that the expected real return on a one-month bill is constant through time, the expected value of $\tilde{\Delta}_t$ in (43) is described by (21). In brief, the statement of (21) is that all the information available at $t-1$ about the expected value of $\tilde{\Delta}_t$ is summarized in the value of the one-month nominal rate R_t set in the market at $t-1$, and all variation through time in R_t mirrors variation in the correctly assessed expected value of $\tilde{\Delta}_t$. Substituting (21) into (43), the model of $\tilde{\Delta}_t$ suggested by the data is

$$\tilde{\Delta}_t = E(\tilde{r}) - R_t + \tilde{\epsilon}_t. \tag{44}$$

The coefficients of determination in Part 1 of Table 6.2 suggest that about 30 percent of the variance of $\tilde{\Delta}_t$ can be attributed to the regression function relationship between $\tilde{\Delta}_t$ and R_t of equation (21); that is, variation through time in the expected value of $\tilde{\Delta}_t$, as mirrored by the variation through time in R_t, accounts for 30 percent of the sample variance of $\tilde{\Delta}_t$. In terms of equation (43), the estimate is that 70 percent of the variance of $\tilde{\Delta}_t$ can be attributed to the disturbance $\tilde{\epsilon}_t$, while 30 percent can be attributed to variation through time in the expected rate of change in purchasing power.

The conclusion drawn from the residual autocorrelations in Table 6.2 and the sample autocorrelations of r_t in Table 6.1 is that the disturbance $\tilde{\epsilon}_t$ in (43) is uncorrelated through time. This is consistent with the hypothesis that, in effect, there is random sampling from the distribution of $\tilde{\epsilon}_t$. The time series of past values is no help in predicting the next value. Quite the opposite sort of behavior characterizes the expected value of $\tilde{\Delta}_t$ in (43). Since variation in R_t through time mirrors variation in the expected value of $\tilde{\Delta}_t$, the time series properties of R_t are the time series properties of $E(\tilde{\Delta}_t | \phi_{t-1})$. The sample autocorrelations of R_t, which we shall not bother to show, are close to 1.0. For the overall pre-controls period, the first 4 sample autocorrelations are all in excess of .93, and only 1 of the first 24 is less than .9. Thus, the autocorrelations of R_t indicate that there is much persistence through time in the level of R_t and thus in the level of the expected value of $\tilde{\Delta}_t$. The time series of past values of R_t has substantial information about future values.

Autocorrelations that are all close to 1.0 are consistent with the representation of R_t as a martingale. This means that at the end of month $t-1$ we can express $\tilde{R}_{t+1}$, the one-month nominal rate to be set at the end of month t, as

$$\tilde{R}_{t+1} = R_t + \tilde{\eta}_t. \tag{45}$$

In words, looking forward from the end of month $t-1$, the value of $\tilde{R}_{t+1}$ to be observed at the end of month t is the one-month nominal rate R_t observed at the end of month $t-1$, plus a change or disturbance $\tilde{\eta}_t$ that has expected value equal to zero and is uncorrelated through time.* The expected value of $\tilde{R}_{t+1}$ at time $t - 1$ is the one-month nominal rate R_t observed at $t - 1$. Thus, the most recent observed value of the one-month nominal rate is the best information about the rate to be observed one month hence.

This discussion helps explain the behavior of the sample autocorrelations of $\tilde{\Delta}_t$ in Table 6.1. As stated in (43), $\tilde{\Delta}_t$ has two components. One component of $\tilde{\Delta}_t$, its expected value, behaves like a martingale; its autocorrelations are close to 1.0 for all lags. The other component of $\tilde{\Delta}_t$, the disturbance $\tilde{\epsilon}_t$, is essentially random noise; its values are uncorrelated through time. The auto-correlations of its expected value cause the autocorrelations of $\tilde{\Delta}_t$ to have approximately the same magnitude for different lags. The uncorrelated disturbance $\tilde{\epsilon}_t$, however, causes the autocorrelations of $\tilde{\Delta}_t$, unlike those of R_t, to be far below 1.0.

The sample autocorrelations of R_t suggest that the expected value of $\tilde{\Delta}_t$ behaves through time much like a martingale. The sample autocorrelations of the month-to-month changes in R_t, shown in Part 3 of Table 6.1, suggest, however, that we can improve on this description of the behavior of $E(\tilde{\Delta}_t | \phi_{t-1})$. For example, the first-order autocorrelations of the changes are consistently negative. From the first-order autocorrelations for the longer periods, the change in R_t might reasonably be represented as

$$\tilde{R}_{t+1} - R_t = -.25(R_t - R_{t-1}) + \tilde{\eta}_t, \tag{46}$$

or as

$$\tilde{R}_{t+1} = R_t - .25(R_t - R_{t-1}) + \tilde{\eta}_t. \tag{47}$$

Thus, the process that generates the nominal rate is no longer just a martingale. Looking forward from time $t - 1$, we now predict that $\tilde{R}_{t+1} - R_t$, the change in the one-month nominal rate from the end of month $t - 1$ to the end of month t, will reverse by 25 percent the change observed from the end of month $t - 2$ to the end of month $t - 1$. In other words, the change in the expected inflation rate from one month to the next reverses itself, on average, by about 25 percent.

From the sample autocorrelations of the changes in R_t in Table 6.1, it is perhaps possible to read further into the behavior through time of the expected rate of change in purchasing power. For example, the autocorrelations are consistently positive for lag $\tau = 4$ and consistently negative for lags $\tau = 7$ and $\tau = 10$. Our purpose, however, is not to develop the most detailed possible description of the behavior of the expected values of $\tilde{\Delta}_t$. The discussion is

---

*Note that a tilde appears over $\tilde{R}_{t+1}$ in equation (45). This is because we are looking forward from time $t - 1$. At t the value of R_{t+1} is known, but at earlier points in time, R_{t+1} is a random variable.

sufficient if the reader appreciates that in our model, variation through time in R_t mirrors variation in the best possible assessment of the expected value of $\tilde{\Delta}_t$.

VIII.   Results for Bills with Longer Maturities

The presentation of theory and tests of bill market efficiency has concentrated so far on one-month bills and one-month rates of change in purchasing power. As far as the theory is concerned, the interval of time over which the variables are measured is arbitrary. The theory applies, for example, to one-week bills and one-week rates of change in purchasing power, or to six-month bills and rates of change in purchasing power. To "generalize" the theory in this way, one simply changes the interpretation of the time interval between successive values of t. In testing the theory, the fact that the CPI is reported monthly limits us to tests based on intervals that cover an integral number of months. We present tests now for one- to six-month intervals. In these tests the interval from $t-1$ to t is $1, 2, \ldots,$ or 6 months; R_t is the 1-, 2-, $\ldots,$ or 6-month nominal return or rate of interest from $t-1$ to t on a bill with $1, 2, \ldots,$ or 6 months to maturity at $t-1$; and the real return $\tilde{r}_t$ and the rate of change in purchasing power $\tilde{\Delta}_t$ are likewise measured for nonoverlapping 1-, 2-, $\ldots,$ or 6-month intervals.

Since the theory and tests are the same for bills of all maturities, the market efficiency hypothesis is that in setting the nominal rate R_t at time $t-1$, the market correctly uses any information about the expected value of $\tilde{\Delta}_t$ which is in the time series of past values $\Delta_{t-1}, \Delta_{t-2}, \ldots$. The model of market equilibrium on which the tests are based is the assumption that the 1-, 2-, $\ldots,$ or 6-month expected real returns on bills with $1, 2, \ldots,$ or 6 months to maturity are constant through time. The tests of these propositions are in Tables 6.3 and 6.4, and the tests are the same as those for one-month bills in Tables 6.1 and 6.2. Results for the one- to three-month versions of the variables are shown for the 1/53–7/71 and 3/59–7/71 periods. Since complete data for four- to six-month bills are only available beginning in March 1959, results for the four- to six-month versions of the variables are only shown for the 3/59–7/71 period.

Implicit in the tests of market efficiency is the assumption that past rates of change in purchasing power have information about expected future rates of change. The autocorrelations of Δ_t in Table 6.3 support this assumption. The autocorrelations are large for all six intervals used to measure Δ_t. But

TABLE 6.3
Sample Autocorrelations of Δ_t and r_t: One- to Six-Month Bills, January 1953–July 1971

PART 1: AUTOCORRELATIONS OF Δ_t

PERIOD	BILL	$\hat{\rho}_1$	$\hat{\rho}_2$	$\hat{\rho}_3$	$\hat{\rho}_4$	$\hat{\rho}_5$	$\hat{\rho}_6$	$\hat{\rho}_7$	$\hat{\rho}_8$	$\hat{\rho}_9$	$\hat{\rho}_{10}$	$\hat{\rho}_{11}$	$\hat{\rho}_{12}$	$\sigma(\hat{\rho}_1)$	$\overline{\Delta}$	$s(\Delta)$	$SR(\Delta)$	$T-1$
1/53–7/71	1	.36	.37	.27	.30	.29	.29	.25	.34	.36	.34	.27	.37	.07	-.00188	.00234	5.26	222
	2	.50	.39	.43	.45	.52	.41	.40	.32	.36	.30	.28	.28	.10	-.00368	.00386	5.59	110
	3	.53	.57	.59	.54	.48	.38	.39	.27	.32	.08	.35	.29	.12	-.00550	.00521	4.24	73
3/59–7/71	1	.40	.39	.32	.36	.43	.44	.34	.40	.44	.40	.34	.47	.08	-.00228	.00211	5.22	148
	2	.55	.50	.66	.57	.58	.56	.53	.60	.55	.49	.54	.56	.12	-.00445	.00348	5.36	73
	3	.58	.74	.64	.70	.66	.65	.65	.58	.73	.42	.84	.55	.14	-.00656	.00485	4.29	49
	4	.67	.72	.71	.71	.63	.76	.61	.73	.70	.65	.54	.82	.17	-.00881	.00628	4.48	36
	5	.84	.78	.74	.73	.76	.77	.89	.83	.94	.79	.14	.11	.19	-.01105	.00735	4.37	29
	6	.86	.83	.74	.81	.90	1.03*	.98	.95	.45	.32	-.07	.23	.21	-.01319	.00857	4.69†	24

PART 2: AUTOCORRELATIONS OF r_t

PERIOD	BILL	$\hat{\rho}_1$	$\hat{\rho}_2$	$\hat{\rho}_3$	$\hat{\rho}_4$	$\hat{\rho}_5$	$\hat{\rho}_6$	$\hat{\rho}_7$	$\hat{\rho}_8$	$\hat{\rho}_9$	$\hat{\rho}_{10}$	$\hat{\rho}_{11}$	$\hat{\rho}_{12}$	$\sigma(\hat{\rho}_1)$	$\overline{r}$	$s(r)$	$SR(r)$	$T-1$
1/53–7/71	1	.09	.13	-.02	-.01	-.02	-.02	-.07	.04	.11	.10	.03	.19	.07	.00074	.00197	6.40†	222
	2	.15	-.09	-.03	.01	.18	.10	.15	-.01	.06	.00	.04	.09	.10	.00185	.00292	5.08	110
	3	.00	.02	.08	.26	.16	-.09	.06	-.01	.08	-.32	.11	.19	.12	.00306	.00371	4.87	73
3/59–7/71	1	.05	.05	-.08	-.07	.06	.10	-.10	.00	.09	.05	-.04	.20	.08	.00090	.00169	5.29	148
	2	.03	-.15	.18	-.06	.00	.10	.07	.14	.08	-.07	.08	.20	.12	.00224	.00236	4.90	73
	3	-.16	.16	-.14	.25	.11	.04	.06	.02	.18	-.33	.36	.10	.14	.00373	.00307	5.07	49
	4	-.17	-.06	.20	.14	-.08	.30	-.22	.17	.16	-.09	-.02	.32	.17	.00514	.00379	4.93	36
	5	.02	-.13	-.03	.03	.15	-.19	.33	-.02	.25	.04	-.69	.13	.19	.00706	.00375	4.45	29
	6	.07	.07	-.05	.26	.11	.43	-.04	.49	-.60	.27	.32	.07	.21	.00882	.00444	4.54	24

*The sample autocorrelations are estimated as linear regression coefficients. Thus, the estimates can be greater than 1.0.

†Studentized range exceeds the .95 fractile of the sampling distribution of the studentized range in samples from a normal population.

SOURCE: Eugene F. Fama, "Short-Term Interest Rates as Predictors of Inflation," *American Economic Review* 65 (June 1975): 280. Reprinted by permission.

TABLE 6.4

Summary Statistics for Regression Tests on One- to Six-Month Bills, January 1953–July 1971

PART 1: $\Delta_t = a_0 + a_1 R_t + e_t$

PERIOD	BILL	a_0	a_1	$s(a_0)$	$s(a_1)$	COEFF. OF DET.	$s(e)$	$\hat{\rho}_1(e)$	$\hat{\rho}_2(e)$	$\hat{\rho}_3(e)$	SR(e)	T
1/53–7/71	1	.00070	−.98	.00030	.10	.29	.00196	.09	.13	−.02	6.54*	223
	2	.00161	−.96	.00066	.11	.42	.00296	.15	−.08	−.03	6.14*	111
	3	.00228	−.92	.00105	.11	.48	.00380	.00	.03	.10	4.72	74
3/59–7/71	1	.00120	−1.09	.00041	.12	.36	.00169	.04	.05	−.08	5.34	149
	2	.00269	−1.08	.00086	.12	.52	.00245	.02	−.16	.14	4.75	74
	3	.00397	−1.03	.00145	.13	.55	.00330	−.16	.12	−.16	5.02	50
	4	.00543	−1.03	.00216	.14	.58	.00413	−.18	−.10	.14	5.33*	37
	5	.00635	−.97	.00236	.12	.68	.00416	.01	−.10	−.02	4.44	30
	6	.00879	−1.01	.00344	.14	.65	.00505	.01	−.01	−.11	4.63*	25

PART 2: $\Delta_t = a_0 + a_1 R_t + a_2 \Delta_{t-1} + e_t$

	BILL	a_0	a_1	a_2	$s(a_0)$	$s(a_1)$	$s(a_2)$	COEFF. OF DET.	$s(e)$	$\hat{\rho}_1(e)$	$\hat{\rho}_2(e)$	$\hat{\rho}_3(e)$	SR(e)	T
1/53–7/71	1	.00059	−.87	.11	.00030	.12	.07	.30	.00195	−.05	.13	−.04	6.36	222
	2	.00115	−.78	.17	.00064	.13	.09	.44	.00280	.03	−.06	.02	5.13	110
	3	.00173	−.79	.11	.00107	.15	.12	.48	.00372	−.06	.07	.05	4.67	73
3/59–7/71	1	.00109	−1.01	.07	.00042	.14	.08	.35	.00169	−.03	.05	−.07	5.31	148
	2	.00252	−1.02	.05	.00094	.18	.12	.51	.00248	−.02	−.16	.15	4.79	73
	3	.00390	−1.06	−.04	.00169	.23	.17	.53	.00334	−.10	.11	−.17	5.02	49
	4	.00520	−.97	.07	.00261	.26	.20	.57	.00423	−.23	−.06	.12	5.15*	36
	5	.00359	−.57	.40	.00301	.27	.23	.71	.00404	−.13	−.08	−.02	4.26	29
	6	.00263	−.39	.58	.00406	.28	.23	.72	.00461	−.29	.18	−.32	4.45	24

*Studentized range exceeds the .95 fractile of the sampling distribution of the studentized range in samples from a normal population.

SOURCE: Eugene F. Fama, "Short-Term Interest Rates as Predictors of Inflation," *American Economic Review* 65 (June 1975): 281. Reprinted by permission.

consistent with the hypotheses that the market is efficient and that the equilibrium expected real returns on bills with different maturities are constant through time, the autocorrelations of the real returns in Table 6.3 are close to zero. Remember that the n-month real return on an n-month bill is approximately the n-month rate of change in purchasing power plus the n-month nominal return on the bill. Thus the evidence from the autocorrelations of Δ_t and r_t in Table 6.3 is that when R_t is added to $\tilde{\Delta}_t$, the substantial autocorrelations of $\tilde{\Delta}_t$ drop to values close to zero. This is consistent with a world where R_t, the n-month nominal rate set at $t-1$, summarizes all the information about the expected value of the rate of change in purchasing power over the n months from $t-1$ to t which is in the time series of past rates of change in purchasing power.

The model gets further support from the regression tests in Table 6.4. Consistent with the hypothesis that expected real returns are constant through time, the values of a_1 for (36) in Part 1 of Table 6.4 are all impressively close to -1.0; none is as far as .1 away from -1.0. Consistent with the hypothesis that the market is efficient, the residual autocorrelations in Part 1 of Table 6.4 are close to zero for bills of all maturities.

The only hint of evidence against the model is in the results for (37) for five- and six-month bills in Part 2 of Table 6.4. As predicted by the model, the values of a_1 and a_2 for one- to four-month bills are close to -1.0 and 0.0, and the residual autocorrelations are close to 0.0. For the five- and six-month bills, the values of a_1 for (37) are far from -1.0 and the values of a_2 are far from 0.0. When one conducts so many different tests for so many different bills, however, some results are likely to turn out badly, even though the model is a good approximation to the world. This argument gains force from the fact that the autocorrelations of the real returns in Table 6.3 and the results for (36) in Part 1 of Table 6.4 do not produce evidence for five- and six-month bills that contradicts the model.

Finally, the fact that the values of the autocorrelations of Δ_t in Table 6.3 increase as the interval used to measure Δ_t increases suggests that past rates of changes in purchasing power contain more information about expected future rates of change the longer the interval used to measure Δ_t. The results in Table 6.4 are consistent with the hypothesis that the nominal rate of interest R_t set in the market at $t-1$ summarizes completely the information about the expected value of $\tilde{\Delta}_t$ which is in the time series of past values. Since the longer the interval covered by Δ_t, the greater the information contained in past values, the information which R_t summarizes varies directly with the maturity of the bill. This shows up in the coefficients of determination in Table 6.4, which increase as the interval covered by Δ_t and R_t increases.

PROBLEM VIII

1. The statements in the preceding paragraph are anomalous. They say that, at a given point in time, there is more information available about the rate of change in purchasing power two, three, or n months ahead than there is about the rate of change in purchasing power one month ahead. In what sense does this mean that the further one looks into the future, the better one can predict inflation? Is the uncertainty about the accuracy of the prediction lower the further one looks ahead?

ANSWER

1. Recall from the discussion of autocorrelations in Chapter 4 that the square of an autocorrelation measures the proportion of the variance of the variable that can be attributed to its linear regression function relationship with the lagged value of the variable. Thus, the larger autocorrelations of Δ_t that are obtained when longer intervals are used to measure Δ_t mean that the longer the interval used to measure Δ_t, the greater the proportion of the variance of Δ_t that can be explained by relationships with lagged values. In this sense, the longer the interval used to measure Δ_t, the more information past values have about future values.

Although a larger proportion of the variance of the two-month rate of change in purchasing power can be explained in terms of past two-month rates of change, the variance of the two-month rate of change is larger than the variance of the one-month rate of change, and the variance of the prediction error is larger for predictions two months ahead than for predictions one month ahead. One can see this most easily in the results for (36) in Part 1 of Table 6.4. The longer the interval covered by Δ_t, the larger the coefficient of determination for the regression of Δ_t on R_t. In other words, R_t summarizes more information about Δ_t as the interval covered by the variables increases. On the other hand, the fact that the residual standard deviation $s(e)$ also increases with the interval covered by Δ_t and R_t means that, as one would expect, predictions of inflation rates are increasingly uncertain the further one tries to look into the future.

IX. Interest Rates as Predictors of Inflation: Comparison with the Results of Others

In a world where equilibrium expected real returns on bills are constant through time, aside from the additive constant $E(\tilde{r})$ in (19), the nominal rate R_t set at time $t - 1$ is in effect the market's prediction of the rate of change in purchasing power from $t - 1$ to t. The coefficients of determination in Part 1 of Table 6.4 indicate that variation through time in these predictions accounts for 30 percent of the variance of the subsequently observed values of Δ_t in the case of one-month bills, and the proportion of the sample variance of Δ_t accounted for by R_t increases to about 65 percent for five- and six-month bills. Thus, nominal interest rates observed at $t - 1$ contain nontrivial information about the rate of change in purchasing power from $t - 1$ to t. Moreover, the evidence on market efficiency suggests that the market's prediction of $\tilde{\Delta}_t$ is the best that can be made on the basis of information available at time $t - 1$; or, more precisely, it is the best that can be done on the basis of information in past rates of change in purchasing power.

The results reported here differ substantially from those of most of the rest of the literature on interest rates and inflation. Irving Fisher (1930) first postulated that interest rates contain predictions of inflation rates; indeed, the hypothesis is usually called the "Fisher effect." But Fisher's empirical work, and that of most others who came after him, suggests that the market does not perform efficiently in predicting inflation. The common finding is that there are no statistically reliable relationships between the interest rates observed in the market at a point in time and the rates of inflation subsequently observed. (For a summary, see Roll 1972.)

Such a result suggests an inefficient market. If the rate of inflation is to some extent predictable, there should be relationships, such as the ones we observe, between interest rates and subsequent inflation rates. If inflation rates are predictable and no such relationships exist, the market is inefficient in the sense that, in setting interest rates, it is not making full use of relevant available information. In such a market, informed traders can reap abnormal returns—that is, expected real returns above equilibrium expected real returns—by trading on the basis of the information about inflation that the market does not fully utilize. In contrast, an efficient market, such as the one we apparently observe, uses all relevant information in setting interest rates, so that trading rules with expected returns higher than equilibrium expected returns do not exist.

I suspect that the negative results on market efficiency obtained by others reflect to a large extent the fact that earlier studies, including of course Fisher's, are based primarily on pre-1953 data. The negative results may to a large extent reflect poor commodity price data. By the same token, the positive results on market efficiency reported here are probably to a nonnegligible extent a consequence of the availability of good data on commodity prices beginning in 1953.

Poor commodity price data might also explain why the empirical literature is replete with evidence in support of the so-called Gibson Paradox, the proposition that there is a positive relationship between the nominal interest rate and the level of commodity prices, instead of the relationship between the interest rate and the rate of change in prices posited by Fisher.* With a poor price index, the Fisherian relationship between the nominal interest rate and the true inflation rate can be obscured by noise and by spurious autocorrelations in measured inflation rates. But over long periods of time (and the Gibson Paradox is usually posited as a long-run phenomenon) even a poor index picks up general movements in prices. Thus, if inflations and deflations tend to persist—an implication of the evidence presented here that $E(\tilde{\Delta}_t | \phi_{t-1})$ is close to a martingale—there may well appear to be a relationship between the level of the interest rate and the measured levels of prices which merely reflects the more fundamental Fisherian relationship between the interest rate and the rate of change of prices that is obscured by poor data. In the relatively clean data of the 1953–1971 period, however, the Fisherian relationship shows up clearly.

X. Extension of the Results to the Period of Price Controls

The results for one- to six-month bills for the pre-controls period are consistent with the hypotheses that the market is efficient and that equilibrium expected real returns on one- to six-month bills are constant through time. The model does not seem to fare so well when the tests are extended into the period of price controls that began in August 1971. Tables 6.5 and 6.6 reproduce the results in Tables 6.3 and 6.4 but for data extended through June 1974. As in Table 6.3, the autocorrelations of Δ_t in Table 6.5 are large, which indicates that there is substantial information about future rates of change in purchasing power in past rates of change. The autocorrelations of the real returns r_t in Table 6.5, are, however, generally positive and substantially larger than the autocorrelations of r_t for the pre-controls period in Table 6.3.

Since the autocorrelations of r_t are a joint test of market efficiency and of the hypothesis that equilibrium expected real returns are constant, we turn to the regression estimates in Table 6.6 for information about whether it is one or both facets of the model that are contradicted by the data. Contrary to the hypothesis that expected real returns are constant through time, the values of a_1 for (36) in Part 1 of Table 6.6 are much different from -1.0. There is also some evidence in the systematically positive residual autocorrelations for (36)

---

*For a discussion of the Gibson Paradox and a review of previous evidence, see Roll (1972). A more recent study is Sargent (1973).

TABLE 6.5
Sample Autocorrelations of Δ_t and r_t: One- to Six-Month Bills, Including Period of Price Controls

PART 1: AUTOCORRELATIONS OF Δ_t

PERIOD	BILL	$\hat\rho_1$	$\hat\rho_2$	$\hat\rho_3$	$\hat\rho_4$	$\hat\rho_5$	$\hat\rho_6$	$\hat\rho_7$	$\hat\rho_8$	$\hat\rho_9$	$\hat\rho_{10}$	$\hat\rho_{11}$	$\hat\rho_{12}$	$\sigma(\hat\rho_1)$	$\bar\Delta$	$s(\Delta)$	$SR(\Delta)$	$T-1$
1/53–6/74	1	.47	.53	.44	.46	.46	.48	.42	.45	.49	.46	.44	.50	.06	−.00233	.00282	8.54*	257
	2	.68	.62	.66	.64	.70	.58	.56	.42	.41	.38	.34	.35	.09	−.00456	.00470	5.59	128
	3	.74	.81	.79	.75	.61	.45	.47	.35	.41	.24	.51	.50	.11	−.00680	.00655	5.13	85
3/59–6/74	1	.50	.56	.50	.52	.58	.62	.51	.50	.55	.52	.53	.60	.07	−.00283	.00277	8.95*	183
	2	.75	.73	.86	.77	.78	.73	.69	.63	.49	.46	.47	.48	.11	−.00554	.00458	5.29	91
	3	.82	.99	.88	.90	.75	.57	.60	.44	.56	.36	.68	.61	.13	−.00830	.00648	5.20*	60
	4	.90	.97	.90	.76	.56	.63	.45	.59	.71	.71	.80	.98	.15	−.01078	.00811	4.61	45
	5	.98	.96	.74	.66	.59	.60	.67	.75	.89	.89	.85	.96	.17	−.01263	.00846	4.55	35
	6	.93	.90	.68	.74	.69	.78	.82	.96	.86	1.07	.93	.92	.19	−.01510	.01026	5.40*	29

PART 2: AUTOCORRELATIONS OF r_t

PERIOD	BILL	$\hat\rho_1$	$\hat\rho_2$	$\hat\rho_3$	$\hat\rho_4$	$\hat\rho_5$	$\hat\rho_6$	$\hat\rho_7$	$\hat\rho_8$	$\hat\rho_9$	$\hat\rho_{10}$	$\hat\rho_{11}$	$\hat\rho_{12}$	$\sigma(\hat\rho_1)$	$\bar r$	$s(r)$	$SR(r)$	$T-1$
1/53–6/74	1	.10	.20	.07	.05	.04	.08	.01	.07	.16	.16	.11	.24	.06	.00056	.00219	8.04*	257
	2	.28	.08	.11	.14	.34	.22	.26	.04	.05	.04	.08	.15	.09	.00143	.00327	5.33	128
	3	.24	.24	.27	.42	.22	−.07	.15	.00	.06	−.36	.18	.18	.11	.00240	.00435	5.30	85
3/59–6/74	1	.09	.21	.11	.08	.15	.23	.07	.07	.20	.18	.15	.31	.07	.00061	.00210	7.61*	183
	2	.32	.19	.37	.23	.39	.35	.34	.25	.10	.07	.21	.35	.11	.00156	.00308	5.43	91
	3	.33	.51	.29	.54	.31	.09	.31	.08	.17	−.31	.47	.18	.13	.00261	.00429	5.20	60
	4	.40	.48	.56	.33	.05	.48	−.17	.19	.38	−.10	.15	.61	.15	.00379	.00520	4.58	45
	5	.47	.51	.15	.38	.11	.01	.03	.01	.56	.60	.33	.72	.17	.00566	.00539	4.32	35
	6	.32	.35	.07	.64	.11	.36	.17	.91	.15	.84	.44	.33	.19	.00708	.00683	5.26*	29

*Studentized range exceeds the .95 fractile of the sampling distribution of the studentized range in samples from a normal population.

TABLE 6.6
Summary Statistics for Regression Tests on One- to Six-Month Bills, Including Period of Price Controls

PART 1: $\Delta_t = a_0 + a_1 R_t + e_t$

PERIOD	BILL	a_0	a_1	$s(a_0)$	$s(a_1)$	COEFF. OF DET.	$s(e)$	$\hat{\rho}_1(e)$	$\hat{\rho}_2(e)$	$\hat{\rho}_3(e)$	$SR(e)$	T
1/53–6/74	1	.00128	−1.25	.00029	.09	.43	.00217	.07	.17	.04	7.45*	258
	2	.00280	−1.23	.00065	.10	.57	.00323	.23	.01	.04	5.73	129
	3	.00427	−1.20	.00108	.10	.61	.00429	.16	.13	.16	5.37	86
3/59–6/74	1	.00212	−1.44	.00041	.11	.48	.00203	−.00	.14	.02	7.32*	184
	2	.00450	−1.41	.00087	.11	.63	.00294	.18	−.02	.14	4.87	92
	3	.00703	−1.40	.00155	.13	.65	.00404	.11	.18	.02	5.31*	61
	4	.01003	−1.43	.00236	.15	.67	.00516	.08	.13	.29	4.97	46
	5	.00975	−1.22	.00296	.15	.66	.00568	.25	.26	−.03	4.20	36
	6	.01242	−1.22	.00378	.15	.68	.00650	.09	.07	−.13	5.32*	30

PART 2: $\Delta_t = a_0 + a_1 R_t + a_2 \Delta_{t-1} + e_t$

BILL	a_0	a_1	a_2	$s(a_0)$	$s(a_1)$	$s(a_2)$	COEFF. OF DET.	$s(e)$	$\hat{\rho}_1(e)$	$\hat{\rho}_2(e)$	$\hat{\rho}_3(e)$	$SR(e)$	T
1/53–6/74													
1	.00115	−1.14	.09	.00030	.12	.06	.43	.00216	−.05	.18	.03	7.57*	257
2	.00197	−.92	.25	.00065	.13	.09	.59	.00305	.03	−.01	.08	5.09	128
3	.00294	−.88	.27	.00114	.16	.11	.63	.00412	−.07	.14	.08	5.03	85
3/59–6/74													
1	.00205	−1.40	.03	.00044	.15	.08	.48	.00204	−.03	.14	.02	7.48*	183
2	.00362	−1.14	.20	.00101	.19	.11	.64	.00292	.01	−.06	.18	4.97	91
3	.00534	−1.05	.26	.00193	.25	.16	.67	.00398	−.14	.25	−.03	4.89	60
4	.00630	−.89	.41	.00292	.29	.18	.70	.00498	−.19	.19	.18	4.91	45
5	.00365	−.46	.67	.00368	.32	.24	.72	.00524	−.05	.28	−.10	4.54	35
6	.00680	−.69	.45	.00523	.36	.28	.69	.00642	−.04	.08	−.24	5.47*	29

*Studentized range exceeds the .95 fractile of the sampling distribution of the studentized range in samples from a normal population.

that the market efficiency hypothesis is in conflict with the evidence. This shows up more clearly in the results for (37) in Part 2 of Table 6.6. The estimates a_2 of the regression coefficient for Δ_{t-1} are all positive and generally large relative to their standard errors. For the period of price controls the nominal rate R_t set at time $t-1$ apparently does not summarize all of the information about the expected value of $\tilde{\Delta}_t$ which is in the most recent observed value Δ_{t-1}.

Thus, neither the market efficiency hypothesis nor the hypothesis that expected real returns are constant through time does well on data that include the period of price controls from August 1971 to June 1974. One can at this point discard the model or the data. I shall argue for the latter. Specifically, I shall argue that the CPI data for the period of price controls are not appropriate for testing the model, and that conclusions about the model should be based on the pre-controls period.

Let me first describe what happens in the data for the period of controls. When controls on different prices were slowly lifted in the last months of 1973 and the first few months of 1974, successive large negative values of Δ_t were observed. As anyone who lived through this period knows, reported monthly inflation rates were extremely high. Interest rates on Treasury bills were high, but not nearly so high as the model would predict. The extreme negative values of Δ_t, when combined with insufficient adjustment of R_t, pull the estimates a_1 in (36) down below the theoretical value -1.0, which shows up so nicely in the tests for the pre-controls period. Since the insufficient adjustment of R_t and the large negative values of Δ_t persist for some time, R_t seems to be ignoring the information in past inflation rates. Thus, the coefficients of Δ_{t-1} in (37) turn out substantially positive, and positive autocorrelation is observed both in real returns and in the residuals from (36). The reason that such a relatively short period can have such a large impact on the results is that the period generates extreme observations. These get heavy weight in least squares estimates, which, after all, are concerned with minimizing sums of squared errors.

The presence of extreme observations or "outliers" is not in itself a basis for concluding that CPI data for the controls period are inappropriate for testing the model. An efficient market does not shut down because inflation rates are extreme. The conclusion that data for the period of controls are inappropriate must be based on the argument that the CPI for this period does not accurately measure true price changes. I think the case is clear. Quoted prices during periods of controls do not reflect true cost of goods to consumers. If the prices of goods are fixed at levels below equilibrium prices, there are shortages, queues, and other distortions that raise the effictive cost of goods to consumers above quoted prices. For example, anyone who waited in line for an hour or more during the winter of 1973-1974, attempting, often futilely, to purchase gasoline at prices fixed below equilibrium levels, was aware that the effective price of gasoline was well above the quoted price. When the quoted price was allowed to rise in successive months of early 1974, pulling the CPI along with it, the gas lines eventually disappeared. The effective price of gasoline, if it rose at all, certainly did not rise as much as the quoted price. Similar statements can be made for other goods.

The argument, then, is that the large increases in the CPI—and, consequently, the extreme negative values of Δ_t observed as price controls were lifted early in 1974—reflect the adjustment of quoted prices to levels more like what consumers were effectively paying during the immediately preceding period of controls. Measured changes in the CPI for this period overstate true price changes. Conversely, measured changes in the CPI during the period of controls but prior to the lifting of controls probably understate true price changes. Thus, one would expect higher interest rates during this period than if one took measured inflation rates at face value. Fama and MacBeth (1974) report a regression of the one-month version of Δ_t on the one-month bill rate for 1953-1972. Their estimate of a_1 in (36) is $-.90$, as compared to $-.98$ for the 1/53-7/71 period in Table 6.2 and -1.25 for the 1/53-6/74 period in Table 6.6. Thus, consistent with our interpretation of the effects of controls, the interest rate overshoots the measured inflation rates in the period (ending in 1972), that includes the controls but not the lifting of controls, while the interest rate undershoots the measured inflation rates for the period (ending in 1974) that includes the lifting of controls.

In any case, it seems safe to argue that the price controls create distortions in the market which make the price data for this period of questionable value for tests of market efficiency. Conclusions about the hypotheses that the market is efficient and that equilibrium expected real returns are constant through time are probably best based on tests for the free-market period 1953-1971. The results in Tables 6.1 to 6.4 indicate that for this period both hypotheses are good approximations to the world.

XI.   Conclusions

The two major conclusions of this chapter are as follows. First, during 1953-1971, the bond market seems to be efficient in the sense that in setting one- to six-month nominal rates of interest, the market correctly uses all the information about future rates of change in purchasing power that is in the time series of past rates of change. Second, one cannot reject the hypothesis that equilibrium expected real returns on one- to six-month bills are constant during the period. When combined with the conclusion that the market is efficient, this means that one also cannot reject the hypothesis that all variation through time in one- to six-month nominal rates of interest mirrors variation in correctly assessed one- to six-month expected rates of change in purchasing power.

For our purposes, the conclusion that the market is efficient is of more interest than the conclusion that expected real returns are constant through time. To test market efficiency, it is always necessary to have a model of market equilibrium. The results indicate that for Treasury bills, and for the 1953–1971 period, the assumption that equilibrium expected real returns are constant is close enough to reality to be a meaningful vehicle for tests of efficiency. But it would have been a matter of indifference if the data had indicated that some other model of market equilibrium were more appropriate, so long as it also yielded meaningful tests of efficiency.

Moreover, our tests of the assumption that expected real returns are constant are narrow in scope. We look for variation in expected real returns that would lead to nonzero autocorrelations of observed real returns, and we look for variation in expected real returns as a linear function of the level of nominal rates. There are many other interesting possibilities that remain untested. For example, equilibrium expected real returns might be related to variation in economic activity, to changes in the rate of change in the money supply, to foreign investment in bills, and so forth. On the other hand, any such variation through time in expected real returns must be random in character or small relative to the variation through time of real returns. Otherwise, it would show up more systematically in the sample autocorrelations of the real returns.

CHAPTER

7

The Two-Parameter Portfolio Model

I. Introduction

In Chapter 2 the two-parameter portfolio model was introduced. We now consider the model in more detail. We proceed in three steps. This chapter discusses portfolio decisions by investors in a two-parameter world. The model is credited to Markowitz (1952; 1959), who is rightfully regarded as the founder of modern portfolio theory. The next chapter considers the implications of the portfolio model for the pricing of securities. That is, if investors make portfolio decisions according to the two-parameter model, what does this imply about the way securities are priced in the capital market? In particular, how does the capital market view risk? In the setting of prices, what is the relationship between expected return and risk? Finally, Chapter 9 presents empirical tests of the expected return-risk relationships developed in Chapter 8.

In discussing the two-parameter portfolio model in this chapter, we first give a general treatment of its major features. We then discuss different aspects of the model in more detail.

II. Normal Distributions, Risk Aversion, and the Efficient Set

A. The Framework

In the most common version of the two-parameter portfolio model, and the only version that we treat here, it is assumed that at time $t = 1$ the investor has wealth w_1 which he must allocate to current consumption c_1 and to an investment $(w_1 - c_1)$ in some portfolio of securities. The value of his portfolio at time $t = 2$ provides his consumption c_2 for time 2. Thus, the investor consumes and invests at time 1, and at time 2 he consumes the market value of the investment made at time 1. Since only one period passes between time 1 and time 2, we call this a one-period model.

The investor's wealth w_1 is the market value of all his resources at time 1. It includes the market value of securities, real estate, and any other assets purchased in previous periods, along with any income from his labor that he receives at time 1. Since we are concerned with the portfolio decision at time 1, to simplify things we assume that the investor's wealth at time 2 derives completely from the market value of the portfolio that he chooses at time 1.

It is assumed that at time 1 an investor can purchase as much or as little of any security as he sees fit, and securities are assumed to be infinitely divisible. It is also assumed that there are no transactions costs (e.g., brokerage fees) in purchasing and selling securities and that any investor can buy or sell as much as he likes of any security without affecting its price. In short, investors are atomistic competitors in frictionless markets, a statement we summarize by saying that the capital market is perfect. Throughout the rest of the book we assume that the capital market is perfect in this sense.

The problem facing the investor at time 1 is to allocate his wealth w_1 to consumption c_1 and to an investment $(w_1 - c_1)$ in some portfolio in such a way as to maximize the satisfaction or welfare that he anticipates from consumption at time 1 and time 2. Consumption at time 2 is, however, a random variable at time 1, since the return from time 1 to time 2 on a portfolio chosen at time 1 is generally unknown at time 1. In formal terms, if the investor chooses current consumption c_1 and invests $(w_1 - c_1)$ in the portfolio p, his wealth and consumption at time 2 are

$$\tilde{c}_2 = \tilde{w}_2 = (w_1 - c_1)(1 + \tilde{R}_p), \tag{1}$$

where the random variable $\tilde{R}_p$ is the return on the portfolio p from time 1 to time 2.* Thus, the investor's problem is to choose an optimal combination of

---

*Since we are discussing a one-period world in this chapter, it is unnecessary to include a time subscript on the portfolio return. As usual, tildes ($\sim$) are used to denote random variables.

current consumption c_1 and a probability distribution on $\tilde{c}_2$. Equivalently, he must choose a value of c_1 and a probability distribution of portfolio return.

B. The Simplifications Obtained When Portfolio Return Distributions Are Normal

It is assumed that the investor can rank all possible combinations of c_1 and probability distributions of $\tilde{c}_2$ according to the level of welfare he perceives that they provide. This assumption is so general, however, that it yields nothing in the way of propositions about observable behavior. We would like to simplify the decision problem so that it involves only a few potentially measurable parameters and yields some simple propositions about how the typical investor behaves with respect to these parameters.

One way to accomplish this goal is to assume that the joint distribution of security returns is multivariate normal, so that probability distributions of portfolio returns are normal (see Chapter 2). The property of normal distributions that simplifies the consumption-investment decision is the fact that any normal distribution can be completely described from knowledge of its mean and standard deviation.* Thus, if the distribution of the return $\tilde{R}_p$ on any portfolio p is normal with mean $E(\tilde{R}_p)$ and standard deviation $\sigma(\tilde{R}_p)$, then from (1) and the properties of the normal distribution we know that the probability distribution of consumption at time 2 obtained with portfolio p is normal with mean and standard deviation

$$E(\tilde{c}_2) = (w_1 - c_1)[1 + E(\tilde{R}_p)] \tag{2}$$

$$\sigma(\tilde{c}_2) = (w_1 - c_1)\,\sigma(\tilde{R}_p). \tag{3}$$

In short, when all portfolio return distributions are normal, knowledge of c_1, $E(\tilde{R}_p)$, and $\sigma(\tilde{R}_p)$ is sufficient to describe completely the combination of current consumption and probability distribution on future consumption associated with any choice of c_1 and portfolio p. If all portfolio return distributions are normal, the investor can rank the different combinations of c_1 and probability distribution on $\tilde{c}_2$ available in terms of the values of c_1, $E(\tilde{R}_p)$, and $\sigma(\tilde{R}_p)$ that they imply.

C. The Simplifications Obtained When Investors Are Risk-averse

The assumption that portfolio return distributions are normal reduces the consumption-investment decision to a three-dimensional problem involving

---

*At this point the reader may want to review the discussion of normal distributions in Chapter 1.

the choice of c_1, $E(\tilde{R}_p)$, and $\sigma(\tilde{R}_p)$. Additional simplifications can be obtained with assumptions about the investor's tastes and, in particular, about his attitudes toward $E(\tilde{R}_p)$ and $\sigma(\tilde{R}_p)$. We assume that for given values of c_1 and $\sigma(\tilde{R}_p)$, the investor prefers more expected portfolio return to less. From equations (2) and (3) we can see that this is equivalent to assuming that for given values of c_1 and $\sigma(\tilde{c}_2)$, the investor prefers more expected consumption at time 2 to less. Next we assume that the investor is risk-averse in the sense that for given values of c_1 and $E(\tilde{R}_p)$, he prefers less standard deviation of portfolio return to more. From equations (2) and (3) we can again see that this is equivalent to assuming that for given values of c_1 and $E(\tilde{c}_2)$, the investor prefers less standard deviation of consumption at time 2 to more. To characterize this assumption by saying that the investor is risk-averse is to assume that the risk of a portfolio can be measured by the standard deviation of its return. This is reasonable with normal portfolio return distributions, since the dispersion of the return distribution, and thus of the distribution of consumption at time 2, can be completely described in terms of the standard deviation of the return.

The assumptions that portfolio return distributions are normal and that the investor likes expected portfolio return but is averse to standard deviation of portfolio return imply the fundamental result of the two-parameter portfolio model. The investor's optimal portfolio is an efficient portfolio, where to be classified as efficient a portfolio must have the property that no other portfolio with the same or higher expected return has lower standard deviation of return.* The argument goes as follows. With normal portfolio return distributions, the consumption-investment decision reduces to choosing c_1, $E(\tilde{R}_p)$, and $\sigma(\tilde{R}_p)$. If the investor's tastes are such that conditional on any given values of c_1 and $\sigma(\tilde{R}_p)$ more expected return is preferred to less, then among all portfolios with a given value of $\sigma(\tilde{R}_p)$ the most preferred portfolio is the one with the largest value of $E(\tilde{R}_p)$. On the other hand, if for any given values of c_1 and $E(\tilde{R}_p)$ less standard deviation of return is preferred to more, then among all portfolios with a given $E(\tilde{R}_p)$ the most preferred portfolio is the one with the smallest value of $\sigma(\tilde{R}_p)$.

Taken together, these two statements say that with normal return distributions, a risk-averse investor only considers a portfolio if it has the largest possible expected return given its standard deviation of return, and if it has the smallest possible standard deviation of return given its expected return. A portfolio that has these two properties is called efficient, and the collection of portfolios that have these two portfolios is called the efficient set. Alterna-

---

*The concept of portfolio efficiency should not be confused with the concept of market efficiency discussed in Chapters 5 and 6. The terminology, if a bit unfortunate, is standard.

tively, the two properties of an efficient portfolio can be summarized in terms of a single property which requires that for a portfolio to be efficient, there must be no other portfolio with the same or higher expected return that has lower standard deviation of return.

D. Geometric Interpretation

All of this has a convenient geometric interpretation. The curves U_1 to U_6 in Figure 7.1 give a possible representation of the investor's tastes for expected return and standard deviation of return, conditional on some value of

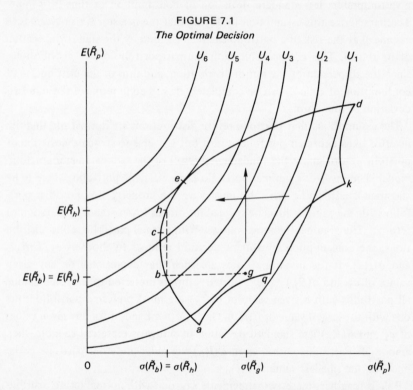

FIGURE 7.1
The Optimal Decision

current consumption c_1. Each of the curves represents combinations of $E(\tilde{R}_p)$ and $\sigma(\tilde{R}_p)$ among which the investor is indifferent; no combination of $E(\tilde{R}_p)$ and $\sigma(\tilde{R}_p)$ along a curve is preferred to any other combination on the curve. The assumptions that the investor likes expected return but is averse to standard deviation of return imply that any such indifference curve must be positively sloped. If the investor regards two portfolios as equivalent in the sense that neither is preferred to the other, the portfolio with the higher standard deviation of return must also have higher expected return. Moreover, with our assumptions about the investor's tastes, higher indifference curves imply more preferred combinations of $E(\tilde{R}_p)$ and $\sigma(\tilde{R}_p)$. Or, as suggested by the arrows in Figure 7.1, the level of the investor's satisfaction increases as we consider combinations of $E(\tilde{R}_p)$ and $\sigma(\tilde{R}_p)$ further upward and/or further to the left in the $E(\tilde{R}_p)$, $\sigma(\tilde{R}_p)$ plane.

Having given a geometric interpretation of the investor's tastes, we now turn to the other ingredient in his decision problem, his portfolio opportunities, the feasible or attainable combinations of expected return and standard deviation of return. We spend considerable space in the rest of this chapter discussing the shapes that the opportunity set can take when plotted in the mean-standard deviation plane, but for the moment let us just assume that the possible combinations of expected return and standard deviation of return are on or within the rather irregularly shaped curve *acdkq* in Figure 7.1. All points on or within the curve are combinations of $E(\tilde{R}_p)$ and $\sigma(\tilde{R}_p)$ attainable with some portfolio, but combinations outside the curve are not attainable.

Given our assumptions about tastes, however, only a small part of the investment opportunity set is relevant. For example, because the investor dislikes standard deviation of return, the portfolio *b* is strictly preferred to the portfolio *g*, since *g* has the same expected return as *b* but higher standard deviation of return. Indeed, the investor's aversion to standard deviation of portfolio return allows us to rule out immediately all portfolios except those along the left boundary of the opportunity set. However, many of the points along the left boundary can also be ruled out as a consequence of the fact that the investor likes expected return. Thus, the portfolio *b* is dominated by the portfolio *h*, which has the same standard deviation of return as *b* but higher expected return.

In short, the assumptions that the investor likes expected return but is averse to standard deviation of return imply that among the investment opportunities shown in Figure 7.1, the only portfolios the investor might possibly choose are those along the positively sloped segment *cd* of the left boundary of the opportunity set. Each of the portfolios along this segment has the efficiency property that no other portfolio with the same or higher expected return has lower standard deviation of return, and only portfolios along *cd* have this property. Thus the segment *cd* is the efficient set of portfolios. When we later consider the geometry of the efficient set in more detail, we find that the efficient set of portfolios is always the positively sloped segment of the upper left boundary of the opportunity set.

Given the representation of the investor's tastes and portfolio opportunities in Figure 7.1, the optimal efficient portfolio is *e*, which is the portfolio that puts the investor on the highest attainable indifference curve. Recall, however, that the indifference curves in Figure 7.1 represent the investor's tastes for $E(\tilde{R}_p)$ and $\sigma(\tilde{R}_p)$ conditional on some assumed value of c_1. The consumption-investment decision, after all, involves choice of an optimal combination of c_1, $E(\tilde{R}_p)$, and $\sigma(\tilde{R}_p)$, and the details of the investor's tastes for $E(\tilde{R}_p)$ and $\sigma(\tilde{R}_p)$ need not be the same for different assumed values of c_1. In terms of Figure 7.1, his indifference curves may be different depending on the value of c_1, and the portfolio that is optimal for one assumed value of c_1 is not necessarily optimal for other values of c_1. Thus, if we wish to think about the solution to the consumption-investment problem in geometric terms, we must, in the general manner of Figure 7.1, determine the optimal portfolio for each possible value of c_1 and then choose the *optimum optimorum*—that is, the value of current consumption c_1 and the associated optimal portfolio that maximizes the investor's welfare.

For our purposes, however, the important result, the one on which we build in this and the following chapters, is that in the assumed framework, the optimum portfolio for any and thus for the optimum choice of c_1 is an efficient portfolio. The next chapter considers the characteristics of market equilibrium in a world where investors make portfolio decisions according to the two-parameter model. It turns out that the measurement of risk and especially the relationships between equilibrium expected returns and risk that are relevant in a two-parameter world are direct implications of the fact that in such a world investors hold efficient portfolios. Chapter 9 then considers whether observed relationships between average returns and risk are in accordance with the predictions of the two-parameter model. These tests can be interpreted as asking whether the prices of securities are in line with the hypothesis that investors hold or attempt to hold efficient portfolios. In short, by the time discussion of the two-parameter model is finished, the dominant role played by the concept of portfolio efficiency and by the characteristics of efficient portfolios will be evident.

Finally, the preceding is an intuitive and rather general discussion of how the tastes of a risk-averse investor combine with the characteristics of his portfolio opportunities to yield the conclusion that the optimal portfolio must be efficient. The characteristics of portfolio opportunities in a world where portfolio return distributions are normal are the subject matter of the rest of this chapter. The geometry of the efficient set is developed, and then risk and the effects of diversification on portfolio risk are discussed.

III. The Geometry of the Efficient Set

We first consider the geometric properties of portfolios that are combinations of two securities or portfolios. The geometric properties of the efficient set of portfolios follow almost directly. The reader is assumed to be familiar with the material of Chapter 2.

A. The Geometry of Combinations of Two
Securities or Portfolios

Let q and s be two securities or portfolios. For later purposes, it is important to keep in mind that either or both q and s can be portfolios. Consider portfolios that are combinations of q and s with the proportion x of portfolio funds $w_1 - c_1$ invested in q and $(1 - x)$ invested in s. The return, expected return, and standard deviation of return for such portfolios are

$$\tilde{R}_p = x\tilde{R}_q + (1 - x)\tilde{R}_s \tag{4}$$

$$E(\tilde{R}_p) = xE(\tilde{R}_q) + (1 - x)E(\tilde{R}_s) \tag{5}$$

$$\sigma(\tilde{R}_p) = [x^2\sigma^2(\tilde{R}_q) + (1 - x)^2\,\sigma^2(\tilde{R}_s) + 2x(1 - x)\,\mathrm{cov}\,(\tilde{R}_q,\tilde{R}_s)]^{1/2}. \tag{6}$$

For current purposes, it is more convenient to express $\sigma(\tilde{R}_p)$ in terms of corr $(\tilde{R}_q,\tilde{R}_s)$, the correlation coefficient between $\tilde{R}_q$ and $\tilde{R}_s$, than in terms of the covariance cov $(\tilde{R}_q,\tilde{R}_s)$. Thus, since

$$\mathrm{corr}\,(\tilde{R}_q,\tilde{R}_s) = \frac{\mathrm{cov}\,(\tilde{R}_q,\tilde{R}_s)}{\sigma(\tilde{R}_q)\,\sigma(\tilde{R}_s)}, \tag{7}$$

equation (6) can be rewritten as

$$\sigma(\tilde{R}_p) = [x^2\sigma^2(\tilde{R}_q) + (1 - x)^2\,\sigma^2(\tilde{R}_s)$$
$$+ 2x(1 - x)\,\mathrm{corr}\,(\tilde{R}_q,\tilde{R}_s)\,\sigma(\tilde{R}_q)\,\sigma(\tilde{R}_s)]^{1/2}. \tag{8}$$

POSITIVELY WEIGHTED COMBINATIONS ($0 \leqslant x \leqslant 1$)

Consider now the extreme and unrealistic case where the correlation coefficient between $\tilde{R}_q$ and $\tilde{R}_s$ is 1.0; that is, there is a perfect positive correlation between $\tilde{R}_q$ and $\tilde{R}_s$, so that the value of $\tilde{R}_q$ is perfectly predictable from the value of $\tilde{R}_s$ (and vice versa). Then (8) becomes

$$\sigma(\tilde{R}_p) = [x^2\sigma^2(\tilde{R}_q) + (1 - x)^2\sigma^2(\tilde{R}_s) + 2x(1 - x)\,\sigma(\tilde{R}_q)\,\sigma(\tilde{R}_s)]^{1/2} \tag{9}$$

$$= |x\sigma(\tilde{R}_q) + (1 - x)\,\sigma(\tilde{R}_s)|, \quad \mathrm{corr}\,(\tilde{R}_q,\tilde{R}_s) = 1.0. \tag{10}$$

The absolute value sign is necessary to ensure that we take the positive root in computing the standard deviation from the variance. Standard deviations must be nonnegative. For the moment, however, we consider only nonnegative values of x and $(1 - x)$. Since $\sigma(\tilde{R}_q)$ and $\sigma(\tilde{R}_s)$ are nonnegative, when x and $(1 - x)$ are nonnegative, the absolute value sign in (10) is unnecessary, and $\sigma(\tilde{R}_p)$ is just the weighted average of the component standard deviations, $\sigma(\tilde{R}_q)$ and $\sigma(\tilde{R}_s)$. Since $E(\tilde{R}_p)$ is always just the weighted average of the component expected returns, $E(\tilde{R}_q)$ and $E(\tilde{R}_s)$, in the case of perfect positive correlation, both $E(\tilde{R}_p)$ and $\sigma(\tilde{R}_p)$ are weighted averages of the expected returns and standard deviations of $\tilde{R}_q$ and $\tilde{R}_s$.

This result has a simple geometric interpretation. Suppose the expected values and standard deviations of $\tilde{R}_q$ and $\tilde{R}_s$ are as shown in Figure 7.2. In terms of equations (5) and (10), point q in Figure 7.2 corresponds to $x = 1.0$

FIGURE 7.2

Geometry of Combinations of Two Securities or Portfolios

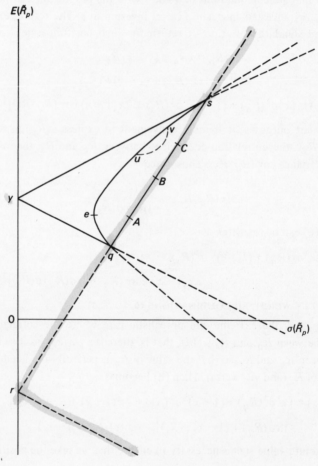

and $(1 - x) = 0.0$, so that all portfolio funds are invested in q; point s corresponds to $x = 0.0$, and $(1 - x) = 1.0$, so that all funds are invested in s. With perfect positive correlation between $\tilde{R}_q$ and $\tilde{R}_s$, any value of x between 1.0 and 0.0 generates a combination of $E(\tilde{R}_p)$ and $\sigma(\tilde{R}_p)$ along the straight line between q and s. For example, point B in Figure 7.2 represents the combination of $E(\tilde{R}_p)$ and $\sigma(\tilde{R}_p)$ obtained with $x = .5$ and $(1 - x) = .5$, that is, when portfolio funds are divided equally between q and s. In this case

$$E(\tilde{R}_B) = .5E(\tilde{R}_q) + .5E(\tilde{R}_s)$$

is just halfway between $E(\tilde{R}_q)$ and $E(\tilde{R}_s)$. From equation (10),

$$\sigma(\tilde{R}_B) = .5\sigma(\tilde{R}_q) + .5\sigma(\tilde{R}_s)$$

is likewise halfway between $\sigma(\tilde{R}_q)$ and $\sigma(\tilde{R}_s)$. Point A in Figure 7.2 represents the combination of $E(\tilde{R}_p)$ and $\sigma(\tilde{R}_p)$ obtained with $x = .75$ and $1 - x = .25$, while C is the portfolio corresponding to $x = .25$ and $1 - x = .75$. Point A is along the straight line between q and s, and it is just one-quarter of the way between q and s. Likewise, portfolio C is three-quarters of the way between q and s along the straight line between q and s.

Suppose now that the expected values and standard deviations of $\tilde{R}_q$ and $\tilde{R}_s$ are as shown in Figure 7.2 but that there is less than perfect positive correlation between the two returns. What can we say about the combinations of $E(\tilde{R}_p)$ and $\sigma(\tilde{R}_p)$ obtained from portfolios of q and s formed in the manner of equation (4)? First of all, the correlation between $\tilde{R}_q$ and $\tilde{R}_s$ has no effect on $E(\tilde{R}_p)$. The expected return on any portfolio of q and s is always just the appropriate weighted average of $E(\tilde{R}_q)$ and $E(\tilde{R}_s)$. From (8), however, we can see that the correlation between $\tilde{R}_q$ and $\tilde{R}_s$ affects the standard deviation of the return on a portfolio of q and s. For given $x(0 < x < 1)$ and given values of $\sigma^2(\tilde{R}_q)$ and $\sigma^2(\tilde{R}_s)$, the largest possible value of $\sigma(\tilde{R}_p)$ occurs when corr $(\tilde{R}_q, \tilde{R}_s) = 1.0$, in which case (10) holds. With less than perfect positive correlation, $\sigma(\tilde{R}_p)$ is less than the quantity given by (10),

$$\sigma(\tilde{R}_p) < x\sigma(\tilde{R}_q) + (1 - x)\sigma(\tilde{R}_s), \quad 0 < x < 1, \quad \text{corr } (\tilde{R}_q, \tilde{R}_s) < 1.0, \quad (11)$$

and for given x and given values of $\sigma^2(\tilde{R}_q)$ and $\sigma^2(\tilde{R}_s)$, $\sigma(\tilde{R}_p)$ is smaller the lower the correlation between $\tilde{R}_q$ and $\tilde{R}_s$.

These results have an important implication. Equation (10) says that when the correlation between the returns on two assets or portfolios like q and s is 1.0, diversification is ineffective in reducing dispersion: the standard deviation of the return on a portfolio which is just a weighted combination of q and s is the corresponding weighted average of $\sigma(\tilde{R}_q)$ and $\sigma(\tilde{R}_s)$. On the other hand, (11) says that when corr $(\tilde{R}_q, \tilde{R}_s) < 1.0$, $\sigma(\tilde{R}_p)$ is less than the weighted average of $\sigma(\tilde{R}_q)$ and $\sigma(\tilde{R}_s)$, and $\sigma(\tilde{R}_p)$ decreases as corr $(\tilde{R}_q, \tilde{R}_s)$ decreases. Thus, when there is less than perfect positive correlation between the returns on two assets or portfolios q and s, diversification is an effective way to reduce dispersion, and it is more effective the further corr $(\tilde{R}_q, \tilde{R}_s)$ is from 1.0.

The opposite extreme from perfect positive correlation is perfect negative correlation, corr $(\tilde{R}_q, \tilde{R}_s) = -1.0$; for given $x(0 < x < 1)$ and given values of $\sigma(\tilde{R}_q)$ and $\sigma(\tilde{R}_s)$, perfect negative correlation gives the smallest possible value of $\sigma(\tilde{R}_p)$. With perfect negative correlation, equation (8) becomes

$$\sigma(\tilde{R}_p) = [x^2 \sigma^2(\tilde{R}_q) + (1 - x)^2 \sigma^2(\tilde{R}_s) - 2x(1 - x) \sigma(\tilde{R}_q) \sigma(\tilde{R}_s)]^{1/2}$$

$$= |x\sigma(\tilde{R}_q) - (1 - x)\sigma(\tilde{R}_s)|, \quad \text{corr} (\tilde{R}_q, \tilde{R}_s) = -1.0. \tag{12}$$

One consequence of perfect negative correlation is that there is a portfolio of q and s, with both x and $(1 - x)$ strictly positive, that has zero standard deviation of return. From (12) we determine that $\sigma(\tilde{R}_p) = 0.0$ when

$$x = \frac{\sigma(\tilde{R}_s)}{\sigma(\tilde{R}_q) + \sigma(\tilde{R}_s)}. \tag{13}$$

Moreover, (12) also implies that when corr $(\tilde{R}_q, \tilde{R}_s) = -1.0$,

$$\sigma(\tilde{R}_p) = x\sigma(\tilde{R}_q) - (1 - x)\sigma(\tilde{R}_s), \quad \text{when } x > \frac{\sigma(\tilde{R}_s)}{\sigma(\tilde{R}_q) + \sigma(\tilde{R}_s)}, \tag{14}$$

$$\sigma(\tilde{R}_p) = (1 - x)\sigma(\tilde{R}_s) - x\sigma(\tilde{R}_q), \quad \text{when } x < \frac{\sigma(\tilde{R}_s)}{\sigma(\tilde{R}_q) + \sigma(\tilde{R}_s)}. \tag{15}$$

In geometric terms, when $x = 1.0$ we are at point q in Figure 7.2. For smaller values of x, the combinations of $E(\tilde{R}_p)$ and $\sigma(\tilde{R}_p)$ obtained are at first described by (5) and (14). Since these equations are both linear in x, we move away from q along a straight line that touches the $E(\tilde{R}_p)$ axis at y when x takes the value given by (13). For still lower values of x, the combinations of $E(\tilde{R}_p)$ and $\sigma(\tilde{R}_p)$ obtained are given by (5) and (15), so that we move along another straight line away from y in the direction of the point s in Figure 7.2, which is reached when $x = 0.0$. Thus when corr $(\tilde{R}_q, \tilde{R}_s) = -1.0$, the two line segments that meet at y on the $E(\tilde{R})$ axis in Figure 7.2 describe the combinations of $E(\tilde{R}_p)$ and $\sigma(\tilde{R}_p)$ obtained by varying x in (4).

For given $x(0 < x < 1)$ and given values of $\sigma^2(\tilde{R}_q)$ and $\sigma^2(\tilde{R}_s)$, the maximum possible value of $\sigma(\tilde{R}_p)$ occurs when $\tilde{R}_q$ and $\tilde{R}_s$ are perfectly positively correlated, while the minimum possible value of $\sigma(\tilde{R}_p)$ occurs when $\tilde{R}_q$ and $\tilde{R}_s$ are perfectly negatively correlated. When $-1 < \text{corr} (\tilde{R}_q, \tilde{R}_s) < 1$, the value of $\sigma(\tilde{R}_p)$ is greater than the value obtained when corr $(\tilde{R}_q, \tilde{R}_s) = -1.0$ and less than the value obtained when corr $(\tilde{R}_q, \tilde{R}_s) = 1.0$. Thus when $-1 < \text{corr} (\tilde{R}_q, \tilde{R}_s) < 1$, the plot of the combinations of $E(\tilde{R}_p)$ and $\sigma(\tilde{R}_p)$ obtained by varying x between 1.0 and 0.0 in (4) is a curve that starts at point q in Figure 7.2 and ends at s. The curve must be to the left of the line between q and s, since this line describes the combinations of $E(\tilde{R}_p)$ and $\sigma(\tilde{R}_p)$ obtained when $\tilde{R}_q$ and $\tilde{R}_s$ are perfectly positively correlated. The curve must also be to the right of the two line segments that describe the combinations of $E(\tilde{R}_p)$ and $\sigma(\tilde{R}_p)$ obtained with perfect negative correlation between $\tilde{R}_q$ and $\tilde{R}_s$. In short, with less than perfect correlation, the combinations of $E(\tilde{R}_p)$ and $\sigma(\tilde{R}_p)$ obtained from portfolios of q and s must lie along a curve somewhat like qes in Figure 7.2.

In fact, the curve traced by portfolios of q and s must have the specific properties exhibited by the curve qes in Figure 7.2. Any positively sloped segment of the curve (like es) must be concave, and any negatively sloped segment (like qe) must be convex.* To establish these properties, suppose first that they do not hold. Thus, suppose that the positively sloped segment of the curve in Figure 7.2 has a convex section like the dashed curve between points u and v. Since u and v are themselves portfolios of q and s, any portfolio of q and s that gives a combination of $E(\tilde{R}_p)$ and $\sigma(\tilde{R}_p)$ along the dashed curve between u and v can be expressed as a portfolio of u and v. But the arguments of the preceding paragraphs imply that portfolios of u and v must plot either along a straight line between u and v (if u and v are perfectly positively correlated) or to the left of the line between u and v (if u and v are less than perfectly positively correlated). Thus, the dashed curve between u and v cannot represent portfolios of u and v, so it cannot represent portfolios of q and s. Successive application of these arguments leads to the conclusion that any positively sloped segment of the curve generated by portfolios of q and s must be concave, while any negatively sloped segment must be convex.

PROBLEM III.A

1. Show that any portfolio of q and s that yields a point between u and v in Figure 7.2 can be expressed as a portfolio of u and v.

ANSWER

1. Let x_u and x_v be the proportions of portfolio funds invested in q to form the portfolios u and v, so that $1 - x_u$ and $1 - x_v$ are the proportions invested in s. Consider any third portfolio k of q and s such that

$$x_u > x_k > x_v.$$

---

*A curve or a segment of a curve is concave if a straight line between any two points is everywhere on or below the curve. A curve or a segment of a curve is convex if a straight line between any two points is everywhere on or above the curve. With strict concavity a straight line between any two points lies below the curve, while with strict convexity a straight line between any two points is above the curve.

There is a value of y, $0 < y < 1$, such that

$$x_k = yx_u + (1 - y)x_v.$$

Thus, the return on portfolio k can be expressed as

$$\begin{aligned}
\tilde{R}_k &= x_k \tilde{R}_q + (1 - x_k)\tilde{R}_s \\
&= [yx_u + (1 - y)x_v]\tilde{R}_q + \{1 - [yx_u + (1 - y)x_v]\}\tilde{R}_s \\
&= y[x_u \tilde{R}_q + (1 - x_u)\tilde{R}_s] + (1 - y)[x_v \tilde{R}_q + (1 - x_v)\tilde{R}_s] \\
&= y\tilde{R}_u + (1 - y)\tilde{R}_v.
\end{aligned}$$

THE ANALYSIS OF SHORT-SELLING

In the preceding discussion, we assumed that x, the proportion of portfolio funds invested in q, was between 0.0 and 1.0, so that $(1 - x)$, the proportion invested in s, was also nonnegative. Suppose, however, that the investor can issue as well as purchase securities. For example, suppose q is the common stock of firm q. At time 1 we allow the investor to issue securities equivalent to the shares of firm q. He might do this by selling a promise to pay at time 2 whatever is the market value of a share of firm q at time 2 plus any dividends paid by the firm at time 2. If the market believes that the investor can deliver on this promise, at time 1 it will pay him the price of a share in firm q for every share that he issues. He can then use the proceeds from the securities he issues to acquire an investment in s in excess of $(w_1 - c_1)$, his own initial portfolio funds.

The mechanism whereby an investor issues a security equivalent to one already existing is a short sale. To sell short the shares of firm q, the investor borrows the shares from someone who owns them at time 1, agreeing to return the shares at time 2 along with any dividends paid at time 2. On borrowing the shares, the investor immediately sells them in the market. At this point he has issued shares in firm q, since both the lender of the shares and the person who purchases them from the short-seller receive returns at time 2 from ownership of the shares. At time 2 the investor pays his debt to the lender of the shares of firm q by repurchasing in the market the shares of q to be returned to the lender.

When he borrows the shares of firm q and sells them in the market at time 1, the investor is said to have a negative or "short" position in the shares. He "covers" his short position when he purchases shares of q at time 2 and returns them to the lender. In contrast, an investor who owns the shares of firm q has a positive or "long" position in the shares. Finally, just as an investor uses a short sale to issue a security equivalent to one that is already outstanding, we can also think of him as short-selling q or s when they are portfolios rather than individual securities. To sell short or "issue" a portfolio, the investor simply sells short each of its component securities in the appropriate proportions.

We now extend the geometric analysis of combinations of two securities or portfolios to allow for short-selling. Note first that if we always consider x to be the proportion of $w_1 - c_1$ invested in q and $(1 - x)$ to be the proportion of $w_1 - c_1$ invested in s, then (4) is always the relevant expression for the return on a portfolio of q and s, and (5) and (6) or (8) are the relevant expressions for the expected value and standard deviation of the portfolio's return.* If x and $(1 - x)$ are both between 0.0 and 1.0, positive amounts are invested in both q and s. A negative value of x implies that q is issued or sold short and the proceeds are used to get an investment in s in excess of $w_1 - c_1$. Likewise, a negative value of $(1 - x)$—and thus a value of x greater than 1.0— implies that s is issued or sold short and the proceeds used to obtain an investment in q greater than $w_1 - c_1$.

Consider now the case where the returns on q and s are perfectly negatively correlated. When corr $(\tilde{R}_q, \tilde{R}_s) = -1.0$, the expected return on a portfolio of q and s is given by (5), and equation (8) for the standard deviation of the portfolio return becomes either (14) or (15), depending on whether x, the proportion of portfolio funds invested in q, is greater or less than the strictly positive quantity given by equation (13). If x is negative—that is, if the portfolio involves issuing or short-selling of q—then (15) is relevant and in Figure 7.2 the combination of $E(\tilde{R}_p)$ and $\sigma(\tilde{R}_p)$ obtained with such a portfolio is somewhere beyond the point s on the dashed extension of the line from the vertical axis through s. On the other hand, if the portfolio involves short-selling of s, so that $(1 - x) < 0$ and $x > 1$, then (14) is relevant and the portfolio plots along the dashed extension of the line from the vertical axis down through point q. Thus, when corr $(\tilde{R}_q, \tilde{R}_s) = -1.0$, all we must do in Figure 7.2 to cover the possibility of short-selling is to extend the two relevant line segments that meet at y on the $E(\tilde{R})$ axis through the points corresponding to q and s.

Consider next the case where there is perfect positive correlation between $\tilde{R}_q$ and $\tilde{R}_s$. As in the case where $0 \leqslant x \leqslant 1$, the combinations of $E(\tilde{R}_p)$ and $\sigma(\tilde{R}_p)$ given by portfolios of q and s where either q or s is sold short are described by equations (5) and (10). Moreover, if as in Figure 7.2, $E(\tilde{R}_s) > E(\tilde{R}_q)$ and $\sigma(\tilde{R}_s) > \sigma(\tilde{R}_q)$, the absolute value sign is unnecessary for $x < 0$. Thus, when q is sold short, the combination of $E(\tilde{R}_p)$ and $\sigma(\tilde{R}_p)$ obtained is

---

*If this point is not obvious, the reader should review the development of the algebra of portfolio theory in Chapter 2. In particular, the development of expressions for the return, expected return, and standard deviation of return on a portfolio does not impose nonnegativity constraints on the proportions of portfolio funds invested in individual securities.

along the dashed extension of the straight line from q through s in Figure 7.2. On the other hand, when s is sold short, so that $x > 1$ and $(1 - x) < 0$, the absolute value sign in (10) becomes necessary when x exceeds the quantity

$$x = \frac{\sigma(\tilde{R}_s)}{\sigma(\tilde{R}_s) - \sigma(\tilde{R}_q)}, \quad \sigma(\tilde{R}_s) > \sigma(\tilde{R}_q), \tag{16}$$

and when x takes the value given in (16), $\sigma(\tilde{R}_p) = 0.0$. Thus, when s is sold short, the combinations of $E(\tilde{R}_p)$ and $\sigma(\tilde{R}_p)$ obtained from portfolios of q and s plot at first along the dashed extension of the straight line from s through q in Figure 7.2. This line hits the $E(\tilde{R})$ axis at r when x takes the value given by (16). For values of x in excess of the quantity given by (16), the absolute value sign in (10) becomes relevant, and the combinations of $E(\tilde{R}_p)$ and $\sigma(\tilde{R}_p)$ obtained with portfolios of q and s plot along the new dashed line that goes downward and to the right from r.

Note that for portfolios that involve short sales of either q and s, the standard deviation of the return on a portfolio of q and s is larger when corr $(\tilde{R}_q, \tilde{R}_s) = -1.0$ than when corr $(\tilde{R}_q, \tilde{R}_s) = 1.0$. In geometric terms, when corr $(\tilde{R}_q, \tilde{R}_s) = -1.0$, the dashed lines in Figure 7.2 generated by portfolios that involve short sales of q or s are to the right of the corresponding dashed lines generated when corr $(\tilde{R}_q, \tilde{R}_s) = 1.0$. This is, of course, the reverse of what is obtained when the proportions x and $(1 - x)$ invested in q and s are both positive. In that case, for given x, the largest possible value of $\sigma(\tilde{R}_p)$ occurs when corr $(\tilde{R}_q, \tilde{R}_s) = 1.0$, while the smallest possible value occurs when corr $(\tilde{R}_q, \tilde{R}_s) = -1.0$.

The reversal in the roles of perfect positive and negative correlation that arises with short-selling is easily explained. If two securities or portfolios are perfectly positively correlated, the return on a short position in one is perfectly negatively correlated with the return on a long position in the other. Likewise, a short sale of either q or s transforms perfect negative correlation into perfect positive correlation. In general, the correlation between the returns on a short and a long position in two securities or portfolios is the negative of the correlation between the returns obtained when both are held long.

With less than perfect correlation, that is, when $-1.0 < $ corr $(\tilde{R}_q, \tilde{R}_s) < 1.0$, then the combinations of $E(\tilde{R}_p)$ and $\sigma(\tilde{R}_p)$ obtained when q is sold short are along the dashed extension of the solid curve through the point s in Figure 7.2, while when s is sold short, we get points along the dashed extension of the curve through q. Without going into the details, which at this point the reader should be able to provide, the dashed extensions of the curve must lie between the dashed extensions of the lines obtained with perfect positive and negative correlation. Again, any positively sloped segment of the curve must be concave, while any negatively sloped segment must be convex.

SOME NUMERICAL EXAMPLES

The preceding analysis can be made more concrete with numerical examples. We first consider portfolios of q and s when $E(\tilde{R}_q) = .01$, $E(\tilde{R}_s) = .02$, and $\sigma(\tilde{R}_q) = \sigma(\tilde{R}_s) = .05$. Plots of $E(\tilde{R}_p)$ against $\sigma(\tilde{R}_p)$ under five different assumptions about the value of corr $(\tilde{R}_q, \tilde{R}_s)$ are in Figure 7.3. The straight

FIGURE 7.3

Plots of $E(\tilde{R}_p)$ Against $\sigma(\tilde{R}_p)$ for Different Values of corr $(\tilde{R}_q, \tilde{R}_s)$ When $E(\tilde{R}_s) > E(\tilde{R}_q)$ and $\sigma(\tilde{R}_q) = \sigma(\tilde{R}_s)$

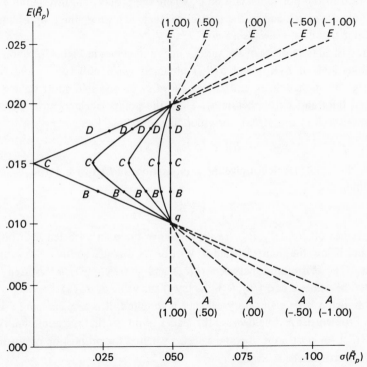

line between q and s shows the combinations of $E(\tilde{R}_p)$ and $\sigma(\tilde{R}_p)$ obtained for values of x between 1.0 and 0.0 when corr $(\tilde{R}_q, \tilde{R}_s) = 1.0$. The first solid curve to the left of this line shows the combinations of $E(\tilde{R}_p)$ and $\sigma(\tilde{R}_p)$ obtained for values of x between 1.0 and 0.0 when corr $(\tilde{R}_q, \tilde{R}_s) = .5$; the second solid curve to the left applies to the case corr $(\tilde{R}_q, R_s) = 0.0$ (that is, $\tilde{R}_q$ and $\tilde{R}_s$ are uncorrelated); the third curve applies to the case corr $(\tilde{R}_q, \tilde{R}_s) = -.5$; and the two straight lines from q and s that meet on the vertical axis show the combinations of $E(\tilde{R}_q)$ and $\sigma(\tilde{R}_p)$ obtained when corr $(\tilde{R}_q, \tilde{R}_s) = -1.0$.

Points labeled with a given uppercase letter in Figure 7.3 show the combinations of $E(\tilde{R}_p)$ and $\sigma(\tilde{R}_p)$ obtained for fixed values of the proportions invested in q and s, but with different assumptions about the value of corr $(\tilde{R}_q, \tilde{R}_s)$. For example, in portfolio B the proportion of $w_1 - c_1$ invested in q is .75, and the proportion invested in s is .25. The expected return on the portfolio is

$$E(\tilde{R}_B) = .75\,E(\tilde{R}_q) + .25\,E(\tilde{R}_s) = .75\,(.01) + .25\,(.02) = .0125,$$

and $E(\tilde{R}_B)$ does not depend on corr $(\tilde{R}_q, \tilde{R}_s)$. However, Figure 7.3 illustrates that $\sigma(\tilde{R}_B)$ decreases as corr $(\tilde{R}_q, \tilde{R}_s)$ decreases. The same phenomenon is observed in the portfolios labeled C, where the proportions invested in q and s are always equal, and in the portfolios labeled D, where the proportions invested in q and s are always .25 and .75.

The dashed extensions of the various lines and curves in Figure 7.3 show the combinations of $E(\tilde{R}_p)$ and $\sigma(\tilde{R}_p)$ obtained when either q is sold short (giving the dashed lines and curves above s) or s is sold short (giving the dashed lines and curves below q). Thus, the points labeled E give the combinations $E(\tilde{R}_E)$ and $\sigma(\tilde{R}_E)$, corresponding to

$$\tilde{R}_E = -.5\,\tilde{R}_q + 1.5\,\tilde{R}_s,$$

while the points labeled A give the combinations of $E(\tilde{R}_A)$ and $\sigma(\tilde{R}_A)$, corresponding to

$$\tilde{R}_A = 1.5\,\tilde{R}_q - .5\,\tilde{R}_s.$$

The values of corr $(\tilde{R}_q, \tilde{R}_s)$ are shown above the points labeled E in Figure 7.3 and below the points labeled A. We can see that when either q or s is sold short, the relationship between $\sigma(\tilde{R}_p)$ and corr$(\tilde{R}_q, \tilde{R}_s)$ is reversed; the higher the value of corr $(\tilde{R}_q, \tilde{R}_s)$, the lower the value of $\sigma(\tilde{R}_p)$.

Although a little elementary calculus is required, it is easy enough to show (and Problem III.A.3 below asks the reader to do so) that the minimum value of $\sigma(\tilde{R}_p)$ for portfolios of q and s occurs when x, the proportion of portfolio funds invested in q, is

$$x = \frac{\sigma^2(\tilde{R}_s) - \text{corr}\,(\tilde{R}_q, \tilde{R}_s)\,\sigma(\tilde{R}_q)\,\sigma(\tilde{R}_s)}{\sigma^2(\tilde{R}_s) + \sigma^2(\tilde{R}_q) - 2\,\text{corr}\,(\tilde{R}_q, \tilde{R}_s)\,\sigma(\tilde{R}_q)\,\sigma(\tilde{R}_s)}. \qquad (17)$$

Thus, in general, the value of x that minimizes $\sigma(\tilde{R}_p)$ varies with the magnitude of $\sigma^2(\tilde{R}_s)$ relative to $\sigma^2(\tilde{R}_q)$; in general, it also depends on the value of corr $(\tilde{R}_q, \tilde{R}_s)$. But $\sigma^2(\tilde{R}_q) = \sigma^2(\tilde{R}_s)$ is the special case where for all values of corr $(\tilde{R}_q, \tilde{R}_s)$ the minimum value of $\sigma(\tilde{R}_p)$ occurs when $x = .5$, that is, when portfolio funds are split equally between q and s. Thus, in Figure 7.3 portfolio C has the minimum value of $\sigma(\tilde{R}_p)$ for all values of corr $(\tilde{R}_q, \tilde{R}_s)$, but this is a peculiar implication of the fact that $\sigma^2(\tilde{R}_q) = \sigma^2(\tilde{R}_s)$.

PROBLEMS III.A

2. When will the value of x in (17) be between 0.0 and 1.0? The answer to this question defines the cases where it is possible to get a portfolio of q and s, with nonnegative proportions invested in both q and s, that has a standard deviation of return less than both $\sigma(\tilde{R}_q)$ and $\sigma(\tilde{R}_s)$.

3. Show that equation (17) does indeed give the value of x that minimizes $\sigma(\tilde{R}_p)$ for portfolios of q and s.

ANSWERS

2. To get

$$x = \frac{\sigma^2(\tilde{R}_s) - \text{corr}(\tilde{R}_q, \tilde{R}_s)\,\sigma(\tilde{R}_q)\,\sigma(\tilde{R}_s)}{\sigma^2(\tilde{R}_s) + \sigma^2(\tilde{R}_q) - 2\,\text{corr}(\tilde{R}_q, \tilde{R}_s)\,\sigma(\tilde{R}_q)\,\sigma(\tilde{R}_s)} < 1,$$

we must have

$$\sigma^2(\tilde{R}_q) - \text{corr}(\tilde{R}_q, \tilde{R}_s)\,\sigma(\tilde{R}_q)\,\sigma(\tilde{R}_s) > 0.$$

Likewise, to get $x > 0$ in (17), we must have

$$\sigma^2(\tilde{R}_s) - \text{corr}(\tilde{R}_q, \tilde{R}_s)\,\sigma(\tilde{R}_q)\,\sigma(\tilde{R}_s) > 0.$$

These two conditions are always satisfied when $\text{corr}(\tilde{R}_q, \tilde{R}_s) \leqslant 0.0$, but for given values of $\sigma(\tilde{R}_q)$ and $\sigma(\tilde{R}_s)$ there will also always be some range of positive values of $\text{corr}(\tilde{R}_q, \tilde{R}_s)$ for which the conditions are satisfied. Chapter 8 will provide an application for this result.

3. The value of x that minimizes $\sigma^2(\tilde{R}_p)$ also minimizes $\sigma(\tilde{R}_p)$. From (8), we have

$$\frac{d\sigma^2(\tilde{R}_p)}{dx} = 2x\sigma^2(\tilde{R}_q) - 2(1 - x)\,\sigma^2(\tilde{R}_s) + 2\,\text{corr}(\tilde{R}_q, \tilde{R}_s)\,\sigma(\tilde{R}_q)\,\sigma(\tilde{R}_s)$$

$$- 4x\,\text{corr}(\tilde{R}_q, \tilde{R}_s)\,\sigma(\tilde{R}_q)\,\sigma(\tilde{R}_s).$$

Setting this expression equal to 0.0 and solving for x yields (17). That (17) yields the value of x which minimizes $\sigma^2(\tilde{R}_p)$ follows from the fact (which we state without proof but which the reader can deduce from the lengthy geometric discussion above) that $\sigma^2(\tilde{R}_p)$ is a convex function of x.

The numerical example in Figure 7.3 is a special case in the sense that $\sigma(\tilde{R}_q)$ and $\sigma(\tilde{R}_s)$ are assumed to be equal. Figure 7.4 shows plots of $E(\tilde{R}_p)$ against $\sigma(\tilde{R}_p)$ for three different assumed values of $\text{corr}(\tilde{R}_q, \tilde{R}_s)$ when $E(\tilde{R}_q) = .01$, $E(\tilde{R}_s) = .02$, $\sigma(\tilde{R}_q) = .04$, and $\sigma(\tilde{R}_s) = .06$. The straight line between q and s (and its dashed extensions) shows the combinations of $E(\tilde{R}_p)$ and $\sigma(\tilde{R}_p)$ ob-

FIGURE 7.4

Plots of $E(\tilde{R}_p)$ Against $\sigma(\tilde{R}_p)$ When $E(\tilde{R}_q) < E(\tilde{R}_s)$ and $\sigma(\tilde{R}_q) < \sigma(\tilde{R}_s)$

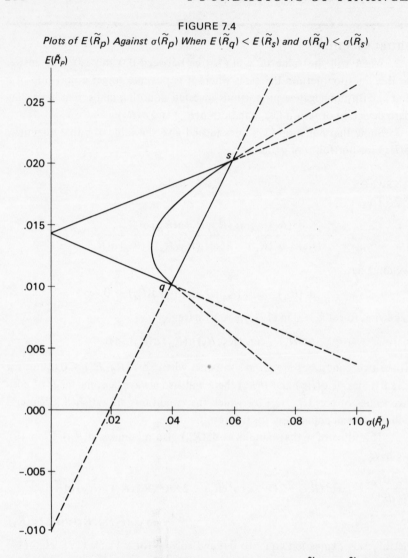

tained when there is perfect positive correlation between $\tilde{R}_q$ and $\tilde{R}_s$. The two lines from q and s that meet on the $E(\tilde{R})$ axis apply when corr $(\tilde{R}_q, \tilde{R}_s) = -1.0$, while the curve in the figure shows the combinations of $E(\tilde{R}_p)$ and $\sigma(\tilde{R}_p)$ obtained when $\tilde{R}_q$ and $\tilde{R}_s$ are uncorrelated. Figure 7.5 shows still a different example in which, as in Figure 7.4, $E(\tilde{R}_q) = .01$ and $E(\tilde{R}_s) = .02$; but in Figure 7.5 the values of $\sigma(\tilde{R}_q)$ and $\sigma(\tilde{R}_s)$ are the reverse of those in Figure 7.4; that is, in Figure 7.5, $\sigma(\tilde{R}_q) = .06$ and $\sigma(\tilde{R}_s) = .04$. Instead of explicitly engaging in further tedium, we leave detailed scrutiny of these two examples to the reader.

Finally, in Figures 7.2–5, the plots of $E(\tilde{R}_p)$ against $\sigma(\tilde{R}_p)$ always seem

FIGURE 7.5

Plots of $E(\widetilde{R}_p)$ Against $\sigma(\widetilde{R}_p)$ When $E(\widetilde{R}_q) < E(\widetilde{R}_s)$ and $\sigma(\widetilde{R}_q) > \sigma(\widetilde{R}_s)$

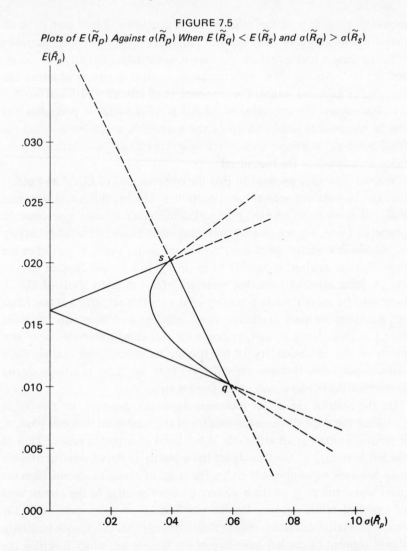

symmetric about the portfolio that minimizes $\sigma(\widetilde{R}_p)$. This is not a peculiarity of the examples. Merton (1972) shows that when $-1.0 < \text{corr}(\widetilde{R}_q, \widetilde{R}_s) < 1.0$, the plot of $E(\widetilde{R}_p)$ against $\sigma(\widetilde{R}_p)$ is a hyperbola. This is interesting but not important for our purposes, so we leave the reader to pursue the details in Merton's excellent treatment of the topic.

B. The Efficient Set: No Risk-free Asset

This discussion of the geometric properties of portfolios that are combinations of two securities or portfolios q and s allows us to determine easily the geometric properties of the efficient set of portfolios. Recall that to be efficient a portfolio must have the dual properties that (a) no other portfolio with the same expected return can have lower standard deviation of return, and (b) no other portfolio with the same standard deviation of return can have higher expected return. The collection of all efficient portfolios is called the efficient set. The collection of feasible portfolios—that is, portfolios that can be obtained as combinations of the n available securities—is called the feasible set or, sometimes, the investment opportunity set. Efficient portfolios are a subset of the feasible set.

Suppose now that we want to plot the combinations of $E(\tilde{R}_p)$ and $\sigma(\tilde{R}_p)$ that can be obtained with efficient portfolios. The portfolios that minimize $\sigma(\tilde{R}_p)$ at given levels of $E(\tilde{R}_p)$ are called minimum variance portfolios. In geometric terms, the set of minimum variance portfolios is the left boundary of the feasible set of portfolios; that is, minimum variance portfolios are those that are as close as possible to the $E(\tilde{R}_p)$ axis at each feasible level of $E(\tilde{R}_p)$. Since efficient portfolios minimize $\sigma(\tilde{R}_p)$ at given levels of $E(\tilde{R}_p)$, they must be along the left boundary of the feasible set; efficient portfolios are minimum variance portfolios. Since efficient portfolios also maximize $E(\tilde{R}_p)$ at given levels of $\sigma(\tilde{R}_p)$, they must plot along positively sloped segments of the left boundary of the feasible set. Thus, there are minimum variance portfolios that are not efficient. They are along negatively sloped portions of the left boundary of the feasible set.

On the basis of the earlier geometric discussion, however, we now argue that once the slope of the left boundary of the feasible set becomes positive, it remains positive at all attainable higher levels of expected return. Thus, if the left boundary of the feasible set has a positively sloped segment, there is only one such segment and it covers the range of expected returns from the point where the slope of the boundary becomes positive to the highest level of expected return on any feasible portfolio. Even more specifically, the earlier geometric discussion implies almost directly that this unique positively sloped segment of the left boundary of the feasible set, which describes the combinations of $E(\tilde{R}_p)$ and $\sigma(\tilde{R}_p)$ available from efficient portfolios, is a concave curve.

For example, the portfolio opportunities available to the investor might be as represented in Figure 7.6. The irregularly shaped solid curve is the boundary of the set of feasible portfolios. The left boundary of the feasible set, which describes the set of minimum variance portfolios, is the solid curve abg. The set of efficient portfolios is the positively sloped concave segment of this boundary from b to g. That the positively sloped segment of the boundary must be a concave curve follows directly from the geometric properties of combinations of two securities or portfolios. For example, the left boundary cannot be as represented by the curves *bcd* and *deg* in Figure 7.6, since it is always possible to form portfolios of *c* and *e*, and these portfolios must plot either on or to the left of the straight line between *c* and *e*, depending on whether corr $(\tilde{R}_c, \tilde{R}_e)$ is equal to or less than 1.0. Such arguments rule out gaps in the boundary of the feasible set, and they also rule out indentations in the left boundary, such as *cde* and *hij*. Indeed, the geometry of combinations of two securities or portfolios implies that the slope of the left boundary of the feasible set of portfolios can change sign once at most. The negatively sloped segment is convex and covers lower levels of expected return, while the positively sloped segment is concave and covers higher levels of expected return.

PROBLEM III.B

1. Show that, in general, any point on the left boundary of the feasible set is unique in the sense that there is only one portfolio with the indicated combination of $E(\tilde{R}_p)$ and $\sigma(\tilde{R}_p)$. What is the exception to this general rule?

ANSWER

1. Suppose there are two portfolios, call them *u* and *v*, such that $E(\tilde{R}_u) = E(\tilde{R}_v)$ and $\sigma(\tilde{R}_u) = \sigma(\tilde{R}_v)$. When corr $(\tilde{R}_u, \tilde{R}_v) < 1.0$, *u* and *v* cannot be on the left boundary of the feasible set, since positively weighted combinations of *u* and *v* have the same expected return but, from (11), lower standard deviation of return than *u* and *v*.

When $0 \leqslant x \leqslant 1$ and corr $(\tilde{R}_u, \tilde{R}_v) = 1.0$, from equation (10)

$$\sigma(\tilde{R}_p) = x\sigma(\tilde{R}_u) + (1 - x)\sigma(\tilde{R}_v) = \sigma(\tilde{R}_u) = \sigma(\tilde{R}_v).$$

Thus, if there are two portfolios that correspond to the same point on the left boundary of the feasible set, not only must the two portfolios have the same expected returns and standard deviations, but their returns must also be perfectly positively correlated.

There are some additional assumptions implicit in the representation of the efficient and feasible sets of portfolios as in Figure 7.6. Since there are no feasible portfolios with $\sigma(\tilde{R}_p) = 0.0$, there are no securities or portfolios whose returns are perfectly negatively correlated. Moreover, since the boundary of the feasible set has no straight line segments, there are no portfolios on the boundary whose returns are perfectly positively correlated. Finally, since the feasible set of portfolios pictured in Figure 7.6 is assumed to have a right boundary, there is an implicit assumption that there is no short-selling

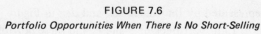

FIGURE 7.6
Portfolio Opportunities When There Is No Short-Selling

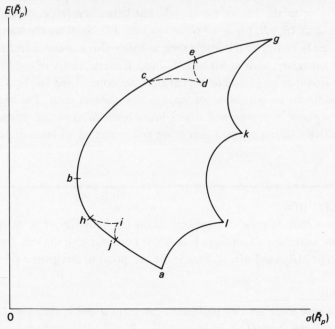

or, at least, that short-selling is not unlimited.* For example, the earlier geometric analysis of portfolios formed as combinations of two securities or portfolios implies that with unlimited short-selling, combinations of portfolios b and g in which b is sold short could be used to get portfolios with arbitrarily large values of $E(\tilde{R}_p)$ and $\sigma(\tilde{R}_p)$. From this we can conclude that if there is unlimited short-selling, the efficient set of portfolios must extend indefinitely upward and to the right in the $E(\tilde{R})$, $\sigma(\tilde{R})$ plane. Likewise, with unlimited short-selling, the left boundary of the feasible set of portfolios extends indefinitely downward and to the right in the $E(\tilde{R})$, $\sigma(\tilde{R})$ plane. One can see this in Figure 7.6 by noting that with combinations of portfolios b and a in which b is sold short, one can get portfolios with arbitrarily small values of $E(\tilde{R}_p)$ and arbitrarily large values of $\sigma(\tilde{R}_p)$.

In fact, Merton (1972) shows that if unlimited short-selling of all securities is allowed, and if it is not possible to obtain a portfolio that has $\sigma(\tilde{R}_p) = 0.0$, then the left boundary of the feasible set of portfolios, the set of minimum variance portfolios, is a hyperbola, and so has the general shape shown in

---

*Using the geometric properties of combinations of two securities or portfolios, the reader can determine that in the absence of short-selling, the irregular curve *alkg* is a possible shape that the right boundary of the feasible set might take.

FIGURE 7.7
Portfolio Opportunities When There Is Short-Selling

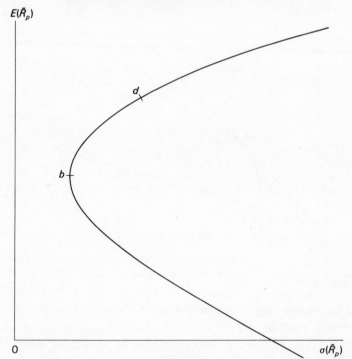

Figure 7.7. The boundary is symmetric about the point b, which is the portfolio that has the smallest possible standard deviation of return. The efficient set of portfolios covers the positively sloped segment of the boundary, the segment that starts at b and extends indefinitely upward and to the right.

From the earlier geometric discussions, the condition that it is not possible to obtain a portfolio that has $\sigma(\tilde{R}_p) = 0.0$ implies that no two securities or portfolios have perfectly negatively correlated returns. With unlimited short-selling, the condition also implies that no two securities or portfolios have perfectly positively correlated returns (see Figure 7.2). Finally, the condition implies that there is no risk-free security, that is, no security j with $\sigma(\tilde{R}_j) = 0.0$.

Models based on the existence of a risk-free asset play an important role in two-parameter theory and especially in the two-parameter models of capital market equilibrium presented in the next chapter. Thus, we now discuss in some detail the effect of a risk-free asset on the investment opportunity set.

C. The Efficient Set with a Risk-free Asset

Suppose the curve bd in Figure 7.8 represents the set of portfolios that

FIGURE 7.8

The Efficient Set with a Risk-Free Security

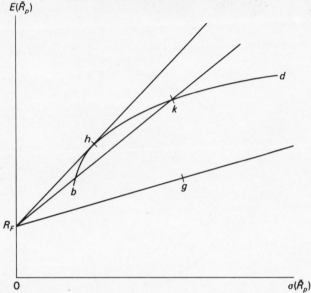

would be efficient in the absence of a risk-free security.* Suppose, however, that there is a risk-free security, call it F, that will pay the sure return R_F if held from time 1 to time 2. Consider portfolios of the risk-free security F and any risky security or portfolio g formed as

$$\tilde{R}_p = xR_F + (1 - x)\tilde{R}_g. \tag{18}$$

With $x = 1.0$, all portfolio funds $w_1 - c_1$ are invested in F, while with $x = 0.0$, all funds are in g. When $1.0 > x > 0.0$, positive proportions of $w_1 - c_1$ are invested in both F and g. When $x < 0.0$, the investor issues or sells F short and uses the proceeds to get an investment in g in excess of $w_1 - c_1$. Equivalently, issuing or short-selling of F can be regarded as borrowing at the rate R_F. Thus, a value of $x < 0.0$ in (18) implies that the investor borrows at the rate R_F and uses the proceeds to get an investment in g in excess of $w_1 - c_1$. In this view, $1.0 > x > 0.0$ implies that the investor lends at the rate R_F. The lending-borrowing interpretation of positions involving F is the one we use almost exclusively here.[†]

---

*Since investors only hold efficient portfolios and since we have finished our discussion of what the entire boundary of the investment opportunity set looks like when there is no risk-free asset, in the remaining geometric discussions we do not bother to show the entire boundary.

[†]Short-selling or issuing of a risky security can also be viewed as borrowing, but at an uncertain rate; and a long position in such a security can likewise be regarded as lending at an uncertain rate. In essence, short or long positions in one security are no different in kind from short and long positions in any other. It is, however, customary to interpret positions in bonds in terms of lending and borrowing, with the terms long and short reserved for positions in common stocks.

The expected return on any portfolio formed according to (18) is

$$E(\tilde{R}_p) = xR_F + (1 - x)E(\tilde{R}_g). \qquad (19)$$

Since $\sigma(\tilde{R}_F) = 0.0$, the standard deviation of the return on any such portfolio is

$$\sigma(\tilde{R}_p) = |1 - x|\sigma(\tilde{R}_g), \qquad (20)$$

and if we restrict attention to values of $x \leqslant 1.0$ (that is, if we do not consider short-selling of g), then

$$\sigma(\tilde{R}_p) = (1 - x)\sigma(\tilde{R}_g), \quad x \leqslant 1.0. \qquad (21)$$

It is perhaps clear from inspection of equations (19) and (21) that the combinations of $E(\tilde{R}_p)$ and $\sigma(\tilde{R}_p)$ obtained from portfolios of F and g plot along a straight line from R_F through g in Figure 7.8. Thus, $x = 1.0$ gives the point R_F on the $E(\tilde{R}_p)$ axis, while $x = 0.0$ is the point g. With $x = .5$,

$$E(\tilde{R}_p) = .5R_F + .5E(\tilde{R}_g)$$

$$\sigma(\tilde{R}_p) = .5\sigma(\tilde{R}_g),$$

which is the combination of $E(\tilde{R}_p)$ and $\sigma(\tilde{R}_p)$ halfway between R_F and g on the straight line between R_F and g. Likewise, with $x = .25$,

$$E(\tilde{R}_p) = .25R_F + .75E(\tilde{R}_g)$$

$$\sigma(\tilde{R}_p) = .75\sigma(\tilde{R}_g),$$

which is the combination of $E(\tilde{R}_p)$ and $\sigma(\tilde{R}_p)$ that is three-fourths of the way between R_F and g on the straight line between R_F and g. Finally, with $x = -.5$, that is, when the portfolio involves borrowing $.5(w_1 - c_1)$ and putting this plus $(w_1 - c_1)$ in g, we have

$$E(\tilde{R}_p) = -.5R_F + 1.5E(\tilde{R}_g)$$

$$\sigma(\tilde{R}_p) = 1.5\sigma(\tilde{R}_g),$$

which is on the extension of the line from R_F through g.

In short, the portfolios obtained from combinations of a riskless security F with any given risky security or portfolio g plot along a straight line from the riskless rate R_F through the point corresponding to g in the $E(\tilde{R}_p)$, $\sigma(\tilde{R}_p)$ plane. Lending portfolios (portfolios with $1.0 \geqslant x \geqslant 0.0$) plot on the line between R_F and g. Borrowing portfolios (portfolios with $x < 0.0$) plot along the extension of the line through g.

PROBLEMS III.C

1. Derive the exact form of the linear relationship between $E(\tilde{R}_p)$ and $\sigma(\tilde{R}_p)$ for portfolios formed according to (18) with $x \leqslant 1.0$.

2. The linear relationships between $E(\tilde{R}_p)$ and $\sigma(\tilde{R}_p)$ that arise from combinations of a risk-free security with a risky security or portfolio bring to mind the linear relationships obtained from combinations of two risky securities or portfolios when the returns on the two are perfectly positively correlated. Show that, in fact, with $x < 1.0$ in (18), the returns on any two portfolios of F and g are perfectly positively correlated. Interpret this result.

ANSWERS

1. First solve (19) and (21) for x to get

$$x = \frac{E(\tilde{R}_p) - E(\tilde{R}_g)}{R_F - E(\tilde{R}_g)}$$

$$x = \frac{\sigma(\tilde{R}_g) - \sigma(\tilde{R}_p)}{\sigma(\tilde{R}_g)}, \quad x \leqslant 1.0.$$

Equating these two expressions for x and solving for $E(\tilde{R}_p)$ yields

$$E(\tilde{R}_p) = R_F + \left(\frac{E(\tilde{R}_g) - R_F}{\sigma(\tilde{R}_g)} \right) \sigma(\tilde{R}_p), \quad x \leqslant 1.0. \tag{22}$$

This is indeed the equation for the line from R_F through g in Figure 7.8, since this line has intercept R_F and slope $(E(\tilde{R}_g) - R_F)/\sigma(\tilde{R}_g)$.

In intuitive terms, equation (22) describes the behavior of the expected return on portfolios formed according to (18) as the proportion x invested in the risk-free security F is decreased and the proportion $1 - x$ invested in g is increased. When one shifts from the risk-free to the risky investment, the expected portfolio return changes at the rate $E(\tilde{R}_g) - R_F$: one exchanges R_F for $E(\tilde{R}_g)$. Equation (21) tells us that such shifts toward larger holdings of the risky investment also cause $\sigma(\tilde{R}_p)$ to increase.

2. Consider two portfolios p and p' formed according to

$$\tilde{R}_p = xR_F + (1 - x)\tilde{R}_g, \quad x < 1.0$$

$$\tilde{R}_{p'} = x'R_F + (1 - x')\tilde{R}_g, \quad x' < 1.0, x \neq x'.$$

Then

$$\begin{aligned}
\text{corr}(\tilde{R}_p, \tilde{R}_{p'}) &= \frac{\text{cov}(\tilde{R}_p, \tilde{R}_{p'})}{\sigma(\tilde{R}_p)\sigma(\tilde{R}_{p'})} \\
&= \frac{\text{cov}[(1 - x)\tilde{R}_g, (1 - x')\tilde{R}_g]}{(1 - x)\sigma(\tilde{R}_g)(1 - x')\sigma(\tilde{R}_g)} \\
&= \frac{(1 - x)(1 - x')\,\text{cov}(\tilde{R}_g, \tilde{R}_g)}{(1 - x)(1 - x')\sigma^2(\tilde{R}_g)} = 1.0.
\end{aligned}$$

In intuitive terms, all the uncertainty in the return on a portfolio of F and g

arises from g. Although the returns on two different portfolios of F and g will not be identical, if both involve positive investment in g, the returns on the portfolios are perfectly positively correlated. It is left to the reader to show that any two portfolios of F and g that both involve a short position in g (that is, $x > 1.0$) are likewise perfectly positively correlated; but if one of the portfolios involves a short position in g while the other involves a long position, their returns are perfectly negatively correlated. Completing the problem in this way completes the analogy between the linear investment opportunities obtained with a risk-free security and those obtained from two positive variance securities or portfolios whose returns are perfectly positively correlated.

How might one best take advantage of the investment opportunities provided by a risk-free security? One can get a lot better results from F than are obtained by combining it with g in Figure 7.8. For example, portfolios of F and k give combinations of $E(\tilde{R}_p)$ and $\sigma(\tilde{R}_p)$ along the straight line from R_F through k. This line clearly dominates the combinations of $E(\tilde{R}_p)$ and $\sigma(\tilde{R}_p)$ along the line from R_F through g. At any given level of $\sigma(\tilde{R}_p)$, the portfolio of F and k has higher expected return than the portfolio of F and g. Combinations of F and k likewise do not make the best possible use of F. In the two-parameter model, since investors like maximum expected return at any given level of standard deviation of return and minimum standard deviation of return at any given level of expected return, the best way to use F is to combine it with a risky portfolio so that the resulting straight line is upward and to the left as much as possible in the $E(\tilde{R}_p)$, $\sigma(\tilde{R}_p)$ plane. In geometric terms, this involves "resting" a line on the curve bd in Figure 7.8. The point h where this line just touches bd is the portfolio of risky securities that one combines with F to get the combinations of $E(\tilde{R}_p)$ and $\sigma(\tilde{R}_p)$ along this line.

The line from R_F through h in Figure 7.8 describes the efficient set of portfolios. Except for h, portfolios along the curve bd are not efficient, since the portfolios along the line from R_F through h have higher expected returns at given levels of standard deviation of return. Thus, efficient portfolios are combinations of F and h, with returns, expected returns, and standard deviations of returns given by

$$\tilde{R}_p = xR_F + (1 - x)\tilde{R}_h \qquad x \leqslant 1.0 \qquad (23)$$

$$E(\tilde{R}_p) = xR_F + (1 - x)E(\tilde{R}_h) \quad x \leqslant 1.0 \qquad (24)$$

$$\sigma(\tilde{R}_p) = (1 - x)\sigma(\tilde{R}_h) \qquad x \leqslant 1.0. \qquad (25)$$

With $x = 1.0$, all funds are invested in F and we are at the point on the $E(\tilde{R}_p)$ axis corresponding to R_F in Figure 7.8. As we consider successively lower values of x, equations (24) and (25) give combinations of $E(\tilde{R}_p)$ and $\sigma(\tilde{R}_p)$ along the line from R_F to h, and we hit the point h when $x = 0.0$. For still lower values of x, we get combinations of $E(\tilde{R}_p)$ and $\sigma(\tilde{R}_p)$ along the extension of the line from R_F through h.

The important point is that with risk-free borrowing and lending, all efficient portfolios are just combinations of the risk-free security F with the one portfolio of risky securities h. Some efficient portfolios, those on the line between R_F and h in Figure 7.8, are lending portfolios. Other efficient portfolios, those on the extension of the line from R_F through h, are borrowing portfolios; that is, the investor borrows at rate R_F and puts both his borrowings and his investment funds $w_1 - c_1$ into h. The only difference between one efficient portfolio and another is in how $w_1 - c_1$ is split between F and h. The portfolio h is the only efficient portfolio of only risky assets, and h is the risky component of every risky efficient portfolio.

In the next chapter, we find that these simplified characteristics of the efficient set when there is risk-free borrowing and lending are important in the analysis of market equilibrium in a world where investors make portfolio decisions in accordance with the two-parameter model.

PROBLEM III.C

3. Suppose there is risk-free lending but not borrowing; that is, suppose that in (23), x is restricted to values between 0.0 and 1.0. What then is the efficient set of portfolios in Figure 7.8?

ANSWER

3. When there is no risk-free borrowing, the portfolios on the line between R_F and h are feasible, since they are lending portfolios, but portfolios on the extension of the line through h are no longer feasible, since they are borrowing portfolios. Thus, when there is no borrowing at the risk-free rate, the efficient set includes portfolios along the line from R_F to h. Efficient portfolios with $\sigma(\tilde{R}_p) > \sigma(\tilde{R}_h)$ are those portfolios above h along the curve bd.

IV. Portfolio Risk, Security Risk, and the Effects of Diversification

Chapter 2 introduced the concepts of security risk and portfolio risk that are relevant in a two-parameter world. We now review these concepts briefly and provide empirical illustrations. The discussion should be useful background for Chapter 8, which is concerned with the relationships between expected return and risk that arise in a two-parameter world. The discussion also expands on some earlier comments concerning the effects of diversification on dispersion of returns.

A. Portfolio Risk and Security Risk in a Two-Parameter World

In the portfolio model, the investor is motivated by a desire to consume. He invests at time 1 in order to consume at time 2. His only concern in his portfolio decision is the probability distribution on consumption at time 2 that it implies. From equation (1) we can see that is is equivalent to say that his only concern in his portfolio decision is the probability distribution of portfolio return that it implies. The investor is only concerned with individual securities in terms of how they affect the distribution of the return on his portfolio.

In a world of normal portfolio return distributions, the distribution of the return on any portfolio can be completely characterized from knowledge of its mean and standard deviation or variance. Thus, to determine the effect of an individual security on the distribution of a portfolio's return, it is sufficient to determine the contribution of the security to the expected value and variance of the return on the portfolio. The return, expected return, and variance of return on a portfolio are

$$\tilde{R}_p = \sum_{i=1}^{n} x_{ip}\tilde{R}_i \tag{26}$$

$$E(\tilde{R}_p) = \sum_{i=1}^{n} x_{ip}E(\tilde{R}_i) \tag{27}$$

$$\sigma^2(\tilde{R}_p) = \sum_{i=1}^{n} \sum_{j=1}^{n} x_{ip}x_{jp}\sigma_{ij}, \tag{28}$$

where $\sigma_{ij} = \text{cov}(\tilde{R}_i, \tilde{R}_j)$, n is the number of securities available, and one portfolio is different from another in terms of the proportions $x_{ip}, i = 1, \ldots, n$, invested in individual securities.

The contribution of security i to $E(\tilde{R}_p)$ is

$$x_{ip}E(\tilde{R}_i),$$

the expected return on the security weighted by x_{ip}, the proportion of portfolio funds $w_1 - c_1$ invested in security i to obtain portfolio p. To highlight the contribution of security i to $\sigma^2(\tilde{R}_p)$, equation (28) is rewritten as

$$\sigma^2(\tilde{R}_p) = \sum_{i=1}^{n} x_{ip}\left(\sum_{j=1}^{n} x_{jp}\sigma_{ij}\right). \tag{29}$$

Thus, the variance of the return on portfolio p is the sum of n terms,

$$x_{ip}\left(\sum_{j=1}^{n} x_{jp}\sigma_{ij}\right), \qquad i = 1, \ldots, n, \qquad (30)$$

each of which represents the contribution of a security to $\sigma^2(\tilde{R}_p)$. This contribution of security i to $\sigma^2(\tilde{R}_p)$ is x_{ip}, the proportion of portfolio funds invested in i, multiplied by $\left(\sum_{j=1}^{n} x_{jp}\sigma_{ij}\right)$, the weighted average of the pairwise covariances between the return on security i and the returns on each of the securities in p, where the weight applied to σ_{ij} is x_{jp}, the proportion of portfolio funds invested in security j to obtain portfolio p.

In the two-parameter model, the risk of a portfolio is measured by the variance of its return. Thus, under one interpretation, the risk of security i in portfolio p might be measured by (30), the contribution of the security to $\sigma^2(\tilde{R}_p)$. It is, however, more convenient to call the weighted average of covariances

$$\sum_{j=1}^{n} x_{jp}\sigma_{ij}, \quad i = 1, \ldots, n, \qquad (31)$$

the risk of security i in portfolio p. Then, from (29), the risk of the portfolio, $\sigma^2(\tilde{R}_p)$, is just the weighted average of the risks of the individual securities.

Several comments ought to emphasize the view of security risks one gets when the object of concern to the investor is the distribution of the return on his portfolio. First, to be precise, one must always talk about the risk of security i in portfolio p, since the risk of a security is different from one portfolio to another. In formal terms, as defined by (31), the risk of security i in portfolio p depends on the return covariances σ_{ij}, $j = 1, \ldots, n$, which are parameters of the joint distribution of security returns and thus are the same from portfolio to portfolio. The risk of i in p also depends on how securities are combined to form p (that is, on the portfolio weights $x_{jp}, j = 1, \ldots, n$), and the combinations are different from one portfolio to another.

Second, an apparently "risky" security (that is, a security that has a positive variance of return) may have positive, zero, or negative risk in a portfolio. Thus, noting that one of the terms in (31) involves $\sigma_{ii} = \sigma^2(\tilde{R}_i)$, we can rewrite (31) as

$$\sum_{j=1}^{n} x_{jp}\sigma_{ij} = x_{ip}\sigma^2(\tilde{R}_i) + \sum_{\substack{j=1 \\ j \neq i}}^{n} x_{jp}\sigma_{ij}. \qquad (32)$$

Although the first term on the right of the equality is positive if x_{ip} is positive, the value of the whole expression can be positive, zero, or negative depending on the value of the weighted average of covariances in the second term on the right of the equality. In short, the risk of a security in a portfolio depends on the covariances between the return on the security and the returns on other securities in the portfolio, as well as on the variance of the return on the security. A security that apparently has high "risk" in terms of the variance of its return may have low risk when viewed as a component of a portfolio.

In fact, inspection of equation (32) suggests that in a portfolio which contains a large number of securities, and where portfolio funds are not concentrated in one or a few of the securities, the risk of a security might depend more on the covariances between the return on the security and the returns on other securities in the portfolio than on the variance of the security's return. Thus, from (32), $\sigma^2(\tilde{R}_i)$ is just one of n terms that determine the risk of security i in p, with the remaining $n - 1$ terms being the pairwise covariances. This, however, does not in itself imply that the covariances in (32) dominate the variance. For this purpose, what constitutes a "large" n depends on the magnitude of $\sigma^2(\tilde{R}_i)$ relative to the σ_{ij}, an empirical issue which the examples that follow are meant to illuminate.

PROBLEMS IV.A

1. Can a security have positive risk in a portfolio and yet make a negative contribution to the risk of the portfolio?

2. Show that the sample mean and variance of the return on a portfolio can be written in forms exactly analogous to (27) and (28). This problem is important for the numerical examples that follow.

ANSWERS

1. The contribution of a security to the variance of the return on a portfolio is given by (30). We have defined the risk of the security in the portfolio as the weighted average of covariances that appear in the parentheses in (30), that is, as (31). Thus, even if the risk of a security in the portfolio is positive, the security makes a negative contribution to the risk of the portfolio if (31) is positive and $x_{ip} < 0.0$; that is, portfolio p involves short-selling of security i.

In intuitive terms, when a security makes a negative contribution to the variance of the return on a portfolio, that security is risk-reducing as far as the portfolio is concerned. In the present example, we see that a security that would make a positive contribution to the risk of a portfolio if held long makes a negative contribution when held short. Thus, a short position in the security is risk-reducing. The sword is, however, double-edged. If the expected return on the security is positive and the security is sold short, then the security also makes a negative contribution to the expected return on the portfolio.

2. With a time series R_{pt}, $t = 1, \ldots, T$, of T observations of the return on portfolio p, the sample variance of the portfolio returns is

$$s^2(R_p) = \frac{\sum_{t=1}^{T}(R_{pt} - \bar{R}_p)^2}{T - 1}, \tag{33}$$

where $\bar{R}_p$, the sample mean of the portfolio returns, is

$$\bar{R}_p = \frac{\sum_{t=1}^{T} R_{pt}}{T}. \tag{34}$$

Since

$$R_{pt} = \sum_{i=1}^{n} x_{ip}R_{it}, \tag{35}$$

$$\bar{R}_p = \frac{\sum_{t=1}^{T}\sum_{i=1}^{n} x_{ip}R_{it}}{T} = \frac{\sum_{i=1}^{n} x_{ip} \sum_{t=1}^{T} R_{it}}{T} = \sum_{i=1}^{n} x_{ip}\bar{R}_i, \tag{36}$$

where $\bar{R}_i$ is the sample mean of the returns on security i. Thus, (33) can be rewritten as

$$
\begin{aligned}
s^2(R_p) &= \frac{\sum_{t=1}^{T}\left(\sum_{i=1}^{n} x_{ip}R_{it} - \sum_{i=1}^{n} x_{ip}\bar{R}_i\right)^2}{T - 1} \\
&= \frac{\sum_{t=1}^{T}\left(\sum_{i=1}^{n} x_{ip}[R_{it} - \bar{R}_i]\right)^2}{T - 1} \\
&= \frac{\sum_{t=1}^{T}\sum_{i=1}^{n}\sum_{j=1}^{n} x_{ip}x_{jp}(R_{it} - \bar{R}_i)(R_{jt} - \bar{R}_j)}{T - 1} \\
&= \sum_{i=1}^{n}\sum_{j=1}^{n} x_{ip}x_{jp}\left(\frac{\sum_{t=1}^{T}(R_{it} - \bar{R}_i)(R_{jt} - \bar{R}_j)}{T - 1}\right)
\end{aligned}
$$

$$s^2(R_p) = \sum_{i=1}^{n}\sum_{j=1}^{n} x_{ip}x_{jp}s_{ij}, \tag{37}$$

where

$$s_{ij} = \frac{\sum_{t=1}^{T}(R_{it} - \bar{R}_i)(R_{jt} - \bar{R}_j)}{T - 1}$$

is the usual (see Chapter 3) sample estimate of the covariance σ_{ij}, and when $i = j$, $s_{ii} = s^2(R_i)$ is the usual sample estimate of the variance $\sigma^2(\tilde{R}_i)$.

Equation (37) says that the sample variance of the return on a portfolio is the weighted average of the sample variances and covariances of security returns, just as equation (28) says that the true variance of the return on a portfolio is the corresponding weighted average of security return variances and covariances. And (36) says that the sample mean of the return on a portfolio is the weighted average of the sample means of the security returns, just as (27) says that the expected portfolio return is the weighted average of the expected security returns.

B. Portfolio Risk and Security Risk: Empirical Examples

Using monthly data for July 1963–June 1968, Table 7.1 shows components of the average monthly return and of the variance of monthly returns on portfolios of increasing numbers of randomly selected securities. Results are presented for ten portfolios, and column (7) of the table shows that the ten portfolios include $N = 1, 2, 3, 4, 5, 6, 10, 15, 25$, and 50 securities. Columns (1) and (2) show that the number of securities in the portfolios is increased by adding securities and redistributing portfolio funds equally across securities, so that in a portfolio of N securities, each security gets the proportion $x_{ip} = 1/N$ of portfolio funds. We use upper case N now to indicate the number of securities that appear in a portfolio with nonzero weights. For a given security and portfolio, the entry in column (3) of Table 7.1 shows $x_{ip}\overline{R}_i$, which equation (36) says is the contribution of security i to the average return on the portfolio. Thus, the average return on the portfolio is the sum of the entries for individual securities in column (3), and for a given portfolio the average portfolio return is shown in column (3) in the line labeled "Totals."

For a given security and portfolio, the entries in columns (4)–(6) show components of the contribution of the security to the sample variance of the return on the portfolio. Thus in direct analogy with equations (29) to (31), equation (37) for the sample variance of the return on portfolio p can be rewritten as

$$s^2(R_p) = \sum_{i=1}^{N} x_{ip}\left(\sum_{j=1}^{N} x_{jp}s_{ij}\right), \tag{38}$$

so that the contribution of security i to the sample variance of the return on p is

$$x_{ip}\left(\sum_{j=1}^{N} x_{jp}s_{ij}\right). \tag{39}$$

If we call the weighted average of sample covariances

$$\sum_{j=1}^{N} x_{jp} s_{ij}, \tag{40}$$

the estimated risk of security i in portfolio p, then, from (38), the estimate of the risk of the portfolio, $s^2(R_p)$, is just the weighted average of the estimates of security risks.

For a given security and portfolio, column (6) of Table 7.1 shows the quantity in expression (39) which is the contribution of the security to the sample variance of the portfolio's return; and the entry on the "Totals" line of column (6) is $s^2(R_p)$. The entries in columns (4) and (5) for a given security break the contribution of the security to $s^2(R_p)$ into a variance component and a weighted average of covariances component. That is, expression (39) is broken down as

$$x_{ip}\left(\sum_{j=1}^{N} x_{jp} s_{ij}\right) = x_{ip}^2 s^2(R_i) + x_{ip} \sum_{\substack{j=1 \\ j \neq i}}^{N} x_{jp} s_{ij}. \tag{41}$$

The entries in the "Totals" line of columns (4) and (5) thus give a breakdown of $s^2(R_p)$ into security return variances and covariances as

$$s^2(R_p) = \sum_{i=1}^{N} x_{ip}^2 s^2(R_i) + \sum_{i=1}^{N} \sum_{\substack{j=1 \\ j \neq i}}^{N} x_{ip} x_{jp} s_{ij}. \tag{42}$$

Several points of interest can be drawn from Table 7.1. Note that as the number of securities in the portfolios increases, the contributions of a security to average portfolio return and to sample variance of portfolio return go down. In the case of $\overline{R}_p$, since the contribution of security i to $\overline{R}_p$ is $x_{ip}\overline{R}_i$ and since we are dealing with portfolios of equally weighted securities, $x_{ip}\overline{R}_i = (1/N)\overline{R}_i$ decreases as N, the number of securities in the portfolio, is increased. Likewise, the contribution of security i to $s^2(\tilde{R}_p)$ is

$$x_{ip}\left(\sum_{j=1}^{N} x_{jp} s_{ij}\right) = \frac{1}{N}\left(\frac{\sum_{j=1}^{N} s_{ij}}{N}\right).$$

Although the estimated risk of security i in the portfolio

$$\sum_{j=1}^{N} x_{jp} s_{ij} = \frac{\sum_{j=1}^{N} s_{ij}}{N}$$

TABLE 7.1
Components of the Sample Mean and Variance of Monthly Returns on Portfolios
of Increasing Numbers of Randomly Selected Securities, July 1963–June 1968

(1) SECURITIES (i)	(2) x_{ip}	(3) $x_{ip}\bar{R}_i$	(4) $x_{ip}^2 s^2(R_i)$	(5) $x_{ip}\sum\limits_{\substack{j=1 \\ j\neq i}}^{N} x_{jp}s_{ij}$	(6) $x_{ip}\sum\limits_{j=1}^{N} x_{jp}s_{ij}$	(7) N
IPL, Inc.	1.000	0.00701	0.012341	0.000000	0.01234	
Totals	1.000	0.00701	0.012341	0.000000	0.01234	1
IPL, Inc.	0.500	0.00351	0.003085	0.000524	0.00361	
Lehigh Portland Cement	0.500	0.00171	0.001376	0.000524	0.00190	2
Totals	1.000	0.00522	0.004462	0.001048	0.00551	
IPL, Inc.	0.333	0.00234	0.001371	0.000274	0.00164	
Lehigh Portland Cement	0.333	0.00114	0.000612	0.000470	0.00108	
Hotel Corp. of America	0.333	0.01186	0.001548	0.000277	0.00183	3
Totals	1.000	0.01534	0.003531	0.001021	0.00455	
IPL, Inc.	0.250	0.00175	0.000771	0.000233	0.00100	
Lehigh Portland Cement	0.250	0.00085	0.000344	0.000432	0.00078	
Hotel Corp. of America	0.250	0.00890	0.000871	0.000370	0.00124	4
Portec, Inc.	0.250	0.00489	0.000622	0.000461	0.00108	
Totals	1.000	0.01639	0.002608	0.001495	0.00410	
IPL, Inc.	0.200	0.00140	0.000494	0.000213	0.00071	
Lehigh Portland Cement	0.200	0.00068	0.000220	0.000296	0.00052	
Hotel Corp. of America	0.200	0.00712	0.000557	0.000280	0.00084	
Portec, Inc.	0.200	0.00391	0.000398	0.000397	0.00080	5
Bristol Myers Co.	0.200	0.00458	0.000142	0.000228	0.00037	
Totals	1.000	0.01769	0.001811	0.001413	0.00322	
IPL, Inc.	0.167	0.00117	0.000343	0.000216	0.00056	
Lehigh Portland Cement	0.167	0.00057	0.000153	0.000265	0.00042	
Hotel Corp. of America	0.167	0.00593	0.000387	0.000234	0.00062	
Portec, Inc.	0.167	0.00326	0.000277	0.000303	0.00058	6
Bristol Myers Co.	0.167	0.00381	0.000098	0.000178	0.00028	
Van Raalte Co.	0.167	0.00347	0.000101	0.000215	0.00032	
Totals	1.000	0.01821	0.001359	0.001411	0.00277	
IPL, Inc.	0.100	0.00070	0.000123	0.000164	0.00029	
Lehigh Portland Cement	0.100	0.00034	0.000055	0.000150	0.00021	
Hotel Corp. of America	0.100	0.00356	0.000139	0.000168	0.00031	
Portec, Inc.	0.100	0.00195	0.000100	0.000181	0.00028	
Bristol Myers Co.	0.100	0.00229	0.000035	0.000106	0.00014	
Van Raalte Co.	0.100	0.00208	0.000036	0.000122	0.00016	10
Ex-Cell-O Corp.	0.100	0.00157	0.000051	0.000164	0.00022	
Keebler Co.	0.100	0.00201	0.000056	0.000191	0.00025	
Canadian Breweries Ltd.	0.100	0.00253	0.000059	0.000018	0.00008	
Gulf, Mobile & Ohio R.R.	0.100	0.00247	0.000061	0.000187	0.00025	
Totals	1.000	0.01949	0.000716	0.001450	0.00217	
IPL, Inc.	0.067	0.00047	0.000055	0.000115	0.00017	
Lehigh Portland Cement	0.067	0.00023	0.000024	0.000108	0.00013	
Hotel Corp. of America	0.067	0.00237	0.000062	0.000123	0.00018	

TABLE 7.1(CONT'D)

Components of the Sample Mean and Variance of Monthly Returns on Portfolios
of Increasing Numbers of Randomly Selected Securities, July 1963–June 1968

(1)	(2)	(3)	(4)	(5)	(6)	(7)
SECURITIES (i)	x_{ip}	$x_{ip}\overline{R}_i$	$x_{ip}^2 s^2(R_i)$	$x_{ip}\sum\limits_{\substack{j=1 \\ j\neq i}}^{N} x_{jp}s_{ij}$	$x_{ip}\sum\limits_{j=1}^{N} x_{jp}s_{ij}$	N
Portec, Inc.	0.067	0.00130	0.000044	0.000127	0.00017	
Bristol Myers Co.	0.067	0.00153	0.000016	0.000067	0.00008	
Van Raalte Co.	0.067	0.00139	0.000016	0.000079	0.00010	
Ex-Cell-O Corp.	0.067	0.00105	0.000023	0.000109	0.00013	
Keebler Co.	0.067	0.00134	0.000025	0.000127	0.00015	
Canadian Breweries Ltd.	0.067	0.00168	0.000026	0.000031	0.00006	15
Gulf, Mobile & Ohio R.R.	0.067	0.00164	0.000027	0.000121	0.00015	
Dana Corp.	0.067	0.00044	0.000011	0.000084	0.00009	
Union Pacific R.R.	0.067	0.00057	0.000011	0.000075	0.00009	
Cyclops Corp.	0.067	0.00063	0.000017	0.000085	0.00010	
Ohio Edison Co.	0.067	0.00046	0.000007	0.000015	0.00002	
Central Foundry	0.067	0.00125	0.000101	0.000221	0.00032	
Totals	1.000	0.01635	0.000464	0.001489	0.00195	
IPL, Inc.	0.040	0.00028	0.000020	0.000059	0.00008	
Lehigh Portland Cement	0.040	0.00014	0.000009	0.000055	0.00006	
Hotel Corp. of America	0.040	0.00142	0.000022	0.000070	0.00009	
Portec, Inc.	0.040	0.00078	0.000016	0.000076	0.00009	
Bristol Myers Co.	0.040	0.00092	0.000006	0.000043	0.00005	
Van Raalte Co.	0.040	0.00083	0.000006	0.000041	0.00005	
Ex-Cell-O Corp.	0.040	0.00063	0.000008	0.000061	0.00007	
Keebler Co.	0.040	0.00080	0.000009	0.000066	0.00007	
Canadian Breweries Ltd.	0.040	0.00101	0.000009	0.000011	0.00002	
Gulf, Mobile & Ohio R.R.	0.040	0.00099	0.000010	0.000068	0.00008	
Dana Corp.	0.040	0.00026	0.000004	0.000045	0.00005	25
Union Pacific R.R.	0.040	0.00034	0.000004	0.000042	0.00005	
Cyclops Corp.	0.040	0.00038	0.000006	0.000049	0.00006	
Ohio Edison Co.	0.040	0.00027	0.000002	0.000014	0.00002	
Central Foundry	0.040	0.00075	0.000036	0.000124	0.00016	
United States Gypsum	0.040	0.00021	0.000007	0.000056	0.00006	
Eversharp Inc.	0.040	0.00013	0.000019	0.000060	0.00008	
Dayton Power & Light Co.	0.040	0.00029	0.000004	0.000034	0.00004	
Cluett, Peabody & Co.	0.040	0.00079	0.000006	0.000038	0.00004	
Washington Gas Light	0.040	−.00000	0.000001	0.000012	0.00001	
Lowenstein, M., & Sons	0.040	0.00076	0.000010	0.000067	0.00008	
International Telephone	0.040	0.00067	0.000006	0.000050	0.00006	
Carpenter Steel Co.	0.040	0.00079	0.000009	0.000045	0.00005	
Greyhound Corp.	0.040	0.00030	0.000006	0.000053	0.00006	
Allegheny Ludlum Steel	0.040	0.00057	0.000006	0.000035	0.00004	
Totals	1.000	0.01431	0.000242	0.001276	0.00152	
IPL, Inc.	0.020	0.00014	0.000005	0.000028	0.00003	
Lehigh Portland Cement	0.020	0.00007	0.000002	0.000032	0.00003	
Hotel Corp. of America	0.020	0.00071	0.000006	0.000046	0.00005	
Portec, Inc.	0.020	0.00039	0.000004	0.000042	0.00005	
Richardson Merrill Inc.	0.020	0.00026	0.000002	0.000017	0.00002	

TABLE 7.1 (CONT'D)

Components of the Sample Mean and Variance of Monthly Returns on Portfolios of Increasing Numbers of Randomly Selected Securities, July 1963–June 1968

(1) SECURITIES (i)	(2) x_{ip}	(3) $x_{ip}\bar{R}_i$	(4) $x_{ip}^2 s^2(R_i)$	(5) $x_{ip}\sum_{\substack{j=1 \\ j \neq i}}^{N} x_{jp}s_{ij}$	(6) $x_{ip}\sum_{j=1}^{N} x_{jp}s_{ij}$	(7) N
Van Raalte Co.	0.020	0.00042	0.000001	0.000021	0.00002	
Ex-Cell-O Corp.	0.020	0.00031	0.000002	0.000034	0.00004	
Keebler Co.	0.020	0.00040	0.000002	0.000031	0.00003	
Canadian Breweries Ltd.	0.020	0.00051	0.000002	0.000000	0.00000	
Gulf, Mobile & Ohio R.R.	0.020	0.00049	0.000002	0.000036	0.00004	
Dana Corp.	0.020	0.00013	0.000001	0.000025	0.00003	
Union Pacific R.R.	0.020	0.00017	0.000001	0.000020	0.00002	
Cyclops Corp.	0.020	0.00019	0.000002	0.000028	0.00003	
Ohio Edison Co.	0.020	0.00014	0.000001	0.000008	0.00001	
Central Foundry	0.020	0.00038	0.000009	0.000066	0.00007	
United States Gypsum	0.020	0.00011	0.000002	0.000030	0.00003	
Eversharp, Inc.	0.020	0.00006	0.000005	0.000033	0.00004	
Dayton Power & Light Co.	0.020	0.00014	0.000001	0.000018	0.00002	
Cluett, Peabody & Co.	0.020	0.00039	0.000002	0.000019	0.00002	
Washington Gas Light	0.020	−.00000	0.000000	0.000005	0.00001	
Lowenstein, M., & Sons	0.020	0.00038	0.000002	0.000035	0.00004	
International Telephone	0.020	0.00034	0.000001	0.000027	0.00003	50
Carpenter Steel Co.	0.020	0.00039	0.000002	0.000027	0.00003	
Greyhound Corp.	0.020	0.00015	0.000002	0.000026	0.00003	
Allegheny Ludlum Steel	0.020	0.00028	0.000001	0.000022	0.00002	
United Airlines Inc.	0.020	0.00042	0.000004	0.000037	0.00004	
Adams Express	0.020	0.00024	0.000000	0.000011	0.00001	
Ambac Industries, Inc.	0.020	0.00057	0.000005	0.000057	0.00006	
Masonite Corp.	0.020	0.00034	0.000003	0.000042	0.00005	
Lehigh Valley Industries	0.020	0.00106	0.000011	0.000040	0.00005	
American Cement Corp.	0.020	0.00031	0.000004	0.000041	0.00004	
Ebasco Industries, Inc.	0.020	0.00032	0.000001	0.000017	0.00002	
Raybestos Manhattan	0.020	0.00022	0.000001	0.000014	0.00002	
Inland Steel Co.	0.020	0.00010	0.000001	0.000028	0.00003	
Sterling Drug Inc.	0.020	0.00033	0.000002	0.000024	0.00003	
Walworth Co.	0.020	0.00040	0.000008	0.000047	0.00005	
Carborundum Co.	0.020	0.00035	0.000003	0.000036	0.00004	
Hudson Bay Mining & Smel.	0.020	0.00017	0.000001	0.000023	0.00002	
MSL Industries, Inc.	0.020	0.00022	0.000002	0.000032	0.00003	
Rohr Corp.	0.020	0.00050	0.000004	0.000027	0.00003	
Certainteed Products Corp.	0.020	0.00038	0.000005	0.000062	0.00007	
Neisner Bros.	0.020	0.00031	0.000002	0.000020	0.00002	
Rexall Drug and Chemical	0.020	0.00040	0.000003	0.000046	0.00005	
Laclede Gas Co.	0.020	0.00000	0.000000	0.000011	0.00001	
Chemetron Corp.	0.020	0.00037	0.000002	0.000038	0.00004	
Washington Gas Light	0.020	−.00000	0.000000	0.000005	0.00001	
Fiscbach and Moore Inc.	0.020	0.00038	0.000002	0.000027	0.00003	
C.I.T. Financial	0.020	0.00009	0.000001	0.000015	0.00002	
Donnelley, R. R., and Sons	0.020	0.00025	0.000001	0.000021	0.00002	
Continental Can Co. Inc.	0.020	0.00029	0.000001	0.000027	0.00003	
Totals	1.000	0.01497	0.000130	0.001426	0.00156	

need not change systematically as N is increased, the contribution of the security to $s^2(R_p)$ goes down with the weight $x_{ip} = 1/N$. In simplest terms, as portfolios become increasingly diversified, as new securities are introduced and the proportions invested in individual securities are reduced, an individual security becomes less important in terms of its effects on portfolio return distributions.

The decreasing importance of the role of an individual security in portfolios of increasing numbers of securities depends, however, on the presumption that smaller and smaller fractions of portfolio funds are invested in the security. If the number of securities is increased but the fraction invested in some security is not decreased, then that security will make the same contribution to average portfolio return and about the same contribution to standard deviation of portfolio return for all portfolio sizes.

One of the facts that comes out of the theoretical discussion of the risks of securities in portfolios is that in a portfolio of many securities, the variance of a security's return is only 1 of N terms that determine the contribution of the security to the variance of the return on the portfolio, with the remaining $N - 1$ terms being the pairwise covariances between the return on the security and the return on each of the other securities in the portfolio. However, we cannot conclude that for any specific "large" N the covariance terms dominate the variance term until we know something about the magnitudes of the security return variances versus the covariances. Table 7.1 provides sample information on this point.

For a given security and portfolio, columns (4) and (5) of Table 7.1 show, respectively, the contribution of the security's sample return variance to the sample variance of the portfolio's return and the contribution of its sample covariances. As one looks across portfolios of increasing numbers of securities, the numbers in both columns (4) and (5) decline, which is just a reflection of the fact that the contribution of an individual security to portfolio risk declines as the number of securities in the portfolios increases and the proportion of portfolio funds invested in an individual security decreases. As one looks across portfolios of increasing numbers of securities, however, one also observes a decline in the magnitude of the numbers in column (4) relative to those in column (5), and this is direct evidence of the declining importance of security return variances relative to covariances as the portfolios become increasingly diversified.

Perhaps the best information on this phenomenon is in the "Totals" rows in Table 7.1. For a given portfolio, the entries in columns (4) and (5) of the "Totals" row show the two components of equation (42) for $s^2(R_p)$; that is, the entry in column (4) of the "Totals" row shows the total contribution of the sample security return variances to $s^2(R_p)$, while the entry in column (5) shows the total contribution of security return covariances to $s^2(R_p)$. Since we are dealing with portfolios of equally weighted securities, equation (42) can be rewritten as

$$s^2(R_p) = \frac{1}{N}\left(\frac{\sum\limits_{i=1}^{N} s^2(R_i)}{N}\right) + \frac{\sum\limits_{\substack{i=1 \\ }}^{N}\sum\limits_{\substack{j=1 \\ j\neq i}}^{N} s_{ij}}{N^2}$$

or

$$s^2(R_p) = \frac{1}{N}\,\overline{s^2(R_i)} + \frac{N-1}{N}\,\overline{s_{ij}}, \tag{43}$$

where $\overline{s^2(R_i)}$ is the average of the N values of $s^2(R_i)$ in the portfolio, and

$$\overline{s_{ij}} = \frac{\sum\limits_{\substack{i=1 \\ }}^{N}\sum\limits_{\substack{j=1 \\ j\neq i}}^{N} s_{ij}}{N(N-1)} \tag{44}$$

is the average of the $N(N-1)$ pairwise covariances s_{ij}.

When N is large, $(N-1)/N$ is close to 1, so that, from (43), the total contribution of covariances to the sample variance of the portfolio return is approximately $\overline{s_{ij}}$, and this average of pairwise covariances should not change in any particular way as a function of N. This point is well illustrated in Table 7.1 where, aside from reflecting the approach of $(N-1)/N$ to 1, the values of

$$\sum\limits_{i=1}^{N} x_{ip} \sum\limits_{\substack{j=1 \\ j\neq i}}^{N} x_{jp} s_{ij} = \frac{N-1}{N}\,\overline{s_{ij}}$$

shown in column (5) of the "Totals" rows do not change with N in any particularly systematic way for portfolios of five or more securities. In short, once the portfolio becomes large, continuing to add securities has little effect on the contribution of security return covariances to the variance of the return on the portfolio.

Quite the opposite conclusion applies to the security return variances. Thus, although $\overline{s^2(R_i)}$ in (43) need not change systematically as N is increased $(1/N)\overline{s^2(R_i)}$, the total contribution of the security return variances to $s^2(R_p)$, declines inexorably as N is increased. This effect is well illustrated in Table 7.1, where the values of

$$\sum\limits_{i=1}^{N} x_{ip}^2 s^2(R_i) = \frac{1}{N}\,\overline{s^2(R_i)}$$

shown in column (6) of the "Totals" rows decline more or less like $1/N$ as N is increased. For example, the values of $(1/N)\overline{s^2(R_i)}$ for the portfolios of 10, 15, 25, and 50 securities are .000716, .000464, .000242, and .000130, respectively.

The net result of the declining contribution of security return variances to $s^2(R_p)$ as N is increased, as compared to the relatively stable contribution of the security return covariances, is that $s^2(R_p)$ becomes more and more a reflection of the covariances. Thus in columns (4) and (5) of the "Totals" rows of Table 7.1, one finds that the covariances account for less than one-fifth of $s^2(R_p)$ when $N = 2$; their contribution to $s^2(R_p)$ is about equal to that of the security return variances when $N = 6$; and when $N = 50$ the security return variances account for less than one-tenth of the value of $s^2(R_p)$.

The fact that it takes a portfolio of 50 securities to get the security return variances down to accounting for less than 10 percent of the value of $s^2(R_p)$ indicates, however, that on average the pairwise covariances between security returns are small relative to security return variances. Thus, from the "Totals" row for the portfolio of 50 securities in Table 7.1 we find that

$$\frac{1}{50}\,\overline{s^2(R_i)} = .00013, \quad \text{so that} \quad \overline{s^2(R_i)} = .00650,$$

while

$$\frac{49}{50}\,\overline{s_{ij}} = .00142, \quad \text{so that} \quad \overline{s_{ij}} = .00145.$$

In short, for these 50 securities, security return variances average about 4.5 times larger than pairwise covariances between security returns. Thus, it takes a portfolio of many securities before the covariances dominate in determining the variance of the return on the portfolio. One would find similar results for other securities and portfolios.

C. The Effects of Diversification

The preceding analysis can be viewed from a different perspective. In particular, the analysis shows how diversification works to reduce the variance of the return on a portfolio. Thus, equation (43) and the examples in Table 7.1 tell us that, aside from reflecting the approach of $(N - 1)/N$ to 1.0, the contribution of the pairwise covariances between the returns on individual securities in a portfolio to the variance of the portfolio's return generally does not change in any systematic way as the number of securities in the portfolio is increased. Equation (43) and the examples of Table 7.1 also tell us, however, that the contribution of security return variances to the variance of the return on the portfolio goes down as the number of securities in the portfolio is increased, and more or less in proportion to $1/N$. With the pairwise covariances making a steady contribution to the variance of the portfolio return, and with the contribution of security return variances declining as the number of securities in the portfolio is increased, the net result is a decline in the variance of the portfolio return, with the decline a direct reflection of the declining contribution of security return variances.

An illustration of the effects of diversification on the variance of portfolio returns is provided by columns (4) to (6) in the "Totals" rows of Table 7.1. For larger values of N, one observes smaller values of $s^2(R_p)$ in column (6), and it is clear from columns (4) and (5) that for $N \geqslant 5$ the decline in $s^2(R_p)$ as N is increased is almost entirely a reflection of the decline in the contribution of security return variances to the variance of portfolio returns.

The effects of diversification on the dispersion of distributions of portfolio returns can perhaps be better appreciated from Figure 7.9, which presents a plot of $s(R_p)$ against N for the portfolios of the random sample of stocks in Table 7.1, but for every value of N from 1 to 50. The important fact illustrated in Figure 7.9 is that most of the effects of diversification on the dispersion of the distribution of the portfolio return occur when the first few securities are added to the portfolio. Once the portfolio has 20 securities,

FIGURE 7.9

The Standard Deviation of Portfolio Return as a Function of the Number of Securities in the Portfolio: First Sample of 50 Randomly Selected Stocks

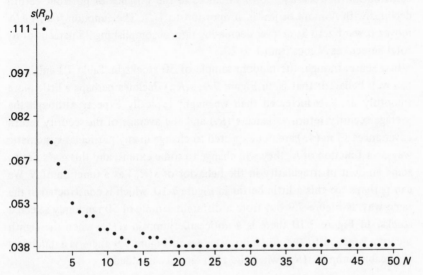

FIGURE 7.10

The Standard Deviation of Portfolio Return as a Function of the Number of Securities in the Portfolio: Second Sample of 50 Randomly Selected Stocks

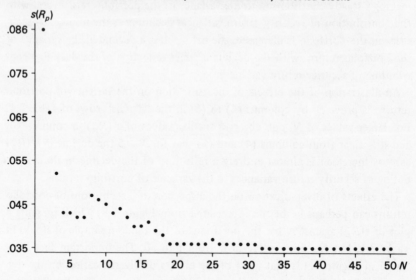

further diversification has little effect. The reason for this phenomenon is evident in equation (43). With portfolios of equally weighted securities, the contribution of security return variances to the variance of portfolio return declines with N more or less in proportion to $1/N$. The function $f(N) = 1/N$ moves toward zero at an ever decreasing rate, accomplishing 95 percent of its total descent as N goes from 1 to 20.

In a sense, though, the random sample of 50 stocks in Table 7.1 might be too well behaved: that is, in Figure 7.9, $s(R_p)$ declines perhaps a little more smoothly as N is increased than we might typically expect. Although the average security return variance $\overline{s^2(R_i)}$ and the average of the security return covariances $\overline{s_{ij}}$ in (43) are not expected to change in any particular systematic way as a function of N, they will change to some extent, and this gives rise to some amount of irregularity in the behavior of $s(R_p)$ as a function of N. We can perhaps see this a little better in Figure 7.10, which is constructed in the same way as Figure 7.9 but from a different sample of 50 randomly selected stocks. In Figure 7.10 there is a noticeable jump in $s(R_p)$ when the eighth security is added to the portfolio, whereas in Figure 7.9 there is a much less noticeable jump in $s(R_p)$ when the 15th security is added.

PROBLEM IV.C

1. Compute the values of $f(N) = 1/N$ for $N = 1, 2, 3, 4, 5, 10, 25, 50, 100$, and $1,000$, and make a rough sketch of the function.

ANSWER

1. Do it!

Finally, when one examines carefully columns (4) and (5) for the portfolio of 50 securities in Table 7.1, it seems that securities with large return variances generally have large average covariances with other securities. The same phenomenon would be observed for other securities and portfolios. A possible explanation is as follows.

One can argue that for measuring the association between the returns on two securities, the correlation between the returns is more relevant than the covariance, since the square of the correlation can be interpreted as the proportion of the variance of the return on either security that can be attributed to its linear association with the return on the other security. The covariance has no such direct interpretation. The correlation is, however, related to the covariance, since the former is

$$\rho(\tilde{R}_i, \tilde{R}_j) = \frac{\text{cov}\,(\tilde{R}_i, \tilde{R}_j)}{\sigma(\tilde{R}_i)\sigma(R_j)}. \tag{44}$$

Alternatively, the covariance is

$$\text{cov}\,(\tilde{R}_i, \tilde{R}_j) = \rho(\tilde{R}_i, \tilde{R}_j)\sigma(\tilde{R}_i)\sigma(\tilde{R}_j). \tag{45}$$

Consider two securities, i and k, whose returns have the same correlation with the return on security j, so that, in terms of proportion of variance explained, the returns on i and k have the same degree of association with the return on j. Nevertheless, equation (45) tells us that if $\sigma(\tilde{R}_i) > \sigma(\tilde{R}_k)$, then $\text{cov}\,(\tilde{R}_i, \tilde{R}_j) > \text{cov}\,(\tilde{R}_k, \tilde{R}_j)$. Thus, although the returns on i and k have the same correlation with the return on j, because the return on i has larger standard deviation than the return on k, it also has larger covariance with the return on j.

Suppose now that there is no systematic relationship between correlations of returns on securities and standard deviations of security returns. Then it follows from the discussion above that there will be a relationship between the standard deviations of security returns and their average covariances with the returns on other securities. As observed in Table 7.1, securities with larger standard deviations of return will tend to have larger average covariances with the returns on other securities.

The observed relationship between standard deviations of security returns and their average covariances with the returns on other securities takes some of the sting out of earlier comments. Thus, in a diversified portfolio of many securities, the contribution of an individual security to the variance of the portfolio's return depends to a greater extent on the security's covariances with the returns on other securities in the portfolios than on the variance of the security's return. Nevertheless, because of the relationship between security return variances and covariances, the variance of a security's return is likely to be a good indication of how the security will contribute to the variance of the return on a diversified portfolio. Similarly, although the variance of the return on a diversified portfolio depends primarily on the covariances between the returns on the securities in the portfolio, the variances of the component security returns are nevertheless likely to be a good indication of the level of the variance of the return on the portfolio. Generally, the larger the variances of component security returns, the larger the variance of the return on the portfolio.

V. Conclusions

We have considered the two-parameter portfolio model in some detail, both theoretical and numerical. We are ready now to consider the characteristics of equilibrium prices and the relationship between expected return and risk in a market where investors make portfolio decisions according to the two-parameter model.

CHAPTER
8

Capital Market Equilibrium in a Two-Parameter World

I. Introduction

Chapter 7 presents a model for portfolio decisions by investors in a world where probability distributions of returns on portfolios are normal. In this two-parameter model, the investor finds it possible to summarize the distribution of the return on any portfolio in terms of its mean and its standard deviation, and he can rank portfolio return distributions solely in terms of the values of these parameters. Moreover, the investor is assumed to like expected portfolio return, but he is risk-averse in the sense that he dislikes standard deviation of portfolio return. These assumptions about the investor's tastes lead to the fundamental result of the two-parameter model—the investor's optimal portfolio is efficient. To be efficient, a portfolio must have the property that no other portfolio with the same or higher expected return has lower standard deviation of return.

This chapter is concerned with the implications of the portfolio model for capital market equilibrium. That is, if investors make portfolio decisions in accordance with the two-parameter model, how will this affect the process of price formation in the capital market? More specifically, if investors try to hold efficient portfolios, what sort of relationships between expected return and risk can we expect to observe in the capital market? The next chapter then considers whether the expected return-risk relationships that characterize the capital market in a two-parameter world are descriptive of the data generated by the real-world capital market.

The first step in the present chapter is to discuss expected return and risk from the viewpoint of an individual investor. We then find that, with a few simplifying assumptions, the type of expected return-risk relationships that apply to individual investors also apply to the market.

II.   The Relationship Between Expected Return and Risk in an Efficient Portfolio

The decision problem facing the investor is precisely as in Chapter 7. At time 1 the investor has wealth w_1 that he must allocate to current consumption c_1 and to an investment $w_1 - c_1$ in some portfolio. The market value of his portfolio at time 2 is then his consumption c_2 at time 2. The consumption-investment decision takes place in a capital market assumed to be perfect or frictionless in the sense that an investor can purchase as much or as little of any security as he sees fit (securities are infinitely divisible), there are no transactions costs in purchasing and selling securities, and any investor can buy or sell as much as he likes of any security without affecting its price. Finally, the investor's decision is assumed to be in accordance with the two-parameter model.

A.   The Risks of Securities and Portfolios

In the two-parameter model, the risk of a portfolio is measured by the standard deviation or, equivalently, by the variance of its return. The logic is that a risk-averse investor is averse to dispersion of portfolio return. With normal portfolio return distributions, dispersion is completely summarized by variance. The risk of a security in a portfolio is then determined by the contribution of the security to the variance of the return on the portfolio.

In formal terms, the return, expected return, and variance of return on a portfolio p are

$$\tilde{R}_p = \sum_{i=1}^{n} x_{ip} \tilde{R}_i \tag{1}$$

$$E(\tilde{R}_p) = \sum_{i=1}^{n} x_{ip} E(\tilde{R}_i) \tag{2}$$

$$\sigma^2(\tilde{R}_p) = \sum_{i=1}^{n} \sum_{j=1}^{n} x_{ip} x_{jp} \sigma_{ij}, \tag{3}$$

where n is the number of securities available for inclusion in portfolios, x_{ip} is the proportion of portfolio funds $w_1 - c_1$ invested in security i in portfolio p, $E(\tilde{R}_i)$ is the expected return on security i, and $\sigma_{ij} = \text{cov}(\tilde{R}_i, \tilde{R}_j)$ is the covariance between the returns on securities i and j.

Rewriting (3) as

$$\sigma^2(\tilde{R}_p) = \sum_{i=1}^{n} x_{ip} \left(\sum_{j=1}^{n} x_{jp} \sigma_{ij} \right) = \sum_{i=1}^{n} x_{ip} \, \text{cov}(\tilde{R}_i, \tilde{R}_p), \tag{4}$$

the contribution of security i to the risk or variance of the return on p is

$$x_{ip} \left(\sum_{j=1}^{n} x_{jp} \sigma_{ij} \right) = x_{ip} \, \text{cov}(\tilde{R}_i, \tilde{R}_p). \tag{5}$$

Thus, one could interpret (5) as the risk of security i in portfolio p. Chapter 7 suggests, however, that it is more convenient to call the weighted average of covariances,

$$\sum_{j=1}^{n} x_{jp} \sigma_{ij} = \text{cov}(\tilde{R}_i, \tilde{R}_p), \tag{6}$$

the risk of security i in p, and we see shortly why this is the more convenient measure of risk. If we interpret (6) as the risk of security i in portfolio p, then from (4) the risk of the portfolio is the weighted average of the risks of individual securities.

We have known since Chapter 2 what the two-parameter model says about the risks of portfolios and the risks of securities in portfolios. We now want to determine what the model says about the relationships between expected return and risk. We find that for any efficient portfolio there is an equation relating the expected return on any security in that portfolio to the risk of the security in the portfolio. More specifically, the mathematical conditions that a portfolio must satisfy to be efficient define the relationship between expected return and risk for individual securities in that portfolio. Much of the rest of this chapter involves developing this point in detail.

B. The Mathematics of Minimum Variance Portfolios

To be efficient, a portfolio must have the property that no other portfolio with the same or higher expected return has lower standard deviation of return. Equivalently, if a portfolio is efficient, then (a) it has the maximum possible expected return given the variance of its return, and (b) it has the smallest possible variance of return given its expected return.

Any portfolio that satisfies condition (a) is called a minimum variance portfolio. Any such minimum variance portfolio can be viewed as the solution to a problem of the form:

$$\text{Minimize} \quad \sigma^2(\tilde{R}_p), \tag{7a}$$
$$\underset{\substack{x_{ip} \\ i=1,\ldots,n}}{}$$

subject to the constraints

$$\sum_{i=1}^{n} x_{ip} E(\tilde{R}_i) = E(\tilde{R}_e) \tag{7b}$$

$$\sum_{i=1}^{n} x_{ip} = 1.0. \tag{7c}$$

Here $E(\tilde{R}_e)$ is some given level of expected return. The problem stated in equations (7a) to (7c) is to choose proportions x_{ip}, $i = 1, \cdots, n$, invested in individual securities that minimize the variance of portfolio return subject to the constraints that expected portfolio return is equal to $E(\tilde{R}_e)$ and that the sum of the proportions invested in individual securities is 1.0.

In geometric terms, suppose the left boundary of the portfolio opportunity set is the solid curve shown in Figure 8.1. (For the moment, the dashed line in the figure is to be ignored.) The minimum variance portfolio with expected return $E(\tilde{R}_e)$ is then a point along this left boundary, say the point e. The solution to (7a) to (7c) is the set of n proportions invested in individual securities that give the minimum variance portfolio with expected return $E(\tilde{R}_e)$. Once these weights are determined, the variance of the portfolio's return is determined, which, in combination with the target value of the expected portfolio return, gives the geometric location of the portfolio.

Every point along the left boundary of the investment opportunity set is a minimum variance portfolio and so can be viewed as the solution to a problem stated in the form of equations (7a-c). One can think of the boundary in Figure 8.1 as determined by the solutions to lots of problems stated in the form of (7a-c). The portfolio e is obtained from the solution to (7a-c) when the target level of expected portfolio return is $E(\tilde{R}_e)$. Other points

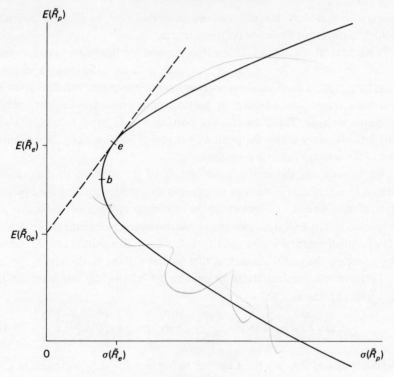

FIGURE 8.1
Minimum Variance Portfolios

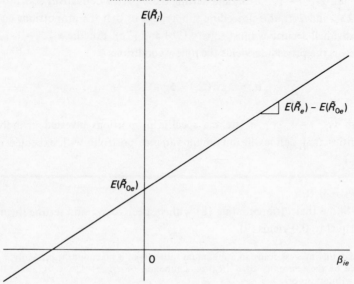

FIGURE 8.2
Relationship Between Expected Return and Risk for Securities in the
Minimum Variance Portfolio e

along the boundary are obtained by re-solving (7a) to (7c) for different values of the target expected portfolio return.

Note that in Figure 8.1 efficient portfolios are minimum variance portfolios, but not all minimum variance portfolios are efficient. An efficient portfolio, like a minimum variance portfolio, minimizes variance given its expected return, but an efficient portfolio also maximizes expected return given its variance. Thus, the efficient portfolios in Figure 8.1 are those along the left boundary above the point b, but points below b along the boundary are also minimum variance portfolios.

We now discuss the mathematical details of the solution to the problem stated in equations (7a–c). The outcome is an equation relating the expected return on a security to its risk in the minimum variance portfolio that has expected return $E(\tilde{R}_e)$. In two places, the discussion uses elementary calculus. The nonmathematical reader can either skip down to equation (16) or, better, try to follow the verbal discussions that accompany the mathematics.

To solve the problem stated in equations (7a) to (7c), first form the Lagrangian expression

$$\sigma^2(\tilde{R}_p) + 2\lambda_e \left[E(\tilde{R}_e) - \sum_{i=1}^{n} x_{ip} E(\tilde{R}_i) \right] + 2\phi_e \left[1 - \sum_{i=1}^{n} x_{ip} \right], \qquad (8)$$

where $2\lambda_e$ and $2\phi_e$ are the Lagrange multipliers for the constraints of (7b) and (7c). The convenience of stating the Lagrange multipliers in this way is soon apparent. Minimizing the variance of portfolio return subject to the constraints of (7b) and (7c) involves differentiating (8) with respect to $2\lambda_e$, $2\phi_e$, and x_{ip}, $i = 1, \ldots, n$, and setting these partial derivatives equal to 0.0.* For $2\lambda_e$ and $2\phi_e$, this procedure simply tells us that the proportions invested in individual securities must satisfy (7b) and (7c). For the x_{ip}, $i = 1, \ldots, n$, however, the procedure yields the n new conditions

$$\sum_{j=1}^{n} x_{je} \sigma_{ij} - \lambda_e E(\tilde{R}_i) - \phi_e = 0.0, \quad i = 1, \ldots, n, \qquad (9)$$

where x_{je}, $j = 1, \ldots, n$, are the specific proportions invested in individual securities that define the minimum variance portfolio with expected return $E(\tilde{R}_e)$.

PROBLEM II.B

1. Show that differentiating (8) with respect to x_{ip} and setting the derivative equal to 0.0 yields (9).

---

*That this process leads to a minimum rather than a maximum is primarily a consequence of the convexity of $\sigma^2(R_p)$ as a function of x_{ip}, $i = 1, \ldots, n$, a fact that we state without proof.

ANSWER

1. As a first step, differentiating (8) with respect to x_{ip} and setting the derivative equal to 0.0 leads to

$$\frac{\partial \sigma^2(\tilde{R}_e)}{\partial x_{ie}} - 2\lambda_e E(\tilde{R}_i) - 2\phi_e = 0.0,$$

where $\partial \sigma^2(\tilde{R}_e)/\partial x_{ie}$ is $\partial \sigma^2(\tilde{R}_p)/\partial x_{ip}$ evaluated at the values $x_{ip} = x_{ie}$, $i = 1, \ldots, n$, that represent the solution to the problem stated in (7a) to (7c). Thus, all we must show is that

$$\frac{\partial \sigma^2(\tilde{R}_p)}{\partial x_{ip}} = 2 \sum_{j=1}^{n} x_{jp} \sigma_{ij}. \tag{10}$$

The most transparent way to establish (10) is to first write $\sigma^2(\tilde{R}_p)$ as

$$\sigma^2(\tilde{R}_p) = \sum_{i=1}^{n} \sum_{j=1}^{n} x_{ip} x_{jp} \sigma_{ij}$$

$$= \begin{bmatrix} x_{1p}^2 \sigma_{11} + x_{1p}x_{2p}\sigma_{12} + x_{1p}x_{3p}\sigma_{13} + \cdots + x_{1p}x_{np}\sigma_{1n} \\ + x_{2p}x_{1p}\sigma_{21} + x_{2p}^2\sigma_{22} + x_{2p}x_{3p}\sigma_{23} + \cdots + x_{2p}x_{np}\sigma_{2n} \\ + x_{3p}x_{1p}\sigma_{31} + x_{3p}x_{2p}\sigma_{32} + x_{3p}^2\sigma_{33} + \cdots + x_{3p}x_{np}\sigma_{3n} \\ \vdots \qquad \vdots \qquad \vdots \qquad \vdots \qquad \vdots \\ + x_{np}x_{1p}\sigma_{n1} + x_{np}x_{2p}\sigma_{n2} + x_{np}x_{3p}\sigma_{n3} + \cdots + x_{np}^2\sigma_{nn} \end{bmatrix}.$$

For any given i, the terms involving x_{ip} are those in the ith row and those in the ith column of this block:

$$\begin{bmatrix} + x_{1p}x_{ip}\sigma_{1i} \\ + x_{2p}x_{ip}\sigma_{2i} \\ \vdots \\ + x_{ip}x_{1p}\sigma_{i1} + x_{ip}x_{2p}\sigma_{i2} + \cdots + x_{ip}^2\sigma_{ii} + \cdots + x_{ip}x_{np}\sigma_{in} \\ \vdots \\ + x_{np}x_{ip}\sigma_{ni} \end{bmatrix}.$$

It is then easy to see that

$$\frac{\partial \sigma^2(\tilde{R}_p)}{\partial x_{ip}} = \sum_{\substack{j=1 \\ j \neq i}}^{n} x_{jp}\sigma_{ij} + \sum_{\substack{j=1 \\ j \neq i}}^{n} x_{jp}\sigma_{ji} + 2x_{ip}\sigma_{ii} = 2 \sum_{j=1}^{n} x_{jp}\sigma_{ij},$$

since $\sigma_{ij} = \sigma_{ji}$. It is now also easy to see why it is convenient to state the Lagrange multipliers in (8) as $2\lambda_e$ and $2\phi_e$ rather than as λ_e and ϕ_e.

The n equations described by (9), along with (7b) and (7c), determine the values of the Lagrange multipliers $2\lambda_e$ and $2\phi_e$ and the proportions invested in individual securities that yield the minimum variance portfolio with expected return $E(\tilde{R}_e)$. Thus, the equations of (9) are conditions on the proportions invested in individual securities that must be met by a minimum variance portfolio. We now show that (9) implies the relationship between the expected return on a security and its risk in the minimum variance portfolio e.

Since (9) holds for every security, it holds for security k

$$\sum_{j=1}^{n} x_{je}\sigma_{kj} - \lambda_e E(\tilde{R}_k) - \phi_e = 0.0, \tag{11}$$

and (9) and (11) together imply

$$\sum_{j=1}^{n} x_{je}\sigma_{kj} - \lambda_e E(\tilde{R}_k) = \sum_{j=1}^{n} x_{je}\sigma_{ij} - \lambda_e E(\tilde{R}_i). \tag{12}$$

Multiplying both sides of (12) by x_{ke} and then summing over k, we get

$$\sigma^2(\tilde{R}_e) - \lambda_e E(\tilde{R}_e) = \sum_{j=1}^{n} x_{je}\sigma_{ij} - \lambda_e E(\tilde{R}_i). \tag{13}$$

PROBLEM II.B

2. Write out the details involved in going from (12) to (13).

ANSWER

2. First multiply both sides of (12) by x_{ke} to get

$$x_{ke} \sum_{j=1}^{n} x_{je}\sigma_{kj} - \lambda_e x_{ke} E(\tilde{R}_k) = x_{ke} \left(\sum_{j=1}^{n} x_{je}\sigma_{ij} - \lambda_e E(\tilde{R}_i) \right). \tag{14}$$

Applying equations (2) and (4) to portfolio e yields, with a change in subscripting,

$$E(\tilde{R}_e) = \sum_{k=1}^{n} x_{ke} E(\tilde{R}_k)$$

$$\sigma^2(\tilde{R}_e) = \sum_{k=1}^{n} x_{ke} \sum_{j=1}^{n} x_{je} \sigma_{kj}.$$

Since none of the terms within the parentheses on the right-hand side of (14) involve security k, and since $\sum_{k=1}^{n} x_{ke} = 1.0$, summing (14) over k yields (13).

We can now rearrange (13) to get

$$E(\tilde{R}_i) - E(\tilde{R}_e) = \frac{1}{\lambda_e} \left(\sum_{j=1}^{n} x_{je} \sigma_{ij} - \sigma^2(\tilde{R}_e) \right), \quad i = 1, \dots, n. \tag{15}$$

Since equation (15) is a direct implication of (9), we can interpret (15) as a condition on the weights x_{je}, $j = 1, \dots, n$, that must be met if these weights describe the minimum variance portfolio that has expected return $E(\tilde{R}_e)$. In determining the weights x_{je}, $j = 1, \dots, n$, that cause (15) to be satisfied for every security i, the risk of portfolio e, $\sigma^2(\tilde{R}_e)$, and the risk of each security in portfolio e, $\sum_{j=1}^{n} x_{je} \sigma_{ij}$, $i = 1, \dots, n$, are also being determined. Once the weights are known, however, we can interpret (15) as the relationship between the expected return on any security i and the risk of the security in the minimum variance portfolio e. The equation says that the difference between the expected return on any security i and the expected return on e is proportional to the difference between the risk of i in e and the risk of e, and where the proportionality factor is $1/\lambda_e$.

To complete the interpretation of the relationship between expected return and risk in the minimum variance portfolio e, we must interpret the quantity $1/\lambda_e$. The Lagrange multiplier $2\lambda_e$ in (8) is the rate of change of the minimum value of $\sigma^2(\tilde{R}_p)$ in (7a) with respect to a small increase in the target value of the expected portfolio return;

$$2\lambda_e = \frac{d\sigma^2(\tilde{R}_e)}{dE(\tilde{R}_e)}.$$

This derivative is related to the slope of the boundary of the opportunity set at the point e in Figure 8.1. If S_e denotes the slope, then

$$S_e = \frac{dE(\tilde{R}_e)}{d\sigma(\tilde{R}_e)};$$

that is, the slope of the boundary at the point e is the rate of change of expected return with respect to a change in the minimum value of the portfolio standard deviation. To show the relationship between λ_e and S_e, we use the chain rule for differentiation to determine that

$$\frac{1}{S_e} = \frac{d\sigma(\tilde{R}_e)}{dE(\tilde{R}_e)} = \frac{d\sigma(\tilde{R}_e)}{d\sigma^2(\tilde{R}_e)} \frac{d\sigma^2(\tilde{R}_e)}{dE(\tilde{R}_e)}$$

$$= \frac{1}{2\sigma(\tilde{R}_e)} \frac{d\sigma^2(\tilde{R}_e)}{dE(\tilde{R}_e)} = \frac{\lambda_e}{\sigma(\tilde{R}_e)},$$

so that

$$\frac{1}{\lambda_e} = \frac{S_e}{\sigma(\tilde{R}_e)}. \tag{16}$$

In words, the proportionality factor $1/\lambda_e$ in the expected return-risk relationship (15) is the slope of the left boundary of the investment opportunity set at the point e in Figure 8.1 divided by the standard deviation of the return on the minimum variance portfolio e.

We can now transform (15) into an expression that has a somewhat more intuitive interpretation and is also more in keeping with the form of the equation used later in empirical tests. Substituting (16) and (6) into (15) and rearranging yields the equation

$$E(\tilde{R}_i) = [E(\tilde{R}_e) - S_e \sigma(\tilde{R}_e)] + \frac{S_e}{\sigma(\tilde{R}_e)} \operatorname{cov}(\tilde{R}_i, \tilde{R}_e). \tag{17}$$

The square brackets are to indicate that the quantity

$$E(\tilde{R}_e) - S_e \sigma(\tilde{R}_e) \equiv E(\tilde{R}_{0e}) \tag{18}$$

has a special interpretation. It is the expected return on any security whose return is uncorrelated and thus has zero covariance with the return on the portfolio e. Using the somewhat mnemonic notation $E(\tilde{R}_{0e})$ for this quantity, the slope of the left boundary of the investment opportunity set at the point corresponding to the portfolio e is

$$S_e = \frac{E(\tilde{R}_e) - E(\tilde{R}_{0e})}{\sigma(\tilde{R}_e)}. \tag{19}$$

PROBLEM II.B

3. What is the geometric interpretation of (18) and (19)?

ANSWER

3. Since S_e is the slope of the boundary of the investment opportunity set at the point e in Figure 8.1, we can see from inspection of the figure that

$E(\tilde{R}_e) - S_e\sigma(\tilde{R}_e)$ is the intersection on the $E(\tilde{R}_p)$ axis of the (dashed) line tangent to the boundary at e. If $E(\tilde{R}_e) - S_e\sigma(\tilde{R}_e)$ is called $E(\tilde{R}_{0e})$ to indicate that it is also the expected return on any security whose return is uncorrelated with the return on e, then it is clear from Figure 8.1 that the slope of the investment opportunity boundary at the point corresponding to the portfolio e is as given by (19).

With (18) and (19), the expected return-risk relationship of (17) becomes

$$E(\tilde{R}_i) = E(\tilde{R}_{0e}) + [E(\tilde{R}_e) - E(\tilde{R}_{0e})]\,\beta_{ie}, \quad i = 1, \ldots, n, \qquad (20)$$

where

$$\beta_{ie} = \frac{\mathrm{cov}\,(\tilde{R}_i, \tilde{R}_e)}{\sigma^2(\tilde{R}_e)} \qquad (21)$$

is the risk of security i in the portfolio e measured relative to the risk of the portfolio.

C. Interpretation of the Results

If the portfolio e is efficient—that is, if as in Figure 8.1 it is along the positively sloped segment of the left boundary of the opportunity set—then (20) has an intuitive interpretation. If e is efficient, then $S_e > 0$, and it follows from (18) that $E(\tilde{R}_e)$ is greater than $E(\tilde{R}_{0e})$. Thus, the term $[E(\tilde{R}_e) - E(\tilde{R}_{0e})]\,\beta_{ie}$ in (20) can be interpreted as the risk premium in the relationship between the expected return on security i and its risk in the portfolio e. Moreover, any security whose return is uncorrelated with the return on e, and so has $\beta_{ie} = 0.0$, is riskless as far as e is concerned, since such a security contributes nothing to $\sigma^2(\tilde{R}_e)$. In these terms, equation (20) says that the expected return on any security i is equal to the expected return on a security that is riskless in e plus a risk premium that is the difference between the expected return on e and $E(\tilde{R}_{0e})$, multiplied by β_{ie}, the risk of security i in e measured relative to the risk of e.

This interpretation of (20) makes sense, however, only when the portfolio e is efficient as well as of minimum variance. If e is minimum variance but inefficient (that is, if it is along the negatively sloped portion of the left boundary of the opportunity set), then $S_e < 0$, and, from (18) and (19), $E(\tilde{R}_e)$ is less than $E(\tilde{R}_{0e})$, so that (20) must be interpreted in terms of risk discounts rather than premiums. Since the investor is only concerned with efficient portfolios, no harm is done if we use the risk premium interpretation of (20).

Figure 8.2 gives a geometric interpretation of the expected return-risk relationship of (20). The figure emphasizes that the relationship between $E(\tilde{R}_i)$ and β_{ie} is linear. It has intercept $E(\tilde{R}_{0e})$ on the $E(\tilde{R}_i)$ axis and slope $E(\tilde{R}_e) - E(\tilde{R}_{0e})$. In geometric terms, the fact that e is a minimum variance portfolio implies that the weights x_{ie}, $i = 1, \ldots, n$ are chosen in such a way that all securities end up with combinations of $E(\tilde{R}_i)$ and β_{ie} that lie along the line in Figure 8.2. Thus, the n available securities would be arrayed at different points along the line.

It is instructive to look at Figures 8.1 and 8.2 from the viewpoint of the investor faced with a two-parameter world. If the boundary of the investment opportunity set is as represented by the solid curve in Figure 8.1, then the efficient portion of the boundary, the segment above the point b, shows the relationship between expected return and portfolio risk that is relevant when the investor is considering which portfolio to choose. Once he chooses some efficient portfolio, say the portfolio e, then equation (20) and Figure 8.2 show the relationship between expected security return and security risk within the portfolio e. Thus, whereas Figure 8.1 shows the trade-offs of expected return for risk among efficient portfolios, Figure 8.2 shows how the expected returns on individual securities are related to their risks in a specific efficient portfolio.

There is a different version of Figure 8.2 and equation (20) for each minimum variance portfolio. Thus, using equations (3) and (6) we can rewrite (21) and (20) as

$$\beta_{ie} \equiv \frac{\text{cov}\,(\tilde{R}_i, \tilde{R}_e)}{\sigma^2(\tilde{R}_e)} = \frac{\displaystyle\sum_{j=1}^{n} x_{je}\,\sigma_{ij}}{\displaystyle\sum_{i=1}^{n}\sum_{j=1}^{n} x_{ie}x_{je}\,\sigma_{ij}} \tag{22}$$

$$E(\tilde{R}_i) = E(\tilde{R}_{0e}) + [E(\tilde{R}_e) - E(\tilde{R}_{0e})]\,\frac{\displaystyle\sum_{j=1}^{n} x_{je}\,\sigma_{ij}}{\displaystyle\sum_{i=1}^{n}\sum_{j=1}^{n} x_{ie}x_{je}\,\sigma_{ij}}. \tag{23}$$

The expected security returns $E(\tilde{R}_i)$, $i = 1, \ldots, n$, and the pairwise security return covariances σ_{ij} $(i, j = 1, \ldots, n)$ are parameters of the joint distribution of security returns and so are the same from one efficient portfolio to another. But the weights x_{je}, $j = 1, \ldots, n$, change from one minimum variance portfolio to another; consequently, the risk of a security is different in different portfolios. Since expected security returns do not change from one minimum variance portfolio to another, the fact that the risks of individual securities change means that the intercept $E(\tilde{R}_{0e})$ and the slope $[E(\tilde{R}_e) -$

$E(\tilde{R}_{0e})]$ in (20) must also change from one minimum variance portfolio to another.

PROBLEMS II.C

1. Discuss in general terms how the intercept $E(\tilde{R}_{0e})$ and the slope $[E(\tilde{R}_e) - E(\tilde{R}_{0e})]$ in (20) change as one considers efficient portfolios with higher levels of expected return.

2. Show that equation (20) applies to portfolios as well as to individual securities. That is, show that for any minimum variance portfolio e and any portfolio p

$$E(\tilde{R}_p) = E(\tilde{R}_{0e}) + [E(\tilde{R}_e) - E(\tilde{R}_{0e})] \beta_{pe}, \qquad (24)$$

where

$$\beta_{pe} = \frac{\text{cov}(\tilde{R}_p, \tilde{R}_e)}{\sigma^2(\tilde{R}_e)}. \qquad (25)$$

3. We interpret the intercept $E(\tilde{R}_{0e})$ in (20) as the expected return on any security whose return is uncorrelated with the return on the portfolio e. It is well to note that $E(\tilde{R}_{0e})$ is indeed the expected return on such a security if one exists, but (20) does not require the existence of such a security. Equation (20) simply says that within an efficient portfolio there is a linear relationship between expected security returns and security risks in that portfolio.

With the result of the preceding problem, however, the reader can easily show that when short-selling of securities is allowed, it is always possible to construct a portfolio whose return is uncorrelated with the return on e, and the expected return on any such portfolio is $E(\tilde{R}_{0e})$. (Show it!) Thus, when short-selling of securities is possible, $E(\tilde{R}_{0e})$ can be interpreted as the expected return on any security or portfolio whose return is uncorrelated with the return on e. The importance of this result becomes clear later.

ANSWERS

1. One can apply equations (17) to (20) to any efficient portfolio. Thus, thinking of e as an arbitrary efficient portfolio, the intercept

$$E(\tilde{R}_{0e}) = E(\tilde{R}_e) - S_e \sigma(\tilde{R}_e)$$

in (20) is always the intercept on the $E(\tilde{R}_p)$ axis of a line tangent to the efficient boundary at the point corresponding to the portfolio e. Since the efficient boundary is positively sloped and concave, this means that $E(\tilde{R}_{0e})$ is higher for efficient portfolios with higher levels of expected return and that $E(\tilde{R}_{0e})$ increases faster than $E(\tilde{R}_e)$, so that the slope $[E(\tilde{R}_e) - E(\tilde{R}_{0e})]$ in (20) declines as one considers portfolios further up along the efficient boundary.

2. First, note that

$$\beta_{pe} = \frac{\text{cov}\,(\tilde{R}_p, \tilde{R}_e)}{\sigma^2(\tilde{R}_e)} = \frac{\text{cov}\left(\sum\limits_{i=1}^{n} x_{ip}\tilde{R}_i, \tilde{R}_e\right)}{\sigma^2(\tilde{R}_e)}$$

$$= \sum\limits_{i=1}^{n} x_{ip}\,\frac{\text{cov}\,(\tilde{R}_i, \tilde{R}_e)}{\sigma^2(\tilde{R}_e)} = \sum\limits_{i=1}^{n} x_{ip}\beta_{ie}. \tag{26}$$

If we now multiply through both sides of (20) by x_{ip} and then sum over i, (24) follows directly.

Thus, equation (20), the relationship between expected security returns and security risks within a minimum variance portfolio, turns out to apply to portfolios as well as to securities. This result is important in the empirical tests of the two-parameter model in the next chapter.

3. It suffices to show that when short-selling is allowed, it is always possible to use any two securities to form a portfolio whose return is uncorrelated with the return on e. The answer to the preceding problem then implies that the expected return on any such portfolio is $E(\tilde{R}_{0e})$.

Let i and j be any two securities and let

$$\tilde{R}_p = x\tilde{R}_i + (1 - x)\tilde{R}_j.$$

From the answer to the preceding problem,

$$\beta_{pe} = x\beta_{ie} + (1 - x)\beta_{je}.$$

It is clear that if the value of x is unrestricted, it is always possible to choose x so that $\beta_{pe} = 0.0$.

Finally, equation (20) is derived from the solution to the variance minimization problem of equations (7a) to (7c). Since the constraints do not include statements about the signs of the proportions of portfolio funds invested in individual securities, unrestricted short-selling of securities is assumed. If short-selling is ruled out and if the proportions are constrained to be nonnegative, the mathematics of the analysis of expected return-risk relationships is more complex. The results, however, are similar. In particular, equation (20), with precisely the same interpretation as above, is the relationship between the expected return on a security and its risk in the portfolio e. As one might expect, however, the relationship only applies to securities that appear in e with nonzero weights. The reader can also determine that if (20) only applies to securities that appear in the minimum variance portfolio e at a nonzero level, then (24), the "portfolio" version of (20), only applies to portfolios of such securities.

III. Market Relationships Between Expected Return and Risk When There Is Risk-free Borrowing and Lending

The preceding can be viewed as a discussion of the relationships between expected return and risk that are relevant for an individual investor in a two-parameter world. When the investor is choosing a portfolio, the relevant relationship between expected return and risk is that described by the curve of efficient portfolios. Once he chooses an efficient portfolio, there is a relationship between expected security returns and their risks in that portfolio which is a direct consequence of the fact that the portfolio is efficient.

It is time, however, to step beyond the analysis of risk and expected return as seen by the individual investor and to consider what a two-parameter world implies about the process of price formation in the capital market. That is, if investors make portfolio decisions at time 1 according to the two-parameter model, what does this imply about the prices of securities that are set in the market at time 1? More specifically, we now know how to talk about expected return and risk from the viewpoint of an investor. What remains to be determined is whether the portfolio decisions of individual investors, considered together, cause securities to be priced in such a way that there are similar expected return-risk relationships that apply to the market.

Note the change in perspective in going from the investor to the market. From the viewpoint of the investor, security prices at time 1 are taken as given. The investor is assumed to be small relative to the market, so that security prices are given parameters in his decision problem. When we look at the two-parameter world from the viewpoint of the market, however, we must recognize that security prices are determined by the decisions of investors. The effect of any investor on prices is negligible, but the portfolio decisions of all investors, considered together, determine prices.

A. Complete Agreement

The task of the market at time 1 is to determine a market-clearing or market equilibrium set of prices, that is, prices where supply equals demand for each security. Once equilibrium prices are determined, the picture of the efficient set facing an investor is determined. The investor considers this picture as showing the relationship between expected portfolio return and portfolio risk. For the purposes of his own investment decision, this view is entirely correct. Given the prices of securities set at time 1, however, each investor's view of the efficient set depends on an assessment of the joint distribution of the time 2 prices or values of securities that may be unique to him.* If disagreement among investors about the joint distribution of security prices at time 2 is substantial, there may be no meaningful sense in which one can talk about expected return and risk from the viewpoint of the market.

One can reasonably argue, however, that investors would only make portfolio decisions according to the two-parameter model if their assessments of the joint distribution of future security prices were descriptively valid. Although we present the two-parameter model in a one-period framework, we have in mind a multiperiod world where, period after period, the investor makes portfolio decisions in accordance with the two-parameter model.† It does not make sense for the investor to behave in this way unless his assessments of portfolio opportunities are accurate. If he is consistently inaccurate, he will come to feel that the whole decision-making framework is of little value.‡ In short, if one assumes that investors make portfolio decision according to the two-parameter model, then one must assume that they can obtain reasonably accurate assessments of the parameters that the model requires as inputs to a portfolio decision. This in turn implies that there is considerable consensus among investors in their assessments of the joint distribution of future values of securities and thus considerable consensus in how they view the efficient set of portfolios.§

Although "considerable consensus" is the general notion we have in mind, such a concept is too vague for a formal model. To make life simple, we assume that the degree of agreement among investors is complete rather than just considerable; that is, at time 1 there is complete agreement among investors with respect to the joint distribution of security values at time 2. Given the equilibrium prices set at time 1, this means that every investor has the same view of the set of efficient portfolios available at time 1. The common

---

*When we talk about the prices or values of securities at time 2, we mean to include any dividends or interest paid on the securities at time 2.

†The conditions under which the two-parameter model applies period after period are discussed in Fama (1970) and Merton (1973). These papers are rather difficult mathematically, and so the topic is not considered in this book, which is meant to be more of an introduction to theory and empirical work. Suffice it to say that the empirical evidence of Fama and MacBeth (1974) seems to be consistent with the conditions required for period-by-period application of the one-period model.

‡The argument is not special to the two-parameter model. Any framework for rational decision-making must assume that accurate assessments of relevant parameters are available. Otherwise, the formal decision-making apparatus has little value.

§It is, of course, reasonable to ask how such a consensus might arise. In a multiperiod framework, the simplest case is when, period after period, the equilibrium current prices of securities and the joint distribution of next period's prices are such that the efficient-set curve facing the investor is the same every period. The empirical relevance of this situation is discussed by Fama and MacBeth (1974).

picture of the efficient set shows the relationship between expected portfolio return and portfolio risk for every investor and thus for the market.

The complete agreement assumption also helps us to determine which of the various portfolios available are efficient. There are two basic approaches. We consider first the simpler approach, which is based on the assumed existence of risk-free borrowing and lending.

B. The Efficient Set When There Is Risk-free Borrowing and Lending

Suppose that at time 1 investors can borrow and lend at a risk-free rate of interest R_F. Like the prices of other securities, the value of the risk-free rate is determined as part of the market-clearing process at time 1. As in the case of other securities, an equilibrium or market-clearing value of R_F implies a value such that supply equals demand; the total quantity that investors want to borrow is equal to the quantity that others want to lend.

FIGURE 8.3

Market Equilibrium with Unrestricted Risk-free Borrowing and Lending

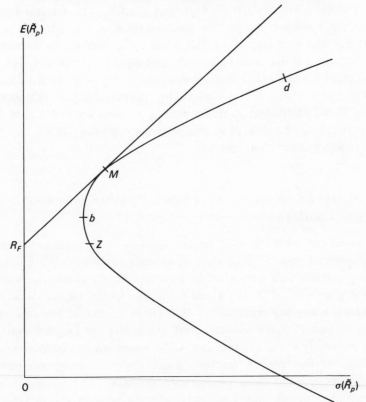

We know from Chapter 7 that with risk-free borrowing and lending the efficient set has a simple form. For example, suppose that the curve from b through d in Figure 8.3 shows the portfolios that would be efficient in the absence of risk-free borrowing and lending. With risk-free borrowing and lending, however, efficient portfolios are along the line from R_F that just sits on or is tangent to the curve, that is, the line from R_F through M in Figure 8.3. Portfolios along this line are combinations of risk-free borrowing or lending with the portfolio M, where the proportion x of portfolio funds is invested in F and $(1 - x)$ is in M. The returns, expected returns, and standard deviations of returns on such portfolios of F and M are

$$\tilde{R}_p = xR_F + (1 - x)\tilde{R}_M \tag{27}$$

$$E(\tilde{R}_p) = xR_F + (1 - x)E(\tilde{R}_M) \tag{28}$$

$$\sigma(\tilde{R}_p) = (1 - x)\sigma(\tilde{R}_M), \quad x \leqslant 1. \tag{29}$$

When $x = 1.0$, all portfolio funds are invested in F; when $x = 0.0$, all funds are in M. Portfolios with $0.0 < x \leqslant 1.0$ are lending portfolios, since such values of x imply that a positive fraction of portfolio funds is lent at the rate R_F. Portfolios with $x < 0.0$ are borrowing portfolios; the investor borrows $-x(w_1 - c_1)$ and puts this plus the portfolio funds $w_1 - c_1$ into M. Lending portfolios give combinations of $E(\tilde{R}_p)$ and $\sigma(\tilde{R}_p)$ that are on the straight line between R_F and M in Figure 8.3. Borrowing portfolios give combinations of $E(\tilde{R}_p)$ and $\sigma(\tilde{R}_p)$ that are along the extension of the line through M. Efficient portfolios differ in terms of how portfolio funds are split between F and M, but all efficient portfolios are just combinations of F and M. M is the only efficient portfolio of all positive variance securities, that is, securities with strictly positive return variances.

C. Market Equilibrium When There Is Risk-free Borrowing and Lending

Consider now what this result implies about the characteristics of a market equilibrium at time 1. Since there is assumed to be complete agreement among investors with respect to the joint distribution of security values at time 2, given a set of security prices and a value for the risk-free rate at time 1, there is a tangency portfolio like M in Figure 8.3 that all investors try to combine with F. Some investors want to combine the tangency portfolio with borrowing at the risk-free rate, while others want to combine it with lending, but the tangency portfolio is the only portfolio of only positive variance securities for which investors enter demands.

Remember, though, that a market equilibrium requires a market-clearing set of prices; a market equilibrium requires that, in aggregate, investors demand all securities and demand them in the proportions in which they are outstanding. Given the nature of the efficient set when there is risk-free borrowing and lending, this market-clearing condition means that a market equilibrium is not attained until the one tangency portfolio that all investors try to combine with risk-free borrowing or lending is a portfolio of all the positive variance securities in the market, where each security is weighted by the ratio of the total market value at time 1 of all its outstanding units to the total market value of all outstanding units of all securities. In short, a market equilibrium is not reached until the tangency portfolio M in Figure 8.3 is the value-weighted version of the market portfolio. In addition, the value of R_F must be such that the aggregates of demands and supplies of loans are equal.

In slightly different terms, given the common assessment by investors of the joint distribution of security values at time 2, a set of prices for securities at time 1 and a value of R_F imply a representation of investment opportunities like that in Figure 8.3. A different risk-free rate and a different set of security prices imply a different picture of investment opportunities, but one that is always similar to Figure 8.3 in the sense that all efficient portfolios are combinations of borrowing or lending with one tangency portfolio of positive variance securities. The tangency portfolio is, however, different for different sets of security prices at time 1 and different values of R_F. A market equilibrium—a set of security prices that clears the securities market and a value of R_F that clears the borrowing-lending market—requires that the tangency portfolio be the value-weighted version of the market portfolio.

Since the market portfolio M is efficient, equation (20), which shows the relationship between expected security returns and their risks in an arbitrary minimum variance portfolio e, can be applied to M. We have

$$E(\tilde{R}_i) = E(\tilde{R}_{0M}) + [E(\tilde{R}_M) - E(\tilde{R}_{0M})]\, \beta_{iM}, \quad i = 1, \ldots, n, \qquad (30)$$

where

$$\beta_{iM} = \frac{\mathrm{cov}\,(\tilde{R}_i, \tilde{R}_M)}{\sigma^2(\tilde{R}_M)} \qquad (31)$$

is the risk of security i in M measured relative to the risk of M, and $E(\tilde{R}_{0M})$ is the expected return on any security or portfolio whose return is uncorrelated with the return on M.

In the present view of the world, there indeed exists a security, F, whose return is uncorrelated with $\tilde{R}_M$. Substituting R_F for $E(\tilde{R}_{0M})$ in (30) yields

$$E(\tilde{R}_i) = R_F + [E(\tilde{R}_M) - R_F]\, \beta_{iM}, \quad i = 1, \ldots, n. \qquad (32)$$

In words, the expected return on any security i is the risk-free rate R_F plus a risk premium which is the risk measure β_{iM} multiplied by the difference between the expected return on M and R_F.

Equation (32) is just (20) applied to M, but the interpretation of (32) goes far beyond that of (20). With the assumption that investors agree on the joint distribution of security values at time 2, and with the assumed existence of risk-free borrowing and lending, it is not happenstance that the value-weighted market portfolio M is efficient. The efficiency of M is a necessary condition for a market equilibrium. With complete agreement and risk-free borrowing and lending, a market equilibrium requires that R_F and the prices of securities at time 1 are set so that M is efficient, which means that R_F and the prices of securities must be set in such a way that (32) holds for every security. Thus, with complete agreement and risk-free borrowing and lending, the expected return-risk relationship (32) is the implication of the two-parameter model for the process of price formation in the capital market at time 1.

PROBLEM III.C

1. In the present model, what is the formal expression for the relationship between the expected return $E(\tilde{R}_e)$ on an efficient portfolio and its risk $\sigma(\tilde{R}_e)$?

ANSWER

1. From inspection of Figure 8.3, the relationship is

$$E(\tilde{R}_e) = R_F + \left[\frac{E(\tilde{R}_M) - R_F}{\sigma(\tilde{R}_M)} \right] \sigma(\tilde{R}_e), \qquad (33)$$

where M is the value-weighted market portfolio, the subscript e indicates an arbitrary efficient portfolio, and

$$\frac{E(\tilde{R}_M) - R_F}{\sigma(\tilde{R}_M)} = S_M \qquad (34)$$

is the slope of the efficient-set at the point corresponding to M and at every other point.

Be clear on the difference between (33) and (32). Equation (33) is the relationship between the expected returns and risks of efficient portfolios, while (32) is the relationship between expected security returns and security risks within the particular efficient portfolio M.

D. Criticisms of the Model

The two-parameter model of market equilibrium discussed above is credited to Sharpe (1964) and Lintner (1965a), and it is usually called the Sharpe-Lintner model. The model is also often called the capital asset pricing model, although we do not use the term here. There are two common criticisms of the model. First, the model says that all investors hold the market portfolio in combination with different amounts of borrowing or lending, and one does not observe that all investors hold the market portfolio. Second, borrowing or lending is never completely risk-free. Any funds borrowed at time 1 must be repaid from the market value of the portfolio at time 2. Since we assume that return distributions are normal and since normal distributions are unbounded, there is always some chance that the borrower cannot deliver in full to the lender. Moreover, in the real-world capital market, the promises of the borrower are usually stated in terms of money. The investor values money, however, only for the "real" consumption (that is, goods and services) that it will buy. Thus, if the purchasing power of money at time 2 is uncertain, at time 1 a contract that pays a perfectly certain amount of money at time 2 is not perfectly certain in "real" terms and so is not considered as risk-free by the investor.*

There are several responses to these criticisms of the Sharpe-Lintner model. I offer just one, and by now it is familiar. Throughout the book I have emphasized that any model proposes a simplified view of the world but that this is not sufficient basis for its rejection. Thus, even though it is not realistic in all of its details, we may be willing to go along with the Sharpe-Lintner model of market equilibrium as long as its implications for equilibrium prices of securities are empirically descriptive. The primary purpose of the Sharpe-Lintner model is to develop testable implications of the two-parameter portfolio model for the process of price formation in the capital market. Despite the fact that in many respects it is oversimplified, the model is vindicated if its implication about equilibrium security prices—in particular, the expected return-risk relationship of (32)—seems to be a good description of real-world data.

The Sharpe-Lintner model is, however, just one view of the implications of the two-parameter portfolio model for the process of price formation in the capital market. There are other two-parameter models of market equilibrium that likewise yield testable propositions concerning how the attempts of

---

*The implication of these comments is that the portfolio model itself should be developed in "real" terms rather than in terms of dollars of consumption at time 1 and time 2. When we speak of "dollars" in the context of the model, we have in mind the general notion of a unit of purchasing power.

investors to hold efficient portfolios affect equilibrium prices of securities, and the testable propositions of these models differ somewhat from those of the Sharpe-Lintner model. When we confront the two-parameter model with real-world data in Chapter 9, we want to be armed with the implications of as many two-parameter models of market equilibrium as possible. In this way we minimize the chance of falsely rejecting the proposition that prices and returns reflect the attempts of investors to hold efficient portfolios when, in fact, the failure of the tests is due to a bad specific model of market equilibrium.

In short, testing the implications of the two-parameter portfolio model for the process of price formation in the capital market requires a two-parameter model of market equilibrium, and such models of market equilibrium require more restrictive assumptions than the portfolio model. If our basic interest is to test whether the process of price formation is dominated by investors concerned with portfolio efficiency, then we want to be aware of the various two-parameter models of market equilibrium that are consistent with this basic proposition.

IV.   Market Relationships Between Expected Return and Risk When Short-Selling of Positive Variance Securities Is Unrestricted

The implications of the Sharpe-Lintner model for the nature of a market equilibrium at time 1 follow from the fact that with complete agreement among investors with respect to the joint distribution of security values at time 2 and with unrestricted risk-free borrowing and lending, all efficient portfolios are combinations of borrowing or lending with one efficient portfolio of positive variance securities. The requirement that all securities be cleared from the market then implies that in a market equilibrium the one efficient portfolio of only positive variance securities is the market portfolio. This line of reasoning does not require that positive variance securities can be sold short. The major alternative to the Sharpe-Lintner model of market equilibrium is less restrictive than the Sharpe-Lintner model in the sense that it does not assume the existence of a risk-free security; but in another sense it is more restrictive, since it assumes that short-selling of positive variance securities is unrestricted. The alternative model is credited primarily to Black (1972).

In the Sharpe-Lintner model, a market equilibrium at time 1 requires the efficiency of the market portfolio. Thus, equation (20), when applied to M, can be interpreted as a condition on equilibrium prices of securities at time 1 rather than as just the expected return-risk relationship that holds for securities within an efficient portfolio. Equivalently, to show that a market equilibrium requires the efficiency of M is to transform (20) into a market equilibrium expected return-risk relationship. The implications of the Black model for equilibrium security prices are likewise based on the efficiency of the market portfolio in a market equilibrium. We now see, however, that the path to showing that a market equilibrium requires the efficiency of M is more tortuous than in the Sharpe-Lintner model.

A. The Efficiency of the Market Portfolio

OVERVIEW

Since the formal arguments quickly get rather involved, we begin with a brief informal discussion of the basis of the efficiency of the market portfolio in the Black model. Suppose that when a market equilibrium is established at time 1, the set of minimum variance portfolios is the solid curve in Figure 8.1. Since the Black model, like the Sharpe-Lintner model, assumes complete agreement among investors with respect to the joint distribution of security prices at time 2, when a market equilibrium is attained at time 1, each investor perceives that Figure 8.1 is the relevant picture of portfolio opportunities. Depending on tastes, each investor then chooses some efficient portfolio, so we can think of investors as choosing different points from along the efficient segment of the curve of minimum variance portfolios, the segment above point b.

A market equilibrium requires that total investor demand for each security be equal to total supply. Equivalently, in a market equilibrium, the portfolio of the efficient portfolios chosen by investors, where each investor's portfolio is weighted by the ratio of his invested wealth to the total invested wealth of all investors, must be the market portfolio M. It follows that to show that a market equilibrium requires that M be efficient, it is sufficient to show that any portfolio of efficient portfolios, with component efficient portfolios receiving positive weights, is itself efficient. This is what we now do.

PROPERTIES OF THE MINIMUM VARIANCE BOUNDARY

Go back to equations (7) to (9). Recall that the n conditions of (9), along with (7b) and (7c), determine the n proportions of portfolio funds invested in individual securities that define the minimum variance portfolio with expected return $E(\tilde{R}_e)$. These $N + 2$ equations also determine the values of the Lagrange multipliers $2\lambda_e$ and $2\phi_e$ for this portfolio. For the moment, however, let us assume that someone gives us the values of λ_e and ϕ_e. Then we can use the n equations of (9) to solve for the values of $x_{ie}, i = 1, \ldots, n$.*

Stating (9) in matrix form, we get

$$\underset{(n \times n)}{A} \underset{(n \times 1)}{X_e} = \lambda_e \underset{(n \times 1)}{E(\tilde{R})} + \phi_e \underset{(n \times 1)}{[1]} , \tag{35}$$

where A is the $n \times n$ matrix of the pairwise security return covariances σ_{ij} $(i, j = 1, \ldots, n)$; X_e is the $n \times 1$ vector of the proportions of portfolio funds invested in individual securities; $E(\tilde{R})$ is the $n \times 1$ vector of expected security returns; and $[1]$ is an $n \times 1$ vector of ones. If D is the inverse of A with typical element d_{ij}, we can solve (35) for X_e to get

$$X_e = \lambda_e DE(\tilde{R}) + \phi_e D[1], \tag{36}$$

$$x_{ie} = \lambda_e \left[\sum_{j=1}^{n} d_{ij} E(\tilde{R}_j) \right] + \phi_e \left[\sum_{j=1}^{n} d_{ij} \right], \quad i = 1, \ldots, n. \tag{37}$$

Thus, if someone gives us the values of λ_e and ϕ_e, the n equations of (37) give the values of the proportions invested in individual securities that define the minimum variance portfolio with expected return $E(\tilde{R}_e)$.

There is a better way to look at equation (37). If we only consider values of λ_e and ϕ_e that are consistent with solutions to the problem stated in equations (7a–c) for different values of the target expected portfolio return $E(\tilde{R}_e)$, then by varying λ_e and ϕ_e in (37) we generate the different values of the proportion of portfolio funds invested in security i $(i = 1, \ldots, n)$ in different minimum variance portfolios. By varying λ_e and ϕ_e through all the feasible values of these Lagrange multipliers, we generate the proportions invested in individual securities in each of the portfolios along the minimum variance boundary. In effect, this is how the boundary is determined, and a better understanding of the process allows us to attain easily the goal of establishing that in a market equilibrium the market portfolio M is efficient.

The problem comes down to identifying the feasible combinations of λ_e and ϕ_e. For λ_e, the answer follows from equation (16) and the discussion in Chapter 7 of the nature of the minimum variance boundary when unlimited short-selling is possible. In particular, the boundary of minimum variance portfolios in Figure 8.1 is a hyperbola that extends indefinitely upward and to the right and indefinitely downward and to the right. As one moves from the point b upward on the boundary, the slope S_e of the curve goes from ∞ toward a finite positive asymptote; when one moves downward from b, S_e goes from $-\infty$ toward a finite negative asymptote. As one moves either

---

*The next paragraph requires a little matrix algebra. The reader should follow along so that the line of reasoning and the notation become familiar, even if the mathematics is not completely comprehensible.

up or down the boundary away from b, $\sigma(\tilde{R}_e)$ increases continuously. With these observations, we can then infer from (16) that $\lambda_e = \sigma(\tilde{R}_e)/S_e$ can take any positive or negative value.

Thus, the set of minimum variance portfolios is generated by varying λ_e in (37) between $-\infty$ and ∞, combining each value of λ_e with the appropriate value of ϕ_e. To determine the appropriate value of ϕ_e, we simply note from (8) that $2\phi_e$ is the Lagrange multiplier for the constraint (7c). For any given λ_e, the appropriate ϕ_e is the value that makes the sum of the n values of x_{ie} equal to 1.0.

With a little new notation, we can now obtain a simple description of how the set of minimum variance portfolios is generated when short-selling of securities is unrestricted. First, define two new portfolios u and v as

$$\tilde{R}_u = \sum_{i=1}^{n} x_{iu}\tilde{R}_i \text{ and } \tilde{R}_v = \sum_{i=1}^{n} x_{iv}\tilde{R}_i, \tag{38}$$

$$x_{iu} = \sum_{j=1}^{n} d_{ij}E(\tilde{R}_j) \Big/ \sum_{i=1}^{n} \sum_{j=1}^{n} d_{ij}E(\tilde{R}_j), \quad i = 1, \ldots, n, \tag{39}$$

$$x_{iv} = \sum_{j=1}^{n} d_{ij} \Big/ \sum_{i=1}^{n} \sum_{j=1}^{n} d_{ij}, \quad i = 1, \ldots, n. \tag{40}$$

From inspection of these two expressions we can see that

$$\sum_{i=1}^{n} x_{iu} = 1.0 \text{ and } \sum_{i=1}^{n} x_{iv} = 1.0, \tag{41}$$

so that u and v are standard portfolios. If we next define

$$y_{eu} = \lambda_e \left[\sum_{i=1}^{n} \sum_{j=1}^{n} d_{ij}E(\tilde{R}_j) \right] \tag{42}$$

$$y_{ev} = \phi_e \left[\sum_{i=1}^{n} \sum_{j=1}^{n} d_{ij} \right], \tag{43}$$

then (37) can be rewritten as

$$x_{ie} = y_{eu}x_{iu} + y_{ev}x_{iv}, \quad i = 1, \ldots, n. \tag{44}$$

Since the double sum in (42) is a constant and so is independent of λ_e, the fact that λ_e can take any value between $-\infty$ and ∞ means that y_{eu} in (44) can take any value between $-\infty$ and ∞. Since the double sum in (43) is a constant and so is independent of ϕ_e, for any given value of y_{eu} in (42) the appropriate value of y_{ev} in (43) involves choosing ϕ_e so that

$$\sum_{i=1}^{n} x_{ie} = 1.0. \tag{45}$$

But from (41) and (44)

$$\sum_{i=1}^{n} x_{ie} = \sum_{i=1}^{n} (y_{eu}x_{iu} + y_{ev}x_{iv}) = y_{eu} + y_{ev}. \tag{46}$$

Thus, to satisfy (45) for any given value of y_{eu} in (44), y_{ev} must be chosen to satisfy

$$y_{eu} + y_{ev} = 1.0. \tag{47}$$

In words, to determine the proportion of portfolio funds invested in security i ($i = 1, \ldots, n$) in different minimum variance portfolios, we simply vary y_{eu} in (44), combining each value of y_{eu} with the value of y_{ev} that satisfies (47). Equivalently, with (44) the return on any minimum variance, portfolio e can be written as

$$\tilde{R}_e = \sum_{i=1}^{n} x_{ie}\tilde{R}_i$$

$$= \sum_{i=1}^{n} (y_{eu}x_{iu} + y_{ev}x_{iv})\tilde{R}_i$$

$$= y_{eu}\left(\sum_{i=1}^{n} x_{iu}\tilde{R}_i\right) + y_{ev}\left(\sum_{i=1}^{n} x_{iv}\tilde{R}_i\right)$$

$$\tilde{R}_e = y_{eu}\tilde{R}_u + y_{ev}\tilde{R}_v. \tag{48}$$

Thus, any minimum variance portfolio e is a combination of the portfolios u and v, where the proportion y_{eu} of portfolio funds is invested in u and $y_{ev} = 1.0 - y_{eu}$ is invested in v. Any such combination of u and v is a minimum variance portfolio and the set of minimum variance portfolios includes all combinations of u and v that satisfy (47).

PROBLEMS IV.A

1. Show that u and v are themselves minimum variance portfolios.

2. Show that v is in fact the minimum variance portfolio b in Figure 8.1.

ANSWERS

1. The portfolio u is a portfolio of u and v with $y_{eu} = 1.0$ and $y_{ev} = 0.0$, and v is a portfolio of u and v with $y_{eu} = 0.0$ and $y_{ev} = 1.0$. Since any combinations of u and v that satisfy (47) are minimum variance portfolios, u and v are minimum variance portfolios.

2. At the point b in Figure 8.1, $\lambda_b = \sigma(\tilde{R}_b)/S_b = 0$, so that, from (37),

$$x_{ib} = \phi_b \sum_{j=1}^{n} d_{ij}.$$

Since ϕ_b must be chosen so that $\sum_{i=1}^{n} x_{ib} = 1$, we can conclude from (40) that $x_{ib} = x_{iv}$. Thus, the portfolio v defined by (40) is the minimum variance portfolio that has the smallest possible return variance.

With these results it is now easy to show that any portfolio of minimum variance portfolios is a minimum variance portfolio. The return on any portfolio p of minimum variance portfolios can be written as

$$\tilde{R}_p = \sum_{e} x_e \tilde{R}_e \tag{49}$$

$$\sum_{e} x_e = 1.0, \tag{50}$$

where x_e is the proportion of portfolio funds invested in minimum variance portfolio e and where the notation $\sum_e$ is meant to indicate that we are taking a sum over some finite number of minimum variance portfolios. Substituting (48) into (49) yields

$$\tilde{R}_p = \sum_{e} x_e (y_{eu} \tilde{R}_u + y_{ev} \tilde{R}_v) = \left(\sum_{e} x_e y_{eu} \right) \tilde{R}_u + \left(\sum_{e} x_e y_{ev} \right) \tilde{R}_v.$$

Any combination of u and v with proportions invested in u and v that sum to 1.0 is a minimum variance portfolio. Thus p is a minimum variance portfolio if

$$\sum_{e} x_e y_{eu} + \sum_{e} x_e y_{ev} = 1.0.$$

But as stated in (48), each of the component portfolios e in (49) is a portfolio of u and v that satisfies (47). Thus, from (50) and (47),

$$\sum_{e} x_e y_{eu} + \sum_{e} x_e y_{ev} = \sum_{e} x_e (y_{eu} + y_{ev}) = \sum_{e} x_e = 1.0.$$

If any portfolio of minimum variance portfolios is a minimum variance portfolio, then any portfolio of efficient portfolios is a minimum variance portfolio, since efficient portfolios are minimum variance portfolios. Moreover, any portfolio of efficient portfolios where the proportions invested in component efficient portfolios are all nonnegative is an efficient portfolio, since such a combination of efficient portfolios is a minimum variance portfolio and it necessarily has an expected return within the range of expected returns covered by the efficient segment of the minimum variance boundary.

MARKET EQUILIBRIUM AND THE MARKET PORTFOLIO

It follows almost directly that with complete agreement among investors concerning the joint distribution of security values at time 2, and with no restrictions on short-selling, a market equilibrium at time 1 implies that the market portfolio M is efficient. A market equilibrium at time 1 requires a set of security prices such that the aggregate demand for each security by investors is equal to the supply of the security. Equivalently, a market equilibrium requires that when one combines the portfolios chosen by investors, weighting each investor's portfolio by the ratio of his invested wealth to the sum of the invested wealths of all investors, then the resulting portfolio is the market portfolio. Since investors choose efficient portfolios, and since the invested wealth of each investor is assumed to be nonnegative, from the above analysis we can conclude that in a market equilibrium the market portfolio is efficient.

In geometric terms, suppose that when a market equilibrium is attained at time 1, minimum variance portfolios are as shown by the solid curve in Figure 8.1. Then the market portfolio M is along the positively sloped segment of the curve, which describes the set of efficient portfolios. Since M is efficient, equation (30) holds, showing the relationship between expected returns on securities and their risks in M. Moreover, since a market equilibrium requires that M is efficient, (30) can be interpreted as a condition on equilibrium security prices. Equivalently, as in the Sharpe-Lintner model, equation (30) can be interpreted in the Black model as the market equilibrium relationship between expected security returns and their risks in M.

The difference between the Sharpe-Lintner model and the Black model is that in the Sharpe-Lintner model the intercept $E(\tilde{R}_{0M})$ in (30) can be identified as the risk-free rate of interest, whereas in the Black model there is no risk-free security, so that $E(\tilde{R}_{0M})$ is the return on any positive variance security that has $\beta_{0M} = 0.0$, that is, on any positive variance security whose return is uncorrelated with the return on M. Remember that since such a security contributes nothing to the variance of the return on M, it is riskless in M even though it is not risk-free in the sense of having a zero variance of return.

B. Efficient Portfolios as Combinations of the Market Portfolio M and the Minimum Variance Portfolio Z

The remaining models of market equilibrium are variants of the Black model in the sense that arguments similar to those above are used to show that a market equilibrium generally requires the market portfolio to be efficient. Before proceeding to these models, however, it is convenient to discuss further the nature of minimum variance and efficient portfolios in a market equilibrium when short-selling of securities is unrestricted. This will improve our perspective both on the Black model and on the variants of the model that are discussed later.

The goal is to show that with unrestricted short-selling, in a market equilibrium any minimum variance portfolio can be expressed as a combination of the market portfolio M and the minimum variance zero-β_{pM} portfolio—that is, the minimum variance portfolio, call it Z, whose return is uncorrelated with the return on M. The first step is to show that the set of minimum variance portfolios can be generated as combinations of any two minimum variance portfolios. Next we show that a minimum variance zero-β_{pM} portfolio always exists. Since M and this zero-β_{pM} portfolio Z are minimum variance portfolios, it then follows that the set of minimum variance portfolios can be generated as combinations of M and Z.

In the preceding section we found that with unrestricted short-selling, any portfolio of minimum variance portfolios is a minimum variance portfolio. Thus, any portfolio of two different minimum variance portfolios is a minimum variance portfolio. Since any two different minimum variance portfolios have different expected returns, with the appropriate weights assigned to these two portfolios we can generate a minimum variance portfolio with any specified level of expected return. It follows that any two minimum variance portfolios can be used to generate the entire set of minimum variance portfolios.

With unrestricted short-selling, in a market equilibrium the market portfolio M is efficient. Thus, one of the two portfolios used to generate minimum variance portfolios can be M. The other can be the minimum variance zero-β_{pM} portfolio Z, as long as we can show that there is indeed a minimum variance portfolio whose return is uncorrelated with the return on M. The existence of such a portfolio is implied by the fact that the range of expected returns covered by minimum variance portfolios is unbounded both from above and from below, so that there is necessarily a minimum variance portfolio with any specified level of expected return. Thus, there is a minimum variance portfolio with expected return equal to $E(\tilde{R}_{0M})$. Since (30) applies to any security or portfolio, any portfolio with expected return equal to $E(\tilde{R}_{0M})$ must have $\beta_{pM} = 0.0$. The existence of the minimum variance zero-β_{pM} portfolio Z is thus established.

In short, the returns on different minimum variance portfolios can be obtained by varying x in

$$\tilde{R}_e = x\tilde{R}_Z + (1 - x)\tilde{R}_M. \tag{51}$$

When minimum variance portfolios are formed in this way, the expected value and variance of the return on a minimum variance portfolio are

$$E(\tilde{R}_e) = xE(\tilde{R}_Z) + (1 - x)E(\tilde{R}_M) \tag{52}$$

$$\sigma^2(\tilde{R}_e) = x^2\sigma^2(\tilde{R}_Z) + (1 - x)^2\sigma^2(\tilde{R}_M), \tag{53}$$

where the absence of the usual covariance term in equation (53) follows from the fact that $\tilde{R}_Z$ and $\tilde{R}_M$ are uncorrelated.

PROBLEMS IV.B

1. Show that the portfolio Z must be below M on the minimum variance boundary; that is, $E(\tilde{R}_Z) < E(\tilde{R}_M)$.

2. Show that the portfolio Z cannot be efficient.

ANSWERS

1. Since M is efficient, $E(\tilde{R}_M) - E(\tilde{R}_{0M})$ in (30) is positive. Since $E(\tilde{R}_Z) = E(\tilde{R}_{0M})$, it follows that Z is below M on the minimum variance boundary.

2. Since $\tilde{R}_Z$ and $\tilde{R}_M$ are uncorrelated, in (51) the portfolio of Z and M that has the smallest possible variance has (from Problem III.A.*3* of Chapter 7),

$$x = \frac{\sigma^2(\tilde{R}_M)}{\sigma^2(\tilde{R}_M) + \sigma^2(\tilde{R}_Z)}.$$

Since this value of x is greater than 0.0 and less than 1.0, it follows that there are portfolios of Z and M formed according to (51) that have smaller variances than either Z or M and that fall between Z and M on the minimum variance boundary. Since $E(\tilde{R}_M) > E(\tilde{R}_Z)$, such portfolios must also have larger expected returns than Z. Thus Z cannot be efficient.

Since $E(\tilde{R}_Z) = E(\tilde{R}_{0M})$, Black (1972) suggests that (30) be rewritten as

$$E(\tilde{R}_i) = E(\tilde{R}_Z) + [E(\tilde{R}_M) - E(\tilde{R}_Z)]\beta_{iM}, \quad i = 1, \dots, n. \tag{54}$$

In words, with unrestricted short-selling, in a market equilibrium the prices of securities are set so that the expected return on any security is the expected return on Z, the minimum variance portfolio whose return is uncorrelated with the return on the market portfolio M, plus a risk premium which is β_{iM}, the risk of security i in M measured relative to the risk of M, times the difference between the expected returns on M and Z.

In geometric terms, the set of minimum variance portfolios available in a market equilibrium might be as shown by the solid curve in Figure 8.4. All

FIGURE 8.4

Market Equilibrium with Unrestricted Short-Selling of Positive Variance Securities

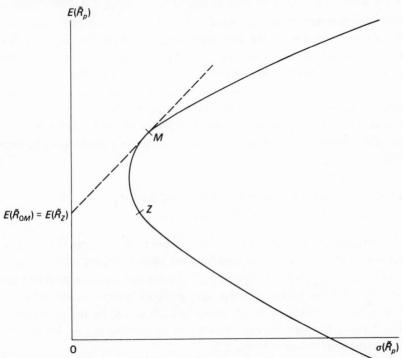

minimum variance portfolios can be obtained as combinations of M and Z. With $x = 1.0$ in (51) we get Z, while with $x = 0.0$ we get M. Portfolios between Z and M on the minimum variance curve have $0 < x < 1$; that is, positive fractions of portfolio funds are invested in both Z and M. Points above M on the curve involve short-selling of Z; that is, $x < 0.0$ in (51). Points below Z involve short-selling of M; that is, $x > 1.0$ and $(1 - x) < 0.0$. The market portfolio is on the efficient segment of the minimum variance curve, but from Problem IV.B.2 above we know that Z is not. Finally, applying the analysis of equations (17) to (19) to M tells us that the (dashed) line tangent to the minimum variance boundary at the point M in Figure 8.4 must intersect the $E(\tilde{R}_p)$ axis at $E(\tilde{R}_Z) = E(\tilde{R}_{oM})$.

V. Variants of the Model of Market Equilibrium When There Is Unrestricted Short-Selling of Positive Variance Securities

There are several other two-parameter models of market equilibrium that are closely related to the Black model presented above. Like the Black model, they assume that short-selling of positive variance securities (securities whose return distributions have positive variances) is unrestricted and that there is complete agreement among investors with respect to the joint distribution of security values at time 2. The key result in each of these models is that in a market equilibrium the market portfolio M is a minimum variance portfolio, so that (30) or (54) can be interpreted as a market equilibrium relationship between the expected returns on securities and their risks in M. These models differ from the Black model in that they assume the existence of a risk-free security, but they also differ from the Sharpe-Lintner model in that they do not allow unrestricted risk-free borrowing and lending at the same interest rate.

A. Market Equilibrium When There Is a Risk-free Security But It Cannot Be Sold Short

For example, Black (1972) discusses a model in which there is a risk-free security F which investors can hold long but cannot sell short. Thus, there is risk-free "lending" but not "borrowing." The risk-free securities might be the securities of firms whose activities have perfectly certain market values at time 2, or they might be bonds issued and guaranteed by the government. In either case, the portfolio opportunities facing investors in a market equilibrium might be as shown in Figure 8.5.

The solid curve in the figure is the set of minimum variance portfolios of only positive variance securities—that is, portfolios which minimize variance at different levels of expected return but are subject to the additional constraint that they not contain any of the risk-free security F. Henceforth, these portfolios are what we refer to when we use the term minimum variance portfolios. These minimum variance portfolios of positive variance securities have the same properties as the minimum variance portfolios of the preceding section. In particular, precisely the same arguments imply that with unrestricted short-selling of positive variance securities, (a) any portfolio of minimum variance portfolios is itself a minimum variance portfolio; (b) any portfolio of positively weighted minimum variance portfolios from along the positively sloped segment of the minimum variance boundary is likewise

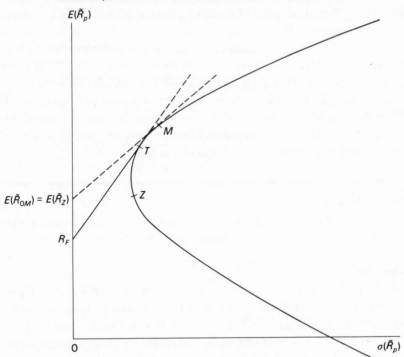

FIGURE 8.5

Market Equilibrium with Risk-free Lending But Not Borrowing

along the positively sloped segment of the boundary; and (c) the set of minimum variance portfolios can be generated as portfolios of any two different minimum variance portfolios.

The set of efficient portfolios in Figure 8.5 includes, first, the portfolios along the line from R_F to the tangency portfolio T. Such portfolios of F and T are lending portfolios; positive fractions of portfolio funds are invested in both F and T. Portfolios along the dashed extension of the line from R_F through T are not feasible, however, since they would require borrowing or short-selling of the risk-free security F. To get efficient portfolios with expected returns greater than $E(\tilde{R}_T)$, one must move from T up along the boundary of minimum variance portfolios of positive variance securities.

In Figure 8.5 the portfolio M, which is now defined as the market portfolio of only positive variance securities, is efficient. In a market equilibrium, this portfolio must be efficient. As always, a market equilibrium requires a set of security prices such that demand equals supply for each security. Equivalently, if one weights the risky component of each investor's portfolio by the ratio of the funds invested by that investor in positive variance securities to the total investment in positive variance securities by all investors, then in a market equilibrium the portfolio of the risky components of investor portfolios must be the market portfolio of positive variance securities. The risky component of any portfolio along the line from R_F to T in Figure 8.5 is the tangency portfolio T. The risky components of other efficient portfolios chosen by investors are the portfolios themselves, the chosen points along the efficient boundary above T. Thus, in a market equilibrium the market portfolio of positive variance securities is a portfolio of efficient minimum variance portfolios where each component portfolio receives a positive weight. When short-selling of positive variance securities is unrestricted, any such portfolio of efficient minimum variance portfolios is efficient.

PROBLEM V.A

1. Show that in general the market portfolio M is above the tangency portfolio T on the curve of minimum variance portfolios.

ANSWER

1. If all investors choose portfolios along the line from R_F to T in Figure 8.5, then in a market equilibrium T must be the market portfolio M. If some investors choose efficient portfolios above T, then in a market equilibrium M is a portfolio of T and portfolios above T along the minimum variance boundary. In this case, which I call the general case, M has higher expected return than T and so is above T on the minimum variance boundary.

With unrestricted short-selling of positive variance securities, the set of minimum variance portfolios of positive variance securities can be generated as combinations of any two minimum variance portfolios. We have just shown that in a market equilibrium, one of these two minimum variance portfolios can be the market portfolio M. Moreover, the arguments of the preceding section can be used to show that there is a minimum variance (but inefficient) zero-β_{pM} portfolio Z of only positive variance securities, so that the set of minimum variance portfolios can be generated from combinations of M and Z.

In the present model, however, $E(\tilde{R}_Z)$ is generally greater than the risk-free rate R_F. As illustrated in Figure 8.5, $E(\tilde{R}_{0M})$ is the intercept on the $E(\tilde{R}_p)$ axis of the dashed line tangent to the minimum variance boundary at the point corresponding to M. As in the preceding section, $E(\tilde{R}_{0M})$ is the expected return on any risky security or on any portfolio of risky securities whose return is uncorrelated with the return on M. In essence, a market equilibrium requires that M be a minimum variance portfolio, which means that (30) applies to each of the securities in M and to portfolios of the securities in M. Since M includes all positive variance securities, (30) applies to all positive variance securities and to portfolios of positive variance securities. The minimum variance zero-β_{pM} portfolio Z is just a special case of such a portfolio; and since $\beta_{ZM} = 0.0$, $E(\tilde{R}_Z) = E(\tilde{R}_{0M})$.

The market portfolio M, however, does not include the risk-free security F. Thus, even though the return on F is uncorrelated with the return on M, there is no reason to expect (30) and (54) to apply to F, and so there is no reason to expect that $R_F = E(\tilde{R}_Z)$. In fact, since the positively sloped segment of the minimum variance boundary is concave, and since M is generally above the tangency portfolio T on the minimum variance boundary, in general $E(\tilde{R}_Z) > R_F$. Only in the special case where M and T coincide do we get $E(\tilde{R}_Z) = R_F$.

We can contrast these results of what might be called the modified Black model with those of the Sharpe-Lintner model. In the Sharpe-Lintner model, there is unrestricted borrowing as well as lending at the risk-free rate R_F. In terms of Figure 8.5, this means that portfolios along the dashed extension of the line from R_F through T are now feasible. Since T is the risky component of every efficient portfolio, in a market equilibrium T must be the market portfolio of positive variance securities M. In this case, although M does not include F, $R_F = E(\tilde{R}_Z) = E(\tilde{R}_{0M})$, since R_F, $E(\tilde{R}_Z)$, and $E(\tilde{R}_{0M})$ all correspond to the intercept on the $E(\tilde{R}_p)$ axis of the line tangent to the minimum variance boundary at the point M. Thus, equation (32) holds for any security or portfolio, and R_F is the expected return on any security or portfolio whose return is uncorrelated with the return on M. In short, in the Sharpe-Lintner model the investment opportunities available in a market equilibrium are as shown in Figure 8.3, whereas in the modified Black model the world is as shown in Figure 8.5.

Finally, we should note one further thing about the modified Black model. In Figure 8.5 any portfolio of positively weighted efficient portfolios, where each component efficient portfolio is T or a portfolio above T on the efficient boundary, is itself an efficient portfolio. Any portfolio of positively weighted efficient portfolios from along the line between F and T is itself efficient. Unlike the Sharpe-Lintner model and the basic Black model, however, in the modified Black model it is not the case that any portfolio of positively weighted efficient portfolios is efficient. For example, portfolios of F and any efficient portfolio above T are inefficient, since such portfolios are always dominated either by portfolios along the line between F and T or by portfolios along the boundary from T through M. In short, the tangency portfolio T is our first instance of what is called a "corner" portfolio. Efficient portfolios below T contain a security, F, which does not appear in portfolios above T. Such corner portfolios appear consistently in the two-parameter models that we consider below.

PROBLEMS V.A

2. In the modified Black model, since there is risk-free lending but not borrowing, there must be a positive amount of the risk-free security F in the market. Show that the market portfolio of both risk-free and positive variance securities is not efficient.

3. In the Sharpe-Lintner model it is usually assumed that the risk-free security is borrowing and lending among investors, so that in a market equilibrium aggregate borrowing is equal to aggregate lending and the net outstanding amount of the risk-free security is zero. How must the model be modified if the values at time 2 of the activities of some firms are perfectly certain at time 1, so that the net outstanding amount of risk-free securities is positive?

ANSWERS

2. In the modified Black model the market portfolio M in Figure 8.5 includes only positive variance securities. The market portfolio of all securities is a portfolio of F and M, where F is weighted by the ratio of the total market value at time 1 of outstanding risk-free securities to the total market value of all outstanding units of all securities, and where M is weighted by the ratio of the total market value of all outstanding units of all positive variance securities to the total market value of all outstanding units of all securities. This combined market portfolio of risk-free and positive variance securities is on the straight line (not shown) between F and M in Figure 8.5, so it is only efficient in the special case where M and T coincide.

3. The Sharpe-Lintner model changes little when the net outstanding amount of risk-free securities is positive rather than zero. In geometric terms, the relevant picture of investment opportunities in a market equilibrium is again Figure 8.3. Now we must say that M is the market portfolio of only positive variance securities, and the solid curve through Z and M is the curve of minimum variance portfolios of positive variance securities. The only new wrinkle in the Sharpe-Lintner model when there is a positive outstanding amount of risk-free securities is that, as in the preceding problem, the market portfolio of risk-free and risky securities is the appropriately weighted combination of F and M, and it would be somewhere on the straight line between R_F and M in Figure 8.3 Unlike the results for the modified Black model in the preceding problem, however, in the Sharpe-Lintner model the market portfolio of all securities, like the market portfolio of only positive variance securities, is efficient.

B.   Market Equilibrium When There Is Risk-free
Borrowing and Lending But at Different Interest Rates

Another variant of the Black model, developed by Brennan (1971), allows for risk-free borrowing and lending, but at different interest rates. The simplest way to set up the Brennan model is to assume that there is risk-free borrowing and lending among investors, so that aggregate borrowing equals lending and there is no net outstanding supply of risk-free securities, but that there is a middleman or broker who exacts a fee from both borrowers and lenders. The same market rate is quoted to borrowers and lenders, but brokerage fees, assumed to be a fixed fraction of the amount borrowed or lent, have the effect of making the rate received by lenders less than the quoted rate, while the rate paid by borrowers is higher than the quoted rate. The assumption of the Brennan model is that there are only brokerage fees in the borrowing-lending market. Positive variance securities can be bought or sold without such transactions costs. Moreover, as in the two variants of the Black model discussed above, short-selling of positive variance securities is unrestricted. Finally, as in all the models of market equilibrium discussed so far, at time 1 there is assumed to be complete agreement among investors with respect to the joint distribution of securities values at time 2.

In the present model, the picture of the investment opportunities available at time 1 might be as shown in Figure 8.6. There are now two different tangency portfolios, T_L and T_B, and three different types of efficient portfolios. The lowest-expected-return efficient portfolios are lending portfolios. These start at the point R_L (the net rate received by lenders) on the vertical axis in Figure 8.6 and go up to the first tangency portfolio T_L on the curve of minimum variance portfolios of positive variance securities. The dashed extension of the line from R_L through T_L does not describe feasible portfolios, since such portfolios imply borrowing at the rate R_L, and borrowers must pay the higher rate R_B. The highest-expected-return efficient portfolios are borrowing portfolios. These are along the solid extension of the line from R_B through the second tangency portfolio T_B. The dashed segment of the line between R_B and T_B does not represent feasible portfolios, since such portfolios imply lending at the rate R_B, and lenders only net the rate R_L. Finally, the remaining efficient portfolios are those between T_B and T_L along the boundary of minimum variance portfolios of positive variance securities.

In Figure 8.6 the market portfolio M is one of the efficient portfolios between T_B and T_L. In a market equilibrium M must indeed be efficient, and the reasoning is similar to that of the modified Black model of the preceding section. In particular, a market equilibrium requires that the portfolio of the

FIGURE 8.6

Market Equilibrium When the Risk-free Borrowing Rate Is Greater Than the Risk-free Lending Rate

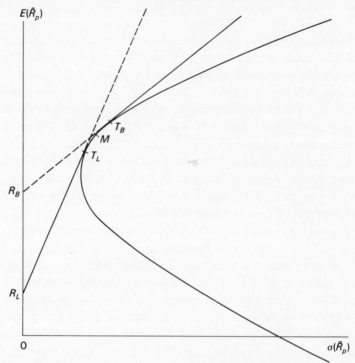

risky components of investor portfolios, where the risky component of each investor's portfolio is weighted by the ratio of his total investment in positive variance securities to the total investment in positive variance securities by all investors, be the market portfolio M. The risky component of every efficient portfolio that involves lending is the tangency portfolio T_L. The risky component of every efficient portfolio that involves borrowing is the tangency portfolio T_B. The risky components of other efficient portfolios are simply the portfolios themselves, that is, points along the efficient boundary between T_L and T_B. Thus, in a market equilibrium, the market portfolio can be expressed as a portfolio of positively weighted efficient portfolios between T_L and T_B. Any such portfolio of efficient portfolios of positive variance securities is efficient; as shown in Figure 8.6, the market portfolio must lie somewhere along the efficient boundary between T_L and T_B. Thus, as in the two-parameter models of market equilibrium discussed in preceding sections, we once again have the result that a market equilibrium requires that the market portfolio be efficient, which means that we can interpret (30) or (54) as the market equilibrium relationship between the expected returns on securities and their risks in M.

PROBLEM V.B

1. Show that $R_L < E(\tilde{R}_{0M}) = E(\tilde{R}_Z) < R_B$.

ANSWER

1. The inequality follows from three facts. First, the order of the portfolios T_L, M, and T_B along the efficient boundary must be as shown in Figure 8.6. Second, the efficient boundary between T_L and T_B is strictly concave. Third, R_L, $E(\tilde{R}_{0M})$, and R_B are, respectively, the intercepts on the $E(\tilde{R}_p)$ axis of lines tangent to the boundary at the points T_L, M, and T_B.

In the Brennan model there are two "corner" portfolios along the efficient boundary, T_L and T_B. Portfolios above T_B on the efficient boundary contain a "security" (borrowing at the rate R_B) which does not appear in any portfolios below T_B on the boundary, while portfolios below T_L on the efficient boundary contain a "security" (lending at the rate R_L) which does not appear in portfolios above T_L on the boundary. Any portfolio of positively weighted portfolios from along the line between R_L and T_L is efficient, and likewise for portfolios of positively weighted portfolios on the curve between T_L and T_B, or for portfolios of efficient portfolios above T_B. But not all portfolios of positively weighted efficient portfolios are efficient. For example, combining risk-free lending at the rate R_L with any minimum variance portfolio above T_L yields an inefficient portfolio.

Finally, note that the borrowing rate R_B and the lending rate R_L do not conform to the expected return-risk equation (54). Since (54) is a relationship between expected return and risk for securities in M, and since M does not include either risk-free borrowing or lending, there is no reason to expect that (54) will apply to these activities.

C. Market Equilibrium When There Is Risk-free Borrowing and Lending But There Are Margin Requirements

The next two-parameter model of market equilibrium is similar to the Black model in that short-selling of positive variance securities is unrestricted, but it is also similar to the Sharpe-Lintner model in that there is risk-free borrowing and lending at a common interest rate. The amount of borrowing, however, is assumed to be restricted to some fixed fraction of an investor's portfolio funds ($w_1 - c_1$). The fraction is the same for all investors, and it is independent of which portfolio of positive variance securities an investor chooses. Finally, at time 1 there is complete agreement among investors with respect to the joint distribution of security values at time 2.

FIGURE 8.7

Market Equilibrium with Risk-free Lending and Margin Requirements on Risk-free Borrowing

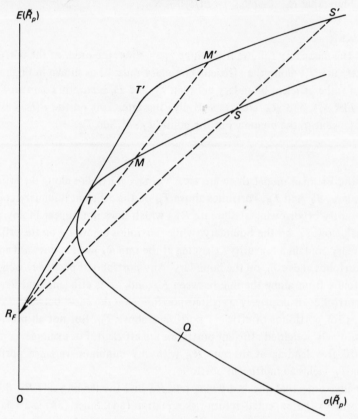

In this model, which we call the restricted borrowing model, the portfolio opportunities facing investors in a market equilibrium might be as shown in Figure 8.7. The solid curve through the points Q and S shows minimum variance portfolios of positive variance securities. Efficient portfolios are first along the line from the risk-free rate R_F through the tangency portfolio T. Portfolios between F and T on the line are combinations of F and T involving different fractions of lending at the rate R_F. Portfolios above T on the line from R_F are borrowing portfolios. The point T' is the portfolio of F and T that involves the maximum allowable fraction of borrowing at the rate R_F. Efficient portfolios along the continuation of the boundary from T' involve combining maximum borrowing with successive minimum variance portfolios of positive variance securities above T on the minimum variance boundary. For example, the efficient portfolio S' involves combining the minimum variance portfolio S with the maximum allowable fraction of borrowing at the risk-free rate R_F.

In Figure 8.7, the market portfolio M of only risky securities is on the minimum variance boundary. In a market equilibrium this must be the case, and the reasoning is similar to that used in the two preceding models. In particular, in a market equilibrium the portfolio of the risky components of investor portfolios, where the risky component of each investor's portfolio is weighted by the ratio of his investment of his own funds in positive variance securities to the total of such investments by all investors, must be the market portfolio M. The risky components of efficient portfolios are the minimum variance portfolio T and portfolios above T on the curve of minimum variance portfolios of only positive variance securities. Any portfolio of positively weighted minimum variance portfolios where the component portfolios are T and minimum variance portfolios above T is a minimum variance portfolio, and in general it is àbove T on the minimum variance boundary. Thus, in a market equilibrium, the market portfolio M is a minimum variance portfolio, and in general it is above the tangency portfolio T on the minimum variance boundary.

For the first time, however, the market portfolio of positive variance securities is not efficient. It is the risky component of the efficient portfolio M', but M itself is not efficient. Nevertheless, as long as M is a minimum variance portfolio, (30) or (54) applies. Moreover, since market equilibrium requires that M be a minimum variance portfolio, we can make the by now familiar comments concerning (30) or (54). Since these are conditions that must hold in a market equilibrium, they can be interpreted as conditions on equilibrium prices, or as market equilibrium relationships between the expected returns on positive variance securities and their risks in M. Again, however, since M does not include risk-free securities, (30) and (54) do not apply to F. In fact, recalling that $E(\tilde{R}_{0M}) = E(\tilde{R}_Z)$ is the intercept on the $E(\tilde{R}_p)$ axis of a line tangent to the curve of minimum variance portfolios at the point M, we can see from Figure 8.7 that in the present model, as in the modified Black model (where there is risk-free lending but not borrowing), the risk-free rate R_F is equal to or less than $E(\tilde{R}_Z)$.

PROBLEM V.C

1. In the restricted borrowing model, when will a market equilibrium imply $R_F = E(\tilde{R}_Z)$?

ANSWER

1. From inspection of Figure 8.7 and the definition of $E(\tilde{R}_{0M}) = E(\tilde{R}_Z)$ in (18), we can see that the condition $R_F = E(\tilde{R}_Z)$ requires that the tangency portfolio T be the market portfolio M. This will happen when the only efficient portfolios investors choose to hold are those along the segment of the efficient boundary from R_F to T'. Then T will be the risky component of every efficient portfolio which any investor holds, so that in a market equilibrium T must be the market portfolio M. In this case the present model and the Sharpe-Lintner model are indistinguishable; (32) is the appropriate market equilibrium condition for both models.

VI.　Comparison of and Comments on the Various Two-Parameter Models of Market Equilibrium

In all the models of market equilibrium considered so far, a market equilibrium requires that the market portfolio M of positive variance securities be a minimum variance portfolio of positive variance securities, and M is always on the positively sloped segment of the minimum variance boundary. In all models but one, the restricted borrowing model of the preceding section, M is also efficient. The fact that a market equilibrium requires that the market portfolio M be a minimum variance portfolio means that when applied to M, equation (20), which is basically a mathematical condition on the proportions of portfolio funds invested in individual securities that must be met by a minimum variance portfolio, can be interpreted as a condition on equilibrium prices. The fact that a market equilibrium requires that M be a minimum variance portfolio means that in a market equilibrium securities must be priced so that (30), which is (20) applied to M, holds for every positive variance security. Thus, (30) can be interpreted as the implication of the various two-parameter models of market equilibrium for equilibrium prices of securities at time 1. Alternatively, (30) can be interpreted as the market equilibrium relationship between the expected return on any positive variance security and its risk in M.

The differences between the various two-parameter models of market equilibrium, in terms of what they say about prices at time 1, center on additional statements that they make about $E(\tilde{R}_{0M})$ in (30). In all models, $E(\tilde{R}_{0M})$ is the intercept on the $E(\tilde{R}_p)$ axis of the line tangent to the curve of minimum variance portfolios at the point corresponding to the market portfolio M. In all models, $E(\tilde{R}_{0M})$ is the expected return on any positive variance security or on any portfolio of positive variance securities whose return is uncorrelated with the return on M. In the Sharpe-Lintner model, in which there is assumed to be unrestricted risk-free borrowing and lending, $E(\tilde{R}_{0M})$ is equal to R_F, the rate of interest that lenders receive and borrowers pay. Thus, in this model the expected return on positive variance zero-β_{iM} securities and on zero-β_{pM} portfolios of positive variance securities is equal to the return on risk-free securities. In the modified Black model, in which there is risk-free lending but not borrowing, in general $E(\tilde{R}_{0M}) > R_F$, where R_F is now the rate on risk-free lending. The same result, $E(\tilde{R}_{0M}) > R_F$, applies to the restricted borrowing model, in which there is borrowing and lending at the common rate R_F but the amount of borrowing is restricted to a fixed fraction of the investor's portfolio funds $w_1 - c_1$. Thus, in these models, positive variance zero-β_{iM} securities and zero-β_{pM} portfolios of positive variance securities have higher expected returns than risk-free securities. Finally, in the Brennan model, in which there is unrestricted risk-free borrowing and lending but the rate paid by borrowers is higher than the rate required by lenders, $R_L < E(\tilde{R}_{0M}) < R_B$, where R_L and R_B are the lending and borrowing rates.

There are, however, basically just two different types of models. First, there is the Sharpe-Lintner model, in which there is assumed to be unrestricted borrowing and lending at a common risk-free rate R_F but in which it is not necessary that positive variance securities can be sold short. Then there is the Black model and variants thereof, in which unrestricted short-selling of positive variance securities is always assumed. In the basic Black model there are no risk-free securities. In the variants of the model there are risk-free securities, but borrowing is either impossible or restricted, or lending and borrowing are subject to transactions costs.

Given that these models consistently assume that short-selling of positive variance securities is unrestricted and that there are no transactions costs in trading such securities, the assumptions that the variants of the Black model then make about the borrowing-lending market are somewhat contrived. For example, in the Brennan model there are transactions costs for risk-free securities such that the risk-free rate paid by borrowers is greater than the rate received by lenders, but there are no transactions costs in trading positive variance securities. In real-world capital markets there are brokerage fees in trading all securities, and in general they are higher on common stocks than on bonds. Thus, although introducing transactions costs seems to move the model in the direction of greater realism, one can argue that quite the opposite is true if such costs are assumed to exist only for risk-free securities, since this has the effect of assuming the reverse of the actual relationship between the costs of trading risk-free and positive variance securities.

In the other two variants of the Black model, either there is no risk-free borrowing, or risk-free borrowing is restricted to some fixed fraction of portfolio funds. Risk-free lending is unrestricted, and there are no restrictions on either long or short positions in positive variance securities. In the real world, of course, it is impossible for an investor to borrow unlimited amounts at a risk-free rate. Nevertheless, restrictions on short-selling of positive variance securities like common stocks are even more severe. In truth, short-selling of common stocks, in the manner in which we use that term, does not exist. We assume that when an investor sells short a security—that is, borrows the security and sells it on the open market—he gets to use the proceeds from the sale to increase his investments in other securities. In reality, when an investor sells a common stock short, not only does he not get the proceeds from the sale of the security (they reside with the broker), but he must also put up collateral as if he were buying the security long. Given that the funds required are the same as in a long position, a real-world short sale of a common stock is in effect a "long" position in the stock, but one where the short-seller arranges to get the negative of the return on the usual type of purchase.

In any case, the point is that although risk-free borrowing is not unrestricted in the real world, it is less restricted than short-selling of positive variance securities like common stocks. Thus, models that incorporate restrictions on borrowing but allow unrestricted short-selling of positive variance securities are a step away from the real world, since they reverse the real relative degrees of restrictiveness in risk-free borrowing and short-selling of positive variance securities.

The Sharpe-Lintner model and the basic Black model are much more consistent in this respect than the variants of the Black model discussed above. In the Sharpe-Lintner model, borrowing and lending at a common risk-free rate are unrestricted, and the implication of the model for market equilibrium, the expected return-risk equation (32), does not require the assumption that positive variance securities can be sold short. Thus, although real-world borrowing is certainly not unrestricted, this model is at least consistent with the fact that real-world borrowing is less restricted than real-world short-selling of positive variance securities. In the basic Black model, risk-free securities are not assumed to exist, and short-selling of positive variance securities is unrestricted. Thus, although the assumption of unrestricted short-selling is unrealistic, this model, unlike its variants, is at least consistent in that it assumes that all available securities can be sold short.

We do not, however, judge the Sharpe-Lintner and Black models on the basis of whether the assumptions of one or the other seem more appealing. Both are to some extent unrealistic, and it is best to choose between them on the basis of which does a better job explaining real-world data on average returns and risk. Indeed, in the empirical tests of the next chapter we do not hesitate to invoke implications of variants of the Black model when these help to explain what is observed in the data. The fact that we do not find the assumptions of these models as pleasing as those of the Sharpe-Lintner and Black models does not mean that the variants of the Black model cannot offer some insight into what we observe in the data. Such insight, as always, is the basis on which we judge whether a model is useful.

VII. Market Equilibrium When There Are No Risk-free Securities and Short-Selling of Positive Variance Securities Is Prohibited

A. Preliminary Discussion

The implications of the Sharpe-Lintner model and the Black model and its variants for equilibrium security prices and for equilibrium relationships between the expected returns on securities and their risks derive from the fact that in these models a market equilibrium requires that M, the market portfolio of positive variance securities, be a minimum variance portfolio and usually an efficient portfolio. Thus, in equilibrium, securities must be priced so that the mathematical relationship between the expected returns on securities and their risks in a minimum variance portfolio applies to M. In the Sharpe-Lintner model the efficiency of M is a consequence of the fact that with unrestricted risk-free borrowing and lending, there is only one efficient portfolio of only positive variance securities, and this portfolio is the risky component of every efficient portfolio. If the market is to clear, this "tangency" portfolio must be M. In the Black model and its variants, the minimum variance property of the market portfolio is a consequence of the facts that (a) in a market equilibrium the portfolio of the risky components of investor portfolios must be the market portfolio; (b) the risky components of investor portfolios are minimum variance portfolios; and (c) with unrestricted short-selling of positive variance securities, any portfolio of minimum variance portfolios is a minimum variance portfolio. All models are also based on the assumption that there is complete agreement among investors with respect to the joint distribution of security prices at time 2.

In addition to the assumption of complete agreement, in the Black model and its variants the key ingredient for the result that M must be a minimum variance portfolio is the assumption that short-selling of positive variance securities is unrestricted, while the key ingredient in the Sharpe-Lintner model is the assumption that risk-free borrowing and lending is unrestricted.

We now examine what we can say about market equilibrium when there are no risk-free securities and there is no short-selling of positive variance securities. We find that in general the market portfolio is neither efficient nor minimum variance.

This result is not necessarily troublesome. In the various two-parameter models, the implications of a model for equilibrium prices of securities are obtained by showing that a market equilibrium requires that some portfolio, with proportions invested in individual securities that are known, is a minimum variance portfolio. Then we say that when applied to this portfolio, equation (20), which otherwise is just a mathematical condition that is met by securities in a minimum variance portfolio, can be interpreted as a condition on security prices that must be met in a market equilibrium. Since it contains all securities and in the proportions in which they are outstanding, the market portfolio is a convenient and appealing candidate for this market equilibrium interpretation of the minimum variance condition. However, the same interpretation of (20) would apply to any portfolio that must be a minimum variance portfolio in a market equilibrium. Unfortunately, at least as the state of the art stands now, when there are no risk-free securities and there is no short-selling of positive variance securities, we cannot identify such portfolios.

This result presents some cause for concern. The basic goal of the empirical work in the next chapter is to test whether security prices and returns behave as if investors choose portfolios in conformance with the two-parameter portfolio model. The goal is to test whether the behavior of prices and returns seems to reflect the attempts of investors to hold efficient portfolios. Such tests require some two-parameter model of market equilibrium. To date, the models of market equilibrium that produce testable propositions about security prices and expected returns require either the assumption that there is unrestricted risk-free borrowing and lending or the assumption that short-selling of positive variance securities is unrestricted. The portfolio model itself requires neither of these assumptions. Thus, in the empirical tests of the next chapter, we run the danger of rejecting the basic proposition that the behavior of returns is as if investors attempt to hold efficient portfolios, when the real problem is that we do not have a suitable two-parameter model of market equilibrium. On the other hand, if the tests turn out well, and we argue in Chapter 9 that they do, then they provide some vindication both for the models of market equilibrium that are used and for the more basic proposition that the prices of securities reflect the attempts of investors to hold efficient portfolios.

B. The Efficient Set Without Short-Selling or Risk-free Securities

When short-selling of positive variance securities is not allowed, the set of minimum variance portfolios is generated by a sequence of "corner" portfolios. For example, in Figure 8.8 the corner portfolios are assumed to be the points a, b, c, d, e, f, g. The portfolio g is the security with the highest expected return, or, if there is more than one security with the highest expected return, g can be a portfolio of these. Moving down the boundary, the next corner portfolio, f, contains all the securities in g plus one security not contained in g. In general, adjacent corner portfolios differ by one security (that is, one of them contains a security not included in the other), but in some cases adjacent corner portfolios differ by two securities (that is, each contains a security not included in the other). Equivalently, as one moves down the minimum variance boundary, each new corner portfolio involves adding a new security to the immediately preceding corner portfolio and/or dropping a security that appears in the immediately preceding corner portfolio.

When short-selling is not allowed, portfolios on the minimum variance boundary that are between two corner portfolios are just combinations of these two adjacent corner portfolios. For example, all the points along the boundary between the corner portfolios d and e in Figure 8.8 are portfolios of d and e. In general, however, only combinations of adjacent corner portfolios are on the minimum variance boundary. For example, combinations of the nonadjacent corner portfolios d and f in Figure 8.8 are not on the minimum variance boundary. This is in contrast with the situation when short-selling is unrestricted. Then any portfolio of minimum variance portfolios is a minimum variance portfolio. In the Black model and its variants, it is this property of minimum variance portfolios that allows us to reason that in a market equilibrium the market portfolio must be a minimum variance portfolio. When short-selling is prohibited, the fact that portfolios of nonadajacent corner portfolios are not minimum variance portfolios allows us to conclude that in general the market portfolio cannot be a minimum variance portfolio.

Thus, suppose that there is complete agreement among investors with respect to the joint distribution of security prices at time 2 and that the common picture of the portfolio opportunities facing investors in a market equilibrium is Figure 8.8. Different investors choose different portfolios from along the efficient or positively sloped segment of the minimum variance boundary. Since Figure 8.8 is supposed to represent a market equilibrium, the portfolio of the portfolios chosen by investors, where the portfolio chosen by an in-

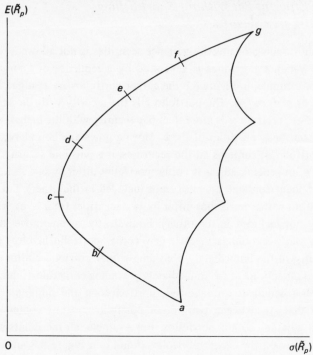

FIGURE 8.8

The Efficient Set When There Is No Short-Selling

vestor is weighted by the ratio of his portfolio funds to the portfolio funds of
all investors, must be the market portfolio. Thus, the market portfolio is a
portfolio of minimum variance portfolios. Unless investors all choose minimum variance portfolios between the same two adjacent corner portfolios,
when short-selling is prohibited such a portfolio of minimum variance portfolios cannot itself be a minimum variance portfolio.

So much for the market portfolio! As discussed above, the cause is not lost
if we can identify some portfolio or portfolios that must be of minimum variance or efficient in a market equilibrium. So far as I know, this task has met
with no success. The problem is that, aside from the general comments above,
we know little about the characteristics of minimum variance portfolios when
short-selling is prohibited. For example, as one moves down the minimum
variance boundary, minimum variance portfolios at first become more diversified; then they become less diversified as one approaches the bottom point
on the boundary, which is the security with the lowest expected return or a
portfolio of securities with the same lowest possible expected return. Beyond
this, however, one can, at the moment, say nothing.

In short, a market equilibrium requires that aggregate investor demand for each security be equal to the outstanding supply of the security. This in turn means that securities must be priced so that each security is in some efficient portfolios that are chosen by investors. These statements fall substantially short of interesting and testable propositions about the nature of capital market equilibrium. For such propositions, we have to rely on the Sharpe-Lintner model and on the Black model and its variants.

VIII. Market Equilibrium: Mathematical Treatment

In the preceding sections, the implications of the two-parameter model for equilibrium prices of securities are derived from a combination of geometric arguments with the properties of minimum variance portfolios. This approach is best for developing an intuitive appreciation for what the portfolio model and the derived two-parameter models of capital market equilibrium are all about. In this section, we consider a more "elegant" (i.e., mathematical) approach which derives market equilibrium prices more or less directly from the solutions to the consumption-investment decision problems that investors are presumed to face. Although this approach obscures some of the more interesting aspects of the model, it is more useful for attacking some questions than the geometric approach of the preceding sections.

The nonmathematical reader who is taking a first pass at this book might skip this section, since the new insights that it provides are not critical to a good understanding of two-parameter theory. The nonmathematical reader who is interested in the new insights can, however, continue on. He can get what he wants from the verbal discussions, especially those of Section VIII.C. The mathematical reader may find the present approach more appealing than that of the preceding sections.

A. *Consumption-Investment Decisions and Equilibrium Prices*

Begin with a few definitions:

> $\tilde{V}_j$ = market value of firm j at time 2. Firms are assumed to have only common stock outstanding at time 1; and $\tilde{V}_j$ is the total market value of the common stock of firm j at time 2, including any dividends paid at time 2. We assume that there is complete agreement among investors with respect to the joint distribution of $\tilde{V}_j, j = 1, \ldots, n$.

P_j = market value of firm j at time 1. Market equilibrium at time 1 involves determination of a set of market-clearing prices P_j for each of the $j = 1, \ldots, n$ firms in the market.

X_{ij} = fraction of P_j and thus of $\tilde{V}_j$ demanded by investor i at time 1. X_{ij} is the fraction of firm j owned by investor i after he chooses his portfolio at time 1. We assume that short-selling of all securities is unrestricted, so that X_{ij} can take positive or negative values.

c_{1i}, c_{2i} = consumption of investor i at times 1 and 2.

$E(\tilde{V}_j)$ = expected market value of firm j at time 2.

$\text{cov}(\tilde{V}_j, \tilde{V}_k)$ = covariance between the market values of firms j and k at time 2, with $\text{cov}(\tilde{V}_j, \tilde{V}_k) = \sigma^2(\tilde{V}_j)$.

The investor's consumption at time 2 is the total value of his holdings in all firms

$$\tilde{c}_{2i} = \sum_{j=1}^{n} X_{ij} \tilde{V}_j, \tag{55}$$

and $\tilde{c}_{2i}$ and $\tilde{V}_j$ are random variables at time 1. The mean and variance of the distribution of $\tilde{c}_{2i}$ are

$$E_i \equiv E(\tilde{c}_{2i}) = \sum_{j=1}^{n} X_{ij} E(\tilde{V}_j) \tag{56}$$

$$\sigma_i^2 \equiv \sigma^2(\tilde{c}_{2i}) = \sum_{j=1}^{n} \sum_{k=1}^{n} X_{ij} X_{ik} \, \text{cov}(\tilde{V}_j, \tilde{V}_k). \tag{57}$$

In the present framework, we assume that the joint distribution of firm values $\tilde{V}_j$, $j = 1, \ldots, n$, is multivariate normal. This in turn means that for any choice of X_{ij}, $j = 1, \ldots, n$, the distribution of $\tilde{c}_{2i}$ is normal. Following the arguments of Chapter 7, the investor's decision problem reduces to a choice of current consumption c_{1i}, expected future consumption E_i, and variance of future consumption σ_i^2. We assume that the tastes of investor i for c_{1i}, E_i, and σ_i^2 can be summarized by a welfare function $G_i(c_{1i}, E_i, \sigma_i^2)$ which is increasing in c_{1i} and E_i but decreasing in σ_i^2. In words, the investor likes consumption at time 1 and expected consumption at time 2, but he is averse to dispersion in the distribution of consumption at time 2. Finally, the welfare function G is assumed to be differentiable at least once in each of its arguments.

The investor's decision problem at time 1 is to choose values of c_{1i} and X_{ij}, $j = 1, \ldots, n$, that maximize his welfare subject to the constraint that the total of his current consumption and his investment in firms is equal to w_{1i}, the market value of his wealth at time 1. In formal terms, the investor must choose c_{1i} and $X_{ij}, j = 1, \ldots, n$, which

$$\text{maximize } G_i(c_{1i}, E_i, \sigma_i^2) \tag{58}$$

subject to the budget constraint

$$w_{1i} = \sum_{j=1}^{n} X_{ij} P_j + c_{1i}. \tag{59}$$

To solve the problem, we form the Lagrangian expression

$$G_i(c_{1i}, E_i, \sigma_i^2) + \lambda_i(w_{1i} - c_{1i} - \sum_{j=1}^{n} X_{ij} P_j),$$

differentiate the expression partially with respect to λ_i, c_{1i}, and $X_{ij}, j = 1, \ldots, n$, and then set these partial derivatives equal to zero. This yields (59) and the $n + 1$ equations

$$\frac{\partial G_i}{\partial c_{1i}} - \lambda_i = 0 \tag{60}$$

$$\frac{\partial G_i}{\partial E_i} E(\tilde{V}_j) + \frac{\partial G_i}{\partial \sigma_i^2} 2 \sum_{k=1}^{n} X_{ik} \, \text{cov}(\tilde{V}_j, \tilde{V}_k) - \lambda_i P_j = 0, \quad j = 1, \ldots, n, \tag{61}$$

where the partial derivatives $\partial G_i/\partial c_{1i}$, $\partial G_i/\partial E_i$ and $\partial G_i/\partial \sigma^2$ are rates of change of welfare with respect to changes in c_{1i}, E_i, and σ_i^2. Substituting (60) into (61), we get

$$\frac{\partial G_i}{\partial E_i} E(\tilde{V}_j) + \frac{\partial G_i}{\partial \sigma_i^2} 2 \sum_{k=1}^{n} X_{ik} \, \text{cov}(\tilde{V}_j, \tilde{V}_k) - \frac{\partial G_i}{\partial c_{1i}} P_j = 0, \quad j = 1, \ldots, n. \tag{62}$$

Each investor is presumed to solve a problem like that stated in (58) and (59). Thus, there is a set of equations like (59), (60), and (62) for each investor i; conditional on some set of values for firms at time 1, these equations determine the optimal values of current consumption and fractions of firms chosen by investor i at time 1. To get the implications of optimal decisions by investors for market equilibrium values of firms at time 1, we shall aggregate (62) across all investors, invoke the market-clearing constraints

$$\sum_{i=1}^{n} X_{ij} = 1, \quad j = 1, \ldots, n, \tag{63}$$

and then solve the resulting aggregate equations for $P_j, j = 1, \ldots, n$. As a first step, we divide through equation (62) by $\partial G_i/\partial \sigma_i^2$, to get

$$\frac{\partial G_i/\partial E_i}{\partial G_i/\partial \sigma_i^2} E(\tilde{V}_j) + 2 \sum_{k=1}^{n} X_{ik} \operatorname{cov}(\tilde{V}_j, \tilde{V}_k) - \frac{\partial G_i/\partial c_{1i}}{\partial G_i/\partial \sigma_i^2} P_j = 0, \quad j = 1, \ldots, n.$$

$$(64)$$

To interpret the two ratios of partial derivatives in (64), first set the differential of G_i equal to zero:

$$\frac{\partial G_i}{\partial c_{1i}} dc_{1i} + \frac{\partial G_i}{\partial E_i} dE_i + \frac{\partial G_i}{\partial \sigma_i^2} d\sigma_i^2 = 0, \tag{65}$$

where dc_{1i}, dE_i and $d\sigma_i^2$ represent "small" changes in c_{1i}, E_i, and σ_i^2. Equation (65) tells us how we can vary current consumption, expected consumption at time 2, and variance of consumption at time 2, while keeping the welfare of investor i constant. The equation allows us to determine marginal rates of substitution of one variable for another; that is, it can be used to determine how any two of the three variables can be varied while keeping the investor's welfare constant. For example, $d\sigma_i^2/dE_i$, the marginal rate of substitution of expected consumption at time 2 for variance of consumption at time 2, is obtained by setting dc_{1i} equal to zero in (65) and then solving to get

$$\frac{d\sigma_i^2}{dE_i} = -\frac{\partial G_i/\partial E_i}{\partial G_i/\partial \sigma_i^2}. \tag{66}$$

Likewise, $d\sigma_i^2/dc_{1i}$, the marginal rate of substitution of consumption at time 1 for variance of consumption at time 2, is obtained by setting dE_i equal to zero and then solving (65) to get

$$\frac{d\sigma_i^2}{dc_{1i}} = -\frac{\partial G_i/\partial c_{1i}}{\partial G_i/\partial \sigma_i^2}. \tag{67}$$

PROBLEM VIII.A

1. Give an intuitive explanation for the minus signs in (66) and (67).

ANSWER

1. The marginal rate of substitution in (66) is concerned with changes dE_i and $d\sigma_i^2$ in the mean and variance of consumption at time 2, holding consumption constant at time 1, that leave welfare unchanged. Since the investor is assumed to like expected consumption ($\partial G_i/\partial E_i > 0$) but to dislike variance of consumption ($\partial G_i/\partial \sigma_i^2 < 0$), keeping welfare constant implies that dE_i and $d\sigma_i^2$ in equation (65) must have the same sign. Since $\partial G_i/\partial E_i$ and $\partial G_i/\partial \sigma_i^2$ have opposite signs, this means that we must have a minus sign on the right of the equality in (66). Similar comments apply to (67).

We can now see that the two ratios of partial derivatives in (64) are the marginal rates of substitution of equations (66) and (67). If we interpret the n equations of (64) as the security demand equations for investor i, we can say that the fraction of the total securities of firm j demanded by investor i depends on the expected market value of the firm at time 2, the covariances of its market value at time 2 with the market values of all firms, the market value of the firm at time 1, and investor i's marginal rates of substitution between mean and variance of consumption at time 2 and between consumption at time 1 and variance of consumption at time 2.

To get an expression for the value of firm j in a market equilibrium, we aggregate the demand equations of (64) across all investors $i, i = 1, \ldots, I$, invoking the market-clearing constraints of (63). The result is

$$-\gamma E(\tilde{V}_j) + 2 \sum_{k=1}^{n} \text{cov}(\tilde{V}_j, \tilde{V}_k) + \delta P_j = 0, \quad j = 1, \ldots, n, \tag{68}$$

where

$$\gamma = \sum_{i=1}^{I} \frac{d\sigma_i^2}{dE_i} \quad \text{and} \quad \delta = \sum_{i=1}^{I} \frac{d\sigma_i^2}{dc_{1i}}. \tag{69}$$

Equation (68) shows the relationship between the market equilibrium value of firm j at time 1, its expected value at time 2, the covariances of its value at time 2 with the values of all firms, and the tastes of investors as summarized by γ and δ. To get an explicit equation for the market equilibrium value of firm j at time 1, we solve (68) for P_j,

$$P_j = \frac{\gamma}{\delta} E(\tilde{V}_j) - \frac{2}{\delta} \sum_{k=1}^{n} \text{cov}(\tilde{V}_j, \tilde{V}_k). \tag{70}$$

A more intuitive version of this pricing equation can be obtained by developing interpretations of γ/δ and $2/\delta$. The aggregate values of all firms at time 1 and time 2 are

$$P_M = \sum_{j=1}^{n} P_j \quad \text{and} \quad \tilde{V}_M = \sum_{j=1}^{n} \tilde{V}_j. \tag{71}$$

P_M and $\tilde{V}_M$ can also be interpreted as the values of invested wealth at time 1 and time 2. The mean and variance of the distribution of $\tilde{V}_M$ are

$$E(\tilde{V}_M) = \sum_{j=1}^{N} E(\tilde{V}_j) \quad \text{and} \quad \sigma^2(\tilde{V}_M) = \sum_{j=1}^{N} \sum_{k=1}^{N} \text{cov}(\tilde{V}_j, \tilde{V}_k). \tag{72}$$

Thus, if we aggregate (70) across firms, we determine that

$$P_M = \frac{\gamma}{\delta} E(\tilde{V}_M) - \frac{2}{\delta} \sigma^2(\tilde{V}_M), \tag{73}$$

$$\frac{2}{\delta} = \frac{\frac{\gamma}{\delta} E(\tilde{V}_M) - P_M}{\sigma^2(\tilde{V}_M)}. \tag{74}$$

With (74), equation (70) can be rewritten as

$$P_j = \frac{\gamma}{\delta} E(\tilde{V}_j) - \left[\frac{\frac{\gamma}{\delta} E(\tilde{V}_M) - P_M}{\sigma^2(\tilde{V}_M)} \right] \sum_{k=1}^{n} \mathrm{cov}\,(\tilde{V}_j, \tilde{V}_k). \tag{75}$$

Or better, using (71) we can determine that

$$\mathrm{cov}\,(\tilde{V}_j, \tilde{V}_M) = \mathrm{cov} \left(\tilde{V}_j, \sum_{k=1}^{n} \tilde{V}_k \right) = \sum_{k=1}^{n} \mathrm{cov}\,(\tilde{V}_j, \tilde{V}_k), \tag{76}$$

so that

$$P_j = \frac{\gamma}{\delta} E(\tilde{V}_j) - \left[\frac{\frac{\gamma}{\delta} E(\tilde{V}_M) - P_M}{\sigma^2(\tilde{V}_M)} \right] \mathrm{cov}\,(\tilde{V}_j, \tilde{V}_M). \tag{77}$$

Better yet, if we let

$$\frac{\gamma}{\delta} = \frac{1}{\theta}, \tag{78}$$

then

$$P_j = \frac{1}{\theta} \left[E(\tilde{V}_j) - \left(\frac{E(\tilde{V}_M) - \theta P_M}{\sigma^2(\tilde{V}_M)} \right) \mathrm{cov}\,(\tilde{V}_j, \tilde{V}_M) \right]. \tag{79}$$

It is an easy matter to develop an interpretation of θ. Suppose there is a firm, call it firm 0, whose market value at time 2 is uncorrelated with $\tilde{V}_M$, so that $\mathrm{cov}\,(\tilde{V}_0, \tilde{V}_M) = 0$. From (79), for this firm we have

$$P_0 = \frac{1}{\theta} E(\tilde{V}_0) \tag{80}$$

so that

$$\theta = \frac{E(\tilde{V}_0)}{P_0} = 1 + E(\tilde{R}_0) = 1 + E(\tilde{R}_{0M}). \tag{81}$$

In words, θ can be interpreted as 1 plus the expected return on the securities of a firm whose market value at time 2 is uncorrelated with the total market value of all firms at time 2. If the market value of a firm at time 2 is uncorrelated with the total market value of all firms, the return on the firm's securities is uncorrelated with the return on the market portfolio. Thus, $E(\tilde{R}_0)$ is $E(\tilde{R}_{0M})$ of preceding sections; that is, $E(\tilde{R}_0) = E(\tilde{R}_{0M})$ is the expected return on any security (or firm) whose return is uncorrelated with the return on the market portfolio M.

PROBLEM VIII.A

2. Show that cov $(\tilde{V}_0, \tilde{V}_M) = 0$ implies cov $(\tilde{R}_0, \tilde{R}_M) = 0$.

ANSWER

2.

$$\text{cov}(\tilde{R}_j, \tilde{R}_M) = \text{cov}\left(\frac{\tilde{V}_j}{P_j} - 1, \frac{\tilde{V}_M}{P_M} - 1\right) = \frac{1}{P_j P_M} \text{cov}(\tilde{V}_j, \tilde{V}_M). \tag{82}$$

It follows that cov $(\tilde{V}_0, \tilde{V}_M) = 0$ implies cov $(\tilde{R}_0, \tilde{R}_M) = 0$.

Substituting (81) into (79), we get

$$P_j = \frac{1}{1 + E(\tilde{R}_{0M})} \left[E(\tilde{V}_j) - \left(\frac{E(\tilde{V}_M) - [1 + E(\tilde{R}_{0M})] P_M}{\sigma^2(\tilde{V}_M)} \right) \text{cov}(\tilde{V}_j, \tilde{V}_M) \right]. \tag{83}$$

This equation has an interesting interpretation. From (72) and (76), we can determine that

$$\sigma^2(\tilde{V}_M) = \sum_{j=1}^n \sum_{k=1}^n \text{cov}(\tilde{V}_j, \tilde{V}_k) = \sum_{j=1}^n \text{cov}(\tilde{V}_j, \tilde{V}_M). \tag{84}$$

Since $\tilde{V}_M$ is the market value of invested wealth at time 2, $\sigma^2(\tilde{V}_M)$ can be interpreted as the risk of invested wealth. Then cov $(\tilde{V}_j, \tilde{V}_M)$ can be interpreted as the risk of the market value of firm j at time 2 in the sense that it is the contribution of the securities of firm j to the risk of market wealth. Thus, (83) says that the market value of firm j at time 1 is determined by first adjusting the expected market value of the firm at time 2 for the risk of the market value of the firm at time 2, then discounting this risk-adjusted expected market value at a rate equal to the expected return on a riskless security, that is, a security which contributes nothing to the risk of market wealth at time 2.

Alternatively, (83) says that a firm sells two things in the capital market at time 1: its expected market value at time 2, $E(\tilde{V}_j)$, and the risk of its market value at time 2, $\text{cov}(\tilde{V}_j, \tilde{V}_M)$. The price at time 1 of a unit of expected market value at time 2 is

$$1/[1 + E(\tilde{R}_{0M})],$$

and the price of a unit of risk is

$$-\left(\frac{E(\tilde{V}_M) - [1 + E(\tilde{R}_{0M})]P_M}{\sigma^2(\tilde{V}_M)}\right)\Big/ [1 + E(\tilde{R}_{0M})].$$

Finally, suppose there is unrestricted risk-free borrowing and lending. Then the value at time 1 of V_F dollars to be delivered for certain at time 2 is, from (83),

$$P_F = \frac{V_F}{[1 + E(\tilde{R}_{0M})]}. \tag{85}$$

Since V_F/P_F is just 1 plus the risk-free rate of interest,

$$1 + E(\tilde{R}_{0M}) = 1 + R_F. \tag{86}$$

In short, we have rederived the Sharpe-Lintner result that $E(\tilde{R}_{0M})$, the expected return on any positive variance security whose return is uncorrelated with the return on the market portfolio M, is equal to the risk-free rate of interest R_F. We simply follow a different approach to the Sharpe-Lintner model here.

Substituting (86) into (83), we get

$$P_j = \frac{1}{1 + R_F}\left[E(\tilde{V}_j) - \left(\frac{E(\tilde{V}_M) - (1 + R_F)P_M}{\sigma^2(\tilde{V}_M)}\right)\text{cov}(\tilde{V}_j, \tilde{V}_M)\right], \quad j = 1, \ldots, n. \tag{87}$$

In words, as in (83), the market value of firm j at time 1 is the present value of the risk-adjusted expected market value of the firm at time 2. In (87), however, the discount rate is the risk-free rate of interest R_F. Thus, in (87) we first adjust $E(\tilde{V}_j)$, the expected market value of the firm at time 2, for the risk of $\tilde{V}_j$, and then discount this risk-adjusted expected value back to time 1 at the risk-free rate.

PROBLEM VIII.A

3. Since it is based on the assumptions of complete agreement and unrestricted short-selling of all securities, (83) must be the market equilibrium pricing equation for the Black model. We earlier interpreted equation (30) in this way. Show that (30) can be obtained from (83). Likewise, show that (32), which we earlier interpreted as the market equilibrium pricing equation for the Sharpe-Lintner model, can be derived from (87).

ANSWER

3. Rearranging (83), we can determine that

$$E(\tilde{R}_j) \equiv \frac{E(\tilde{V}_j) - P_j}{P_j} = E(\tilde{R}_{0M}) + \left(\frac{E(\tilde{V}_M) - [1 + E(\tilde{R}_{0M})]P_M}{\sigma^2(\tilde{V}_M)}\right)\frac{\text{cov}(\tilde{V}_j, \tilde{V}_M)}{P_j}.$$

(88)

Since

$$\tilde{V}_M = P_M(1 + \tilde{R}_M),$$

$$E(\tilde{V}_M) = P_M[1 + E(\tilde{R}_M)] \quad \text{and} \quad \sigma^2(\tilde{V}_M) = P_M^2\sigma^2(\tilde{R}_M).$$

Thus, equation (88) can be rewritten as

$$E(\tilde{R}_j) = E(\tilde{R}_{0M}) + \left[\frac{E(\tilde{R}_M) - E(\tilde{R}_{0M})}{\sigma^2(\tilde{R}_M)}\right]\frac{\text{cov}(\tilde{V}_j, \tilde{V}_M)}{P_j P_M}.$$

Then from (82) it follows that

$$E(\tilde{R}_j) = E(\tilde{R}_{0M}) + \left[\frac{E(\tilde{R}_M) - E(\tilde{R}_{0M})}{\sigma^2(\tilde{R}_M)}\right]\text{cov}(\tilde{R}_j, \tilde{R}_M),$$

which is just (30).

Thus, (83) and (30) are equivalent statements about the implications of the Black model for market equilibrium prices. Equation (83) states the equilibrium condition in terms of prices, whereas (30) states the equilibrium condition in terms of expected returns. Likewise, when the preceding analysis is applied to (87), we get (32) as the implied market equilibrium condition for expected returns in the Sharpe-Lintner model. Thus, (87) and (32) are equivalent statements of the implications of the Sharpe-Lintner model for market equilibrium prices and expected returns.

B. Counting Equations and Unknowns

As the first-order conditions for a solution to the maximization problem stated in (58) and (59), equations (59) to (61) determine optimal values of current consumption c_{1i} and fractions X_{ij} $(j = 1, \ldots, n)$ of firms demanded by investor i at time 1, conditional on some set of market values $P_j(j = 1, \ldots, n)$ of firms at time 1. Thus, equations (59) to (61) are the conditions for investor equilibrium, and there is a set of such equations for each investor. The conditions for a market equilibrium are the n market-clearing equations of (63). When these are appended to the conditions for investor equilibrium, we have a system of equations which determine the n market equilibrium values of firms at time 1, as well as the equilibrium fractions of firms demanded by individual investors and the equilibrium consumptions of individual investors at time 1.

The conditions for investor equilibrium given by (59) to (61) are $n + 2$ equations in $n + 1$ unknowns, c_{1i} and $X_{ij}(j = 1, \ldots, n)$. One of the n demand equations of (61) is redundant. Given the optimal value of c_{1i} and of $n - 1$ of the X_{ij}, the nth fraction X_{ij} can be implied from the budget constraint of (59). Thus, we can arbitrarily drop one of the n demand equations of (61), and the remaining $n - 1$ equations along with (59) and (60) determine c_{1i} and $X_{ij}(j = 1, \ldots, n)$.

There is one remaining puzzle. When the n equations of (63) are appended to the system obtained when (59) to (61) are applied to each investor, we have a sufficient number of equations to determine the market equilibrium values of each of the n firms in the market. In most models of market equilibrium, we usually can only determine relative prices. Here we seem to be able to determine all n security prices. In fact, the model does determine relative prices only. There are $n + 1$ goods in the market at time 1: the n common stocks of individual firms plus current consumption. The model determines the prices of the common stocks in terms of—that is, in units of—current consumption, so that current consumption is the numeraire.

C. Market Equilibrium Without Complete Agreement

The models of market equilibrium discussed so far are based on the assumption that there is complete agreement among investors with respect to the joint distribution of the market values of firms at time 2. This assumption is not a necessary ingredient for a market equilibrium. A market equilibrium simply requires a set of market-clearing values of firms at time 1. Equilibrium prices set at time 1 must cause equation (63) to be met for each security.

The method used above to derive equations (83) and (87) allows us to develop explicit pricing equations for a two-parameter world where complete agreement among investors is not assumed. Although the pricing equations are similar in form to those obtained with complete agreement, the equations obtained when complete agreement is not assumed contain parameters that cannot be estimated from market data. We conclude that meaningful empirical tests of the two-parameter model probably must be based on models of market equilibrium that assume complete agreement.

When the complete agreement assumption is dropped, the statement of the decision problem facing the investor at time 1 is to a large extent unchanged. Each investor is assumed to behave as if the joint distribution of the market values of firms at time 2 were multivariate normal, but each investor assesses his own values for the parameters of the distribution, and the assessed values of the parameters are different from one investor to another. The investor still behaves as if he were solving the maximization problem stated in (58) and (59), but now, instead of (56) and (57), the equations for the expected value and variance of his consumption at time 2 are

$$E_i \equiv E(\tilde{c}_{2i}) = \sum_{j=1}^{n} X_{ij} E_i(\tilde{V}_j) \tag{89}$$

$$\sigma_i^2 = \sigma^2(\tilde{c}_{2i}) = \sum_{j=1}^{n} \sum_{k=1}^{n} X_{ij} X_{ik} \operatorname{cov}_i (\tilde{V}_j, \tilde{V}_k); \tag{90}$$

that is, $E_i(\tilde{V}_j)$ and $\operatorname{cov}_i (\tilde{V}_j, \tilde{V}_k)$ now contain i subscripts to indicate that they are the assessments of investor i.

The conditions for a solution to the investor's expected utility maximization problem are again (59) to (61), but in (61) we substitute $E_i(\tilde{V}_j)$ and $\operatorname{cov}_i (\tilde{V}_j, \tilde{V}_k)$ for $E(\tilde{V}_j)$ and $\operatorname{cov} (\tilde{V}_j, \tilde{V}_k)$. Then, following the steps that lead from (61) to (64) and substituting (66) and (67) into (64), in the absence of complete agreement, the security demand equations for investor i are

$$-\frac{d\sigma_i^2}{dE_i} E_i(\tilde{V}_j) + 2 \sum_{k=1}^{n} X_{ik} \operatorname{cov}_i (\tilde{V}_j, \tilde{V}_k) + \frac{d\sigma_i^2}{dc_{1i}} P_j = 0, \quad j = 1, \ldots, n.$$

$$\tag{91}$$

To get an expression for the value of firm j in a market equilibrium, we aggregate the demand equations of (91) across all investors $i, i = 1, \ldots, I$, and then solve for P_j as

$$P_j = \frac{\displaystyle\sum_{i=1}^{I} \frac{d\sigma_i^2}{dE_i} E_i(\tilde{V}_j)}{\delta} - \frac{2}{\delta} \sum_{k=1}^{n} \sum_{i=1}^{n} X_{ik} \operatorname{cov}_i (\tilde{V}_j, \tilde{V}_k), \tag{92}$$

where δ is as defined in (69). Equation (92) is similar in form to the pricing equation (70) obtained when complete agreement is assumed. The common assessed expected market value $E(\tilde{V}_j)$ of firm j at time 2 that appears in (70) is replaced in (92) by a weighted average of the expected values assessed by individual investors, with $E_i(\tilde{V}_j)$ weighted by investor i's marginal rate of substitution of expected consumption at time 2 for variance of consumption at time 2. Likewise, the sum of covariances between the market value of firm j at time 2 and the market values of all firms that appears in (70) is replaced by a weighted average of investor-assessed covariances, with investor i's assessment of $\operatorname{cov}_i (\tilde{V}_j, \tilde{V}_k)$, weighted by the fraction of firm k that he holds. The similarity of (70) and (92) is apparent when one notes that (92) reduces to (70) when complete agreement is assumed; that is, (70) can be obtained from (92) by dropping the i subscripts that appear on $E_i(\tilde{V}_j)$ and $\text{cov}_i(\tilde{V}_j, \tilde{V}_k)$ in (92) and then making use of (69) and (63).

The analogy between the pricing equations obtained with and without the complete agreement assumption can be pressed even further by developing (92) into an equation similar to (79). Since

$$\text{cov}_i(\tilde{V}_j, \tilde{c}_{2i}) = \text{cov}_i\left(\tilde{V}_j, \sum_{k=1}^{n} X_{ik}\tilde{V}_k\right) = \sum_{k=1}^{n} X_{ik}\,\text{cov}_i(\tilde{V}_j, \tilde{V}_k), \quad (93)$$

we can rewrite (92) as

$$P_j = \frac{\displaystyle\sum_{i=1}^{I} \frac{d\sigma_i^2}{dE_i} E_i(\tilde{V}_j)}{\delta} - \frac{2}{\delta} \sum_{i=1}^{I} \text{cov}_i(\tilde{V}_j, \tilde{c}_{2i}). \quad (94)$$

If we sum (94) across firms and then solve the resulting expression for $2/\delta$, we get

$$\frac{2}{\delta} = \frac{\displaystyle\frac{\sum_{i=1}^{I} \frac{d\sigma_i^2}{dE_i} E_i(\tilde{V}_M)}{\delta} - P_M}{\displaystyle\sum_{i=1}^{I} \text{cov}_i(\tilde{V}_M, \tilde{c}_{2i})}, \quad (95)$$

where $E_i(\tilde{V}_M)$ is investor i's assessment of expected market wealth at time 2, and $\text{cov}_i(\tilde{V}_M, \tilde{c}_{2i})$ is investor i's assessment of the covariance between market wealth and his consumption at time 2. Substituting (95) into (94), we get

$$P_j = \frac{1}{\delta}\left[\sum_{i=1}^{I} \frac{d\sigma_i^2}{dE_i} E_i(\tilde{V}_j) - \left(\frac{\displaystyle\sum_{i=1}^{I} \frac{d\sigma_i^2}{dE_i} E_i(\tilde{V}_M) - \delta P_M}{\displaystyle\sum_{i=1}^{I} \text{cov}_i(\tilde{V}_M, \tilde{c}_{2i})}\right) \sum_{i=1}^{I} \text{cov}_i(\tilde{V}_j, \tilde{c}_{2i})\right].$$

Multiplying and dividing through this expression by γ of (69) and then making use of the definition of θ in (78), we get

$$P_j = \frac{1}{\theta} \left[\frac{\sum\limits_{i=1}^{I} \frac{d\sigma_i^2}{dE_i} E_i(\tilde{V}_j)}{\sum\limits_{i=1}^{I} \frac{d\sigma_i^2}{dE_i}} - \left(\frac{\frac{\sum\limits_{i=1}^{I} \frac{d\sigma_i^2}{dE_i} E_i(\tilde{V}_M)}{\sum\limits_{i=1}^{I} \frac{d\sigma_i^2}{dE_i}} - \theta P_M}{\sum\limits_{i=1}^{I} \text{cov}_i(\tilde{V}_M, \tilde{c}_{2i})} \right) \sum\limits_{i=1}^{I} \text{cov}_i(\tilde{V}_j, \tilde{c}_{2i}) \right].$$

$$(96)$$

Since market wealth at time 2 is also aggregate consumption at time 2, that is, since

$$\tilde{V}_M = \sum_{j=1}^{n} \tilde{V}_j = \sum_{i=1}^{I} \tilde{c}_{2i}, \tag{97}$$

with the assumption of complete agreement we would have

$$\sum_{i=1}^{I} \text{cov}(\tilde{V}_M, \tilde{c}_{2i}) = \text{cov}\left(\tilde{V}_M, \sum_{i=1}^{I} \tilde{c}_{2i}\right) = \sigma^2(\tilde{V}_M) \tag{98}$$

$$\sum_{i=1}^{I} \text{cov}(\tilde{V}_j, \tilde{c}_{2i}) = \text{cov}\left(\tilde{V}_j, \sum_{i=1}^{I} \tilde{c}_{2i}\right) = \text{cov}(\tilde{V}_j, \tilde{V}_M). \tag{99}$$

Thus, with complete agreement, (96) reduces to (79), and this makes it clear that the pricing equations obtained with and without complete agreement again have the same form.

In the absence of complete agreement, however, one cannot reduce the sum of covariances

$$\sum_{i=1}^{I} \text{cov}_i(\tilde{V}_M, \tilde{c}_{2i}) \tag{100}$$

to $\sigma^2(\tilde{V}_M)$ in the manner of (98). The i subscripts that appear on the covariances in (100) prevent us from interpreting this expression as anything but the sum across investors of each investor's perceived covariance between his consumption at time 2 and aggregate consumption or market wealth at time 2. Likewise, in the absence of complete agreement, the i subscripts on the individual covariances in

$$\sum_{i=1}^{I} \text{cov}_i(\tilde{V}_j, \tilde{c}_{2i}) \tag{101}$$

prevent us from reducing this sum to $\text{cov}(\tilde{V}_j, \tilde{V}_M)$ in the manner of (99).

Nevertheless, it is possible to develop an interpretation of (96) which is similar to the interpretation of the pricing equations obtained when complete agreement is assumed. Thus, if we interpret $\text{cov}_i(\tilde{V}_M, \tilde{c}_{2i})$ as investor i's perception of the risk of his consumption at time 2 relative to aggregate consumption, then we can interpret the sum of covariances in (100) as aggregate risk, but keeping in mind that this aggregate risk is not perceived by any particular market participant. Likewise, since

$$\sum_{j=1}^{n} \sum_{i=1}^{I} \text{cov}_i(\tilde{V}_j, \tilde{c}_{2i}) = \sum_{i=1}^{I} \text{cov}_i\left(\sum_{j=1}^{n} \tilde{V}_j, \tilde{c}_{2i}\right) = \sum_{i=1}^{I} \text{cov}_i(\tilde{V}_M, \tilde{c}_{2i}),$$

we can interpret the sum of covariances in (101) as the risk of firm j (although again this risk is not perceived by any particular investor) since it is the contribution of the securities of firm j to what we have called aggregate risk.

With these interpretations of the two sums of covariances in (96), we can then say that this pricing equation represents the market value of firm j at time 1 as $1/\theta$ multiplied by the risk-adjusted weighted average of investor expectations of the value of the firm at time 2. Moreover, we can interpret θ as 1 plus a weighted average of investor-expected returns on a firm that is "riskless" in the sense that its risk, as measured by the sum of covariances in (101), is zero, even though none of the individual terms of (101) need be equal to zero. Specifically, with such a firm, call it firm 0, we can determine from (96) that

$$\theta = \frac{\sum_{i=1}^{I} \dfrac{d\sigma_i^2}{dE_i} \dfrac{E_i(\tilde{V}_0)}{P_0}}{\sum_{i=1}^{I} \dfrac{d\sigma_i^2}{dE_i}} = 1 + \frac{\sum_{i=1}^{I} \dfrac{d\sigma_i^2}{dE_i} E_i(\tilde{R}_0)}{\sum_{i=1}^{I} \dfrac{d\sigma_i^2}{dE_i}}.$$

Better yet, if there is borrowing and lending, and all investors perceive such borrowing and lending to be risk-free, so that there is complete agreement with respect to risk-free securities, then

$$\theta = \frac{\sum_{i=1}^{I} \dfrac{d\sigma_i^2}{dE_i} \dfrac{V_F}{P_F}}{\sum_{i=1}^{I} \dfrac{d\sigma_i^2}{dE_i}} = \frac{V_F}{P_F} = 1 + R_F.$$

Substituting $1 + R_F$ for θ in (96), we get

$$P_j = \frac{1}{1+R_F} \times$$

$$\left[\frac{\sum\limits_{i=1}^{I} \frac{d\sigma_i^2}{dE_i} E_i(\tilde{V}_j)}{\sum\limits_{i=1}^{I} \frac{d\sigma_i^2}{dE_i}} - \left(\frac{\frac{\sum\limits_{i=1}^{I} \frac{d\sigma_i^2}{dE_i} E_i(\tilde{V}_M)}{\sum\limits_{i=1}^{I} \frac{d\sigma_i^2}{dE_i}} - (1+R_F)P_M}{\sum\limits_{i=1}^{I} \mathrm{cov}_i(\tilde{V}_M, \tilde{c}_{2i})} \right) \sum\limits_{i=1}^{I} \mathrm{cov}_i(\tilde{V}_j, \tilde{c}_{2i}) \right].$$

$$(102)$$

It is clear that (102) is an equation for the market value of firm j at time 1 which is in the same form as equation (87), the pricing equation that is obtained when there is complete agreement and risk-free borrowing and lending.

IX. Conclusions

Having pricing equations which have the same form and similar interpretations as those obtained under the assumption of complete agreement does not mean, however, that empirical tests of the implications of the two-parameter model for the process of price formation in the capital market can be based on models in which complete agreement is not assumed. Empirical tests require that the quantities that appear in pricing equations be estimable from observable market data. The expected values and covariances that appear in (96) or (102) are investor assessments of parameters that vary from one investor to another. It is not even logical to talk about estimates of these assessments obtained from market data.

In contrast, with complete agreement the assessed values of the parameters $E(\tilde{V}_j)$, $\mathrm{cov}(\tilde{V}_j, \tilde{V}_M)$, $E(\tilde{V}_M)$, and $\sigma^2(\tilde{V}_M)$ that appear in the pricing equations (83) and (87) are common to all investors, and they are presumed to be based on correct perception of the joint distribution of the market values of firms at time 2. The fact that assessments are assumed to be common to all investors and that investor perceptions are assumed to be correct allows us to go from theory to data. This is the subject of the next and last chapter.

CHAPTER

9

The Two-Parameter Model: Empirical Tests

I. Introduction

In the two-parameter portfolio model of Chapter 7 the capital market is perfect, distributions of returns on all portfolios are normal, and investors are risk-averse. These assumptions imply that the optimal portfolio for any investor is efficient in the sense that no other portfolio with the same or higher expected return has lower variance of return. In Chapter 8 we studied how the presumed attempts of investors to hold efficient portfolios are reflected in the process of price formation in the capital market. In the present chapter we test these implications of the two-parameter model for the behavior of returns on securities and portfolios.

The results that we report are from Fama and MacBeth (1973). A detailed discussion of the problems that arise in tests of the two-parameter model was first given by Miller and Scholes (1972). The first empirical study to provide solutions to these problems was Black, Jensen, and Scholes (1972). The approach of Fama and MacBeth is similar to that of Black, Jensen, and Scholes.

II. Testing the Model: General Discussion

All of the testable two-parameter models of market equilibrium discussed in Chapter 8 have a common implication: Market equilibrium requires that the value-weighted market portfolio M be a minimum variance portfolio and, generally, an efficient portfolio. This means that the mathematical condition that defines a minimum variance portfolio necessarily applies to M, so that the expected return from time 1 to time 2 on any positive variance security* i is

$$E(\tilde{R}_i) = E(\tilde{R}_{0M}) + [E(\tilde{R}_M) - E(\tilde{R}_{0M})]\, \beta_{iM}, \quad i = 1, \ldots, n. \tag{1}$$

As in Chapter 8, n is the number of positive variance securities in the market; $E(\tilde{R}_i)$ and $E(\tilde{R}_M)$ are the expected returns on security i and on the market portfolio M; $E(\tilde{R}_{0M})$ is the expected return on any positive variance security or any portfolio of such securities whose return is uncorrelated with the return on M; and

$$\beta_{iM} = \frac{\mathrm{cov}\,(\tilde{R}_i, \tilde{R}_M)}{\sigma^2(\tilde{R}_M)} \tag{2}$$

is the risk of security i in the market portfolio M measured relative to the risk of M.

The fact that a market equilibrium requires that M be a minimum variance portfolio transforms (1) from a condition on portfolio weights that must be met if a portfolio is to minimize variance at a given level of expected return to a condition on equilibrium prices and expected returns. Since a market equilibrium requires that M be minimum variance, prices must be set in such a way that (1) holds for every positive variance security. The purpose of this chapter is to test whether actual average returns conform to the implications of this expected return-risk relationship.

A. Hypotheses about Expected Returns

Most of the testable implications of (1) can be noted from inspection. First, the equation says that securities are priced so that the relationship between the expected return on security i and its risk in M, β_{iM}, is linear. Second, since β_{iM} is the only measure of risk that appears in (1), it is the only measure of risk that we need in order to explain differences among the ex-

---

*Positive variance securities are securities whose return distributions have strictly positive variances.

pected returns on securities. Third, since the models of market equilibrium say that securities must be priced so that M is on the positively sloped segment of the boundary of minimum variance portfolios, in a market equilibrium $E(\tilde{R}_M) > E(\tilde{R}_{0M})$; that is, securities are priced so that (1) implies a positive relationship between the expected return on any security and its risk in M.

Finally, we also test the implications of the various models of market equilibrium for the expected returns on securities and portfolios that have $\beta_{iM} = 0.0$. In the Sharpe-Lintner model there is unrestricted borrowing and lending at a common risk-free rate R_F, and R_F is also the expected return $E(\tilde{R}_{0M})$ on any positive variance securities and portfolios that have $\beta_{iM} = 0.0$. In the basic Black model there are no risk-free securities, but all zero-β_{iM} securities and portfolios have the common expected return $E(\tilde{R}_{0M})$. In the variants of the Black model there are risk-free securities, but there are restrictions on the amount of borrowing at the risk-free rate. In one variant there is no borrowing at the risk-free rate, while in another borrowing is limited to a fixed fraction of the investor's portfolio funds. In either case (1) is the relevant market equilibrium condition for the expected returns on positive variance securities, so that $E(\tilde{R}_{0M})$ is the expected return on all positive variance securities and portfolios that have $\beta_{im} = 0.0$. In these models, however, R_F is less than $E(\tilde{R}_{0M})$.

Tests of the implications of the Sharpe-Lintner model for expected returns on positive variance securities and portfolios that have $\beta_{iM} = 0.0$ against the corresponding implications of the "restricted borrowing" variants of the Black model are tests of differing implications of different models of market equilibrium. Of course, it is well to know which of the various models of market equilibrium best describes the world. However, we are more interested in the general question of whether the behavior of returns is consistent with a world where investors attempt to hold efficient portfolios. This is the fundamental empirical question of the two-parameter model. To give it testable content, some model of market equilibrium is required. We must know specifically what it means to say that the prices of securities reflect the attempts of investors to hold efficient portfolios. Finding which model of market equilibrium works best is important but secondary to the fundamental issue.

B. Competing Hypotheses

To test the implications drawn from (1) concerning the pricing of securities in a two-parameter world, we need an alternative hypothesis about expected returns that includes (1) as a special case but allows us to reject (1) if it is inappropriate. We propose the following:

$$E(\tilde{R}_i) = E(\tilde{R}_{0M}) + [E(\tilde{R}_M) - E(\tilde{R}_{0M})] \beta_{iM} + q\beta_{iM}^2 + d\sigma(\tilde{\epsilon}_i). \qquad (3)$$

This representation of the expected return on security i includes two explanatory variables, β_{iM}^2 and $\sigma(\tilde{\epsilon}_i)$, that do not appear in (1). The quadratic term β_{iM}^2 is included to test the proposition of (1) that the expected return-risk relationship is linear in β_{iM}. If this proposition is true, then q in (3) is zero. Likewise, $\sigma(\tilde{\epsilon}_i)$ is meant to be some measure of the "risk" of security i which is not an exact function of β_{iM}. It is included in (3) to test the proposition of (1) that β_{iM} is the only measure of risk needed to explain the expected return on security i. If this proposition is correct, then d, the coefficient of $\sigma(\tilde{\epsilon}_i)$ in (3), is zero.

The measure of "non-β_{iM} risk," $\sigma(\tilde{\epsilon}_i)$, that we propose to use in (3) comes out of the market model of Chapters 3 and 4. The two-parameter model assumes that the joint distribution of security returns is multivariate normal. This implies that the joint distribution of the return on any security and the return on the market portfolio M is bivariate normal. Bivariate normality implies a market model relationship between $\tilde{R}_i$ and $\tilde{R}_M$ of the form

$$\tilde{R}_i = \alpha_{iM} + \beta_{iM}\tilde{R}_M + \tilde{\epsilon}_i, \quad i = 1, \ldots, n, \qquad (4)$$

where

$$\alpha_{iM} = E(\tilde{R}_i) - \beta_{iM}E(\tilde{R}_M), \qquad (5)$$

β_{iM} is the relative risk measure of (2), and $\tilde{\epsilon}_i$ is a random disturbance that has expected value equal to zero and is independent of $\tilde{R}_M$. Since $\tilde{\epsilon}_i$ and $\tilde{R}_M$ are independent,

$$\sigma^2(\tilde{R}_i) = \beta_{iM}^2\sigma^2(\tilde{R}_M) + \sigma^2(\tilde{\epsilon}_i). \qquad (6)$$

Portfolio theory implies a world where the pricing of securities reflects the attempts of investors to hold efficient portfolios. An alternative model, completely antithetical to portfolio theory, says that the pricing of securities is dominated by investors who hold single-security portfolios. Given a market of risk-averse investors, this model says that a security's expected return is positively related to the variance of its return rather than to β_{iM}. We can see from (6) that the variance of the return on security i can be split into two components. One depends directly on β_{iM}, but the other, the disturbance variance $\sigma^2(\tilde{\epsilon}_i)$, does not. Thus, under the alternative model, $\sigma^2(\tilde{\epsilon}_i)$ or, equivalently, the standard deviation of the disturbance, $\sigma(\tilde{\epsilon}_i)$, is a measure of the non-β_{iM} risk of security i, and $\sigma(\tilde{\epsilon}_i)$ is the measure that appears in (3).

C. The Portfolio Approach to the Tests

To test whether the coefficients q and d in (3) are, as implied by (1), equal to zero, we need estimates of these coefficients. We obtain them by forming portfolios whose returns have expected values equal to q or d and whose expected returns reflect only the effects of β_{iM}^2 or of $\sigma(\tilde{\epsilon}_i)$ in (3). We can then compute the time series of the returns on these portfolios and test whether the mean returns are different from zero.

Specifically, multiply through (3) by the portfolio weight x_{ip} and sum over i to get

$$E(\tilde{R}_p) = \sum_{i=1}^{n} x_{ip} E(\tilde{R}_i) = E(\tilde{R}_{0M}) \sum_{i=1}^{n} x_{ip} + [E(\tilde{R}_M) - E(\tilde{R}_{0M})] \sum_{i=1}^{n} x_{ip} \beta_{iM}$$

$$+ q \sum_{i=1}^{n} x_{ip} \beta_{iM}^2 + d \sum_{i=1}^{n} x_{ip} \sigma(\tilde{\epsilon}_i). \tag{7}$$

To get a portfolio that has expected return equal to q, we choose the x_{ip} in such a way that the weighted average of β_{iM}^2 is 1.0, and all other variables that appear in (3) are "zeroed out." Thus, we choose $x_{ip}, i = 1, \ldots, n$, so that

$$\sum_{i=1}^{n} x_{ip} = 0 \tag{8a}$$

$$\sum_{i=1}^{n} x_{ip} \beta_{iM} = 0 \tag{8b}$$

$$\sum_{i=1}^{n} x_{ip} \beta_{iM}^2 = 1 \tag{8c}$$

$$\sum_{i=1}^{n} x_{ip} \sigma(\tilde{\epsilon}_i) = 0. \tag{8d}$$

To get a portfolio that has expected return equal to d, we choose another set of x_{ip} in such a way that the weighted average of the $\sigma(\tilde{\epsilon}_i)$ is 1.0 but all other variables in (3) are "zeroed out." This implies choosing the x_{ip} so that

$$\sum_{i=1}^{n} x_{ip} = 0 \tag{9a}$$

$$\sum_{i=1}^{n} x_{ip} \beta_{iM} = 0 \tag{9b}$$

$$\sum_{i=1}^{n} x_{ip} \beta_{iM}^2 = 0 \tag{9c}$$

$$\sum_{i=1}^{n} x_{ip} \sigma(\tilde{\epsilon}_i) = 1. \tag{9d}$$

From (8b) and (9b) we see that the portfolios described by equations (8) and (9) are zero-β_{pM} portfolios; that is, they are portfolios that have $\beta_{pM} = \sum_{i=1}^{n} x_{ip}\beta_{iM} = 0.0$. From (8a) and (9a) we see that they are also "zero investment" portfolios: the investor puts up no personal funds but rather obtains long positions in some securities ($x_{ip} > 0$) by taking short positions ($x_{ip} < 0$) in others. This is in contrast to a "standard portfolio," where the sum of the weights invested in individual securities is 1.

PROBLEMS II.C

1. Does condition (8d) imply a portfolio whose return is perfectly correlated with the return on M, that is, a portfolio whose market model disturbance is always zero?

2. Use equation (7) to show that equation (3) is only a legitimate representation of expected returns on securities when q and d in (3) are equal to zero.

ANSWERS

1. Equation (8d) is a condition on the weighted average of the standard deviations of market model disturbances for individual securities. It implies nothing in particular about the market model disturbance for the resulting portfolio. Thus, if we multiply through (4) by x_{ip} and sum over i, the market model disturbance for the resulting portfolio is

$$\tilde{\epsilon}_p = \sum_{i=1}^{n} x_{ip}\tilde{\epsilon}_i,$$

which has standard deviation

$$\sigma(\tilde{\epsilon}_p) = \left[\sum_{i=1}^{n} \sum_{j=1}^{n} x_{ip}x_{jp} \text{ cov}(\tilde{\epsilon}_i, \tilde{\epsilon}_j)\right]^{1/2}.$$

It is then clear that the constraint on the portfolio weights described by (8d) does not imply $\sigma(\tilde{\epsilon}_p) = 0$.

In the same vein, note that equation (8c) implies nothing about the value of β_{pM}^2 that results when a portfolio is formed according to the equations of (8). Indeed, since (8b) implies $\beta_{pM} = 0.0$, it implies $\beta_{pM}^2 = 0$, while (8c) says that the x_{ip} must be chosen so that the weighted average of the β_{iM}^2 of individual securities is 1.

2. If x_{ip} in (7) is set equal to x_{iM}, we have the market portfolio M with $E(\tilde{R}_p) = E(\tilde{R}_M)$. Equation (7) will only lead us to this conclusion when q and d are both equal to zero. Thus, strictly speaking, (3) is only a legitimate representation of expected returns on securities when it reduces to (1). To make the notation in (3) rigorous, we could change $E(\tilde{R}_{0M})$ to, say, h and $[E(\tilde{R}_M) - E(\tilde{R}_{0M})]$ to, say, k. The notation in (3), however, maintains a convenient analogy with (1), and switching to a more rigorous notation would not change anything that follows.

The equations of (8) impose four constraints on the weights given to individual securities in the portfolio whose expected return concentrates on the effects of nonlinearities. Since the number of available securities n is much greater than four, there are many portfolios that satisfy (8). We are not indifferent among them. We use the average return on the chosen portfolio to test the hypothesis that the nonlinearity coefficient q in (3) is zero. To make the most reliable possible inference, we want the portfolio whose average return gives the most reliable estimate of q. This means choosing the portfolio that has the smallest variance of return among all portfolios that satisfy (8). Likewise, to make the most reliable inference about the hypothesis that the coefficient d of $\sigma(\tilde{\epsilon}_i)$ in (3) is zero, we want the portfolio that has the smallest variance of return among all portfolios where the weights applied to individual securities satisfy (9).

D. Least Squares Coefficients as Portfolio Returns

Finding the portfolios that have these properties seems a formidable task, but the approach generally taken is straightforward.

INFORMAL DISCUSSION

Let us recognize that we use data for many time periods (actually months) to test the implications of (1). Let us represent the return on security i for month t as

$$\tilde{R}_{it} = \tilde{\gamma}_{it} + \tilde{\gamma}_{2t}\beta_{iM} + \tilde{\gamma}_{3t}\beta_{iM}^2 + \tilde{\gamma}_{4t}\sigma(\tilde{\epsilon}_i) + \tilde{\eta}_{it}, \quad i = 1, \ldots, n. \quad (10)$$

Suppose we know the values of β_{iM}, β_{iM}^2 and $\sigma(\tilde{\epsilon}_i)$ for each of the securities in the market, and suppose we take $\tilde{\gamma}_{1t}$, $\tilde{\gamma}_{2t}$, $\tilde{\gamma}_{3t}$, and $\tilde{\gamma}_{4t}$ to be the least squares coefficients from a multiple regression of the n security returns for month t on the n combinations of β_{iM}, β_{iM}^2, and $\sigma(\tilde{\epsilon}_i)$. Then $\tilde{\gamma}_{3t}$ and $\tilde{\gamma}_{4t}$ are the returns for month t on portfolios that, respectively, conform to the constraints of (8) and (9). Under certain assumptions about the disturbances $\tilde{\eta}_{it}$ for different securities, the least squares values of $\tilde{\gamma}_{3t}$ and $\tilde{\gamma}_{4t}$ are also the returns for month t on the portfolios with the smallest possible return variances among all portfolios that satisfy (8) and (9).

Note that, although we usually think of "least squares" as a method of estimation, we do not use the term "estimates" when talking about the least squares values of $\tilde{\gamma}_{3t}$ and $\tilde{\gamma}_{4t}$ in (10). The appropriate view is that the least squares method just provides a convenient way to obtain portfolio returns that have the desired properties.

We now discuss more formally the properties claimed for the least squares values of $\tilde{\gamma}_{3t}$ and $\tilde{\gamma}_{4t}$. In the process, we uncover interesting properties of the least squares values of $\tilde{\gamma}_{1t}$ and $\tilde{\gamma}_{2t}$ in (10). Unfortunately, any reasonably concise exposition of the arguments requires some matrix algebra. The mathematically disinclined can skip down to the discussion that follows equation (22).

FORMAL DISCUSSION

Let

$$\underline{\tilde{R}}_t = \begin{pmatrix} \tilde{R}_{1t} \\ \vdots \\ \tilde{R}_{nt} \end{pmatrix} \tag{11}$$

be the $(n \times 1)$ vector of returns on individual securities for month t. Let

$$\underline{C} = \begin{pmatrix} 1 & \beta_{1M} & \beta_{1M}^2 & \sigma(\tilde{\epsilon}_1) \\ \vdots & \vdots & \vdots & \vdots \\ 1 & \beta_{nM} & \beta_{nM}^2 & \sigma(\tilde{\epsilon}_n) \end{pmatrix} \tag{12}$$

be the $(n \times 4)$ matrix of the values of the explanatory variables in (10). Let

$$\underline{\tilde{\eta}}_t = \begin{pmatrix} \tilde{\eta}_{1t} \\ \vdots \\ \tilde{\eta}_{nt} \end{pmatrix} \tag{13}$$

be the $(n \times 1)$ vector of security return disturbances for month t in (10), and let

$$\underline{\tilde{\gamma}}_t = \begin{pmatrix} \tilde{\gamma}_{1t} \\ \tilde{\gamma}_{2t} \\ \tilde{\gamma}_{3t} \\ \tilde{\gamma}_{4t} \end{pmatrix} \tag{14}$$

be the (4×1) vector of the least squares values of $\tilde{\gamma}_{1t}$, $\tilde{\gamma}_{2t}$, $\tilde{\gamma}_{3t}$, and $\tilde{\gamma}_{4t}$ for month t. Then the matrix representation of (10) is

$$\tilde{\underline{R}}_t = \underline{C}\,\tilde{\underline{\gamma}}_t + \tilde{\underline{\eta}}_t. \tag{15}$$

The least squares value of $\tilde{\underline{\gamma}}_t$ is*

$$\tilde{\underline{\gamma}}_t = (\underline{C}'\underline{C})^{-1}\underline{C}'\tilde{\underline{R}}_t. \tag{16}$$

Equivalently, if we define the $(4 \times n)$ matrix

$$\underline{X} = (\underline{C}'\underline{C})^{-1}\underline{C}', \tag{17}$$

then

$$\tilde{\underline{\gamma}}_t = \underline{X}R_t \tag{18}$$

or

$$\tilde{\gamma}_{jt} = \sum_{i=1}^{n} x_{ij}\tilde{R}_{it}, \quad j = 1, 2, 3, 4, \tag{19}$$

where x_{ij} is the element of row j ($j = 1, 2, 3, 4$) and column i ($i = 1, \ldots, n$) of $\underline{X}$. This is the reverse of the more common notation, where the first subscript on x would refer to a row of the matrix $\underline{X}$, and the second subscript would refer to a column. The choice here reflects the fact that we shall interpret x_{ij} as the portfolio weight assigned to security i to get the least squares value of the portfolio return $\tilde{\gamma}_{jt}$. In the notation for portfolio weights it is our practice to use the first subscript to refer to the security and the second to refer to the portfolio.

Equation (19) says that the least squares value of $\tilde{\gamma}_{jt}$ is the return on a portfolio where the weights assigned to the n individual securities are the n elements of the jth row of the matrix $\underline{X}$. To determine the properties of the $\tilde{\gamma}_{jt}$, we study the properties of $\underline{X}$. Note first that

$$\underline{X}\,\underline{C} = (\underline{C}'\underline{C})^{-1}\underline{C}'\underline{C} = \underline{I}, \tag{20}$$

where $\underline{I}$ is the (4×4) identity matrix; that is, $\underline{I}$ has 1's along its diagonal and 0's elsewhere. From (12), the first column of $\underline{C}$ is an $(n \times 1)$ vector of 1's. Thus from (12) and (20), it follows that

$$\sum_{i=1}^{n} x_{ij} = \begin{cases} 1 \text{ for } j = 1 \\ 0 \text{ for } j = 2, 3, 4 \end{cases}. \tag{21}$$

In words, the least squares value of $\tilde{\gamma}_{1t}$ in (19) is the return on a standard portfolio, that is, a portfolio where the sum of the weights assigned to individual securities is 1. The least squares values of $\tilde{\gamma}_{2t}$, $\tilde{\gamma}_{3t}$, and $\tilde{\gamma}_{4t}$ given by (19) are returns on zero-investment portfolios, that is, portfolios where the sum of the weights assigned to individual securities is zero.

*See, for example, Theil (1971, chap. 3).

Next note that if c_{ki} is the element of row i and column k of $\underline{C}$, then (20) can be written as

$$\sum_{i=1}^{n} x_{ij} c_{ki} = \begin{cases} 1 \text{ for } j = k \\ 0 \text{ for } j \neq k \end{cases}. \tag{22}$$

From (19), x_{ij}, $i = 1, \ldots, n$ are the weights applied to individual security returns to get the least squares values of $\tilde{\gamma}_{jt}$, $j = 1, 2, 3, 4$. If we enumerate (22) for $j = 3$ and $k = 1, 2, 3, 4$, we find that the least squares value of $\tilde{\gamma}_{3t}$ is the return on a portfolio that satisfies the constraints of (8), and thus it has expected return equal to q, the coefficient of β_{iM}^2 in (3). Likewise, enumeration of (22) for $j = 4$ and $k = 1, 2, 3, 4$ shows that the least squares value of $\tilde{\gamma}_{4t}$ is the return on a portfolio where the proportions invested in individual securities satisfy the constraints of (9), so that the portfolio has expected return equal to d, the coefficient of $\sigma(\tilde{\epsilon}_i)$ in (3). Thus, if for each month t we calculate the cross-sectional regression of security returns on β_{iM}, β_{iM}^2, and $\sigma(\tilde{\epsilon}_i)$, the means of the times series of the least squares values of $\tilde{\gamma}_{3t}$ and $\tilde{\gamma}_{4t}$ can be used to test the propositions of (1) that the relationship between the expected returns on securities and their risks in M is linear, and that β_{iM} is the only measure of risk needed to explain differences between the expected returns on different securities.

E. Getting the Most Powerful Tests: General Discussion

TESTING $E(\tilde{R}_M) > E(\tilde{R}_{0M})$ AND $E(\tilde{R}_{0M}) = R_F$

If we enumerate (22) for $j = 1$ and $j = 2$, we find that the least squares values of $\tilde{\gamma}_{1t}$ and $\tilde{\gamma}_{2t}$ in (10) are also the returns on portfolios that have desirable properties. The weights x_{i1}, $i = 1, \ldots, n$, applied to individual security returns to get $\tilde{\gamma}_{1t}$, satisfy

$$\sum_{i=1}^{n} x_{i1} = 1 \tag{23a}$$

$$\sum_{i=1}^{n} x_{i1} \beta_{iM} = 0 \tag{23b}$$

$$\sum_{i=1}^{n} x_{i1} \beta_{iM}^2 = 0 \tag{23c}$$

$$\sum_{i=1}^{n} x_{i1} \sigma(\tilde{\epsilon}_i) = 0. \tag{23d}$$

In words, (23a) says that the least squares value of $\tilde{\gamma}_{1t}$ is the return on a standard portfolio; (23b) says that the β_{pM} of this portfolio is zero; and (23c) and (23d) say that the weights invested in individual securities are also chosen so as to "zero out" any effects of β_{iM}^2 and $\sigma(\tilde{\epsilon}_i)$ on expected returns. In terms of (3) or (7), the least squares value of $\tilde{\gamma}_{1t}$ is the return on a portfolio where securities are weighted so that $E(\tilde{\gamma}_{1t}) = E(\tilde{R}_{0M})$. The mean of the time series of $\tilde{\gamma}_{1t}$ can be used to test the proposition of the Sharpe-Lintner model that $E(\tilde{R}_{0M})$, the expected return on any positive variance security or portfolio whose return is uncorrelated with the return on M, is equal to the risk-free rate R_F.

Likewise, (22) says that the weights applied to individual security returns to get $\tilde{\gamma}_{2t}$ in (19) satisfy

$$\sum_{i=1}^{n} x_{i2} = 0 \tag{24a}$$

$$\sum_{i=1}^{n} x_{i2}\,\beta_{iM} = 1 \tag{24b}$$

$$\sum_{i=1}^{n} x_{i2}\,\beta_{iM}^2 = 0 \tag{24c}$$

$$\sum_{i=1}^{n} x_{i2}\,\sigma(\tilde{\epsilon}_i) = 0. \tag{24d}$$

Thus the least squares value of $\tilde{\gamma}_{2t}$ is the return on a zero-investment portfolio that has $\beta_{pM} = 1$ and that zeroes out any effects of β_{iM}^2 and $\sigma(\tilde{\epsilon}_i)$ on expected returns. If we substitute the conditions described by (24) into (7), we find that the expected value of $\tilde{\gamma}_{2t}$ is $E(\tilde{R}_M) - E(\tilde{R}_{0M})$. We can, then, use the mean value of the time series of $\tilde{\gamma}_{2t}$ to test the proposition that $E(\tilde{R}_M) > E(\tilde{R}_{0M})$.

Tests of the hypotheses that $E(\tilde{R}_{0M}) = R_F$ and $E(\tilde{R}_M) > E(\tilde{R}_{0M})$ are not of great interest, however, unless q and d in (3) are equal to zero. The hypothesis that $E(\tilde{R}_M) > E(\tilde{R}_{0M})$ is concerned with whether M is on the positively sloped segment of the minimum variance boundary. The proposition that $E(\tilde{R}_{0M}) = R_F$ is concerned with whether M is at the point on the positively sloped segment of the boundary where a straight line from R_F is tangent to the boundary. Tests of these two propositions only make sense when the data are consistent with the hypothesis that M is somewhere on the minimum variance boundary; that is, the data must be consistent with the propositions that the relationship between the expected returns on securities and their risks in M is linear ($q = 0.0$) and that β_{iM} is the only measure of risk needed to explain expected security returns ($d = 0.0$).

If the data are consistent with the hypothesis that q and d in (3) are zero, then the time series of the least squares values of $\tilde{\gamma}_{1t}$ and $\tilde{\gamma}_{2t}$ in (10) provide the basis for tests of the hypotheses that $E(\tilde{R}_{0M}) = R_F$ and $E(\tilde{R}_M) > E(\tilde{R}_{0M})$. The inferences obtained, however, are not likely to be the most reliable possible. From (23), the least squares value of $\tilde{\gamma}_{1t}$ in (10) is the return on a standard portfolio that has $\beta_{pM} = 0.0$ and that also zeroes out any effects of β_{iM}^2 and $\sigma(\tilde{\epsilon}_i)$ on expected returns; the portfolio weights satisfy (23c) and (23d) as well as (23a) and (23b). If q and d in (3) are zero, then when testing the hypothesis that $E(\tilde{R}_{0M}) = R_F$, we do not have to worry about zeroing out the effects of β_{iM}^2 and $\sigma(\tilde{\epsilon}_i)$. If the constraints of (23c) and (23d) do not need to be met, we can probably find a standard zero-β_{pM} portfolio that has a smaller variance of return than any standard zero-β_{pM} portfolio that also satisfies (23c) and (23d). Likewise, although the least squares value of $\tilde{\gamma}_{2t}$ in (10) is the return on a zero-investment portfolio that has $\beta_{pM} = 1.0$ and expected return equal to $E(\tilde{R}_M) - E(\tilde{R}_{0M})$, it is also a portfolio that satisfies the constraints of (24c) and (24d). If the tests indicate that these constraints can be ignored, we can probably find a portfolio that has a smaller variance of return and so provides more reliable tests of the hypothesis that $E(\tilde{R}_M) > E(\tilde{R}_{0M})$.

One way to obtain portfolio returns appropriate for testing the hypotheses that $E(\tilde{R}_M) > E(\tilde{R}_{0M})$ and $E(\tilde{R}_{0M}) = R_F$, while ignoring possibly redundant constraints, is from cross-sectional regressions of security returns on their β_{iM}. Consider

$$\tilde{R}_{it} = \tilde{\gamma}_{1t} + \tilde{\gamma}_{2t}\beta_{iM} + \tilde{\eta}_{it}, \quad i = 1, \ldots, n. \tag{25}$$

If $\tilde{\gamma}_{1t}$ is defined as the intercept in the least squares regression of the n values of $\tilde{R}_{it}$ for month t on the corresponding n values of β_{iM}, then $\tilde{\gamma}_{1t}$ is the return on a standard zero-β_{pM} portfolio, but one that imposes no particular constraints on the weighted averages of β_{iM}^2 and $\sigma(\tilde{\epsilon}_i)$. The weights assigned to individual security returns satisfy (23a) and (23b) but not (23c) and (23d). If q and d in (7) are equal to zero, the expected return on this portfolio is $E(\tilde{R}_{0M})$. If we calculate the time series of cross-sectional regressions described by (25), the mean of the resulting time series of $\tilde{\gamma}_{1t}$ can be used to test the Sharpe-Lintner proposition that $E(\tilde{R}_{0M}) = R_F$. Likewise, the least squares value of $\tilde{\gamma}_{2t}$ in (25) is the return on a zero-investment portfolio that has $\beta_{pM} = 1.0$ but imposes no particular constraints on the weighted averages of β_{iM}^2 and $\sigma(\tilde{\epsilon}_i)$. The weights assigned to individual security returns satisfy (24a) and (24b) but not (24c) and (24d). If q and d in (7) are zero, the expected value of $\tilde{\gamma}_{2t}$ is $E(\tilde{R}_M) - E(\tilde{R}_{0M})$, and the mean of the time series of $\tilde{\gamma}_{2t}$ can be used to test the hypothesis that $E(\tilde{R}_M) > E(\tilde{R}_{0M})$.

PROBLEM II.E

1. The expected return-risk equation (1) holds for portfolios as well as for individual securities. (See Problem II.C.*2* of Chapter 8.) The least squares value of $\tilde{\gamma}_{2t}$ in (25) is the return on a portfolio that has $\beta_{pM} = 1.0$. Why is the expected return on this portfolio $E(\tilde{R}_M) - E(\tilde{R}_{0M})$ rather than $E(\tilde{R}_M)$, as (1) would seem to imply?

ANSWER

1. Multiplying through (1) by x_{ip} and summing over i yields

$$\sum_{i=1}^{n} x_{ip} E(\tilde{R}_i) = E(\tilde{R}_{0M}) \sum_{i=1}^{n} x_{ip} + [E(\tilde{R}_M) - E(\tilde{R}_{0M})] \sum_{i=1}^{n} x_{ip} \beta_{iM}$$

$$E(\tilde{R}_p) = E(\tilde{R}_{0M}) \sum_{i=1}^{n} x_{ip} + [E(\tilde{R}_M) - E(\tilde{R}_{0M})] \beta_{pM}.$$

The expected return on any standard portfolio ($\Sigma x_{ip} = 1.0$) that has $\beta_{pM} = 1.0$ is $E(\tilde{R}_M)$, but the expected return on a zero-investment portfolio ($\Sigma x_{ip} = 0$) that has $\beta_{pM} = 1.0$ is $E(\tilde{R}_M) - E(\tilde{R}_{0M})$.

TESTING FOR THE EFFECTS OF NONLINEARITIES AND NON-β_{iM} RISKS

The idea that better tests can be obtained when irrelevant constraints are ignored also applies to tests of the propositions that the coefficients q and d in (3) are equal to zero. The least squares value of $\tilde{\gamma}_{3t}$ in

$$\tilde{R}_{it} = \tilde{\gamma}_{1t} + \tilde{\gamma}_{2t} \beta_{iM} + \tilde{\gamma}_{3t} \beta_{iM}^2 + \tilde{\eta}_{it}, \quad i = 1, \ldots, n, \tag{26}$$

is the return on a zero-investment portfolio that has $\beta_{pM} = 0.0$ and where the weighted average of β_{iM}^2 is 1.0. Hence the portfolio satisfies the constraints of (8a), (8b), and (8c), but the constraint of (8d) is ignored. If d in (3) is zero, then from (7) and (8a–c) we can determine that $E(\tilde{\gamma}_{3t}) = q$. Thus, the mean of the time series of the portfolio return $\tilde{\gamma}_{3t}$ can be used to test the proposition that the nonlinearity coefficient q in (3) is zero.

Finally, if q in (3) is zero, there is no need to "zero out" the effects of β_{iM}^2 when testing the proposition that β_{iM} is the only measure of risk needed to explain differences among expected security returns. To test the proposition that d in (3) is zero, we can form a portfolio that satisfies (9a), (9b), and (9d) but ignores (9c). One such portfolio is given by the least squares value of $\tilde{\gamma}_{4t}$ in

$$\tilde{R}_{it} = \tilde{\gamma}_{1t} + \tilde{\gamma}_{2t} \beta_{iM} + \tilde{\gamma}_{4t} \sigma(\tilde{\epsilon}_i) + \tilde{\eta}_{it}, \quad i = 1, \ldots, n. \tag{27}$$

When q in (3) is zero, the mean of the time series of the $\tilde{\gamma}_{4t}$ can be used to test the hypothesis that $\sigma(\tilde{\epsilon}_i)$ contributes nothing to the explanation of differences in expected security returns.

We have claimed, without proof, some properties for the least squares values of the various $\tilde{\gamma}_{jt}$ in (25) to (27). To establish these properties, we would repeat the arguments of equations (11) to (22), deleting some explanatory variables from the matrix $\underline{C}$ of (12). For example, to establish the properties claimed for $\tilde{\gamma}_{3t}$ in (26), one would delete the column of $\underline{C}$ corresponding to $\sigma(\tilde{\epsilon}_i)$. The analysis that leads to (22) would then imply that the least squares value of $\tilde{\gamma}_{3t}$ satisfies the conditions of (8a-c); but since $\sigma(\tilde{\epsilon}_i)$ is not included as an explanatory variable, the relevant version of (22) implies no constraint, like (8d), on the weighted average of the $\sigma(\tilde{\epsilon}_i)$. In short, when one deletes $\sigma(\tilde{\epsilon}_i)$ and/or β_{iM}^2 from (10), the analysis of (11) to (22) still applies, but the least squares procedure only imposes constraints on variables that are explicitly included in the return equation.

In this respect, there is nothing special about equations (10) and (25) to (27). Anytime one does a cross-sectional regression of security returns on their β_{iM} and on other variables, an analysis similar to (11) to (22) leads to the conclusion that the least squares intercept is the return on a standard portfolio that has $\beta_{pM} = 0.0$ and that zeros out the effects of other variables. The least squares value of the coefficient of any other variable is the return on a zero-investment portfolio where the weights assigned to individual securities have the effect of setting the weighted average of the values of the variable for different securities equal to 1, while zeroing out the effects of all other variables. An excellent example of this general property of cross-sectional risk-return regressions, outside the context of the concerns of this chapter, is provided by Black and Scholes (1974).

PROBLEMS II.E

2. The least squares values of $\tilde{\gamma}_{1t}$ and $\tilde{\gamma}_{2t}$ in (25) can be written as

$$\tilde{\gamma}_{2t} = \frac{\sum_{i=1}^{n} (\tilde{R}_{it} - \bar{\tilde{R}}_t)(\beta_{iM} - \bar{\beta}_M)}{\sum_{i=1}^{n} (\beta_{iM} - \bar{\beta}_M)^2} \tag{28}$$

$$\tilde{\gamma}_{1t} = \bar{\tilde{R}}_t - \tilde{\gamma}_{2t}\bar{\beta}_M, \tag{29}$$

where $\bar{\tilde{R}}_t$ is the average of the returns on the n securities for month t and $\bar{\beta}_M$ is the average of the β_{iM}. Use (28) and (29) to show that the least squares value of $\tilde{\gamma}_{1t}$ in (25) is the return on a standard portfolio that has $\beta_{pM} = 0.0$, while $\tilde{\gamma}_{2t}$ is the return on a zero-investment portfolio that has $\beta_{pM} =$

1.0. The analysis above has already discussed these properties of $\tilde{\gamma}_{1t}$ and $\tilde{\gamma}_{2t}$. The present approach, however, does not require the matrix algebra of equations (11) to (22), and it is better for the second task of this problem, which is to interpret the weights assigned to individual securities in $\tilde{\gamma}_{1t}$ and $\tilde{\gamma}_{2t}$ of (25).

3. Tests of the propositions that q and d in (3) are zero are tests of the proposition that M is on the minimum variance boundary. Do these tests make sense if $E(\tilde{R}_M) - E(\tilde{R}_{0M}) \leqslant 0.0$?

ANSWERS

2. First rewrite (28) as

$$\tilde{\gamma}_{2t} = \sum_{i=1}^{n} \left(\frac{\beta_{iM} - \bar{\beta}_M}{\sum_{i=1}^{n} (\beta_{iM} - \bar{\beta}_M)^2} \right) \tilde{R}_{it} - \sum_{i=1}^{n} \left(\frac{\beta_{iM} - \bar{\beta}_M}{\sum_{i=1}^{n} (\beta_{iM} - \bar{\beta}_M)^2} \right) \tilde{\bar{R}}_t$$

$$= \sum_{i=1}^{n} \left(\frac{\beta_{iM} - \bar{\beta}_M}{\sum_{i=1}^{n} (\beta_{iM} - \bar{\beta}_M)^2} \right) \tilde{R}_{it}. \tag{30}$$

With (30), (29) can be developed as follows:

$$\tilde{\gamma}_{1t} = \tilde{\bar{R}}_t - \sum_{i=1}^{n} \left(\frac{(\beta_{iM} - \bar{\beta}_M)\bar{\beta}_M}{\sum_{i=1}^{n} (\beta_{iM} - \bar{\beta}_M)^2} \right) \tilde{R}_{it}$$

$$= \sum_{i=1}^{n} \left(\frac{1}{n} - \frac{(\beta_{iM} - \bar{\beta}_M)\bar{\beta}_M}{\sum_{i=1}^{n} (\beta_{iM} - \bar{\beta}_M)^2} \right) \tilde{R}_{it}, \tag{31}$$

and

$$\sum_{i=1}^{n} \left(\frac{1}{n} - \frac{(\beta_{iM} - \bar{\beta}_M)\bar{\beta}_M}{\sum_{i=1}^{n} (\beta_{iM} - \bar{\beta}_M)^2} \right) = 1 - \sum_{i=1}^{n} \frac{(\beta_{iM} - \bar{\beta}_M)\bar{\beta}_M}{\sum_{i=1}^{n} (\beta_{iM} - \bar{\beta}_M)^2} = 1. \tag{32}$$

Equation (31) says that $\tilde{\gamma}_{1t}$ is a weighted average of the returns on individual securities for month t, while (32) says that the sum of the weights applied to individual securities is 1.0. Thus $\tilde{\gamma}_{1t}$ is the return on a standard portfolio. As for any portfolio, this portfolio has a β_{pM} which is just a weighted average of the β_{iM} for individual securities. Since the appropriate weights are given by the expression within the brackets of (31), the value of β_{pM} for $\tilde{\gamma}_{1t}$ is

$$\sum_{i=1}^{n} \left(\frac{1}{n} - \frac{(\beta_{iM} - \bar{\beta}_M)\bar{\beta}_M}{\sum_{i=1}^{n} (\beta_{iM} - \bar{\beta}_M)^2} \right) \beta_{iM} = \bar{\beta}_M - \frac{\sum_{i=1}^{n} \beta_{iM}^2 - n\bar{\beta}_M^2}{\sum_{i=1}^{n} (\beta_{iM} - \bar{\beta}_M)^2} \bar{\beta}_M = 0.$$

To interpret the weights assigned to individual security returns in $\tilde{\gamma}_{1t}$, note from (31) that the first term in any weight is $1/n$, which implies equal weights for individual securities. The second term adjusts these equal weights according to the difference between β_{iM} and $\bar{\beta}_M$. The effect is to lower the investment in securities with above-average values of β_{iM} and increase the investment in securities with below-average values of β_{iM}. Thus, securities with values of β_{iM} close to $\bar{\beta}_M$ get a weight approximately equal to $1/n$. Securities with high values of β_{iM} are sold short, with proceeds from short sales used to increase the investment in securities with low values of β_{iM}.

A similar analysis shows that $\tilde{\gamma}_{2t}$, as defined by (28), is the return on a zero-investment portfolio that has $\beta_{pM} = 1.0$. We can see from (30) that the sum of the weights assigned to individual security returns in $\tilde{\gamma}_{2t}$ is zero, so that $\tilde{\gamma}_{2t}$ is the return on a zero-investment portfolio. We can then use the weights in (30) to determine that β_{pM} for $\tilde{\gamma}_{2t}$ is

$$\sum_{i=1}^{n} \left(\frac{\beta_{iM} - \bar{\beta}_M}{\sum_{i=1}^{n} (\beta_{iM} - \bar{\beta}_M)^2} \right) \beta_{iM} = \frac{\sum_{i=1}^{n} \beta_{iM}^2 - n\bar{\beta}_M^2}{\sum_{i=1}^{n} (\beta_{iM} - \bar{\beta}_M)^2} = 1.0.$$

Since $\tilde{\gamma}_{2t}$ is the return on a zero-investment portfolio, the investor puts up no money of his own; rather, he sells some securities short and uses the proceeds to buy others. From (30) we can see that $\tilde{\gamma}_{2t}$ involves short positions in securities with below-average values of β_{iM} and long positions in securities with above-average values of β_{iM}, which reverses the general pattern of weights assigned to individual securities in $\tilde{\gamma}_{1t}$.

3. All the models of market equilibrium say that M is on the positively sloped segment of the minimum variance boundary, so that $E(\tilde{R}_M) > E(\tilde{R}_{0M})$. If this is not true, then tests of the linearity and non-β_{iM} risk propositions implied by (1) are not of great interest.

If $E(\tilde{R}_M) > E(\tilde{R}_{0M})$ in (1), then when testing the propositions that q and d in (3) are zero, it is necessary to form portfolios that zero out the effects of β_{iM} on expected returns. Including β_{iM} in the cross-sectional regressions guarantees this result. The least squares values of $\tilde{\gamma}_{3t}$ and $\tilde{\gamma}_{4t}$ in (10), (26), and (27) are the returns on portfolios that have $\beta_{pM} = 0.0$.

F. The Reliability of the Least Squares Portfolio Returns

We have shown that the least squares values of the various $\tilde{\gamma}_{jt}$ in equations (10) and (25) to (27) are the returns on portfolios that concentrate on the effects on expected returns of the different variables in (3). We have, however, provided no justification for the presumption that the least squares values of the $\tilde{\gamma}_{jt}$ are also the returns on the portfolios that have the smallest possible return variances among portfolios that concentrate on the effects of the different variables on expected returns. Providing some justification for the "smallest variance" properties of the least squares approach is important, since it will imply that the least squares portfolio returns provide more reliable inferences about the various hypotheses than other portfolios we might use. Unfortunately, the arguments require more statistical sophistication than is generally assumed in this book. The reader should nevertheless be able to grasp the sense of the discussion, especially when we eventually make comparisons of the reliability of the least squares $\tilde{\gamma}_{jt}$ of (10), (25), (26), and (27).

The "smallest variance" property of the least squares portfolio returns follows from an assumption on the properties of the disturbances $\tilde{\eta}_{it}$ in equations (10), (25), (26), and (27). For example, if the disturbance $\tilde{\eta}_{it}$ in (10) is independent from one security to another and if the distribution of $\tilde{\eta}_{it}$ is the same for all securities, then a slightly sophisticated appeal to the Gauss-Markov theorem* can be used to imply that the least squares values of $\tilde{\gamma}_{1t}, \tilde{\gamma}_{2t}, \tilde{\gamma}_{3t}$, and $\tilde{\gamma}_{4t}$ are the returns on the portfolios that have the smallest possible return variances among portfolios that satisfy, respectively, the constraints on portfolio weights described by (23), (24), (8), and (9).

The Gauss-Markov theorem concerns the properties of the least squares estimators of the coefficients in a regression where the estimators are based on a sample from the process of interest. The trick in applying the theorem in the present case is to note that although the least squares $\tilde{\gamma}_{jt}$ are portfolio returns that are computed from the entire population of returns for month t, the process itself generates returns each month, so that the population of time periods from which the $\tilde{\gamma}_{jt}$ are drawn is in principle infinite. In this view, we can regard $\tilde{\gamma}_{jt}$ as an estimator of $E(\tilde{\gamma}_j)$. Given the appropriate properties of the disturbances, the Gauss-Markov theorem then says that the least squares value of $\tilde{\gamma}_{jt}$ minimizes the variance of $\tilde{\gamma}_{jt} - E(\tilde{\gamma}_j)$, the error in $\tilde{\gamma}_{jt}$ as an estimator of $E(\tilde{\gamma}_j)$. For any given $\tilde{\gamma}_{jt}$, this is precisely the variance we wish to minimize.

---

*See, for example, Theil (1971, p. 119) for a general discussion of the Gauss-Markov Theorem.

With these formalities behind us, we can now look at things from a more intuitive perspective. In effect, when applied to (10), the least squares procedure attempts to find portfolio returns $\tilde{\gamma}_{1t}$, $\tilde{\gamma}_{2t}$, $\tilde{\gamma}_{3t}$, and $\tilde{\gamma}_{4t}$ that have the smallest variances subject to the constraints of (23), (24), (8), and (9), but where the search is carried out under the assumption that the disturbances $\tilde{\eta}_{it}$ for different securities are independent and identically distributed.

Analogous comments apply to the least squares values of $\tilde{\gamma}_{jt}$ in (25) to (27). For example, when applied to (26), the least squares approach searches for the values of $\tilde{\gamma}_{1t}$, $\tilde{\gamma}_{2t}$, and $\tilde{\gamma}_{3t}$ that have the smallest possible variances subject to the constraints of (23), (24), and (8). Since $\sigma(\tilde{\epsilon}_i)$ does not appear as an explanatory variable in (26), the constraints (23d), (24d), and (8d) are ignored. Since there are fewer constraints on the portfolio weights, we expect that the least squares portfolio returns $\tilde{\gamma}_{1t}$, $\tilde{\gamma}_{2t}$, and $\tilde{\gamma}_{3t}$ obtained from (26) will have smaller variances than the $\tilde{\gamma}_{1t}$, $\tilde{\gamma}_{2t}$, and $\tilde{\gamma}_{3t}$ obtained from (10). Likewise, when applied to (27), the least squares approach tries to find the smallest variances $\tilde{\gamma}_{1t}$, $\tilde{\gamma}_{2t}$, and $\tilde{\gamma}_{4t}$ that satisfy the constraints of (23), (24), and (9), except that the constraints (23c), (24c), and (9c) on the weighted average of the β_{iM}^2 are ignored. Again, we expect that ignoring these constraints will lead to $\tilde{\gamma}_{1t}$, $\tilde{\gamma}_{2t}$, and $\tilde{\gamma}_{4t}$ which have smaller variances than those obtained from (10). Finally, when applied to (25), the least squares approach searches for $\tilde{\gamma}_{1t}$ and $\tilde{\gamma}_{2t}$ which have the smallest possible variances, subject only to the constraints of (23a) and (23b) for $\tilde{\gamma}_{1t}$ and (24a) and (24b) for $\tilde{\gamma}_{2t}$. Because fewer constraints are imposed on the portfolio weights, we expect the $\tilde{\gamma}_{1t}$ and $\tilde{\gamma}_{2t}$ obtained from (25) to have smaller variances than the $\tilde{\gamma}_{1t}$ and $\tilde{\gamma}_{2t}$ obtained from (10), (26), and (27).

In searching for the smallest variance values of the $\tilde{\gamma}_{jt}$, the least squares approach makes the same assumption about the disturbances $\tilde{\eta}_{it}$ in (25) to (27) that is made for (10). The $\tilde{\eta}_{it}$ are assumed to be independent and identically distributed across securities i. This assumption, like any assumption, is not a completely accurate description of the world. To the extent that it is inaccurate, the least squares approach can be misled in its search for smallest variance portfolio returns. Moreover, since the extent to which the assumption is valid is likely to be different for (10), (25), (26), and (27), we might find that adding and dropping constraints does not, in fact, have the predicted effects on the variances of the resulting portfolio returns. There is, however, no need to speculate. We carry out time series of cross-sectional regressions for each of the equations (10), (25), (26), and (27). We can compute the variances of the time series of given $\tilde{\gamma}_{jt}$ in different equations and use these variances to decide which equation provides the most reliable inferences about any given hypothesis.

G. Capital Market Efficiency: The Behavior of Returns Through Time

The tests discussed so far propose to use average values of the $\tilde{\gamma}_{jt}$ in equations (10) and (25) to (27) in order to test the propositions of the two-parameter model about expected returns. It is also possible to obtain tests based on the period-by-period behavior of the $\tilde{\gamma}_{jt}$. The analysis takes us back to the market efficiency concept introduced in Chapter 5.

The models of capital market equilibrium of Chapter 8 assume a perfect capital market in which information available at any time is costlessly available to all investors. Moreover, the complete agreement assumption of these models says that at any time $t-1$, investors agree on the implications of the available information for the joint distribution of security prices at time t. From here it is a short and logical step to assume that the market is also efficient in the sense that the common assessment of the joint distribution of security prices makes full and correct use of all information available at $t-1$.*

In the notation of Chapter 5, market efficiency says that

$$\phi_{t-1}^m = \phi_{t-1}, \tag{32}$$

$$f_m(p_{1t}, \ldots, p_{nt} \mid \phi_{t-1}^m) = f(p_{1t}, \ldots, p_{nt} \mid \phi_{t-1}), \tag{33}$$

where ϕ_{t-1}^m is the information used by the market in setting prices at $t-1$, ϕ_{t-1} is the information available at $t-1$, $f_m(p_{1t}, \ldots, p_{nt} \mid \phi_{t-1}^m)$ is the joint distribution of security prices for time t assessed by the market at $t-1$, and $f(p_{1t}, \ldots, p_{nt} \mid \phi_{t-1})$ is the true joint distribution implied by ϕ_{t-1}. Equations (32) and (33) say that in assessing the joint distribution of prices for t, the market correctly uses all information available at $t-1$.

If the market correctly uses all information in assessing the joint distribution of security prices for time t, then when prices are set at $t-1$,

$$E_m(\tilde{R}_{it} \mid \phi_{t-1}^m) = E(\tilde{R}_{it} \mid \phi_{t-1}), \quad i = 1, \ldots, n, \tag{34}$$

the market's perception of the expected return on security i from $t-1$ to t is the true expected return. If the market sets prices at $t-1$ so that the market portfolio M is on the minimum variance boundary, then

$$E_m(\tilde{R}_{it} \mid \phi_{t-1}^m) = E_m(\tilde{R}_{0Mt} \mid \phi_{t-1}^m)$$

$$+ [E_m(\tilde{R}_{Mt} \mid \phi_{t-1}^m) - E_m(\tilde{R}_{0Mt}^m \mid \phi_{t-1}^m)] \, \beta_{iM}$$

---

*This use of the word "efficient" is not to be confused with portfolio efficiency. The terminology is unfortunately standard.

$$= E(\tilde{R}_{it} | \phi_{t-1}) = E(\tilde{R}_{0Mt} | \phi_{t-1})$$
$$+ [E(\tilde{R}_{Mt} | \phi_{t-1}) - E(\tilde{R}_{0Mt} | \phi_{t-1})] \beta_{iM}. \qquad (35)$$

In words, the market's view of the expected return-risk relationship for securities in M is the correct view.*

The general implication of (35) is that there is no way to use information available at $t - 1$ to make meaningful predictions about how the returns on securities at time t will deviate from the expected return-risk relationship for securities in M that characterizes the various models of market equilibrium. Thus, if (35) is valid, then in (10) and (26), $E(\tilde{\gamma}_{3t} | \phi_{t-1}) = 0$. If the market correctly uses all the available information ϕ_{t-1} in setting prices at $t - 1$, and if prices are set so that the market's expected returns conform to the two-parameter model, then there is no way to use information in ϕ_{t-1} as the basis of a correct assessment that the relationship between the expected returns on securities and their risks in M is nonlinear. Likewise, if (35) is valid, then in (10) and (27), $E(\tilde{\gamma}_{4t} | \phi_{t-1}) = 0$, and in (10) and (25) to (27), $E(\tilde{\eta}_{it} | \phi_{t-1}) = 0$; that is, there is no way to use information in ϕ_{t-1} as the basis of correct non-zero assessments of the means of the distributions of the non-β_{iM} risk coefficient $\tilde{\gamma}_{4t}$ and of the disturbances $\tilde{\eta}_{it}$.

In testing these hypotheses about $\tilde{\gamma}_{3t}$, $\tilde{\gamma}_{4t}$, and the $\tilde{\eta}_{it}$, we concentrate on one subset of ϕ_{t-1}, the time series of past values of $\tilde{\gamma}_{3t}$, $\tilde{\gamma}_{4t}$, and $\tilde{\eta}_{it}$. As summarized by (35), capital market efficiency in the two-parameter model implies that there is no way to use the period-by-period behavior of past values of $\tilde{\gamma}_{3t}$ as the basis of correct nonzero assessments of expected future values of $\tilde{\gamma}_{3t}$; the sequence of past values carries no information about expected future values. Likewise, the time series of past values of $\tilde{\gamma}_{4t}$ and $\tilde{\eta}_{it}$ have no information about the expected future values of these variables. Recall from Chapters 4 and 5 that serial correlations are a natural way to test whether the expected future values of a random variable depend on past values. If (35) is valid, the autocorrelations of $\tilde{\gamma}_{3t}$, $\tilde{\gamma}_{4t}$, and $\tilde{\eta}_{it}$ are zero for all lags. We use sample autocorrelations to test these propositions.

The hypothesis that the capital market is efficient and that the market sets prices at time $t - 1$ so that the market portfolio M is on the positively sloped segment of the boundary of minimum variance portfolios has implications for the behavior of $\tilde{\gamma}_{2t}$ in (10) and (25) to (27). In each of these equations, $\tilde{\gamma}_{2t}$ is a portfolio return with expected value equal to $E(\tilde{R}_M) - E(\tilde{R}_{0M})$. If securities are priced so that the market perceives M to be on the positively sloped

---

*Since β_{iM} depends on the joint distribution of prices at time t, we should also note that (32) and (33) imply $\beta_{iM}(\phi_{t-1}^m) = \beta_{iM}(\phi_{t-1})$; that is, the market correctly uses all information in assessing the risk of any security in the market portfolio M. For the moment, however, we choose not to complicate the notation in the text in this way. A detailed discussion of problems that arise in assessing risk measures comes later.

segment of the minimum variance boundary, and if the market is efficient, then $E(\tilde{R}_{Mt}|\phi_{t-1}) - E(\tilde{R}_{oMt}|\phi_{t-1}) = E(\tilde{\gamma}_{2t}|\phi_{t-1}) > 0.0$; there is no way to use any information available at $t-1$ as the basis of a correct negative assessment of the expected value of $\tilde{\gamma}_{2t}$. We test only a specialized form of this hypothesis. We assume that $E(\tilde{R}_{Mt}|\phi_{t-1}) - E(\tilde{R}_{oMt}|\phi_{t-1})$ is not only positive but constant through time. We then test this proposition with sample auto-correlations of $\tilde{\gamma}_{2t}$, all of which should be indistinguishable from zero if the proposition is valid.

Finally, in equations (10) and (25) to (27) the least squares values of $\tilde{\gamma}_{1t}$ are the returns on standard zero-β_{pM} portfolios. If the Sharpe-Lintner version of the two-parameter model is valid, $E_m(\tilde{R}_{oMt}|\phi_{t-1}^m) = R_{Ft}$; that is the market sets prices so that it perceives the expected return on any security or portfolio whose return is uncorrelated with the return on M to be equal to R_{Ft}. If the market correctly uses available information, $E_m(\tilde{R}_{oMt}|\phi_{t-1}^m) = E(\tilde{R}_{oMt}|\phi_{t-1}) = R_{Ft}$; the true expected return on zero-β_{iM} securities and portfolios is R_{Ft}. One implication of this is that the time series of past values of $\tilde{\gamma}_{1t} - R_{Ft}$ cannot be used as the basis of correct nonzero assessments of expected future values of $\tilde{\gamma}_{1t} - R_{Ft}$, which in turn implies that the auto-correlations of $\tilde{\gamma}_{1t} - R_{Ft}$ are zero for all lags.

Introducing the concept of market efficiency has not produced hypotheses about expected returns that are different from those developed in the initial discussion of (1). Equation (35), after all, is just the expected return-risk equation (1) with some additional notation whose purpose is to emphasize the characteristics of the pricing process in an efficient market. Discussing market efficiency in the context of the two-parameter model has, however, made us aware of tests that were not apparent in the initial discussion of (1). The tests that came out of the discussion of (1) involve using averages of the least squares values of $\tilde{\gamma}_{1t}$, $\tilde{\gamma}_{2t}$, $\tilde{\gamma}_{3t}$, and $\tilde{\gamma}_{4t}$ in equations (10) and (25) to (27) to test the propositions of (1) about the expected values of these variables. The discussion of market efficiency leads to tests based on the period-by-period behavior of the variables.

III. Details of the Methodology

The least squares values of the $\tilde{\gamma}_{jt}$ in equations (10) and (25) to (27) give us the inputs for testing the implications of a two-parameter world for expected returns. Empirical realities, however, present us with unavoidable complications. We assume above that the values of the risk measures β_{iM} and $\sigma(\tilde{\epsilon}_i)$ of different securities are known. In fact they must be estimated from return data. We also assume that the components of the returns on the market portfolio M, the returns on all investment assets, and their corresponding value weights are available. In fact, the empirical tests deal only with common stocks on the New York Stock Exchange, and in the absence of the appropriate value weights, an equally weighted portfolio of these stocks, the portfolio we have heretofore called m, is used instead of M. We discuss first the problems that this causes and then the problems that arise from using estimates of risk measures.

A. Application of the Approach to the Equally Weighted Market Portfolio m

The role of the value-weighted market portfolio in the preceding analysis can be played by any portfolio that must be efficient, or at least minimum variance, when a market equilibrium is established at time $t-1$. Although the supposition has no rigorous justification, suppose a market equilibrium requires that m, the equally weighted portfolio of NYSE stocks, be a minimum variance portfolio. Then the expected return-risk equation for a minimum variance portfolio applies to m. For any security i in m, we have

$$E(\tilde{R}_{it}) = E(\tilde{R}_{0mt}) + [E(\tilde{R}_{mt}) - E(\tilde{R}_{0mt})]\,\beta_{im}, \qquad (36)$$

where

$$\beta_{im} = \frac{\mathrm{cov}\,(\tilde{R}_i, \tilde{R}_m)}{\sigma^2(\tilde{R}_m)} \qquad (37)$$

is the risk of security i in m measured relative to the risk or variance of the portfolio's return, and $E(\tilde{R}_{0mt})$ is the expected return on any security in m, or any portfolios of the securities in m, whose return is uncorrelated with the return on m.

Like (1), equation (36) is linear in the risk measure β_{im}; β_{im} is the only measure of the risk security i that appears in (36); and if we assume that m is along the positively sloped segment of the minimum variance boundary, then $[E(\tilde{R}_{mt}) - E(\tilde{R}_{0mt})] > 0$, so that (36) implies a positive relationship between the expected returns on securities and their risk in m. In short, the testable implications of (36) are the same as those of (1), the expected return-risk equation implied by the fact that a market equilibrium requires that the value-weighted market portfolio M be a minimum variance portfolio.

Moreover, the approach described in Section II for testing whether M is a minimum variance portfolio can be used to test whether the pricing of NYSE common stocks is consistent with the proposition that m is a minimum variance portfolio. Thus, consider

$$\tilde{R}_{it} = \tilde{\gamma}_{1t} + \tilde{\gamma}_{2t}\beta_{im} + \tilde{\gamma}_{3t}\beta_{im}^2 + \tilde{\gamma}_{4t}\sigma(\tilde{\epsilon}_i) + \tilde{\eta}_{it} \tag{38}$$

$$\tilde{R}_{it} = \tilde{\gamma}_{1t} + \tilde{\gamma}_{2t}\beta_{im} + \tilde{\gamma}_{3t}\beta_{im}^2 + \tilde{\eta}_{it} \tag{39}$$

$$\tilde{R}_{it} = \tilde{\gamma}_{1t} + \tilde{\gamma}_{2t}\beta_{im} + \tilde{\gamma}_{4t}\sigma(\tilde{\epsilon}_i) + \tilde{\eta}_{it} \tag{40}$$

$$\tilde{R}_{it} = \tilde{\gamma}_{1t} + \tilde{\gamma}_{2t}\beta_{im} + \tilde{\eta}_{it}, \tag{41}$$

where $\sigma(\tilde{\epsilon}_i)$ is now the standard deviation of the disturbance in the market model relationship between $\tilde{R}_{it}$ and $\tilde{R}_{mt}$,

$$\tilde{R}_{it} = \alpha_{im} + \beta_{im}\tilde{R}_{mt} + \tilde{\epsilon}_{it} \tag{42}$$

$$\alpha_{im} = E(\tilde{R}_{it}) - \beta_{iM}E(\tilde{R}_{mt}), \tag{43}$$

and where the assumption that the joint distribution of security returns is multivariate normal implies all the properties of (42) discussed in Chapters 3 and 4.

Equations (38) to (41) are just (10) and (25) to (27), but with β_{im}, β_{im}^2, and the new version of $\sigma(\tilde{\epsilon}_i)$ used as explanatory variables. If the same substitution of explanatory variables is made in the matrix $\underline{C}$ of (12), then the analysis of (11) to (22) implies that the least squares values of the $\tilde{\gamma}_{jt}$ in (38) to (41), obtained from cross-sectional regressions of security returns on the relevant explanatory variables, are the returns on portfolios that have properties analogous to the least squares values of the $\tilde{\gamma}_{jt}$ in equations (10) and (25) to (27). For example, the least squares value of $\tilde{\gamma}_{1t}$ in (38) is the return on a standard portfolio that has $\beta_{pm} = 0.0$; $\tilde{\gamma}_{2t}$ is the return on a zero-investment portfolio where the weighted average value of β_{im} is 1.0; $\tilde{\gamma}_{3t}$ is the return on a zero-investment portfolio where the weighted average value of β_{im}^2 is 1.0; and $\tilde{\gamma}_{4t}$ is the return on a zero-investment portfolio where the weighted average of $\sigma(\tilde{\epsilon}_i)$ for individual securities is 1.0. As in equations (10) and (25) to (27), the least squares value of a given $\tilde{\gamma}_{jt}$ in (38) to (41) focuses on the effects of the explanatory variable of interest by choosing portfolio weights that zero out the effects of other explanatory variables in the equation. Moreover, as in equations (10) and (25) to (27), if the $\tilde{\eta}_{it}$ in (38) to (41) are independent and identically distributed for different securities i, the least squares $\tilde{\gamma}_{jt}$ are the "smallest variance" portfolios that focus on different explanatory variables in the manner described above, so they provide the most reliable tests of the proposition that securities are priced so that m is a minimum variance portfolio. The only problem with all of this is that we don't have a model of market equilibrium that tells us that m must be a minimum variance portfolio.

Given that m is to be used in the tests, there are two justifications. First, in empirical work one usually must settle for proxies for the variables called for by a theory. The equally weighted portfolio of NYSE stocks, m, might be viewed as a proxy for M, the value-weighted portfolio of all investment assests. This tack is, however, open to valid arguments as to whether m is a reasonable proxy for M. An equally weighted portfolio is rather different from a value-weighted portfolio. More important, although investment in NYSE stocks is a large fraction of the total investment in the common stocks of publicly held companies, the NYSE does not cover investments in bonds, privately held real estate, and consumer durables, which together are a much larger fraction of invested wealth than common stocks.

The second approach to justifying the use of m in the tests is to say that since m is a diversified portfolio of many securities, perhaps it is reasonable to assume that it is "close enough" to a minimum variance portfolio to be a meaningful basis for tests of the two-parameter model. For those with tastes for rigor (and I include myself in that group), this approach is unaesthetic. Nevertheless, from the viewpoint of the empiricist (and I also include myself in that group), the approach can provide its own justification. If the testable hypotheses drawn from (36) are upheld by the data, then it seems reasonable to conclude both that the two-parameter model is a meaningful approxima- tion of how securities are priced in the capital market and that securities are priced so that the equally weighted portfolio m of NYSE stocks is a minimum variance portfolio.

Finally, there is an important exception to the statement that (1) and (36) have the same testable implications, and the exception acquires some impor- tance in the empirical results. The Sharpe-Lintner hypothesis that $E(\tilde{R}_{0Mt}) = R_{Ft}$ cannot be applied to the portfolio m. Even if the Sharpe-Lintner model is the relevant view of the world, it is not the case that $E(\tilde{R}_{0mt}) = R_{Ft}$. Recall that $E(\tilde{R}_{0Mt})$ is the intercept on the $E(\tilde{R}_p)$ axis of the line tangent to the boundary of minimum variance portfolios of positive variance securities at the point corresponding to the value-weighted market portfolio M. In the Sharpe-Lintner model, a market equilibrium requires that this intercept also be the risk-free rate of interest R_{Ft}. If the equally weighted portfolio m is also a minimum variance portfolio, then $E(\tilde{R}_{0mt})$ is the intercept on the $E(\tilde{R}_p)$ axis of the line tangent to the minimum variance boundary at the point corresponding to m. Since m and M are not the same portfolio, $E(\tilde{R}_{0mt}) \neq E(\tilde{R}_{0Mt}) = R_{Ft}$. We shall have more to say later about where $E(\tilde{R}_{0mt})$ is likely to be relative to R_{Ft}.

B. The Portfolio Approach to Estimating Risk Measures

To test the implications of (36), we must still face another serious problem. Equation (36) is in terms of the true values of the risk measure β_{im}, and empirical tests require that estimates b_{im} be used.

ESTIMATES OF RISK FROM THE MARKET MODEL

One approach is to build on the assumption underlying the two-parameter model that the joint distribution of security returns is multivariate normal. This means that the joint distribution of the return on any security and the return on the portfolio m is bivariate normal. If the bivariate normal joint distribution of $\tilde{R}_{it}$ and $\tilde{R}_{mt}$ is also the same or stationary through time, then the market model of (42) and the methods of Chapters 3 and 4 can be used to estimate β_{im} and to assess the sampling properties of the estimates. We should note, however, that empirical realities have forced on us an assumption—that the joint distribution of $\tilde{R}_{it}$ and $\tilde{R}_{mt}$ is stationary through time—which is not required by the two-parameter model. If we are to use the methods of Chapters 3 and 4 to estimate β_{im}, the stationarity assumption is required, at least for the sampling period to be used in the estimation.

It is interesting at this point to recall the discussion of the complete agreement assumption in Chapter 8. We argued there that this assumption is a sensible approximation to the world when the joint distribution of security returns is the same through time. Then history leads investors to a correct consensus about the joint distribution of future returns. We are now arguing that the stationarity assumption is a necessary ingredient for successful tests of the two-parameter model. Thus, although this assumption is not an explicit part of two-parameter theory, it makes the assumptions of the theory more palatable, and it is pretty much a precondition for tests of the theory.

THE ERRORS-IN-THE-VARIABLES PROBLEM

The most direct approach to the tests would seem to be to obtain estimates b_{im} of the β_{im} of individual securities, plug these into equations (38) to (41), and then proceed. The problem with such a brute force approach is that any estimate b_{im} differs from the true β_{im} by an estimation error. If the errors are typically large, there is a serious "errors-in-the-variables" problem.

There is a large statistical literature on the errors-in-the-variables problem that we do not need to consider in any formal way here. In intuitive terms, the problem centers on the fact that if a proxy explanatory variable is used in a least squares regression (e.g., b_{im} rather than β_{im}), the computed coefficients do not have the same properties as if the true explanatory variable were used. For example, the least squares value of $\tilde{\gamma}_{1t}$ for (41) is the return for month t on a zero-β_{pm} portfolio; the true value of β_{pm} for this portfolio is zero. Suppose, however, that we substitute estimates b_{im} for the true values of β_{im} that appear in (41) and then carry out the cross-sectional regression. It will then turn out that the least squares value of $\tilde{\gamma}_{1t}$ is the return on a standard portfolio where the weights assigned to individual securities are such that the weighted average of the b_{im} is zero; that is, $\tilde{\gamma}_{1t}$ is the return on a zero-b_{pm} portfolio. Since each of the b_{im} is just an estimate of the corresponding true β_{im}, $\tilde{\gamma}_{1t}$ is not the return on a portfolio where the true β_{pm} is zero.

The arguments are quite general. If one uses estimates instead of the true values of the explanatory variables that appear in (38) to (41), then the analysis of equations (11) to (22) will imply that the least squares values of the $\tilde{\gamma}_{jt}$ are portfolio returns that focus on the effects of given explanatory variables while zeroing out the effects of others. All the focusing and zeroing out, however, will be in terms of the estimates rather than the true values of the explanatory variables. To the extent that the estimates differ from the true values of the explanatory variables, the least squares portfolio returns are out of focus for the purpose of testing the implications of (36).

PROBLEM III.B

1. We have long known that for any portfolio p,

$$\beta_{pm} = \frac{\text{cov}(\tilde{R}_p, \tilde{R}_m)}{\sigma^2(\tilde{R}_m)} = \sum_{i=1}^{n} x_{ip} \frac{\text{cov}(\tilde{R}_i, \tilde{R}_m)}{\sigma^2(\tilde{R}_m)} = \sum_{i=1}^{n} x_{ip} \beta_{im}.$$

Show that the same relationship holds between the estimates b_{pm} and the b_{im} of individual securities.

ANSWER

1. For any portfolio p,

$$\bar{R}_p = \frac{\sum_{t=1}^{T} R_{pt}}{T} = \frac{\sum_{t=1}^{T} \sum_{i=1}^{n} x_{ip} R_{it}}{T} = \sum_{i=1}^{n} x_{ip} \frac{\sum_{t=1}^{T} R_{it}}{T} = \sum_{i=1}^{n} x_{ip} \bar{R}_i.$$

Thus,

$$b_{pm} = \frac{\sum_{t=1}^{T} (R_{pt} - \bar{R}_p)(R_{mt} - \bar{R}_m)}{\sum_{t=1}^{T} (R_{mt} - \bar{R}_m)^2}$$

$$= \frac{\sum_{t=1}^{T} \left(\sum_{i=1}^{n} x_{ip} R_{it} - \sum_{i=1}^{n} x_{ip} \bar{R}_i \right)(R_{mt} - \bar{R}_m)}{\sum_{t=1}^{T} (R_{mt} - \bar{R}_m)^2}$$

$$= \sum_{i=1}^{n} x_{ip} \frac{\sum_{t=1}^{T} (R_{it} - \bar{R}_i)(R_{mt} - \bar{R}_m)}{\sum_{t=1}^{T} (R_{mt} - \bar{R}_m)^2}$$

$$b_{pm} = \sum_{i=1}^{n} x_{ip} b_{im}.$$

The general idea behind the solution to the errors-in-the-variables problem is direct. We try to minimize the problem by reducing the errors in the estimates of the risk measures. Since, from Chapter 3, the sampling variance of $\tilde{b}_{im}$ as an estimator of β_{im} is

$$\sigma^2(\tilde{b}_{im}) = \frac{\sigma^2(\tilde{\epsilon}_i)}{\sum_{t=1}^{T} (R_{mt} - \bar{R}_m)^2}, \tag{44}$$

it would seem that one way to accomplish this goal is to compute b_{im} from long time series of monthly returns. This ensures that the sum of squares in the denominator of (44) is large, so that $\sigma^2(\tilde{b}_{im})$ is small. We know from Chapter 4, however, that this approach leans too heavily on the assumption that the value of β_{im} is stationary through time. The values of β_{im} of individual securities do wander slightly through time, and the optimal period for estimation from monthly data is roughly 5–10 years. Recall from Chapter 4 that with 5–10 years of monthly data, the estimates b_{im} leave substantial uncertainty about the true values; that is, the errors in the b_{im} of individual securities are likely to be large relative to the true β_{im}.

An alternative approach to reducing the errors in estimates of risk measures is to work on the numerator in (44), that is, to reduce $\sigma^2(\tilde{\epsilon}_i)$, the variance of the market model disturbance. The way we do this is to work with portfolios rather than individual securities. To see the basis of the approach, recall that multivariate normality of security returns implies that the joint distribution of the return on any portfolio p and the return on the portfolio m is bivariate normal, so that there are market model relationships like (42) for portfolios as well as for individual securities. For any portfolio p, we have

$$\tilde{R}_{pt} = \alpha_{pm} + \beta_{pm} \tilde{R}_{mt} + \tilde{\epsilon}_{pt}. \tag{45}$$

The portfolio return disturbance $\tilde{\epsilon}_{pt}$ in (45) is, however, just the weighted average of security return disturbances $\tilde{\epsilon}_{it}$. To the extent that the $\tilde{\epsilon}_{it}$ for different securities are less than perfectly positively correlated, there is a "diversification effect," and $\sigma^2(\tilde{\epsilon}_p)$ can be expected to be smaller than the $\sigma^2(\tilde{\epsilon}_i)$ of individual securities. The result is that $\sigma^2(\tilde{b}_{pm})$ is generally smaller for portfolios than for individual securities. This means that the errors-in-the-variables problem is likely to be less serious if tests of (36) are carried out in terms of portfolios rather than individual securities.

In brief, then, the intention is to calculate the least squares values of the coefficients $\tilde{\gamma}_{jt}$ in (38) to (41) and to use these to test the various hypotheses implied by (36) about the relationship between expected return and risk within the portfolio m. In place of the returns on individual securities that appear on the left of these equations, we substitute returns on portfolios; and the security risk measures β_{im} that appear on the right in these equations are replaced by estimates b_{pm} relevant for the portfolios that appear on the left of the equations.

CHOOSING PORTFOLIOS AND THE REGRESSION PHENOMENON

We present evidence shortly that the estimates b_{pm} for portfolios are indeed much more reliable than those for individual securities. The portfolio approach, however, also raises problems that center in large part on how the portfolios used in the analysis are chosen. When securities are combined into portfolios, some of the information in the data about the relationship between risk and expected return is lost. For example, if the allocation of securities to portfolios is random, and if the portfolios formed contain many securities, the portfolios will have b_{pm} much more closely concentrated about one than individual securities, which means that we can expect to observe only a narrow range of the expected return-risk relationship. In the extreme case where all the portfolio risk measures turn out to have about the same value, forming portfolios destroys all of the information about the expected return-risk relationship that is potentially contained in the security return data.

To reduce the loss of information caused by working with portfolios, one forms portfolios in such a way as to guarantee that a wide range of b_{pm} is obtained. This is done by allocating securities to portfolios on the basis of ranked values of b_{im}. If naïvely executed, however, such a procedure could result in what is called a "regression phenomenon." When one ranks the b_{im} of all securities, one is to some extent ranking the estimation errors in the b_{im}. A large positive estimation error is likely to result in a high b_{im}, while the reverse is true of a large negative estimation error. Forming portfolios on the basis of ranked b_{im} thus causes bunching of positive and negative sampling errors within portfolios, especially at the extremes of the b_{im} range. The result is that the larger values of b_{pm} would tend to overestimate the true β_{pm}, while the lower b_{pm} would tend to be underestimated.

The regression phenomenon can be avoided by forming portfolios from ranked b_{im} computed from data for one time period, but then using a subsequent period to obtain the b_{pm} for these portfolios that are used in the tests. The errors in the estimates from the fresh data are likely to be independent of the estimation errors for the portfolio formation period, so that in the new portfolio b_{pm} there is no regression phenomenon. We also expect that when fresh data are used, the extreme b_{pm} will be less extreme than for the period of portfolio formation. In the new data there will be some tendency for all the b_{pm} to "regress" toward 1, that is, to become less extreme. This is the basis of the term "regression phenomenon."

The errors-in-the-variables problem and the regression phenomenon that arises when the portfolio approach is used to solve it were first pointed out by Blume (1968). The portfolio approach is used by Black, Jensen, and Scholes (1972), who offer a solution to the resulting regression phenomenon which is similar to that of Fama and MacBeth (1973). The approach presented here is that of Fama and MacBeth.

DETAILS OF THE APPROACH

The specifics of the Fama-MacBeth approach are as follows. Let n be the total number of securities to be allocated to portfolios, and let int $(n/20)$ be the largest integer equal to or less than $n/20$. Using the first four years (1926–1929) of monthly return data, 20 portfolios of NYSE stocks are formed on the basis of ranked b_{im} for individual securities. The middle 18 portfolios each have int $(n/20)$ securities. If n is even, the first and last portfolios each have int $(n/20) + \frac{1}{2} [n - 20 \text{ int } (2/20)]$ securities. The last (highest b_{pm}) portfolio gets an additional security if n is odd.

The following five years (1930–1934) of data are then used to recompute the b_{im}, and these are averaged across securities within portfolios to obtain 20 initial portfolio b_{pmt} for the risk-return tests. Thus, within portfolios, equal weights are applied to individual securities. The subscript t is added to b_{pmt} to indicate that for each month t of the following four years (1935–1938) these b_{pmt} are recomputed as simple averages of individual security b_{im}, thus adjusting the portfolio b_{pmt} month-by-month to allow for delisting of individual securities. The component values of b_{im} for securities are themselves updated yearly; that is, they are recomputed from monthly returns from 1930 through 1935, 1936, or 1937.

The month-by-month returns on the 20 portfolios, with equal weighting of individual securities each month, are also computed for the four-year period 1935–1938. For each month t of this period, the least squares method is used to compute γ_{jt} in*

---

*Since we are talking about results for a given historical period, the tildes that heretofore appeared are henceforth dropped.

$$R_{pt} = \gamma_{1t} + \gamma_{2t}b_{pm,t-1} + \gamma_{3t}b_{pm,t-1}^2 + \gamma_{4t}\bar{s}_{p,t-1}(e_i) + \eta_{pt} \tag{46}$$

$$R_{pt} = \gamma_{1t} + \gamma_{2t}b_{pm,t-1} + \gamma_{3t}b_{pm,t-1}^2 + \eta_{pt} \tag{47}$$

$$R_{pt} = \gamma_{1t} + \gamma_{2t}b_{pm,t-1} + \gamma_{4t}\bar{s}_{p,t-1}(e_i) + \eta_{pt} \tag{48}$$

$$R_{pt} = \gamma_{1t} + \gamma_{2t}b_{pm,t-1} + \eta_{pt}, \quad p = 1, 2, \ldots, 20. \tag{49}$$

The explanatory variable $b_{pm,t-1}$ is the average b_{im} for securities in portfolio p discussed above; $b_{pm,t-1}^2$ is the average of the squared values of these b_{im} and is thus somewhat mislabeled; and $\bar{s}_{p,t-1}(e_i)$ is likewise the average of $s(e_i)$ for securities in portfolio p. The $s(e_i)$ are sample standard deviations of market model residuals for individual securities; that is, they are the usual estimates of $\sigma(\tilde{e}_i)$ in (42). They are computed from data for the same period as the component b_{im} of $b_{pm,t-1}$; and, like these b_{im}, they are updated annually.

Equations (46) to (49) are equations (38) to (41) averaged across the securities in a portfolio, with estimates $b_{pm,t-1}, b_{pm,t-1}^2$, and $\bar{s}_{p,t-1}(e_i)$ used as explanatory variables. The results from these equations, the time series of month-by-month values of $\gamma_{1t}, \gamma_{2t}, \gamma_{3t}$, and γ_{4t} for the four-year period 1935–1938 are the inputs for the tests of the implications of (36) for this period. To get results for other periods, the general steps described above are repeated. Specifically, seven years of data are used to form portfolios; the next five years are used to compute initial values of the explanatory variables; and then the least squares values of the γ_{jt} are computed month-by-month for the following four-year period.

The nine different portfolio formation periods (all except the first are seven years in length), initial five-year estimation periods, and testing periods (all except the last are four years in length) are shown in Table 9.1. Fama and MacBeth explain the choice of four-year testing periods as a balance of computation costs against the desire to reform portfolios frequently. The choice of seven-year portfolio formation periods and five- to eight-year periods for the estimates $b_{pm,t-1}$ reflects the desire to balance the statistical power obtained with a large sample from a stationary process against potential problems caused by any nonconstancy of the β_{im}. The choices here are in line with the results of Gonedes (1973). His results also led Fama and MacBeth to require that to be included in a portfolio, a security available in the first month of a testing period must also have data for all five years of the preceding estimation period and for at least four years of the portfolio formation period. The total number of securities available in the first month of each testing period and the number (n) of securities meeting the data requirement are shown in Table 9.1.

Finally, all the tests are "predictive" in the sense that the explanatory

TABLE 9.1

Portfolio Formation, Estimation, and Testing Periods

	1	2	3	4	5	6	7	8	9
Portfolio formation period	1926–29	1927–33	1931–37	1935–41	1939–45	1943–49	1947–53	1951–57	1955–61
Initial estimation period	1930–34	1934–38	1938–42	1942–46	1946–50	1950–54	1954–58	1958–62	1962–66
Testing period	1935–38	1939–42	1943–46	1947–50	1951–54	1955–58	1959–62	1963–66	1967–68
No. of stocks listed	710	779	804	908	1,011	1,053	1,065	1,162	1,261
No. of stocks (n) used	435	576	607	704	751	802	856	858	845

SOURCE: Eugene F. Fama and James D. MacBeth, "Risk, Return, and Equilibrium: Empirical Tests," *Journal of Political Economy* 71 (May–June 1973): 618–619.

variables $b_{pm,t-1}$, $b_{pm,t-1}^2$ and $\bar{s}_{p,t-1}(e_i)$ that appear in (46) to (49) are computed from a period prior to the month of the returns, the R_{pt} that appear on the left-hand side of these equations. Thus, in computing the least squares values of the γ_{jt} in (46) to (49), we are looking at the relationships between returns for month t and estimates of risk measures that were available at the beginning of the month. Having emphasized the predictive nature of the tests, we can simplify the notation by henceforth referring to the explanatory variables in (46) to (49) as b_{pm}, b_{pm}^2 and $\bar{s}_p(e_i)$.

SOME EVIDENCE ON THE EFFECTIVENESS OF THE PORTFOLIO APPROACH

Table 9.2 shows the values of the 20 portfolio b_{pm} and their standard errors $s(b_{pm})$ for each of the nine five-year estimation periods of Table 9.1. Also shown are $\hat{\rho}(R_p, R_m)^2$, the coefficient of determination between R_{pt} and R_{mt}; $s(R_p)$, the standard deviation of R_{pt}; $s(e_p)$, the standard deviation of the portfolio residuals from the market model, not to be confused with $\bar{s}_p(e_i)$, the average of the residual standard deviations for individual securities in p, which is also shown. The b_{pm} and $\bar{s}_p(e_i)$ are the explanatory variables in (46) to (49) for the first month of the testing periods following the estimation periods shown.

Since the estimate of the variance of a b_{im} or a b_{pm} is

$$s^2(b) = \frac{s^2(e)}{\displaystyle\sum_{t=1}^{T} (R_{mt} - \bar{R}_m)^2}, \tag{50}$$

we can see that if data from a given period are used to compute b_{im} for securities and b_{pm} for portfolios, the denominator in the expression for $s^2(b)$ is the same for all of the estimates, while the numerator is just the relevant sample variance of the market model residuals for the security or portfolio. Thus, the fact that in Table 9.2 $s(e_p)$ is generally on the order of one-third to one-seventh $\bar{s}_p(e_i)$ implies that $s(b_p)$ is one-third to one-seventh $s(b_i)$. Estimates of β_{pm} for portfolios are indeed more reliable than the estimates of the β_{im} of individual securities.

Note, however, that if the market model disturbances $\tilde{e}_{it}$ were independent from security to security, the "effects of diversification" in reducing $s(e_p)$ would be about the same for all portfolios. More precisely, the ratio $s(e_p)/\bar{s}_p(e_i)$ would be about the same for all portfolios, so that the relative increase in the precision of the risk estimates obtained by using portfolios rather than individual securities would be about the same for all portfolios. We argue later, however, that the market model disturbances for securities are interdependent, and the interdependence is strongest among high-β_{im} securities and among low-β_{im} securities. For the moment we note that this shows

TABLE 9.2

Sample Statistics for Estimation Periods.

PORTFOLIO

ESTIMATION PERIOD 1930–1934

STATISTIC	1	2	3	4	5	6	7	8	9	10	11	12	13	14	15	16	17	18	19	20
b_{pm}	.693	.702	.771	.840	.863	.892	.917	.935	.977	.983	1.014	1.058	1.059	1.063	1.106	1.143	1.149	1.255	1.280	1.291
$s(b_{pm})$	.031	.030	.023	.034	.031	.025	.033	.026	.024	.020	.033	.025	.037	.030	.032	.026	.040	.044	.028	.033
$\hat{\rho}(R_p, R_m)^2$	.89	.90	.95	.91	.93	.96	.93	.96	.97	.98	.94	.97	.93	.96	.95	.97	.93	.93	.97	.96
$s(R_p)$	.136	.139	.147	.163	.166	.170	.177	.178	.185	.185	.194	.200	.204	.202	.210	.216	.221	.238	.241	.245
$s(e_p)$	.045	.043	.033	.048	.044	.036	.047	.038	.034	.029	.047	.036	.053	.043	.045	.037	.057	.063	.039	.047
$\bar{s}_p(e_i)$	.173	.156	.137	.158	.143	.162	.175	.176	.148	.164	.179	.161	.203	.185	.187	.174	.203	.243	.194	.205
$s(e_p)/\sqrt{s_p(e_i)}$	.26	.28	.24	.30	.31	.22	.26	.21	.22	.17	.26	.22	.26	.23	.24	.21	.28	.25	.20	.22

ESTIMATION PERIOD 1934–1938

STATISTIC	1	2	3	4	5	6	7	8	9	10	11	12	13	14	15	16	17	18	19	20
b_{pm}	.322	.508	.651	.674	.695	.792	.921	.942	.970	1.005	1.046	1.122	1.181	1.192	1.196	1.295	1.335	1.396	1.445	1.458
$s(b_{pm})$	.027	.027	.025	.023	.028	.026	.032	.029	.034	.027	.028	.031	.035	.028	.029	.032	.032	.053	.039	.053
$\hat{\rho}(R_p, R_m)^2$	.709	.861	.921	.936	.912	.941	.932	.946	.933	.958	.959	.956	.951	.969	.966	.966	.967	.922	.958	.927
$s(R_p)$	.040	.058	.072	.074	.077	.087	.101	.103	.106	.109	.113	.122	.128	.128	.129	.140	.144	.154	.156	.160
$s(e_p)$	.022	.022	.020	.019	.023	.021	.026	.024	.028	.022	.023	.026	.029	.023	.024	.026	.026	.043	.032	.043
$\bar{s}_p(e_i)$	.085	.075	.083	.078	.090	.095	.109	.106	.111	.097	.094	.124	.120	.122	.132	.125	.129	.158	.145	.170
$s(e_p)/\sqrt{s_p(e_i)}$	.259	.293	.241	.244	.256	.221	.238	.226	.252	.227	.245	.210	.242	.188	.182	.208	.202	.272	.221	.253

ESTIMATION PERIOD 1938–1942

STATISTIC	1	2	3	4	5	6	7	8	9	10	11	12	13	14	15	16	17	18	19	20
b_{pm}	.335	.470	.588	.633	.768	.781	.798	.899	.981	1.057	1.084	1.129	1.206	1.241	1.255	1.257	1.261	1.331	1.560	1.627
$s(b_{pm})$	.032	.039	.038	.026	.026	.025	.034	.025	.023	.025	.015	.018	.025	.039	.038	.025	.033	.037	.050	.080
$\hat{\rho}(R_p, R_m)^2$	.65	.71	.80	.91	.94	.94	.90	.96	.97	.97	.99	.99	.97	.94	.95	.98	.96	.96	.94	.87
$s(R_p)$	.044	.059	.070	.070	.084	.085	.089	.097	.106	.114	.116	.121	.130	.135	.137	.135	.136	.144	.171	.185
$s(e_p)$	.026	.032	.031	.022	.021	.020	.028	.020	.019	.020	.012	.015	.021	.032	.031	.020	.027	.030	.041	.066
$\bar{s}_p(e_i)$	.071	.066	.083	.073	.072	.087	.083	.088	.085	.100	.098	.104	.116	.135	.123	.119	.103	.107	.148	.181
$s(e_p)/\sqrt{s_p(e_i)}$	.36	.48	.37	.30	.29	.22	.33	.22	.22	.20	.12	.14	.18	.23	.25	.16	.26	.28	.27	.36

ESTIMATION PERIOD 1942-1946

b_{pm}	1.661	1.631	1.473	1.316	1.312	1.254	1.038	1.010	.952	.949	.894	.805	.792	.770	.721	.707	.628	.593	.537	.467
$s(b_{pm})$	.077	.083	.084	.041	.039	.034	.030	.040	.036	.031	.040	.028	.035	.035	.032	.027	.037	.044	.041	.045
$\hat{\rho}(R_p, R_m)^2$	.887	.867	.839	.945	.951	.958	.954	.917	.923	.942	.896	.934	.898	.889	.898	.919	.829	.753	.745	.645
$s(R_p)$	.106	.105	.097	.081	.081	.077	.064	.063	.060	.059	.057	.050	.050	.049	.046	.044	.041	.041	.037	.035
$s(e_p)$	.036	.038	.039	.019	.018	.016	.014	.018	.016	.014	.018	.013	.016	.016	.015	.013	.017	.020	.019	.021
$\bar{s}_p(e_i)$	.122	.117	.134	.086	.083	.096	.077	.085	.074	.073	.069	.062	.064	.064	.063	.058	.058	.063	.055	.055
$s(e_p)/\bar{s}_p(e_i)$	.295	.325	.291	.221	.217	.167	.182	.212	.216	.192	.261	.210	.250	.250	.238	.224	.293	.317	.345	.382

ESTIMATION PERIOD 1946-1950

b_{pm}	1.479	1.434	1.349	1.325	1.243	1.184	1.075	1.052	1.027	1.002	.955	.937	.919	.857	.812	.810	.745	.694	.608	.538
$s(b_{pm})$	.086	.052	.049	.034	.035	.030	.037	.027	.030	.027	.028	.033	.032	.025	.029	.028	.032	.033	.041	.040
$\hat{\rho}(R_p, R_m)^2$	.83	.93	.93	.96	.96	.96	.93	.96	.95	.96	.95	.93	.93	.95	.93	.93	.90	.88	.79	.76
$s(R_p)$	.084	.077	.073	.070	.066	.063	.058	.056	.055	.053	.051	.050	.049	.046	.044	.043	.041	.038	.035	.032
$s(e_p)$	.034	.021	.020	.013	.014	.012	.015	.011	.012	.011	.011	.013	.013	.010	.012	.011	.013	.013	.016	.016
$\bar{s}_p(e_i)$	.102	.078	.082	.066	.071	.070	.069	.069	.069	.064	.064	.067	.062	.058	.059	.052	.053	.053	.052	.049
$s(e_p)/\bar{s}_p(e_i)$	.33	.26	.24	.19	.19	.17	.21	.15	.17	.17	.17	.19	.20	.17	.20	.21	.24	.24	.30	.32

ESTIMATION PERIOD 1950-1954

b_{pm}	1.527	1.478	1.324	1.295	1.235	1.186	1.134	1.131	1.123	1.117	1.014	.996	.950	.929	.784	.777	.751	.694	.590	.418
$s(b_{pm})$	.086	.058	.046	.045	.049	.037	.033	.044	.027	.039	.029	.035	.038	.050	.035	.038	.037	.045	.047	.042
$\hat{\rho}(R_p, R_m)^2$	.841	.917	.934	.933	.915	.944	.952	.919	.968	.934	.954	.933	.913	.856	.895	.878	.872	.798	.723	.629
$s(R_p)$	.060	.056	.050	.049	.047	.044	.042	.043	.041	.042	.038	.037	.036	.036	.030	.030	.029	.028	.025	.019
$s(e_p)$	.024	.016	.013	.013	.014	.010	.009	.012	.007	.011	.008	.010	.011	.014	.010	.010	.010	.013	.013	.012
$\bar{s}_p(e_i)$	.088	.076	.068	.065	.064	.064	.060	.066	.057	.066	.057	.054	.053	.052	.051	.051	.048	.046	.044	.040
$s(e_p)/\bar{s}_p(e_i)$	.273	.210	.192	.200	.219	.156	.150	.182	.123	.167	.140	.185	.208	.269	.196	.196	.208	.283	.295	.300

TABLE 9.2 (CONT'D)

STATISTIC		PORTFOLIO																		
	1	2	3	4	5	6	7	8	9	10	11	12	13	14	15	16	17	18	19	20
	ESTIMATION PERIOD 1954–1958																			
b_{pm}	.457	.544	.614	.637	.768	.859	.924	.972	.993	1.007	1.021	1.091	1.098	1.116	1.238	1.247	1.258	1.392	1.450	1.587
$s(b_{pm})$	.042	.047	.045	.041	.034	.035	.034	.038	.037	.034	.033	.040	.040	.042	.045	.038	.042	.065	.049	.064
$\hat{\rho}(R_p, R_m)^2$	.66	.69	.76	.80	.90	.91	.92	.92	.92	.94	.94	.93	.93	.92	.93	.95	.94	.89	.94	.91
$s(R_p)$	.020	.023	.025	.025	.028	.032	.034	.036	.036	.036	.037	.040	.040	.041	.045	.045	.045	.052	.052	.058
$s(e_p)$	.011	.013	.012	.011	.009	.009	.009	.010	.010	.009	.009	.011	.011	.011	.012	.010	.011	.017	.013	.017
$\bar{s}_p(e_j)$	.045	.046	.049	.047	.053	.056	.057	.055	.065	.062	.063	.063	.067	.067	.066	.070	.064	.076	.071	.081
$s(e_p)/\bar{s}_p(e_j)$	.24	.28	.24	.23	.16	.16	.15	.18	.15	.14	.14	.17	.16	.16	.18	.14	.17	.22	.18	.20
	ESTIMATIÓN PERIOD 1958–1962																			
b_{pm}	.626	.635	.719	.801	.817	.860	.920	.950	.975	.995	1.013	1.019	1.037	1.048	1.069	1.081	1.092	1.098	1.269	1.388
$s(b_{pm})$	.043	.048	.039	.046	.047	.033	.037	.038	.032	.037	.038	.031	.036	.033	.036	.038	.045	.045	.048	.065
$\hat{\rho}(R_p, R_m)^2$	.783	.745	.851	.835	.838	.920	.913	.915	.939	.925	.922	.948	.934	.945	.936	.931	.907	.910	.922	.886
$s(R_p)$	.030	.031	.033	.037	.038	.038	.041	.042	.043	.044	.045	.045	.046	.046	.047	.048	.049	.049	.056	.063
$s(e_p)$	.014	.016	.013	.015	.015	.011	.012	.012	.011	.012	.013	.010	.012	.011	.012	.013	.015	.015	.016	.021
$\bar{s}_p(e_j)$	.049	.052	.056	.059	.064	.061	.070	.069	.068	.064	.069	.066	.067	.062	.070	.072	.076	.068	.070	.078
$s(e_p)/\bar{s}_p(e_j)$	.286	.308	.232	.254	.234	.180	.171	.174	.162	.188	.188	.152	.179	.177	.171	.180	.197	.220	.228	.269
	ESTIMATION PERIOD 1962–1966																			
b_{pm}	.514	.625	.665	.697	.791	.812	.843	.888	.916	.940	.941	.943	.976	1.062	1.070	1.216	1.291	1.316	1.365	1.486
$s(b_{pm})$	.042	.046	.050	.040	.032	.032	.034	.033	.029	.034	.032	.030	.038	.036	.036	.041	.032	.046	.052	.056
$\hat{\rho}(R_p, R_m)^2$	.72	.75	.75	.84	.91	.92	.91	.92	.94	.93	.94	.94	.92	.93	.94	.94	.96	.93	.92	.92
$s(R_p)$	.025	.030	.032	.032	.035	.036	.037	.039	.039	.041	.041	.041	.043	.046	.046	.053	.055	.057	.060	.065
$s(e_p)$	.013	.015	.016	.013	.010	.010	.011	.011	.009	.011	.010	.010	.012	.012	.012	.013	.010	.015	.017	.018
$\bar{s}_p(e_j)$	.053	.046	.046	.053	.057	.057	.059	.057	.055	.060	.053	.056	.064	.062	.067	.075	.068	.071	.076	.089
$s(e_p)/\bar{s}_p(e_j)$	.24	.32	.34	.24	.17	.17	.18	.19	.16	.18	.18	.17	.18	.19	.17	.17	.14	.21	.22	.20

SOURCE: Eugene F. Fama and James D. MacBeth, "Risk, Return, and Equilibrium: Empirical Tests," *Journal of Political Economy* 71 (May–June 1973): 620–621.

up in Table 9.2 in terms of ratios $s(e_p)/\bar{s}_p(e_i)$ that are always highest at the extremes of the b_{pm} range and lowest for b_{pm} close to 1. Since these ratios are generally less than .33, however, interdependence among the market model disturbances for different securities does not destroy the value of using portfolios to reduce the dispersion of the errors in estimates of risk measures.

PROBLEMS III.B

2. What is the formal basis for the statement that if the market model disturbances $\tilde{e}_{it}$ were independent from security to security, then the ratio $s(e_p)/\bar{s}_p(e_i)$ would be about the same for all portfolios?

3. Make some specific comments about the reliability of the b_{pm} of portfolios versus the b_{im} of individual securities. Don't be afraid to look back at the results in Chapter 4.

4. With the switch from securities to portfolios, are there any dramatic changes in the interpretation of the least squares values of γ_{1t}, γ_{2t}, γ_{3t}, and γ_{4t} in (46) to (49) as portfolio returns?

ANSWERS

2. The disturbance in the market model relationship between the return on portfolio p and the return on the portfolio m is related to the corresponding market model disturbances for the securities in p according to

$$\tilde{e}_{pt} = \sum_{i=1}^{K} x_{ip} \tilde{e}_{it},$$

where K is the number of securities in the portfolio. In the Fama-MacBeth tests, K is approximately the same for all portfolios and there is equal weighting of securities within portfolios. Thus, if the $\tilde{e}_{it}$ were independent across securities,

$$\sigma^2(\tilde{e}_p) = \sum_{i=1}^{K} x_{ip}^2 \sigma^2(\tilde{e}_i) = \frac{1}{K}\,\overline{\sigma^2(\tilde{e}_i)},$$

where $\overline{\sigma^2(\tilde{e}_i)}$ is the average of the $\sigma^2(\tilde{e}_i)$ for the K securities in the portfolio p. Since this analysis would be the same for all the Fama-MacBeth portfolios if within each portfolio the $\tilde{e}_{it}$ were independent across securities, then for each portfolio $\sigma^2(\tilde{e}_p)$ would be the fraction $1/K$ of the average of the $\sigma^2(\tilde{e}_i)$ for individual securities. This statement also holds (at least approximately) for the ratio $\sigma(\tilde{e}_p)/\overline{\sigma(\tilde{e}_i)}$ if within given portfolios the values of $\sigma^2(\tilde{e}_i)$ for individual securities are not too different.

The evidence in Table 9.2 suggests, however, that the simple expression above for $\sigma^2(\tilde{e}_p)$ is not valid. Within portfolios that have b_{pm} much different from 1, there must on average be positive covariances between the $\tilde{e}_{it}$ of different securities which cause the $\sigma^2(\tilde{e}_p)$ for these portfolios to be greater than implied by the expression above.

3. To get a more direct appreciation for the effectiveness of the portfolio approach in increasing the reliability of the risk estimates, one can compare the $s(b_{pm})$ for portfolios in Table 9.2 with the $s(b_i)$ for individual securities in Tables 4.3 and 4.4. In Table 9.2, the $s(b_{pm})$ for portfolios for the five-year period 1962-1966 range from about .03, when b_{pm} is close to 1, up to .056 for the portfolio with the highest b_{pm}. Except for the portfolios with the highest b_{pm}, the values of the $s(b_{pm})$ are generally about 4 percent of the values of b_{pm}. On the other hand, in Tables 4.3 and 4.4, the $s(b_{im})$ for individual securities range from .110 to .522. In Table 4.3 $s(b_{im})$ is, on average, about 25 percent as large as b_{im}, whereas in Table 4.4, $s(b_i)$ is on average about 22 percent as large as b_{im}. In short, for individual securities the estimation error in b_{im} is likely to be a substantial fraction of the estimate, whereas for portfolios the estimation error is likely to be a small fraction of the estimate.

4. The least squares values of the γ_{jt} in (46) to (49) are the returns on portfolios, but they are portfolios of the 20 component portfolios used in the computations. Moreover, the least squares values of the γ_{jt} in (46) to (49) have the same properties as the least squares values of the γ_{jt} in (38) to (41), except that for (46) to (49), the properties of the γ_{jt} must be stated in terms of the 20 component portfolios and the b_{pm}, b_{pm}^2, and $\bar{s}_p(e_i)$ for these 20 portfolios. For example, the least squares value of γ_{1t} in (46) is the return on a standard portfolio of the 20 component portfolios, where the weights assigned to the component portfolios yield zero-weighted average values of the 20 values of b_{pm}, the 20 b_{pm}^2, and the 20 $\bar{s}_p(e_i)$. To substantiate these claims, the reader can work through the analysis of (11) to (22), substituting the estimates b_{pm}, b_{pm}^2, and $\bar{s}_p(e_i)$ for β_{iM}, β_{iM}^2 and $\sigma(\tilde{e}_i)$.

IV. Results

A. *Preliminary Discussion*

THE MONTHLY RECORD

We are ready to consider the results of the tests of the two-parameter model. As a warm-up, Table 9.3 shows the month-by-month record of the least squares values of γ_{1t} and γ_{2t} in (49). The table also shows the month-by-month values of $\rho(R_{pt}, b_{pm})^2$, the coefficient of determination, adjusted

TABLE 9.3
The Month-by-Month Record of the Relationship Between Return and Risk on the NYSE, $R_{pt} = \gamma_{1t} + \gamma_{2t}b_{pm} + \eta_{pt}$

t	γ_{1t}	γ_{2t}	$\rho(R_{pt}, b_{pm})^2$	t	γ_{1t}	γ_{2t}	$\rho(R_{pt}, b_{pm})^2$
3501	0.0064	−0.0413	0.007	3903	0.0152	−0.1880	0.931
3502	0.0369	−0.0997	0.328	3904	−0.0074	0.0072	−0.033
3503	−0.0657	−0.0126	−0.045	3905	0.0683	0.0147	0.032
3504	−0.0007	0.1040	0.192	3906	0.0321	−0.1213	0.944
3505	0.1129	−0.0889	0.151	3907	0.0138	0.1202	0.834
3506	0.0277	0.0105	−0.051	3908	−0.0212	−0.0827	0.656
3507	−0.0348	0.1370	0.191	3909	−0.2040	0.6295	0.758
3508	−0.0092	0.0973	0.085	3910	0.0737	−0.0899	0.689
3509	−0.0790	0.0945	0.174	3911	0.0427	−0.1312	0.855
3510	−0.0142	0.0869	0.185	3912	0.0526	−0.0433	0.298
3511	0.1585	0.0060	−0.055	4001	0.0319	−0.0543	0.458
3512	0.0472	0.0021	−0.055	4002	0.0242	0.0069	−0.042
3601	0.0368	0.1342	0.125	4003	0.0318	−0.0076	−0.024
3602	0.0471	0.0047	−0.054	4004	0.0058	0.0038	−0.053
3603	0.0165	−0.0219	−0.039	4005	−0.1816	−0.0898	0.765
3604	0.0179	−0.1398	0.436	4006	0.0424	0.0333	0.184
3605	0.1004	−0.0433	0.024	4007	0.0346	−0.0010	−0.055
3606	0.0102	−0.0096	−0.048	4008	0.0022	0.0226	0.134
3607	0.0397	0.0292	−0.029	4009	−0.0014	0.0365	0.140
3608	0.0159	0.0098	−0.051	4010	−0.0190	0.0692	0.647
3609	0.0247	0.0113	−0.043	4011	0.0140	−0.0206	0.042
3610	0.0133	0.0458	0.042	4012	0.0232	−0.0438	0.334
3611	−0.0841	0.1763	0.341	4101	−0.0110	0.0118	−0.044
3612	−0.0626	0.0905	0.219	4102	−0.0181	−0.0010	−0.055
3701	−0.0530	0.1400	0.265	4103	0.0023	0.0165	0.045
3702	−0.0197	0.0572	0.050	4104	0.0063	−0.0609	0.594
3703	−0.0792	0.0898	0.248	4105	−0.0301	0.0432	0.504
3704	0.0170	−0.1279	0.641	4106	0.0135	0.0518	0.335
3705	0.0055	−0.0295	−0.012	4107	0.0357	0.0987	0.562
3706	−0.0599	−0.0220	−0.014	4108	0.0079	−0.0163	0.152
3707	−0.0489	0.1531	0.481	4109	0.0416	−0.0624	0.561
3708	−0.0134	−0.0449	0.129	4110	−0.0328	−0.0386	0.234
3709	−0.0738	−0.1197	0.630	4111	−0.0096	−0.0258	0.119
3710	−0.0675	−0.0333	0.061	4112	−0.0260	−0.0623	0.479
3711	−0.0380	−0.0659	0.183	4201	−0.0768	0.2445	0.426
3712	0.0110	−0.1122	0.374	4202	−0.0395	0.0240	0.165
3801	0.0305	0.0144	−0.043	4203	−0.0778	0.0266	0.019
3802	0.0200	0.0365	0.005	4204	−0.0225	−0.0226	0.066
3803	−0.1642	−0.1357	0.457	4205	0.0960	−0.0633	0.447
3804	0.1524	0.0786	−0.028	4206	0.0360	−0.0126	0.017
3805	0.0682	−0.1338	0.362	4207	0.0207	0.0274	0.273
3806	0.0405	0.2677	0.694	4208	0.0205	0.0083	−0.037
3807	0.0461	0.0746	0.091	4209	−0.0281	0.0859	0.417
3808	−0.0666	−0.0053	−0.051	4210	−0.0022	0.1036	0.635
3809	−0.0208	0.0085	−0.047	4211	0.0679	−0.0865	0.661
3810	−0.0869	0.2235	0.368	4212	0.0316	0.0001	−0.056
3811	0.0079	−0.0520	0.048	4301	−0.0064	0.1840	0.661
3812	0.0722	−0.0380	0.013	4302	−0.0967	0.2402	0.622
3901	0.0195	−0.0946	0.841	4303	0.0395	0.0746	0.352
3902	0.0406	0.0000	−0.056	4304	−0.0244	0.0631	0.667

TABLE 9.3 (CONT'D)

t	γ_{1t}	γ_{2t}	$\rho(R_{pt}, b_{pm})^2$	t	γ_{1t}	γ_{2t}	$\rho(R_{pt}, b_{pm})^2$
4305	0.0105	0.0759	0.469	4709	−0.0120	0.0188	0.265
4306	0.0441	−0.0357	0.289	4710	0.0147	0.0189	0.366
4307	0.0295	−0.0950	0.786	4711	0.0016	−0.0284	0.289
4308	0.0247	−0.0222	0.282	4712	0.0097	0.0132	0.078
4309	0.0140	0.0222	0.327	4801	−0.0435	0.0249	0.432
4310	0.0092	−0.0133	0.033	4802	−0.0109	−0.0507	0.879
4311	0.0115	−0.1024	0.847	4803	0.0307	0.0684	0.551
4312	0.0239	0.0720	0.713	4804	0.0140	0.0272	0.338
4401	−0.0025	0.0495	0.466	4805	0.0310	0.0614	0.668
4402	0.0011	0.0125	0.031	4806	−0.0226	0.0064	−0.017
4403	0.0115	0.0335	0.462	4807	−0.0272	−0.0256	0.202
4404	0.0038	−0.0348	0.694	4808	0.0095	−0.0089	0.063
4405	0.0359	0.0319	0.299	4809	−0.0106	−0.0350	0.717
4406	−0.0122	0.1177	0.779	4810	0.0306	0.0240	0.384
4407	0.0204	−0.0355	0.752	4811	−0.0182	−0.0903	0.863
4408	0.0029	0.0259	0.219	4812	0.0278	−0.0160	0.125
4409	−0.0008	−0.0019	−0.047	4901	0.0236	−0.0046	−0.032
4410	0.0229	−0.0233	0.333	4902	0.0152	−0.0582	0.736
4411	0.0103	0.0138	0.093	4903	0.0155	0.0448	0.563
4412	−0.0057	0.0778	0.679	4904	0.0265	−0.0594	0.839
4501	0.0171	0.0269	0.236	4905	0.0302	−0.0735	0.875
4502	0.0117	0.0770	0.783	4906	0.0174	−0.0230	0.430
4503	−0.0021	−0.0551	0.587	4907	0.0429	0.0190	0.201
4504	0.0332	0.0577	0.605	4908	0.0288	−0.0051	−0.029
4505	0.0137	0.0174	0.109	4909	0.0237	0.0203	0.209
4506	−0.0528	0.0877	0.688	4910	0.0088	0.0312	0.418
4507	−0.0026	−0.0290	0.570	4911	0.0208	−0.0118	0.060
4508	0.0599	0.0037	−0.051	4912	0.0237	0.0470	0.631
4509	0.0339	0.0272	0.380	5001	−0.0235	0.0603	0.799
4510	0.0622	0.0023	−0.054	5002	0.0153	−0.0009	−0.055
4511	0.0227	0.0720	0.687	5003	0.0087	−0.0105	0.072
4512	−0.0308	0.0633	0.109	5004	−0.0156	0.0646	0.587
4601	−0.0065	0.1036	0.659	5005	0.0156	0.0201	0.135
4602	−0.0169	−0.0518	0.799	5006	−0.0362	−0.0399	0.712
4603	0.0883	−0.0303	0.200	5007	−0.0933	0.1501	0.735
4604	0.0546	−0.0029	−0.052	5008	0.0487	0.0044	−0.046
4605	0.0226	0.0318	0.310	5009	0.0509	0.0037	−0.049
4606	−0.0418	−0.0070	−0.008	5010	−0.0032	−0.0001	−0.056
4607	0.0000	−0.0427	0.661	5011	−0.0068	0.0397	0.435
4608	−0.0291	−0.0477	0.695	5012	−0.0377	0.1200	0.875
4609	−0.0517	−0.0839	0.896	5101	0.0379	0.0382	0.266
4610	−0.0181	0.0104	0.036	5102	0.0331	−0.0239	0.333
4611	0.0182	−0.0190	0.192	5103	0.0190	−0.0544	0.774
4612	0.0548	−0.0116	0.004	5104	−0.0004	0.0420	0.384
4701	−0.0208	0.0543	0.653	5105	0.0162	−0.0413	0.524
4702	−0.0101	0.0026	−0.038	5106	0.0252	−0.0727	0.894
4703	0.0019	−0.0311	0.756	5107	0.0135	0.0498	0.601
4704	−0.0254	−0.0584	0.767	5108	0.0143	0.0366	0.344
4705	0.0119	−0.0494	0.858	5109	−0.0108	0.0317	0.570
4706	0.0438	0.0173	0.121	5110	−0.0105	−0.0126	0.107
4707	0.0093	0.0538	0.616	5111	0.0047	0.0018	−0.049
4708	−0.0083	−0.0082	0.028	5112	0.0347	−0.0206	0.180

TABLE 9.3 (CONT'D)

t	γ_{1t}	γ_{2t}	$\rho(R_{pt},b_{pm})^2$	t	γ_{1t}	γ_{2t}	$\rho(R_{pt},b_{pm})^2$
5201	0.0145	0.0013	−0.054	5605	−0.0210	−0.0207	0.398
5202	−0.0120	−0.0095	0.029	5606	0.0229	−0.0022	−0.052
5203	0.0197	0.0111	0.049	5607	0.0375	0.0019	−0.051
5204	−0.0204	−0.0267	0.377	5608	−0.0038	−0.0130	0.124
5205	0.0201	0.0036	−0.037	5609	−0.0344	0.0001	−0.056
5206	0.0030	0.0296	0.454	5610	0.0129	−0.0062	−0.028
5207	0.0199	−0.0075	−0.003	5611	0.0087	0.0042	−0.043
5208	0.0218	−0.0248	0.403	5612	0.0180	0.0002	−0.055
5209	0.0019	−0.0199	0.301	5701	−0.0035	0.0060	−0.032
5210	−0.0065	−0.0053	−0.016	5702	0.0114	−0.0346	0.500
5211	0.0338	0.0228	0.220	5703	0.0102	0.0120	0.025
5212	0.0164	0.0054	−0.033	5704	0.0254	0.0010	−0.055
5301	−0.0033	0.0291	0.274	5705	0.0131	0.0082	0.014
5302	0.0075	0.0027	−0.051	5706	0.0007	−0.0044	−0.042
5303	0.0145	−0.0261	0.180	5707	0.0184	−0.0118	0.013
5304	−0.0150	−0.0070	−0.012	5708	0.0003	−0.0506	0.740
5305	−0.0103	0.0175	0.222	5709	0.0127	−0.0646	0.747
5306	0.0039	−0.0353	0.671	5710	0.0370	−0.1023	0.824
5307	0.0289	−0.0128	0.102	5711	0.0300	−0.0119	0.058
5308	0.0452	−0.0993	0.875	5712	0.0364	−0.0876	0.833
5309	0.0259	−0.0375	0.461	5801	0.0037	0.1024	0.856
5310	0.0128	0.0261	0.368	5802	0.0400	−0.0518	0.609
5311	0.0270	−0.0067	−0.034	5803	0.0394	−0.0017	−0.053
5312	0.0462	−0.0618	0.775	5804	0.0197	0.0111	−0.019
5401	−0.0008	0.0743	0.866	5805	−0.0033	0.0404	0.410
5402	0.0127	−0.0004	−0.055	5806	0.0006	0.0317	0.497
5403	0.0282	0.0016	−0.054	5807	0.0017	0.0547	0.740
5404	0.0228	−0.0026	−0.051	5808	0.0104	0.0216	0.224
5405	0.0044	0.0388	0.431	5809	−0.0065	0.0607	0.693
5406	0.0190	−0.0065	−0.033	5810	−0.0066	0.0361	0.258
5407	0.0341	0.0359	0.280	5811	0.0384	−0.0002	−0.056
5408	−0.0070	−0.0032	−0.046	5812	0.0497	−0.0096	−0.003
5409	0.0431	0.0035	−0.048	5901	0.0157	0.0260	0.153
5410	−0.0031	−0.0026	−0.048	5902	0.0139	0.0120	0.030
5411	0.0465	0.0491	0.504	5903	0.0071	0.0038	−0.048
5412	−0.0321	0.1222	0.888	5904	0.0122	0.0125	0.043
5501	−0.0004	0.0162	0.111	5905	0.0037	0.0054	−0.030
5502	−0.0063	0.0463	0.497	5906	−0.0131	0.0177	0.119
5503	−0.0021	0.0053	−0.032	5907	0.0356	−0.0057	0.001
5504	0.0451	−0.0230	0.194	5908	0.0345	−0.0483	0.783
5505	0.0009	0.0059	−0.037	5909	−0.0247	−0.0203	0.271
5506	0.0250	0.0102	0.001	5910	0.0064	0.0145	0.128
5507	0.0107	−0.0005	−0.055	5911	0.0202	−0.0069	−0.034
5508	0.0094	−0.0057	−0.035	5912	0.0091	0.0133	0.114
5509	−0.0265	0.0187	0.113	6001	−0.0184	−0.0205	0.136
5510	0.0002	−0.0164	0.208	6002	0.0175	−0.0110	0.030
5511	0.0412	0.0139	0.040	6003	0.0270	−0.0520	0.690
5512	0.0025	0.0188	0.095	6004	0.0335	−0.0548	0.723
5601	−0.0063	−0.0152	0.113	6005	0.0216	−0.0030	−0.048
5602	0.0292	0.0056	−0.031	6006	0.0559	−0.0354	0.332
5603	0.0493	0.0039	−0.047	6007	0.0098	−0.0262	0.536
5604	−0.0035	0.0088	−0.010	6008	0.0422	−0.0059	−0.029

TABLE 9.3 (CONT'D)

t	γ_{1t}	γ_{2t}	$\rho(R_{pt}, b_{pm})^2$	t	γ_{1t}	γ_{2t}	$\rho(R_{pt}, b_{pm})^2$
6009	−0.0146	−0.0440	0.627	6408	0.0147	−0.0236	0.193
6010	0.0156	−0.0362	0.663	6409	−0.0491	0.0914	0.748
6011	0.0435	−0.0019	−0.052	6410	0.0055	0.0122	0.009
6012	0.0477	−0.0110	0.009	6411	0.0531	−0.0543	0.414
6101	0.0269	0.0547	0.535	6412	0.0181	−0.0276	0.304
6102	0.0356	0.0243	0.222	6501	0.0344	0.0231	0.171
6103	0.0164	0.0291	0.218	6502	−0.0084	0.0373	0.266
6104	0.0158	−0.0106	−0.007	6503	−0.0006	0.0060	−0.048
6105	0.0016	0.0398	0.565	6504	−0.0198	0.0578	0.423
6106	0.0063	−0.0452	0.582	6505	−0.0019	−0.0066	−0.028
6107	0.0220	−0.0072	−0.001	6506	−0.0094	−0.0627	0.670
6108	0.0603	−0.0385	0.319	6507	−0.0445	0.0773	0.715
6109	0.0183	−0.0463	0.709	6508	−0.0201	0.0599	0.602
6110	0.0603	−0.0381	0.426	6509	−0.0161	0.0487	0.234
6111	0.0619	−0.0171	0.097	6510	−0.0496	0.0978	0.645
6112	−0.0314	0.0295	0.300	6511	−0.0429	0.0718	0.388
6201	−0.0580	0.0538	0.699	6512	−0.0530	0.0903	0.493
6202	0.0249	−0.0079	−0.016	6601	−0.0241	0.0720	0.405
6203	0.0034	−0.0087	0.002	6602	−0.0507	0.0637	0.560
6204	−0.0257	−0.0411	0.753	6603	−0.0063	−0.0139	0.068
6205	−0.0709	−0.0226	0.199	6604	−0.0602	0.0933	0.717
6206	−0.0540	−0.0277	0.373	6605	0.0257	−0.0991	0.832
6207	0.0511	0.0090	−0.009	6606	−0.0379	0.0317	0.295
6208	0.0067	0.0151	0.079	6607	0.0132	−0.0252	0.143
6209	−0.0184	−0.0392	0.595	6608	−0.0436	−0.0486	0.456
6210	−0.0207	0.0032	−0.038	6609	0.0494	−0.0638	0.679
6211	0.0305	0.1051	0.819	6610	0.0728	−0.0500	0.373
6212	0.0320	−0.0402	0.662	6611	−0.0353	0.0611	0.408
6301	0.0197	0.0615	0.461	6612	−0.0001	0.0141	0.001
6302	−0.0174	0.0061	−0.038	6701	−0.0049	0.1371	0.818
6303	−0.0053	0.0274	0.287	6702	0.0154	−0.0027	−0.050
6304	0.0225	0.0174	0.040	6703	0.0149	0.0373	0.216
6305	−0.0349	0.0695	0.610	6704	0.0292	0.0060	−0.026
6306	−0.0116	−0.0041	−0.044	6705	−0.0328	0.0154	0.024
6307	0.0142	−0.0220	0.059	6706	−0.0139	0.0640	0.621
6308	−0.0084	0.0603	0.485	6707	0.0315	0.0398	0.308
6309	0.0168	−0.0344	0.236	6708	−0.0069	0.0102	0.001
6310	−0.0011	0.0219	0.156	6709	0.0202	0.0093	−0.018
6311	−0.0273	0.0230	0.080	6710	−0.0272	−0.0125	0.014
6312	−0.0213	0.0313	0.248	6711	0.0084	−0.0032	−0.048
6401	−0.0303	0.0558	0.464	6712	0.0109	0.0445	0.368
6402	−0.0423	0.0728	0.590	6801	0.0501	−0.0561	−0.414
6403	−0.0479	0.0815	0.547	6802	0.0171	−0.0577	0.549
6404	0.0405	−0.0394	0.168	6803	−0.0224	0.0146	0.101
6405	−0.0171	0.0309	0.302	6804	−0.0005	0.1127	0.838
6406	0.0095	0.0076	−0.029	6805	0.0184	0.0378	0.142
6407	0.0340	−0.0049	−0.050	6806	0.1000	−0.0809	0.730

for degrees of freedom, in the regression of the 20 portfolio returns for month t on the corresponding b_{pm}. Table 9.3 can be viewed as the monthly record of the relationship between return and risk on the New York Stock Exchange and, as such, has several points of interest.

First, the strength of the relationship, as measured by $\rho(R_{pt}, b_{pm})^2$, seems on average low and quite variable from month to month. There are many months when $\rho(R_{pt}, b_{pm})^2$ is negative.* Second, there are many months (149 out of 402) when γ_{1t} is negative, and, more interesting, there are many months (185 out of 402) when γ_{2t} is negative, so that for these months there is a negative relationship between return and risk. The variability of the γ_{1t} and γ_{2t} and the low $\rho(R_{pt}, b_{pm})^2$ indicate that if one were to plot risk-return lines (R_{pt} against b_{pm}), one would find that the characteristics of the lines (intercept γ_{1t} and slope γ_{2t}) change dramatically from month to month and that there is substantial dispersion of points, the 20 portfolio returns, about any given line.

None of this is particularly surprising nor, in itself, contrary to the two-parameter model. All of the hypotheses drawn from the model are statements about the relationship between expected returns and risk, and not about the relationships between return and risk. Thus, it may well be the case that risk, as measured by b_{pm}, does not account for much of the differences among the returns on the 20 portfolios for any given month. If securities are priced according to the theory, however, and if they are priced so that m is a minimum variance portfolio, then β_{pm} should be sufficient to explain differences among the expected returns on the 20 portfolios.

Moreover, it is not at all surprising that γ_{1t} and γ_{2t} are quite variable from month to month. The least squares values of γ_{1t} and γ_{2t} are the returns on portfolios of NYSE stocks. We have known since Chapter 1 that even highly diversified portfolios of NYSE stocks show substantial variability of monthly returns. Thus, we expect γ_{2t} to be quite variable through time and even negative in a large fraction of months. The hypothesis that there is a positive relationship between expected return and risk is nevertheless upheld as long as $E(\tilde{\gamma}_{2t}) > 0$, that is, as long as "on average" there is a positive relationship between return and risk.

Since the hypotheses of the model concern relationships between expected returns and risk, we have to do some manipulation of the time series of γ_{1t} and γ_{2t} in Table 9.3 to get tests of these hypotheses. In essence, average values of γ_{1t} and γ_{2t} and summary measures of the time series properties of γ_{1t} and γ_{2t} are the basis of the relevant tests. Moreover, to test all of the

---

*Negative values of the coefficient of determination are possible when the coefficient is adjusted for degrees of freedom.

different hypotheses, we need to do similar manipulations of the time series of the least squares values of the γ_{jt} in (46) to (48).

THE NATURE OF THE TESTS

The major tests are summarized in Table 9.4. Results are presented for ten periods: the overall period 1935–June 1968; three long subperiods, 1935–1945, 1946–1955, and 1956–June 1968; and six subperiods, which, except for the first and last, cover five years each. Results are presented for each of the equations (46) to (49). For each period and equation, the table shows: $\overline{\gamma}_j$, the average of the month-by-month least squares values of γ_{jt}; $s(\gamma_j)$, the sample standard deviation of the monthly γ_{jt}; $\overline{\rho}^2$ and $s(\rho^2)$, the mean and the standard deviation of month-by-month coefficients of determination for the regressions of the 20 portfolio returns on the relevant risk measures.

The table also shows first-order autocorrelations of the various monthly γ_{jt}, where the autocorrelations are computed either about the sample mean of γ_{jt}, in which case they are labeled $\hat{\rho}(\gamma_{jt})$, or about an assumed mean of zero, in which case they are labeled $\hat{\rho}_0(\hat{\rho}_{jt})$. The reasons for doing this are discussed below. Finally, t-statistics for testing the hypothesis that $E(\widetilde{\gamma}_{jt}) = 0$ are presented. These t-statistics are

$$t(\overline{\gamma}_j) = \frac{\overline{\gamma}_j}{s(\gamma_j)/\sqrt{T}}, \tag{51}$$

where T is the number of months in the period. If successive values of $\widetilde{\gamma}_{jt}$ are independent and identically distributed normal random variables, the t-statistic of (51) is a drawing from the student distribution with $T - 1$ degrees of freedom. Since the time periods in Table 9.4 are all five years or longer, $T - 1$ is always greater than 59 and the student distribution is well approximated by the unit normal distribution.

B.   Tests of the Major Hypotheses

TESTS BASED ON AVERAGE RETURNS

Consider first the proposition that if securities are priced so that m is a minimum variance portfolio, then no measure of risk, in addition to β_{im}, is needed to explain expected returns. The results in Panels C and D of Table 9.4 are consistent with this hypothesis. For both (48) and (46), the t-statistics for the mean values of γ_{4t}, the coefficient of $\overline{s}_p(e_i)$, are small, and the signs of the $t(\overline{\gamma}_4)$ for subperiods are randomly positive and negative. Thus, one cannot reject the hypothesis that in both (48) and (46), $E(\widetilde{\gamma}_{4t}) = 0$.

Likewise, the results in Panels B and D of Table 9.4 do not reject the proposition that the relationship between expected return and β_{im} is linear. In

TABLE 9.4
Tests of the Two-Parameter Model

PERIOD	$\bar{\gamma}_1$	$\bar{\gamma}_2$	$\bar{\gamma}_3$	$\bar{\gamma}_4$	$\bar{\gamma}_1 - R_f$	$s(\gamma_1)$	$s(\gamma_2)$	$s(\gamma_3)$	$s(\gamma_4)$	$\hat{\rho}_0(\gamma_1 - R_f)$	$\hat{\rho}_0(\gamma_2)$	$\hat{\rho}_0(\gamma_3)$	$\hat{\rho}_0(\gamma_4)$	$t(\bar{\gamma}_1)$	$t(\bar{\gamma}_2)$	$t(\bar{\gamma}_3)$	$t(\bar{\gamma}_4)$	$t(\bar{\gamma}_1 - R_f)$	$\bar{\rho}^2$	$s(\rho^2)$
Panel A:																				
									$R_{pt} = \gamma_{1t} + \gamma_{2t} b_{pm} + \eta_{pt}$											
1935–6/68	.0061	.0085			.0048	.038	.066			.15	.02			3.24	2.57			2.55	.29	.30
1935–45	.0039	.0163			.0037	.052	.098			.10	–.03			.86	1.92			.82	.29	.29
1946–55	.0087	.0027			.0078	.026	.041			.18	.07			3.71	.70			3.31	.31	.32
1956–6/68	.0060	.0062			.0034	.030	.044			.27	.15			2.45	1.73			1.39	.28	.29
1935–40	.0024	.0109			.0023	.064	.116			.07	–.09			.32	.79			.31	.23	.30
1941–45	.0056	.0229			.0054	.034	.069			.23	.15			1.27	2.55			1.22	.37	.28
1946–50	.0050	.0029			.0044	.031	.047			.20	.04			1.27	.48			1.10	.39	.33
1951–55	.0123	.0024			.0111	.019	.035			.37	.08			5.06	.53			4.56	.24	.29
1956–60	.0148	–.0059			.0128	.020	.034			.37	.18			5.68	–1.37			4.89	.22	.31
1961–6/68	.0001	.0143			–.0029	.034	.048			.22	.09			.03	2.81			–.80	.32	.27
Panel B:																				
									$R_{pt} = \gamma_{1t} + \gamma_{2t} b_{pm} + \gamma_{3t} b_{pm}^2 + \eta_{pt}$											
1935–6/68	.0049	.0105	–.0008		.0036	.052	.118	.056		.03	–.11	–.11		1.92	1.79	–.29		1.42	.32	.31
1935–45	.0074	.0079	.0040		.0073	.061	.139	.074		–.10	–.31	–.21		1.39	.65	.61		1.36	.32	.30
1946–55	–.0002	.0217	–.0087		–.0012	.036	.095	.034		.04	.00	.00		–.07	2.51	–2.83		–.38	.36	.32
1956–6/68	.0069	.0040	.0013		.0043	.054	.116	.053		.17	.07	.03		1.56	.42	.29		.97	.30	.30
1935–40	.0013	.0141	–.0017		.0012	.069	.160	.075		–.13	–.36	–.35		.16	.75	–.19		.14	.24	.30
1941–45	.0148	.0004	.0108		.0146	.050	.111	.073		–.04	–.19	–.04		2.28	.03	1.15		2.24	.39	.29
1946–50	–.0008	.0152	–.0051		–.0015	.037	.104	.032		.14	.04	.00		–.18	1.14	–1.24		–.32	.44	.32
1951–55	.0004	.0281	–.0122		–.0008	.030	.085	.035		–.17	–.14	–.01		.10	2.55	–2.72		–.20	.28	.29
1956–60	.0128	–.0015	–.0020		.0108	.030	.072	.029		.35	.11	.26		3.38	–.16	–.54		2.84	.25	.31
1961–6/68	.0029	.0077	.0034		–.0000	.066	.138	.064		.14	.06	–.01		.42	.53	.51		–.01	.34	.29

TABLE 9.4 (CONT'D)

Tests of the Two-Parameter Model

PERIOD	$\bar{\gamma}_1$	$\bar{\gamma}_2$	$\bar{\gamma}_3$	$\bar{\gamma}_4$	$\gamma_1 - R_f$	$s(\gamma_1)$	$s(\gamma_2)$	$s(\gamma_3)$	$s(\gamma_4)$	$\hat{\rho}_0(\gamma_1 - R_f)$	$\hat{\rho}_0(\gamma_2)$	$\hat{\rho}_0(\gamma_3)$	$\hat{\rho}_0(\gamma_4)$	$t(\bar{\gamma}_1)$	$t(\bar{\gamma}_2)$	$t(\bar{\gamma}_3)$	$t(\bar{\gamma}_4)$	$t(\bar{\gamma}_1 - R_f)$	$\bar{\rho}^2$	$s(\rho^2)$
Panel C:																				
$R_{pt} = \gamma_{1t} + \gamma_{2t}b_{pm} + \gamma_{4t}\bar{s}_p(e_i) + \eta_{pt}$																				
1935–6/68	.0054	.0072		.0198	.0041	.052	.065		.868	.04	−.12		−.04	2.10	2.20		.46	1.59	.32	.31
1935–45	.0017	.0104		.0841	.0015	.073	.083		.921	−.00	−.26		−.08	.26	1.41		1.05	.24	.32	.31
1946–55	.0110	.0075		−.1052	.0100	.032	.056		.609	.08	.02		−.20	3.78	1.47		−1.89	3.46	.34	.32
1956–6/68	.0042	.0041		.0633	.0016	.040	.052		.984	.12	.08		.03	1.28	.96		.79	.50	.30	.29
1935–40	.0036	.0119		−.0170	.0035	.082	.105		.744	−.03	−.26		−.18	.37	.97		−.19	.36	.25	.30
1941–45	−.0006	.0085		.2053	−.0009	.061	.052		1.091	.07	−.29		−.02	−.08	1.25		1.46	−.11	.41	.30
1946–50	.0069	.0081		−.0920	.0062	.034	.066		.504	.14	.06		−.02	1.56	.95		−1.41	1.40	.42	.33
1951–55	.0150	.0069		−.1185	.0138	.029	.043		.702	.06	−.18		−.32	4.05	1.24		−1.31	3.72	.27	.29
1956–60	.0127	−.0081		.0728	.0107	.037	.045		1.164	.15	.15		.21	2.68	−1.40		.48	2.26	.26	.30
1961–6/68	−.0014	.0122		.0570	−.0044	.042	.055		.850	.10	.00		−.19	−.32	2.12		.64	−.98	.33	.27
Panel D:																				
$R_{pt} = \gamma_{1t} + \gamma_{2t}b_{pm} + \gamma_{3t}b_{pm}^2 + \gamma_{4t}\bar{s}_p(e_i) + \eta_{pt}$																				
1935–6/68	.0020	.0114	−.0026	.0516	.0008	.075	.123	.060	.929	−.09	−.09	−.12	−.10	.55	1.85	−.86	1.11	.20	.34	.31
1935–45	.0011	.0118	−.0009	.0817	.0010	.103	.146	.079	1.003	−.20	−.23	−.24	−.15	.13	.94	−.14	.94	.11	.34	.31
1946–55	.0017	.0209	−.0076	−.0378	.0008	.042	.096	.038	.619	−.10	−.00	−.01	−.20	.44	2.39	−2.16	−.67	.20	.36	.32
1956–6/68	.0031	.0034	−.0000	.0966	.0005	.065	.122	.055	1.061	.12	.03	.01	−.05	.59	.34	−.00	1.11	.10	.32	.29
1935–40	.0009	.0156	−.0029	.0025	.0008	.112	.171	.085	.826	−.16	−.23	−.26	−.12	.07	.78	−.29	.03	.06	.26	.30
1941–45	.0015	.0073	.0014	.1767	.0012	.092	.109	.072	1.181	−.28	−.21	−.22	−.18	.12	.52	.15	1.16	.10	.43	.31
1946–50	.0011	.0141	−.0040	−.0313	.0004	.047	.106	.042	.590	−.10	.03	−.01	−.12	.18	1.03	−.73	−.41	.07	.44	.33
1951–55	.0023	.0277	−.0112	−.0443	.0011	.037	.085	.034	.651	−.11	−.13	−.01	−.28	.48	2.53	−2.54	−.53	.23	.29	.30
1956–60	.0103	−.0047	−.0020	.0979	.0083	.049	.078	.032	1.286	−.16	.19	−.01	.02	1.63	−.47	−.49	.59	1.31	.28	.30
1961–6/68	−.0017	.0088	.0013	.0957	−.0046	.073	.144	.066	.887	.20	.00	.01	−.15	−.21	.58	.19	1.02	−.60	.35	.29

SOURCE: Eugene F. Fama and James D. MacBeth, "Risk, Return, and Equilibrium: Empirical Tests," *Journal of Political Economy* 71 (May–June 1973): 622–623.

Panel B, the value of $t(\bar{\gamma}_3)$ for the overall period 1935–June 1968 is only $-.29$. In the subperiods, there are four positive values of $\bar{\gamma}_3$ and five negative values. In the five-year subperiods, $t(\bar{\gamma}_3)$ for 1951–1955 is approximately -2.7, but for subperiods that do not cover 1951–1955 the values of $t(\bar{\gamma}_3)$ are much closer to zero. There is likewise no systematic evidence in Panel D against the hypothesis that $E(\tilde{\gamma}_{3t}) = 0$. Thus, one cannot reject the hypothesis that b_{pm}^2 contributes nothing to the description of expected returns.

Since the evidence is consistent with (36)—that is, with the propositions that the relationship between expected return and β_{im} is linear and that β_{im} is the only measure of risk needed to explain differences among expected returns—we cannot reject the hypothesis that securities are priced so that m is a minimum variance portfolio. The data are also consistent with the hypothesis that m is on the positively sloped segment of the minimum variance boundary, so that the trade-off of expected return for risk in m is positive. For the overall period 1935–June 1968, $t(\bar{\gamma}_2)$ is large for all models. Except for 1956–1960, the values of $t(\bar{\gamma}_2)$ are also systematically positive in the subperiods, but not so systematically large.

The small values of $t(\bar{\gamma}_2)$ for subperiods reflect the substantial month-to-month variability of γ_{2t}. For example, in Panel A we find that for equation (49) during 1935–1940, $\bar{\gamma}_2 = .0109$. For this period the average incremental return per unit of b_{im} is almost 1.1 percent per month. On average, bearing risk produced substantial rewards. Nevertheless, because of the variability of γ_{2t}—in this period, $s(\gamma_2)$ is 11.6 percent per month—$t(\bar{\gamma}_2)$ is only .79. It takes the statistical power of the large sample for the overall period, that is, a large value of T in (51), before values of $\bar{\gamma}_2$ that are large in practical terms also yield large t-statistics.

At least with the sample for the overall period, $t(\bar{\gamma}_2)$ achieves values supportive of the conclusion that there is a statistically observable positive relationship between expected return and risk. This is not the case with respect to $t(\bar{\gamma}_3)$ and $t(\bar{\gamma}_4)$. Even or indeed especially for the overall period, these t-statistics are close to zero. This makes us somewhat more confident of the conclusions that the relationship between expected return and risk is linear and that β_{im} is the only measure of risk needed to explain differences among expected returns.

In short, the tests on average returns are consistent with the hypothesis that securities are priced so that the portfolio m is on the positively sloped segment of the minimum variance boundary.

TESTS BASED ON THE TIME-SERIES BEHAVIOR OF RETURNS

The autocorrelations in Table 9.4 are also consistent with what would be expected from a market where securities are priced according to (36) and where, in addition, the market is efficient. The autocorrelations of γ_{3t} and

γ_{4t}, computed about means that are assumed to be zero, test the proposition that there is no information in the time series of past values of γ_{3t} and γ_{4t} that ever warrants nonzero assessments of expected future values. Consistent with this proposition, $\hat{\rho}_0(\gamma_3)$ and $\hat{\rho}_0(\gamma_4)$ in Table 9.4 are always low in terms of explanatory power and generally low in terms of statistical significance.

Recall from Chapter 4 that the proportion of the variance of a variable explained by first-order autocorrelation is estimated by the square of the estimated first-order coefficient. In all cases, $\hat{\rho}_0(\gamma_3)^2$ and $\hat{\rho}_0(\gamma_4)^2$ are small. As for statistical significance, if the true autocorrelation is zero, the standard deviation of the sample coefficient can be approximated by $\sigma(\hat{\rho}) = 1/\sqrt{T}$. For the overall period, $\sigma(\hat{\rho})$ is approximately .05, while for the ten- and five-year subperiods, $\sigma(\hat{\rho})$ is approximately .09 and .13, respectively. Thus, the values of $\hat{\rho}_0(\gamma_{3t})$ and $\hat{\rho}_0(\gamma_{4t})$ are generally also statistically close to zero. There are exceptions to this statement, but they involve primarily periods that include the 1935-1940 subperiod, and the results for these periods are not independent. Moreover, even though the true autocorrelation may be close to zero, some autocorrelations are expected to be large on a purely chance basis when many sample autocorrelations are computed.

The proposition that securities are priced so that m is on the positively sloped segment of the minimum variance boundary only says that $E(\tilde{\gamma}_{2t}) = [E(\tilde{R}_{mt}) - E(\tilde{R}_{0mt})] > 0$; the model does not hypothesize a specific value of $E(\tilde{\gamma}_{2t})$. If we are willing to assume that the equilibrium expected value of the risk premium is constant through time, then sample autocorrelations of γ_{2t}, computed about the sample mean of γ_{2t}, test the proposition that the time series of past values of γ_{2t} never warrants an assessment of the expected future value of $\tilde{\gamma}_{2t}$, which is different from the assumed constant equilibrium expected value of γ_{2t}. Since the sample values of $\hat{\rho}(\gamma_{2t})$ in Table 9.4 are small, both statistically and in terms of explanatory power, the proposition is not rejected by the evidence.

Market efficiency in a world where securities are priced so that m is a minimum variance portfolio also implies that the disturbances $\tilde{\eta}_{pt}$ in (46) to (49) should be uncorrelated through time. If this is not the case, then the time series of past values of $\tilde{\eta}_{pt}$ can be used as the basis of correct nonzero assessments of expected future values, which means that the future expected return on the portfolio is not simply as predicted by the expected return-risk relationship (36). In this case, if the market is trying to price securities according to (36), then it is inefficient in the sense that it is ignoring information in past returns.

Fama and MacBeth do not show autocorrelations for the η_{pt}, but they report that, like the autocorrelations of the γ_{jt}, those of the η_{pt} are close to zero. They also compute higher-order autocorrelations for the γ_{jt} and η_{pt}, that is, autocorrelations for lags greater than one, and they report that these are likewise never systematically large.

EVIDENCE ON THE RELIABILITY OF THE γ_{jt} OF DIFFERENT RETURN EQUATIONS

Since the results from (46) to (49) are mutually consistent, we need not be too concerned with determining which version of a particular γ_{jt} provides the most reliable test of a specific implication of (36). Nevertheless, it is interesting to note that the results in Table 9.4 are consistent with our earlier discussion of reliability. Thus, for any given j, the least squares γ_{jt} in (46), (47), (48), or (49) is the return on a portfolio that focuses on one testable implication of (36), while "zeroing out" the effects of any other explanatory variables that appear in (46), (47), (48), or (49). The fewer the explanatory variables in an equation, the fewer "zeroing out" constraints imposed on the least squares procedure in its search for a "smallest variance" γ_{jt}. Thus, the search is likely to be more successful.

For example, in each of the equations (46) to (49), the least squares γ_{2t} is the return on a portfolio that has $b_{pm} = 1.0$ and that zeroes out the effects of any other variables that appear in the return equation. In Panel A of Table 9.4, we find indeed that the less constrained γ_{2t} of (49) has standard deviations $s(\gamma_2)$ much smaller than the $s(\gamma_2)$ from (46) or (47) in Panels B and D, and usually at least a little smaller than $s(\gamma_2)$ from (48). Similar comparisons can be carried out, by the reader, between the values of $s(\gamma_3)$ in Panels B and D of Table 9.4 and between the values of $s(\gamma_4)$ in Panels C and D.

PROBLEM IV.B

1. How can one explain the fact that $s(\gamma_2)$ increases more when one goes from Panel A to Panel B than when one goes from Panel A to Panel C?

ANSWER

1. When an additional variable is included in a return equation, its effect on $s(\gamma_2)$ depends on the strength of the relationship between the additional variable, b_{pm}^2 or $\bar{s}_p(e_i)$, and b_{pm}. If the relationship is strong, then the additional constraint that the weighted average of the 20 values of b_{pm}^2 or $\bar{s}_p(e_i)$ must be zero is a strong constraint on the way the 20 component portfolios can be combined to get the smallest variance portfolio that has $b_{pm} = 1.0$. The evidence from the $s(\gamma_2)$ in Table 9.4 is that the relationship between b_{pm} and b_{pm}^2 is (obviously) strong, but the relationship between b_{pm} and $\bar{s}_p(e_i)$ is not so strong. The statistically sophisticated reader recognizes that this is just an intuitive discussion of the statistical phenomenon called multicollinearity.

C. The Sharpe-Lintner Hypothesis

STATISTICAL CONSIDERATIONS

In the Sharpe-Lintner model of market equilibrium there is unrestricted borrowing and lending at the risk-free rate of interest R_{Ft}. The testable implication of this assumption is that the expected return on any security or portfolio whose return is uncorrelated with the return on the market portfolio M is R_{Ft}. If we are willing to assume that m, the equally weighted portfolio of NYSE stocks, is a good proxy for M, the value-weighted portfolio of all investment assets, then Table 9.4 contains tests of the Sharpe-Lintner hypothesis. Thus, the least squares value of γ_{1t} for (49) is the return on a standard portfolio where the weights assigned to the 20 component Fama-MacBeth portfolios yield a weighted average value of the 20 component b_{pm} equal to zero. The least squares values of γ_{1t} for (46), (47), and (48) are likewise the returns on zero-b_{pm} portfolios, but these portfolios are constructed under the additional constraints that the weighted average of the 20 b_{pm}^2 must be zero [(46) and (47)] and/or the weighted average of the 20 component $\bar{s}_p(e_i)$ must be zero [(46) and (48)].

Since we could not reject the linearity and non-β risk hypotheses of the two-parameter model, we are free to choose any of the return models as the basis of the tests of the Sharpe-Lintner hypothesis. That is, in constructing a zero-b_{pm} portfolio, there is no need to "zero out" the effects of non-linearities and non-β risk on expected returns; we can make our decision about the Sharpe-Lintner hypothesis by determining which return model seems to provide the most convincing evidence. As judged by the values of $s(\gamma_1)$, the most reliable tests are indeed from the simplest model (49), and in these the hypothesis takes a sound thumping. For the overall period, the value of $t(\overline{\gamma_1 - R_F})$ in Panel A of Table 9.4 is 2.55, which is reliably different from zero. In practical terms, the average value of $\gamma_{1t} - R_F$ for 1935–June 1968 is .0048; on average, the premium in the return on the zero-b_{pm} portfolio produced by the least squares computations is almost half of one percent per month. In the results from (49), there is only one subperiod, 1961–June 1968, when the Sharpe-Lintner hypothesis does well. In all other subperiods, and especially those covering 1951–1960, the premium of γ_{1t} over R_{Ft} is substantial.

On the basis of tests similar to those of Fama and MacBeth, Black, Jensen, and Scholes (1972) and Friend and Blume (1970) likewise come to a negative conclusion with respect to the Sharpe-Lintner hypothesis.

THEORETICAL CONSIDERATIONS

Under the assumption that m, the equally weighted portfolio of NYSE stocks, is an adequate proxy for M, the value-weighted portfolio of all investment assets, there are at least two versions of the two-parameter model consistent with the preceding evidence; that is, there are at least two models of market equilibrium in which $E(\tilde{R}_{0Mt})$, the expected return on zero-β positive variance securities and portfolios, is greater than the risk-free rate R_{Ft}.

Thus, in the restricted borrowing version of the Black model there is risk-free lending at the rate R_{Ft}, but there is no risk-free borrowing. The picture of market equilibrium is Figure 8.5. The value-weighted market portfolio M is efficient, but it is above the tangency portfolio T on the efficient boundary. As a consequence, $E(\tilde{R}_{0Mt})$, which is just the intercept on the $E(\tilde{R}_{pt})$ axis of the line tangent to the boundary at M, is greater than R_{Ft}. Similarly, in the "margin" version of the model, there is unrestricted risk-free lending, but risk-free borrowing is restricted to some fixed fraction of portfolio funds. Market equilibrium is as pictured in Figure 8.7. The market portfolio M is one of the minimum variance portfolios of positive variance securities; but since it is above the tangency portfolio T on the minimum variance boundary, we again have the condition $E(\tilde{R}_{0Mt}) > R_{Ft}$. Since there are at least two models of market equilibrium that are consistent with the evidence, rejection of the Sharpe-Lintner model is not a telling blow to two-parameter theory.

There is, however, good reason to believe that the Fama-MacBeth tests of the Sharpe-Lintner hypothesis are inappropriate, and the arguments that follow apply equally to the results of Black, Jensen, and Scholes (1972) and Friend and Blume (1970). In particular, there is good evidence that m is not

FIGURE 9.1

A View of the Sharpe-Lintner Model That Is Consistent with the Empirical Evidence

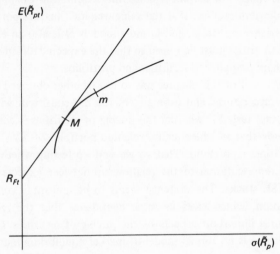

a good proxy for M. Lawrence Fisher (1966) reports that the standard deviation of the return on a value-weighted portfolio of NYSE stocks is about 80 percent as large as the standard deviation of the return on an equally weighted portfolio of NYSE stocks. NYSE stocks would be among the more risky securities in a market portfolio that included all investment assets. Thus, there is little doubt that m, the equally weighted portfolio of NYSE stocks, is substantially more risky than M, the value-weighted portfolio of all investment assets. In this light, the empirical evidence might be interpreted as consistent with the picture of market equilibrium shown in Figure 9.1. The portfolio m is along the positively sloped segment of the boundary of minimum variance portfolios of positive variance securities, but m is pictured as substantially more risky than M. The overall view of market equilibrium is that of the Sharpe-Lintner model.

In truth, all we can really say at this time is that the literature has not yet produced a meaningful test of the Sharpe-Lintner hypothesis.

V.   Some Applications of the Measured Risk-Return Relationships

The general objective of this chapter is to test the implications of the portfolio model of Chapters 2 and 7 for the pricing of securities in the capital market. We want to test whether the pricing of securities reflects the attempts of investors to hold efficient portfolios. To give this hypothesis testable content, we need some specific model of market equilibrium. The testable implication of the models of market equilibrium presented in Chapter 8 is that a market equilibrium requires that the value-weighted market portfolio M be a minimum variance portfolio, and in most models M is also an efficient portfolio. Thus, securities must be priced so that the expected return-risk equation (1) of this chapter applies to securities and portfolios.

The original goal of this chapter was to test whether observed relationships between average returns and estimates of risk are consistent with (1). What we have in fact tested is whether the pricing of securities is consistent with the hypothesis that m, the equally weighted portfolio of NYSE stocks, is a minimum variance portfolio. That is, we end up testing whether (36) is an appropriate representation of the relationship between expected return and risk for NYSE stocks. The evidence seems to be uniformly consistent with this proposition, which gives us some confidence that the two-parameter model captures important aspects of the pricing of securities. On the other hand, since there is no formal model of market equilibrium that tells us that securities are priced so that m is a minimum variance portfolio, it is not clear how much support for the two-parameter model should be imputed to the results.

Like all the empirical issues raised in this book, this is an issue that the reader can judge. My task is completed if I have presented a reasonably coherent introduction to the theory and evidence. I shall, however, now try to bias the reader's judgment with respect to the usefulness of the risk-return tests with a brief discussion of some of the applications that have been made of the results.

The applications use the month-by-month relationships between risk and return obtained from the preceding results (a) to test the efficiency of the capital market in adjusting prices to specific types of new information and (b) to measure the performance of managed portfolios. Before discussing these applications, however, we must develop a better understanding of the nature of the measured risk-return relationships that come out of the preceding results.

A. A Two-Factor Market Model

We found in Chapter 3 that if the joint distribution of security returns is multivariate normal, the joint distribution of the return on any security and the return on any portfolio is bivariate normal. Although we need not go into the details,* multivariate normality of security returns also implies that the joint distribution of the return on any security and the returns on any two (or three, or four or $n - 1$) portfolios is multivariate normal.

We are interested in a specific application of this result. As in Chapter 8, let Z be the minimum variance portfolio of positive variance securities whose return is uncorrelated with the return on the market portfolio M. With multivariate normality of security returns, the joint distribution of the return on any security i and the returns on Z and M is multivariate (trivariate) normal, which can be shown to imply a relationship among $\tilde{R}_{it}, \tilde{R}_{Zt}$, and $\tilde{R}_{Mt}$ of the form

$$\tilde{R}_{it} = \alpha_i + \beta_{iZ}\tilde{R}_{Zt} + \beta_{iM}\tilde{R}_{Mt} + \tilde{\eta}_{it}, \tag{52}$$

where

$$\alpha_i = E(\tilde{R}_{it}) - \beta_{iZ}E(\tilde{R}_{Zt}) - \beta_{iM}E(\tilde{R}_{Mt}), \tag{53}$$

$$\beta_{iZ} = \frac{\text{cov}(\tilde{R}_i, \tilde{R}_Z)}{\sigma^2(\tilde{R}_Z)}, \text{ and } \beta_{im} = \frac{\text{cov}(\tilde{R}_i, \tilde{R}_M)}{\sigma^2(\tilde{R}_M)}, \tag{54}$$

*Those interested can consult Anderson (1958, chaps. 1–2) or Cramer (1946, chaps. 21, 24).

and where the disturbance $\tilde{\eta}_{it}$ has expected value equal to zero and is independent of $\tilde{R}_{Zt}$ and $\tilde{R}_{Mt}$.

Note that β_{iZ} is the risk of security i in the portfolio Z, measured relative to the risk or variance of the return on Z, just as β_{iM} is the risk of security i in M measured relative to the risk of M. That the coefficients in (52) correspond to these risk measures is a special consequence of the fact that $\tilde{R}_{Zt}$ and $\tilde{R}_{Mt}$ are uncorrelated. Note also that (52) can be interpreted as a "two-factor" version of the market model of (4). In (52) the return on security i is related to the returns on the portfolios Z and M, whereas in (4) only M is used. Finally, it is also important to note that if security returns have a multivariate normal distribution, then the market models of (4) and (52) are both valid representations of the return on security i.

The fact that Z is the minimum variance zero-β_{pM} portfolio will soon be shown to imply that

$$\beta_{iZ} = 1 - \beta_{iM}. \tag{55}$$

Thus, (52) can be rewritten as

$$\tilde{R}_{it} = \alpha_i + (1 - \beta_{iM})\tilde{R}_{Zt} + \beta_{iM}\tilde{R}_{Mt} + \tilde{\eta}_{it} \tag{56a}$$

$$= \alpha_i + \tilde{R}_{Zt} + \beta_{iM}(\tilde{R}_{Mt} - \tilde{R}_{Zt}) + \tilde{\eta}_{it}. \tag{56b}$$

If the world is as described by any of the models of market equilibrium of Chapter 8—that is, if the relationship between expected return and risk in M is as described by (1)—then for every security i, $\alpha_i = 0.0$ and (56a–b) become

$$\tilde{R}_{it} = (1 - \beta_{iM})\tilde{R}_{Zt} + \beta_{iM}\tilde{R}_{Mt} + \tilde{\eta}_{it} \tag{57a}$$

$$\tilde{R}_{it} = \tilde{R}_{Zt} + \beta_{iM}(\tilde{R}_{Mt} - \tilde{R}_{Zt}) + \tilde{\eta}_{it}. \tag{57b}$$

PROBLEMS V.A

1. Show that if Z is the minimum variance zero-β_{pM} portfolio, then (55) holds.

2. Show that in (56)

$$\sum_{i=1}^{n} x_{iM}\alpha_i = 0, \qquad \sum_{i=1}^{n} x_{iM}\tilde{\eta}_{it} = 0.$$

3. Interpret the constant α_i and the disturbance $\tilde{\epsilon}_{it}$ in the one-factor market model of (4) in terms of quantities from the two-factor model of (57).

4. Assume that the equally weighted portfolio m of NYSE stocks is a minimum variance portfolio, and let z be the minimum variance portfolio whose return is uncorrelated with the return on m. Show that the return on any NYSE stock can then be expressed as

$$\tilde{R}_{it} = (1 - \beta_{im})\tilde{R}_{zt} + \beta_{im}\tilde{R}_{mt} + \tilde{\eta}_{it} \qquad (58a)$$

$$\tilde{R}_{it} = \tilde{R}_{zt} + \beta_{im}(\tilde{R}_{mt} - \tilde{R}_{zt}) + \tilde{\eta}_{it}, \qquad (58b)$$

where $\tilde{\eta}_{it}$ has expected value equal to zero and is independent of $\tilde{R}_{zt}$ and $\tilde{R}_{mt}$.

ANSWERS

1. The minimum variance zero-β_{pM} portfolio Z is given by the set of weights $x_{iZ}, i = 1, \cdots, n$, that constitute the solution to the problem

$$\min \sigma^2(\tilde{R}_Z) = \min \sum_{i=1}^{n} \sum_{j=1}^{n} x_{iZ}x_{jZ}\sigma_{ij}$$

subject to the constraints

$$\beta_{ZM} = \sum_{i=1}^{n} x_{iZ}\beta_{iM} = 0 \text{ and } \sum_{i=1}^{n} x_{iZ} = 1.$$

The Lagrangian expression for this problem can be written as

$$\sigma^2(\tilde{R}_Z) + 2\lambda_1\left(0 - \sum_{i=1}^{n} x_{iZ}\beta_{iM}\right) + 2\lambda_2\left(1 - \sum_{i=1}^{n} x_{iZ}\right).$$

Differentiating this expression with respect to x_{iZ}, and then setting the derivative equal to zero, we get

$$\sum_{j=1}^{n} x_{jZ}\sigma_{ij} - \lambda_1\beta_{iM} - \lambda_2 = 0, \qquad i = 1, \cdots, n, \qquad (59)$$

or

$$\text{cov}(\tilde{R}_i, \tilde{R}_Z) = \lambda_1\beta_{iM} + \lambda_2. \qquad (60)$$

If we multiply through (59) or (60) by x_{iZ} and then sum over i, we find that

$$\sigma^2(\tilde{R}_Z) = \lambda_2. \qquad (61)$$

If we multiply through (60) by x_{iM} and sum over i, we find that

$$0 = \text{cov}(\tilde{R}_M, \tilde{R}_Z) = \lambda_1 + \lambda_2,$$

which, with (61), implies

$$\lambda_1 = -\lambda_2 = -\sigma^2(\tilde{R}_Z). \qquad (62)$$

With (61) and (62), (60) becomes

$$\text{cov}(\tilde{R}_i, \tilde{R}_Z) = -\sigma^2(\tilde{R}_Z)\beta_{iM} + \sigma^2(\tilde{R}_Z),$$

so that

$$\beta_{iZ} = \frac{\text{cov}(\tilde{R}_i, \tilde{R}_Z)}{\sigma^2(\tilde{R}_Z)} = 1 - \beta_{iM}.$$

2. Multiply through (56) by x_{iM} and then sum over i to get

$$\tilde{R}_{Mt} = \sum_{i=1}^{n} x_{iM}\alpha_i + \tilde{R}_{Mt} + \sum_{i=1}^{n} x_{iM}\tilde{\eta}_{it}.$$

Since the α_i are constants and the $\tilde{\eta}_{it}$ are random variables, the two weighted averages must separately be equal to zero. The fact that the weighted sum of the disturbances must be zero implies that the $\tilde{\eta}_{it}$ of different securities cannot be independent. Recall the similar result that we found in Section II.C of Chapter 3 for the disturbances from the one-factor market model of (4).

3. If we take expected values in (4) and (57a), we find that the intercept α_i in the one-factor market model is

$$\alpha_i = (1 - \beta_{iM})E(\tilde{R}_Z). \tag{63}$$

If we substitute (63) into (4) and then subtract (57a) from (4), we find that the disturbance $\tilde{\epsilon}_{it}$ in the one-factor model of (4) is related to $\tilde{R}_{Zt}$ and the disturbance $\tilde{\eta}_{it}$ in the two-factor model according to

$$\tilde{\epsilon}_{it} = (1 - \beta_{iM})[\tilde{R}_{Zt} - E(\tilde{R}_{Zt})] + \tilde{\eta}_{it}. \tag{64}$$

Thus, in the one-factor market model of (4), there is an "omitted variable," $\tilde{R}_{Zt}$, which shows up in the disturbance $\tilde{\epsilon}_{it}$. Since $\tilde{R}_{Zt}$ and $\tilde{R}_{Mt}$ are uncorrelated, the omitted variable does not lead to any particular statistical problems in (4). Since $\tilde{R}_{Zt}$ and $\tilde{\eta}_{it}$ are independent, $\sigma^2(\tilde{\eta}_{it}) \leqslant \sigma^2(\tilde{\epsilon}_{it})$; that is, the two-factor model necessarily "explains" at least as much of $\sigma^2(\tilde{R}_{it})$ as the one-factor model. The improvement in explanatory power that one gets from including $\tilde{R}_{Zt}$ in the equation depends on the size of the variance of $\tilde{R}_{Zt}$ relative to that of $\tilde{\eta}_{it}$.

Finally, the presence of the common variable $\tilde{R}_{Zt}$ in the disturbance $\tilde{\epsilon}_{it}$ tends to produce correlation between the one-factor market model disturbances of different securities. From (64) we can see that the presence of $\tilde{R}_{Zt}$ in $\tilde{\epsilon}_{it}$ will tend to produce positive correlation between the $\tilde{\epsilon}_{it}$ of securities that have values of β_{iM} on the same side of 1.0 and negative correlation between the $\tilde{\epsilon}_{it}$ of securities that have values of β_{iM} on opposite sides of 1.0. We can also see from (64) that these effects are larger the further the values of β_{iM} are from 1. This may explain our earlier observation (Table 9.2) that when portfolios are formed from securities with very high or very low values of β, there is a smaller reduction in the variance of the one-factor market model disturbances than when portfolios are formed from securities with values of β closer to 1.

4. Multivariate normality of security returns implies that there is a relationship between $\tilde{R}_{it}$, $\tilde{R}_{zt}$, and $\tilde{R}_{mt}$ in the form of (52), with coefficients given by (53) and (54), but where one simply substitutes z for Z and m for M. The same substitutions in Problem V.A.*1* produce the conclusion that

$$\beta_{iz} = \frac{\text{cov}\,(\tilde{R}_i, \tilde{R}_z)}{\sigma^2(\tilde{R}_z)} = 1 - \beta_{im}, \tag{65}$$

so that the step from (52) to (56) is valid. If securities are priced so that m is a minimum variance portfolio, then (36) applies to securities in m, from which it follows that the constant α_i in the relevant version of (56) is zero for securities in m; that is, the returns on securities in m can be represented as in (58). Finally, substitution of z for Z and m for M also allows us to apply the results of Problems V.A.2 and 3 to the two-factor market model relationship between $\tilde{R}_{it}, \tilde{R}_{zt}$, and $\tilde{R}_{mt}$.

We might emphasize that all of the properties ascribed to (56) are implications of multivariate normality and of the fact that Z is the minimum variance portfolio whose return is uncorrelated with the return on M. In adding the assumption that securities are priced according to some two-parameter model of market equilibrium, we get the implication that α_i is zero for all securities. In the applications, however, this additional implication is important.

B. Market Efficiency and the Two-Factor Models

We found in Chapter 8 that in the Black model and its variants, in a market equilibrium the returns on all minimum variance portfolios can be expressed as combinations of Z and M:

$$\tilde{R}_{et} = x_e \tilde{R}_{Zt} + (1 - x_e)\tilde{R}_{Mt}, \tag{66}$$

where x_e and $(1 - x_e)$ are the proportions invested in Z and M to get the minimum variance portfolio e. With (66) we can determine that

$$\beta_{eM} = \frac{\text{cov}\,(\tilde{R}_e, \tilde{R}_M)}{\sigma^2(\tilde{R}_M)}$$

$$= \frac{\text{cov}\,(x_e \tilde{R}_Z + (1 - x_e)\tilde{R}_M, \tilde{R}_M)}{\sigma^2(\tilde{R}_M)} = \frac{(1 - x_e)\sigma^2(\tilde{R}_M)}{\sigma^2(\tilde{R}_M)} = 1 - x_e.$$

Thus (66) can be rewritten as

$$\tilde{R}_{et} = (1 - \beta_{eM})\tilde{R}_{Zt} + \beta_{eM}\tilde{R}_{Mt} = \tilde{R}_{Zt} + \beta_{eM}(\tilde{R}_{Mt} - \tilde{R}_{Zt}). \tag{67}$$

Equation (67) says that there is an exact relationship between the return on any minimum variance portfolio e, its β_{eM}, the return on the minimum variance zero-β_{pM} portfolio Z, and the return on the market portfolio M. Equations (57) say that there is a similar risk-return relationship for any security i, except that the relationship is not exact; it is subject to a disturbance $\tilde{n}_{it}$. In intuitive terms, $\tilde{R}_{Zt}$ and $\tilde{R}_{Mt}$ capture the effects of marketwide factors on

$\tilde{R}_{it}$, while factors more specific to the prospects of security i show up in $\tilde{\eta}_{it}$. The applications discussed below are concerned with the efficiency of the market in adjusting security prices to information specific to the prospects of security i. Thus, they are concerned with testing the implications of market efficiency for the properties of $\tilde{\eta}_{it}$. By applying (35) to (57) we determine that if the market is efficient, and if market equilibrium is characterized by the expected return-risk equation (1), then in (57),

$$E(\tilde{\eta}_{it}|\phi_{t-1}) = 0. \tag{68}$$

In words, there is no way to use ϕ_{t-1}, the set of information available at $t-1$, or any subset of ϕ_{t-1}, as the basis of a correct nonzero assessment of the expected value of the disturbance $\tilde{\eta}_{it}$ in (57).

The applications discussed below test whether (68) is a correct description of the world. One set of tests is concerned with whether (68) holds with respect to particular items of company-specific information. For example, if a merger is announced by firm i at $t-1$, can it be used as the basis of a correct nonzero assessment of the expected value of $\tilde{\eta}_{it}$ for that firm's stock? If the market is efficient the answer to this question is, of course, no. The price of the stock of firm i will fully adjust at $t-1$ to any information in a merger, so that at time t the deviation of $\tilde{\eta}_{it}$ from zero cannot be predicted from the information available at $t-1$.

The other types of tests of market efficiency are concerned with the performance of managed portfolios. These tests ask whether portfolio managers can use any of the information available at $t-1$ to make correct nonzero assessments of the expected values of the $\tilde{\eta}_{it}$ of different securities. In practical terms, are the portfolio managers able to utilize information available at $t-1$ to choose portfolios that on average have higher returns at t than the combinations of Z and M that have the same level of risk? A positive answer to this question would imply an inefficient market: it is possible to use information available at $t-1$ to predict how the disturbance $\tilde{\eta}_{it}$ for some securities will differ from zero.

The preceding is, of course, similar in tone to most of Chapter 5. To test market efficiency, some model of market equilibrium is required. The two-parameter models of market equilibrium are more sophisticated than those used in Chapter 5, but the approach to testing market efficiency is the same.

C. Market Efficiency and Company-Specific Information

As usual, in carrying out the tests of market efficiency discussed above, some concessions must be made to the data. First, to date, the tests of the market's reaction to company-specific information are based on the proposition that m, the equally weighted portfolio of NYSE stocks, is a minimum variance portfolio. Thus, the expected return equation is (36), and (58) is the corresponding version of the two-factor market model. Given that m is a minimum variance portfolio, the switch from M to m is legitimate, and the approach to tests of market efficiency based on m is precisely the same as that based on M.

The second concession made to the data is in the definition of z, the minimum variance zero-β_{pm} portfolio in (58). In the tests to date, R_{zt} is taken to be γ_{1t} of (49), that is, the intercept in the least squares regression of the 20 Fama-MacBeth portfolio returns on the estimates of β_{pm} for these portfolios. Recall that the least squares γ_{1t} is the return on a portfolio that has an estimated value of β_{pm} equal to zero, but the true β_{pm} of this portfolio is not zero. Moreover, even ignoring the loss of information caused by the fact that the regressions are carried out on portfolios rather than individual securities, and even ignoring the fact that we use estimates b_{pm} rather than the true values β_{pm}, the least squares γ_{1t} is only the minimum variance zero-β_{pm} portfolio when the disturbances $\tilde{\eta}_{it}$ in (41) are independent and identically distributed across securities. In short, γ_{1t} from (49) is a proxy for R_{zt} in (58).

The mechanics of the approach to tests of market efficiency based on the two-factor model of (58) are in most respects identical to the mechanics of the approach based on the one-factor model, as described in Chapter 5. In brief, instead of examining the behavior of the average and cumulative average residuals from the one-factor model in months surrounding an event of interest, one examines the behavior of the average and cumulative average η_{it} from

$$R_{it} = R_{zt} + b_{im}(R_{mt} - R_{zt}) + \eta_{it}, \tag{69}$$

which is (58) but with the estimate b_{im} substituted for the true value β_{im} and with the understanding that R_{zt} is the least squares value of γ_{1t} in (49).

Thus, Ball (1972) uses average and cumulative average values of η_{it} in (69) to study the reaction of the market to changes in accounting techniques by firms. He finds that there is no unusual subsequent behavior in the returns on the shares of firms carrying out such changes, in the sense that average and cumulative average values of η_{it} do not depart much from zero in the months following the accounting change. Moreover, in cases where the accounting changes have no real effect on the net returns to the firm, there is no unusual behavior of share returns before or after the accounting change. Ball interprets this as evidence that the market reacts efficiently to any information in a change in accounting techniques, and the market is not misled when such a change has no information content.

Mandelker (1974) uses more or less the same technique to study the behavior of the returns on both acquiring and acquired firms in a merger. He finds that acquired firms experience abnormal returns when a merger is announced (cumulative average values of η_{it} that reach about .15, or 15 percent, by the time the merger takes place). The acquiring firms, however, do not on average experience abnormal returns at any time reasonably close to the release of information about the merger. Mandelker interprets this as evidence that any gains from mergers go to the acquired firms. One possible explanation is that the synergy in a merger is in many cases improved management of the acquired firm. If the acquisitions market for poorly managed firms is perfectly competitive, competition among acquiring firms will cause all the gains from the merger (removal of the poor management of the acquired firm) to be passed on to the shareholders of the acquired firm.

In another study that uses more or less the same techniques, Ibbotson (1974) finds that when a firm goes public for the first time—that is, when a firm makes its first public issue of common stock—the stock is on average underpriced by the underwriters. From the date of issue to the end of the month of issue, the average value of η_{it} in (69) for such securities is about .14. Thus, there is an "abnormal" average return of 14 percent in the month of issue. As a result, during the 1960s, the period that Ibbotson studies, new issues were typically oversubscribed and had to be rationed by underwriters to their customers. Ibbotson admits that he has no good explanation for this phenomenon. More important for the issue of capital market efficiency, he does find that once a newly public security is available in the open market (after it passes from the hands of the underwriter), the market for it seems to be efficient; that is, once they are available in the open market, the average η_{it} for these securities are not significantly different from zero.

Although it probably has no major effect on his results, there is one problem in Ibbotson's work that should be mentioned. When firms first go public, their shares are almost always traded in the over-the-counter market. Even if (58) is a valid risk-return relationship, it refers only to NYSE common stocks, and in principle it should only be the basis of tests of efficiency for NYSE stocks. For Ibbotson's data, this is probably not an important criticism. The 14 percent average initial underpricing that he observes is so large that it would probably be significant under any method of analysis. Moroever, the variability of the returns on securities newly gone public is generally so large that the method of abstracting from the effects of risk has little impact on the results.

Finally, Jaffe (1974) uses (69) to study the returns on insider trading—that is, trading by company managers and directors in the shares of their own firms. He finds that, on average, the η_{it} in (69) are negative subsequent to heavy sales by insiders and positive subsequent to heavy purchases. Strictly speaking, this is evidence of market inefficiency: insiders typically have information that the market has not utilized in setting prices. In itself, it is not surprising that insiders can beat the market. However, Jaffe also finds that correct nonzero assessments of the expected values of future $\tilde{\eta}_{it}$ can be made on the basis of Securities and Exchange Commission publications of insider activity. This is somewhat more impressive evidence of a market inefficiency. As far as I know, Jaffe's is the only test of market efficiency that finds that the market ignores some obviously publicly available information in setting prices.

PROBLEM V.C

1. In fact, the tests of market efficiency discussed above are based on the η_{it} from

$$R_{it} = \gamma_{1t} + \gamma_{2t}b_{im} + \eta_{it}, \tag{70}$$

where γ_{1t} and γ_{2t} are the (generally Fama-MacBeth) least squares values from (49). Given that R_{zt} in (69) is taken to be γ_{1t} in (49), when will the η_{it} in (69) and (70) be identical?

ANSWER

1. Suppose the 20 Fama-MacBeth portfolios include all the stocks on the NYSE. Then, multiplying through (49) by 1/20 and summing over p leads to

$$\frac{1}{20} \sum_{p=1}^{20} R_{pt} = R_{zt} + \gamma_{2t} \frac{1}{20} \sum_{p=1}^{20} b_{pm} + \frac{1}{20} \sum_{p=1}^{20} \eta_{pt}$$

$$R_{mt} - R_{zt} = \gamma_{2t}.$$

Here we make use of the facts that (a) if the 20 portfolios include all NYSE stocks, the average of the 20 portfolio returns is R_{mt} and the average of the b_{pm} is 1; (b) the sum of the residuals in any least squares regression is zero. We find, then, that the least squares value of γ_{2t} in (49) is $R_{mt} - R_{zt}$, so that the η_{it} in (69) and (70) are identical.

In fact, because of the data requirements imposed on the securities included in the 20 portfolios, the Fama-MacBeth portfolios cover most but not all of the stocks on the NYSE for month t. Fama-MacBeth indicate, however, that the average of their 20 portfolio returns is always quite close to R_{mt}, and the average of their b_{pm} is close to 1. Thus, the relationships between (69) and (70) developed above hold to a close approximation.

D. Portfolio Selection and Performance Evaluation

GENERAL COMMENTS

In an efficient market and with securities priced according to the Black model, portfolio selection is a simple matter. All efficient portfolios are combinations of the market portfolio M and the minimum variance zero-β_{pM} portfolio Z. The investor simply chooses the combination of Z and M that has the desired combination of mean and standard deviation of return.

Some investors and portfolio managers may feel, however, that the market is inefficient. They feel that they have more information or are better able to evaluate existing information than the market. If securities are priced according to the Black model, it is, in principle, easy to test whether in fact particular investors and portfolio managers can beat the market. The returns on minimum variance portfolios are related to their β_{eM} as in (67). There is a corresponding risk-return relationship, (57), for individual securities and for nonminimum variance portfolios, which is the same as (67), except that it is subject to a disturbance $\tilde{\eta}_{it}$. If the market is efficient, (68) holds and there is no way to use information available at $t-1$ to predict how $\tilde{\eta}_{it}$ will differ from zero. If the market is inefficient, however, and if some investors are shrewd enough to capitalize on the inefficiency, then we should find that the securities and portfolios they choose have measurably higher average returns than the combinations of Z and M that have the same level of β_{pM}. In other words, such investors should be able to use information available at $t-1$ to assess correct nonzero expected values for the $\tilde{\eta}_{it}$ in (57).

If we take the position that m, the equally weighted portfolio of NYSE stocks, is a minimum variance portfolio, then the statements above apply, but with the usual change from Z to z and M to m, and where we talk in terms of the disturbances from (58) rather than (57). However, there is also a more substantive change. Since (58) refers to NYSE stocks, we should only use it to evaluate security and portfolio selections of NYSE stocks.

THE INVESTMENT PERFORMANCE OF MUTUAL FUNDS

The major application of these ideas, in Jensen (1968; 1969), is based on the Sharpe-Lintner model of market equilibrium. In this model, one substitutes the risk-free rate R_{Ft} for $\tilde{R}_{Zt}$ in (66) and (67), so that (67) becomes

$$\tilde{R}_{et} = (1 - \beta_{eM})R_{Ft} + \beta_{eM}\tilde{R}_{Mt} = R_{Ft} + (\tilde{R}_{Mt} - R_{Ft})\beta_{eM}. \tag{71}$$

Moreover, from Problem V.A.*3* we know that if we are in the Sharpe-Lintner world, the intercept α_i in the one-factor market model is

$$\alpha_i = R_{Ft}(1 - \beta_{iM}), \tag{72}$$

so that (4) can be rewritten as

$$\tilde{R}_{it} = R_{Ft}(1 - \beta_{iM}) + \beta_{iM}\tilde{R}_{Mt} + \tilde{\epsilon}_{it}. \tag{73}$$

If the market is efficient,

$$E(\tilde{\epsilon}_{it}|\phi_{t-1}) = 0; \tag{74}$$

that is, there is no way to use any information available at $t-1$ as the basis of a correct nonzero assessment of the expected value of $\tilde{\epsilon}_{it}$.

Jensen tries to use the performance of mutual fund portfolios to find contradictions of (74). He tests whether mutual funds, or particular funds, seem to have access to information that allows them to earn higher average returns (positive average $\tilde{\epsilon}_{pt}$) than they would get simply by buying the combinations of F and M that have the same level of β_{pM} as their chosen portfolios. As usual, some concessions must be made to the data. He must use estimates of β_{pM} for mutual fund portfolios, and he must choose a proxy for the market portfolio M. He chooses the Standard and Poor's value-weighted index of NYSE stocks.

Jensen uses the risk-return framework described above to evaluate the performance of 115 mutual funds over the ten-year period 1955–1964. The general question to be answered is whether mutual fund managers have any special insights or information that allows them to earn average returns above the norm provided by the Sharpe-Lintner model. But Jensen attacks the question on several levels. First, can the funds generally do well enough to compensate investors for loading charges, management fees, and other costs that might be avoided by simply choosing the combination of the risk-free asset F and the market portfolio M with risk level comparable to that of the fund's actual portfolio? The answer seems to be an emphatic no. As far as net returns to investors are concerned, in 89 out of 115 cases the fund's average return for the ten-year period was below what would have been obtained from the combination of F and M with the same level of b_{pM}, and on average the investor's wealth after ten years of holding mutual funds is about 15 percent less than if he held the appropriate combinations of F and M.

The loading charge that an investor pays on buying into a fund is usually a salesman's commission that the fund itself never gets to invest. One might ask whether, if one ignores loading charges—that is, if one assumes no such charges are paid by the investor—fund managers can earn returns sufficiently above the norm to cover other expenses that are presumably more directly related to the management of the fund portfolios. Again, the answer seems to be no. When loading charges are ignored in computing returns, the average returns for 72 out of 115 funds are still below what would have been obtained from the combinations of F and M with the same level of b_{pM}, and on average the investor's wealth after ten years is about 9 percent less than if he held the appropriate combinations of F and M.

Finally, as a somewhat stronger test of market efficiency, one would like to know whether, ignoring all expenses, fund managements show any ability to pick securities that outperform the norm. Unfortunately, this question cannot be answered with precision for individual funds, since data on brokerage commissions are not published regularly. But Jensen suggests that available evidence indicates that the answer to the question is negative. Specifically, adding back all other published expenses of funds to their returns, the average returns for 58 out of 115 funds were below those for the corresponding combinations of F and M, and average wealth was about 2.5 percent less. Part of this result is due to the absence of a correction for brokerage commissions. Estimating these commissions from average portfolio turnover rates for all funds for 1953–1958 and adding them to returns for all funds just about wipes out the deficit that the funds have vis-à-vis the relevant naïve combinations of F and M, which is consistent with the proposition that the fund managers do not have access to special information.

Although mutual fund managers generally do not seem to have access to information not already fully reflected in prices, perhaps there are individual funds that consistently do better than the norm, thus providing at least some evidence against market efficiency. If there are such funds, however, they escape Jensen's search. For example, returns above the norm for individual funds in one subperiod do not seem to be associated with performance above the norm by those same funds in other subperiods.

VI. Conclusion

There is much more that could be said about how the two-parameter models of market equilibrium can and have been used to test market efficiency (cf. Ellert 1975). We could also go into much more detail on how the models can be used to evaluate the performance of managed portfolios (cf. Fama 1972). I hope, however, that the book has given the reader the base of sophistication that will enable him to continue investigation of these topics in the original literature.

References

Alexander, Sidney S. 1961. "Price Movements in Speculative Markets: Trends or Random Walks." *Industrial Management Review* 2 (May): 7–26; Reprinted in Cootner (ed.), 199–218.

———. 1964. "Price Movements in Speculative Markets: Trends or Random Walks. No. 2." In Cootner (ed.), 338–372.

Anderson, T. W. 1958. *An Introduction to Multivariate Statistical Analysis.* New York: John Wiley.

Arrow, Kenneth J. 1964. "The Role of Securities in the Optimal Allocation of Risk-Bearing." *Review of Economic Studies* 31 (April): 91–96.

Bachelier, Louis. 1900. *Théorie de la speculation.* Paris: Gauthier-Villars. Reprinted in Cootner (ed.), 17–78.

Ball, Ray. 1972. "Changes in Accounting Techniques and Stock Prices." Ph.D. dissertation, University of Chicago.

Ball, Ray, and Brown, Phillip. 1968. "An Empirical Evaluation of Accounting Income Numbers." *Journal of Accounting Research* 6 (Autumn): 159–178.

Black, Fischer. 1972. "Capital Market Equilibrium with Restricted Borrowing." *Journal of Business* 45 (July): 444–454.

Black, Fischer, and Scholes, Myron. 1973. "The Pricing of Options and Corporate Liabilities." *Journal of Political Economy* 81 (May–June): 637–654.

———. 1974. "The Effects of Dividend Yield and Dividend Policy on Common Stock Prices and Returns." *Journal of Financial Economics* 1 (May): 1–22.

Black, Fischer; Jensen, Michael; and Scholes, Myron. 1972. "The Capital Asset Pricing Model: Some Empirical Tests." In Jensen (ed.), 79–121.

Blattberg, Robert, and Gonedes, Nicholas. 1974. "A Comparison of the Stable and Student Distributions as Statistical Models for Stock Prices." *Journal of Business* 47 (April): 244–280.

Blattberg, Robert, and Sargent, Thomas. 1971. "Regression with Non-Gaussian Disturbances: Some Sampling Results." *Econometrica* 39 (May): 501–510.

Blume, Marshall. 1968. "The Assessment of Portfolio Performance." Ph.D. dissertation, University of Chicago, Graduate School of Business.

———. 1970. "Portfolio Theory: A Step Toward Its Practical Application." *Journal of Business* 43 (April): 152–173. This is an informative summary of Blume (1968).

———. 1971. "On the Assessment of Risk." *Journal of Finance* 26 (March): 1–10.

Brennan, Michael J. 1971. "Capital Market Equilibrium with Divergent Borrowing and Lending Rates." *Journal of Financial and Quantitative Analysis* 6 (December): 1197–1205.

Cass, David, and Stiglitz, Joseph. 1970. "The Structure of Investor Preferences and Asset Returns, and Separability in Portfolio Allocation: A Contribution to the Pure Theory of Mutual Funds." *Journal of Economic Theory* 2 (June): 122–160.

Cootner, Paul, ed. 1964. *The Random Character of Stock Market Prices*. Cambridge: MIT.

Cramer, Harald. 1946. *Mathematical Methods of Statistics*. Princeton: Princeton University Press.

Douglas, George W. 1969. "Risk in the Equity Markets: An Empirical Appraisal of Market Efficiency." *Yale Economic Essays* 9 (Spring): 3–45.

Ellert, James. 1975. "Anti-Trust Enforcement and Behavior of Stock Prices." Ph.D. dissertation, University of Chicago.

Fama, Eugene F. 1965. "The Behavior of Stock Market Prices." *Journal of Business* 38 (January): 34–105.

———. 1968. "Risk, Return, and Equilibrium: Some Clarifying Comments." *Journal of Finance* 23 (March): 29–40.

———. 1970a. "Multiperiod Consumption-Investment Decisions." *American Economic Review* 60 (March): 163–174.

———. 1970b. "Efficient Capital Markets: A Review of Theory and Empirical Work." *Journal of Finance* 25 (May): 383–417.

———. 1971. "Risk, Return, and Equilibrium." *Journal of Political Economy* 79 (January–February): 30–55.

———. 1972. "Components of Investment Performance." *Journal of Finance* 27 (June): 551–567.

———. 1973. "A Note on the Market Model and the Two-Parameter Model." *Journal of Finance* 28 (December): 1181–1185.

———. 1975. "Short-Term Interest Rates as Predictors of Inflation." *American Economic Review* 65 (June): 269–282.

Fama, Eugene F., and Blume, Marshall. 1966. "Filter Rules and Stock Market Trading Profits." *Journal of Business* 39 (special supp., January): 226–241.

Fama, Eugene F., and MacBeth, James D. 1973. "Risk, Return, and Equilibrium: Empirical Tests." *Journal of Political Economy* 71 (May–June): 607–636.

———. 1974*a*. "Tests of the Multiperiod Two-Parameter Model." *Journal of Financial Economics* 1 (May): 43–66.

———. 1974*b*. "Long-Term Growth in a Short-Term Market." *Journal of Finance* 29 (June): 857–885.

Fama, Eugene F., and Miller, Merton. 1972. *The Theory of Finance*. New York: Holt, Rinehart and Winston.

Fama, Eugene F., and Roll, Richard. 1968. "Some Properties of Symmetric Stable Distributions." *Journal of the American Statistical Association* 63 (September): 817–836.

———. 1971. "Parameter Estimates for Symmetric Stable Distributions." *Journal of the American Statistical Association* 66 (June): 331–338.

Fama, Eugene F.; Fisher, Lawrence; Jensen, Michael; and Roll, Richard. 1969. "The Adjustment of Stock Prices to New Information." *International Economic Review* 10 (February): 1–21.

Fisher, Irving. 1930. *The Theory of Interest*. Reprint. New York: Augustus M. Kelley, 1965.

Fisher, Lawrence. 1966. "Some New Stock Market Indices." *Journal of Business* 49 (supp., January): 191–225.

———. 1970. "The Estimation of Systematic Risk: Some New Findings." *Proceedings of the Seminar on the Analysis of Security Prices*, University of Chicago, May.

Friend, Irwin, and Blume, Marshall. 1970. "Measurement of Portfolio Performance under Uncertainty." *American Economic Review* 60 (September): 561–575.

Gonedes, Nicholas. 1973. "Evidence on the Information Content of Accounting Numbers: Accounting-Based and Market-Based Estimates of Systematic Risk." *Journal of Financial and Quantitative Analysis* 8 (June): 407–444.

Ibbotson, Roger. 1974. "Price Performance of Common Stock New Issues." Ph.D. dissertation, University of Chicago.

Jacob, Nancy. 1971. "The Measurement of Systematic Risk for Securities and Portfolios: Some Empirical Results." *Journal of Financial and Quantitative Analysis* 6 (March): 815–834.

Jaffe, Jeffrey F. 1974. "Special Information and Insider Trading." *Journal of Business* 47 (July): 410–428.

Jensen, Michael. 1968. "The Performance of Mutual Funds in the Period 1945–64." *Journal of Finance* 23 (May): 389–416.

———. 1969. "Risk, the Pricing of Capital Assets, and the Evaluation of Investment Portfolios." *Journal of Business* 42 (April): 167–247.

———. 1972. "Capital Markets: Theory and Evidence." *Bell Journal of Economics and Management Science* 3 (Autumn): 357–398.

Jensen, Michael, ed. 1972. *Studies in the Theory of Capital Markets*. New York: Praeger, 1972.

Johnston, John. 1972. *Econometric Methods*. 2nd ed. New York: McGraw-Hill.

Kendall, M. G., and Stuart, A. S. 1968. *The Advanced Theory of Statistics, vol. 3, Design & Analysis & Time Series*. 2nd ed. New York: Hafner.

King, Benjamin F. 1966. "Market and Industry Factors in Stock Price Behavior." *Journal of Business* 39 (supp., January): 139–190.

Lintner, John. 1956. "Distribution of Incomes of Corporations among Dividends, Retained Earnings, and Taxes." *American Economic Review* 46 (May): 97–113.

———. 1965a. "The Valuation of Risk Assets and the Selection of Risky Investments in Stock Portfolios and Capital Budgets." *Review of Economics and Statistics* 47 (February): 13–37.

———. 1965b. "Security Prices, Risk, and Maximal Gains from Diversification." Journal of Finance 20 (December): 587–616.

———. 1969. "The Aggregation of Investors' Diverse Judgments and Preferences in Purely Competitive Securities Markets." *Journal of Financial and Quantitative Analysis* 4 (December): 347–400.

Lorie, James H., and Niederhoffer, Victor. 1968. "Predictive and Statistical Properties of Insider Trading." *Journal of Law and Economics* 11 (April): 35–51.

Mandelbrot, Benoit. 1963. "The Variation of Certain Speculative Prices." *Journal of Business* 36 (October): 394–419.

———. 1966. "Forecasts of Future Prices, Unbiased Markets, and Martingale Models." *Journal of Business* 39 (special supp., January): 242–255.

Mandelker, Gershon. 1974. "Risk and Return: The Case of Merging Firms." *Journal of Financial Economics* 1 (December): 303–335.

Markowitz, Harry. 1952. "Portfolio Selection." *Journal of Finance* 7 (March): 77–91.

———. 1959. *Portfolio Selection: Efficient Diversification of Investments.* New York: John Wiley.

Mayers, David. 1972. "Nonmarketable Assets and Capital Market Equilibrium under Uncertainty." In Jensen (ed.), 223–248.

Merton, Robert C. 1972. "An Analytic Derivation of the Efficient Portfolio Frontier." *Journal of Financial and Quantitative Analysis* 7 (September): 1151–1172.

———. 1973. "An Intertemporal Capital Asset Pricing Model." *Econometrica* 41 (September): 867–887.

Miller, Merton, and Scholes, Myron. 1972. "Rates of Return in Relation to Risk: A Re-examination of Some Recent Findings." In Jensen (ed.), 47–78.

Mossin, Jan. 1966. "Equilibrium in a Capital Asset Market." *Econometrica* 34 (October): 768–783.

Niederhoffer, Victor, and Osborne, M. F. M. 1966. "Market Making and Reversal on the Stock Exchange." *Journal of the American Statistical Association* 61 (December): 897–916.

Officer, Robert R. 1971. "A Time Series Examination of the Market Factor of the New York Stock Exchange." Ph.D. dissertation, University of Chicago.

Osborne, M. F. M. 1959. "Brownian Motion in the Stock Market." *Operations Research* 7 (March–April): 145–173. Reprinted in Cootner (ed.), 100–128.

Roberts, Harry V. 1959. "Stock Market 'Patterns' and Financial Analysis:

Methodological Suggestions." *Journal of Finance* 14 (March 1959): 1–10.

Roll, Richard. 1970. *The Behavior of Interest Rates*. New York: Basic Books.

———. 1972. "Interest Rates on Monetary Assets and Commodity Price Index Changes." *Journal of Finance* 27 (May): 251–277.

Samuelson, Paul A. 1965. "Proof That Properly Anticipated Prices Fluctuate Randomly." *Industrial Management Review* 6 (Spring): 41–49.

Sargent, Thomas J. 1973. "Interest Rates and Prices in the Long Run: A Study of the Gibson Paradox." *Journal of Money, Credit, and Banking* 5 (February): 385–449.

Scholes, Myron. 1972. "The Market for Securities: Substitution versus Price Pressure and the Effects of Information on Share Prices." *Journal of Business* 45 (April): 179–211.

Sharpe, William F. 1964. "Capital Asset Prices: A Theory of Market Equilibrium under Conditions of Risk." *Journal of Finance* 19 (September). 425–442.

Theil, Henri. 1971. *Principles of Econometrics*. New York: John Wiley.

Tobin, James. 1958. "Liquidity Preference as Behavior towards Risk." *Review of Economic Studies* 25 (February): 65–85.

U. S. Bureau of Labor Statistics. 1971. *Handbook of Methods for Surveys and Studies*. BLS Bulletin no. 1458.

Index

Alexander, Sidney S., 140–142
Anderson, T. W., $63n$, 77, 91, $371n$
Autocorrelations: market-efficiency
tests based on, 144–151; of returns
and residuals, 114–120

Bachelier, Louis, 17–18
Ball, Ray, 165, 377
Bivariate normality (bivariate normal
distribution): implications of,
market model coefficient estimators and, 109–112; market model
and, 66–77; of pairwise security
and portfolio returns, 65–66
Black, Fischer, 278, 286, 288, 320,
333, 348, 368, 369
Black model of market equilibrium,
278–279, 284, 285, 288, 291,
299–301, 303, 322
Blattberg, Robert, 26, 38
Blume, Marshall, 15, 33, 43, 131,
132, 141, 348, 368, 369

Borrowing and lending, risk-free, *see*
Risk-free borrowing and lending
Brennan, Michael J., 293
Brennan model of market equilib-
rium, 293–295, 299
Brown, Phillip, 165

Capital market, efficient, *see* Efficiency of capital market
Center for Research in Security
Prices (CRSP) returns, 12
Central-limit theorem, distributions
of returns and, 18, 20, 26, 38
Coefficients of determination, 100,
106
Complete agreement assumption:
market equilibrium model with,
271–273, 338; market equilibrium
model without, 314–319
Confidence intervals, estimators of
market model and, 92–94
Consumer Price Index (CPI),
171–172, 186–188, 209–210

Cootner, Paul, 151
Corner portfolios, 291–292, 303, 304
Cramer, Harold, 63n, 77, 91, 371n

Daily returns: distributions of, 21–26; distributions of monthly returns and, 26, 27, 30–33; stable nonnormal, 26–27
Distributions: sampling, of estimators of market model, 84–91; of stock market returns, *see* Distributions of stock market returns; "t," *see* "t" distributions
Distributions of stock market returns, 17–38; Bachelier-Osborne model of, 17–18; daily, *see* Daily returns; monthly, 26–38; normal, *see* Normal distributions; stable nonnormal, 26–27

Efficiency of capital market, 133–168; autocorrelations as bases of tests of, 144–151; behavior of returns through time and, two-parameter model test, 338–340; chartists' veiw of, 139–141; company-specific information and, 376–379; FFJR (Fama, Fisher, Jensen, and Roll) study of, 154–165; filter tests and, 141–142; formal discussion of, 134–137; introduction to, 133–134; market-equilibrium models and, *see* Market equilibrium; market model and tests of, 151–166; splits and adjustment of stock prices to new information and, 154–164; tests of, 136–166; two-factor models and, 375–376
Efficiency of market portfolio, market equilibrium and, 279–284
Efficiency of Treasury bill market,

170, 171, 174–211; behavior of $\tilde{\Delta}_t$ and, 197–200; for bills with maturities longer than a month, 200–204; data on, 186–188; general description of, 176–177; inflation and, theory of, 175–178; interest rates as predictors of inflation and, 176, 180–184, 204–206; major results for one-month bills and, 188–197; market-equilibrium model and, 178–179; price controls and, 206–210; testable implications of, when equilibrium expected real return is constant through time, 179–186; tests of, summary and reinterpretation of, 184–186; in uncertain world, 175–178; in world of perfect foresight, 175
Efficient portfolios, 215–218, 232; as combinations of market portfolio M and minimum variance portfolio Z, 285–287; expected return-risk relationship in an, two-parameter model, 258–270
Efficient set of portfolios: combinations of two securities or portfolios and, geometry of, 219–31; definition of, 215–216; geometry of, 219–240; risk-free assets and, 231–240; risk-free borrowing and lending and, 273–274; short-selling and, 233–236; without short-selling or risk-free securities, 303–305
Ellert, James, 382
Empirical tests of two-parameter models, 320–382; applications of the measured risk-return relationships and, 370–382; based on average returns as, 362–365; based on time-series behavior of returns, 365–367; competing hypotheses and, 322–323; efficiency of capital market and, behavior of returns through time, 338–340; equally weighted market portfolio m and, 341–343; errors-in-the-variables problem and, 344–347; Fama-MacBeth approach to regression phenomenon and, 348–351; getting

the most powerful, 329–335; hypotheses about expected returns and, 321–322; introduction to, 320; least squares coefficients as portfolio returns and, 326–329; least squares portfolio returns and, reliability of, 336–337; methodological details of, 340–356; monthly record and results of, 356–362; portfolio approach to, 323–326, 348–356; portfolio approach to estimating risk measures and, 343–356; regression phenomenon, choosing portfolios, and, 347–348; results of, 356–370; risk measures and, 340–356; selection of portfolios and performance evaluation and, 380–382; Sharpe-Lintner hypothesis and, 368–370
Equilibrium, market, *see* Market equilibrium
Estimated regression function, 99; fit of, 104–106
Estimates, market model, 99–132; assumptions underlying, evidence on the, 124–128; autocorrelations of returns and residuals and, 114–120; coefficient estimators and, testing assumptions underlying 109–120; fit of estimated regression function and, 104–106; for IBM common stock, 101–104; for larger and smaller firms, 121–124; parameter, comparison of prewar and postwar, 128–131; reliability of, for IBM common stock, 106–108; reliability of risk estimates, 131–132; stationarity and random sampling and, 112–120
Estimators of market model, 77–98; algebraic properties of, 81–84; Bayesian approach to reliability of, 96–98; bivariate normality and, 109–112; classical approach to reliability of, 92–96; coefficient, testing the assumptions underlying, 109–120; equations for, 79–81; generality of the procedures for, 78; reliability of, 91–98; sampling

distributions of, 84–91; summary of equations and properties of, 99–101; "t" distributions of the standardized, 87–91; unbiasedness of, 84–87
Expected real return on Treasury bills, market efficiency tests and, 179–186, 192–197
Expected returns: constant, as model of market equilibrium, 142–151; market relationships between risk and, when short-selling of positive variance securities is unrestricted, 278–301; market relationships between risk and, when there is risk-free borrowing and lending, 271–278; positive, as model of market equilibrium, 137–142; relationship between risk and, in an efficient portfolio, 258–270; two-parameter models and, empirical tests, 321–322

Fama, Eugene F., 21, 26, 30, 33n, 141–142, 145, 154, 169n, 210, 272n, 320, 348, 349, 366–369, 382
Filter rules, tests of, 141–142
Fisher, Irving, 186, 205, 206
Fisher, Lawrence, 132, 154, 370
"Fisher effect," 205
Friend, Irwin, 368, 369

Gibson Paradox, 205–206
Gonedes, Nicholas, 38, 132, 349

Hypothesis testing, classical, market-model estimators' reliability and, 94–96

Ibbotson, Roger, 378
Indexes of stock market returns, 13
Inflation: efficiency and, in Treasury
    bill market, 175–178; nominal in-
    terest rate as predictor of, 180–
    184; returns on Treasury bills and,
    in an uncertain world, 175–176;
    short-term interest rates as predic-
    tors of, 176, 180–184, 204–206
Interest rates: market equilibrium
    when there is risk-free borrowing
    and lending but at different,
    293–295, 298–301; nominal, as
    predictor of inflation, 180–184,
    204–206; short-term, as predictors
    of inflation, 176, 180–184,
    204–206

Jaffe, Jeffrey F., 166, 378–379
Jensen, Michael, 154, 320, 348, 368,
    369, 380–382

King, Benjamin F., 15, 131

Least squares coefficients, as port-
    folio returns, 326–329
Lintner, John, 162, 277
Lorie, James H., 166n

MacBeth, James D., 210, 272n, 320,
    348, 349, 366–369
Mandelbrot, Benoit, 26
Mandelker, Gershon, 166, 377–378
Margin requirements, market equilib-
    rium when there is risk-free bor-
    rowing and lending but there are,
    295–297
Market equilibrium: bill market ef-
    ficiency tests and, 179–186; Black
    model of, 278–279, 284, 285, 288,
    291, 299–301, 303, 322; Brennan
    model of, 293–295, 299; without
    complete agreement assumption,
    314–319; constant-expected-
    returns model of, 142–151; effi-
    ciency of capital market and, 135–
    166; efficiency of market for one-
    month Treasury bills and model of,
    178–179; efficiency of market
    portfolio and, 279–287; efficient
    portfolios as combinations of the
    market portfolio M and the
    minimum variance portfolio Z and,
    285–287; empirical tests of two-
    parameter models and, *see*
    Empirical tests of two-parameter
    models; expected return-risk rela-
    tionships and, when short-selling of
    positive variance securities is un-
    restricted, 278–301; expected
    return-risk relationships and, when
    there is risk-free borrowing and
    lending, 271–278; market model
    and, 151–166; market portfolio
    and, 284; mathematical treatment
    of, 305–319; with no risk-free
    securities and when short-selling of
    positive variance securities is pro-
    hibited, 301–305, positive-
    expected-returns model of, 137–
    142; risk-free borrowing and lend-
    ing and, 274–276; with risk-free
    borrowing and lending but at
    different interest rates, 293–295;
    with risk-free borrowing and lend-
    ing but with margin requirements,
    295–297; with risk-free lending but
    not borrowing, 288–292; with risk-
    free security that cannot be sold
    short, 288–292; Sharpe-Lintner
    model of, 277–279, 284, 291, 298–
    301, 322, 343, 368–370, 380, 381;
    two-parameter models of, compari-
    son of and comments on various,
    298–301; in two-parameter world,
    257–319
Market model, 63–132; bivariate nor-

mality and, 66–77; in empirical
literature, 76–77; equilibrium of
market and, 151–154; estimators
of, *see* Estimators of market
model; market-efficiency tests and,
151–166; properties of, 66–69, 73–
77; risk estimates from, two-
parameter model and, 344; splits
and the adjustment of stock prices
to new information and (FFJR
study), 154–164; two-factor,
371–376
Market portfolio: efficiency of, 279–
284; efficient portfolios as combinations of minimum variance
portfolio Z and, 285–287;
market equilibrium and, 284
Markets, *see* Capital market
Markowitz, Harry, 62, 212
Means, 4–5; normal distributions
characterized by their standard
deviations and, 6–7; of portfolio's
return, 44–48; sample, 7–9
Merton, Robert C., 231, 234, 272*n*
Miller, Merton, 320
Minimum variance portfolios,
260–267; properties of boundary
of, 279–284
Models (statistical models): market,
see Market model; reality and,
11–12
Monthly returns, 26–38; definition
of, 12–13; indexes or portfolios of,
13; studentized ranges for, 33, 34
Multivariate normal distribution:
properties of, 64–65; of returns on
securities, 63–66
Mutual funds, investment performance of, 380–382

Neiderhoffer, Victor, 166
Normal distributions, 4; bivariate,
market model and, 66–77;
bivariate, of pairwise security and
portfolio returns, 65–66; multivariate, of returns on securities,

63–66; studentized range and
inferences about, 9–10; studentized
range as test for, 8–11; two-
parameter portfolio model and,
214
NYSE common stocks, returns on,
see Returns on NYSE common
stocks

Officer, Robert R., 15–17, 33, 43
Osborne, M. F. M., 17–18, 166

Portfolio returns, 41–62; bivariate
normality of pairwise security returns and, 65–66; distribution of,
41–62; diversification's effect on
variance of, 252–256; efficiency of
portfolios and, *see* Efficient set of
portfolios; as function of returns
on securities, 41–43; multivariate
normal, returns on securities and
normal, 63–64; standard deviation
of, 44; tests of two-parameter
model based on average, 362–365;
tests of two-parameter model based
on time-series behavior of, 365–
367; two-parameter models of, *see*
Two-parameter models of portfolio
returns; variance of, 44, 48–58
Portfolio risk: security risk and, 58–
62; security risk and, in two-
parameter world, 240–252; two-
parameter model and relationship
between expected return and,
258–270
Portfolios: corner, 291–292, 303,
304; efficient, *see* Efficient portfolios; efficient set of, *see* Efficient
set of portfolios; geometry of combinations of two securities or, 219–
231; market, *see* Market portfolios;
minimum variance, *see* Minimum
variance portfolios; performance
evaluation and selection of,
380–382; regression phenomenon

Portfolios *(continued)*
and choosing, empirical tests of
two-parameter model, 347–348;
returns on, *see* Portfolio returns;
set of, *see* Efficient set of portfolios; short-selling and geometric
analysis of two securities or portfolios, 224–231; of stock market
returns, 13
Positive variance securities, short-
selling of: prohibited, market
equilibrium with no risk-free
securities and, 301–305; unrestricted, market equilibrium with,
278–301

Random variables, 3–4; mean or expected value of, 4–5; variance of, 5
Regression function, estimated, 99;
fit of, 104–106
Regression phenomenon: choosing
portfolios and, in empirical tests of
two-parameter model, 347–348;
Fama-MacBeth approach to,
348–351
Residuals: autocorrelations of returns and, 114–120; market
model, splits and the adjustment
of stock prices to new information,
154–165; times series plots of
returns and, 113–115
Return variability, *see* Variability of
returns
Returns on NYSE common stocks
(stock market returns): average,
14; daily, *see* Daily returns; definition of, 12–13; distributions of, *see*
Distributions of stock market returns; indexes or portfolios of, 13;
monthly, *see* Monthly returns;
risks or market sensitivities of,
evidence on the, 121–132; variability of, *see* Variability of returns
Returns on portfolio, *see* Portfolio
returns
Returns on securities: bivariate
normal distribution of, 65–66;
expected, *see* Expected returns;

multivariate normal distribution of,
63–66; *see also* Returns on NYSE
common stocks
Returns on Treasury bills: real,
market efficiency and, 179–180;
real and nominal, on one-month
bills, 170–174
Risk aversion, two-parameter portfolio model and, 214–216, 218
Risk estimates, reliability of, 131–132
Risk-free assets or securities, efficient set of portfolios and,
231–240
Risk-free borrowing and lending:
efficient set of portfolios when
there is, 273–274; market equilibrium when there is, 274–276;
market equilibrium with, but at
different interest rates, 293–295,
298–301; market equilibrium with,
with margin requirements, 295–
297; market relationships between
expected return and risk when
there is, 271–278
Risk-free lending but not borrowing,
market equilibrium with, 288–292,
298–301
Risk-free securities: efficient set of
portfolios without short-selling or,
303–305; market equilibrium with
no, and prohibited short-selling of
positive variance securities,
301–305
Risk measures, empirical tests of
two-parameter models and,
340–356
Risk-return relationships: applications of the measured, 370–382;
in efficient portfolio, 258–270
Risks: of NYSE common stocks, evidence on, 121–132; portfolio, *see*
Portfolio risk; security, *see* Security risk
Roll, Richard, 26, 33n, 154, 186,
205, 206n

Sample means, 9; standard deviation
and, 7–8

Sampling, random, *see* Random sampling

Sampling distributions of estimators of market model, 84–91

Sargent, Thomas J., 26, 206*n*

Scholes, Myron, 165–166, 320, 333, 348, 368, 369

Security risk: portfolio risk and, 58–62; portfolio risk and, in two-parameter model, 240–252, 258–259; *see also* Risk-free securities

Sharpe, William F., 277

Sharpe-Lintner model, 277–279, 284, 291, 298–301, 322, 343, 368–370, 380, 381

Short-selling: combinations of two securities or portfolios and, geometric analysis, 224–231; efficient set of portfolios and, 233–236; efficient set of portfolios without risk-free securities or, 303–305; market equilibrium when there is a risk-free security but it cannot be sold short, 288–292, 298–301; of positive variance securities, *see* Positive variance securities, short-selling of

Splits, adjustment of stock prices to new information and, 154–164

Standard deviation, 5; normal distributions characterized by their means and, 6–7; of portfolio's return, 44; sample mean and, 7–8

Standard errors, of coefficient estimators of market model, 87–89

Stock market returns, *see* Returns on NYSE common stocks

Stock splits, *see* Splits

Studentized range (SR): for daily returns, 24–26; definition of, 8; inferences about normality from the, 9–11; probability distributions for sample statistics and, 8–9

Theil, Henri, 91, 328*n*, 336*n*

Time-series behavior of returns, tests of two-parameter model based on, 365–367

Treasury bills: efficiency of market for, *see* Efficiency of Treasury bill market; market for, 169–174; real and nominal returns on one-month, 170–174; returns on, *see* Returns on Treasury bills

Two-factor market model, 371–376

Two-parameter models of portfolio returns, 58, 212–382; market equilibrium in, 257–319 (*see also* Market equilibrium); complete agreement assumption in, 271–273; diversification and, 252–256; efficient set of portfolios and, *see* Efficient set of portfolios; empirical tests of, *see* Empirical tests of two-parameter models; framework of, 213–214; geometric interpretation of, 216–218; introduction to, 212; market relationships between expected return and risk in, when short-selling of positive variance securities is unrestricted, 278–301; market relationships between expected return and risk in, when there is risk-free borrowing and lending, 271–278; normal distribution and, 214; portfolio risk and security risk in world of, 240–252; risk aversion of investors and, 214–216, 218; risk-expected return relationship in efficient portfolio in, 258–270

U.S. Treasury bills, *see* Treasury bills

"t" distributions, of standardized estimators of the market model, 87–91

Variability of returns, 14–15; history of, 15–17

Variance of portfolio's return, 44, 48–58